CROSS COUNTRY

Short taxying on landing, Valparaiso, 1921

photo: Hans Frey

CROSS COUNTRY

Being extracts from the letters of J. L., H. G. and C. T. Travers and their family; and from the log-books of H. G. Travers; with background material, linking narrative and some pages of reminiscence by E. Travers.

James Lindsay Travers, O.B.E., F.R.Ae.S., A.M.I.C.E.   1883–1924
Herbert Gardner Travers, D.S.C.   1891–1958
Charles Tindal Travers, A.F.C.   1898–1969

Hothersall & Travers

First published 1990 by Hothersall & Travers, P.O. Box 149, Sittingbourne, Kent,
ME9 8AW, England
© E. Travers 1989. All Rights Reserved Author & Publisher 1989

This book made and printed in Great Britain by
Butler & Tanner Ltd,
Frome and London

Cover design by E. Travers

ISBN 0 9515461 0 4

To
C. F.
who kept me on course

CONTENTS

BOOK ONE

INTRODUCTION

London River

THERE is no way of finding out all that Jim saw and heard on his voyages to and from Australia and during his time there.

The Exhibition he so much enjoyed, for instance. One keeps thinking about that Exhibition and of what fascinating machinery may have been there. What farm and factory machinery, what pumps and windmills. Perhaps Hargraves' famous box-kite was there; it had certainly been at Stanwell Park, near Sydney, in 1894, in the decade when Hargraves became famous and when Australia was already flying-mad. In the days before television the major shows and exhibitions were the shop-windows of new projects and ideas. And the pattern fits.

Jim went out to Australia as a frail boy who stammered badly, a boy who appeared to be nervous but who was, in fact, almost without physical fear; a boy who had missed much formal education due to severe childhood illness but who was albeit intensely interested in the world about him and eager for knowledge in all practical matters.

'When he went out,' said Jay, the sister who was to tell me most about him, – 'when he went out none of us had ever heard a word about it, but when he came home again, all he could talk about was flying. It was something that happened in Australia. We never knew what it was.'

Jim had been sent to Australia to grow strong; his parents hoped that he might have an improvement in health and, at the same time, spend an enjoyable two years amongst his many cousins. But Australia worked her magic. Australia made him. At one time I conjectured that perhaps the great distances involved in his journeyings plus the effect of space and light on an imaginative boy who had spent much of his childhood in the sickroom – ephemeral notions, other-worldly ideas, had played their part. But the more I read his early letters, the more I

saw his practical diagrams accompanying them, the more I am sure
that the right mind was in the right place at the right time.

And when he came home again, all that he could talk about was
flying.

Jim was by no means the first member of the Travers family to go to
Australia – 'to go out' it was called in our family. The Travers had
travelled and settled there for generations as, for hundreds of years,
they had travelled and traded round the world from the City of
London.

Like so many other English families they had arrived in England
with the Conquest. John de Travers, who arrived with the Conquest,
'planted English soyle', married the Saxon daughter and heiress of one
of his 'captives' and settled quietly in a Saxon house on English soil
and farmed there; generations lived quietly on the same land at Horton
Hall on the borders of Cheshire and Lancashire.

My father, H. G. Travers, who had a happy sense of the continuity
of things, sometimes spoke of Horton Hall as the 'Old House' and I
was in my 'teens before I realized that he had never actually lived in the
'Old House' himself and that it was indeed old – sacked, ruined, fallen
down – in the Middle Ages. Not only had my father never lived in the
'Old House' he did not even know precisely where it had stood. He had
searched once in the lovely land around Preston but had found only an
outcrop of stones, mason's marks still on them, nothing certain.

Like many another once-conquering family we were out-manoeuvred
ourselves, got on the wrong side in the Wars of the Roses, and
came South to the City of London and to Devonshire. It was many
generations before the Travers family put their trust in land again.

There were numerous Travers in London during Tudor times and
by the start of the 17th Century, through energetic trading, we had
become prosperous. Recorded in the Vellum Book of the Honourable
Artillery Company are (1614) Philip Travers, (1626) James Travers,
(1642) Philip Travers and (1660) Giles Travers. All these, save James,
were officers in the London Trained Bands. These men were not only
all members of the same trading family they were all merchants in the
true sense: i.e. with permission to trade abroad.

We were early and vigorous members of the Hanseatic League.
Memories of the terrible days of the Danegeld remained long in
England and the Hanseatic League, that affinity of trading nations,

was formed to keep the Danes out of the City of London. My father used to say that the trade was all from London River, the ships all from Devonshire; that we were 'Merchant Venturers, the trade all in our own ships' and that we 'were long before the East India Company.' It was scarcely surprising, therefore, that we adopted the sign of the SHIP, battling home through a heavy sea, as our TRADE MARK. And what fine little ships they were, those Salcombe-built schooners, with names such as *The Spy, Jane, Saucy Jack, Susan, The Scud, Revel, Fortune, Torch, Maria* and *Black Cat,* which brought into London River the commodities in which we traded: spices, sugar, wine, (we were the first importers of Madeira), dried fruits in great variety from the Mediterannean, for we were Shippers, Importers & Merchant Grocers, selling only to the Wholesalers and with a system of Riders, later called Travellers, carrying samples in their saddle-bags throughout England, We also traded in tea and coffee.

During the 17th Century we joined forces with the remarkable Smith family and resumed trading, in a joint venture with them, after the Great Fire at the sign of The Cannon by LONDON STONE.

One Ledger, which was preserved for many years in the firm's archives, was opened in 1709. At that time Joseph Smith was head of the firm. It is probable that it was the same Joseph Smith who was the owner of ground rents in Savannah; certainly his two sons, Benjamin and Samuel, were the owners of that property – 'a great part of the City of Savannah' – but they, being in strong sympathy with the American Cause, made no claim for compensation for loss on the Declaration of Independence in 1776. They could afford to be magnanimous for the family was by then immensely rich. The Smiths and the Travers had married into each other's families and a tremendous web of wealth and influence controlled and supported their lives. Samuel Smith's son, William, was first cousin to Joseph Travers, – Samuel's sister Elizabeth having married Benjamin Travers, Joseph's father. The cousins were joint owners of the firm in the late 18th Century. The two men were united by strong family ties, by partnership in business and by their detestation of the Slave Trade.

William Smith did something about it, by becoming a Member of Parliament and actively campaigning against slavery. He was in the House for 46 years, representing Sudbury and Chelmsford for eighteen years and the rest as Member for Norwich. His was the leading

Dissenting voice in the House. He was the first avowed Nonconformist to take his seat in the House of Commons. He fought for the abolition of the Slave Trade, for Catholic Emancipation, for the repeal of the Corporation and Tests Acts and of all other disabilities affecting Dissenters.

The first of a set of verses written about him at the time runs:

> 'At length when the candles burn low in their sockets,
> 'Up jumps William Smith with his hands in his pockets,
> 'On a course of morality fearlessly enters,
> 'With all the opinions of all the Dissenters.'

All this fine reforming zeal needed a great deal of money – so, too, did the Smith's increasingly grand social life. The money was supplied by the partnership in business of Joseph Travers and William Smith and although Joseph Travers entirely agreed with and supported William Smith's reforming ambitions he had, to put it bluntly, been doing the work of both men for years and years and was getting a little tired of the fact.

William Smith extracted all the money he needed from the firm but he was always absent. The family history refers politely to 'a considerable difference of opinion'. The rights and wrongs of the case were circularized in the most amazingly frank manner, arbitration was called for, and right was found to be with Joseph Travers. He was awarded the St Swithin's Lane property (which contained the dwelling house where the Travers family had lived since the removal of the firm from the old sign in Cannon Street in the 1790's) – more importantly the counting house and it's contents, the warehouse at St Swithin's Lane and the ships, spice mills, warehousing, and wine vaults further down the River. William Smith was awarded a part of the firm's capital in severance with which he started business elsewhere in the City in June 1813, styling his new firm Smith & Kemble. The family divided as a result of the blazing row, the Travers Smiths, Leigh Smiths and so on siding with William Smith and the Smith Travers remaining within the Travers network.

The separation took place in June, 1813, by which time Joseph had his son, John, in partnership with him, so he then styled the firm Joseph Travers & Son. (Later Joseph Travers & Sons).

John Travers became head of the business on the death of his father in 1821 and continued as such for the rest of his life. He was a man of great energies. Apart from his work in the family firm he espoused many causes: he joined and actively assisted Rowland Hill's Committee to bring about the introduction of the Penny Post; the emancipation of British Jewry was also a cause for which he fought; (the Rothschilds were near neighbours in St Swithin's Lane). The City Office of the Reform League was at 19 St Swithin's Lane and in later days the counting house of Messrs Travers was the London centre of the Corn Law League; he also strove all his life against the adulteration of foodstuffs, although whether it was he who publicly burned a shipment of tea – declaring it to be inferior, adulterated and unfit for human consumption – or whether it was his son, also John Travers, who did so, I am unclear.

He married Maria Lindsay, daughter of Dr James Lindsay, D.D. Dr Lindsay kept a small school at Bow at which John had been a pupil. John and Maria produced sixteen children, some of whom I will mention briefly as they are relevant to this story.

Two of the daughters married Cambridge men, becoming Augusta 'Gussie' Burn and Maria Lindsay Dixon respectively. Emma married Samson Lloyd of Warwick Priory and their daughter, also Emma, married a Lloyd cousin which gave two Emma Lloyd's in quick succession; Louie married Roy Butler and they emigrated to Australia; Alice married Count Borgstrom, a Swedish banker then living in Helsingfors. (Helsinki). – But it was Anne, 'Aunt Annie', who married Charles Tindal of Fir Grove in Hampshire, Yattendon in Berkshire and Ramornie Cattle Station on the Clarence River in New South Wales who was to keep the long sea-lanes open for so long to the Travers family.

Of the sons John Ingram remained in the firm, overworked himself and died aged 46. Archibald, 'Uncle Archie', also stayed with the firm all his life, living in bachelor quarters at St Swithin's Lane until the 1850's when the firm returned once more to Cannon Street and he took up occupancy there. He was one of the few Travers men to live to see old age. He amassed an excellent small library in his rooms at Cannon Street, company for his lonely evenings. Samuel Smith Travers entered the firm but was bought out of the family partnership at his own request and on very generous terms. He went out to Melbourne, where he built a fine house overlooking the Harbour. It later became Admiralty House, Melbourne. He then went on to van Diemen's Land – Tasmania – where he settled.

James Lindsay Travers started with the firm, but he had been born in Budleigh Salteron, where the air was clean. London fogs, the dirt and grime of the place, the unhealthy mists which blew from the River, did not suit him: always weak-chested, he became ill each winter in London. He tried to escape to Devonshire as often as he could and in the winter – to Madeira. Finally he and Joseph Travers & Sons parted by mutual consent, the firm buying him out on comfortable terms.

He had married Anna Wansey, member of a once-noted Warminster cloth-milling family and the couple, still searching for health, settled at St Leonard's-on-Sea in Sussex, a newly fashionable resort for the bronchitic and for those weary of London life. They produced several sons and a daughter, their son James Lindsay being born at St Leonard's-on-Sea in December, 1846. Since his name echoes his father's name I shall refer to the Sussex-born James Lindsay Travers as 'J.L.T.' for the rest of this book, in order to avoid confusion. Later in life he was to acquire family nick-names, among them 'Lill' – short for Lindsay and 'Bones', because he was always thin.

Although St Leonard's-on-Sea was preferable to London, James Lindsay Travers continued to be ill each winter. At length, having heard such good reports of the Australian climate from his brother and married sisters, he and his family emigrated there in 1852.

A shadow was cast over what should have been a happy adventure for their daughter, Jessie, died at Madeira on the voyage out. On reaching Australia the family settled in Sydney. They had a strong stone-built house near the Harbour and the comforts of the day. The young sons ran wild along the waterfront, on and off the trading vessels, on and off ships from England, from Nova Scotia and the Americas or from China – looking, seeing, – hearing sometimes the strangest of tales. J.L.T. remembered those days on Sydney Harbour all his life. They were to him an idyllic time. But the idyll lasted only a few short years for his father, who had at last discovered marvellous health and happiness in the Australian climate, was seldom out of the saddle. He rode many long miles visiting family and friends. Returning home one dark night he attempted to swim his horse across a river in torrent: his horse, alone, gained the further bank.

His widow did not remain in Sydney for very long afterwards for as soon as news of the tragedy had spread among the family her sister-in-law, Aunt Annie (Travers) Tindal, invited her up to Ramornie, on the Clarence, and for her and her boys to make their home there. Anna Travers did not arrive at Ramornie empty-handed for as well as tea-chests full of books, which had gone out with them from England, she brought with her a large number of treasures and curios which her husband had bought from the Masters of the sailing vessels who traded into Sydney Harbour from the China Seas: inlaid boxes with secret locks and panels, carvings of jade and of ivory and a number of Oriental jars, of which the two most magnificent were blue and white, about three feet tall, and were known in the family as the Ali-Baba jars. Life at Ramornie must have been one of great changes for the boys who had run wild along the Sydney waterfront, for Aunt Annie Tindal was a splendid woman who as well as her ordinary wifely duties – and she had a large family of her own – ran a school for all the station children.

It must have been a good life. No formal school, perhaps, but a well-stocked schoolroom with a terrestrial globe, (which had come originally from St Swithin's Lane), a Black's Atlas of the World, chests full of books, and Aunt Annie's sympathetic mind to guide the morning's work. As the boys grew older there were long days in the saddle: by the time he was 17 or so J.L.T. was working as a stockrider for his Uncle Charles Tindal.

In the evenings or at other times when he was not working J.L.T. was an avid reader. He particularly loved Dickens; it was said that he knew much of Dickens by heart. I have held in my hands an 1850 Edition of David Copperfield which survived from those Australian days and have tried to imagine, as Adam Lindsay Gordon helps one to imagine, lamplit evenings on the station after a hard day in the saddle, boots loosened, perhaps a pipe burning, the scent of the wattle in the dusk – with another world, another civilization, adventures on another planet it could have seemed – contained in the leather-bound book in one's hand.

J.L.T. had been five years old when he had left England but he remembered nothing of England. He had become an Australian. Then, when he was twenty-seven years old his Uncle Archie, no doubt having received intimations of mortality, sent for him and for his brother Jack, inviting them both to join Joseph Travers & Sons in the City of London.

(Their youngest brother, Geoffrey, had gone to England some years earlier to be brought up by his Aunt and Godmother, Emmie (Travers)

Lloyd, with his cousins at Warwick Priory. Eventually Geoffrey entered St Bartholomew's Medical School and on qualifying returned to Australia, where he practised in Melbourne. Geoffrey was in London, however, for several of J.L.T.'s first years in the City.)

Although the bachelor Uncle Archie was guardian, guide and mentor to the two newcomers to the firm – they lived with him in his rooms – the rest of the family was also most hospitable.

Aunt Alice Borgstrom invited them over to Finland, to the Borgstrom's beautiful summer island home of Turholm; they went, too, to the Lloyd's at Warwick Priory on several occasions. At first J.L.T.'s lack of the normal classical and games – playing education of the day made him feel reserved and different; but he was a superb horseman – a tall, thin, straight-backed young man who could 'ride anything lapped in a hide' – and the Lloyd's loved him. When they asked him down to Warwickshire for some hunting he at first protested that he would not be able, but they lent him the right clothes and put him up on some good horses and he went like a bird, jumping fences, it was said, that had never been jumped before. He became Godfather to, and later Trustee of, the Lloyd's second son, George. (Grandson of Aunt Emma, son of cousin Emma and later to become 1st Lord Lloyd of Dolobran). George Lloyd, in adult life, sometimes looked in to see J.L.T. at Cannon Street. He was inspired by his cousin Jim's early flying adventures to wish to learn to fly himself but this, sadly, he was not free to do until he was in his early fifties. Whatever the delights of lovely Turholm or of the Warwickshire hunting-field the place J.L.T. loved to visit most of all was Fir Grove, in Hampshire.

J.L.T. must indeed have felt as if he were going home when he went to Fir Grove, for the Aunt Annie Tindal who had welcomed him to Ramornie now extended the same warm welcome to 'dearest Lill' to Fir Grove.

Uncle Charles Tindal was a man of wealth and successful enterprise. Apart from his business life he took an active part in local affairs, being among other things a benefactor of Wellington College. Aunt Annie Tindal loved to fill the house with family and with neighbours, with children's parties, dancing classes, small dances: her organizing ability was considerable and her energy prodigious. Among the neighbours who were usually included in the Fir Grove invitations were Mrs Gardner, a widow, of Gothick Cottage, and her son and daughter, Herbert and Emmie.

Mrs Gardner had been born Emma Elizabeth Prescott, daughter of Frederick Prescott, a City banker of Threadneedle Street and Cornhill and of Theobalds House in Hertfordshire. (Theobalds House had been built by an earlier generation of Prescotts on the site of an ancient house).

Her mother had been a Russell, of Cheshunt. Cheshunt House and it's Park lay next door to Theobalds. Cheshunt – otherwise Chessunt, Chestnut, Cestrehunt or it's really old name, Brantyngeshay – where the Russells lived, had formerly belonged to the Cromwells, an earlier Russell having married the daughter of the house, Maria Cromwell, direct descendant of the Lord Protector via Henry Cromwell.

The Russells were a wild lot, a farming family originally from Wiltshire. In fair weather they caught or shot everything that moved in the Park. One of their trophies which has survived and which is still in his original glass case is a stoat-in-ermine which they caught in the winter of 1836, in the great snowstorm of that year, and this stoat-in-ermine was at Cheshunt, only fifteen miles from the City of London. In wet weather the Russells stayed indoors and shot the eyes out of the Cromwell portraits, which caused trouble when, in due course, the Bush cousins (equally descended from Cromwell), claimed the contents of the house as part of their inheritance.

The Prescotts were not wild. They were, indeed, the very essence of probity, decency and good order. Elizabeth Oliveria Russell may well have been glad to have escaped some of the stormier goings-on at Cheshunt when she married Frederick Prescott, the boy next door, and settled down with him at Theobalds to the calm and happy sort of life which the Prescotts always seemed able to achieve.

Frederick and Elizabeth Oliveria produced a large family, of whom the sons all grew up to be sound, safe, sensible men who went into the family Bank. The daughters did not all marry, among them being Olive, whose Tallulah Bankhead voice and devastating wit figured in family gatherings well into this century. One daughter married Mr Barker, of Stanlake Park, Berkshire. Another daughter, born on 14th February, 1826, was Emma Elizabeth. Emma Elizabeth remembered her childhood at Theobalds as a happy one, excepting only the winter cold. She learned to endure cold early in life for the Georgian architecture of Theobalds, with it's large drawing room windows, was cruel in winter to the girls of the family, whose budding or still child-like figures were draped, according to the fashion of the day, in damp muslin. Those twin fashions, of architecture and of dress, ensured only the survival of the fittest.

When his children were grown and when his eldest brother had assumed his (rightful) place in sole possession of Theobalds – Frederick Prescott moved his family into London, where they had a small house in Oxford Square. They were a sociable family who enjoyed entertaining and from her parents' house in London Emma Prescott met, and married by Special Licence in April, 1853, Herbert Calthorpe Gardner, a Captain in the East India Company. The young Captain and his bride sailed for India and their first child, baptized Herbert Prescott, was born the following year. By the time their second child was due, in late May, 1857, the Indian Mutiny was already raging.

Emma Gardner had been visiting some friends and was warned not to return to the Cantonment but to flee at once. Although she was so heavily pregnant she, her small son and his ayah, and some of the other Military wives, all crowded into a bullock cart. For a time Captain Gardner cantered beside them, giving cheerful words of encouragement to his distraught and weeping wife: then he turned his horse and was gone.

A little later on, as the refugees were attempting greater speed, a wheel came off the bullock cart and the passengers, bruised and frightened, descended into the road. It was at that place, in a dry ditch beside the road at Umballah, that Mrs Gardner gave birth to her daughter; even as she did so a stray mutineer, eager for loot, tore the rings from her fingers.

Colonel and Mrs Holland were the Good Samaritans who took Mrs Gardner and her children, and their ayah, into their home and who helped them, after much difficulty, to England. She went of course to her father's house, to the Prescott house in Oxford Square. The baby girl born in the ditch was baptized Emma Louisa.

Captain Gardner was not murdered, for his men remained loyal to him, but he became ill during the weeks following the mutiny and died – still in India – from natural causes.

Emma Louisa, always called Emmie, was brought up almost wholly by her Mother, her Prescott grandparents and the rest of the Prescott family and whether it was this influence or her own intrinsic nature one cannot tell, but she certainly maintained the Prescott steadiness and calm for the rest of her life. Her childhood was one of variety for she and her brother accompanied their Mother on numerous visits around the large and kindly family to which they belonged and they stayed, often for months at a time, with her Barker cousins at Stanlake Park, Berkshire, the Bush cousins at Lamerton and the Prescott and Russell cousins at Theobalds and Cheshunt Park.

When young Herbert Prescott Gardner gained a Foundationer place at Wellington College, Sir George Prescott wrote to the boy's Mother (his first cousin) and in a letter of great charm and seeming casualness offered her money which, he wrote, he had found lying idle, with which to buy herself her own house: and this, in due course, she did, settling on Gothick Cottage, close to Wellington College.

Among the local families who extended a welcome to the widow and her two children were, as has already been written, the Tindals of Fir Grove who were now and for the time being back from the Clarence River. Their daughter Anne Grant Tindal was about the same age as Emmie Gardner and the two girls became great companions. When Mrs Tindal arranged dancing classes and, later on, dances at Fir Grove, Emmie was usually invited. What a happy preparation for marriage it must have been: to know and to immensely like the family into which she was eventually to marry. When Emmie was sixteen her Prescott Grandfather sent her to study at Queen's College, London. She was at Queen's College for two years. She was very happy there and wrote her Mother a number of reassuring letters, particularly concerning the excellence of the food: '. . . I am always hungry at meal time but I have as much as ever I want to eat . . . breakfast consisting of tea or coffee, bread and butter and ham. . . . from 12 to 1.30 is a running luncheon, cut bread and butter and cheese, as much as we choose to eat . . . 5.30 is dinner I generally have two helpings of meat and pudding and vegetables, always very good except when the mutton is tough. . . . beer or claret to drink. 7 to 8 silence hour in study. No work may be done from dinner to 7. 8.15. tea or coffee and bread and butter. . . .' and the work: '. . . we have such fun with the Professors, they make us laugh so . . .'

In more severe mood and away from school she wrote criticizing her brother and her Aunt Barker at Stanlake: '. . . I can't think how Herbert and Auntie can go riding about in that fashion. The other day it was so cold they must nearly have been buried in the snow and now it is so hot they must get quite baked and besides they must know every road by heart now, and as to Auntie riding that horrid little black thing, I should think it nearly pulled her arm out of the socket. . . .'

Later the same year, in August of 1873, she wrote to her Mother from Stanlake, where she was staying, a letter which may now be seen as prophetic.

'. . . Georgy (Barker) was chatting away to-day "after England" he said, "you get to Scotland and after Scotland there are the rocks and then a long bit of sea and then a little bit of Iceland and then?" - "the North Pole", said I. – "And then?" – "Why, nowhere after that, you have to come back again," I couldn't help feeling what an insignificant thing the world was compared to the whole universe and when Georgy asked why we couldn't get away at the North Pole I could only wish we were able . . .'

As Emmie grew up her father's family, the Gardners, took kindly interest in her and she travelled to Cromarty for long, happy summers with her Uncle, General Sir William Gardner, a widower, and his daughter, her cousin Harriet; to the Cornwall cousins in Gloucestershire and to the Gooch cousins in East Anglia. Her cousin Katie Gooch was a youthful companion with whom she was to stay on terms of affectionate friendship for the rest of her life.

However the younger generation of Prescotts had by now discovered Switzerland, a country which they came to love almost as much as their own, and they took Emmie with them on expeditions to the mountains. Wherever she went her Grandfather Prescott's letters of encouragement, or of restraint, followed her, and when she decided that she would like to do something useful with her life and enrolled at the Evelina in order to train as a childrens' hospital nurse, he begged her to re-consider.

At different times I have been told that she and J.L.T. met 'at Wellington' or 'at the Tindal's'. The latter is more likely, for J.L.T. frequently visited his Fir Grove cousins from London and, as Jay said, he often saw her in the company of his young cousin, Anne Grant Tindal. But he proposed to her at Wellington, at a small dinner party given by one of the Housemaster's.

They were married in 1882.

For the early years of their married life their home was in London, at 18, Neverne Road and it was at that address that their four eldest children were born. Emmie was not as strong as she looked – or perhaps she was too brave to consider her own feelings overmuch; whatever the cause she lost several of her babies and carried only one of them, her second son, to full term.

Her first-born, Olivera, usually called Vera or V., was only a seven month's baby when she was born on the 4th February, 1883 and on 8th November of the same year Emmie produced twin boys. Her Mother, now always known as Grannie Gardner or Grannie, had moved in with them for this, the second, confinement. The boys were born in a caul and it was said that it was Grannie Gardner's prompt action which ensured that there was one survivor, the other being stillborn. The baby was baptized James Lindsay, for his father and Grandfather. Among his family he was often called Jem but to everyone else he was, for the rest of his life, Jim Travers.

Grannie Gardner was a born nurse and J.L.T., who both liked and admired his mother-in-law, persuaded her to sell Gothick Cottage and to move in with them permanently. She was to remain in her daughter's household for the next twenty-five years. Jessie (Jay) was born in April 1886 and Herbert (Herbie or H.O. or H.) in April, 1891 – such a cold late spring in 1891, the baby very late and the rest of the family, with the children's Nurse, already removed to a much larger house which J.L.T. had built for them all on the North Downs, above Warlingham in Surrey.

Aunt Maria Lindsay Dixon, agreeing to be Godmother to Herbert – 'your boy No 2' – wrote to Emmie from Reid's Hotel in Madeira on April 28th 1891:

'... I hear from Madre that your boy No 2 is such a fine child and that you are doing well. I am so very glad. I have a litttle Madeira frock for the little fellow – a ruler for Jem and two very ordinary costume dolls for Vera and Jessie. I hope to be in London about Whit Monday! ... it is good that I shall see you all before you move to the new home. You will enjoy the garden and the country and the Downs.... The scenery here is lovely and flowers a constant delight ... Funchal is thinning out now ... this Hotel is nearly empty ... best love dear from the old Auntie, M. Lindsay Dixon.'

The family, when at last they were all settled in at 'Woottonga', did 'enjoy the garden and the country and the Downs'. J.L.T. and Emmie both did much to make a wonderfully happy home; among the delights of Woottonga which the children were to remember all their lives was a humpy which J.L.T. had built for them in the garden, for it was haven, sanctuary, fortress or playhouse according to whim or the plan of the day; and the maze of secret little tracks which the children had made themselves all over their thirty acres and which they called their 'dog-paths'.

The house itself was solidly built, typical of the period, and with such an abundance of white paint, so many gables, dormers and garden doors, and such a solid, roomy coach house and stables as to keep a full-time painter and handyman, a coachman, John – 'I was born in the Cotswolds, Miss Jessie, where the Thames rises,' – two gardeners and a boy, fully occupied throughout the year. Their German governess, 'dear Fraulie', stayed with them for many years and their Nurse, 'Nanny', until they were grown.

Their youngest daughter, Alice Borgstrom, was born at Woottonga in September 1893 and their youngest son, Charles Tindal, was born there in July, 1898.

It is probable that the only two people for which Woottonga was not in every respect perfect were J.L.T. and his eldest daughter, V. For V loved London and the social whirl which a London child, fond of dancing classes and parties, could enjoy; her pallor had been one of the main reasons for the move to the country but she was still pale and was to remain pale all her life; and she missed London.

J.L.T. had shouldered a burden which had perhaps seemed easy when he had first lifted it but which was to become increasingly heavy with the years: the committment to catching, six days a week and for the rest of his working life, the morning train from Warlingham to Cannon Street. He had, after all, been an Australian stockrider until he was twenty-seven years old.

Occasionally, (Jay told me) – he would fume against the smallness of England and the English landscape, the small enclosures, the narrow parcels of land, the little hedges – and at those times of exasperation he would go out into the garden and crack his great stockwhip until it sounded to the echo, like a rifle-shot, along the North Downs. He had not felt cramped in London for there, always, was London River: London River, which led to every quarter of the globe.

In his children's schoolroom there was a map of Australia which covered one wall and he would point out to them places which he remembered and trace for them the long miles he had travelled: 'We knew the map of Australia,' Jay told me, 'better than the map of England'.

Herbert Prescott Gardner, H. P. Gardner, Emmie's brother, was an energetic sort of fellow who did not believe that life should ever be allowed to become dull. He constantly sought means of enlivening the lot of those around him and with his quips, doggerel verses and practical jokes afforded himself in the process plenty of amusement along the way.

He was athletic and excelled at both swimming and gymnastics, winning a number of medals for his skill in these two pastimes. After leaving Wellington he tried a variety of openings. His Prescott uncles did not take him into their Bank – but then, perhaps he had no wish to go. His uncle Charles A. Prescott wrote from 62, Threadneedle Street on 18th November, 1872 to H.P.G.'s Mother: '... It might be possible for Herbert (H.P.G.) to get a clerkship with some under-writers at Lloyds but it would not be easy – he ought to get some business experience first, either at an Insurance Company as clerk or in some Merchant's house, he might then join some underwriters as clerk (not as clerk to Lloyds which I should not recommend,) with an eventual prospect of a partnership and there is a fair sort of pros-pect in this ... but (he) must make up his mind to a life in London and not to overmuch holiday for some time ... of course it would not do for (him) to leave school this year unless he has got something to do....'

In the event the Stillwell's, (cousins of the Travers'), took him on at their Mincing Lane Tea Importing Office, from which office he wrote hilarious letters to Emmie, the letters adorned and decorated by him with inky pictures of a trumpeter in a pointed hat and with pointed, out-turning feet, mincing coquettishly along ... In June, 1881, he engaged with Charles Tindal as Secretary and Sub-Manager to the Australian Meat Company at their London Office, on a quarterly salary, the hours being 9–6 on weekdays and 9–2 on Saturdays ... later, again, we find him with an office job in the Liverpool Office of Joseph Travers & Sons.

He met, in Liverpool, a very jolly doctor's family and became engaged to their daughter, Adelaide, but when he asked her to wait for him while he went out to Australia to make his fortune in the goldfields, she broke off the engagement. He did not attempt any gold prospecting when he reached Australia but took instead a job with Charles Tindal at the Meat Packing Factory at Ramornie, on the Clarence. (The A.M.C. was the originator of canned beef shipments to England. They were later taken over by Liebig).

After a spell on the Clarence H. P. Gardner returned to England and went to J.L.T. for some capital to start again for Australia on his own account and J.L.T., who was naturally sympathetic to anyone with enough gumption to 'go out', gladly advanced him his first capital. H. P. Gardner was too sensible to attempt any fortune-hunting in the goldfields. He took, instead, a much more sound course of action by buying land in Queensland. He chose well. It was good land and he began to farm there, working those hours that few besides farmers know. Later on he took in a working partner but the arrangement proved unsatisfactory and was dissolved after some years.

After his initial labour in building a dwelling house at Dingyarra, near Cressbrook and in breaking the ground there to plant a farm, H. P. Gardner returned to England every two or three years to visit his Mother and other members of his family and, it may be said, to obtain a fresh infusion of capital from his brother-in-law. He was never able to repay more than a fraction of the interest – and none of the capital – to his backer and in 1897 J.L.T. wrote off all loans. He subsequently made gifts of money to H. P. Gardner including meeting all medical and nursing home expenses in about 1911 or so when H.P.G., who had by then married, brought his wife to England and she became very seriously ill on the way.

The two men remained on the best of terms throughout their lives. Apart from the fact that H. P. Gardner was by all accounts a most likeable, good-humoured man, J.L.T.'s devotion to Emmie would have been the mainspring of his generosity, for his loyalty to Emmie certainly extended to the brother of whom she was so fond.

Jim, the survivor of 7-month twins, had been dogged by ill-health throughout his infancy and childhood. At the age of eight he had gone down with one of the killer-diseases of the day, scarlet-fever, to which he would probably have succumbed had it not been for his superb Grandmother; she had barrier-nursed him in his room, and that in a house full of other children, and nobody else in the house caught the infection. The two were closeted for weeks while Jim went through his fevers and deliriums . . . 'we didn't see either of them for so long,' Jay told me, 'it was as though they had both moved away. . . .'

Grannie Gardner was not only an able nurse she was an entertaining companion, with tales and adventures to describe such as might interest an imaginative boy and take his mind out of the sickroom.

She told him of how, returning to London with her parents in their coach when she had been a girl not yet grown, they had been held up by armed highwaymen as they had crossed Hounslow Heath. She described how the leader of the highwaymen's gang, on meeting Frederick Prescott's quizzical gaze by the light of the lantern held high, – had backed away, apologizing for 'disturbing the quality', and had put up his weapons and let the family continue their journey unmolested.

She told him, too, about Sir George Cayley, – not a cousin but some sort of connexion by marriage – and of his experiments with flying machines and gliding boats. All this and much more she told Jim but never, never of the Mutiny. At length he recovered from his illness and was strong enough to get up and to come downstairs. I have seen a photograph, taken in convalescence, of Jim's wan little face, framed as it was with a straggle of fair curls: he looked deathly weak.

There was usually in those days a legacy to scarlet-fever: some children went bald, some went blind. Jim's legacy was a stammer. As a result of this he was not sent to preparatory school but studied at home; thus he was also able, in his spare time from lessons, to learn much practical skill in the Woottonga workshop.

As a young man J.L.T. had learnt carpentry at Ramornie; he was a stickler for the most suitable wood for any particular purpose and for the correct joining of that wood: never use a nail when you can use a screw, never a screw when you can use glue, was the watchword. The hours in the Woottonga workshop were hours which Jim thoroughly enjoyed and made use of and he learnt from his father, and from the Woottonga carpenter, much that was sound.

As soon as Jim was old enough he was sent to Wellington College, Berkshire. J.L.T. had enormous respect for the formal education which he had not experienced himself. Sadly, Jim's stammer proved such a handicap that it was decided to remove him from school. Wellington had liked him and if his stammer could be cured within a year or two they would take him back. After leaving Wellington various doctors, tutors and small private schools tried to help. The stammer seemed to go away and then, at the least excitement, returned to stifle him just when he had a bright idea or some constructive contribution to make.

He was happy enough at The Tower, Dovercourt, Essex, where he was for a term or so in 1897; his letters home from that address, although a schoolboy's letters with half his mind at home and half at school, already show his interest in the sea, in drawing, in windmills and in wind-power: '. . . I have thought of a lovely plan for the windmill. If you want to put the windmill out of gear you put the tail round square and then the turntable will turn round and the sails won't catch the wind. I have a horrid pen to write with I think the rails of the WD railway better be taken up. Your loving son Jem Travers.'

The WD was the 'Warlingham District' and was a miniature railway which ran in the garden at Woottonga. And later: '. . . I hope you are all well at home including the animals. Phisiology is very interesting. That 7s 6d. will be better at home as I will only spend it here. . . . Have you done anything to the windmill or begun the schooner yet. I am getting on all right here and I am very happy. Please ask if I can have my paintbox here. I have drawn a picture of the schooner on her beam ends. There is a book in the school library called Practical Seamanship. It is very interesting as it explains names for different parts of the ship and shows diagrams of different knots and splices and rocks and lots of other things. To-morrow we will have half-term examinations . . .'

I have been told that he went out to Australia, a brief trip only, when he was fifteen, mainly for the therapeutic effects of the long sea voyage. If that was so, he probably went out with his uncle Geoffrey and stayed with him in Melbourne before coming home again in the care of one of the numerous Travers or Tindal relatives who seemed to make the journey so frequently in the latter part of the last century. I have found no reference to the voyage in any of the mass of Australian letters. He was certainly in England, and having another shot at Wellington, in 1898. H. P. Gardner wrote to Emmie on 29th April, 1898, from Queensland: '. . . What a business all the measles at Wellington seems to have been. I hope Jim got past it this time . . .' But on the 9th June, 1898, Mr Davenport wrote to J.L.T. from Wellington College: 'I must apologize for not having answered your letter before in reference to Jim Travers, but I thought it well to let him have a little longer trial before writing my opinion about his improvement in speaking . . . he is not in my form but is under me as Tutor and I have many opportunities of observing him. At first I thought him much improved – but I am sorry to say I fear he has gone back again and at times he is quite as bad as ever he was trying to get his words out. I have given your hints to his Form Master – who I am sure is very patient with Travers, but he finds great difficulty in getting any answers from him. This stammering is of course a serious drawback to the boy and we shall be very glad to assist you so far as we can, in helping him to get over it.'

Emmie's cousin Sir George Prescott wrote to her on January 23rd, 1899: '. . . I am glad to hear that Jim is better . . .' But Jim was not better and when, at the turn of the year and the turn of the century, H. P. Gardner – after another sortie to Woottonga – was preparing to go home again, he took Jim back to Queensland with him.

It was – and everyone knew it at the time – a last throw for Jim. If Jim was ever to join Joseph Travers & Sons, as surely he would one day, he must – said J.L.T. – first of all grow more strong. What finer way to grow strong than by the space and sense of freedom of Australian life: let the Australian sun warm him through and through, let him ride all day and sleep under the stars of the Southern Cross; let him forget all about sick-rooms and pills and potions; above all, let him rid himself once and for all of his incapacitating stammer. A few years in Australia would surely do the trick. Surely.

The bread which J.L.T. had cast upon the waters of his brother-in-law's farming ambitions was to be returned an hundredfold by the care, kindness and companionship which H. P. Gardner was to show his young nephew over the course of the following two years.

As uncle and nephew made their way, by train and boat, across to the other side of the world, the letters describing their lives began to arrive at Woottonga: such a small stream of letters home from Jim, such long reports from H. P. Gardner – his letters all part of the flood-tide which he was to send to England throughout the greater part of his adult life: letters which dealt with the world political scene, with the local political scene, with births, deaths and marriages, with the price of wheat, milk, cattle and horses; about his crops – grapes, peaches, figs, melons, barley, lucerne; about his silky oaks and liquorice and honey-bees; about the Church built at Cressbrook; about the movement of shipping around the Australian coast and world-wide; about the new railway that was coming; about dams and rivers; about wars and rumours of wars; and always with a continuing interest in

Jim, Charles and Herbert Travers, circa November 1899. Studio portrait

his numerous family in England; and all these letters, millions and millions of words, in a steep, difficult hand that must have become more and more exhausting to him as he continued his labour of love at the end of the hot, hard-working days and all down the long, homesick years.

Jim's few letters home, the first of which was written soon after they had crossed the Channel, were always short. On 'the last day of the Century' he wrote to his sisters from Naples: 'My dear girls, We are sending you some stamps and postcards ... it is awfully fine here, there are lots of boats all round the ship with people selling cameos, mandolines, photographs, walking sticks, flowers and fruit, besides guides without number, each with half a dozen pamphlets. I have taken several photographs of different things in the town....'

H. P. Gardner to Grannie Gardner:

Canadian Australian Steamship Line, R.M.S. *Arangi,* off the Clarence River 7th Feby 1900: I am sending a line by this boat and wonder whether Jim's letter from Sydney or this from Brisbane will reach you first ... we were three days there and Jim and I explored the town. He thinks Sydney a fine place, lots of electric trains, and steamers. We went up the harbour to Parramatta and another day to Bondi on the coast and again to see the Bushmen's contingent and their horses....

H. P. Gardner from Dingyarra, February 1900: ... Jim has been promoted to a grey mare with more life in her than '*Eagle*' and he highly approves of the change but he does not like holding her in and likes to feel himself going through the air ...

The Butler's had a nearby station at Kilcoy. The Kilcoy Butler's were members of the same family into which Aunt Louie Travers had married. H. P. Gardner from Kilcoy, 2nd March, 1900: 'Jim is making himself quite at home here and has been out for two rides to-day, with Chris Butler, the same age as Jessie.... One of the men here caught a 20 lb cod and we had part of it for tea. It was very good. Great news to-day about the relief of Ladysmith ...'

H. P. Gardner to V.: '... Jim is still at Kilcoy ... and I can't get him back again. He has been out mustering and having lots of fun. I expect picnics and I daresay some shooting. I am going over to fetch him on Saturday. Chris Butler has taken him in hand in riding and Rosie Butler in photography but he has not written to me about his goings on. It is horribly dry about here now and we have to scoop away the sand in the creek to get water, but our Bullocks will be taken away shortly and so we shall be lighter stocked. I have been round the country buying milkers and have bought 75 and have heard of 30 more so if I can get a New South Wales family up to do the milking we shall be able to start with nearly 200 milkers ... we saved some nice hay to-day. The second cutting of lucerne since I have been back ...'

Jim to his Mother, April 20th, 1900: '... I am staying at Kilcoy because it is Frank Butler's Easter holidays, he goes to school in Brisbane. I am trying shooting at ducks, there are a lot here in the swamps. In the evenings we go out after possums if there is a good moon ... there is a splendid bathing hole in Kilcoy Creek ... we have been playing Vingt-Un this evening ... On Monday we went up to Staghurst, in the mountains, and met the M'Connels....'

H. P. Gardner to Emmie, 3rd May, 1900: '... Jim is very well and is finding his bags too short for him, I must get them let down a bit. I have pretty nearly got over my tumble and was riding about yesterday and to-day ... I am getting the place a bit ship-shape now. Weeds cut down ... 4th May: Jim has gone ... to get some horses and I must finish this now as the Cressbrook carpenter is just finishing boarding the milk scalding house and will take the mail in for me.... Things are getting autumnal now and it is dark by 5.30 and leaves are falling off the peach and mulberry trees, but the weather is delightful. I must go to the pig yard where about 7 or 8 families of young pigs arrived yesterday and the Mothers have to be sorted as they have a playful way of eating any that don't belong to them. Ever Yr affectionate brother, H. P. Gardner. Many happy returns of the 23rd.'

H. P. Gardner to his Mother, 10th May, 1900: '... Jim has been out with us the last two days getting logs and poles for our extended cowshed. We had to go some distance off so took our lunch and boiled the billy. He has ridden most of our horses now so as to give his especial one a spell and is at present giving vivid pictorial scenes of bush life from memory for the edification of Woottonga!'

H. P. Gardner to V., 24th May, 1900: '... Jim is busy writing home so I suppose he will tell you all the news. He has been printing some of his photos and some have come out very well ... (he) is off with Dorothea M'Connel to-morrow to meet the Butlers in the mountains at Staghurst. Did he tell you about his killing a dead snake the other day. We were riding along and I saw a black snake which I knew Peile had killed the day before and called out to him. He tumbled off his horse and seized a huge stick and advanced very cautiously until right on top of the dangerous reptile and raised his weapon to give it a mighty blow but then observed it was covered with ants. . . . He is growing very fast and seems much stronger than he was and is very well. He is fond of riding and likes to go at a hard gallop whenever he gets the chance, but he has never given his horse a sore back and only had one tumble at Kilcoy. Although he was run away with twice by one of our horses. . . .'

H. P. Gardner to Jessie, 7th June 1900: 'Jim is struggling with his mail letter as the days are so much alike one another he finds it hard to make up any news. He has been firing away with his rifle and has just got up his second 200 cartridges . . . After great persuasion he induced the housekeeper to wake him up at six o'clock this morning and went out and got in the milking cows and the horses before breakfast, but to-morrow he is going to ride with Dorothea M'Connel to Mt Brisbane so I am afraid he will not continue his good deeds . . . Last Saturday the Commissioners enquiring into the railway came through Cressbrook and I went in to give evidence. . . . Our new housekeeper makes lots of butter as we keep Sunday evening's milk and set it. On the other days we send twice a day to the factory. Jim has been intending to write to Grannie for several mails. . . . We are wondering whether Roberts will cable old Kruger. There was great excitement over the relief of Mafeking. . . . I am sorry to hear of the goings-on when the Fir Grove cousins were at Woottonga! . . . I have not got Jim any spurs yet for fear he would go to bed in them and tear the sheets. He was making honey toffey yesterday and I got some in my mouth and could not open it for about half an hour. . . . Give my love to all. I will have a horse ready for you to ride when you come out.'

H. P. Gardner to Emmie, 19th July 1900: 'Thank you for various letters. I hope you have found a suitable cook in course of time . . . Jim has been talking about gilding and has been to see the carpenter about it. We are having very cold nights here now, about 26 in the verandah at 7 a.m. I saw some ice that had been thrown off a dish lying in the grass at about 11 o'clock yesterday . . . The holidays are over and Jim is back here again and working at a sieve for the corn mill and a heliograph signal to start and stop the engine. He was driving the engine nearly all day to-day which is a job he likes. He has quite got over his cold but these very cold mornings I do not call him until the sun is well up.... What terrible news from Pekin. There was a capital letter from Dr Morrison in the last *Times* I got.... I must finish this to-morrow at dinner-time as I am sleepy.' And on 20th July: 'Jim has been down at the creek all the morning making the water run through the pigs' drinking place instead of outside as it would much prefer.... The place looks very nice and green now as there are about forty acres of barley coming right up to the garden fence....'

Jim to Emmie on July 26th: '... Dad told me in his letter that I must write longer letters. I hope this one will be longer than the others.... The little dog Spot the fox terrier has been eating eggs lately. We found him trying to drive a hen off its nest to get the egg which the hen had just laid, so he has been chained up and he is very sad about it ...' (this was the only slight hint in any of Jim's letters of nostalgia for home. He had been devoted to all the family dogs and especially so to his own rough-coated terrier, Brush).

From the same letter to his Mother: '... We've had rather a trouble with the stove pipe, it got choked with wood tar from the soot. We had to make a fresh angle at the top of the pipe, yesterday we had to go and kill a dying horse in Labour's paddock....'

So, by the regular Mail Steamers, the letters from Australia came home: H. P. Gardner's lengthy epistles, Jim's brief notes.

Although he was based with his Uncle at Dingyarra, Jim made long stays with the Butler's (connexions) at Kilcoy; with the Tindal's at Ramornie; with the Livingstone-Learmonth's at Groongal. (Although Groongal was mainly a sheep-station, Somerset Livingstone-Learmonth also bred a lot of good horses there. 'I saw Some Learmonth in Brisbane' – H. P. Gardner wrote home, 'he has just sold some horses to go racing in Batavia.') – With his Uncle Geoffrey and Aunt Ida and their two boys, Lindsay and Geoffrey, 'Barley and Fuzz' in Melbourne; then South again to more Travers cousins in Tasmania; back again some months later to Groongal, to Somerset and Janet Livingstone-Learmonth. Janet was the daughter of J.L.T.'s favourite cousin, Laurie Travers, and a grand-daughter of Samuel Smith Travers, who had settled in Australia in the first half of the 19th Century.

Jim remained in Queensland, however, for the greater part of 1900. On 16th August of that year H. P. Gardner wrote to Grannie Gardner: '... Jim and I were in Brisbane last week at the Show which he said was awfully fine. He was poking about among the machinery all day and we went to the theatre at night and saw Trilby, A Royal Divorce and a Circus. I bought an Ayrshire bull there and am going to Esk to-morrow to get him from the train. . . .'

On 23rd August Jim wrote home from Dingyarra: '. . . We killed a bullock this evening and skinned him. We will cut him up and salt him to-morrow. Uncle Herbert got a lawn mower at the Exhibition and I have been mowing the lawn and trimming up the beds and paths around the house. We worked the engine on Tuesday to cut chaff and ground corn in the new mill. On Monday I finished packing the engine which I started last week. I went out for a ride with George the boy at the factory. We saw a lot of kangaroos on Sunday. . . . It will be very much changed at home when I come back with all those new houses built. It is beginning to get warm again now.'

H. P. Gardner to his Mother, 21st November 1900: '. . . Jim has been at the milk factory since Tuesday making tins and boxes and investigating all the machinery, separator, vacuum pan and helping put in the new Boiler so he is quite the engineer now and gets his moleskins very black. He wants to stop here over the Christmas holidays when the Butlers and M'Connels are up. He has just asked me to look at his bedroom window which is festooned with huge sprays of liquorice in flower. . . . When they measured him at the factory in his boots he was $5'9\frac{1}{2}''$ but I have just put him up against the verandah wall without boots: it is $5'8\frac{1}{4}''$. . . . What a nice lot of fruit there seems to be this year at Woottonga. We are anxiously looking at our figs and grapes but the melons will be very late I am afraid. I hope Alice's puppy got over it's chill and arrived safely. . . . I think Jim would like to take his mare away with him. He is never done singing her praises. Of course I always run her down for the fun . . . love to all and Happy New Year. It seems a long time since last Xmas Day.'

Jim to his parents, November 29th, 1900: '. . . Uncle Herbert seems to think I had better go down to Uncle Geoff by steamer, about the end of January. I have written to him telling him this and saying I will write later, if it will suit him, about the steamer, etc., etc. Some photographic materials which I ordered last week came on Tuesday costing 13/1d
i.e. 2 films 7/–
  2 sheets of Invicta 1/9
  2 tubes of chloride of gold 3/4

I think I can do better with Invicta paper than Bromide as the latter is very wasteful until you are practised in using it. There are tons of Peaches here and the figs (will) soon be ripe. It is very dry and we are wanting rain very badly. We are getting along with the new bails. I don't think there is any more news . . .'

H. P. Gardner to his Mother, 9th December, 1900: '. . . Jim is at Kilcoy, he went for a day and they kept him saying I must go over and fetch him . . . I should like to have George Litton's account of China first hand. What a graphic account that was of Dr Morrison's of the siege of Pekin.

The cyclamens are coming along splendidly and will be the envy of everybody directly. It was good of Alice to write to me and tell me about the Puppy. I hope he is middling obedient. Puppies are no fun if they are quite obedient. . . .' and again on 30th November 1900: 'Jim is just off to Cressbrook and then he may perhaps go to Kilcoy to pilot Rosie Butler back to Cressbrook . . .'

And again on 20th December 1900: '. . . our railway has just passed the lower house and now has to get through the upper house, but I don't know where the funds for making it will come from . . .' and from Esk on 28th December 1900: '. . . The Govt. have voted £5000 – to make a start on our Railway. . . .'

Jim had been ploughing during December with twelve horses to a new disc plough – hot, hard work. But now, in the New Year, the fun started again.

H. P. Gardner to his Mother on 4th January 1901: '. . . Jim has been at Cressbrook for a week and they have been riding and picknicking all about. They come in here to-morrow evening and go back by moonlight. It is still very hot and dry. We have no water across the road and have to bring the cattle over to drink in holes scooped out of the creek bed and our milk has gone down. . . . I am wiring down to Geoff to know whether he can take Jim if he leaves about the 18th. Jim says he is going to come back later on. I shall be very glad if he does . . .'

H. P. Gardner to his Mother on 11th January 1901: '. . . Jim is out with David (Butler) cleaning the engine. They went down to the Lagoon for a bathe yesterday afternoon and took the gun to try and get some ducks. Jim confessed they were talking so much they stumbled on the ducks unawares and they flew off. . . . It is getting dryer than ever.

Rain threatens every day but never falls or starts and stops. We have to take feed for our horses to Esk when they go down as there is no grass there and then pump water into a trough to give them a drink which takes some time as they drink faster than one can pump.... I think Jim will probably leave Brisbane on the 18th or 19th for Melbourne and I will wire Geoff when he starts and what boat. I shall be very sorry to lose him he is such a general favourite. I hope he will come back later on....'

Jim wrote home by the same mail, 11th January 1901:

'David Butler is staying here, he came yesterday and will probably stay until Monday when I will go back with him and say good-bye to the Butlers at Kilcoy before I go South. On Monday Uncle Herbert and myself and all the Cressbrook folk went for a picnic halfway between here and Colinton to meet the Colinton people. We had great fun and came home by moonlight. I am not stammering at all; and I think I shall be rid of it altogether by the time I get home.'

After visiting Uncle Geoffrey and Aunt Ida he went on down to Tasmania and wrote to his father from Sandy Bay, Hobart, an undated letter: '... I am sorry I did not write last mail. It is awfully jolly here, we are out in the boat almost every day. Cousin Beatrice is awfully kind and all the cousins are very nice. Margaret and Bertie have an awfully good stamp collection. I have been making a model yacht for the boy, about the same size as the one at home. We went up Mt. Wellington last Tuesday. It is higher than Snowdon and very rough climbing, all rocks. Yesterday and the day before I went out fishing with the Butlers cousins, all day, almost all whiting, some flathead and perch.... I had a letter from Uncle Herbert saying Cousin Paul Bush was in command of the *St. George* and couldn't I get him to take me up to Queensland with him. But I should think it would be better if I went only to Sydney and then to Cousin Somes and Ramornie and then home as Uncle Geoff says it's too hot for me in Queensland in summer ...'

After Tasmania he was back with Uncle Geoffrey and waiting to make another visit to Groongal: 'I will be going to Cousin Somes when my cold is better ... Uncle Geoff says I can't go to Cousin Somes until I'm a bit better. I wrote to Cousin Paul Bush on the *St George* (H.M.S. *St George*) and he wrote back and said he could only see me at 12 o'clock to-day, (I only got his letter at 11 o'clock.) I telegraphed back and said his letter had arrived too late. He goes out into the harbour to-morrow and goes away to Brisbane on the day after. You seem to contradict yourselves almost every mail. You said that I had better not get home in the cold weather, one mail, while last mail you said you expected me home in November. As far as I can see I shall be coming home at the end of August, but I can't say how long either Cousin Some or Cousin Charlie want me to stay with them. . . . We have had a great week of festivities here. We saw all the processions and went over the foreign warships in the bay. . . .'

Up at Dingyarra, H. P. Gardner was still struggling with the difficulties of local transport. On 16th May 1901 he wrote to his Mother: 'We have sent an engine over to Tim Coleman to fill his ensilage silo and I thought I would try to take it over the creek and they were going all right but the river stopped the horses while the hind wheels were still in the creek and we could not move it with thirteen horses as the trace chains began breaking, however a friendly team of 18 Bullocks going along the road came to our assistance and pulled it out. I shall stick to the old road over the bridge next time . . .'

By the end of May Jim was back with the Livingstone-Learmonths at Groongal.

J. Livingstone-Learmonth to Emmie, June 3rd 1901: 'My dear Emmie, I thought you might like a line to hear how Jim is. He has been here about a week now, and really looks better, and fatter. I never saw such a keen boy, and is exactly like Lindsay (J.L.T.) on horseback. He takes to the life like a duck to water. His stuttering is nothing like as bad as I had thought it was, and when he is interested or excited over anything he is as right as ninepence, and the same as anyone else. . . . He is awfully good to the children, too, and they admire him immensely.

'I think it won't be very long before we shall make a start home, in another 6 weeks or so. Som isn't happy here now and though I shall feel leaving very much, it is the only thing to be done, under the circumstances. . . .'

Jim appreciated the orderly way Groongal was managed. He wrote to his father on 16th June, 1901: '. . . I am having a fine time here, generally get up at half past six in the morning and go out riding with the manager, Mr Kayle. They have got windmills all over the run to water the sheep with. On Monday Mr Kayle and a gentleman called

Mr Mathews and myself went out to a new one they have just put up, it is called an Aer motor all made of iron. I went up the windmill 35 ft high and down the well 60 ft deep, they have two tanks each holding 10,000 gallons. The one windmill waters four paddocks. On Tuesday we went out and saw the wool shed on the way out to see some ewes, they have got sheep shearing machines there. I am practising on my banjo and Mr Walker, a gent who was staying here, taught me a new breakdown which I am trying to master. I think if I could read music I could learn much faster. . . .'

After Groongal he spent some more happy weeks at Ramornie and wrote from there on 12th July, 1901: '. . . I have just been here a little under a week, I came here last Saturday. I came up from Sydney to Grafton in the steamer '*City of Grafton*'. It was fairly rough and I was rather sick. . . . I have been out rowing on the river – yesterday and to-day and I made a pump to bale out the boat with, out of an old piece of zinc gutter-piping – it works very well. I have settled to go up to Uncle Herbert's for a week or two and then go home by British India from Brisbane. I will go from here to Brisbane by boat – leave my heavy luggage there and go up to Uncle Herbert's for a fortnight. . . . P.S. I shan't go up to Uncle H.'s for three weeks or so yet.'

And a second typewritten letter from Ramornie, on 19th July, 1901: 'I am learning to write on Cousin Charlie's typewriter and I have been copying out letters for him. I have been out riding with the stockmen several times this week; on Monday we went out and took some Bullocks out of the River paddock and put them into O M C and took some out of O M C and put them into a paddock called Middle Thompson's, then we went into the home run after some horses which we didn't find. On Wednesday Cousin Charlie, a stockman and myself went out and marked up the line for a new fence through the home run. . . . I have been out rowing on the river this morning, I rowed over the first falls to the foot of the second falls up the river . . . Uncle Herbert has written to Cousin Charlie suggesting that I should go home by the White Star Line, but whether he means the Aberdeen or the Suevic Pisic launch I don't know. He also said that he had £100 – of mine so I am all right in the money line. I think I shall stick to the former idea of going by the British India, if there is a boat to suit; Cousin Charlie has written to them to ask particulars etc . . .'

*   *   *

Jim to his father from Ramornie, July 27th, 1901: 'Yesterday we went out mustering in the home run. There was a fellow here who says he knew you very well; he says he remembers you riding a horse called Turvill, and you had a quart pot tied on in front of the saddle and every time the horse bucked it scraped your wrist. He said that you had a mare called Saucy Sally. One of Morrow's sons got ill suddenly the week before last but he improved sufficiently for them to take him down to Grafton. They took him down in a boat. I have been trying to make a small windmill. The other day I rowed a good long way up the river over the first, second and third falls. To-day we went out, Cousin Charlie and myself, a little way down the river and Cousin Charlie took some photos. Cousin Charlie is going to take me to Yougalbar next Saturday. I wrote a detective story on the typewriter the other day. I can't think of anything else to say.'

In the event Jim was never to visit Yougalbar, that strange and extravagant cast-iron mansion, (which belonged to some cousins of the Tindals, not of the Travers') – for a tiresome duty, to give evidence at the trial of a thief, a former servant in the bachelor-quarters at Groongal – obliged him to alter his plans. 'I can't get out of it, though,' he wrote, 'it is rather upsetting to my plans, and perhaps, I shall not be able to get home as early as I had wished, I shall be home by the end of September I think. I shall have to start to-morrow and just miss going to Gordon-Brook and Yougalbar with Cousin Charlie. I am practising Shorthand and the Banjo and I go out almost every day with the men riding about after cattle. Yesterday I rode over to the Works with a letter and the manager showed me over the Bone Mill and the Extract Room – they were very interesting. It seems such a shame to see it all lying idle. I don't think there is any more news to tell. I have been making Bullets this morning out of old tea-lead.'

Up at Dingyarra, the coming of the Railway was still H. P. Gardner's main pre-occupation: 'We had our Minister for Railways round last Friday going over the route of the Railway,' he wrote home, 'they have £10,000 – down on the estimate for starting it so I hope it will begin. I was pumping water to fill our tank over the road at the time and he professed himself much interested. I wish Jim had been there....'

*   *   *

Jim, having returned to Groongal out of duty now found himself reluctant to leave. To his father from Groongal, 1st September, 1901: 'I have decided not to go to Gyppsland for several reasons, first I don't think it's worth it, second I had rather stay here, third it will save pounds.

'They have started shearing here and I've been up to the shed almost every day. It's very interesting for wool pricing, dumping etc. Yesterday I went over to Wyvern, the next station. Their engine had smashed so they had to send to Sydney for a new one. It came yesterday, there were a whole crowd of shearers and roustabouts to haul it out of the train. They are putting all the telephones on new posts here so I went out with the blacksmith the other day who was doing it.'

Still at the Livingstone-Learmonths, Jim wrote to his parents on 18th September 1901: 'I have had a grand week out rabbiting – one day we caught 109 in one day. We had lovely weather for camping, it was not too cold at nights and not too hot in the day. The river is rising and several steamers have been up and down lately, they take the wool down from Togeramane, the next station over the river. Shearing is getting along, they will be at it about a fortnight longer. We had some splendid rain about three weeks ago, but Cousin Some says that the outlook for the summer is very bad, unless there is some more rain soon. I think of coming by the '*China*' P & O or the '*Oruba*', Orient, I will write to Uncle Herbert and get him to send my money to Uncle Geoff to get my ticket by whichever he thinks best. I have got a little under £90 – so Uncle Herbert says.'

H. P. Gardner to Emmie on 27th September 1901: 'I had a letter on Sunday from Jim saying he wanted Geoff to get his ticket from P & O or Orient and asking me to send his money to Geoff, which I did the same day ...'

So the idyll ended and Jim came home.

Although there had been a growing self-confidence one does not sense, in his letters, any sudden change, any particular moment of inspiration – rather, perhaps, a tendency or trend: much as he loves to ride, he will always forsake his horse to look at an engine; much as he loves the river, he will always come ashore to look at a windmill; much as he enjoyed carpentry, he is now more interested in the use of

James Lindsay Travers I = Anna Wansey   H. C. Gardner = Emma Elizabeth Prescott
(Grannie Gardner 1826–1919)

James Lindsay Travers II 'J.L.T.' born 1846 = Emma Louisa Gardner 'Emmie' born 1857

Gladys Olivera 'V' born 1883

HERBERT GARDNER
TRAVERS
'H.' born 1891

JAMES LINDSAY TRAVERS
III
'Jim' born 1883

Alice Borgstrom 'Alie' born 1893

Jessie 'Jay' born 1886

CHARLES TINDAL TRAVERS
Charles born 1898

metal. Not just the home-made baler-pump made out of old zinc gutter-piping but in the marvellous Aer motor, all made of iron.

Whether he had seen or heard anything of Lawrence Hargraves one cannot now be sure – but it is likely. What is certain is that his interest was in powered flight. There had always been balloons about, said Jay when reminiscing about her brother, and he had never shown much interest in them. The inspiration had taken place in Australia. 'We never knew what it was,' said Jay '– it was something that happened in Australia.'

When he came home again he was two inches taller and transformed in health. What did it matter if his stammer was never completely cured: he was full of ideas, full of energy and could talk of nothing but flying. And the money for his trip, the money invested in Ding-yarra, the money which had launched Dr Geoffrey Travers in Melbourne and, a generation earlier, Samuel Smith Travers in Tasmania, James Lindsay Travers in Sydney and much else besides, all of it had come, in the first instance, from trade into London River.

1

THE ISLE OF SHEPPEY

1902–1912

Jim goes to King's College London – to I.C.E – to Legros & Knowles – to Eastchurch where he builds Shed to house the engine he designs – appointed Assistant Draughtsman to Lt-Col. R.E. Capper at Farnborough – appointed Assistant to Professor Huntington at Eastchurch – takes his Ticket at Hendon – appointed Designer and Assistant to Horace Short to design and build Short Brothers first twin-engine machine, S. 39 – re-designs S. 27 to twin-engine status – instructs Members of Territorial Balloon Company at Eastchurch.

JIM had been very much missed during his two years away, for, in that affectionate family, he was, of them all, perhaps the most beloved. His home-coming was a time-mark for all the family and many incidents were dated by ' . . . when Jim was in Australia' or ' . . . after Jim came home . . .' It was strange that one of his greatest supporters at the start of his career was his father. Strange – because the main idea of despatching Jim to Australia had been to give him health and strength for life in the City of London.

The strong excitement of his inspiration and plans for the future were too powerful to be gainsaid, however, and they overcame all earlier decisions. From the moment that Jim came home from Australia and made his thoughts and wishes known, J.L.T. was the most loyal and admiring of his son's backers – the first to discount the City as a dull treadmill, the first to look forward to the age of flight,

Jim began to build at once and it is sad that none of his early flying machines survived, for they might now be interesting specimens in the museums which are devoted to such exhibits. When the machines would not take off, or took off only to descend to earth a few yards further on, they were dismantled and the parts where suitable re-used to a new design. One of his machines, which Jay remembered, was a multi-plane with bicycle-wheel-assisted take off. Pedalling at a furious rate – the family assembled to watch – he did indeed take off and flew for a good many yards at a low height, bouncing and porpoising along until the structure collapsed. He did not seem to notice his many cuts and bruises but picked up the wreckage, said: '*I know what's wrong*,' and rushed off at once to the Woottonga workshop for yet another re-build.

Eventually, in spite of his inventiveness and capacity for perserverance, he realized that he was not going to achieve anything worthwhile without some serious engineering study. His education had been slight: barely a year, altogether, at Wellington, odd terms here and there of private tuition. He had taken no examinations of national standing. In order to matriculate, therefore, he went to a crammer's, Mr Webb's, and in due course was admitted to the Engineering Faculty of King's College London, as a matriculated student. He entered King's College in the Michaelmas Term of 1902 when he was eighteen years old. (He was nineteen in November of the same year). The Engineering Course was tough and Jim certainly found it to be so. Reading the summary report on him contained in the King's College Register, one is made aware of his considerable struggles. Although in his first term he obtained 'Very Good' in Divinity, Mathematics, Natural Philosophy, Practical Chemistry, Chemistry, Geology, Drawing, Civil Engineering and Workshop & Lab., by the Easter Term of 1903 his Tutors were stating that he 'Must pass the College Matric. before proceeding to the 2nd Year.' After that his reports became more variable, so that while he passed in many subjects, including doing well in Heat Engineering, he often failed in other subjects. He may not have been their most brilliant student – nor their best prepared student – but his application can have been second to none and he struggled on. By all accounts he was very happy and during his hard-working years at King's College he seemed to have found the ideal mix of theory and practice in his studies. In 1903 he was awarded a Certificate of Distinction in Engineering Drawing and in 1904 a Certificate of Merit for the Workshop.

Professor Huntington was Professor of Metallurgy and although Jim did not take Metallurgy he worked in the Metallurgy Laboratory as an option in the Engineering course. He therefore came very much under the Professor's influence. Professor Huntington told J.L.T. that he thought highly of Jim and admired his original – and often visionary – thought. Their mutual regard was no doubt due in part to the fact that they were both air-minded men. Huntington's interest had at first been in ballooning only and he took his Aero Club

Aeronaut's (Balloon) Certificate on July 14th, 1905, becoming only the second in this country to do so, C. F. Pollock having been the first. It is noteworthy that when in due course the Professor was converted to the idea of heavier-than-air flying it was Jim whom he invited to help him with the design of his machine.

Having failed to obtain a Degree from King's College London and wishing to continue his engineering training, Jim left King's after the January Term of 1906 and went to Legros & Knowles Engineering Works in Willesden.

The Legros, both father and his engineer son, were extraordinarily talented men. The father, Alphonse Legros, who was born at Dijon in 1837, worked as a house decorator and scene painter before buying himself out of conscription and coming to England in 1863. He became a naturalized Englishman and married an Englishwoman, a girl from Westmorland. He was a most versatile artist: a painter, sculptor, etcher, medallist and draughtsman – a finished draughtsman in chalk, silver-point etc. His work hung in many galleries and museums and some of his paintings, notably *The Angelus*, was reproduced widely. He was appointed Slade Professor of Art at University College, London, a Chair he held for seventeen years. The son, Lucien Alphonse Legros, was even more widely gifted than his father; he had, moreover, a talent so often found in the French, that of embodying the practical and the beautiful within one work.

L. A. Legros was born in 1865 and was educated wholly in London: at University College School, at University College, London and at the City & Guilds of London Institute. His interest, skill and his enormous talent lay across much of the known spectrum of engineering. From Who's Who in Engineering one may read that he was apprenticed to Hunter & English, General Engineers; was an improver with the London & South Western Railway; a journeyman with Hick, Hargreaves & Co., Assistant Works Manager with the London Portland Cement Co; on the staff of Professor (Sir) Alex. Kennedy, LL. D, F. R. S. for two years; Engineer to the Gas Traction Company, tramway vehicles and construction in England and on the Continent; and Engineer to Wicks Rotary Type Casting Co. Ltd; and all this before it was noted that he was the manufacturer of the Iris Motor Car.

L. A. Legros, in partnership with Mr G. J. F. Knowles as Managing Partner, were the makers of the Iris Motor Car. The firm of Legros

& Knowles described themselves as 'installing plant, designing and manufacturing motor cars, launches, lorries, and other motor-propelled vehicles.' L. A. Legros was later to be decorated by the King, and to be elected to Membership of many learned Societies, both in England and in France. His work and later on, his war-work, particularly in the Munitions Inventions Department, was prodigious.

However there is little doubt that the Iris Motor Car was the work for which he was most popularly known. It was the Iris Car which was to set a standard of engineering which was equalled only, some years later, by A. C. and by Rolls-Royce. Legros' dream was of a perfect engine with perfect transmission of power. Such a motor-car, with every part working to perfection, should run silently. Although the tag 'IT RUNS IN SILENCE' was often used by the car's afficianados the car was in fact named for the goddess 'IRIS'.

(My father, H. G. Travers, who visited the Iris Works on several occasions and who heard much talk of the Works from Jim and from some of the other apprentices, often claimed that 'IT RUNS IN SILENCE' was the more apt derivation, even if not the true one.)

With references from Professor Huntington and from Mr J. W. Jacomb-Hood, – a Warlingham neighbour who was a Member of I. C. E. and who had in that same year of 1906 supported the Election of L. A. Legros to Membership of I. C. E. – Jim joined the other Legros & Knowles apprentices at Willesden.

He lived economically in digs with two or three of the others, but they were seldom at home. When not in the Workshop or, in the evening, out at the theatre or concert hall, they were out 'on a chassis' or 'on a car'. It was the age of the horseless carriage and just as the rider had once been 'on a horse' so he was now 'on a car' and as he was soon to be 'on a flying machine.'

They were always busy. Among the other apprentices were Thorne, John Daman and Sammy Gibbens. Geoffrey de Havilland, whose elder brother, Ivon, had been Designer at the Iris Works shortly before his early death, was also an apprentice there. They were a band of dedicated young engineers and although at that time aero and motor engineers were like-minded and often interchangeable people for three, at least, of the Iris men, Jim, Gibbens and de Havilland, flying was the prime ambition.

*   *   *

November 11, 1905.] THE AUTOMOTOR JOURNAL. 1377

THE 1906 LEGROS AND KNOWLES "IRIS" CARS.—PART I.

Fig. 1.—The new Legros and Knowles "Iris" Chassis. View, from the "off" side, of the 25-30-h.p. Model.

The new Legros and Knowles 'Iris' Chassis

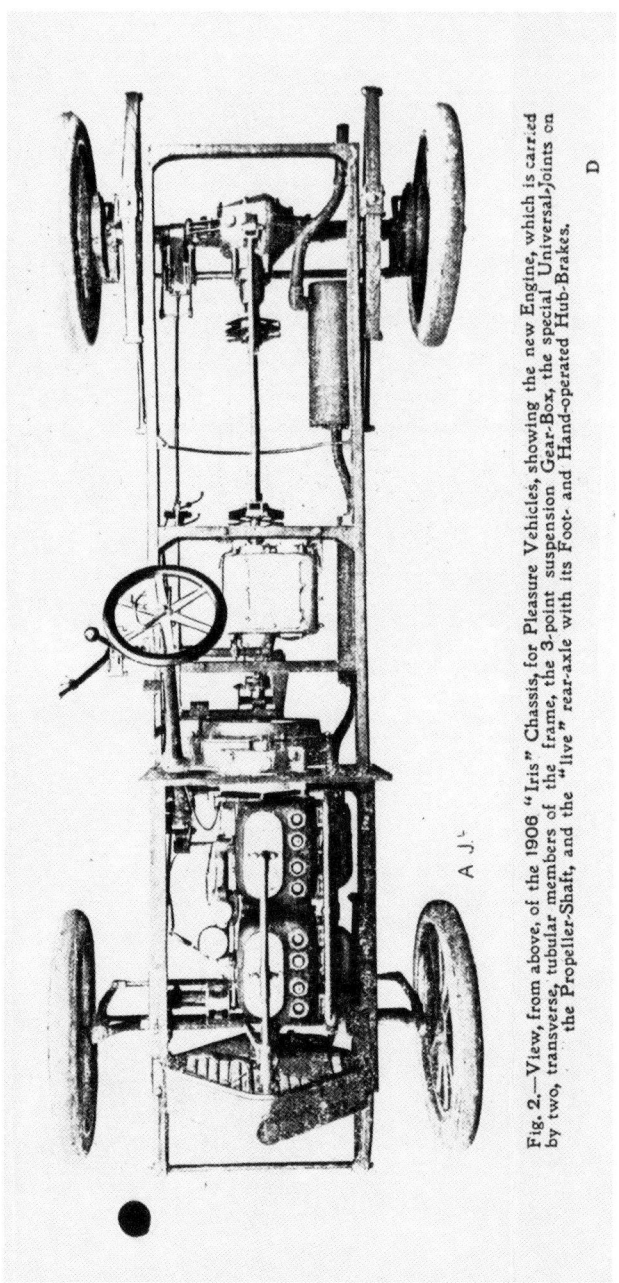

Fig. 2.—View, from above, of the 1906 "Iris" Chassis, for Pleasure Vehicles, showing the new Engine, which is carried by two, transverse, tubular members of the frame, the 3-point suspension Gear-Box, the special Universal Joints on the Propeller-Shaft, and the "live" rear-axle with its Foot- and Hand-operated Hub-Brakes.

A.J.

D

View, from above, of the 1906 'Iris' Chassis

Fig. 3.—The 1906 Legros and Knowles Chassis. View showing the distinctive appearance of the new 25-30-h.p. and 35-40-h.p. Touring Cars—the shape of the Radiator, the position of the Circulating-Pump, and the special construction of the Tubular Front-Axle.

The 1906 Legros and Knowles Chassis

Fig. 4.—Rear View of the new "Iris" Chassis, giving an excellent general idea of the special Live-Axle construction—which enables the Differential-Gear to be removed easily—the full Elliptic Side-Springs, and the double Brake-system for the Driving Wheels.

Rear view of the new 'Iris' Chassis

There was nothing new in 1906 about the idea of flying: it was in how best to achieve it that the excitement, the challenge and the problems lay. At the start of the century the aviators, no matter how innovative they may have been, followed or were inspired by earlier aviators of differing schools. Thus: the balloonists, the parachutists, the rocket-men, the gliding afficianados, the ornithopter-lovers and the kite-men. All schools had their following, the numerous strains of aviation almost as different as were the various types of ships.

Alexander Graham Bell, one of the greatest of all inventors, may perhaps, with his huge multi-plane, have been inspired by the troop-carrying war-canoes of the sky, described by Longfellow in *Hiawatha*, the poem which was written at Wolfville, Nova Scotia and which was first published in 1855. Bell had his summer home at Baddeck, Nova Scotia, and his multi-plane was built in the garden there.

One may, I think, suppose that Jim was inspired by the Hargrave Box-kite and by the Hargrave Rotary Engine of 1897, one of the earliest rotary engines. So that when, in 1906, Santos-Dumont flew in a box-kite of his own design but modelled, as he wrote so charmingly, on Hargrave's idea, it would have been proof to Jim that development was taking place along the right lines.

Now he began to be impatient to leave the Iris Works and start building. Yet it was at the Iris Works that the greatest excellence in English engineering was practised. So he stayed to continue learning, working harder than ever, – seldom in his digs – a young, slight, exhausted-looking little figure, stammering when rushed or excited and hard to find. At the Works. Out on a car. At the theatre. Over to Le Mans. A typical letter, from Jim to his Mother, describes one motor trip of those days: ' ... I ought to have written before ... Gibbens just got his car out for the first time on Saturday night, on Sunday morning we went to Burnham where Gibbens' uncle lives, it is about 35 miles the other side of Bristol. We had lunch there and arrived back here at about 3.30 on Monday morning ... We went into the Works as usual yesterday. The Berlynes had asked me to go to the Hammersmith Theatre with them last night so went although we were both rather tired, it was great fun ... I did not think Gibbens would get his car going on Saturday or I would have let you know; I hoped you would expect me when you saw me. It was raining pretty nearly all the way back from Bristol and we had no mudguards and only one proper seat, the driver's. Sammy drove and Thorne and I had to hang on. The car went splendidly, no trouble at all. I am very sorry we did not telegraph on Saturday afternoon. I hope you were not worried. . . . Tell Jess I am sorry I did not turn up. . . .' It was just a chassis without covering. On another day his brother, Herbert ('H'), wrote to Jay: ' . . . How is poor old Jemmy? It must have been rather a smart piece of work getting over to France, seeing the Grand Prix and returning between 5 o'clock one morning and breakfast the next. . . .'

It was not only his immediate family who would have liked to have seen more of him. Many of the aunts and cousins hoped he would look in, hoped he would visit for a meal, for a weekend, for a month. They all loved him and wanted to see him: the Livingstone-Learmonths, now settled in England again, in Hampshire; the Prescotts, now at Brantyngeshay, near Chilworth; Aunt Alice Borgstrom, in Helsingfors, whose favourite great-nephew he was; and Emmie's cousins the Earl and Countess of Drogheda, who wanted him to come for a long visit, as his sisters were to do a year or two later, to gorgeous Moore Abbey in County Kildare. Later – only a few years later – Lord and Lady Drogheda were to be of the greatest possible help to aviation, as they were among the leaders of fashionable society to be in the watching crowds at Hendon on many occasions.

But Jim was busy – too busy to accept social invitations – and the Iris car was proving itself. Jim wrote a postcard to Charles, now aged nine and at his first prep. school near Tunbridge Wells, on July 8th, 1907: 'In the their heat yesterday at Brooklands the Iris cars were 1st and 2nd and the rest nowhere. In the final Colonel Howell's car was second only a length and a half behind the winning Napier. All the men of the Iris works got the morning off to see the races and they get the afternoon off . . .'

Then, in 1907, circumstances changed radically for the Travers family.

J.L.T. came home to Warlingham one evening from Cannon Street as he had done six days a week for the past sixteen years and, at the dinner table, announced to his family that he would not be returning to Joseph Travers & Sons on the morrow. Or ever again. There had been a Meeting of the Directors, of whom he was one, to appoint a new Director. All Directors were appointed from within the firm and J.L.T. knew and disliked the man whom his fellow-Directors wished to appoint. He disliked the man's policies even more than the man himself and thought him thoroughly unsound. He made the matter a point of principle, threatening to resign if the man was brought onto the Board of Directors. His resignation was accepted.

He and Emmie were not penniless. Far from it. But they had lived extravagantly for many years and would undoubtedly have saved more if they had expected such a blow to fall. J.L.T. had never forgotten the generosity of Charles and Annie Tindal at Ramornie and at Fir Grove, nor that of Uncle Archie – who had given him his first real opportunity to earn money by working hard when he had been a young man; throughout his prosperous years, therefore, he had tried to put back at least as much as had been given to him – often to hospitals in the names of his own children – as well as to numerous other good causes; there is no record of all the people to whom he had given a helping hand, but they were many.

He and Emmie, too, had enjoyed themselves hugely at Woottonga, with open house to family and friends and with a stream of visitors, perpetuating the happy sort of life which they had both known in their youth at the Tindals. They had added, some years after the house was built, a large room and had given dances there for the girls. One way and another they had had a lot of fun. Now they settled down to retrench. The upkeep on Woottonga was like a leak in a tank. Woottonga must go. J.L.T. took out a mortgage on that and other Warlingham property and built 'a horrid little house which we all hated' (according to Jay), in the corner of one of his fields. He twisted the knife in the family wound by calling the house HORTON;

Before the re-organization of their lives could mop up all his resources J.L.T. put aside one thousand pounds for Jim's engine. This was an engine which Jim had been thinking about and was longing to start building.

Eastchurch was the place to be, with it's fine gliding hill close to the sea. Francis McClean, who had a cottage and some land there, had put up a Shed and was tinkering about with flying experiments. Egerton, too, was there, working with McClean in his Shed. Jim bought a few acres of land from McClean and soon put up his own Shed. This was the first Shed at Eastchurch, other than McClean's own, but it was soon to be followed by those of Egerton, Cecil Grace, Professor Huntington – later by Jezzi and by many others. These six men were the first pioneer builders at Eastchurch. It was several years later that Short Brothers, Moore-Brabazon and others joined the Eastchurch brigade.

Jim worked away at his engine in the Eastchurch Shed in his spare time only – for he was still at the Iris Works at the start of 1908. In February, 1908, he passed the Associate Membership examination for entry to I.C.E. and in March was admitted as a Student in the Institution of Civil Engineers on the recommendation of a Member of I.C.E., Professor D. S. Capper.

At Warlingham, things were not going as planned. Knowing how much he had spent on Woottonga, J.L.T. made the classic mistake of asking too high a price when he hoped to sell. The only people who were seriously interested were the Swans. Sir Joseph Swan, who had simultaneously with Thomas Edison (although unbeknownst to each other) – invented the modern electric light bulb, the 'EDISWAN' bulb – was a difficult man to deal with and Lady Swan was worse. They could not make up their minds about Woottonga: they would buy, they wouldn't buy, perhaps they would buy later on, perhaps they would rent and so on and so on. They wanted to live in Woottonga but they would decide nothing, sign nothing, and all this when dealing with a man of the stamp of J.L.T., who was always totally straight-forward and direct, a man whose word was his bond and to whom to think was to act. Horton was not ready to live in and the future of Woottonga remained unsettled.

Weary of it all, J.L.T. took himself off to Australia for a year, taking V. with him. They were both so alike, father and eldest daughter, in liking a well-ordered, well-organized life. The confusion at home was quite intolerable.

By leaving Emmie to cope on her own J.L.T. did the best thing that he could have done. Emmie's method was quieter than his and often more effective. Her vaguely-muddled manner, her seeming for-getfulness of the things she thought it wise to ignore – her very quietness, the quietness of equilibrium and balance, masked a mind like a blade while her sweet face and steady eyes inspired trust and friendship.

While J.L.T. and V. went out, voyaging in a leisurely fashion via the Cape, he enjoying the cold sea-water baths every morning and feeling more cheerful every day, both of them enjoying new acquaint-anceships and bridge-parties in the evening, Emmie, in a few short

Travers family mechanized: (l. to r.) Jim, Jay at steering wheel of family de Dion Bouton, Alie on running board, Emmie, H. and Charles. Outside coach house at Woottonga, circa 1908

months, had watched over the completion of the work at Horton and had seen the workmen out, had found a flat near the twin essentials of life – the Army & Navy Stores and Victoria Station – for her 82-year-old Mother (Grannie Gardner) and had installed her there in modest comfort, had organized the removal from Woottonga to Horton and, with her exquisite tact, had persuaded Sir Joseph Swan to sign a lease on Woottonga. Horton was cramped after Woottonga but Emmie would have been content with much less than Horton in order to stay in England. Her only dread was that J.L.T., who had sometimes expressed nostalgic longings for the land of his boyhood, would settle in Australia, (he had spoken lovingly of the Darling Downs), and summon her to join him there. Hot countries were, to her, where horrid things happened. Hot countries were best avoided. She determined to make Horton as comfortable and as cheerful as she could and in a letter to Charles, reminding him that the name of the house was different, strove to remind him how much was just as before.

In the event J.L.T. and V. did not stay away for as long as they had planned. After visiting Geoffrey and Ida at Elsternwick, spending some weeks in Sydney and in the Blue Mountains, voyaging up the coast to Brisbane and visiting the H.P. Gardners at Dingyarra – a disappointing stay there as there had been a winter of hard frosts and the grass was burnt and brown and the cattle in a bad way – a sortie to the Darling Downs to look at some land, a visit to the Travers Tindals at Spring Grove, a visit to cousin Charles Tindal at Ramornie, a further visit to Geoffrey and Ida, from whence they hoped to visit Roy and Louie Butler at Gippsland, and then stay with cousin Laurie Travers in Melbourne for the Cup before going down to Tasmania – out of the blue came very worrying news from Emmie. The firm was in a bad way. They had followed the policies of the new director and J.L.T. had the melancholy satisfaction of having been proved right in the matter. There were also more expenses in connexion with their rearranged life than he had foreseen.

He wrote to Emmie on 6th October, 1908: ' ... The news of J.T. & Sons passing the usual interim dividend is very serious, and I am afraid also that the repairs to Woottonga cost much more than I anticipated. I wish that I had not come out, but it can't be helped now. We shall come back in the *Marathon* and be home I hope about the middle or end of January.... The weather has turned quite hot and the dust is blowing in clouds. This is very pretty country and we are having a very good trip, but I am worrying about you all, I am afraid you must be penniless. . . . '

The anxiety to get back to England with all possible speed made him decide to take an earlier boat and he wrote on the 19th October, 1908: ' . . . We have taken our passages by the *Moravian* sailing on the 11th of next month, and due in London on the 1st or 2nd of January, 1909. We had first pick of the cabins and the ship ought not to be very full at this time of year. I hope the Swans will pay their rent all right, but I mistrust them somehow.

Of course we are not going to Tasmania now and I don't think we shall go to Gippsland. Roy is, I believe, in Melbourne now, and Aunt Louie is coming here soon on her way to England by the *China*, leaving here on the 10th of next month . . . I am anxious to get back to see you all again and also to hear how things are going on at 119. It makes me very uneasy to hear of our shares falling to 18s. We must try not to sell any more at that price, but are they going lower still? I fear the losses at Singapore must have been enormous, mainly due to that silly ass Frank. I am sorry to hear he has come into a fortune. . . . '

That 'silly ass Frank' was J.L.T.'s third cousin, whom he had brought into the firm at the special request of the young man's father – an action he regretted as soon as it was done.

So J.L.T. came hurrying back from Australia in order to straighten out financial matters at home. Emmie was relieved to learn that her husband had not bought an inch of Australian land, not even any of the magical Darling Downs. But it had been a close call. Emmie had made Horton thoroughly comfortable and they settled down to live there as economically as was possible.

Jim had spent a fruitful time while his father and eldest sister had been away: at the Iris Works; at I.C.E. – and in every spare minute of his time, in his lonely Shed at Eastchurch. There was an extensive railway service over Sheppey in those days and a station at Eastchurch, so that Jim usually ran up and down by train – but if train-times did not suit he would motor down. 'Motor' down was a generic term. He had a variety of motorized tricycles and motor-bikes and sometimes the use of a chassis. Occasionally old King's College friends would accompany him – more often he was alone. He had taken a Primus stove down to the Shed and would brew up tea and if he was working late – would fry sausages or bacon or make hot sandwiches to keep himself going.

The building of his engine was such a spare-time activity that although he had begun work on it in the summer of 1907 it was not finally completed until the start of 1909 – by which time he was no longer so often alone at Eastchurch. He had never made any secret of what he was doing and there were many keen to join him. Sheds proliferated. Serious, eager young designers flocked to Eastchurch. Some worked in secret with doors locked against all comers. Many, including Jim, never locked their Sheds when they were at work. All could come and see what he was trying to achieve and what were his latest ideas. All was progress. Among the inventors was a man who often looked in to see how Jim was getting along and having one day asked Jim to explain a new idea rushed back to his own Shed and, according to Jay, not only copied the idea but took out a Patent on it. Jim did not mind in the slightest degree that anyone else should use his ideas. He often used the ideas of others. Most progress was, after all, only derivation from earlier solutions to problems. But he may have regretted the matter of the Patent.

His philosophy at that stage was akin to that of Hargraves – who never took out Patents on any of his inventions – or to that of Santos-Dumont who, when he showed and flew his *Parasol* at the 2nd Paris Air Show in September/October, 1909, proclaimed 'that this is my design and the whole world is free to copy it.'

Jay, however, was furious at the thought of anyone 'stealing Jim's ideas and claiming them.' She was still cross about it sixty years later. Jim's engine is now in the Science Museum, South Kensington, to which Museum my father took it after Jim's death; and I am grateful to Mr Andrew Nahum for the following description of the engine:

'*Travers Experimental Rotary Engine.*
This design was an experimental 3-cylinder rotary engine of about half a litre total cylinder capacity made by J. L. Travers in 1908/9. A significant feature of this design was that each cylinder had a single valve in the cylinder head, mechanically operated by a push rod and rocker arm actuated by a scroll cam gear. This valve served both as exit of exhaust gases and inlet of fresh air. (This single valve system was later used in the Gnome Monosaupape type of engines.)
   The engine also features a very early form of direct petrol injection. The fuel was supplied through an injector nozzle in each inlet port, and timed by means of a rotary distributor. Fuel was led to the distributor through a pipe which passed inside the hollow fixed crankshaft extension by means of which the engine was mounted.

The cylinders are of steel, and each carries side flanges, and a quadrant flange, so that, when all bolted together, these flanges form each a third part of the 'crankcase,' the back plate thus formed being reinforced by a clamping ring.

No provision is made for taking off the power developed.

The pistons are of cast iron, and domed, their diameter being 4 in, and stroke 3 in.'

Mr Nahum commented to me in his letter, of 1983, that: '... it certainly represents a very early application of direct fuel injection to a petrol engine.'

Great changes were taking place in aviation in 1909, even before Bleriot's Channel crossing sharpened public interest in the subject of flight.

As early as February of that year the brothers Horace, Eustace and Oswald Short began building the Wright biplane under Licence at Shellbeach at Sheppey, thus becoming the first airframe manufacturers in England. And Cody flew at Farnborough. Those of us who revere the name of Avro recall being told that A. V. Roe first flew in 1908; but it was not an officially recognized flight; Cody made the first officially recognized flight in 1908; however he did not make his flight of 'over a mile' until May, 1909.

Jim was still at the Iris Works early in 1909, but by April he had joined Lieut-Colonel R. E. Capper, R. E., at the R. E. Balloon Factory, Farnborough, as Assistant and Draughtsman. If he was hoping for some flying at Farnborough he was, I think, disappointed. He wrote a card to his Mother from his digs in South Farnborough on April 29th, 1909: ' ... Am staying with John Daman next week end. Saw him last night at I.C.E.Also Le Gros, Knowles, Huntington, who says he will try to fix up an aeroplane job later on for me. Nodded at Morcombe. Did not risk shaking his finger ...'

The handwriting is so poor that it suggests there may have been an injury to Jim's hand, not to Morcombe's.

Lieut-Colonel Capper who, as early as 1904, had tried to persuade the War Office to take powered flight in general and that of the Wright brothers in particular, seriously, and who had made a trip to the United States in order to observe and report on the Wright brothers' flights, was to prove the ideal friend to S. F. Cody, just as Cody was to prove the greatest of benefactors to British aviation.

Cody was a showman and showmanship was needed in order to launch the idea – and to persuade people of the normality of the idea, of powered flight. Particularly the idea of powered flight onto the seafaring and cavalry minds of the Admiralty and the War Office respectively. A single detail of Cody's behaviour – that he tied his aeroplane to a tree at Farnborough, that he hitched up his horse, as any cavalryman may do, after dismounting, was tremendously in his favour.

Jim's digs in South Farnborough were near the Drawing Office. He was working chiefly on wind balances for wind tunnel but when the working day was over, in the balmy May evenings, there was the possibility of at least observing a flight. He wrote to J.L.T. on 'Wednesday night. 6 p.m. 1 Woodleigh Villas, Canterbury Road, South Farnborough, Hants . . . I don't expect I shall be home next weekend and my month will be up on Wednesday . . . I hope this job will last on or else lead to something else . . . I have been down to Cody's Shed every night this week but he has not attempted a flight yet.'

However on the 14th May Cody did 'attempt a flight' and flew for over a mile in the sturdily beautiful British Army Aeroplane No 1.

Professor Huntington was as good as his word – that he would try to fix up an aeroplane job for Jim – for he then offered Jim the post of his Assistant in his flying experiments and in the design of his own aeroplane at Eastchurch. Huntington was still at King's College London and Jim, after leaving Farnborough, returned to full-time employ at the Iris Works. Therefore the two men must have worked on their joint project at Eastchurch on Sundays and in any other available spare time.

Jim wrote to Emmie from Willesden on July 16th, 1909: 'I went down to Dover last weekend in case Latham came over. I went on a chassis. Things are fairly busy at the Works. I expect I shall be home on Saturday. . . .'

Poor Latham.

He had not come over. He so very nearly became the first man to fly the English Channel – he was so very nearly the first and would have claimed the £1,000 Prize offered by the *Daily Mail* for the crossing. He would have secured an even more illustrious name in the history of aviation than that which he already holds. As is well known Louis Bleriot took the prize and to him must rightly go all honour and glory.

Betty Baird, of the Royal Canadian Geographical Society, wrote in
the December 1983/January 1984 *Canadian Geographic* an article which
dealt not only with Louis Bleriot but with the other members of his
family who had emigrated from France and gone homesteading in
Canada before Louis' famous flight. The emigrants had included Louis'
Mother and one gathers that Louis was left by the rest of his family
to his own – inexplicable – devices:

> Louis Bleriot's famous flight was on July 25 1909. The Frenchman flew a
> crude monoplane across the Channel from the outskirts of Calais to Dover.
> The distance was 37·8 Km (23·4 miles.) Flight time: $36\frac{1}{2}$ minutes. Not only did
> this feat make aviation history, it earned Bleriot the £1,000 prize offered by
> the London *Daily Mail* for the first air crossing of the Channel. The money
> was a life-saver. Bleriot – an impulsive, reckless man with a red walrus
> moustache and prominent nose – was an engineer who struck it rich with the
> invention of an automobile headlight and such motoring gadgetry as foot
> warmers and luminous licence plates. He poured that wealth into aviation and,
> according to his niece, Sister Jackie Bleriot, was down to his last sou that July
> morning.
>
> As early as 1896 Louis had been tinkering with airplane designs. Ten years
> later he set up one of the first airplane factories in France, and began flying
> soon after...

It is possible that Huntington was building his aeroplane, originally,
with a view to making an attempt in the channel crossing, for Jim
wrote home: ' ... now that Bleriot's done it we don't think that we
will bother.... '

Although Jim was now yearning after aviation more than ever and
had an advanced idea for a monoplane burning in his brain, he
nevertheless remained at Legros & Knowles until November 1909.
the I R I S Works had been good to Jim and he had given of his best
to the firm from whom he had learnt so much. The Iris Car had become
after it's early somewhat crude design a superb car. Each of the various
models, particularly since 1906, had been engineered, built and tested
with exquisite care; not only was the engine and transmission of simple
design, the whole had been made with careful thought of the suitability
of a particular metal to each part of the construction. Since 1906 the
chassis had been revised and restructured to a form which ensured
massive strength.

The car had had great success, not only showing a surprising turn
of foot at Brooklands but, far more importantly, in the numerous road
trials, often over atrocious roads, in which it had been entered. The

following is a quotation from the Iris Company's own 'introduction' to their car and for which I am indebted to the B P Library of Motoring:

> But of all the Iris successes the biggest and the one to clinch its already great reputation was the 2,000 miles non-stop run in October 1909 which was, in many ways, a feat unparalleled in automobilism. It is true that of the making of automobile records there is no end; and nothing has been more abused; therefore, the Iris Company was most particular that everything should be strictly official and under the certificate of the Royal Automobile Club. The car used was an ordinary standard 25 H. P. touring Iris with four up; and the test was a non-stop run over 2,066 miles on the road under all conditions. As it happened the conditions climatically turned out to be of the worst; but the car went through without a single engine-stoppage the whole way, running for 138 hours without a hitch. Such a test involves hundreds of minor possibilities, which may spoil any record, but the Iris defeated them all; and as a well-known motor journalist wrote at the time, 'such an official test places the Iris car upon a pinnacle not hitherto reached by any of its competitors ... etc. etc ...

J.L.T. had spent the summer of 1909 in Finland with his old Aunt Alice Borgstrom. She was getting old – was one of the few surviving Travers aunts of her generation – and had grown more sentimental than the Travers aunts usually were. She wrote affectionately to Emmie on 25th July about 'her dearest Lill & how sweet he was with his children,' Jay and Alie had accompanied him, and 'how pleased he was to hear of dear Jem getting employment.'

Huntington put up his own Shed at Eastchurch near McClean's original Shed. Although Jim spent nearly every spare minute and most weekends at Eastchurch he was not free to live there wholly until he left the Iris Works, which he did in November 1909, after the completion of the road trials in October of that year. Aunt Gussie Burn wrote to Jay from St Chad's, Cambridge, on December 19th:

> When you write next tell me what Jim's new job is not in the air I hope. Though I daresay he would like to be floating about if he can sail down here there is plenty of room on the rifle range for an Antoinette thing to sit down on....

J.L.T. was delighted that Professor Huntington had asked Jim to help him with the design of his aeroplane and at this further advancement of his son's career he also took an increasing interest in aviation, the first manifestation of this being that he straight away put up another and much larger Shed at Eastchurch on his own account. It

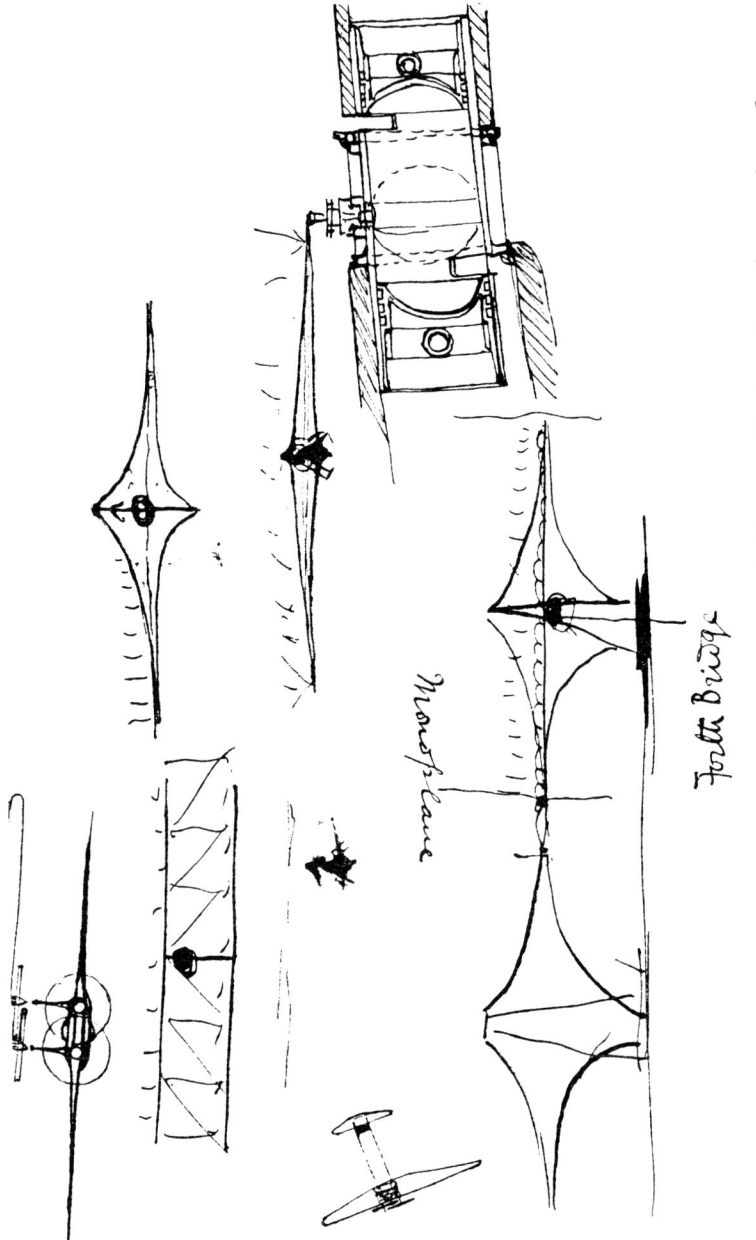

Monoplane

Forth Bridge

Back of an envelope, like all the best ideas. Jim's twin-engine, twin-boom, mid-wing all-metal monoplane of 1910 gave a hint of some later designs to come from Fokker, Junkers and Lockheed

was near Jim's original Shed. 'Jim's Shed.' 'Dad's Shed.' Whenever I asked Jay where anything had been built the answer was in either of the above.

The second Travers Shed was to be for Jim's aeroplane, the aeroplane that so far was an idea only. Jim had sketched a few basic lines of it on the unwritten sections of a letter from one of his Cambridge aunts: 'The Forth Bridge'. The Forth Bridge – repeated, divided, segmented, altered, became: 'The Monoplane.' It was to be a twin-engined all-metal monoplane of monocoque construction. He was not ever to build it. Eventually, with a colleague, he did build a monoplane but it was to a more crude design and he never finished it.

It is a temptation to wonder what an aeroplane manufacturing company Jim might have built up had he not been obliged to earn his own living or if his father's resources had been those of ten years earlier; but when one realized that the extremely tough Short brothers had started with less than Jim and the equally tough de Havilland with roughly the same, the answer must be that Jim was not by nature a business man and that unless his father had been young and energetic enough to have taken on the business side of things, no amount of capital would have secured a commercially successful venture. Although capable of great thrift and self-denial, squandering little on himself, Jim nevertheless squandered his ideas; aviation was the Great Cause; all must share in its advances, excitements and discoveries. That is not the way of the business man.

Of course the monoplane idea was not new. The Bleriot Monoplane had first flown in 1907. The beautiful little Antoinette was so well known than an invalid lady, in her eighties, was confident of Jim being able to sail one down to Cambridge and to sit it down on the rifle range there. The idea of monocoque was only just starting to come in, however, and at the Olympia Aero Show in March, 1910, a Humber monoplane designed by Hubert Le Blon was shown. It was described as 'the first departure from openwork trellis work fuselage, for its body was a tapering cylinder of thin wood bound with tape.' But in the summer of 1909 when Jim first began to sketch out his monocoque monoplane it was certainly an advance on what had gone before.

Development was so rapid and invention and discovery so wide-spread that those early days of heavier-than-air flight now seem to the casual reader like a frenzy. They also seem to have been remarkably international; again and again one surprises the pioneer outside the land of his birth; indeed it is an amusing game to find out just how very few became prophets in their own country. Which came first? The naturally adventurous spirit, the explorer, who might well become air-minded? Or the man removed from his usual landscape by circumstances and who might, as a consequence, see all with fresh eyes?

Lawrence Hargraves, the Australian born in England; Hiram Maxim – later Sir Hiram – the American living in England; Jose Weiss, the Austrian living in London; Santos-Dumont, the French-Brazilian living in France; Hubert Latham, the bi-lingual Oxford-educated son of an English father and French Mother; S. F. Cody, the American living in England and who became naturalized here shortly before his death in 1913; the Dutchman, Anthony Fokker, much of whose work was done in Germany; Jezzi – where was he from? – that precise, dapper and charming little man, who lived and worked in London, built his first machine at Bexley, and later designed, built and flew at Eastchurch; the Farman brothers, Maurice and Henry – later spelt Henri – of English parentage and birth and of French domicile and of whom both countries should be equally proud: these are some of the names which spring to mind. Even the Wright brothers, one learns, were not taken seriously in the United States until Wilbur had flown successfully at Le Mans and elsewhere and until their aircraft were in production by Short Brothers at Shellbeach. More recently, one thinks of the Sicilian, Bellanca, whose work in the United States was so beautiful – who will easily forget the Bellanca Racer? Then the Norwegian, Noorduyn, another designer who made his international name in the States and whose NORSEMAN was such a classic of peace and war and of Northern bush flying.

The list goes on.

It is doubtful if anyone kept any record of when they flew and on what aeroplane; they were all so busy; also, they talked less of 'flying' than of 'flying experiments'; in Jim's Candidature Notes for I.C.E. he records his activities for 1909 as follows: 'Assistant to Professor A. K. Huntington in aviation experiments at Eastchurch,' and in 1910 as 'private aviation experiments on rotary petrol motors having a single valve, and experiments on monoplane construction. Early flying experiments.'

The early flying experiments were legion but, alas, undefined. Jay summed it up neatly for me when I asked her when Jim had learned to fly. 'He never had to learn, my dear,' she said reprovingly, 'he could always fly,' and adding ' – they all taught themselves in those days.' And through her mind's eye one could almost see the multi-plane at Woottonga, with the pedal-assisted take-off, the swooping hops and bounces. He had taught himself to fly.

Emmie spent the summer of 1910 with Aunt Alice Borgstrom in Finland, warming herself in the sun, drinking rather a lot of mead, 'the Romans' drink,' and writing somewhat incoherent letters home; J.L.T. spent much of the summer of 1910 in visiting Eastchurch.

The fact that Professor Huntington, now flying quite often in the machine which he and Jim had designed and which Short Brothers had built, thought highly of Jim; the fact that aviation was developing so rapidly – all these things and others made him decide that Jim should not be obliged to sleep in his Shed indefinitely.

Accordingly he commissioned William Harbrow of South Bermondsey, on 31st May, 1910, to build a bungalow to his own design; since Harbrow, as stated on his address-stamp, specialized in building: Churches, Schools, Hospitals, Bungalows, Pavilions, Stables etc., J.L.T.'s nice Australian-type corrugated-iron design was well suited to his skill. I have the original plans and they are excellent if by excellent one means suitable for their purpose. The building was small and economical of space, yet the centrally-placed living room was 24′ × 18′, thus giving room for a table large enough on which to spread out maps or charts, or on which to slope a drawing-board. In modern parlance, the bungalow was 'purpose-built.'

In 1910, when the Aero Club became the *Royal Aero Club*, J.L.T. made the bungalow available to them for use as their headquarters at Eastchurch. On the list of names of founder members of the Royal Aero Club were those of J.L.T. and of Jim.

Although some of the old free and easy days disappeared with the establishment of the Royal Aero Club at Eastchurch good things were also started at that time. J.T.C. Moore-Brabazon, (Lrd Brabazon of Tara), brought in much organization and regulation, including the idea of properly certificated pilots. Inventor-experimenter pilots, such as Jim, thought it rather an extravagance; however the rules having been agreed he saw the necessity of obtaining a certificate and did so the following year, as soon as he felt that he could afford the cost, becoming No. 86.

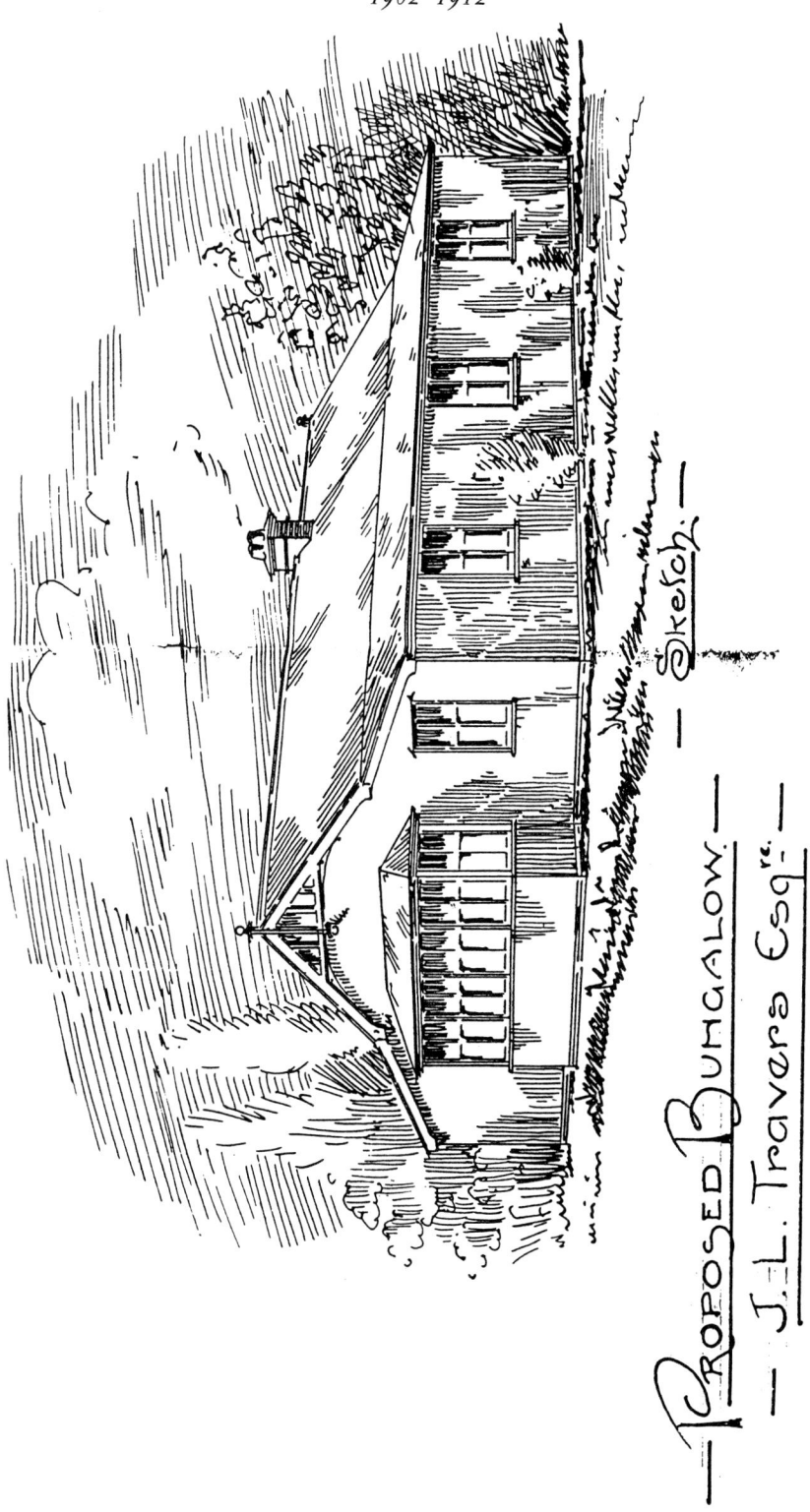

Wm. Harbrow's Sketch for J. L. T.'s Bungalow at Eastchurch

As late as February, 1911, he had not yet saved, or perhaps set aside, enough money to become a certificated pilot; he was still spending most of his time working on the completion of his second engine – an engine which never ran as satisfactorily as had the first; it was a Gnome Rotary with his own modifications and with which, with the three-bladed steel airscrews which he had drawn but which he never in the event made – he hoped to power the monoplane on which he and Arthur Q. Cooper were working. Although living and working in his Shed he continued to keep an eye on his father's bungalow.

He wrote home on 15th February, 1911:

'My dear Mummy,

Thank you for your letter of Saturday last, it is very interesting about Sir Joseph. We are using Vulcanite for the petrol valve now. We have not quite finished the new petrol valve yet, all the castings have come for it and the gear wheels which drive it but the new pistons and the cylinders which have been ground out will not arrive before the end of the week.

We have been drawing out a gear wheel to drive the oil pump. The engine cannot possibly be ready to try again before the middle of next week. Jezzi was down here on Saturday and Sunday but it was too windy for Cooper to try for his certificate and I don't suppose I shall have a try on the machine until he has got it.

I had a card from H. this morning and he thinks that perhaps he has sold the old gas-engine. We are tuning up Jezzi's engine, it won't run quite as fast as it should. Tell Dad that the door to the bungalow is all right and that we had a fire there the other day ...'

H. was Herbert. The family habit of referring to each other by initials remained throughout their lives.

H. had enjoyed long months of travelling, very slowly, around the world, but mails had been regular and he had been kept in touch, albeit belatedly, with what was going on at home. On a postcard home from Tasmania, dated 16th April, 1910, he had written: 'Here's to a long flight!' – Referring no doubt to one of Jim's flying 'experiments.'

Harald Penrose wrote in his British Aviation volume *The Pioneer Years*: ' ... if Brooklands, Larkhill and Hendon had become flourishing centres of instruction to a rapidly increasing number attracted to flying, the home of the Royal Aero Club at Eastchurch was accepting a new distinction. The first pilots of the Royal Navy were receiving tuition there.... The Naval contingent reported at Eastchurch on March 1st, (1911) with six months leave of absence on full pay. Lieuts. R. Gregory, C. R. Samson, A. M. Longmore and Lieut. E. L. Gerrard of the Royal Marines. By May 2nd all had their R. A. C. certificates ...'

It was the generous Cockburn who was their instructor, free gratis.

Only four years earlier, on March 7th, 1907, Lord Tweedmouth, First Lord of the Admiralty, had written to the Wright brothers: 'I have consulted my expert advisers with regard to the your suggestion as to the employment of aeroplanes and I regret to have to tell you, after the careful consideration of the Board, that the Admiralty, whilst thanking you for so kindly bringing the proposals to their notice, are of opinion that they would not be of any practical use to the Naval service.'

So the eventual arrival of the Naval contingent at Eastchurch for flying training was a vindication for poor Captain Bacon, who had resigned over the matter of Naval aviation, and for the far-sighted persistence of Captain H. Murray Sueter, who had taken over from Captain Bacon.

Naval aviation had at last begun.

Possibly encouraged by the boost to aviation which the arrival of the first Naval trainee-pilots had helped to ensure, Jim decided that he must now take his Certificate. He went to Hendon in April, 1911, moving into digs at 9a Colindale Avenue. He sent a postcard home from there on 13th April:

I went up with Gresswell last night for about a quarter of an hour, and if fine will go out alone to-night when the wind has dropped a bit. Another of the pupils got his Certificate last night. What do you think of Prier's flight?' – (Prier had flown to Paris from London in under 4 hours) – 'I will let you know when I start flying properly. Lots of flying here yesterday ...' and a month later: 'I am quite well – and have not yet fixed up about learning the Bleriot, they are such an unbusinesslike crowd. I have been trying to get a definite arrangement with G-W. I may fix it this afternoon. I got Jezzi's cheque and acknowledged same ...

When at Eastchurch Jim had put in hours of work helping Jezzi with design changes to Jezzi's tractor machine, some of the improvements being a tapered fuselage and streamlined undercarriage struts. This was the machine that Jim was referring to when he wrote home in February that 'I don't suppose I shall have a try on it until he (Cooper) has got his certificate.' (It is even possible that it was the fact of having to queue up for so long at Eastchurch to take his Certificate that made Jim hurry things along by going to Hendon.)

Jezzi's cheque was probably in recognition of Jim's help in the Jezzi Tractor machine for Jezzi was by all accounts the most courteous and straight-dealing of men.

Emmie had been spending a long month with her Mother and with some of the Prescott uncles and aunts in rooms at Queen Square, Bath, from whence reams of letters were despatched to all her family, wherever they might be. Towards the end of several pages to Alie, at St. Chad's, Cambridge, and dated 20th May, Emmie wrote:

. . . by the way did they tell you that Jim got his Certificate (pilot's) on Saturday. Someone had smashed the school machine and the mechanics were so busy getting ready for Friday's show. That he could not get it mended – and on Saturday the mechanics never turned up til 11 o'clock. However he got it mended and on Saturday afternoon there was no one to help him out with it. However he commandeered someone – press men – and he got Perrin and Delacombe to observe him and Grahame-White – who had just taken up Lord Curzon – and he looped the loop and did ten figures of 8 at 300 ft high – and they all came and shook hands with him. Now he wants to learn the Bleriot but can't come to terms. Prier has gone to the Bristol School. The Gordon Bennett is to be held at Eastchurch – which will mean a big crowd for the week and I suppose better train service. The Naval men have Dad's Shed but I don't know about Jim's. He and H. are to be there this week end. I hope H. won't smash himself up on his motor bike. I had to make up a Bridge 4 last night and couldn't help listening to some ladies doing the dog patience one was learning; and I lost count of all the cards. . . . I taught Aunt O. (Olive Prescott) the dog patience. I think she likes it. She cheats dreadfully sometimes looking under to see which card she will turn up. . . .

Into Emmie's peaceful pool of family and card-playing and taking the waters at Bath, J.L.T.'s letter to her of 30th May must have arrived like a sling-shot.

It began quietly enough, mentioning that he had let his other house, Court Lees, to the Jacomb-Hoods and is glad that she approves; after various news of the garden he went on: ' ... We had Ben Travers* and his daughter here to-day for lunch and dinner, I am afraid they were rather bored, but we did our best, and Vera managed things very well. Jem went up to town this morning and I asked him to order a fly from Hewetts to meet B.T. and his daughter, and I walked down to the station to meet them. But there was no fly and Jem had evidently forgotten all about it, I really felt very much annoyed. The morning was hot and the roads dusty, and we had to toil up the hill. Jem has a great idea now that he would like to fly at Hendon under Grahame-White, taking up passengers. He thinks he might make money in that way, but I do not like the idea for many reasons, I have told him so very plainly. He must realize that at the age of 27, he must earn his own living, and not shift about from one thing to another. And above all I don't want him to break his neck, which he will probably do if he goes in for flying pure and simple. . . .'

Jim's peccadillo in forgetting to order the fly – if indeed he had forgotten to order it – and the consequent annoyance and embarrassment to his father in front of stuffy old Cousin Ben, is not enough to explain the irritability in that letter. J.L.T. had never before written so crossly about the son whom he adored and nor did he, so far as I know, ever criticize him in such a way again. It is really a letter full of anxiety: what will become of the young man, with his hard-won engineering training and his visionary ideas, if he goes in for 'taking up passengers'. He need not have been so anxious. Jim was too full of inventiveness ever to have been content with 'flying pure and simple.'

There had been a big Meeting at Hendon in May and Jim may well have been impressed by the money which could be earned by taking up passengers at such a Meeting, money such as he needed in order to continue with the work which really mattered to him: his aviation experiments. He had written home earlier of trying to get a definite arrangement 'with G-W.' But G-W was now going abroad – off to the United States on a tour – so Jim's plans of flying for him had to remain in abeyance.

One senses that Jim was in a state of great creative energy, constantly frustrated, when in early June, 1911, Horace Short asked him to join Shorts as his Assistant and Designer.

* Uncle of the Ben Travers who became a playwright.

C. C. Turner wrote in *Flight* in June 1911:

'The English are a hero-worshipping nation, the latest evidence of this fact being the glorification of the individual flying man. Take the crowd at Brooklands or at Hendon on any day, and it may be said that they give all their attention to the prowess shown by flyers and spare not a thought for the students and experimenters who have designed and produced the machines. In England, the names of the big flying men are everything, but no one ever thinks about the pioneers. Bleriot is popular because he flew across the Channel, a very much smaller achievement than his heroic struggles with his early machines. Wilbur Wright, if he flew publicly in England, would have to turn somersaults in the air before he could get what they call in theatrical circles 'a hand.' And who in England cares a rap about Lawrence Hargraves, Glenn Curtiss or the designers of the beautiful Antoinette monoplane? Even Cody is never given credit for his long battle with the kite, and the designing of his aeroplane; and if, during a flight, he fails to go up at least a 1,000 ft, he is almost ridiculed!

As for the French, while they praise daring and skill, they never lose sight of the designer of the machine. As far as this country is concerned, the evil effect of the hero-worshipping habit is that designers and inventors receive no encouragement. . . .' There must indeed have been, as the writer concluded: ' . . . men in this country to-day who have ideas that are languishing simply for want of a little financial support.'

Horace Short was not the type to languish, in this country or anywhere else. His drive, his high standards of workmanship in whatever job he tackled – his strength, too, when dealing with others – all ensured his eventual success; but 1911 was a crucial year for him, with so many new inventors and designers around and such a fever of competition for the small amount of patronage. Shorts had gained a reputation for first-class and knowledgeable workmanship over many years of balloon-building. They were styled Aeronautical Engineers to the Aero Club, but their designs had all been for balloons. More recently they had built the Wright biplane under licence, the Short-Wright, and it was typical of their flair for business that they should have founded their aeroplane construction company, Short Bros., before Horace Short had seen the aeroplane they were to build.

They had joined the Eastchurch brigade from another part of Sheppey in 1910 and were seeking to expand their business by dint of their hard work and shrewd dealing. Although Horace Short was a man of enormous brain-power and intelligence, capable of flexibility and ingenuity, he had worked largely to the designs of others in his aeroplane construction business and Jim was the first designer whom he had brought into the firm. Horace Short certainly had an engineering background and much practical experience, but he was not a trained engineer. He had sought Richard Fairey's engineering help with the re-build (and almost re-design) of a Dunne monoplane for the Blair Atholl Syndicate earlier in the year. Now, once again, he turned to a trained engineer for help in his present difficulty. For Shorts had a problem and the reason for seeking Jim's help was soon apparent. They had been struggling for months with the design of their first twin-engined aeroplane and it had defeated them. Time was running out, for McClean, who had placed the order before going out to the Pacific for six months to watch an eclipse, was due home at Eastchurch in a month's time and nothing was ready.

'Shorts just couldn't do it,' my father used to remark, when I questioned him about those old days, for he had made many visits to Eastchurch in the summer of 1911 and he knew the score – 'they were stumped.'

It was typical of Shorts that they had closed with McClean – as they had closed with the Wright brothers – and worried about details later. They certainly had brilliant business sense.

Cecil Grace had been one of the earliest flyers on Sheppey and it was he, who in April, 1910, had ordered the machine which became S.27. S.27 became the prototype of a number of Short-Sommer Boxkites which were known generically as the S.27's. It was a single-engined machine but when, on December 22nd, 1910, Grace was tragically lost when attempting a double crossing of the Channel, McClean decided that the time had come to seek the greater safety of two engines. As Mc-Clean placed his order for the twin-engined machine with Shorts after Grace's loss the date of the order was either late December, 1910, or – more likely – early January, 1911, before he, McClean, set out for Fiji.

The idea of twin-engines may then have been unusual but it was not entirely new. Maxim and others had built twin-engined machines, mostly non-flying, and on 27th September, 1910, Roger Sommer had made a successful flight on the twin-engined Farman-type machine which he had designed and built himself.

Horace Short had almost certainly made a start on his own on the design of S.39, first of the Short twin-engined machines, in the spring of 1911. There were drawings of a twin-engined aeroplane, said by one visitor to be 'really lovely' – but in lieu of any actual aeroplane – at the Short stand at the Olympia Aero Show in March, 1911. The aeroplane, it was regretfully announced, was not yet ready.

There are no records that I can find of any design drawings as early as March, 1911, and the drawings shown at Olympia were undoubtedly what are usually known as 'artist's impressions.' Whether S.39 subsequently bore any resemblance to the drawings shown at Olympia is not clear; it is doubtful, as S.39 was constantly being altered, particularly after Jim joined the firm. ' ... doing a good lot of talking with Short,' he wrote home – the result of the talking usually being further alterations to the design of S.39.

Personally I doubt if Jim was ever really happy with S.39, even when she eventually flew successfully. But for Shorts, of course, it was a milestone in the history of the firm, as it was their first aeroplane of 'in-house' design.

Jim wrote to his Mother on 10th June, 1911:

' ... I got here all right on Tuesday night and started with Short on Wednesday morning.

I have been drawing – and flying with the Naval Officers – and superintending alterations to machines and doing a good lot of talking with Short.

I have done no flying myself yet.

There is an apprentice of Shorts living at the Post Office, we have meals together – name Chataway.

Short generally lends us his old car to come up and down to lunch or sometimes to tea.

I have not seen anything of Sammy since I saw him at Brooklands on Easter Monday – he said he might be coming down here soon for a few days.

I hope you are recovering from your stay at Bath.

I am feeling very fit. ...'

Five days after the above letter things began to buzz among the Naval pilots with Samson's attempt, on a single-engined, long-winged version of S.27, to make a non-stop cross-country flight from Eastchurch to Brooklands.

Jim wrote home on 18th June, 1911: ' ... I have been having a most exciting time. Lieut. Samson flew from here to Brooklands on

Thursday. I started off with Lieuts. Longmore and Gerrard and two mechanics, lots of spare parts etc. about 3 o'clock on Thursday afternoon.

'After giving us a bit of a start Samson started on Short No. 38 and passed us between Maidstone and Tonbridge flying at about 2,200 feet. We went on after waiting at Tonbridge for about an hour and called for telegrams at Reigate. We got one from Samson to say he had come down to Horley.

'So we found him fairly soon and discovered that he had come down owing to his engine failing, in coming down in a ditch he had broken a wire which we repaired. We then decided that it was too late to start and Samson and I slept under the machine, having previously tied it down in case of the wind getting up. The other chaps took the car into Reigate and slept in a pub. Early (4.30 a.m.) next morning 'Friday' Samson started off to renew his flight to Brooklands, (we having tested his engine.) We started off in pursuit on the car and arrived at the track at about 6.30. We had to wait until 9 before we got any news of him and then got a wire to say he had landed near Maidenhead, he had not recognized the track and gone on. So we went off again only to find when we got there that he had flown back to Brooklands.

'So we had to retrace our steps back to Brooklands and discovered him there at last about 12 a.m. Friday.

'We spent all Saturday there. And as there was no chance of the weather improving I and the mechanics came back here on Saturday night on the car – doing the journey in 4 hours.

'The wind has been too strong as yet to bring the machine back – Longmore will probably bring her back.

'I have been very busy to-day hurrying on the new twin-engine machine which should be finished in about a month. My digs here are very comfortable. Sammy came to see me while I was away so I missed him.

'I am getting on splendidly. . . .'

(Jim lived for a short time at Eastchurch Post Office – the digs he referred to.)

A footnote to Samson's cross-country flight, which set a British duration record of 4 hours 58 minutes and which, with all its diversions, was excitedly reported in the columns of *The Aeroplane* and *Flight*, was

Jim's bill for expenses: 'Expenses per Mr Travers re Brooklands Trip: £6-10-7½.' This sum included the cost of '2 Telegrammes, (Horley & Reigate) at 1/-' (From Short Bros Archive, courtesy Mr Gordon Bruce).

The new twin-engine machine, over which Shorts had agonized since January, was of course S.39. Although considered experimental, many features of S.39 were taken from earlier aeroplanes, in particular the chain-driven propellors, as in the Wright machine. ' . . . There are two A.1. ideas coming along that I shall try . . .' Jim wrote home.

The power was from 2 × 50 h.p. Gnome engines and they were mounted in tandem, the rear engine driving a pusher or true propellor by direct drive but the power of the forward engine being taken up by two tractor propellors – airscrews – one on each side of the fuselage and driven by chains from the engine.

Barnes, in his masterly book on Short's Aircraft, described it thus:

> 'S.39 was structurally the same as the Farman-Sommer-type Short biplane of 1911 apart from nacelle and power plant arrangement; it had a stronger chassis laterally braced by struts, three rudders below the tailplane and a front elevator carried on inset pivots by booms pitched closer together than normal. . . . The cockpit contained two seats side by side. . . .'

Although Horace Short may have improved on some of the aeroplanes which he had built, it is likely that Jim would have improved the design of S.39's chassis still further as it was subsequently described in the aviation press as 'absolutely colossal' – exactly the description applied four years earlier to the chassis design of the Iris car.

One of Jim's design problems – and this was something which my father often discussed at home twenty-five years later – were the methods Jim used for the take-off of power. Although Jim had used the Renold's chain-drive on S.39. he was never entirely happy with the chain-drive; it had been a feature of Iris Car design which had been abandoned in 1906 by their designers and when he made his second twin-engined aeroplane he, too, abandoned chain-drive in favour of direct drive.

For the time being, however, Shorts had been saved from embarrassing failure.

Jim had written home on 18th June: ' . . . hurrying on the new twin-engine machine which should be finished in about a month,' – yet S.39, 'The Triple Twin' – with her triple propellors and twin-engines, was not flown by the man who had commissioned her, her owner, Francis McClean, until 18th September of that year. Although McClean, on his return from the Pacific, had flown at Eastchurch in late July, he was far from well and suffered spasmodic bouts of sciatica well into September – so it may have been for reasons of indifferent health quite as much as the fact that his machine was not ready within the six months, which delayed the first testing of S.39 until 18th September. By which time Jim had completed the re-design of the Tractor Biplane and was working all hours on the second twin-engine machine.

One is aware of there being three main strands to Jim's life and work at that time.

The first was the drawing board and workshop strand, containing the design changes he was making to aeroplanes in the course of building and the bright ideas which came to him along the way. The bright ideas were legion, many of them recurring in different forms until he could use them or persuade others to do so. Among his bright ideas was a 'sort of graph' which kept a continuous record, not only of the hour and the minute, but of wind-speed, barometric pressure, altitude and so forth; this was in pursuit of accurate information so that, should there be a crash, the cause of such a crash or information relating to it could be analyzed scientifically. He actually built this instrument and as it seems to have been one of his few inventions on which Shorts did not seek to take out a patent one may guess that either they did not know about it or else, perhaps, not being pilots themselves, they were unaware of the importance of Jim's early flight recorder.*

The second strand in Jim's life seems to have been his determination to get as much flying practice as possible. Often such practice was reported. Thus, from *Flight* of August 5th: 'On Tuesday morning, Mr Whittaker's Farman was out, piloted by Mr Travers, who gave quite a good account of himself in the course of a twenty minutes' flight, making circular flights and figures of eight at a height of about 40 ft.' And from the same journal of August 12th: 'Lieut Longmore followed in the afternoon with several hours flying, and at the same time, Mr Travers, of Messrs Short Bros., was also flying. The latter flies exceedingly well considering he has had but little experience, and he is evidently cut out for the work.'

* Both Eustace and Oswald Short learnt to fly very much later in life.

'Maclean taking me off to Sheerness in the new "Triple Twin" 100 HP three propellors, two engines' – Jim. Eastchurch 1911

The *Aeroplane* viewed the flying practice in a more sporting manner, and in their issue of 17th August reported that on 8th August: 'Lieut. C. R. Samson and J. L. Travers out taking early morning exercise before 7 a.m., both putting in about an hour's work. Later, naval machines again busy, Lieuts. Samson and Longmore putting up good flights.' And that on Wednesday August 9th: 'The Hon. Maurice Egerton, Lieuts. Samson and Longmore, and Travers, all on Shorts, taking exercise between 5 and 8 a.m. (Famine in eggs and bacon etc. predicted at Eastchurch if this practise continues.) Two machines over the village in quick succession, and Eastchurchites, awakened from slumbers, wondered vaguely whether war had been declared, and they were being honoured by a visit from our friends the enemy. Mr Egerton, flying close upon two hours, made right across island and out over North Sea for considerable distance. Lieut. Samson and J. L. Travers, both remaining aloft well over the hour, went over Elmley, Leysdown, Harty, Teynham etc., former at 2,000 ft, latter at about

800 ft. . . . In evening, naval men, who never let a change of flying slip, all busily engaged between 6 and 8.30 p.m. J. L. Travers was also out for several short flights. Makings of a very nasty accident while Profesor Huntington doing trials over the dykes, Engine failed, letting him down into dyke. Upper plane of machine still usable. Professor got off lightly, minus a tooth or two.' And on Saturday 12th August: 'Lieuts Samson and Gregory, with J. L. Travers, out before 6 a.m. Fortunate to get in good flights before breakfast, for afterwards wind rose considerably and with heat throughout the day, made atmosphere very tricky. Another accident, (unusual at Eastchurch). Strange smash-up of Dunne monoplane; pancaked from about 40 ft. Much dis-sembling into component parts, without damage to pilot.'

The above extracts, culled from numerous reports in *Flight* and *The Aeroplane*, give the flavour of the time: the constant practice by the handful of pilots, fewer than a dozen on most days; the reliance on favourable weather; the continuing search for improvement; the attitude to their machines, which at times seems to have been akin to that of a rider to his horse; for example: ' . . . Valentine again arrived on Deperdussin, landing very neatly close to one of the sheds. had flown from Burnham, sixteen miles, in a side wind, in 18 mins 20 secs. After seeing his machine safe for the night, he returned to Town by train . . .' 'Safe for the night' suggests food, water and a comfortable stable, such as befits a trusty steed.

The third strand in Jim's life was little known about. The conversion of the aeroplane to use on water was not of course new as an idea; but very little had thus far been done, or rather, had been done by men who were too far ahead of their time. One reads of De Lana's giant flying boat of 1670, of Sir George Cayley's gliders of the 1850s, which, although landplanes, were built with boat-like fuselages; and of how, in the late 19th Century, Frank Reade designed big ocean-going flying-boats, with rotors for hovering over trouble spots and propellors for straight-and-level flight.

The French pioneer, Benaud, designed an amphibious two-seat monoplane intended to take off from, and to land on, water.

Gabriel Voisin, brother pioneer of Charles Voisin, produced a glider on floats for Ernest Archdeacon in 1905; then Voisin and Bleriot collaborated in a float-glider, which proved unsuccessful, but Bleriot, now inspired, produced his own successful version of it, Bleriot III, in 1906.

Another great pioneer Frenchman, Henri Fabre, made a powered aeroplane which could take off from and land on water; he first flew this in 1910. And on 27th January, 1911, Glenn Curtiss had taken off from water, flown a mile, and landed on water at San Diego, California. Short Brothers, who were later to produce some of the world's most beautiful flying-boats themselves, started in a quiet and severely practical way in this field. As usual it was Horace Short's keen eye for business which led them in the right direction.

Although the future of the four Naval pilots was still uncertain 'Twixt Wind & Water', as C. G. Grey described them in his long and sympathetic essay, it was reasonable to hope that the Admiralty, particularly with the support of Admiral Prince Louis of Battenberg, now in command at Sheerness and a frequent spectator at Eastchurch himself – would relent and establish a Naval flying service.

Confident that it was only a question of time, Horace Short, with his usual shrewd judgment, asked Jim to design methods of adapting landplanes for use on water.

As Jim was employed by Shorts as their Designer his work and the Patents on it were the property of Short Brothers. Thus the following Patents, taken out by the brothers Short in 1911, may be presumed to be Jim's work.

No. 22,407 H. L., A. E. and H. O. Short.
A cascade of hydrofoils arranged below the floats of seaplanes and hinged horizontally for flight, but when extended will create hydrodynamic forces lifting the nose more powerfully than the foil. The hydrofoil angle is alterable by automatic device. Tail vanes can be utilized to hold the machine in trim during water manoeuvres and

No. 22,408 H. L., A. E. and H. O. Short.
Instead of the rectangular box of vanes of the previous patent, the hydrofoils are set to an acute V to cushion the shock of landing.

In Jim's own Notes he had written: 'Work on aeroplanes and floating devices.'

Although Shorts' first twin-engine machine, S.39, had been so much praised – 'the star turn' of Eastchurch was how one writer described the machine, and although much was learnt during the project, Jim was already striving for something better and had drawn sketch-schemes for a successor long before S.39 was first flown by McClean on the 18th September.

Jim was reported on 7th September, 1911, as 'busy in one of the sheds ... engaged on work of a special nature ...' The work of a special nature would probably have been work on the design drawings of a rebuild to twin-engine status of S.27 – one of Jim's rather better A.1. ideas and an idea which McClean had liked so much that he had placed the order for the machine with Shorts. Although, of course, ordered from Shorts, it was understood that the second twin-engine machine was Jim's 'baby' and McClean promised that he, Jim, could test it in due course.

The first of the generic S.27's, as has already been described, was ordered by Cecil Grace in 1910; after Grace's loss McClean acquired from Shorts the second S.27 which Grace had ordered. McClean had spent many happy hours flying his single-engined 50 h.p.-Gnome powered S.27 during the early January days before he had left for his Pacific jaunt. He had taken up a number of passengers, including Jim, and the latter had flown her once or twice. It was an aeroplane which they both liked.

Jim worked on the re-build to twin-engine status throughout September and saw through the completion of the work by 11th October; partly, perhaps, for reasons of financial economy but at least as much for reasons of economy of his precious time – Jim moved out of his digs in Eastchurch Post Office and back into his own original Shed, which, with a little help, he made more comfortable. Oswald Short, who had been sharing the Post Office digs with Jim, now also moved into Jim's Shed. If one questions why Oswald did not remain in the Post Office digs or remove to even more comfortable quarters in his brother's house, the answer is not difficult to find. Oswald had assisted his brother Eustace in balloon building in their early days and had worked at Shellbeach under Horace for several years before the firm moved to Eastchurch. His work had always been under direction. There had been no designing involved. To move Oswald alongside Jim – the man with the flair for new ideas and the engineering training to put those ideas into effect – was an astute move over which I see Horace Short's guiding hand. Jim, the enthusiast, frank and friendly, would have no ideas not imparted to Oswald, no schemes not discussed and worried over with his companion. It was better than an apprenticeship for Oswald. However, since Jim liked Oswald and got along well with him, it was also a perfectly happy arrangement.

Jim sent a postcard home in September: 'I and Oswald Short are living down in the Shed. The A. I. R. have paid up £10. We are having a bath put in also a sink and white distemper all through. New twin-engine job a great success. Maclean took me up on her on Sunday. I have not been flying at all, only drawing. Lots of work; as the electric light is being put in and several new designs are . . .' the writing ends. Across the top of the postcard he had written: 'Thank you for your letters. Sorry not to have answered or to have thanked you for the biscuits, *Punch* etc. I am writing to Cousin Harry.'

There is no doubt that he was busy – so busy that even the first flight of Short's twin-engined aeroplane rated a total of only fifteen words in reference.

At the very end of October he wrote home again:

Aero Club Flying Grounds, Eastchurch.
Dear Dad,

Oswald Short, the youngest brother, just the same age as myself, is living here in the shed with me. We are halving all expenses and we think it will come cheaper than the P. O. and more convenient. We have closed up the door from the office into the shed and converted the office into a bedroom with a fitted bunk and wardrobe.

My old bedroom is the bathroom, scullery and storeroom with a bath in one corner and a door through into the shed, a sink and a large cupboard . . .

. . . all the rooms are being distempered white, which looks very nice and clean, the place looks habitable and cosy. We cook breakfast and they do all the catering letting us know in detail each week how much has been spent. I use the car much less and economise that way as well, and I see more of the Naval men. Oswald Short is (a) very decent chap and we hit it off very well together.

I hope when things are fixed I will be able to fetch you down here on the car to see it.

Maclean took me up on the new twin-engine machine (27 altered) – I was originally told that I was to fly it but when it came to the point Maclean, (who after all was paying for it) couldn't resist taking it up himself. I have done an awfull lot of work on the machine, drawing,

'Early days of flying' at Eastchurch
photo: Jim Travers.

scheming and hurrying the job through. I hope you are all right. I may be home next week end.

Your loving son, Jim.

Jim's disappointment at not testing his newest work is bitterly clear in that letter.

An 'awfull lot of work, drawing, scheming and hurrying the job through.'

S.27 twin-engine, as well as having the same 'absolutely colossal' chassis as S.39, had various fitted instruments, among them an engine-speed indicator and aneroid barometer – although not, as yet, a black box. But the greatest improvement was the direct drive instead of the chain-drive, with the result that the power of the 2 × 50 h.p. Gnome engines was used more efficiently.

The 'Tandem Twin' or 'Vacuum Cleaner' was an instant success and marked a turning-point and upsurge in Short Brothers' career.

H. P. Gardner had written to Emmie in September:

... I was glad to hear that Jim has got a job with Short and hope he will do so well he will take him in as a partner . . .' Jim had certainly done well enough to be taken in as a partner but when, after the acclaim of the Triple Twin and the even greater acclaim of the Tandem Twin, no partnership was offered, Jim would have realized that no such partnership would ever come his way.

The Short brothers, with their unity of purpose and family solidarity, born of a tough start in life, would not have wanted any additional name on their registration of designs at the Patent Office.

During October an interesting letter reached *The Aeroplane* from Winnipeg:

> Sir, News just to hand about the double-engined 'Short' biplane, and thought I would inform you that I have been designing a similar machine for the past six weeks, (plane actually commenced on Sunday August 20th.) I hope to send you the plans for inspection in a few weeks, but meantime I'd like you to know that I have not copied. My machine is a 'headless' biplane, both engines being in front of pilot. Congratulations on the paper. It's a 'stunner.'
>
> Geo. Mac Williams

Although Mr Mac Williams must have been referring to S.39, it is of note that he took twin-engine design beyond that of S.27 Tandem Twin; for engines in front of, or alongside, pilot, became the norm for many years.

Less spectacular than the two twin-engine machines, but nevertheless innovative, was the 70 h.p. Short on which Jim did a lot of work and which he test-flew in late November. It was adapted specifically for instructional use, with side-by-side seats, and he began to instruct members of the Territorial Balloon Company in early December.

He wrote home on 3rd December in general terms, without any reference to his new occupation, and sounding rather cross.

3rd December 1911. R Ae C. Grounds, Eastchurch.
My dear Mummy,
    Thank you for your letter and the cuttings of Dunne's letter and Masson Burst's article. Dunne always manages to keep himself to the fore by all that sort of letter writing and speech making etc., but his flying and actual performance are rotten.
    I think Short is in a very good position with regard to the navy and I think it is certain that he will have an order for some machines fairly soon.

We get on very well in our rooms here and our meals are decently cooked etc. and the place kept clean. We have been working overtime until 9 o'clock every day last week and that means 8 in the morning until 9 in the evening with $1\frac{1}{2}$ hours for lunch and $\frac{1}{2}$ for tea at 5 o'clock; so there is not much time to spare, I started to overhaul the car but I can't get on with it.

I hope Dad is well and that you are not overdoing yourself.

Love to yourselves and Jessie and Herbert.

Your loving son, Jim.

Flight reported as follows in the issue of 2nd December, 1911: 'On Sunday, Mr Travers, who is to instruct the Territorial Balloon Company in the art of flying, was out testing the new 70 h.p. Gnome-engined Short biplane which has been specially prepared for their instruction.' and in British Notes of the Week in the same issue: 'The good work which is being done with a very scanty equipment by the London Balloon Co. of the Territorials will be considerably benefited by the use of the two Short biplanes which have been placed at its disposal by a well-known member of the Royal Aero Club at the club's grounds at Eastchurch. Some fourteen members have volunteered to go through a course of training, and for those who cannot afford to spend the necessary three weeks or a month at Eastchurch arrangements are being made for special instruction to be given during weekends. The generous lender of the aeroplanes has undertaken to look after their maintenance.'

And from *Flight* of December 9th:

On Monday and Tuesday, Mr S. P. Cockerell and Mr V. A. Barrington Kennett, both of the Territorial Balloon Company, put in their first practice, under Mr Travers' guidance, on the 70 h.p. Short biplane. Mr Cockerell, by the way, already has his R. Ae. C. pilot certificate, and judging from his first performance at Eastchurch is cut out for a really good flyer. Mr Barrington Kennett had his first experience of piloting from the passenger pilot seat of the new machine, from which, by a special dual control, a pupil is able to take charge at the will of the instructor.

And from the issue of December 23rd:

Saturday was an excellent flying day, and no time was wasted by the Eastchurch aviators. Travers was out early on the Short 70 h.p. machine, making a very pretty flight against a clear blue sky. Afterwards he made several tuition flights with Mr Cutler and Mr D. W. Barton, of the Territorial Balloon Section, both of whom took charge of the machine several times through the dual control.'

So the great year of 1911 drew to a close.

With the collapse of her mooring mast in Cavendish Dock of Naval Airship No 1, the poor MAYFLY, (about whom so many offensive remarks had been made – May-not-fly, May-never-fly etc., etc.) the opportunity for the four Naval pilots to be actually employed as pilots was at last assured. 'Twixt Wind & Water' C. G. Grey had written. Fortunately 'Wind' triumphed and the Navy, at last, had wings.

J. L. T. had placed his bungalow at the disposal of the Naval pilots and from the winter of 1911–1912 it became known as the 'Navy bungalow.' No doubt the Admiralty eventually leased the building from J. L. T. I can find no record among family letters of what arrangement was made. However it has been established that he did not sell his property at Eastchurch until 1918. (To the Air Ministry.)

The Memorial at Eastchurch proclaims that it was, in 1909, the first home of British aviation.

The Farnborough brigade might dispute such a claim and put the place nearer home and the date a year or so earlier. That is a matter for aviation historians to argue and I am sure they will do so indefinitely.

There is no doubt that Eastchurch, whether first or only close second, was vital to the rapid expansion of British aviation, both from land and sea; and that the very name of Eastchurch formed, as it were, it's own magnetic field to attract many of the best and brightest men of the day.

Among the very best, at that or at any other time, was Francis – later Sir Francis – McClean.

For it was McClean who, by taking over Grace's posthumous S.27 and continuing to order aeroplanes from Horace Short, did so much to enable Short Brothers to survive and expand: to cross the thinnest cat-ice of survival to the firm ground of a sound business venture.

It was McClean who lent his aeroplanes to the Admiralty, for six months and more, in order that the four Naval pilots could be trained without cost to the country; and it was he 'the well-known member of the Royal Aero Club,' who also lent aeroplanes cost-of-maintenance free, to the Territorial Balloon Company for their training.

It was McClean who ordered the first two twin-engined aeroplanes from Shorts, with all the opportunity for research and experiment which such an order afforded; and it was McClean who, on seeing Jim's ideas for 'floating devices' – ordered from Shorts the 70 h.p.

Tractor Biplane on floats. And it was McClean who, with typical generosity, parted with plots and parcels of land around his cottage, thus enabling the inventors to put up their Sheds and work in peace, Short Brothers to expand their factory, and the Royal Aero Club to establish their flying grounds there.

2

WAR IN THE AIR – WEATHER PERMITTING

1912–1913

Tractor Biplane great success – Jim decides to leave Short's – applies for Australian job – joins Graham-White at Hendon – flies on Wake Up England Mission around South Coast on Waterplane – takes part in Illuminated Display and Night Flying at Hendon – applies for Navy, Army or Breuget – accepted first civilian pilot into Navy.

THE Tractor Biplane was originally a landplane and the adaptation to seaplane was by means of a central float mounted under the land-carriage, laterally stabilized by strut-mounted airbag floats. It first flew as a landplane in early January, 1912. Jim sent a typically brief postcard home to his Mother:

Eastchurch. Wednesday 17 Jan. Just a line to let you know I am quite well, lots of flying last week – since Sunday afternoon however the wind has been too strong, rain as well, very cold here yesterday, and to-day. Oswald Short gone off to town last night so am alone. Not such a press of work for me now 2 draughtsmen have arrived. Tractor Biplane great success.
Thank you for socks and magazines. Yours. J. L. T. Jim.

Emmie's letter to her youngest daughter at St Chad's, Cambridge, was typically long and the following is a short extract:
Warlingham. January 19th. My dear Ali, I have just had a line from Jim, quite well, lots of flying. Short has 2 new draughtsmen so Jim is not quite so pressed for work. He had to do all the drawing before, have you seen the Graphic this week. It has a good account of Samson's flight from the battleship, with pictures. You might get it and send it on to Uncle Geoff. Glen Huntly Rd., Elsterwick, Melbourne. I sent Jim a waistcoat from Jaegers. They had not much choice as they make them for the Ski ing season but I shd not think that is over, we heard from 3 people just back home after 3 weeks. . . .

Although it was perhaps not wholly true – as H. G. Travers claimed that it was – that Jim did all the 'work' while Short 'ran up and down to London, taking out patents and seeing people' – nevertheless there was probably a good deal of truth in his memory of those days. Jim had, after all, been appointed 'Assistant & Designer' not Assistant Designer to Shorts, so the division of their work, Jim doing all the design drawing and Short dealing with all the business and selling side of which he was so much a master, was quite in accordance with what might now be called the 'job description'.

After seven months of almost unremitting toil, for Jim had had only two or three week ends at home and one day in London during those seven months, – he could at last take life a little more steadily. He had lived in adequate though somewhat primitive conditions. He had economized to every ha'penny of his pay and to every minute of his precious time. He had been up early, flying, and up late, drawing. He had yarned 'doing a good lot of talking' with Horace Short and to him Jim had poured out his ideas, his rich, inventive genius.

For the first time for months, he had time to attend a lecture; Emmie wrote to Charles, mentioning the fact, on 26th January: '... Jimmy went up to London last week and stayed a night at the flat. He came up for a lecture on bird flight by Hawker – the one who writes in *Flight* – Jim said the lecture was good and he met a good many people he knew. He and V. went to see something – and they and H. O. went to something else in the evening and John Daman turned up and they yarned and drew plans ...'

By early February Jim was ready to leave Shorts and had applied for a more lucrative job.

He must have gradually realized during his time with them that they would never acknowledge the work which had done so much to launch them as an independent designing firm (– distinct from manufacturers of other people's designs, Wright, Sommer, Bleriot, Grace, Huntington etc.) – nor credit him with the hours of sound engineering instruction which he had given to Oswald Short. His fine ideals of all invention being shared, the ideals with which he had started out, the ideal of a rich pool of knowledge from which everyone could dip, was equally thwarted.

He had no quarrel with Short. Far from it. He liked and admired the man, It was just that he had now taken the measure of Horace

Short's exclusive power and powers of exclusion. As with the twin-engined machines, so with the Tractor Biplane; so with all his work on floating devices, now in Oswald Short's hands.

Quiet as ever and quietly job-hunting, Jim continued to instruct. From *Flight* of 3rd February: 'A number of the Territorial London Balloon Company were also down for the week-end in charge of 2nd-Lieuts. Cockerell and Barrington Kennett, and under the excellent tutelage of Travers some good flying was got through ...' He wrote home on 5th February, 1912: 'Royal Aero Club & Ground, Eastchurch, Isle of Sheppey: Dear Mummy, Thank you very much for the vests and the letter. I went to see some of Legros' paintings and drawings at a place in Bond Street with John Daman the other day. I was a little disappointed. Herbert came down here for the weekend so you will hear a lot of my news from him. He was able to get in a little skating with a fellow called Fowler, – who also had skates – there was no flying as the wind was too strong. I have sent in an application for the Australian job. It is said that they have over a hundred applications for it, of course, a lot of these would be no good, but it shows there is some competition for it. Short cannot pay as much as that though he might pay £300 in a years time if I can continue to stick on with him – which is doubtful, love to Jess and Dad. Your loving son   Jim'.

On February 10th Emmie wrote to Charles from St Chad's, Cambridge, where she was staying for some weeks: '... I am glad you had such good skating. I remember skating on flooded marshes near the sea at Budleigh Salterton ... it was very good sport. ... Herbert went down to Sheppey last weekend and he and one other who had skates found a pond to skate on and then they rigged up a sort of sledge with a sail and tried toboganning down the gliding hill – but there was not enough snow. ... It is a lovely morning so I suppose our later winter is over. I found the thermometer in the verandah had registered 12 degrees of frost one day while I was away ... Jim had applied for one of the Australian appointments. He heard that there had been more than 100 applications ...'

The Australian appointment in question had been advertised through the 'Official Notices to Members' of 'The Royal Aero Club of the U.K.' The following announcement is quoted in full from the advertisement in *Flight* of January 20th, 1912, *Flight* being the official organ of the Royal Aero Club:

Australian Commonwealth.

A letter has been received from the Australian Commonwealth Offices for-
warding a copy of the instructions received from the Commonwealth Government, which are as follows:

> Proposed to appoint two expert mechanics and aviators, Defence Depart-
> ment, salary per annum £400- including all allowances, except travelling;
> applications to be invited by advertisement, receivable by you up to and
> including February 1st; candidates to state nature of qualifications and experi-
> ence, military experience, whether born or domiciled Australia, age, married
> or single.
>
> Commonwealth accept no responsibility for accidents. Applications also
> invited Australia.
>
> Successful candidate will be appointed for 12 months probation on con-
> clusion of which, if satisfactory, appointment may be confirmed. Obtain
> tenders or quotations from approved firms, two monoplanes and two biplanes
> and necessary spare parts. Successful tenderers to put two aviators through
> course of instruction in manufacture of machines and aviation, suffciently
> familiarize them with machines and enable them to make all necessary repairs;
> tenderers submit schedule prices for supply extra parts.
>
> The aviators must be British subjects and the aeroplanes of British make.

Other than his lack of military experience, Jim would have fulfilled the
qualifications for such a wide-ranging and interesting job to perfection;
unfortunately the offer was withdrawn, as Emmie was to mention in
a letter to Alie of March 23rd.

Jim, in the intense cold of Sheppey, continued to work in his Shed
for Shorts, to keep his eyes and ears open for a better job and, whenever
the weather was flyable, to instruct.

From *Flight* of March 2nd: 'Saturday was a very busy day, all the
available machines being in constant use. Sergeant Cutler, of the
Territorial Balloon Company, gained his pilot's certificate by a well-
made flight during which he reached an elevation of some 300 feet.
He was officially observed by Mr Frank McClean, Lieut. L'Strange
Malone, R N, and Mr J. L. Travers, the instructor. He is the first
Territorial pupil to gain his certificate at the Eastchurch Aerodrome,
but others are well on the way to doing so, and Sergeants Hedley,
Hubbard and Meredith may shortly be expected to qualify for their
'tickets.' Lieut. V. A. Barrington Kennett was down for the day and
also flew for the last half of his pilot's certificate test on the Short dual-
control biplane, completing the course in an excellent manner and
landing very neatly.'

Later, from the same issue of *Flight*: 'Mr Frank McClean, to whose generosity and energy the whole of the present forward state and activity at Eastchurch may be traced, visited the aerodrome on Saturday, and flew on the Short T 70 h.p. tractor biplane, which looked very fast when flying with the other machines,' and 'On Sunday Travers and the Territorials were out flying in a dead calm atmosphere, which prevailed between 7 and 10 o'clock a.m., Meredith making several very neat figures of eight. After this the wind began to get up and further flying for beginners was not considered advisable. ...'

On March 23rd Emmie wrote to Alie, at St Chad's:

> ... Jimmy turned up Wednesday. Having come to town to tell McClean of the smash up of the school machine by Barton, a pupil. (no one hurt.) Maclean and Bidder who is in with him and also a pupil of Jim's had to consult whether the pupils might use the newer machine. They said of course Jim might but that was not to the point. Maclean is an awfully decent man and very good natured but disgusted with the Government and cannot keep the territorials going for ever. So Jim is anxious to find out the terms on which Government is going to take civilians. The Australian plan is off until they hear what England means to do. On Friday afternoon Jim called on Bidder who is at the Vickers Maxim Works Westminster and he said they had settled to let them use the new machine and wanted Jim to go down at once – as some men were going ...

– after describing a recent concert she had heard (Emmie was an insatiable concert-goer), she adds as a postscript: 'I wonder if there is a ladies rifle shooting club at Cambridge which you could join. C. T. has been doing quite well this term.'

Jim probably left Shorts in about April of 1912.

I can find no precise record of the date, only circumstantial information on the subject, – indeed, not only does there seem to be no known date on which he left Shorts there equally seems to have been no recorded date, other than in the Travers family letters, when he started with the firm. Aviation historians who have studied the archive of Short Brothers back to the firm's earliest beginnings tell me that nowhere is there any mention of Jim's work as their Designer; nor is there even any mention of his name, other, of course, than on the quaint 'Bill for expenses' and which must surely have included the whole support party for the Samson cross country flight.

Yet it is not as though he had never been, for his work, all those thousands of drawings, all those scores of 'A.1.' ideas – all was appropriated by Shorts and became embodied in their fund of knowledge, thus helping to make them the magnificent firm which they were and still are. None of it went to waste. As for Jim: he was their Designer for a vital six months. He certainly stayed for eight. Everything else is a mystery.

Emmie was staying with her Mother and some of the Prescott Aunts at 18, Queen Square, Bath, for a few weeks in May of 1912. They were taking the cure. Bath was not Emmie's favourite place, but she was a dutiful daughter and of an age when such a family-loving woman will be leant on by the older generation. J. L. T. wrote to her there from Warlingham on the 18th May and from the content and tone of his letter one gathers that Jim had been at home for a while:

The boys have gone to Eastchurch to-day, Jem by train and Herby on his mo-bike, Jem left mid-day and Herbe about 3 ... The girls went to a picnic this afternoon. I have been cutting grass nearly all day. Yesterday Jem and I worked at the tool shed. It will take about 4 or 5 days more to finish it, but I think it will be very useful when it is done and not too much in evidence ...

On the same day Emmie wrote to Alie at St Chad's: '... Can you write to Jim Morse Code as he has to practice it and all sorts of signalling also. I copy this from an officer's note book. Said to be an easy way of learning Morse. Does it strike you in that light.

Bath was in great excitement yesterday.

The *Daily Mail* is sending a Mission round the country to wake up England – on an aeroplane. It was due mid-day and arrived 6.30. Miss Harris invited me to the top of the house to see it, but it was only 3 military kites one above another. In another place was a box kite which looked very like a biplane fighting against the wind.

Next week Grahame-White, Hamel, Hucks etc. are coming here. It is the Bath and West of England Show and also Race Week. So Dr B will not let Grannie have her Wednesday bath as the Bath Chair men may be jovial. ...'

Although J. L. T. did not like his dearest Emmie to spend too much time propping up her Mother and her elderly Aunts, he thoroughly approved of her going off on what seemed to him more pleasurable jaunts, particularly with Alie, as her next trip was planned to be: off to Helsingfors, via some time in Copenhagen. But she was still at Warlingham on June 15th and wrote to Alie, at St Chad's, on that day: ' ... Jim is piloting for Grahame-White until he hears from the War Office. He has sent in his papers. H.O. has settled to get a new Bradbury and his old bike goes in part payment. The Bradbury's take these hills well. ... '

Although it had been Bleriot who had done so much to expand Hendon by putting up his factory there, in three hangars in 1910, by 1912 it was Grahame-White who was the most famous entrepreneur operating out of Hendon. Grahame-White had asked Jim to do some flying for him and Jim, still waiting to hear from the War Office, was glad to accept. In June he was flying again and how cheerful he sounded in his letter to his Mother, short though it was, on June 17th 1912 from his digs in Annesley Avenue, Hendon:

I have been here a week to-day and I have had a little flying. On Friday I made two flights on the School Farman and on Saturday morning on another Farman and on Sunday evening I did some flying. I feel as if it does me good to get on a machine again, even if it is only a rotten old School machine, (strong enough only too heavy.) We were out quite early this morning, about 4.30.

There is not much for me to do but I get paid for it, and I think I am going to do some Hydro aeroplaning with Grahame-White on the sea somewhere, he is going to have a yacht and has ordered some new machines from France which will be over soon, perhaps at the end of the week – if I am chosen for the job and I think it is likely it ought to be great sport and very good experience. I am reading up navigation and practising morse code with the pupils, some Army officers are very good and have taught me some good tips ...

Although one would not have expected anyone such as Jim, who so intensely disliked publicity and noise, to have got along with the archetypal publicist, Grahame-White, nevertheless he did so; and his months of flying for 'G-W', which included instructing, giving passenger-flights, racing, hydro aeroplaning for the WAKE UP ENGLAND campaign, and all the rest of it, proved to be of the greatest interest and enjoyment to him.

Claude Grahame-White was a hustler of the old school: able, energetic and inclined to sharp practice. He had, for example, only won the Statue of Liberty Prize of October, 1910, by a series of technicalities, lodging a complaint against the true winner, Mr J. B. Moisant and then accepting the Royal Aero Club's further complaint against De Lesseps. He had been sued successfully by the Wright brothers for infringement of their patent in his 'own' aeroplane design; and, after repeatedly flying his aeroplane against the watching crowds at Hendon – only pulling away when within twenty feet of them – had been roundly rebuked for this unnecessary showmanship and dangerous flying by C. G. Grey in a long article in *The Aeroplane*.

He had made a successful and money-spinning tour in the United States in 1911 and on his return had checked in at the office of *The Aeroplane* to let them know of his success and, no doubt, to remind them that he was in business in England again and waited to be reported upon.

Yet for most people the other side of the coin predominated and for them the name of Grahame-White meant all that was adventurous, skilful and daring in aviation. Large numbers of people were inspired by him to learn to fly and the Grahame-White organization was there to encourage and to teach them.

Although his was only one of the several schools at Hendon it does seem to have been the best known and people who had scarcely seen an aeroplane had heard of the name of Grahame-White. The Bleriot, the Caudron, the Deperdussin and later, the Beatty, never seemed to have quite the same familiarity to the general public.

Jim had joined, when he joined the Grahame-White enterprise, a lively young crowd of pilots and he sounded hapy from the start; among his companions were some of those whose names were legendary: Hamel, Nardini, Verrier, Richard Gates, Marcel Desoutter, Louis Noel and Turner. Although Jim was doing a certain amount of instructing he was not, in the early days and by his own account, overloaded. He would have had time to read the pages of *The Aeroplane* and it is unlikely that he would have missed the news: '... that a new Short Hydro Aeroplane, officially known as S. 43, has been delivered to the Naval Wing of the Royal Flying Corps by the Short Brothers.'

The Aeroplane reported from the Grahame-White School at Hendon on 27th June: 'In morning Captain Salmond and Mr Fuller doing straights on Sommer with Mr Travers, Captain Halahan and Mr Cholmondeley having lessons in passenger seat,' and on 28th June: 'No school work. ... Mr Travers flew F.7 from S. Tottenham to Chingford, M. Noel having gone to the Farman works at Billancourt to bring over a new machine ...'

Jay wrote a long letter to her Mother on June 30th; after much Warlingham news of the Rose Show, games of golf, the men of the family being invited over to the cricketing week at Tunbridge Wells, and so on, she wrote: "This afternoon Jim came home. It was jolly seeing him and Dad was awfully pleased. He flew Noel's machine from Tottenham – but being rather misty landed at Chingford where the Whitleys came across him and asked him to stay the same night which he did and was very grateful as otherwise he would have had to sleep under the plane. He said they were awfully kind. Jimmy went back again this afternoon. ..."

Subsequently *The Aeroplane* reported on June 30th: 'No school work. Mr Travers flew F.7 to Hendon. Good exhibition flying.' And a little later: 'Mr J. L. Travers did good work on one of the old G-W school "busses", and one hopes to see him on something modern ere long, for he is really quite first class. ... Taking it all round,' (it was The Ladies Day at Hendon and a special occasion,) – 'it was a very entertaining day, and the spread of enthusiasm among the people was again proved by the number of the original 10,000 who hung on till nearly dark to see all the flying they could.'

The programmes on some of those special days at Hendon bore a similarity to the programmes at a gymkhana, for they were a mixture of display, entertainment and competition.

Races were the thing. There is a photograph of him (reproduced in *Flight*) with Lewis Turner, Verrier and Hamel at the start of one of the numerous cross-country races and he later piloted Grahame-White on a round-England race.

Grahame-White, energetic and intensely patriotic, was pursuing the WAKE UP ENGLAND campaign with his customary skill and show-manship; he had long wanted England to have a properly trained and equipped flying corps and the WAKE UP ENGLAND campaign was helpful publicity for his cause. His idea of visiting South Coast resorts with his hydro-aeroplanes suitably emblazoned was typical of his flamboyant nature; the two hydro aeroplanes which he used, and which have already been mentioned by Jim as having been ordered from France, were an Henri Farman and a Paulhan Curtiss. (*Flight* had reported as early as February 4th 1911 that 'Mr Glenn Curtiss succeeded in rising from the water at San Diego, California, on the 27th ult. after flying for half a mile he came down again on the water, and turning round, rose again, flew for a distance of about a mile, finally coming to rest at practically the point from which he started.')

The *Aeroplane* reported in it's Continental Notes for early July, 1912, that: 'During the week Mr Grahame-White and M. Noel both made trial flights to Buc on the formers' 3-seater 70 h.p. Gnome Farman. This machine is intended for hydro-aeroplaning.'

In the same issue of the *Aeroplane* it was reported that something more ambitious was being tested on the lake of Geneva: '... M. Sommer intends shortly to test a hydro Aerobus on the lake of Geneva. It is a biplane with 100 h.p. engine. The two large floats have been constructed by Tellier. It is intended to fly with 6 passengers ...'

The WAKE UP ENGLAND campaign was successful and England, even if not waking up enough to her peril for Grahame-White's liking, certainly woke up to the joys of the waterplane during the summer of 1912.

As for Jim, the seaplane flying and handling experience was, for him, a delight and a chance to extend and multiply knowledge on a subject which had long attracted him. It became a sphere of knowledge which he was to make especially his own.

He flew Grahame-White's Henri Farman up and down the South Coast that summer, giving passenger flights from the beaches at Eastbourne, Bexhill, Hastings, Brighton and Cowes, Isle of Wight.

Grahame-White, on the Paulhan Curtiss, was the supporting or back-up machine; Jim appears to have remained as the constant 'Hydro aeroplane' pilot for the tour but other pilots, among them Richard Gates, Noel and Verrier, are noted as having joined the tour from time to time.

*   *   *

'Mr Travers and the Farman Waterplane, Eastbourne August 2nd, 1912'

photo: R. W. Vieler

H. G. Wells' account of his own first flight on 5th August, 1912, is so interesting and evocative, that I asked the Exctrs of the H. G. Wells Estate for their permission to reprint it, and am grateful to them for their kindness in letting me do so.

From *An Englishman Looks at the World*, published by Cassell & Co. 1914.

Hitherto my only flights have been flights of imagination, but this morning I flew. I spent about ten or fifteen minutes in the air; we went out to sea, soared up, came back over the land, circled higher, planed steeply down to the water, and I landed with the conviction that I had had only the foretaste of a great store of hitherto unexpected pleasures. At the first chance I will go up again, and I will go higher and further.

... ...

Sixteen years ago, in the days of Langley and Lilienthal, I was one of the few journalists who believed and wrote that flying was possible; it affected my reputation unfavourably, and produced in the few discouraged pioneers of those days a quite touching gratitude.

... ...

That was only sixteen years ago, and it is amusing to recall how cautiously even we out-and-out believers did our prophesying. I was quite a desperate fellow; I said outright that in my lifetime we should see men flying. But I qualified that by repeating that for many years to come it would be an enterprise only for quite fantastic daring and skill.

... ...

The waterplane in which I soared over Eastbourne this morning with Mr Grahame-White was as steady as a motor-car running on asphalt.

... ...

I had heard a great deal of talk about the deafening uproar of the engine. I counted a headache among my chances. There again reason reinforced conjecture. When in the early morning Mr Travers came from Brighton in this Farman in which I flew I could hear the hum of the great insect when it still seemed abreast of Beachy Head, and a good two miles away.

... ...

And so it was I went up into the air at Eastbourne with the impression that flying was still an uncomfortable, experimental, and slightly heroic thing to do, and came down to the cheerful gathering crowd upon the sands again with the knowledge that it is a thing achieved for everyone. It will get much cheaper, no doubt, and much swifter, and he improved in a dozen ways – we MUST get self-starting engines, for example, for both our aeroplanes and motor-cars – but it is available to-day for anyone who can reach it. An invalid lady of seventy could have enjoyed all that I did if only one could have got her into the passenger's seat. Getting there was a little difficult, it is rue; the waterplane was out in the surf, and I was carried to it on a boatman's back, and then had to clamber carefully through the wires, but that is a matter of detail. ...

It was not only H. G. Wells, among the famous writers of the day, who was so enchanted by the idea of flying.

Rudyard Kipling came on the scene in, perhaps, a somewhat surprising capacity: he was elected Chairman of the Safety Devices Committee, which was formed in 1910, and early on he suggested to the Committee that safety clothing should be invented for the protection of aviators again the risk of fire. His short story, *With the Night Mail*, published some years later, was a fine tale and one of informed prophecy.

The flying displays at Hendon had been taking place all summer; still the crowds clamoured for more and still Grahame-White and his merry band of aviators sought new ways to interest and to entertain them. The climax came in September, with the 'Grand Illuminated Night Flying and Firework Display.' This followed on the military manœuvres at which, it was reported: 'somewhere about two dozen aeroplanes detailed to take part in the manœuvres now being carried out in East Anglia, with many of them flying under secret orders. . . .' So at last, with much due to the influence of Admiral Prince Louis of Battenberg and to Mr Winston Churchill, the aeroplane became recognized as an essential part of any fighting force. *Flight* could have some claim to have prodded Mr Churchill, but it was prodding – if that is what it was – a man who was already proceeding steadily in the right direction. From the second leader in *Flight* of 9th December, 1911: 'Since his translation to the Admiralty, Mr Winston Churchill has given so much evidence of his thoroughness and sincerity in the best interests of our naval supremacy that we would urgently point out to him the importance of without delay putting the Navy into a position of strength in respect of aeroplanes. There need be no wild plunging, but an immediate start is badly wanted . . .'

The manœuvres in East Anglia were much appreciated by *Flight*, who commented: '. . . valuable information as to the 'enemy's' movements have already been obtained by the aerial observers, while the pilots have had a number of exciting experiences . . .' The exciting experiences were mostly: being brought down by gusty or strong winds, or by ignition or other engine trouble.

In December of 1911 Major R. Baden-Powell had asked, through the columns of *Flight* 'The question that I should like to see authoritatively answered is: "Are military aeroplanes likely to be used at night?" '

In September of 1912 at Hendon his question was authoritatively answered. *Flight* gave an advance notice of 'A unique programme ... There will be the usual exhibition flights from 3 o'clock 'weather permitting – of course; and at 7.30 p.m. will commence the first illuminated flying fete.' The Hendon Aerodrome Programme for Thursday evening, September 26th, announced: 'War in the Air ... 8 p.m. (weather permitting). The lighting effects will be carried out on a most extensive and hitherto unsurpassed scale, and the Aerodrome will present a perfect blaze of light. Each of the aeroplanes, which will be piloted by well-known Aviators, will carry a powerful searchlight, in addition to side and rear lights and they will also be outlined with hundreds of tiny electric lights supplied from portable accumulators carried in the body of the machine. On the roofs of the hangars there will be powerful naval searchlights to guide the Airmen flying in the darkness above and the pylons which mark out the $1\frac{1}{2}$ miles' speed course will also be brilliantly illuminated. The various enclosures and the bandstand will also be fitted with many hundreds of coloured lanterns and the Aerodrome will present a remarkably novel and beautiful scene.

'During the evening there will be a display of fire balloons and fireworks, illustrating "War in the Air", and the effect produced cannot fail to prove extremely interesting and impressive. Among the Aviators who will pilot the illuminated machines are Messrs C. Grahame-White, R. T. Gates, Marcel Desoutter, Lewis Turner, Jules Nardini, Louis Noel and J. L. Travers.

'On the Saturday following (September 28th), the Naval and Military Meeting will be held.'

The military manœuvres, the illuminated night flying, the talk of armaments, the rumours that Germany was spoiling for a fight, all these things produced in the aviators of 1912 a certain dangerous excitement.

The Italians had been among the first to drop bombs from an aeroplane but such an obviously bright idea soon caught on. In January, 1912, Lieut. Samson – with the aid of a Walker hand-held bomb release, did bomb-dropping practise at Eastchurch. (Eastchurch had, in December 1911, been formally established as the Naval Flying School; J.L.T.'s bungalow becoming their Officer's Mess.)

Many and various were the theories on bomb-dropping and Jim,

too, was working on his own design for a bomb-sighter. Emmie
mentioned the fact in a letter to Alie written on October 2nd:

Horton, Warlingham. ... Yesterday was a lovely day here until
about 5 – just when Jim was going to fly – down came the rain ...
Jim went up to Hendon again and I expect managed his flying to try
the sighter. He was going on to Salisbury Plain to see what he could
of the camp – five miles from the nearest station. It has turned very
cold. Jim has been writing another paper and typed it and sent it to
the *Aeroplane*. ...

Looking back over the previous year one can easily see how Jim was
drawn to Service flying rather than to any other. The first four Naval
pilots, – Samson admittedly rather loud but Longmore quiet, charming
and immensely able, the very best of pilots – they had all been good
advertisements for Service life.

Then again the certainty that hydro-aeroplaning must come in as a
regular feature of Naval flying was an attraction. It was after all a well-
known and inescapable fact of the times that it was impossible to put
a flat top on a ship.

WAKE UP ENGLAND and the waking up at last to the necessity of
having a Central Flying School, (opened, in June, at Upavon); the
frequent contact with Service pupils, both Naval and Military, and the
discussions with Service flyers which must surely have taken place
about the use of the aeroplane in modern warfare, the possibility, too,
of scientific advance, – how much all this would have appealed to Jim.
He had come a long way since at the age of sixteen, in Queensland,
he had tried to regulate the pump-engine by means of a heliograph.

He was still flying for Grahame-White but the summer was over;
the weather had permitted war in the air to take place; manœuvres,
too, were over. Jim worked away at his bomb-sighter and with the
darkening October evenings, sometimes flew with a lighted aeroplane.
Emmie wrote to Alie: '... Jim came home for the night on Thursday
about 4 he flew in rather a high wind and later about 5.30 and again
with a lighted plane. I believe Friday's *Standard* has a good notice. He
has not been able to try his bomb dropping sighter yet: but has taken
out a patent. ...'

That Jim of all people should seek to take out a Patent shows that
he had learned, from Horace Short, a little of the ways of the world.
I was unprepared for what I found at the Patent Office when I called

there in 1985 to enquire about Jim's bombsight. There was little difficulty in discovering their numbers, 21,855 and 28,673 and their brief descriptions, 'Title of apparatus for use in dropping bombs/despatches or the like from aircraft,' and, 'Sight for use in dropping bombs from aircraft' respectively.

The helpful staff directed me to the books wherein I could expect to find the detailed descriptions and, of course, Jim's drawings. There was nothing. A senior member of staff also examined the books. All reference and cross-reference to these numbers seemed to have been removed. Yet the books themselves were undamaged and the pages had not been torn out. They were just not there. It gave me an eerie feeling. Where had they gone? Who had them? Who had used the knowledge and perhaps the 'A.1.' ideas, of Jim's bombsight?

The senior staff member told me then that it would be reasonable to assume that they had 'gone into Copyright' and that if they had, he added, 'It is most unlikely that anyone could ever get them out.' So be it. I hope that they may have been helpful to this country during the second war for they were, according to some, too far ahead of their time for the first.

Mr Alexander had been playing golf for weeks with J.L.T. at Warlingham and the two elderly gentlemen decided on a whim to make a trip to Hendon: '... Mr A and Dad went a pilgrimage,' Wrote Emmie, '– to Hendon getting there at 5 and leaving at 5.30 not having asked for Jim and having seen nothing. ...' Sad.

Jim, the weakling child, near to death more than once, had had a run of pretty good health since his Australian days. Although always liable to colds and chest infections he usually threw them off easily. His life style – overwork and an exceptional amount of exposure to cold when 'on an aeroplane' – there cannot have been much that he did not know about the wind-chill factor – now, at last, caught up with him; about the time of his twenty-ninth birthday in November, 1912, he went down with what was probably a chest illness. Emmie nursed him at home; as soon as he was convalescent he began applying for work again.

Emmie wrote to Alie on November 22nd:

... Jim is much better but awfully pulled down. He went out yesterday and twice to-day. But yesterday he had 3 Letters. The most important being from the War Office to the effect that they wished

him to join Upavon 'forthwith' – commanded to do so by the Lords
and to go on to one of the naval depots. So he is just waiting to hear
which day. He is of course very glad as it is what he wanted. By a
strange coincidence, the second letter was from the army aircraft,
Aldershot, offering him a post as 2nd draughtsman combined with
pilot, and the 3rd from the Breguet people, some view of a job.
... The Swans' (their next-door neighbours, tenants and eventually
purchasers of Woottonga had grown, after an unpromising start, into
kindly friends), – 'the Swans have asked the 4 in to tea to-morrow to
meet a sister or neice of Mr Morcom. As V. will be here she and Jess
will go and possibly Jim – but H. is engaged to Jezzi at Sheppey for
the week end. I shall discourage any trip further than that until the
summer – or spring – so don't expect him. ...'

Jim joined Upavon as 'commanded' and gained maximum marks for
theory in his qualifying examination at the Central Flying School for
entry into the Naval Wing of the Royal Flying Corps. But there was
an unforeseen problem.

Emmie wrote to Charles on December 6th; although her letter
began full of news of a wonderful Tetrazzini concert which Uncle
Henry Prescott had taken the girls to, most of the letter concerned the
snag about Jim's entry into the Naval Wing.

'... Jimmy came back from Upavon, having passed the exam. In
the principal he was bracketed top – but when he went to the Admiralty
to enquire what he was to do the Captain in charge said the admiralty
had decided to admit no civilians except as naval volunteers – at least
this man THOUGHT so – but is to let Jim know as soon as he hears.

'So Jim has gone down to-day to try to see Samson. If this is the
case Jim will probably apply for the Farnboro post which he had
refused and take the army air corps with it but he much prefers the
navy ...

'Herbert had a good run to Eastchurch and back last week end. It
was raining hard on Sunday evening, but he had TWO suits of clothes
under overalls and kept warm and dry. ...'

The hard core of Naval Officers, most of whom should have known
better, had always disliked and continued to dislike the aviators in
their midst; they did their best to discredit, disallow and, when possible,
to disown any Naval pilot; as late as 1918 such was still the case. It

was fortunate for Naval flying that the bright stars, Admiral Prince Louis of Battenberg, Captain Bacon, Captain Murray Sueter and others of equal foresight, held sway. There were notable civilians, too, the most famous perhaps being Winston Churchill, whom Jim had taken on a passenger flight from Eastchurch a year or so before. (Sir Winston 'remembered the flight well' his Secretary assured me in a letter of 1959, when I wrote to Chartwell for confirmation of the flight over Sheppey 'an early flight but not his first'.)

Guidance seemed to be needed and J.L.T. turned to an acquaintance of his, the M.P. Mr W. Joynson-Hicks, for advice and help. *Hansard* records that in January, 1913: 'Mr Joynson-Hicks asked the First Lord of the Admiralty whether, in view of the fact that the list of Lieutenants in the Navy is over 100 short, he proposes still further to increase this shortage by appointing naval lieutenants to the Royal Flying Corps; and, if not, how he proposed to obtain sufficient pilots for the permanent establishment of the Naval Wing of the Royal Flying Corps?'

To this clever question Mr Churchill gave a thoroughly satisfactory answer; it was a written answer, of 15th January:

> Lieutenants of the Royal Navy will be appointed to the Royal Flying Corps in such numbers as may be necessary, due regard being had to the requirements of the Service in other directions. In addition to naval lieutenants, Royal Marine officers and officers of other branches of the Royal Navy, and officers of the Royal Naval Reserve and Royal Naval Volunteer Reserve will be appointed to the Royal Flying Corps, and civilian aviators will be accepted in such numbers as may be necessary, being granted commissions in the Reserve Forces. It is also expected that a certain number of competent pilots may be obtained from warrant officers and men of the Royal Navy and Royal Marines.

So it was done.

Civilian aviators will be accepted in such numbers as may be necessary, and the first civilian aviator to be accepted into the Naval Wing of the Royal Flying Corps was Jim. The first 'Direct Entry', he was styled, and commissioned as a Sub-Lieutenant.

3

COMING HOME THROUGH THE RAIN

1891–1916

Schooldays – Around the World in Eighteen Months – Cannon Street
Eastchurch – H. A. C. – Wounded – R. N. A. S. Training.

HERBERT GARDNER TRAVERS, variously called Herbert, Herbie,
or more usually just 'H.' or his nickname 'H. O.', was sufficiently
different to Jim that when he did eventually become a pilot, fulfilling
a long-felt wish in doing so, the whole family was surprised.

He looked so different to Jim. Whereas Jim had been a frail child
who grew up to have poor physique – a slight, hollow-chested young
man with mousey, or dark, hair, H. was a large, late baby who grew
into a fine-looking, tall, blond athlete. He was the pride and joy of
their nurse, 'Nanny', for he did her so much credit; he grew at a
prodigious rate and appeared to go through infancy and boyhood with
perfect ease. He loved ships, as did his eldest brother, but after all that
was an age when most boys loved ships. Staying at Newquay with his
Mother's Cornish cousins, when he was about nine, he spent most of
the holiday with his model boats.

'. . . I am not sending the sails,' he wrote home to his Grandmother,
'. . . as they are all done except one. We went out in a boat yesterday
on the river Camel and sailed the *Mayflower* and the *Seagull*.'

When Jim went to Australia his only fear was that Jim might meet
a pirate ship on the voyage and Jim, writing home to his sisters Vera
and Jay from Dingyarra, wrote: ' . . . I am sending you out some of
the photographs I have taken here and on the voyage. Give the one
of the German warships to Herbert and the yacht and the boats and
the steamer for his ship collection . . .'

At his preparatory school, Gore Court, near Maidstone, Kent, he
spent all his spare time in the carpenter's shop making a one-man lake-
going vessel. All in all he was a thoroughly happy, normal sort of boy,
very good-natured and even-tempered, average in everything until he
entered Wellington in the autumn of 1904, at the age of thirteen.

His Headmaster was Dr Pollock and his housemaster was Mr Bevir so that, in the parlance of Wellington, he was 'in Bevir's Dormitory.'

J. M. Bevir wrote to Emmie on October 7th, 1904: 'I thought that you would like a line from me. He seems to me to get on very well in the house, but I am afraid he feels the strain of his form rather heavy. He is rather a nervous child, and I think the wear and tear of public school life may tell on him a little to begin with. For the moment he has got a cold, as most of us have, but that is nothing serious and will soon pass.'

Mr Bevir liked him, and understood him, and was to make many sympathetic comments on him in his brief notes home to J. L. T. or to Emmie. Certainly he understood him and was probably the first to realize that H.'s sweet nature and apparently placid calm hid 'rather a nervous child.' Less than a year later Jay wrote to Grannie Gardner: ' . . . Herbe came home on Tuesday morning about 10 minutes to 9. He seems very well and has a very good report. Dr Pollock puts 'I like what I have seen of him', and Mr Bevir: 'Has done good work.' Mr Wright his form master says 'He has done exceedingly good work . . .'

Unfortunately for his scholastic career, H. continued to grow; he was well over six feet tall before his fourteenth birthday and could easily have passed for a seventeen-year-old.

Gradually the discrepancy of height to age began to tell against him; his age tended to be forgotten when the young man, towering above the other boys, nowhere to hide, was unable to answer with the knowledge and the assurance which his appearance suggested. But Wellington was an athletic school; not only the usual football and rifle-shooting common to most boys schools but running, in particular cross country running, was a feature of Wellington in those days. Many of the longer runs were organized in the form of hare hunting, although no hares were hunted and no hounds were kept; human boys played every part in the 'Hunt'. There were the hares, the M H or Master of the Hunt, the G H or Gentlemen of the Hunt and the 'squealers', or main body of the field, smaller or younger boys all desperately trying to keep up. Of the many runs H. told me about, I remember best the Big Kingsley of 14 miles, the Little Kingsley of 12 miles, the Eversley and the Fleet; he showed me the route of some of the runs when we drove around the School grounds in 1936. I remember sandy paths through clumps of pine and silver birch, rolling common and grass land and a long sweep of grass in front of the School itself.

Cross country running became his great interest and his descriptions of his many runs usually filled most of his letters home; the following extracts give I think a great flavour of his schooldays; however since many of his letters were undated they may or may not be in chronological order.

23rd July 1905.

I was first last week. Bevirs is still an unbeaten Dormitory at cricket. Top of the second league. Yesterday we started a match with the Orange which is top of the first. Will the J J be in running condition by the 1st August? Because I might expect to see J L T (Jim) in it at the station Warlingham on the same and aforesaid date. . . . Kennedy has started this morning in the Diedrich and went to the Brighton races. He saw McDonnell's Napier which you and I saw in Guildford last autumn; also the Lee-Guinness' Darracq. The 120 h.p. Mercedes and many others he also saw and a racing motorboat. . . .

And again to Emmie, dated only 'Sunday':

. . . We ran the Fleet yesterday, for once in a way the hares Jones and Lovelace did not go out of their way. I ran at the back with the other G H's as a funny sensation. . . . Lotbiniere had strained a tendon. . . . I did not run in but dragged the weary ones. The order was Burridge, Lindsay, Burke, Jones, Bateman etc., a good heavy, about twelve altogether. The distance was 13 or 14 miles. I am going over to the Tindalls to-day. There is a man-eating rat in the Beresford. It ate part of one chap's ear. They had ratters and a ferret up there yesterday . . . The rat has eaten many bedclothes and books and bitten several other people. They have not caught it yet.

31st March '07.

Thanks awfully for the food. It is really awfully decent of you to send me such a lot. . . . Yesterday afternoon the Big Kingsley was run also the Little Kingsley. Big Kingsley order Lawrence, Smith, Burridge, Gordon, Field major, Bublis major etc . . . etc . . . Little Kingsley order Travers major, Barkworth, Field minor, Gaysford etc., etc. For this there were 104 entries. I hope to see Jemmy to-day. I am going over to the Tindalls from 12.30 to 8 to-day. I get a pot worth a £1 for getting the Little Kingsley . . .

An undated letter:

My dear Jemmy, I am glad that your exam. is over. I daresay you will hear from the others that I am going to be a hare in the Eversley. A day or two after the Eversley we are going to run against the United Hospitals, six College runners against six men from United Hospitals. I have been over to Kingsleys twice this last week. There was a qualifying little side on Thursday. I had to lope along at the back and drag the stragglers. About four squealers hanging on you, two each side, they are very small and light for the most part . . .

To Emmie, May 1st, 1908:

. . . I arrived down here all right. Two mechanics went with me on the bus to Paddington. They had a can of petrol and two trade numbers with them. So I marked them down and saw them take a huge Aerial. I saw a good many collegemen at Paddington . . . I was strolling down the train when somebody yelled out to me and I saw John Fraser and Hayland. It was a ripping corridor and we had a cosy little party. Fraser and Hayland had been separately to The Merry Widow and were both very full of it. I have got Simpson's room at the further end of the top floor. Chichester has not recovered since last term and has had a doctor's certificate to require a journey. He is going with his sister to the Italian lakes. . .

July 4th

. . . Thursday a week ago I had improved in shooting and went to Bisley. I have fallen off again now, though . . . Battenberg has got a rifle belonging to an old member of the eight . . . He made 62 for the Junior Eight yesterday. Wasn't it good. . . . I am in the Combermere tent at camp. I am the only one in this house going . . .

December 10th:

. . . We are going to run the Bagshot on Saturday next. We are in a serious dilemma as there should be five gentlemen in a hunt to conduct one properly, and we can only raise three. . . . Again please remember that I don't want to go to any dances or entertainments next holidays. Simpson goes to Klosters next holidays where the *Bystander* says the ice run for luges is faster than that of Davos this year . . . Battenberg is going to Madrid where he will get the sun he so much loves. Exams begin to-morrow. I am determined to play golf this hols . . .

December 14th:

. . . I am glad to say that we have got pretty well into the swing of exams now; and have only another week of a somewhat long term. Randall, in the Combermere, and Chichester minor in this house have been elected into the Racquet Eight.... Friday and Saturday were lovely days, a clear sky and a drying wind. We ran the Bagshot on Saturday ... We took them across country a good lot and everyone agreed that it was a most sporting course. The field was small in numbers, eighteen, but few dropped out. Hayder the MH led the hounds and they gained one minute on us. Neither Lindsay nor I (the hares) had trained at all, but Lindsay's wind went in a most unlooked-for manner. I had hardly trained for three weeks, but I had been for some long walks and I was much surprised to find myself in A1 condition. Poynder came first in the hounds ...

And to his sister, Jay:

I am very sorry you can't come down on Saturday ... After the awful weather last week yesterday evening seemed quite pleasant but did you feel it cold and wintry about 9 o'clock? The butter was excellent, likewise the honey also, which we broached on Sunday evening. The eggs we will start this morning. I thought Alice and Mummy looked awfully nice when they came down on Saturday. Foxy was very decent and had us into the royal room to tea. The eight is composed as follows: R. F. Morrison, Craddock, Ham, Fox, Ebden, Prettyman, Battenberg, Parr, Kenton-Parker and Sykes. I am writing this letter during exams. I am not supposed to be doing work, only reading an extra book. The examinations going on at present are higher maths and German conversation neither of which I do. We are all in the gym. I have got Fraser on my right. Sometimes I have Battenberg on my left. I have got J. Colbourne and Allen in front ... I get photo-ed with Battenberg for the pot....

So, with running and rifle-shooting and a little cricket and football, his schooldays passed. He was in the team which lost 31-nil to a team from the 2nd Battalion, The Gloucestershire Regiment and, a month before he left school, he won the run against South London Harriers. Wellington gave it's young men a great deal of freedom; H. was able to visit his Tindal cousins at Fir Grove frequently, and he went to Brooklands and several times to call on Jim at his 'diggings' in Willesden. But it was the freedom of striking out on a cross-country course which was the greatest blessing of Wellington. It gave him a love of finding his way across country, a sense of direction, an idea of looking at the sky and learning the weather, of looking for landmarks and plotting a straight course; the skills he learnt on his cross-country days became the skills he was to live by: they never left him.

It is a well-known fact that schoolboys are a cruelly treated lot, perpetually half-starved; it will always be so. When a young War-lingham neighbour, Dick Jacomb Hood, went away to school his mother told Vera that 'Dick, who had only been at Winchester a few days, had written an urgent letter for a ham a few tongues several pots of jam and a tin of sardines.' H., at Wellington and growing apace, was in similar need of commissariat from home. Jay, who continued to keep hens after the move from Woottonga to Horton, kept him supplied with boxes of eggs at regular intervals and Emmie sent honey, marmalade, butter, jam and home-made cake; he shared such good things with others in desperate need, amongst whom was Battenberg. Bevir's was by all accounts a frank and friendly – if noisy – sort of house; people got along well with each other in Bevir's and most of them discussed their families and the doings at home.

It is probable that H. spoke of Jim's flying experiments, ideas and ambitions and, particularly in H.'s last year at school, when Jim was so much at Eastchurch, this might have been of particular interest to Battenberg, correctly Prince George of Battenberg, whose father, Admiral Prince Louis of Battenberg, was then in Command at Sheer-ness. Certainly when the Admiral and others of the Royal Party visited Eastchurch repeatedly in 1911, their flights were reported in *Flight* and in *The Aeroplane* and Prince George was noted as being keenly inter-ested in Short's aeroplanes and as spending much time in studying them in the Sheds.

H. had wanted to enter Sandhurst; however, when, after he got his Remove, his new Form Master told him that his maths were too poor for him to even try for the Entrance Examination to Sandhurst, H. felt somewhat at a loss. He had counted on a career in the Army and now had no idea what to do with his life. He was 17 nearly 18 and would have to come to a decision. It is sad but true that some Form Masters seem not to care about crushing youthful ambition, for it surely would have been quite possible to give a normally intelligent young man further Maths study.

J. L. T., always practical, proposed that H. should go round the world, spending some long time in Australia, and then decide about a career when he came home.

H. wrote to his father from Wellington on March 20th, 1909:

I think your proposal about going to Australia is excellent, especially as I have not seen much of the world and do not therefore know what to be. I don't know how long it will last, but at present I fancy civil engineering. My ideas are somewhat like a weathercock or rather a barometer for if they don't change with the wind they probably change with the weather. . . .

He left school at the end of the Easter Term in 1909 and about the time, April 1st, of his 18th birthday. Of his numerous school friends only one, R. F. Pretyman, was to have any apparent influence on him and that influence was later on in his life. The cross-country runs themselves were, I am sure, the greatest influence on his thought patterns and his subsequent career – more than any human being ever was; through the runs, too, he had tasted the joy of success, winning – as he had reported home – the Little Kingsley in 1907 and getting second place in the Big Kingsley in 1908.

By early May he was aboard TSS *Miltiades* of the Aberdeen Line and outward bound for Australia. He had letters to his father's family in Australia, to his Mother's cousins in British Columbia, and one hundred pounds in his pocket; like so many of the Travers family, he was 'going out.' He may have been less well-found than his predecessors but he would not, I think, have changed places with a king.

Unlike Jim, who had difficulty in making up a letter, H. was able to write easily and at length; however, there is no room in this book to quote more than a sentence or two from the long descriptions which he sent home of his round-the-world trip. On leaving London River, he saw 'a lot of warships at Sheerness, and *Indomitable* and some other cruisers,' and further round the coast and still fast on the Goodwin Sands – her masts at an unbelievable rake – the poor *Mahratta*, broken in two. She was of the Brocklebank Line and had been homeward bound from Calcutta when she was wrecked: '. . . they saved most of a very valuable cargo and all the passengers'.

Miltiades came in close under the cliff at Dover and she took fresh

vegetables on board and then hugged the coast down Channel to
Plymouth. His first letter home was written 'off Start Point' from
where the coast of Devonshire looked 'awfully pretty.'

He was the youngest of the few passengers and they and the Ship's
Officers were all kind to him; he sat at a table with the young Ship's
Doctor, who 'had been round the world twice and to Germany
and France,' and an R A M C. doctor who was voyaging out to the
Cape. Most of the passengers left the ship at the Cape and H. went
ashore for a few hours to visit his Mother's cousins Tom and Harriet
Price. Tom took him up to the Kloof and Harriet subsequently
wrote to Emmie: '. . . What a fine tall fellow Herbert is, we were only
sorry he staid such a short time here and we could not do more for
him . . .'

He had taken a small quantity of reading matter: *Fruit Ranching in
British Columbia*, the *Queen's Letters* and *Marcus Aurelius* amongst them.
'Please tell Granny,' he wrote home, 'that the Queen's letters get on
slowly but well. When I asked P. E. to get me Marcus Aurelius I never
realised what a treasure it was . . .'

Miltiades called at Melbourne before continuing up the coast to Sydney,
Newcastle and Brisbane and in Melbourne H. spent a day or so with
his Uncle Geoffrey and Aunt Ida Travers. Geoffrey had bought a new
car and H. helped him work on it: 'After lunch we decided to improve
his compression if you can improve anything that is absolutely new
. . . then we scraped the piston head which he said had been pre-
igniting slightly in spite of no compression. The results seemed excellent though we did not try her on the road . . .' He had a brief glimpse
of Melbourne and was invited for a long visit later on.

On leaving Melbourne his ship and another raced to the Heads. He
wrote to Alie on 29th June: '. . . Did you hear about our race with
the *Pericles*? The *Pericles* from Sydney homeward bound arrived in
Melbourne one hour before we did; and started out of Melbourne half
an hour before us. Some of our engineers had been over there the
night before and had a very fierce argument about the speeds attainable
by their respective craft. When we got into the bay the *Pericles* was
just visible on the horizon, a quarter of a mile before the Heads we
were so close that you could have thrown a cricket ball from one to
the other. We did not pass her as the channel was rather narrow. It

was not a bad piece of work, was it? Remembering that it is only forty miles from Melbourne to the Heads....'

In the same letter, from Sydney, he wrote: 'We are now lying alongside Dalgety's New Wharf discharging and taking in cargoes. If you had seen the weird variation of things which we brought out it would tickle you immensely. Anchors for boats, sheets of galvanized iron, motor cars, tins of paint and oils, sewing machines, barrels of rum, typewriters, copying machines, bottles of Perrier, and 400-gallon water tanks by the dozen. At present they are mainly taking in lards and fats for soap....'

And by the same mail to J. L. T. and Emmie: '... I got permission from the skipper to continue my passage up to Brisbane in this boat, which saves hotel fees, cabs, etc. The boat stays here from Friday morning last till Thursday morning next, when we go on to Newcastle to take in frozen meat. So I'm seeing something of Sydney now. It certainly is a pretty place.... Yesterday I went up the Paramatta. It was a glorious day and I think the Paramatta absolutely knocks spots out of any other part of Sydney ...'

And to Charles on 9th July 1909: ' ... After a week in Sydney we called in at Newcastle. It is a rich coaling town. There were lots of sailing ships in the harbour with no crews. Their crews had deserted and gone up country. They were beautiful boats, lots of them, and it seemed such a pity that they should be lying there doing nothing....'

He left the *Miltiades* at Brisbane, having had a most interesting, if typically slow, voyage out.

The H. P. Gardners, Uncle Herbert and Aunt Ethel, welcomed him at Dingyarra, and Uncle Herbert soon put him up on some of the quieter horses and taught him to drive the sulky. There followed days of meeting friends, cousins and neighbours from all around, of picnics and swimming expeditions, interspersed with him helping with the chores around Dingyarra. He learned fast. 'We rode over about 4 miles to milk some cows that were in one of M'Connell's paddocks. It took the whole day. I know it did, every time I stooped down.... On Wednesday we drove, Uncle H and I, to Eske. He let me hold the reins most of the way there and all the way back. We had Mr Stanley Hudson's horse *Caesar* in Uncle H's sulky. About five Justices from miles around had come in to licence a man to keep a billiard saloon.... When we got back yesterday we found Edgar, Elspeth, Kathleen M'C and another girl. We are going over to have a picnic to-day at the Bunyip Hole. So far I have chopped wood each day before brekker to make me warm. I awoke naturally at six this morning, not bad.'

And to Emmie from Dingyarra on July 16th: 'I suppose Dad has by this time returned from Finland or at any rate will have when my epistle reaches home ... Since the moment I closed my last week's letter I have had an absolutely tremendous time. A1 is not the word, not good enough. It was absolutely copper-bottomed. ... On Friday afternoon last Uncle H drove me over in the trap to meet the Somersets and both (families of) M'Connells at the Bunyip Hole. We had a jolly picnic which resulted in my being asked up to Mt. Brisbane by Mr E. M'C. I drove back in another trap with one of the Eric M'C's on my knee and a jolly drive but I could not for the life of me see what track we were driving along. ...' The next day they are at Cressbrook again: '*Music*, Aunt E's horse, was in the trap. I rode *Black Ben*. In the afternoon with the same turnout we visited Cressbrook. They all assembled outside that door to laugh at me. Thanks to Mr Kirk's tuition on the day before they were very good and did not laugh at all. The next day I rode over again on *Black Ben*. We drove out to meet the Butlers, the two parsons' sons and Judith and Ursula rode. Mrs M'C who is very nice, Molly and Chris B. were there. Frank arrived afterwards. I rode back that night. According to special request I rode over again the next day. I and Judith and the two parson's sons rode to the new tunnel, some M'C's drove. Uncle H. arrived in the afternoon with Aunt Ethel, there were also present Mr Tom Moore, Mrs Marsden, Dr Mason Stuart and Mr and Mrs Fraser and family, engineer for the new line. The tunnel is through three hundred yards of solid rock and the work is very slow. We went along below and then along the single plank above ... The next day there was another picnic, and then we climbed up a rocky gully to the dam. It was perfectly glorious, steep and rocky with most lovely ferns. The Butlers were to have been at the top but they weren't. Jock and Edgar arrived later. Jock is now managing at Warrumba. Coming back I was racing Judith who was on *Puck* her pony and I nearly came off. She is Alice's age. Well after that I should have gone back to Dingyarra which I did, but I had had such a pressing invitation to go and make a four at tennis at Warrumba that I went in the afternoon though it was raining. ...'

*   *   *

So the days of August and September hurried by; he helped enlarge the asparagus bed and make a strawberry bed; he fenced the garden 'to keep old *Eagle* out'; he went over to the German neighbours at Mt. Beppo to bring back a strayed Dingyarra calf; he stayed with the M'Connels and the Butlers; he rode and picnicked and swam; and when October came, he took a job. It was his first paid job. 'I am keeping myself,' he wrote home.

He wrote to his father from Emu Creek, Colinton, Queensland, on 21st October, 1909:

'... I am getting rather to like this place; one good reason being that it is high up and therefore cooler and less humid than Dingyarra. This last week I have been working on a different plan. They have got a new hand. He is an old Army man; been through the Boer War and three years in India, finally being discharged with "Conduct exemplary". He has had three years in Canada, farming, and therefore knows something of agriculture.

'He is a poor milker, but fairly good with a plough; and he is a pleasant chap to work alongside....' To work alongside a pleasant chap made all the difference in the world to H's day, a day that began punctually at six and finished, as a rule, at sundown. He groomed and harnessed the horses and hoed thistles and fed the pig and cut ironbark logs 5″ thick and with them built calf pens, a hut and a dairy; he moved out of his tent and lived in one room of the two-roomed hut when it was built. 'Another week has slipped by and it is mail night again. I am writing on my knee and by moonlight as the other three fill up the dining room table. I am still driving the wagon in the morning and the Gloster-Canadian drives in the evening. I have been promoted to the more dashing pair as we take a heavier load in the morning. 6 cans weigh a good deal ... $676\frac{1}{2}$ lbs that is the weight of the milk alone. The cans are big and heavy and the total load cannot be far short of $\frac{3}{4}$ ton. The events of the day go like clock work so the news is not extensive....'

He enjoyed his jackaroo-ing days; but when he had earned enough to top up his supply of money, he left in order to continue his travels. He made another short visit to Dingyarra in November, partly in order to say his good-byes, partly in order to return the little mare *Black Bess* which Uncle Herbert had lent him for his own use and to wean her from her foal. Uncle Herbert pressed him to return to

Dingyarra the following April and May, but H., was undecided; there was so much of the world still to be seen and, as he confided to Alie, he 'wished Queensland was not so beastly hot.'

Then he went down to his second cousin Archie Tindal's cattle station, Gunjan, Texas, Queensland.

'I had a good trip down,' he wrote, 'I stopped at the North Australian in Ipswich. I stopped on Friday night at the Railway Hotel, Inglewood. It was on 3/- supper bed and breakfast. Not extravagant. I got here at about 4 o'clock on Saturday; the roads were wet and heavy and it was all delightfully cool. I was the only passenger. I had lunch at the pub at Limevale with the bank manager from Texas, a decent quiet sort of johny ... When I was in Ipswich I went to an open air biograph show, entrance 6d. Very good value for the tanner, too. This afternoon we took a short row up the river which being in flood is very pretty. The willows are a mass of green. It is very pleasant and cool here and mosquitoes and fleas are at present conspicuous by their absence.'

And to Jay on 12th December 1909: 'Gunyan, by Inglewood.
' ... I have only 12 minutes in which to catch the post so I hope you will excuse a bad scrawl. I did not get a chance for a ride until a day or two ago when I went over with Archie to the Spur. The Spur is the silver mine near here; Silverspur is the full name and it is said to be as rich as Broken Hill. . . . If that's true it must be worth something – but they are paying no dividend at present (like many other good things.) Archie said he had heard they were badly managed. I should think they must be. . . . All the horses here are very nice and we are taking about half a dozen down to Ramornie on the 16th. I don't know how I shall get down, I expect I shall be very sore or perhaps past that stage. 36 miles a day at a jog and a walk is far more tiring than cantering and walking. The river here is quite a fine bit of water, to-day we got 10 ducks. . . .'

H. 'got down' to Ramornie all right and was there for Christmas 1909 and for several weeks afterwards. Ramornie was now owned and run by Charles Tindal junior; he and his wife and family made H. welcome there and persuaded him to stay longer than he had originally planned; each new station, each new part of the country had fresh delights; no matter how happy he was in any one spot he was happier still to be moving on.

'You must have missed Herbert very much at Christmas,' Alice Borgstrom wrote to Emmie from Helsingfors on 6th January, 'does he think of returning to England or is he thinking of Australia, and Jem is as keen as ever about aeroplanes. It is well to have a hobby ...'

He loved Ramornie, the station on which his father had grown up; life was still good along the Clarence River and among many jaunts during his visit there he went up the river in the *Revenge*: ' ... The *Revenge* is the light rowing boat and it holds just 4. ... We tied up just above the mouth of Main Creek. Here we fished till about 12.30 and then rowed some way above Bullock Falls and had lunch. The river is lovely. Steep banks coming down to rocky edges, pools, little harbours where you can steer in the boat and fish. Great flat rocks partly in the shade and partly in the sun, and the clearest, cleanest water to bathe in. I have just had a water-melon. It was grand. Later: It was raining all yesterday and to-day. Coz Charles has fears of an old fashioned season, as he calls it, which means floods. The River is down again. Will write from Sydney....'

Edith Tindal wrote to Emmie from Ramornie on January 14th:

... have been so busy with our large party of young people that I have not been able to write to anybody. We were so glad Herbert was able to come down with Archie and have much enjoyed having him – he is such a dear Boy he has quite won both our hearts. I hope he has enjoyed himself but he leaves us next Tuesday 18th I am sorry to say. He looks and seems very well and is most long suffering with 'the kids' otherwise the school boys – they 'cheek' him to an unlimited extent and he takes it all with a smile and pays them out when the chance comes.... You must be feeling really settled in the new home now. I hope the garden will soon be as pretty as the old one, but it takes some time for shrubs etc. to grow up....

Herbert is talking of the Blue Mountains when he leaves here – he is lucky to be able to see everything as he is doing....

To 'see everything' was indeed H.'s main ambition and in order to do this he sought a mode of transport which would give him greater independence than would travel by horse, boat or train. He decided to try and continue his journeyings by motor bike.

He wrote to his father on Monday January 31st from the Carrington Hotel, Katoomba: '... I am writing this after getting in by the 8 o'clock mail train from Sydney. . . . I have been thinking it over and have come to the conclusion that the only way to see the country between Sydney and Melbourne to Victoria and to see Tasmania is to get a motor bike. A really first class one, new, a Triumph for instance. I have counted the possible expenses and have come to the conclusion that it would also be cheaper. Even selling it so low as half price at the end of six months. So I went to the Triumph people here and asked them whether it would be possible for them to have a written agreement to buy back the bike at half price at the end of six months. They said certainly they would as they could always get £48-for a half year old Triumph. That is about $\frac{3}{4}$ price – they would be willing to buy back in any case at half price and as much more as they could get from anyone. I have heard from other people that there are good roads between here and Melbourne. I am writing to Uncle Geoff. to ask his permission after all I am out here to enjoy myself and to see the country and that seems to combine the two. I am much stronger than when I left home which would improve things from yours and Mum's point of view. . . .'

After Sydney and the Blue Mountains, with a day trip with a young friend to see over Hawkesbury, ('the College is a fine big place containing about 200 students . . . the vines grown in German fashion in bunches on sticks about 3′ from the ground,') – he at last reached the haven of his Uncle Geoffrey's and Aunt Ida's house in Elsternwick, Melbourne.

He wrote to Emmie from there on 15th February: 'Here I am, safe and sound in Melbourne. I hope you got my postcards last week saying how much I enjoyed the Blue Mountains. They were really beautiful. Last Monday week I took the early train from Katoomba to Blackheath and walked to the Horseshoe Falls and Jovetts Leap where the heights are absolutely dizzy; I took the train back to Sydney that night. The next day I had a short ride in the domain and got a little knocked off the price of the motor bike. . . .'

It may well be that that was the first Emmie had heard about the bike for in a later letter he hopes that he 'has not given her a start about the motor bike.'

'. . . I fixed up about the bike and dispatched it and myself by the mail train and in the evening for Melbourne. I went second as they are exactly the same as 1st and I saved 30/- on an ordinary ticket and

40/- on a sleeping berth. My ticket was £2-11-5d and the cheapest boat ticket is £2-15-od. The carriages are exceedingly clean and comfortable and especially so on the Victorian half. My carriage companions were a decent crowd. Two very quiet mechanics a fat old man who got out not far from Sydney and three senior cadets going from Lithgow in the Blue Mountains to Melbourne to receive from Kitchener the flag given by Lady Dudley for the smartest Company in the Commonwealth. . . .'

His original idea had been to motor bike the journey from Sydney to Melbourne, but Uncle Geoffrey had vetoed the idea. 'Uncle Geoff. met me at Spencer Street,' H. continued, 'I wheeled the bike round to the Melbourne Garage took off the wrapping and rode away to Elsternwick. I went to the Yenckens on Sunday and they were very kind to me. Yesterday Ted and I went on our bikes to the Richmond Garage where he had a felt washer put on his engine bearing as she was throwing oil. Then we rode to the Bank of Australasia where the man was very pleased to see me thinking me dead and buried. From there we went on to the Melbourne Garage where we paid 1/- to see the Bleriot Monoplane. The first real flying aeroplane I have ever seen, and a most beautiful piece of workmanship.

I expect I gave you a start about the bike, but that is the fault of only having one mail per week. . . . The machine has beautiful spring forks and a lovely padded and sprung saddle, extra big tyres. I am to see Dr Stanley, president of the motor bikist's club or the autocycle club. He is going to put me onto the best roads. Dr S. has been all over Victoria and as Uncle Geoff says a better knowledge of the place than any other motorcyclist in the State.

As I have £15- left in Sydney and £76- here (I have been strongly advised to go 2nd as far as Vancouver as the people are more sociable) – I have lots to get about here with. . . .'

It may well have been on the advice of the expert Dr Stanley that H. decided to change his first motor bike for a better one. At all events, only three weeks after reaching Elsternwick he wrote to V: '. . . The new motor bike the $3\frac{1}{2}$ h.p. Twin Peugeot with the Brooks seat is a great success. The spring forks are absolutely marvellous. The spokes, tyres and rims are the sort usually fitted to the 5 h.p.' He had been into Melbourne every evening, hurrying up Browns to get it finished and when it was ready he toured the Western Plains and much else of Victoria on this splendid machine; sometimes he travelled alone, some-

Uncle Geoff and Aunt Ida with the Peugeot, Melbourne, 1910
photo: H. G. Travers

times in company with Dr Stanley and other motor bikists; he kept detailed records of all trips. He noted average speeds, maximum speeds, time elapsed, distance covered, the cost per mile down to the nearest farthing and petrol and oil consumption to the fluid ounce. He posted the information to Charles, now eleven and a half and at his prep. school, The Wells House.

(Although Charles would undoubtedly have been interested he, at that time, was already so interested in flight that in a letter to his Mother on 20th March that year, a scant letter of school news, the drift of his mind was already apparent, for his letter was illustrated with drawings with such titles as: 'monoplane gliding to ground,' 'Jimmy in aeroplane garb,' and 'my new pattern paper bird glides in flight.')

In April H. went down to Tasmania, where he visited most of his Tasmanian cousins, Travers' and Butlers, and toured extensively, covering a total of 810 miles there before returning to Elsternwick. He had written to V. on March 1st: '... I hear from Uncle Herbert that you may let Horton and meet me in British Columbia. That would be high jinks; but I do not know when I shall arrive there although I expect it will be some time in the late spring or early summer ...'

By May his plans were crystallizing and he wrote to Emmie: '... I will let you know by the next mail or mail after whether I go around by Japan or not: and will let you know my addresses . . .' He did not, in the event, 'go around by Japan.' After a week or two in New Zealand he set out 2nd class in the *Atua* to go 'round the islands.'

The Union Steamship Company's *Atua* was a twin-screw vessel of 3,444 tons gross/1,895 net. She was built by D. J. Dunlop & Co. of Glasgow in 1906. Her service speed was 12 knots.

H. did not refer to crossing the Pacific, only to 'going round the islands.' Among the many islands that he visited and from whence literally scores of picture postcards arrived in England were Tonga, Fiji and Samoa; he loved the cheerful islanders and admired their skill in handling their fast canoes or in riding a great rolling wave on a narrow board.

Among his fellow passengers aboard *Auta* were a group of circus people and vaudeville artists returning to San Francisco; they were an hilarious crowd – many of their antics, songs and monologues remembered by H. for the rest of his life. After a few days in San Fransisco, where H. was able to spend some time ashore, the voyage continued – beating back in such a slow, slow boat across the Pacific to the Hawaiian Islands, thence Eastwards again to Canada. The boat was cramped and by the time they reached Vancouver H. was glad to step ashore, in spite of the pall of smoke over city and harbour.

'At last we are getting out,' he wrote to Alie on July 27th, 'We had an excellent run from Honolulu: and lots of fun. Vancouver is covered in smoke from bush fires only they call them forest fires here. . . .'

He had a number of introductions in Vancouver and certainly took up some of them, including one to a Mr Berry, who: 'has been very good to me, getting me an introduction to the Phoenix Salmon Cannery: who used to supply J. T. & Sons . . .' he wrote to Alie on the 4th August. After a couple of weeks around Vancouver he went up the Fraser Valley to the country of his Cornwall kinsmen in the South Cariboo. The original Cornwall brothers, Clement and Henry, were already legendary by 1910; which of their descendants H. met is unclear, probably Gilly and Henry, sons of the original settlers. The first two Cornwalls in that part of the world were younger sons of the Reverend Alan Gardner Cornwall of Ashcroft House in Gloucestershire. Clement had graduated from Magdalene College, Cambridge in 1858 and Henry from Trinity College, Cambridge in 1861. They had originally gone out to British Columbia to look for gold in the Cariboo, but on meeting so many exhausted, starving men returning, men who were empty-handed, penniless, – their feet cut to ribbons – the brothers decided to buy land instead; eventually they jointly acquired some six and a half thousand acres and in due course bought scores of horses, mules and cattle with which, by degrees, they established their ranch; they built a hostelry, a sort of road-house or coaching-inn and called it 'ASHCROFT MANOR'. They missed, it was said, the sights and sounds of the English hunting field and as a result had a draft of hounds shipped out to them from the Quorn. With this small pack they hunted coyotes – with a Red Indian, a magnificent horseman, as whipper-in and anyone who cared to join in as the field. One day in the Nicola Valley a bunch of over-exuberant cowboys, on sighting the hunted fox (coyote), yelled: 'There goes the son of a b----!' and rode over hounds. At this heinous crime Mr Cornwall took his hounds home and never took them out again, the Cornwall Hunt being immediately disbanded.

These and other legends of the Cornwall cousins abounded and H. heard many of them as he journeyed about and visited in that part of British Columbia. He adored the country: 'The most glorious I have ever seen,' he wrote.

He made his way along to Sicamous, thence by C. P. R. across the Rockies, then went down to the Yoho before going up to Banff, where he had an appointment with Ralph Rutherford. He and Rutherford had a cordial lunch together in Banff before seeing over the newly-planted Rutherford Fruit Ranch.

Although H. spoke of going on up to Edmonton he may have abandoned the idea, as he was beginning, as he continued Eastwards, to think of home; at some time on these travels he met men who had been with the Fur Brigade but I cannot find any reference to him travelling any great distance by canoe himself. The tales of the Brigade fascinated him and he included some postcard pictures of the voyageurs in his collection.

Now he was restless for home. 'I may come home by the *Laurentic*,' he had written from Banff. The *Laurentic* was 'a crack White Star boat' and in such a boat it was only a week's voyage from Montreal to Southampton.

H. was home in early October of 1910.

He had been away for eighteen months. He was now $19\frac{1}{2}$ years old and still could not decide what he wanted to do in life; but on the other side of the world, down in the Melbourne Garage, he had seen the Bleriot Monoplane: ' . . . the first real flying aeroplane I have ever seen.'

To Jim he had written, on a postcard and perhaps more tellingly, 'I have SEEN the Bleriot!'

Joseph Travers & Sons Ltd had room for the young son of a former director and present, still substantial, shareholder. H. started at Cannon Street within a day or so of his return to England. He remained with the firm until August, 1914.

The life of the river, London River, fascinated him and the life of J. T. & Sons – the traditions of the firm and the language of commerce, with every detail of quantity and quality carefully recorded, was absorbing to him. He had not expected to enjoy office life but enjoy it he did, at least while he was learning how the business was run and how their products were shipped, handled, milled and sold to the wholesalers: tea, wines and spices from the East – commodities, to a greater or lesser extent, always in demand. He was not always at either the office at Cannon Street or at Wapping, where the wine vaults and bonded warehouses stood, but crossed the River to Bankside, to No 54 Bankside, where some of the spice mills and the almond and fruit cleaning plant lay. Bankside had been acquired in the early 1900's, largely at J. L. T.'s instigation, who considered it important that the firm should increase its premises on the South bank of the River, it already having a great amount of space on the North bank, mainly at St Catherine's Dock, (the 'A' Building), and extensive warehousing at Wapping; and in 1910 No 54 Bankside was still thought to be pretty modern and up-to-date, with the latest in mechanical equipment and in hygiene and safety precautions. The wharfage on the South bank was mainly at Surrey Docks. Older readers may remember the white-painted name T R A V E R S on the long black roofs of the Travers Wharf there. H. lived at home in Warlingham and went up to 119 Cannon Street every morning as his father had done. He finished work at 6 o'clock on weekdays and at 4 o'clock on Saturdays: ' . . . Herbert gets up early and goes to bed early and sticks to his work like a man,' his father wrote to Emmie. But, as so often before, it was his old housemaster, Mr Bevir, who saw the truth with kindly perspicacity: ' . . . he is not suited to a sedentary life,' he wrote, 'it was a pity about the Army. His chance may come later on.' Emmie, too, thought that he looked drawn and weary; their doctor, Dr Ross Todd, prescribed stout for lunch, which H. took with mingled glee and embarrassment, as his senior, with whom he lunched, had signed the pledge and was strictly teetotal.

In the summer of 1911 and when H. had been at Cannon Street for some months, he often went down to Eastchurch, either by train or on his newly-acquired motor-bike, in order to see and to hear what was going on in the Sheds. He treasured the memory of these mysterious excursions and years later used to say how he would 'buy a loaf of bread and a pound or two of sausages, go down to Jim's Shed and fry up supper for them all on the Primus stove,' while Jim and Horace Short would talk far into the night, seemingly oblivious of their listener: Jim, stammering out his ideas, Short, with his great head – and here H. would indicate Disney Land, – nodding attention, both men in their conversation taking design and development far beyond that which had so far been achieved or was even, at that time, possible of achievement. Jet propulsion, they agreed one evening, must come; but metals, then, 'were not good enough'. When these heady conversations came at last to an end and Horace Short returned to his own home, there was always room in the Shed, on a spare bunk or a workbench, for H. to sleep the remainder of the night away.

He took such a delight in touring or, as he put it: 'seeing something of the country', that he filled every holiday with expeditions; one such was referred to by J. L. T. in a letter to Emmie, then in Finland, in July of 1912: 'Your letter to Herbert came yesterday morning. I am very glad you had such a good passage. Herby's holiday begins on Monday (to-morrow). He started off on his mo-bike yesterday evening about 7. intending to camp the night with Jem at Hendon and make an early start this morning for Malvern Wells and come back on Monday. He hopes to spend at any rate part of his holiday with Fraser whose steamer was due in L'pool yesterday. . . .'

And from Cousin Siss Tindal, following what must have been a week-end visit to Fir Grove, Eversley, in late October: '. . . what a pleasure it was to us all to see Herbert again, and I think to Father most of all – he was so good in talking to Father – long yarns. What a dear boy he is, you must be proud of him. . . .'

*　　*　　*

It is tempting to wonder, with the benefit of hindsight, why H. apparently made no effort to learn to fly in those pre-War years; for his interest extended beyond what Jim was doing: he knew Jezzi well, was keenly interested in the Blair Atholl Syndicate and had been to Farnborough to meet and talk with S. F. Cody. It is possible that the cause was that any of his small supply of spare cash would have gone to maintain his motor-bike, the motor-bike which helped to give him such delightful independence of movement; but there may have been another and a subtler reason – the family tradition of 'giving a fellow elbow-room', of not poaching another's preserves. Aeroplanes were Jim's stunt and although H. was interested in them he would have been careful, whether at Farnborough, Hendon, Brooklands or Eastchurch, not to be intrusive or a nuisance to anyone.

It was not until war seemed inevitable, in the summer of 1914 and after the murder at Sarajevo, that H. went to Hendon. He was already a Territorial private soldier with the Honourable Artillery Company, as were so many other young men in the City; in going to Hendon it was as though he realized that a golden opportunity of learning to fly had been just about to slip through his fingers. What chance conversation or newspaper article, what remark, direct or overheard, led him as though on an impulse to Hendon, one can only guess. For I never heard him say what it was and his family, without a doubt, were surprised by his action.

Charles was in Camp that summer and Emmie wrote to him in telegraphese and on a postcard, on 31st July:

To Prte. C. T. Travers, Gresham's School, No. 1 Battalion, O.T.C. Tidworth Pennings, Andover:
Thanks for the card. Can we see your lines in the photograph? The country is much more hilly than I had imagined. – Note from Jim just come – All the machines ordered off to East Coast – War scare. Bat boats engines under repair. So he is going at first to have another – and fetch the B. B. afterwards. The dutch ports are closed to foreign vessels. I wonder if Germany will try for Holland or Denmark. The govt. have sunk their Irish differences. Jessie enjoyed her motor drive to Woodhall Spa. A. is again busy all day at the Boy Scouts. H. has had 2 lessons at Hendon. He is in digs there now to get the early morning and evening before and after the city – Your boxes came 3/8

excess weight. They have not been charged before – I hope you are having nice weather. Yrs. E.L.T.

H. wrote to Charles the following day from Warlingham:

1/8/14

My dear Charlie,

I expect Mummy has told you that I joined the Beatty School at Hendon last week, and have been having some lessons in the mornings and evenings. There are two machines, both dual control, there at present. One is a Wright biplane with an American 40 h.p. Wright engine – 4 cyl. vertical and the other is also a Wright biplane with either a 50 Gnome or a 50 Gyro. They have two complete engine bearers and use these engines alternately. The Handley Page mono: was smashed up by a pupil the other day; and another pupil when completing his brevet tests with a glide into the wind landed the Gyro on the iron fence at the edge of the ground to the detriment of the machine. So we have now only the old Wright engine bus. The machine is quite new, blinkers and dual wheel control, but the engine has been running for 3 years and done 60,000 miles.

The three times I have been up so far have all been with Watts, who took his ticket at the Caudron School and is now putting in time doing extra flying as instructor. He is quite a decent man.

The Graham White School have only one machine between 20 pupils; the Caudron, one between about 12 the 2 spare machines in each case are smashed. Beatty has two more machines with 80 Gyros coming forward from the Handley Page works. After the Bank Holiday Meeting they will start school work again and I shall try and get diggs at Hendon. Your affect. brother Herbert. P.S. I hear Jem has flown to the East Coast on a/c of the war scare. Things are pretty serious. I hope the H.A.C. are not mobilized before I get my ticket!'

One cannot help but feel sad for Grahame-White who, in spite of all his driving energy, patriotism and publicity stunts, started the Great War at Hendon with only two machines and one of them smashed. It had been Grahame-White who in 1912 had preached the necessity of a large and well-trained flying corps. There were probably plenty of Grahame-White aeroplanes building in his Workshops at Hendon but on the 1st of August there was only one: airworthy and available for his School.

*   *   *

H. had not moved fast enough to take his ticket before mobilization; he would certainly have liked to have taken his ticket from the Beatty School, for George W. Beatty, a 26-year-old from New Jersey, was a remarkable man who already held a number of unusual aviation records: an altitude record with a passenger, of 10,700 ft. (with a 35 h.p. Wright machine), and a deliberate and successful first landing in New York, on which occasion he landed in Central Park. He had been taught to fly by Orville Wright, had bought one Wright machine and had built five others, one of which was his school machine at Hendon.

C. G. Grey wrote of the August 1913 Meeting at Hendon: 'It is not more than a few weeks since Mr George W. Beatty came to Hendon, but he is already an established institution there. I own that when he first arrived, his machine, which is a home-made affair of the type designed by the late Wilbur Wright and his brother Orville, gave me cold shivers to look at, and when he did his hair-raising banks on it many of us expected it to fold up in the air. Still, there was never any doubt about his ability as a flyer, nor about the pushing power of his Gyro engine, which for its size is one of the most powerful and certainly the noisiest in all Hendon....'

Beatty was a business-like young man, too, and he and H. had a proper written agreement; this agreement was eventually to lapse, as the war scare and then mobilization heralded the start of the Great War.

After mobilization H. remained in London and wrote to Emmie from his Grandmother's flat on the 9th August:

I expect you have seen in the papers that permission has been obtained to increase the strength of the HAC to a full battalion, which means that we have about 580 new recruits. As a result we shall probably either stay at Headquarters until they have settled down a bit or else move into barracks such as Tower, Duke of York's, or for some infanters, Aldershot.... Please ask Dad to lock up my Tilling shares and agreement with Beatty. I was on to the latter on the 'phone this afternoon. It will be quite all right and I will resume my tuition whenever I may return....

H. remained in London for the first month of the war, his address, on 12th September, being 'Pte H. G. Travers, Machine Gun Section, Hon. Artillery Company, Armoury Buildings, Finsbury, E.C.' But everything was uncertain and unformed as it has a way of being at the start of any hostilities. 'Whenever I may return' was the operative phrase.

In *The Honourable Artillery Company in The Great War*, edited by C. Goold Walker and published in 1930, some of the events in which H. took part are described:

> During the first few weeks after the outbreak of the war, while the trained men were guarding railways and waterworks in London, large bodies of recruits were being rapidly put through the mill and so successful were Officers and N. C. O.'s that as early as 12th September, 1914, the 1st Battalion were inspected at Armoury House by His Majesty the King. By that time the Battalion were 1,000 strong.... We then marched past the King and so out of Headquarters on our way to the greatest of Wars. Although at the time we expected to remain in England for at least three months' training, within a week we were actually in France....

To his father H, wrote: '... I thought the King looked awfully tired.' Emmie, unaware of H.'s imminent departure, wrote to him on 16th September: '... I am writing on chance that you may be still at Rainham as the papers say that the 1st Battalion H A C marched straight down after the inspection on Saturday. I suppose the machine guns went with them. I am glad if so as you will get more practice but I wonder what you do about clothes.

Shall I send you some decent thick socks and shirts and anything warm. You must want some clean things. I sent two coloured hankies to the H A C Headquarters. Send a postcard. Charlie went back to school to-day. Jim is trying to get sent to the front with the naval brigade. He says engineers will be the last to be sent. I see Spenser-Grey has gone and Samson has his full Commandership. I believe the Navy will have their turn afterwards. It generally has been so....'

Further extracts from the history of the 1st Battalion, H. A. C. run as follows:

> ... on Wednesday the 16th orders arrived for 800 men and 29 officers to leave on Friday the 18th for overseas, in two trains at 6.25 a.m. and 8.30 a.m. At that time we had no equipment, no rifles and no ammunition, and our transport was composed of an extraordinary collection of vehicles, including Pickford covered vans, a Frederick Gorringe delivery cart, a four-wheeled milk cart, and a huge tank on wheels used by one of the London Borough Councils for watering the streets. (This was to serve as a watercart.)
>
> The equipment arrived about 5 p.m. and the rifles at about 10 p.m. and the issue of these could not be completed til 1 a.m. on Friday the 18th. Col Treffry was to leave with the right half-Battalion at 3.15 a.m. and Major Hanson with

H. A. C. Machine Gun, B. E. F. France, 1914.
H. G. Travers H A C Gunn H A C Goodall H A C

photo: Macnamara H A C

the left half about an hour later. At 2.30 a.m. the confusion in the transport lines was dreadful, owing to the difficulty of hooking up and loading up in the dark. The Transport Officer, however, was quite cheerful and declared his intention of leaving on time, which by some miracle he did. The only animal missing was Captain Ward's charger, which refused to be handled, and was left careering wildly over the Park. Both half-Battalions got away on time and entrained at Purfleet at 6.30 and 8.30 a.m. respectively. At 4 p.m. the 1st H.A.C. left Southampton on board the s.s. *Westmeath* for an unknown destination, that is to say, under sealed orders which were opened at sea. . . .

The *Westmeathians* were to become a select band of men.

H. to J.L.T. on Monday 12th October, 1914: '764 Machine Gun Section, 1st Battalion, Hon. Artillery Coy, B.E.F. . . . Just a short letter to let you know I am pretty comfortable and enjoying life. I suppose by this time it is getting chilly at home. Here the weather is perfect. There was a sharp frost last night, but as we are billeted in a kindergarten we manage to keep very snug. The mid-day sun is quite warm. They are inoculating us for typhoid. I suppose it is a sensible precaution. . . . We went out for a short march this morning for exercise – it is topping to get going on the French roads. The country is sufficiently undulating to avoid monotony, and when you get away from the alluvial river valley it is sandy and covered with pines and heather, very much like the country between Bagshot and Coll. Not very rich perhaps but the Frenchmen seem able to make things grow in clearings between the trees. The only thing really desirable would be a good light 2-seater or an aeroplane. The roads are first class and the evenings are perfect. . . . There used to be an aerodrome here but I believe it is closed now, anyhow I have not seen any machines about lately. We have very little news here. The French papers are very vague. I imagine from what I saw in an old *Daily Mail* that Spenser Grey did pretty well with Marix and another wasn't it. I see that Bevir wants to know of any O.W.'s I will drop him a line. . . .'

(Commander Spenser-Grey and Lieut Marix had indeed done pretty well, destroying the Dusseldorf Shed and Zeppelin on the 10th October. From Naval Aeroplane H.Q. Ostende Commander Samson sent a signal describing the action to the Central Office, Naval Wing, R.F.C. The signal concluded: '. . . The attack was carried out in the face of a heavy fire at a low altitude; the aeroplane was repeatedly hit by shrapnel but the pilot was able to return to Antwerp. There can be no doubt that the Zeppelin was completely destroyed.')

To return to the H.A.C.
The Goold-Walker History continues:

... On October 25th news was received that Nos. 2 and 3 Companies were leaving Nantes and St. Nazaire respectively. The same day Captain Ward and No. 3 Company passed through Le Mans, and Captain Cole followed two days later with No. 4 Company. Major Cooper and Lieuts. Schiff and Blake, with two platoons of No. 1 Company, also left for Abbeville. On the 27th Corpl. Smart of the transport died from injuries received from his horse falling on him. This was our first casualty.

We were at this time issued with new S.A.A. carts, water-carts and G.S. wagons in place of our nondescript collection, the Commandant saying we could not proceed to the front with such vehicles. The Battalion left Le Mans at 7.45 a.m. on October 31st, travelling via Rouen. There were all sorts of rumours as to our destination and everyone was very excited by the fact that at length we were moving nearer the front, some of the younger bloods declaring that the war would be over before we moved.

Major Cooper and the other half of No. 1 Company rejoined at Abbeville, where we received orders to go on to St. Omer. While waiting to detrain at that place we heard that the London Scottish had been in action that morning. Probably we should have been sent in as the London Scottish were, had H.Q. arrived at St. Omer with the transport, machine guns and reserve ammunition in time. At St. Omer we were under Brigadier-General Chichester, and occupied our time trench digging in the neighbourhood of Blendecques. This trench system was supposed to be part of a reserve line, in case the front line was driven in round Ypres.

On November 3rd Col. Treffry met General Lambton, Military Secretary to the Commander-in-Chief, and suggested that, before the H.A.C. were put in the line, they should go into reserve and be gradually worked up, so as to accustom the men to shell and rifle fire. He also told him that as yet many of the men had had no opportunity of firing their rifles. General Lambton seemed much surprised, and the next day the Battalion had the use of the 200-yards range under the town walls.

Almost immediately, however, orders were received to proceed by motor-buses to Bailleul.

It seemed curious that we should be moved up to the front line in buses belonging to the London General Omnibus Company. We arrived safely without any incident, and the C.O. was ordered to General Moreland, commanding the 5th Division....

H. wrote to Emmie on 4th November:

I wrote from the train coming up here but the letter got mushed up and unreadable so could not send it. I should most awfully like to say how we came here & from where but of course it is absolutely forbidden. It took us some time getting up.... There is plenty of

Jezzi's favourite game going on here. Coming home through the rain I thought I saw Prettyman. But of course we were marching down the road in form so I could not stop and fall out and speak to him.

There are lots of interesting things (true) I should like to tell you. I am sure I shall not remember them all.

The more I see of the A.S.C. & R.F.C. & R.N.D. the more I am convinced that I stayed at Cannon St. too long. Tell Dad that I never expected to see beet growing at such close quarters. Cousin Char was awfully decent and sent me some chocolate and socks both of which were very acceptable. I am about full up with socks now for a bit. I am told that if we get moved a little further up we shall find that disinfectant, soap, candles, matches and chocolate are very scarce, not much of any one thing at a time. When we are moving we can only take what we can carry in addition to some underthings, greatcoat, blankets, munitions of war, food, washing materials, etc. It is beastly having to scrap stuff that is still quite new and good. I may not have much opportunity of writing for the next few days so you will know I am quite fit unless you hear I have caught cold. I will try and write to the flat and Coz Char. I enclose a short letter for Jem's birthday.

Emmie no doubt forwarded H.'s covering letter as well as the birthday letter, to Jim, for Jim wrote to her from Calshot Naval Air Station on Nov 11th 1914: '... Thanks awfully for Herbert's letter, he seems quite cheerful. I am sorry he did not start flying sooner, but I don't think anybody realized he was so keen on it. It is blowing up a bit from the SW. but we did an early patrol all right.... Herbert's reference to Jezzi's favourite game, it is dominoes, I think....'

The H.A.C. History continues:

'On November 7th the C.O. took the 1st and 4th Companies for a route march across the Belgian frontier. The battle seemed to have eased down, but many shells could be seen bursting around Mount Kemmel. Orders were then received to proceed by route march to Estaires the same afternoon and report to the headquarters of the Lahore Division of the Indian Corps. Two days later we received orders to proceed to Les Lobes and report to the Headquarters of the 8th Infantry Brigade. We arrived there at 3 p.m., the men being billeted in outhouses and farms. Just before we reached billets General Sir John French reviewed the Battalion as it marched past. The Commander-in-Chief, after remarking that the men of the 1st H.A.C. must average six feet in height, asked the O.C. if there was anything he could do for him. Now it so happened that our two machine guns had been lent to the 1st Division and had not been returned. The circumstances were these: when matters were so critical at the first Battle of Ypres a staff officer arrived at the Solferino Barracks at St Omer and asked Col. Treffry if he could lend him some machine guns for the 1st Division, who were hard put to it. The C. O. naturally said, "Anything I have is at your disposal"; Capt. Holliday immediately paraded guns, men and ammunition. The staff officer, however, said he only wanted the guns and ammunition (much to Capt. Holliday's and the men's disgust) and he took them off in a car, promising that they should be returned in two days. As they had not been returned the C. O. now explained the circumstances. The Commander-in-Chief thereupon instructed Gen. Lambton to arrange for the guns to be returned to us forthwith. Three days later our two old machine guns turned up and also two new ones, much to Capt. Holliday's joy and that of his gunners.

On November 10th Gen. Sir James Wilcocks, commanding the Indian Corps, inspected the Battalion. He informed Col. Treffry that Gen. French wished the H. A. C. to go into the trenches by companies attached to a regular battalion as a start, so as to be gradually educated to the particular kind of warfare obtaining, and afterwards as a separate unit. While attached to the 8th Brigade (Brig.-Gen. Bowes, Comdg.) at Les Lobes the Battalion was employed mostly in digging trenches in the neighbourhood of Rouge Croix and Croix Barbe, close behind the firing line. While assembling for one of these night operations an amusing incident occurred which has been chronicled elsewhere. The 4th Middlesex arrived at the rendezvous and found the H. A. C. already there. They were very anxious to know who we were, and when they found out they said, "Oh, yes, you are all volunteers and pay two guineas to come out. You must be blooming well balmy."

On November 13th we were shelled while trench digging. This was the first experience our men had of shelling and machine-gun fire, and the next day, while No. 3 Company were engaged in trench digging, a shell landed among a section, killing one man, Pte. F. J. Milne, and wounding eight others. We were lucky not to have had more casualties, as we were digging in full view of the Germans and not more than 1,000 yards from their front line.

On November 16th we left at 6.45 a.m. and, after a very trying march in torrents of rain, reached Bailleul at 2 p.m. and went into billets.

Gen. Smith-Dorrien inspected the Battalion on November 21st, and after his inspection watched the Battalion march past him in fours. Major Cooper with 'A' Company then went into the front line, attached to the 4th Middlesex. . . .'

In a scrap of a letter H. wrote home:
'. . . We are now at the front and there seems to be a perpetual cannonade – aeroplanes constantly passing. We often see the little white puffs from the anti-aircraft shrapnel. The weather has changed again and the last three nights have been very heavy frosts. It is very

cold at night in the wood but better than the wet. The sergeant is just off with the letters to the Censor ...'

And to Emmie: 'France. 22/11/14.... I have 35 seconds to write a line to thank you for the warm pants before the letters get the Censor. They arrived in the nick of time. Everybody was frozen solid last night. This at the 3rd frost we have had hot water bottles indoors! We have been at the front for 10 days now, some of our men in reserve trenches. But the M.G. not yet. Love to all at home and at the flat. Will write again as soon as possible but have not always the opportunity....'

The H.A.C. History continues:

> We remained at Neuve Eglise until the 27th, each Company doing two turns in the front line trenches. Their sector was immediately opposite Messines, only 500 yards separating them from the German trenches, the River Douve flowing between....
>
> We had a few casualties while opposite Messines, among them being Sgt. A.E. Thomas, who had been a keen member of the H.A.C. for some years.
>
> We moved in the afternoon of November 27th to billets at Westoutre, and later to Sherpenberg.
>
> December 3rd was a great day. A king of England, for the first time for 171 years, was with his Army in the field. His Majesty arrived outside 'C' Company's billet, accompanied by the Corps Commander (Gen. Smith-Dorrien), the Divisional Commander (Gen. Haldane), and Brig.-Gen Bowes. The Battalion was drawn up in line along the road facing the billets, and as the King passed down the line each company in succession gave him the H.A.C. 'Regimental Fire.'
>
> His Majesty then went into the sergeants' hut, and chatted with the sergeants, and also talked to some of the men in another hut. The Prince of Wales, who accompanied His Majesty, also inspected the huts. After the inspection, and on our way back to the Royal car, the King enquired as to the number of casualties we had suffered and expressed his great pleasure that we had had so few and that the men looked so well. He then shook hands with the C.O. and said, 'Colonel, I am delighted to have had a look at my Battalion again, and under active service conditions, and I am very glad that your casualties have been so light. I am informed that the H.A.C. is doing extremely well, and that your General is very pleased with you. I shall continue to watch your doings with the greatest of interest, and I wish you all possible luck.'
>
> 'A' and 'D' Companies then marched off to report to the 2nd Royal Scots and proceed to the front line trenches north of Kemmel. 'B' and 'C' Companies, with the Battalion Headquarters, marched off to Shrapnel Farm, alongside Kemmel Chateau, in support. The Brigade was relieved on December 6th and returned to Westoutre. Everyone was feeling rather done, and Capt. Walsh was of great assistance. He somehow managed to secure a cart and brought

in several men whose feet had given out. Corpl. Fabian, a pre-war member of the Regiment, was killed during this term in the trenches – a great loss. . . .

We returned to the line on December 9th, to take over from the Royal Scots Fusiliers the sector in front of Spanbrock Moelen, going in for the first time as a Battalion, and remained in the trenches until the 12th. The weather was awful, frost and snow at intervals, but mostly continuous rain. One began to realize why the British troops of the Duke of York's expedition swore so horribly in Flanders. The trenches we took over were known as the 'F' trenches of Kemmel, and lay to the right of the line held by the 3rd Division, facing almost the centre of the famous Wytschaete-Messines Ridge, and immediately opposite the Spur of Spanbrock Moelen, which was one of the strongest centres of resistance of the German Line on the Ridge, and, unfortunately for us, dominated the 'F' trenches completely. On the right was the 5th Division, and on the left of the 3rd Division were the French, the right of whose line was then opposite the Hollendischur Spur. However, as the British Army increased it took over from the French northwards towards Ypres. Our trenches had been made by the French, and were nothing but ditches full of liquid mud; there was no wire in front, and no material of any kind, nor were there any communication trenches. The only way the front line could be approached was over the open through a sea of mud, and across a bullet-swept area. Bullets came through the parapets as though they had been butter. In some of the trenches, the parapet was only breast high, and in order to get cover during the daytime the men had to sit in the mud on the floor of the trench, and very often a man would find himself sitting on the chest of a mutely protesting Frenchman who had been lying there for a month or six weeks. The German line, on an average, was about 100 yards distant and dominating.

We were relieved by the Royal Scots Fusiliers on December 12th, and went into billets at Locre. Several officers were down. The Adjutant was very ill. Capts. Whyte and Gibson, Lieut. Byron and the Doctor were all sick, and a great number of men were suffering from exhaustion, exposure and frostbite. It turned out afterwards that this turn at the trenches cost the Battalion 12 officers and 250 men . . .

'Herbert is a lucky dog to be going to the front,' Jim had written home in September.

The H.A.C. History continues:

. . . On December 14th two battalions of the 8th Brigade, the 2nd Royal Scots and 1st Gordon Highlanders, received orders to attack at Petit Bois, and the machine-gun section of the H.A.C. were to assist in covering the advance. This operation was not very successful owing to the appalling state of the ground, the men having to wade through mud to the attack, and the battalions lost very heavily, capturing only one short line of trench. We had four men wounded in our machine-gun section, and I heard afterwards from the Divisional Commander, and also from the Corps Commander, that they had done extraordinarily well.

H. was firing his machine-gun during the action described above when, he later said, 'it jambed and exploded' – it may itself have been hit – sending spent shells and a quantity of jagged metal from the shattered gun back into his right hand, wrist and arm below the shoulder. For the rest of his life he never forgot the long wait by his wrecked machine-gun, icy-cold, as he was, with shock and loss of blood and in increasing pain until, eventually, a Quaker stretcher-party waded through the mud, under enemy fire, and brought him in. 'Those good people,' he called the Quakers, whenever he mentioned their name thereafter. After the field-dressing station he was sent back to Dunkerque. He must have made light of his injuries in messages home for Emmie sent a brief undated letter to Alie: 'Herbert's hand is getting better and he seems to have some companions in the Dunkerk hospital . . .'

He was soon back in England, however, and was admitted to the 3rd General Base Hospital, Oxford. J.L.T. went down to see him on the 21st December, one week after H. was wounded.

'It was jolly seeing Dad yesterday,' H. wrote to his Mother, 'I hardly expected to see him so soon. He said I might expect to see Charlie to-morrow.

I heard from Jezzi this morning. He has little business to attend to, no aeroplanes, all his bachelor friends have enlisted in something or other. I will write to him now. Glad you got back safely. . . . P.S. Some small pieces of wood and one small piece of metal were pulled out this morning.'

Thereafter and for almost a year H.'s left-handed writing, his 'spider walking all over the paper', sent the news and views from his hospital bed, or rather, from various hospital beds.

The slowness with which proper surgical treatment was carried out is distressing to read about, even at this distance in time, accustomed as one has become to the rapid effectiveness of antibiotics and to better radiography and screening techniques. Charles was prompt in his offers of help and in good advice. If H. was only at Oxford he should come home where he would be properly looked after and he, Charles, could get a fast train home; the response of a warm-hearted young brother, then aged 16. Because Emmie was often busy with her work for the Soldiers & Sailors Families Association she and J.L.T. seem to have taken turn and turn about in writing news of H. He was moved from

Oxford to Milton Hill, Steventon, and J.L.T. wrote to Emmie, who was visiting there, in early January: ' ... I have just returned. What I waited was to get the Drs advice as to getting a London Surgeon's opinion on Herby's case. Dr E. said quite decidedly – not at present. Later on when the wound was clean and healing he thought perhaps a specialist might help to get back the use of the wrist. He was glad to hear that H.O. could move his fingers. ... I hope you will stay as long as you can with Herbert. We are getting on all right here. ...'

Jay wrote to Emmie on 10th January: ' ... I am awfully glad you are down with H.O. and I know you will do everything that is possible. I will send eggs as often as I can. ...'

A month later Aunt Lucy Prescott, her wires slightly crossed, wrote to Emmie: ' ... I am glad Herbert is better. I shall be gladder still to hear he has got rid of all foreign bodies from his arm. How can he manage to fly with a bad arm? Surely he'll want both his *wing bones* to use freely. Or are the feathers sprouting already instead of his arm. They say Nature makes up for deficiencies of wounds etc. etc. ...'

Milton Hill was a beautiful small hospital which had been donated to the war effort by the Mortimer Singer family. H. had a comfortable, spotlessly clean room all to himself, with glorious South views over Park and golf course. He sat there, 'done up like an Egyptian mummy' in 'a longer, stiffer wooden splint tied on very tight. This is not comfortable. But everything else is ...' He again and again praised the care and kindness of the doctors and nurses. But he was ill. 'Invalidy' – Jay described his appearance. His arm was still full of mud and dirty metal, suppurating and unhealthy. He protested that he did not feel much pain, only a feeling of his arm 'having been worried'. Again and again J.L.T. and Emmie talked of second opinions. Again they were advised to wait. He went to the theatre for removal of foreign bodies but it was later known that they fished about in his wrist for small pieces of metal and left much uninvestigated. The likelihood of him losing his arm was much in Emmie's mind after one visit, in March, 1915.

H.'s spirits might have been much lower had it not been for the visit of his old school friend, Pretyman. R.F. Pretyman, now serving with No 3 Squadron, was the man whom he thought he had seen when he had been coming home through the rain, marching down the road in form near Bailleul in November. After Pretyman's visit he wrote home: '...Pretyman says they are awfully short of good pilots ...'

In April Jim had become engaged to be married to Nancy, daughter of Major and Mrs Edwards of The Grange, Bembridge, Isle of Wight, and the wedding was fixed for June. V., at Macdonald College in Canada, was disappointed not to be able to be there, for weddings, garden-parties, gatherings of attractive and well-dressed people were the scenes and occasions which she loved best in life: ... 'you must tell me all about it', she wrote home, 'I expect H.O. will be best man ...'

There was in fact some doubt as to whether H. would be well enough to attend in any capacity, but in May, Milton Hill, believing that there was no more that they could do for him, sent him to convalesce at Blenheim Palace, where he soon improved enough in general health to be able to wander slowly in the peaceful grounds: 'the jolly walks,' he called them – and from time to time to be taken for short motor-drives or out to tea by the Marriotts, old Warlingham friends who now lived in Woodstock and who showed him much kindness.

Jim had asked his cousin Ben, now also a pilot, to be best man if H. was unable to be present; but in the event all went well, for conformity's sake, and Jim subsequently wrote home: ' ... H.O. performed his duties as best man splendidly ...'

After attending his brother's wedding H. was told to report to the War Hospital, Croydon. Once again his wounds were bursting out. However, J.L.T. and Emmie had watched their son's sufferings long enough, and always having had especial confidence in Guy's Hospital, asked that he be transferred there, at their own expense, of course. The reply to their request was curt:

'War Hospital, Croydon. 29.7.15.
'Dear Sir, I regret I am unable to arrange the transfer of Pte. H.G. Travers to Guys Hospital. Yours sincerely,' – and a signature that I shall not quote, but it was that of a Lt Col R.A.M.C.

J.L.T. and Emmie continued to fight for H.'s removal to Guy's and after considerable obstruction they did at last obtain his transfer there. The Guy's surgeons must have been really thorough in excavating and cleaning his wounds, and in removing the further, numerous, foreign bodies which had been such a drain on his general health. After his time in their hands his wounds soon healed. Emmie received a postcard from Guy's in October: 'From the Sister-in-Charge, Bright Ward, Guy's Hospital, S E. 7.10.15. Your son has asked me to send you this p.c. to say he has had his operation and is quite comfortable this evening. Sister-in-Charge.'

Thereafter H. made a speedy convalescence and although his upper arm remained as thin as a stick for the rest of his life, for nothing could restore the muscle which had been torn and shot away from it, he recovered, in spite of contracted tendons, the almost normal use of his hand. Milton Hill doctors had predicted as much.

After almost a year out of things he was anxious to get back, preferably as a pilot. He sought Jim's advice, which he took, and as a result was granted a temporary commission as a pilot in the Royal Naval Air Service as a Provisional Flight Sub Lieutenant. The date of his appointment was 14th December 1915; precisely one year after he had been wounded. He was back and would soon be flying. He resigned from the H.A.C. but felt proud, always, of his time in their ranks and particularly so of having been a *Westmeathian*.

He was posted to Eastbourne on the 4th January 1916. He reported there a day or so early, as was customary, and wrote to Emmie on 3rd January.

'Royal Naval Air Station, Trinity Place, Eastbourne....

The wind has been fresh to-day: too fresh. This afternoon we had a run with some basset hounds for exercise ... I am afraid the postage on the two lots of gear will come to a good lot but it is better than buying the stuff again down here....'

The first entry in his first log-book was on 5th January 1916: Wind Direction & Velocity: W.5. Machine Type & No: Maurice Farman #3002. Pilot: Lloyd. Time in Air: Minutes 9. Height: 300/400 ft. Course: Two circuits Eastbourne Aerodrome and two landings. Remarks: Accompanied Mr Lloyd as passenger. Hands placed lightly on controls. Bumpy.

The first 9 minutes were from 11.12 until 11.21. He flew again on the afternoon of the same day, from 4.5 to 4.20 p.m. on the same machine and with the same Pilot, but this time they were at 2,000 ft and their course was N. from aerodrome past Polegate and return and his Remarks: 'Accompanied Mr Lloyd as passenger. Took no part whatever in controls. Machine very steady above 800.'

M. Farman Shorthorn. The 'Mechanical Cow'. This m/c is one of the two last surviving of this type worldwide

photo: courtesy National Aeronautical Collection, Rockcliffe, Ottawa

On the 8th January he did some circuits on the same machine but this time the Pilot was Hackman. On the 9th January, with Wind at NW.1 he flew with Hackman and then Lloyd for a total of 6 circuits on M. Farman #3001. His total flying time for week ending 9th January for 57 minutes. On the 10th January with the wind at N.W.4 he flew again with Lloyd on M. Farman #3001: 'Course. 3 circuits aerodrome and 3 landings. Remarks: Instruction; had control of machine 2nd and 3rd circuits and landings.'

He wrote to Jay on the 11th January:

Please thank Dad for his letter which arrived here this evening. We have had some grand weather in patches and my total time up so far has been 1 hr 23 mins.

To-day there was nothing doing so six of us went to the rifle range. I shot with an automatic pistol for the first time. They are very pretty weapons. After that we had some rifle practice at 200.... We have plenty of pupils (about 28) of all sorts here, most of them are rattling good fellows. The Canadians are very keen.... The C.O. is a live man. I am very lucky to be under a decent (sub) acting flight commander. Both he and the W.O. who does most of the instruction are sound, good, pilots. The W.O. Mr Lloyd makes most perfect landings.

As you know I am being taught on a 'mechanical cow' (M.F.).

To-day on the range Lloyd and I tied top so we shot it off with 5 rounds....

He flew again on the 14th January, with the Wind at N.N.W.3. on M. Farman #3002 with Lloyd, one flight of 13 minutes, the next of 4 minutes. And again on 16th January with the Wind at N.W.2. for 10 minutes at 300 ft and made two landings. Later the same morning on the same machine, #3002, he flew again with Lloyd, this time for 7 minutes at 300/400 ft. Later on the same morning he went solo. He flew for 10 minutes at a 1,000 ft, doing figures of 8 round the aerodrome on #3002; he noted in his Remarks column: 'made first solo flight landing too fast but no damage done'. He made a further solo flight half an hour later, flying at 600 ft on the same machine. The week closed; his total recorded flying time was 141 minutes of which the last 25 minutes were solo.

One week later he flew again, doing a refresher solo on #3002; later the same morning he had his first passenger flight (with Hackman) on B.E.2.C #1184, at 300 ft; then at 11.50 the same morning he flew for

28 minutes at 1,600 ft on M. F. #3002, doing figures of 8 round the gasworks and to the N. E. of the aerodrome. It was his qualifying flight. His Remarks record: 'Solo. Ticket Flight. Bumpy up to 800. Very steady 800/1600. Qualified.' He had done 64 minutes solo. Later the same day he flew M. F. #3001 solo off to have a look at Pevensey Castle. Remarks: 'This machine was lower powered than #3002.' On the 26th January, with the Wind at W.2. he was Lt Newberry's passenger on Curtiss 3374 out to the Downs and back. H.'s Remarks: 'Compared M. F. this machine is nose heavy and quick on lateral control. She also carries Stb'd helm.'

He wrote to Emmie on the 28th January: 'Thanks very much for your postcard.... Very little flying since I last wrote. Could you send me my "Aviation", "Map-Reading", "The Manual of R.F.C. Training" both parts, Woods' "Strength and Elasticity of Structural Members". I am afraid this is a big list but if you could include the Old report of the Aircraft factory too it might be useful. I would come home and fetch them but I do not want to miss any flying (and) not ask for leave as soon as this.

'I am afraid you have had a very anxious time lately – don't overwork yourself, Mum.... By the way you were right, about turning into or with the wind.'

On the 29th January, with Wind S.E.1. he again flew with Lt Newberry on Curtiss 3374, receiving instruction and landing on the downs. Later the same day he flew M. F. #3001 solo round Beachy Head, Polegate Woods, Willingdon and return. Remarks: 'Thick clouds from 1000 to 2000. But very steady above.' Later the same day, with Wind S.W.2. he flew M. F. #3007 solo round Bexhill, making two circuits of the town. Remarks: 'Engine stopped when coming down over Pevensey 2800 ft. Forced landing. Machine dismantled.'

The week ending 7th February he had no flying.

On the 8th February, with the Wind: W.5. he flew M. F. #3002 near the aerodrome at 1,950 ft. Remarks: 'Wind coming over Beachy Head gusty and bumpy. Landing over corner big shed. Too much engine & too fast. n.d.d.'

On the 9th February he was out again on the Curtiss 3374 with Lt Newberry; they landed near Wilmington 3 times; later the same day, with the Wind: N.3. he went solo on Curtiss 3392, keeping near the aerodrome. Remarks: 'first solo on a Curtiss: machine climbs slowly at first. $1\frac{1}{2}$ S turns to land.' In the afternoon of the same day, with

Wind: N.W.2. he flew the same machine at 2,500 ft. Remarks: 'This machine with a 4 bladed prop. climbs slowly at first; S turns (3) to land.'

Later the same day he flew Curtiss 3347 to 2,000 ft with the Wind: N.W.3. for 26 minutes. Remarks: '(2 bladed prop) climbs well. engine started missing badly would not climb above this height. left wing apt to drop.'

On the 12th February Lt Newberry took him up for a short flight on Bristol 1224 near the aerodrome. Remarks: '1st passenger flight on Bristol.' On the afternoon of the same day, with the Wind: N.N.W.2. he went solo on the same machine for 26 minutes flying at 4,300 ft over Beachy Head. Remarks: '1st solo on Bristol. perfect day. 1st experience of Gnome engine. climb 45 level 54.' Later on the same afternoon Lt McMinnies took him up on B.E.2.C 1187 for 22 minutes, practising bomb-dropping over Langley Pt & target N. of field. On the 19th February Lt Jamieson took him up for 51 minutes on B.E.2.C. 1184 with Wind: N.W.6. They flew N.W. from the aerodrome to Hailsham then W. to Lewes & return. Remarks: 'used this flight for observation practice. Wind very bumpy near ground. Steady about 3000.'

On the 20th February with the Wind: S.E.2., H. flew Bristol 1224 for 31 minutes at 3,600 ft near the aerodrome. Remarks: 'Rain Hail & snow at 3600 & all way down to 900. could not see. came in.' But he took off again on the same machine about an hour later, at noon, and climbed to 4,100 ft near the aerodrome and Beachy Head. Remarks: 'When between B'hy Head & Town ran out of petrol. landed in field near aerodrome filled up & returned.' At 3.20 on the same afternoon he took the same machine up to 5,150 ft for 40 minutes over Beachy Head. Remarks: 'small clouds at 4,500 ft. 5150 Highest yet reached. weather perfect. cold.'

He did some more practise landings on the same machine during the remainder of the afternoon and on the following morning, with the Wind: E.S.E.5 was up again on Bristol 1224, climbing to 5100 over Beachy Head Road. spotting gunfire. getting more confidence. wind steady.' He did some more practise landings and then went up again with Scott as Pilot over the aerodrome. Remarks: 'Was to spot gunfire but snowstorm sent us down.'

He was at Eastchurch for one day, the 25th February, although still stationed at Eastbourne. His log-book records: 'Wind N.E.3. Bristol

1218. 6 minutes. 800 ft. Round Eastchurch (Isle of Sheppey). Remarks: 'Testing strange machine. Bad get off. good landing.' He had probably been sent to Eastchurch in order to learn to find his way back to Eastbourne for on the next day he returned to his own Station.

'26/2/16.Wind:E.S.E.4.Bristol Tractor 1218 A. 88 minutes. 2,900 ft. From Eastchurch 215°. Passed Headcorn & Robertsbridge. To Eastbourne. Remarks: 1st long cross country. steered a compass course & checked by ma/c passing. Snow on ground & 3 Snowstorms in the air prevented machine from going higher. lost 300 ft in one snowstorm. Engine started 1075 revs. afterwards dropped 1050.'

Back at Eastbourne, he made a number of further flights on Bristol Tractor A 1218 around the aerodrome, testing the engine, cleaning the petrol supply; he really does not seem to have liked the machine at all. On the 1st March he remarked: 'Experimenting with needle valve. cut down petrol too much. came into aerodrome too flat.'

Later on the same afternoon he went up with Jamieson as Pilot on Bleriot 3215. The Wind: S.2. and they were up for 7 minutes at 180 ft over the aerodrome. Remarks: 'Machine could hardly get away from very heavy ground & climbed slowly. First experience as passenger on monoplane.'

Later the same afternoon, with Wind: S.E.1. he went solo on Bleriot 3214 for 8 minutes at 1,100 ft over the aerodrome. Remarks: 'First solo on Bleriot. weather perfect. Found no difficulty in getting off or landing. made turns of large radius. (petrol 22 1200 revs. climbs 45 level 54.)' By now the light had gone but the following morning, 2nd March, with the Wind. N.E.2. he was up again, on Bleriot 3236 this time, practising landings. On the afternoon of the 2nd March he went up with Lloyd as Pilot on Maurice Farman 3001, his dear old 'mechanical cow', to do a bit of bomb-dropping practice. Their course was: 'Pevensey Castle, Hurstmonceux Castle, Gardner Street, Dallington Church, Ashburnham House, Battle Abbey, Pevensey Castle, aerodrome.' Remarks: 'Bomb dropping practice. Floods to starboard. Country getting hilly. Fired two Very's lights. large woods & lake. The rain clouds were not above 1,000 ft making observation very difficult.'

On Monday, 6th March, with the Wind:N.5. he was sent out solo to drop a bomb at Dallington. He was on Bristol Tractor A 1218, the machine which he had brought from Eastchurch. 'Course: Compass Co.N. This was wrong because Dallington was objective. When 1 mile due E. Hailsham forced landing. Remarks: Set out solo for Dallington to drop 1 bomb (Very's light). Engine doing 1050 at start afterwards 1060. At Hailsham dropped to 1000 then 950. Came down in good stubble field (Woodland's farm). 1 spiral and S turn good landing phoned for assistance. L. M. Young found partial air lock in petrol feed.'

He wrote to Emmie on 13th March:

Thank you for your letter just arrived. I have been away most of this week.

On Monday I had a forced landing engine trouble about 9 miles away but picked out a good field and flew back in the afternoon. On Tuesday I went out in a car to help another fellow who had had his forced landing about 20 miles away. On Thursday I went over to Shoreham as a passenger to fetch another machine but spent 2 days thawing it up. So went back on Saturday night and flew over again on Sunday and brought it back. I am very fit and hope everyone at home is also. . . . Please thank J. for cuffs. I will write soon. They are very warm and just right . . .

He had done a lot of practice on Bleriot 3214 and really liked the machine. One of his Remarks was: 'These machines are much easier to land without engine than with it. Owing to electric light knife switch being used instead of small press button.'

On the 9th March he was flying alone on Curtiss 3356 near Shoreham Aerodrome when, at 200 ft: 'Engine cut out completely at 150 feet on edge aerodrome (low tension trouble). Turn back quickly. Engine cut in again. made good landing. Right wing down in air.'

The following day he tested the machine with a new magneto. 'Very good.'

On the 12th March McMinnies took him up on Henry Farman 1519, for 30 minutes at 3,200 ft near the aerodrome: Remarks: 'First passenger flight on Henry Farman. visibility good. weather perfect.'

Later the same morning he took up Bleriot 3214 near the aerodrome. Remarks: 'Engine ran well on ground but missed in air. Missing became worse so came in.'

In the afternoon he went up in B.E.2.C. with Mc Minnies and they went to Polegate, Lewes and Shoreham. Remarks: 'Engine rev counter came adrift at Polegate. Slightly misty.'

On the same afternoon he took up Curtiss 3356 for 61 minutes. This must have been the flight he mentioned to his Mother. Course: 'Shoreham to N. Brighton, Lewes, Glynde, Polegate Eastbourne. Remarks: Black clouds drifted up from E. & ground was invisible at 2000 ft. Climbed to 3000. Comp. Co100°. Came below clouds near Lewes & again took compass course 130°. Very dark low clouds when landing at Eastbourne. Good landing. Climb 50 level 60 K.'

On the 15th March he was once again struggling with Bristol 1218, which he took up for 18 minutes to 2,000 ft near Eastbourne aerodrome. Remarks: 'Testing engine 1100 revs at first later dropped to 1080. Cut down petrol from 4 turns to $1\frac{1}{4}$ (slowly) Revs dropped to 1050. Came down & found mag distributor brush crooked. Weather perfect.' He tested 1218's engine again on the 16th. Remarks: 'Testing engine. 1080 revs steady. Petrol 2 turns.'

Later on during the morning of the 16th March he went solo on B.E.2.C., flying for 23 minutes and taking the machine to 3,600 ft, near Eastbourne aerodrome and over Polegate, Elm Town & Pevensey. Remarks: 'First solo on B.E.2.C. Hands off controls from 2000 up. Came down in large circles hands off.'

On the 18th March he was once again up on Bristol 1218 for 12 minutes, testing the engine over the aerodrome at 500 ft; Remarks: 'Testing engine 1080 revs.'

But at 10.35 on the same morning he took Henry Farman 1519 up solo for 28 minutes at 2,500 ft over the aerodrome. Remarks: 'First solo on Henry Farman. Takes left rudder (opposite to tractor Gnomes). Very flyable machine answers controls.' He had landed at 11.03 and an hour later, at 12.04, he took up his first passenger, Grove, for 41 minutes on Henry Farman 1519; they stayed near the aerodrome, in good weather, observing some live bomb dropping. In the evening of the same day, at 6 o'clock, he went up again on Henry Farman 1519 alone. Remarks: 'Practising turns. machine very pleasant to handle.'

He was transferred to Eastchurch, to the Gunnery School, and first flew there on 1st April, his 25th birthday, on Maurice Farman Longhorn 3005 with F. S. L. Kidner as passenger. Remarks: 'Machine rather underpowered. 75 HP engine. Weather good.' At 4 o'clock on the same day he went up on Maurice Farman Shorthorn 8471 with F. S. L. Dornton as Pilot. Remarks: 'First passenger flight on Shorthorn.' Ten minutes after landing the role was reversed and he took up F. S. L. Dornton as passenger on the same machine. Remarks: 'First solo on Shorthorn a very slow machine. Climbs 40 K Level 48 K.'

On the 2nd April, with the Wind: N.E.4. he went down to Eastbourne on Curtiss 3420 with F. S. L. J. D. Scott as Pilot; they flew down at 6,000 ft. Remarks: 'Weather clear. picked out Leeds Castle. Headcorn. Cranbrook. Robertsbridge.'

On the 4th April, with Wind: N.W.4. he returned to Eastchurch from Eastbourne on Morane 3236 Parasol, with F. L. Marsden as Pilot. They flew at 3,100 ft and the journey took 60 minutes exactly, (as the journey down in the Curtiss had done.) Remarks: 'first passenger flight on Morane. Hazy atmosphere. Cold on face. angle of view good.'

At 5 o'clock the same evening he went up on Maurice Farman Longhorn A70, with F. S. L. McClelland as Pilot, flying at 2,000 ft over Eastchurch. Remarks: 'Flying over mirror at 2000 ft. average error 35 feet passed out.'

On the 5th April he went up on Maurice Farman Longhorn 2005, with F. S. L. Saunders as Pilot, to practise dummy bomb dropping at Eastchurch. Remarks: 'Bumpy to 1000. Steady at 2000. Bomb rack jammed at 1 bomb which was within radius.' An hour later, with a passenger, he flew Maurice Farman Longhorn 8474 to continue practise. Remarks: 'Bumpy: not too bumpy for flying but too bumpy for bombsight work.'

On the 6th April, with the Wind: E.4 and with F. L. Newberry as Pilot, he went up on Maurice Farman Shorthorn 70 'Gunbus' from Eastchurch to Leysdown and back. Remarks: 'Firing Lewis Gun at surface target. passed.'

He continued with dummy bomb dropping practise on the 8th and again on the 10th April, taking it in turns with the other Pilots to fly Maurice Farman Shorthorn 8471, 8470 and Maurice Farman Longhorn 70. He went on early patrol with F. S. L. Whittier on the 13th in a B.E.2.C., over Eastchurch, W. Westgate, N. Dover, N. Folkestone and E. Detling. Remarks: 'A perfect morning. Wind increased in strength & clouds appeared 6.30 A.M. Progress was then very slow.'

On the 15th he flew the solo machine Curtiss Tractor 3361 near the aerodrome. Remarks: 'Clumsy landing on rough ground broke one chassis wire only.'

And on the 16th April, with F. S. L. Newman as Pilot, went up on Curtiss Tractor 3420. Remarks: 'Came down for petrol.' He flew again the same morning on the same machine, at 6,000 ft round the Isle of Sheppey. Remarks: 'Wind gusty up to 3000 ft.'

On the 20th April with Wind: S.W.3. he went up on Maurice Farman Gunbus 8110 with F. S. L. Pizey as Pilot, flying at 500 ft to Leysdown. Remarks: 'Lewis gun firing at Kite target.'

On the 21st April he flew Bleriot Parasol 1538 for 11 minutes at 1,600 ft. Remarks: 'First solo on this type. Climbs 55 K. level 62 K. a very pleasant machine in the air; view very good. machine in good condition.'

Later the same morning he took up Curtiss Tractor 3381 for 9 minutes at 1,200 ft. Remarks: 'Engine running very irregularly. Came down.'

In the afternoon he flew B.E.2.C. 1168 for 30 minutes at 2,500 ft. Remarks: 'A very good machine. clouds at 2,500 ft. Engine rather harsh.' On the 22nd he flew Curtiss 3420 locally, on the 23rd Bleriot Parasol 1538 locally, practising landings with and without engine. Remarks: 'Bumpy landing without engine.' and 'Good landing used a little engine.' Again on the 23rd he went up on Maurice Farman Longhorn 3005, with F. S. L. Taylor as Pilot. Remarks: 'Trying to get height for mirror – no good.' On the 24th he flew B.E.2.C. 1124 on a cross country to Rochford with Wind: S.W.7. Course: 'Eastchurch to Rochford via Grain, Lower Hope, and Rayleigh.' Remarks: 'A very gusty wind, full of bumps. A very tail heavy machine. Interesting but tiring journey.' He picked up a Pilot at Rochford, F. S. L. Sproat, who flew them both back to Eastchurch.

On the 25th April he flew Bleriot Parasol 1544 for 10 minutes and again for 49 minutes. Remarks: 'solo over mirror practise at 1000.' and 'solo over mirror loading pistol single handed.'

They were pleased with him at the Gunnery School and thought him ready to transfer to Dover. The next stage had begun. Leaving Eastchurch must have been very like leaving home for H. He had known the aerodrome and had watched the flying there for years. He had skated on the dykes and tobogganed and snow-sailed down the gliding hill. The R. N. A. S. Officers' Mess was the very same iron bungalow that his father had put up in 1910.

Dover was certainly going to be different.

He first flew there on the 28th April with the Wind N.$\frac{1}{2}$ on B.E.2.C.

998, taking off at 7.10 a.m. and flying at 1,500 ft for 15 minutes locally over Dover. Remarks: 'a small difficult aerodrome with deep gullies and valleys on all sides. a very good slow landing.'

On the evening of the same day, taking off at 6.50 p.m., he flew Avro 1478 for 15 minutes at 1,500 ft, this time with the Wind: N.N.E.3. Remarks: '1st solo on Avro. a very perfect machine. very slow landing. slight bump. climbs 45 K. level 60 K.'

On the 30th April he flew Avro 1478 again for some more local practice. Landed. Took off again on the same machine at 12 noon, flying for 25 minutes at 2,500 ft. Remarks: 'Big explosion in engine. Cut off petrol & switch. Brought machine down quickly good landing in football field near to aerodrome.'

On the 1st of May he flew B.E.2.C. to Eastchurch via Canterbury, flying at 5,000 ft the flight taking 30 minutes. He returned the same afternoon at 6,000 ft via Cranbrook and Folkestone. Compass Co. 140°. He landed at Folkestone taking off again at 6.10 p.m. to complete his journey to Dover. On the 3rd May he went solo on Morane Parasol 3242, flying locally and practising landings. Remarks: '1st solo on this type of machine & 1st experience of Le Rhone engine, which runs sweetly & throttles down well. Morane does not seem to have a great deal of lateral control. otherwise a pleasant fine weather machine. climbs well. visibility good.'

On the 4th May he flew Morane Parasol 3242 locally for 20 minutes; subsequently took off on Morane Parasol 3249 for a further 20 minutes. Remarks: 'This machine was slightly different to 3242 having no elastic on fore and aft control.' Later the same afternoon, at 4.20 p.m., he took off on 3249 to fly from Dover to Eastbourne. He recorded the Wind as S.1 on ground. Remarks: 'Wind veered with increased height until no progress was made at 7500. Clumsy landing at Eastbourne.' He recorded the Wind: S.W.8/9 at 7500. He then flew from Eastbourne to Folkestone. Remarks: 'Again bumpy behind Dungeness. V. good landing.' He took off from Folkestone at 7.15 pm to return to Dover. Remarks: 'rough time getting off.'

He continued to fly Morane Parasols, both 3249 and 3242, on the 5th, 6th, 10th and 11th May, mostly in very bumpy conditions and with numerous practise landings. On the 11th Remarks: 'Bumpy. flying over mirror. could not reload pistol.'

On the 12th May, on a fine, still evening, 'no wind,' he took off

H. G. Travers, early 1916. Studio portrait

solo on Bristol 'Bullet', flying locally over Dover. Remarks: '1st solo in this type of machine. Perfect evening: so found her very pleasant to handle. Owing to faulty switch made a fast but otherwise good landing.'

Later the same evening he wrote to Alie and how pleased she must have been to notice that his handwriting, which had been right-handed again for nearly six months, was now quite excellent.

12/5/16.   19, Waterloo Crescent, Dover.
... I sent you a card this evening which was rather brief but I was in a hurry. We get no leave from this station until 'khaki leave' i.e.: 4 days to get khaki before we leave for the other side.

My No 2 monkey jacket is getting very filthy and so are my breeks. I shall not need blue when I get over the other side.

This is a most curious town. No one allowed in or out. We are all supposed to carry passes. The place is quite stiff with soldiers and sailors. We do not see anyone outside the mess. We get a fair amount of flying: but must leave any news of that sort until I see you.... How is Charlie getting on? Ask him to write and let me know how he goes. Also if he wants anything.

I sent Granny a photo.

Hope she liked it. She wrote such a nice letter to me thanking me.

Yours ever, Herbert Travers.

Such a formal letter, quite unlike his normal jolly and rumbustious style. The other side was drawing near and he knew only too well what it felt like when your luck ran out and things went against you, over on the other side.

On the 16th May he was up again on Morane Parasol 3249, flying non-stop Dover, Ashford, Maidstone, Detling, Dover.

Remarks: 'A perfect morning. reached 6500 in 15 mins at 55 K where she flies level at 63 K. tried to get to 10,000 but could not get there. She was flying without any climb for 20 minutes at 60 K below which she did not seem steady.'

On the 17th May he tested Morane Parasol 3248 over Dover. Remarks: 'Local Dover. Testing. Flies rt wing down.' He continued to fly for the rest of the day, mostly on 3242, doing some dummy bomb dropping over St Margaret's Bay. Remarks: 'Dummy bomb dropping. Line good. Elevation (lever sight) very poor.' He also tested Bleriot 3219 and at 6.45 p.m. took off solo on Nieuport 3165. Remarks: '1st solo on Nieuport. Machine is very handy. But at 55 K did not appear to climb quickly. Carburration very poor & engine is either over-revving or cuts out altogether.'

On the 18th May he was up early, taking off at 4.56 a.m. on Morane Parasol 3248 and taking her up to 6,500 for 19 mins; he also made two short local flights on Bleriot 3219 before breakfast and a third at 11.10 a.m. At 6.45 p.m. with the Wind E.4. he took Nieuport 3165 up to 3,000 ft for 20 minutes. The following morning he took Nieuport 3165 up again, this time for 50 minutes, for a final practise 'handling & landing.' It was his final practise. From now on he was on his own.

The C. O. of R. N. Aeroplane Station, Dover, duly confirmed in H.'s log-book: 'Instruction completed. 42 hours solo. All types. specially Scouts. Ready for Service abroad. 19/V/16.'

It was time for khaki leave.

4

SAY IT AGAIN TO-MORROW

1916–1917

Dunkerque – Reconnaisance Patrols – WING TIP – Seconded R.F.C. and to
Vert Galand – Bertangles – Marieux – Disposition of Squadrons.

H. was transferred to Dunkerque on the 25th May 1916. For the first
few days he made some local flights on a Clerget 110 powered Nieuport,
3930; on the first flight the 'Engine would not stop after landing.
"Brought up" in soft ground. no damage.'; subsequently did a flight
with Fletcher as passenger, Fletcher being a 'Bomb sight expert'.

He settled in happily at Dunkerque and wrote to Emmie on 29th
May:

> #1 Wing R N A S Dunkirk (or Dunkerque)
> 29/5/16.
>
> . . . One of the fellows is going across this afternoon so I am asking
> him to take this to post.
>
> I had a grand trip across (not by the air route) and find everything
> here in good condition.
>
> Everyone rather tired after a mutual strafe lasting for a whole week.
> The Huns must be the same for they have not worried us since I have
> been here. I am lucky to have a Nieuport, a 2-seater converted to a
> single-seater for my own.
>
> I have not flown her yet. I am having some new wires put in.
> However there are other Nieuports here and I had a flip or two the
> other day.
>
> Have not been over the lines yet. I am under a Canadian Nurlock.
>
> Haskins is C.O. but has been quite inoffensive. Groves left the day
> I came.
>
> Chambers is to be C.O. here.
>
> Under Ft. Comm. Nurlock is Flt.Lt. Bell – a Queenslander and a
> splendid man. I believe he knows the M'Connells and may be one of

that crowd. . . . This morning he took a passenger up the lines in a two-seater 2-gun bus and attacked 2 Aviatiks.

The passengers gun jambed but they brought down one Hun. . . .

Can you ask Alice to send me 1 towel, 1 pr pyjamas and wd you send me an old pair puttees. . . . P.S. The weather here is gorgeous to-day. But has been cold. Could you send me any old coloured sweaters of mine.

On the 2nd June he was up on 80 Standard Nieuport 3962 and on the 3rd June went off on a fighting patrol, with F. S. L. Mack as Pilot, as 110 Clerget Nieuport 3918. They flew at 8,200 feet. Remarks: 'Fighting patrol up to trenches. nothing seen.'

He took possession of his own single-seat Nieuport that day and at 6 p.m. took off on 80 h.p. Standard Nieuport 3184 for a patrol lasting an hour and a quarter. He accompanied F.Lt. Hinchelwood (on another machine). They flew: 'Out to sea and Furnes, Nieuport, Dixmunde Ypres & back to coast.' They flew at 11,000 ft. Remarks: 'This is height record and first fighting patrol.'

The following morning, with Wind S.W.2., he took off at 7.40 a.m. alone on 3184; it was the first of many such patrols alone. He made Remarks: 'This machine is fitted with 2 guns in top plane.

Climbs down to 43 K   1140 revs.
   ,,   57 K   1140 revs.
   flies level   65 K   1200 revs.'

On the 10th, with Wind N.W.2. he took 80 Le Rhone Nieuport 3184 standard single seater for a short patrol but 'visibility bad too misty for patrol'.

He wrote to Emmie on the 12th:

Wing R N A S c/o G P O London.

. . . Thanks so much for your last letter. Tell Dad the breeches are a great success and that I wear them every day. They look very fine and just match the local sand – but are getting rather greasy round the knees now. We are having a cold wet spell. Have got a cabin to myself now in a new hut. Very like the room at Coll; a window with a ventilating top.

Several lockers made from petrol can boxes, a bed I made myself which is very comfortable.

(There followed a diagram):

AA   two baulks of timber
BB   three long slats
CC   strip of canvas
DDD   eleven light cross pieces
M   a mattress, very comfortable

They have distempered the matchboard with an artistic shade of light green. Very restful to the eye, and the floor is stop-rotted. These huts are sent over in sections and consequently there are occasional and unintentional ventilations. The 'Tishs' are about 8 feet high. At present I am alone but probably someone will be put in on top of me soon.

The French soldiers are very handy.

One of them was in here yesterday morning with two 75 m/gun cartridges worked up into flower vases, most beautiful engraving, but I let the other fellows buy them. They would only add to the clobber already at home. One French air mechanic the other day had just finished a most beautiful scale model of a Morane Parasol in brass. But I think he was making it for himself or for his people. It was perfect and every control and the engine worked properly.

By the way, in several of the men's letters lately they say they have had their letters home charged for. Have the Post Office charged you for those I have sent? Tell me if they do because it should not be so and we are trying to collect as much evidence as possible so as to have the matter put right.

It was very nice of J to make me those socks. As a matter of fact I am putting on all the warm clothes I can lay my hands on.

If that particular pair have gone elsewhere I will get Alice to send me one of the several pairs from the flat. Do you know if there is a 'ship's dirty clothes bag' you know – a canvas thing? at home. If there is I would like Alice to send it out to me with some thick underthings which she has of mine at the flat.

When I next have to move I will find that I have a lot of gear here and no where to stow it. . . . I am getting very cold. Best of luck and love to all. . . .

By the 10th June he had headed the page in his log-book: 'Dunkerque. St. Pol.' And on the page thus headed the Remarks column in the log were written in his smallest writing, for there was more happening on his flights. He was not only doing more adventurous patrols but was undertaking them in increasingly cold conditions; it may have been the month of June but at heights of 10,000 ft and above and at speeds of 40 K–60 K the cold was intense; he was a tall man, 6′ 3″, and his head and shoulders were well clear of even the scant protection of the light frame and doped fabric of his Nieuport.

16.6.16. 11.20 am. Wind N.E.5. Nieuport 3184. Time in air: 1 hour. Height 10,000. Course: out to sea to Nieuport. Remarks: Clouds 5000. Dutch frontier visible.

17.6.16. 12.55 pm. Wind N.E.4. 3184. Time in air: 2 hours. Height: 12,000 feet. out to sea to Zeebrugge, Ostende, St Pierre Capelle. 1st Flight over enemy country. also height record. distant shelling. chased fast machine.

18.6.16. 6.35 pm. Wind N.3. 3184. Time in air: 1 hr 35 mins. 11,400 (later 10,500) Ostende, solo reconnaissance & fighting patrol. Fought Fokker monoplane off Nieuport. Fired one drum and forced him down in spin.

On the 22nd June in 'no wind' he was up for an hour and a half on 3184 to 11,800 ft: 'Ostende, to accompany reconnaissance. v.g. landing.' He landed at 7.30 a.m. and went up again at 11.50 a.m., with Wind N.E.1. for 1 hour and 35 minutes to 12,000 feet. 'Fighter to accompany photography. lost track of convoy, who did not come over.'

He did not fly on the 23rd June but wrote to Emmie, describing the attractive homestead he and his fellow-pilots had made at #1 Wing Royal Naval Air Service.

My dear Mum,
Thanks so much for the stockings, socks and canvas bag. I expect by this time you will have heard from V. or even seen her. Give her my love if she is at home. You ask about leave. I expect to get some in about 2 months time. But for the moment it has been stopped so mine may come later.

We had a very chilly spell of weather then one or two fine days and then some more clouds – hut hot and oppressive to-day. We are an excellent mess here. Much better than any at home stations. Omelettes etc. for breakfast, cold salad for lunch and a very excellent dinner as a rule. Have been taking exercise this morning by driving in 4″ × 4″ stakes for a fence round our new hut. It will be quite pretty when finished, a verandah with a broad, flat rail round it to sit on. 12 ft × 20 or so inside tiled with old bricks. Two hydrangeas in pots and lots of little things in flower boxes. A gunroom inside painted white all round stiff paper up to about 4 feet on the walls, a stained (stoprot) floor with mats.

We have done all this ourselves on bad days and on off times.

I wonder if Charlie Harris has to pay postage on his parcels. It must be rather mad expense if he does – and any how Mrs H. must pay for the clean stuff going out. Could you send me a pair of old sheets and a pillow slip. The blankets here are clean compared to Eastchurch but a sheet would be nicer in the hot weather. I have a servant now – share him with three or four other people. He also has loading up to do in the Mess. But he cleans boots, makes the bed, tidies the cabin, gets hot water and that sort of thing.

Cousin Char very kindly sent me a parcel. But one feels you have received it on false pretences for we are so comfortably installed and equipped.

It is so hot that it must break in a thunderstorm soon. It is raining a little already. Please thank Dad and J for their letters and give my love to everyone at home. Your loving son, Herbert.

It was the lull, too, before the start of the Battle of the Somme, the battle which was more terrible than are most wars.

On the 25th June he flew Nieuport 3963 for a reconnaissance of 2 hours and 10 minutes, but on 1st July was back again on 3184 doing some long patrols. On the 2nd July he was up at 7.20 a.m. on 3181. He recorded 'Local engine giving trouble. Bent axle landing without engine.' He went up again on the same machine for several short flights, recording 'This engine was Warneford's* & very old but good.' He changed plugs from R.E.V. to K.L.G. and continued to test the machine on 2nd and again on the 3rd. On the 7th (his log-book now headed 'St Pol.Dunkerque') he went out on a long patrol on 3181. Remarks: 'Fighting patrols accompanying reconnaissance. Out to sea off Lombartgyde. Machine climbs very well. Fighting patrol accompanying artillery spotting machine.' On the 8th he was up again on 3181 for $2\frac{1}{2}$ hours, flying for part of the time at nearly 14,000 feet. On the 9th he continued to patrol between Ostende & Nieuport, flying for 2 hours 45 minutes at 14,200 feet. On the 15th he was up again on

* Flight Sub Lieut. R. A. J. Warneford, V. C.

3181, this time as fighter to accompany photography, but visibility was very bad and he returned, having not been above 6,000 feet.

On the 18th, with Wind N.2. he went up again on 3181 but stayed up for just 15 minutes at 3,500 feet, as once again visibility was very bad and he returned. On the 19th with Wind N.N.E.2, he had just taken off on 3181, at 3.20 p.m. when, at 200 feet: 'Engine stopped. Forced landing in sea. Machine destroyed.' Warneford's 'very old but good' engine had gone to a watery grave.

The following day he was up again on his original Nieuport 3184, as fighter cover for a convoy; and later on the same evening went up on her again, patrolling alone. Remarks: 'Middelkerke 13000 in 40 mins.' He reached 13,500 feet on that flight. On the 31st July he took off on 3184 at 3.10 p.m. flying at 13,000 ft for an hour and 50 minutes. Remarks: 'to accompany photography. Knocke & Zeebrugge. plenty A.A. Fired Lewis at a Bosche.'

On the 2nd August, at 7.10 on an evening of 'light air', he took off on Sopwith Pup 9496 with an 80 h.p. Clerget engine. He patrolled for an hour and three-quarters and reached 15,000 feet. Remarks: 'Fighting patrol. N'port, Dixmunde, Ypres, Kemmel. Height record. spinning nose dive engine pulled her out.'

On the 3rd August, with Wind N.N.W.3. he went up at 5.35 a.m. on Nieuport 3184 for 1 hour 15 minutes, flying at 11,000 feet. Remarks: 'Zepp. patrol 3 × 16 lb bombs. Nieuport much haze & clouds.' At 2.10 p.m. on the same day, with the wind veering and abating slightly, he went up on Sopwith Pup 9496 for an hour at 13,000 feet. Remarks: 'Fighting patrol after Huns near Bergue Nieuport Dixmunde. another good landing.'

On the 9th August he took off at 4.50 a.m. on 3184. Remarks: 'Zepp. patrol 3 × 16 lb bombs. Off Ostende for 30 mins. nothing doing.'

Later on the same morning he spent 15 minutes doing a test flight on Nieuport 8517, landing at 7.30 a.m.; and at 3.50 p.m. he took up 3184 for 1 hour and 25 minutes as 'Fighter to accompany reconnaissance Ostende.'

Should one wonder whether the repeated patrols over the same stretches of coast and country ever became monotonous one has only to re-read the log-books; for no two aeroplanes of a type were alike, the difference between types was tremendous, and the other variables – of weather, wind, visibility, barometric pressure, temperature and so on, allowed of no falling off in a pilot's concentration and of no falling off in his luck, irrespective, of course, of the greatest variable of all, whether or not he attacked or was attacked by an enemy machine and the outcome of such battle.

It was scarcely surprising that the R.N.A.S. songs, sung so cheerfully around a Mess piano, often joked about Death and listed the numerous faults in their aeroplanes likely to lead to it; of the many such songs I believe that #1 Wing's variant of 'Wrap me up in my Tarpaulin Jacket' listed more faulty aeroplanes per verse than did any other.

On the 10th August H. took up Nieuport 'Baby' for some local practice. Remarks: 'A most priceless machine to fly: landed 3 ft up: smashed tail skid.' He continued to practise on the Baby on the 11th. Remarks: '3 landings. pretty fair.' On the 12th August he took off on Sopwith 'Pup' 9496 for a flight of 1 hour 40 minutes. He flew at 16,000 feet. Remarks: 'Fighter after Hun. not seen. Gravelines, Bergues, Furnes, Nieuport, Dixmunde, Ypres, Furnes. Bumpy.'

He flew Nieuport 3963 on the 18th as 'Fighter with photography' and on the 19th was back on the Nieuport 'Baby'. He really liked this machine and often spoke of her in later years. On the 19th he flew 'Baby' 3986 for 45 minutes. Remarks: 'Weather reconnaissance. Middelkerke. Good landing. nice machine.' At 5.45 p.m. the same day he went up again on a Nieuport Baby, this time 3992. Remarks: 'Test flight. good machine. Lewis gun double feed.' He flew her again on the following day, in 'dense clouds off Middelkerke' and on the 22nd August flew Nieuport '15 metre' Baby Type '17 Bis' 3958 for 10 minutes. He remarked that it was his '1st flight on this type.' The 'priceless' Baby – his all-time favourite land-machine of the Great War.

He continued to patrol on various other Nieuports and on 1st September flew the 'Baby' 17 Bis 3958 again. Remarks: 'Heavy clouds. Test flight.' He flew her again on 6th September. Remarks: 'Fighter with spotter. Gun jammed while testing. returned. cured jam. set out again & picked up spotter.'

Then it was time for his leave. They sent him home for ten days.

When he went back to Dunkerque/St Pol after his first leave, he went back once more into the thick of things; the battle of second Somme, that terrible wearing-down battle, had not yet been won – if such a battle, with its extravagant loss of men and material – can ever be said to have been won. But there had been one Dunkerque triumph whilst H. had been at home: the enemy gun battery in the Ostende area, a massive emplacement of four 28-cm guns, the TIRPITZ BATTERY, known as 'T.4.', – had at last been pin-pointed by a photo-graphic/reconnaissance patrol.

T.4. had an effective range of 35,000 yards and had been a menace to Allied shipping in the Channel and to the British monitors; now it was only a matter of time before T.4. could be destroyed and #1 Wing were jubilant.

But the patrolling, the chasing and engaging the enemy and all the seemingly endless reconnaissance still went on. H. went back to Dunkerque/St Pol on the 21st September on a Sopwith Strutter. He recorded Wind. N.W.3. Sopwith #$1\frac{1}{2}$ Strutter 5084. Solo. 55 minutes. 7,500 ft. Dover to Dunkerque. 1st flight on this type of machine & 1st cross Channel. good landing.'

The next day he was up flying Nieuport Baby 17 bis 3958 for $2\frac{1}{4}$ hrs, reaching 16,000 ft. Remarks: 'Fighter with spotter. Patrolling between N'port & Ostende. good landing.' The same afternoon he was up again patrolling the same area on the Baby and the following day, 23rd September, went up on Baby 3957 for an hour and forty minutes. Remarks: 'Fighter with spotter near Ostende. Dived & attacked enemy seaplane at 6,000 ft. Fight ended at 4,000 ft $1\frac{1}{2}$ miles off Ostende.'

On the 24th September he went up in the late afternoon on Nieuport Baby 3957 for an hour and 35 minutes. Remarks: 'Dixmunde, Nieuport, Ostende & return. Chasing 6 Huns. not seen. Heavy layer of clouds at 6,000. good entry.' On the 25th September, still on his favourite Baby 3957, patrolling. Remarks: 'Middelkerke. Ghistelles Accompany photography. afterwards a fighting patrol.' And on the 26th September, on the same machine: 'Ypres Kemmel Dixmunde Chasing reported enemy machine.'

On the 28th, again on 3957: 'Zeebrugge & Ostende. accompany photo reconnaissance. Clouds.'

And on the 29th September, still on Baby 3957: '16 miles out to sea off Nieuport. Fleet patrol. clouds.'

On the 2nd October he took off early, at 5.20 a.m., again on Baby 3957; like most of the previous week's flights, it was of over two hours. Remarks: 'Anti-Zepp patrol. chased ?Schotte Lang off Dutch

Island of Schowen. lost in clouds. Bruges. Heavy A.A.' On the 4th
October he was Gazetted Flt.Lieut. to date from 1st October.

On the 16th October he flew Sopwith Pup, 80 Le Rhone engine
5187. Remarks: 'Test flight & anti-Hun patrol ... 3 attempts to land.
Bumpy.' The next day, on the Pup 5187, he remarked: 'Fighter to
accompany photography. heavy clouds. all returned.' He continued to
do long patrols on the Pup for the remainder of the week, on one
occasion mentioning engine trouble, but seems to have glided in. On
the 23rd October he delivered Nieuport Baby 3986, 80 h.p. Le Rhone,
to Petite Synthe; later the same day delivering Sopwith Pup 5194 to
'French aerodrome', and later again the same day took off on Sopwith
Pup 5187. Remarks: 'Fighter patrol. Ostende. Zeebrugge. Dived down
& attacked enemy seaplane at 4000 feet. Tracers into fuselage. Gun
jambed temporarily.'

On the 26th October he was on the move again, this time to Vert
Galand. He flew over on Sopwith Pup N.5194; this was the first time
he used the prefix N. for Navy before the registration number of his
machine. His course was: 'Dunkerque, St. Omer, Heodin, Dallons,
Vert Galand. Remarks: Steered a compass course 230°: For new Squadron attd. R.F.C. 23rd Squadron. only machine to arrive out of six.'

The enemy had been busy on the way.

The enemy were busy everywhere and the R.F.C. had requested
further R.F.C. Squadrons and urgent help from the R.N.A.S. Whether
the prefix 'N' was by command or by custom I do not know but it
emphasizes, if emphasis is necessary, the invaluable – probably the
decisive – help which the Navy were giving the Army in those long
and terrible months of trench warfare.

On the 1st November he was on Sopwith Pup N5187; he took off
at 8 a.m. with Wind: S.W.3 on the ground and W.7 at 12,000 feet: he
flew the same machine two or three times a day on most days for nearly
a fortnight. Some of his Remarks: 'Ostende, Zeebrugge. accompany
reconnaissance.' 'Hostile aircraft patrol Nieuport, Dixmunde out to
sea. bad visibility.' 'Fighter patrol with attempted reconnaissance. very
bad visibility.' 'Test flight – Nieuport – Very hazy in patches.' 'Huffing
match with Canon Voisins. Local.' 'Reconnaissance Nieuport. engine
& visibility bad.' 'Patrol. forced landing. Malo. High tension lead
off.' 'Testing returned machine. Very low clouds.' 'Fighter to meet
bombers. visibility nil. recrossed lines at 250 feet.' On the 16th
November he took off at 10.10 a.m. on Sopwith Scout N.5181, 80 h.p.

Le Rhone engine and led a formation on patrol. 'Course: Dunkerque, St. Omer, St. Pol, Doullens, Vert Galand. Remarks: A very hazy day. Acted as leader to six machines who kept good formation & landed together. Other pilots were Thom, Breadner, Booker, Todd & Casey.' He continued to patrol, often in atrocious visibility, on the Scout with an 80 h.p. Le Rhone engine or on the $1\frac{1}{2}$ Strutter with a 110 h.p. Clerget engine, up and down the coast. On the 26th November, flying the Scout/Le Rhone 5187, he Remarks: 'Dutch coast & Ostende. hazy. dropped grenades near Ostende trawler.'

When the weather was too bad for patrolling, he often tested machines locally, testing Sopwith Scout 5198 on the 7th December and a S.P.A.D., a new machine to him, later on the same morning: 'S.P.A.D. 9611 140 h.p. Hispano Suiza. Remarks: Test flight. local. Haze low clouds bad visibility.'

The low cloud, the bad visibility, the uncertainty of all machines, other than the Nieuport Baby 17 Bis – all was recorded; but he had not mentioned the severe cold for many weeks. Suddenly, in his record for 18th December, one is again reminded of its severity.

'18/12/16. Time: 2.15 pm. Wind: S.W.1. Sopwith Scout 5187 80 Hp Le Rhone. Time in air: 1 hr 25 mins. 14000 ft. Course: Fighter patrol. Local & Mariakerke. Remarks: Compass again froze. Nose frost bitten.'

They gave him 12 days leave to recover. Emmie wrote to Alie: 'He has frosted his poor little nose.' He had also frosted the edges of his ears; they went a different colour to the rest of his ears for the remainder of his life.

In December 1916 #1 Wing R.N.A.S. brought out *Wing Tip*, an hilarious occasional publication, most of the humour directed inwards but with a few pieces capable of being appreciated by outsiders. Apart from the 'Weather Forecast for 1917', or 'A Comedy in Flanders', with 'Dresses and uniforms supplied by Messrs Gieve; Army Ordnance Store; and Individual Enterprise & Co, Properties by an ungrateful Government and Orchestra under the direction of M. Clerget le Rhone', there were numerous articles and verses; but the advertisements were almost the best. viz.:

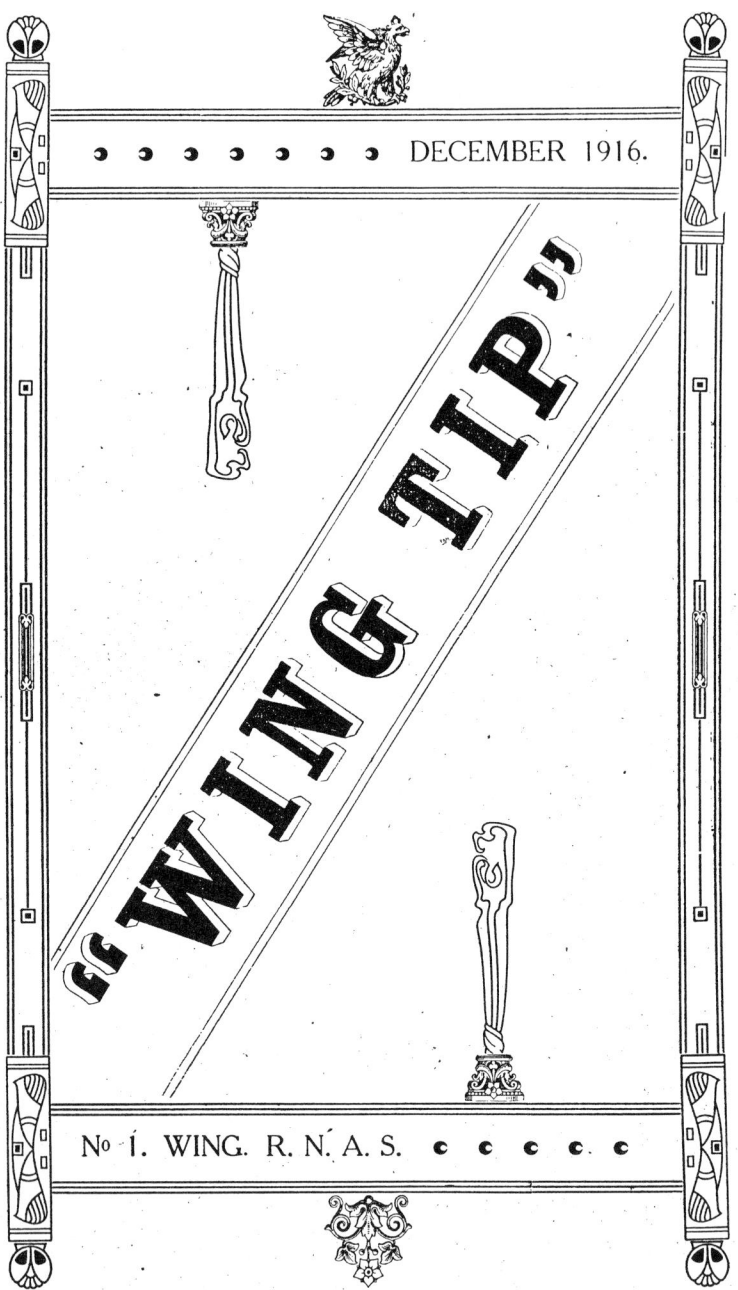

WING TIP

We're Here! We're Here! We're Here!

THE REDSKINS

We want YOU some, but we want your MONEY more.

Poker! Roulette!! Baccarat!!!

Vingt et Un!!!! Petits Chevaux!!!!!

COME RIGHT ALONG.

SKINNEM, FLEECE & CO.

This was a dig at the lively Canadian element among the pilots.

or the

SCHOOL OF LANGUAGE

Under the able management of Professors MACK and CASEY.

Do YOU play GOLF? – Then take our course and learn to address the ball.

Do YOU travel by TAXI? – Then take our course and argue with the driver on EQUAL TERMS.

Do YOU ever feel lost for a word? – Then take our course and you will never have that feeling.

WE can teach YOU to BEAT a BARGEE.

WE can teach YOU to CUT OUT a COLONEL.

OUR motto: – SAY IT AGAIN TO-MORROW.

or

UNIVERSAL R.N.A.S. BANKERS

Randvoll House.

Remember that it's war-time!! Be Patriotic!!

Don't draw all your pay, but leave it with us

and

SEE WHAT HAPPENS!!!

Our motto: – SIMPLICITAS.

Or D'Albiac's interesting prose piece:

FRAGMENT OF AN ANCIENT TABLET

unearthed by Professor Jaydal Byack during the excavations on the site of a new dug-out.

Now it came to pass in the Great War that the tribe of the Mahn-it-taws rose up and took counsel together, that they might lay waste and ravage the land between Nu-pawht and Zy-Bruggy, which had been wrested from their friends and allies, the Bel-juns, by the Boshanduns, a fierce and warlike tribe living between the Kil Kanal, a large river on their Northern boundary, much used by their ships of war, and the Ahl-lief-frunt, a line of deep excavations which could only be crossed under great danger and peril – thunderbolts, sticks which spat flame and objects, apple-like in shape which hurled themselves into fragments, living there and deeply resenting all intruders, whom they used to kill or maim, few escaping injury.

They first assaulted Tee-faw but were unable to take it, whereupon their leaders again rose and took counsel together, saying: 'It is not meet that we waste our time upon such an insignificant object; let us therefore treat it with scorn and surely it will surrender to us of its own accord.'

Whereupon they then approached unto the territory which lies between Nu-pawht and Zy-bru-gy, formerly in the possession of the Bel-juns, and hurled huge rocks, threat that they might break the bones of the Boshanduns; and great was the noise thereof.

But it came to pass that Tee-faw arose in its might, waxing wroth at the impudence of the Mahn-it-taws and in its turn belched flame and heaved great rocks high into the air; whereupon the Mahn-it-taws grew afraid and betook themselves in headlong flight for their own territory and there planned new plans wherewith they might discommode the Boshan-duns and Tee-faw.

Meanwhile the Boshan-duns summoned large birds of prey, called in their tongue Towb, El-ve-jee and Foh-ker which passing over the Mahn-it-taws dropped rocks; whereat the Mahn-it-taws again grew exceeding afraid and summoned in their turn the tribe of the Ahren-ayess with their birds called Beybis. Puhpease and divers other names, to chase away the Birds of the Boshan-duns.

Whereat the Ahren-ayess rejoiced exceedingly, chasing the Towbs, El-ve-jees and Foh-kers and striking them to earth with flame and thunder.

The Mahn-it-taws thereafter brought unto them gifts of Feyr-rets, Kyp-pahs, Pah-triges and the like and returned to their homes.

On the 8th January 1917 he took off on Sopwith Scout 5189 with an 80 h.p. Le Rhone engine, from Dunkirk to Clairmarais. Remarks: 'Engine conked over No 20 Squadron R.F.C. successful forced landing.' On the 11th January he attempted to take the same machine from Clairmarais to Le Ponchel. Remarks: 'Engine conked & picked up 11 times finally stopping. Good forced landing on stubble field.' On the 12th January, in bad snow conditions but only a light S.W. wind, he made yet another attempt to continue his journey on 5189. Course: 'Le Ponchel to Au Bon Air. Remarks: Low clouds. Engine cut out again forced landing on plough. snow. Turned over. 5 miles from Vert Galand.' Although he later flew many other Sopwith Scouts, there is no further reference to 5189.

On the 15th January he is back on Nieuport 17 Bis 8750, flying from Vert Galand to Dunkirk. Remarks: 'Very thick & snowy.' In the afternoon he took 8750 to Aircraft Depot from French Aerodrome, so presumably he had paused at a French Aerodrome on account of the weather. The snow was heavy and flying was impossible for many days; he next flew on the 27th January and subsequently records 'With No 3 Squadron R N A S to Vert Galand. Somme Area.'

He tested Sopwith Scout 80 h.p. Le Rhone 5188 locally and flew a lot of practice formations on her during the first ten days of February.

The spirit of 'say it again to-morrow' infused the R N A S Squadrons; the phrase summed up the pilots' own clear knowledge of what they faced each day, it summed up their hope that their own endurance would not fail them. That which had begun in comedy became, in due course, both a plea and a prayer.

On the 8th February, on 5188, H. was in pursuit of hostile aircraft. On the 10th and 11th, still on Sopwith Scout 5188, he was on Line Patrol Martenpincle – Sailly au Bois, and on the 14th, on Scout 6175, on the same Line Patrol for 2 hours and 10 minutes at a height of 17,000 feet. He does not record this as his personal height record but it is the first record of 17,000 feet in his log-books. On the 15th February with Wind N.E.5. he was out on Sopwith Scout 6175 for 2 hours 35 minutes. Remarks: 'Offensive Patrol. Tranloy Gruillers Miramont Gommecourt.' Later the same day, on the same machine, in pursuit of hostile aircraft over Albert Colincamp Bailleulmont. On the 16th February, still on Scout 6175, he was up for 3 hours, flying at 14,000 feet. Remarks: 'Offensive Patrol. Boudersess Transley Bapaume Miramont Our 5 attacked by 9 Huns. One Hun crashed at Miramont Probably by (?) Beamish or Glen. My m/c damaged.'

He did not fly for several days, probably because his machine was being repaired, for he was up on 6175 again on the 26th February, for 2 hrs 10 mins at 12,000 feet. Remarks: 'Accompany F.E.'s 18 Squadron Puiselet Fabines Hermines Reconnaissance.' On the following day, still on 6175: 'To Loiseville (No 3 Moranes) to accompany for Photographic.' He returned later the same day: 'return to Vert Galand – Felt pretty good.'

Charles was now in France with the R.F.C.; I will quote some of his letters a little later on. H. called on him during early March and the two brothers had a fine reunion, cheering to them both. Charles wrote to Jim of the meeting at No 10 Squadron, who must then have been at Chateau du Reveillon.

But to return to H's log-book; on the 1st March, on 6175 again, he flew from Vert Galand to Bertangles, taking 5 minutes for the flight; later on that day, on the same machine, flew again: 'Bertangles to Arras near Cambrai & L. Fighter with F.E.'s 18 Squadron. kept good formation.' On the 4th March, still on 6175 and at 13,000 feet: 'Bertangles to Hermies. Cambrai. Escort to No 18 Squadron. attacked by Huns near Bapaume.'

The page of his log-book which starts on the 6th March is headed: 'Bertangles – Marieux.'

By March the enemy had brought into service their new 'Albatros' and 'Halberstadt' fighters. These machines were awesome foes, with their twin synchronized machine-guns. On the 6th March, still on 6175, he was up for an hour and a half on an Offensive Patrol. Remarks: 'Bapaume. Ardingles. Ina Wire broke in the air.' On the 11th March, once again up to 17,000 feet and on 6175: 'Offensive Patrol. Vaux Hermies Pronville Bapaume Shot down 2-seater Albatros near Hermies. Forced down single seater Albatros near Pronville. Fired 120 rounds into another 2 seater Albatros. Scraped with A90 near Bapaume.'

He flew again uneventfully on the 13th March and on the 15th March did another patrol, still on 6175: 'Patrol just over lines Bapaume, Achiet Borquay.' On the 17th March, with Wind: W.N.W.3. he was up for two and a half hours on 6175. Remarks: 'Offensive Patrol. Shot down Albatros Scout. Pronville. Shot observer in Type L 2-seater Bapaume & 2 other small fights.' (Morane–Saulnier Type L).

On the 22nd March, with Wind: E.6. he was up again on 6175. The ink in the log-book entry has been thinned, or it was perhaps rained on, so that it is barely legible: 'Escort to 18 Squadron. 5 miles beyond Cambrai hit by A.A. Very cold.' He was out early again on the 24th on 6175, patrolling N.E. Arras Douai Leus sector.

He had a new engine fitted to 6175, tested this on the 25th March and on 28th March moved to a new aerodrome.

It was new and it was nasty. He records on the 28th March that he flew there at 7.45 a.m.: 'Bertangles to new aerodrome at Marieux. Small & bad & dirty.'

On the same day, at 11.55 a.m., he took up Sopwith Scout 6169 for a flight of an hour and a half. Remarks: 'In charge Command "A" Flight No 3 Squadron. Escort to F.E.'s. Bad weather. Towards Cambrai. Led formation "A" flight.'

On the 31st March 1917, before the Battle of Arras, the following units of R.F.C. and Naval Squadrons were disposed as follows:
H.Q., R.F.C., St Andre-aux-Bois.
G.H.Q. Wing (9th Wing), Fienvillers (attached G.H.Q. for special duties; comprised following squadrons: 35, 27, 55, 57, 70, 19, 66).
1 Brigade, at Chateau du Reveillon. This included 1st Wing (2, 5, 10, 16 Squadrons). 10th Wing (25, 40, 43, Naval 8, Squadrons).
11 Brigade, at Cassel. This included: 2nd Wing (53, 6, 42, 46, 21 Squadrons); 11th Wing (1, 20, 41, 45 Squadrons).
111 Brigade, at Chateau de Sains. This included: 12th Wing (8, 59, 12, 13 Squadrons); 13th Wing (11, 29, 48, 60, 100 Naval 6, Squadrons).
1V Brigade, at Misery. This included: 3rd Wing (7, 9, 34, 52 Squadrons); 14th Wing (22, 24, 54, Naval 1 Squadrons).
V Brigade, at Albert. This included: 15th Wing (4, 3, 15 Squadrons); 22nd Wing (18, 23, 32, Naval 3 Squadrons).
There were also Balloon Wings, Aircraft Parks for 1st, 2nd, 3rd, 4th and 5th Armies, six Air Ammunition Columns, two Aircraft Depots (at St Omer and at Candas) and Engine Repair Shops at Rouen.

On the 2nd April he took off at 6.10 a.m. on Sopwith Scout 6169; he flew at a height of 14,000 feet, with Wind: W.7. at that height, for 2 hrs 35 mins. Remarks: 'Led line "Hindenburg" patrol A Flight Fontaine Les Croisville Havincourt attacked 2-seater Albatross over Havincourt–Noyelles. Gun jammed landed in a gully,' and he recorded also that at '2.10: 20 landed in our lines. Pilot name Meixner.' Pilot Meixner duly obeyed the polite courtesy of one who has landed behind an adversary's lines and autographed the end paper of the victor's log-book; his large signature is still clear to-day. There was one less Albatros. (The enemy constructed, during the winter of 1916–1917, a new defensive system some miles behind his own lines; it ran from near Arras south-eastwards for about 12 miles to Queant, thence westwards of Cambrai towards St Quentin. This was the Hindenberg Line.)
On the 3rd April H. was up again, with Wind: W.7. on a patrol of

2 hrs 10 mins at 14,000 ft. Remarks: 'Defensive patrol Sailly St Misel–Ardingles. Many clouds. V. cold. led patrol.'

On the 5th April, with the wind abating and backing, he was up on 6169 again to 15,000. Remarks: 'Offensive patrol. Cambrai Marquion. Dense haze.' Later the same day he was up on 6169 again for an hour and a quarter to 8,000 ft. Remarks: 'Escort to B.E.'s, who did not reach objective Marquion.'

On the 7th April he took off at 5.5 p.m. on Sopwith Scout N.6169 80hp Le Rhone and flew at 17,000 ft for an hour and 50 minutes. Remarks: 'Offensive patrol. Havincourt Cambrai Econst St Quentin Croixelles Dived 17,000 to 10,000 feet at 2-seater Albatros. Casey & I attacked. both had 5 stoppages. Flight followed well & arrived back complete.'

On the 8th he was up on the same machine for an hour and a half. Remarks: 'Escort to Bombers B.E.'s nr Pronville attacked by 3 shot down German ?Nieuport ?Albatros.' H. was flying at 7,500 ft on that occasion.

On the 11th April he was up on N.6169 for 2 hours and 10 minutes. Remarks: 'Offensive patrol behind Hindenburg Line. vis: fair to poor. No H.A. & bad weather.' On the 13th he flew N.6169 as 'Escort to F.E.'s Epinoy. No H.A.' and later the same day flew the same machine on an Offensive Patrol along the Cambrai road, but again there were no hostile aeroplanes about. On the 14th he was out escorting a photographic patrol and on the 16th he flew N.5194 for two and a half hours on an Offensive Patrol over Cambrai Epinoy and Havin-court. 'No H.A. near.'

On the 20th April he was back on 6169 gain, flying an offensive Patrol of three hours. Remarks: 'O.P. Dense clouds & haze landed at St. Just – Paul Schmitts. Wind: N.7. at 10000' – but he had flown 'mostly at 14000 ft.'

On the 21st April, on 6169, he flew another Offensive Patrol. Remarks: 'O.P. Many H.A. Shot Albatros Sct. & one other scrap nr. Coqueville.' He has recorded his altitude as 14,000 ft dropping to 6,000 ft, so he had presumably dived at the hostile aeroplane.

On the 22nd April he took off on 6169 on an evening patrol of two and a half hours. Remarks: 'Escort F.E.'s Cambrai Town Hall Many H.A. All F.E.'s returned.'

On the 23rd April, with Wind now down to N.E.4. he flew for 2 hrs 25 minutes. His altitude again varied dramatically, this time from

14,000 ft down to 4,000 ft. Remarks: 'O.P. Broke up 2 hostile reconnaissance. Shot down 2 Albatros Scouts.' He had taken off at 5.40 a.m. landing at five minutes past eight. But at 10 o'clock that morning he took off again in pursuit of H.A. in company with Breadner. Remarks: 'Pursuit H.A. Chased 2 engine H.A/C to coast. In company with Flt.Lt. Breadner who hit his engine. Landed near Hun at Vonn.'

H. returned to Marieux from Vonn at one o'clock the same day. On the 24th April, with Wind: N.E.5. he took off at 3.30 p.m. on his reliable N.6169. Remarks: 'O.P. attacked 2-seater D.F.W. Casey myself & Malone brought him down in our lines near Doignies.' He had gone up to 18,500 ft on that flight. The pilot of the downed machine, Haase, duly signed H.'s log-book, beneath the signature of Meixner.

On the 25th April he was up testing N.6202 for 10 minutes and at 10.30 the same morning took off on N.6169 80 Le Rhone again, this time to an advanced landing ground at Freinecourt; returning from thence to Marieux in the afternoon. On the 26th April he attempted an offensive patrol but low clouds forced him down and he returned again to Marieux. However, at 6.05 p.m. that evening he took off again, with Wind: N.E.3. Remarks: 'O.P. with F.E.'s below. Dived on one H.A. & got mixed up with 5 in turn. Shots through centre front, left rear lower, rt. front lower spars. Came down to 2000 feet over Cambrai.' (He had been flying at 16,500 feet.) N.6169 had been shot up and was in need of extensive repair, but he had got back unharmed.

On the 28th April, therefore, he took off on N.6162, for 1 hour and twenty minutes. Remarks: 'Escort to attempted recon. did not cross lines.'

He was up early on the 29th April, on N.6175 and flew for 2 hours and 20 minutes. Remarks: 'Escort to F.E.'s. near S.E. Cambrai. Scrapping into Le Cateau 8000 ft All F.E.'s returned.'

In the afternoon of the same day he tested his repaired 'N.6169'. But reported 'Badly rt wing down.' Another test the same evening showed her still to be 'Still a little rt wing down.'

The next day they gave him a new machine, N.6183, which he flew from Candas to Marieux, and on the 1st May he flew another new machine, N.6477, from Dunkirk to Marieux.

On the 5th May he had his first flight on a Sopwith Triplane, N.5356, with a 130 h.p. Clerget engine. He flew her at 4,000 ft from the Aircraft Depot, Dunkirk, to an unspecified French Aerodrome; later the same day on to Furnes.

The following day he ferried a Sopwith Camel over to Furnes, N.517 with a 130 Clerget; it was his first trip on 'Camel'. He continued to fly the Camel for several days, back to Dunkirk to retrieve his gun, locally over Dunkirk, over to Furnes as fast as he could, climbing to 15,000 ft in 18 minutes, then back to No 1 Wing, Dunkirk, climbing to 17,000 in 25 minutes.

On the 8th May he delivered Sopwith Triplane N.5365 130 h.p. Clerget engine, to Furnes. Remarks: 'N.A.D. to Furnes. Delivery. no room for my legs in machine.'

On the 9th May he tested Sopwith Camel N.517 for an hour, recording that he reached 10,000 feet in 11 minutes and 19,000 in 33 minutes. He then pursued a hostile aircraft but was not seen. He spent the next week both testing the Camel and the Triplane (it took him 36 minutes to get the Triplane to 19,000 feet), and from time to time pursuing hostile aircraft. On the 16th, 18th and 19th May he was variously at N.A.D. Dunkirk and Furnes, testing his gun, getting it fixed, and testing again, on N.517. He also flew Sopwith Pup N.9928 on the 19th, doing more gun testing.

On the 20th he flew N.517 to N.A.D. Dunkirk and the same day took Sopwith Camel N.6330 from Dunkirk to G.H.Q. R.F.C. St Andre. Flew locally at St Andre for a couple of days and on the 23rd May flew A.V.M. Farquhar from St Andre to N.A.D. Dunkirk.

Later that day he flew De Havilland 4 N.190 h.p. Rolls Royce engine, for 55 minutes at 6,000 feet. Remarks: 'St. Pol. Local. Trial trip. 1st solo on this type.' It was the first De Havilland machine that he had flown. The 23rd May 1917 was a memorable day.

On the 25th May he delivered Sopwith Camel N.6332 to St Omer, and on the 27th May flew Capt. Lambe, D.S.O., R.N. to G.H.Q., R.F.C. St Andre from St Pol in Sopwith 1½ Strutter N.5172, 110 Clerget. On the following day, 28th May, he took the Strutter from St Andre to Marieux by himself, a flight of half an hour.

He was waiting to go on leave. He was ready for some leave. Except for the twelve days' frostbite leave in early January he had had no change since September of 1916; and it had been a long winter.

There was also the matter of his decoration, which he had heard about in a surprising way.

He wrote to Alie on the 12th May: My dear Sloper, Many thanks for your letter which arrived just before I left the old squadron. Whenever it is (my) turn to write to you it always seems as if I want something done. Well, I have been told that I may be in England shortly on leave, or duty – I am not sure which – but the point is this:

I had a signal this morning from Charlie's most senior general congratulating me on being awarded the D.S.C. That's the first and last I have heard about it but I suppose somebody has given it to me. Now be a good old thing Sloper and have a ribbon, not too wide, put on my two blue monkey jackets and if there is an odd six inches it will do for the Khaki. Don't have it on a tin background, it looks far more natural sewn straight onto the cloth.

The weather is hot enough here, it must be beastly in London.

Later another one from the Commodore – to the same effect so there can be no doubt now.

Will write more later or perhaps see you. Good old thing, I am glad you had that 'spells' at Bath with Mum. Chas and I take off our hats to you for the way you are sticking to it at home.

love to Granny, Your loving brother Herbert.

There can have been few recipients of the D.S.C. more delighted with the Award or more surprised to have received it, than was H. He wrote to his father in similarly light-hearted vein on the 25th May:

c/o Headquarters Mail Office, R.N.A.S. Dunkirk. My dear Dad, Hope you got my last letters. Had to write from various places round the country. As I expect you heard I have been doing quiet jobs for the last 3 weeks. Hope to get some leave soon. Was with Charlie's old instructor Fairbairn a few nights ago, – and must agree with Charles. He is a tophole fellow & certainly has had plenty of experiences.

Wish I had leave while Charles was home. Hope to get back anyhow before he leaves the country. As a matter of fact it was promised me when I left the old squadron. . . .

I have had some most interesting letters to open. They were all in a bunch together. One was from the topmost general another from my Brigadier another from the Commodore & one from my C.O. – Charlie's old instructor & other pilots (where I was staying on Monday) would not hear of my having a decoration without putting the ribbon up so took my jacket round to a farm near & got one of the milkmaids to sew it on! Then two letters: one from Jem & one from Chas. V. wrote to me, also Alice. And last but not least the Fleet Pay. demanding an income tax return.

Love to Mum & anyone at home.

Your dootiful son

Herbert.

P.S. as you may judge from the above rot, the rest I have enjoyed for the past few weeks has done me no end of good – so long.

By the way – Do I address you J.P.?

H. continued to fly the Sopwith Camel and the $1\frac{1}{2}$ Strutter locally at Dunkerque, dong various climb tests and gun tests, until the 3rd June. Then they gave him 14 days leave.

Later on in 1917 he was posted to a Home Station, but for the time being he must return to France. He flew back off leave on the 21st June. His log-book records on Sopwith Camel 3797 with 150 A.R.I. engine, and that he flew in a light Westerly wind at 8,000 feet, taking 1 hour 45 minutes for the trip from Brooklands to N.A.D. Dunkerque. But his letter to Emmie of 25th June suggests that he enjoyed himself on the way.

'Did you see me paying you a visit last Thursday morning? You were right on my course but I passed over rather high up. Then on to Jess. I zummed around Leeds Castle a couple of times – I believe she is near there. But was not feeling really full out. I am being employed here for a bit, but it is quite likely that I shall be over in England again soon for a few months. I am very well. It was jolly to see you all. Wish I could have stayed longer.'

During the next few days he tested a number of aircraft. Sopwith Triplane N.5472, Sopwith Pup N.6189, Sopwith Camel N.6372, Sopwith Pup N.6182, Sopwith Triplane N.5429. another Triplane N.5427; this last he described as 'bad machine'. He again tested Sopwith Triplane N.5427, N.5354, N.6304 and a Sopwith Pup, N.6171. He broke off this work to take off on Pup N.6478 in pursuit of hostile aircraft on the 2nd July, but lost them in clouds over Nieuport and returned to Base.

He continued to test on the 3rd and on the 4th July, while taking up Rev. Southern for what appears to have been a joy-ride, since no course is mentioned, Remarks: 'engine partly conked. Very thick weather.' The aeroplane was D.H.4. N.5972, with 275 h.p. Rolls Royce engine. He continued to test and they must have ironed out the problems for on the 5th July he delivered N.5972 to No 2 Squadron at a French aerodrome. He returned and subsequently tested five further aircraft that day.

On the 6th July he records testing Sopwith Camel N.6330. Remarks: 'Induced vacuum feed only worked partially.' And on the same morning went up on another Camel B.3806 with an A.R.I. engine, taking her to 16,000 feet. Remarks: 'Oxygen test. All used in 5 mins.' His first oxygen test. He continued to test four different Sopwith Triplanes on the evening of the 6th and morning of the 7th July, but once again a hostile aircraft appeared. H. then took off on a Pup N.6168 80 Le Rhone and pursued the enemy from Dunkerque to 'over London'. He landed at Eastbourne and later the same day flew from Eastbourne to Dunkerque. He continued to test and on the 11th July, with Wind backing from East to North, took up Sopwith Camel B.3806 to 18,000 ft for an oxygen test. He remarked: 'Very cold.' He then took a Pup N.6206 to Bray Dunes & return: then flew the Rev. Southern from Calais to St Pol in a Sopwith $1\frac{1}{2}$ Strutter N.9663.

On the 12th he tested Sopwith Triplane N.5360. Remarks: 'Very out of truth. readjusted slow climb.' The next day the same machine made a 'better climb'. On the 14th July Triplane N.524 was briefly described as: 'poor'. He continued to test on the 14th, again on the 15th and on 16th flew Camel B.3822 'To Petite Synthe'. On the 17th July he flew a Pup N.6468 'To Furnes. chased A.A. no Huns. landed Furnes and returned to depot.'

So H.'s first log-book closes. He records his 'Solo on land machines: 307 hours 30 minutes. In France: 265 hrs. 30 min. Combats: 25. Enemy aircraft brought down: seven. Made to land on our side of lines – half share in two.'

He lists twenty-three different types on which he has flown; but nowhere is there mention of his first exhilarating flight at the Beatty School, on the aeroplane hand-built by Beatty to a design supplied by the Wright Brothers.

5

THE WING IS TO GO

1898–1916

Charles at Gresham's – Sandhurst – Worcestershire Regt. – R.F.C. – his first
cross-country – France – 10 Squadron – injured – 84 Squadron – peace

CHARLES would probably have sought a career in aviation even had
there been no war but he would, most likely, have studied engineering
first or as an adjunct to it.

In the event he arrived at No 3 Reserve Squadron in October
1916 via the OTC at Gresham's, six months in 'E' Company, RMC
Sandhurst and thence, after passing out of Sandhurst on 16th August
1916, with a commission as 2nd Lieutenant in the 1st Worcestershire
Regiment. He had asked Jim's advice all along; at one time he had
thought of an engineering apprenticeship with Whites of Cowes, but
it was a seven-year apprenticeship which Jim had advised against, as
it was war-time; no doubt Charles was thinking of amphibious flying
in due course at Cowes. Jim asked Colonel Warner and other cousins
what steps they thought Charles should take and relayed on their ideas
to Charles, who did as he was advised, putting in for those regiments,
Wiltshires, Royal West Kents and Lincolnshires, from whom second-
ment to the Royal Flying Corps might be obtained.

Charles' letters home, youthful and enthusiastic, were full of practical detail and gave no hint of the horrors of war. That was not his
style. He was always a steady character, very calm and steady, like his
Mother. I have often thought that he, of all three brothers, would
have been most successful in the City; Joseph Travers & Sons would
have prospered under such a sound and unflappable character; he
loved the City, too, and took great pride in being a Member of the
Fishmonger's Company; but such a career was not to be. The aeroplane
had claimed him early in life, ever since, when he, Charles, was only
3 years old, Jim had come home from Australia talking of nothing but
flying.

Charles, probably 1916. Studio portrait

photo: Gabel

The first of his RFC letters, like the majority of his letters through-out his life, were written to Alie. It was headed Royal Flying Corps, Shoreham-by-Sea, where he was in No 19 Reserve Squadron.

Nov. 9th 1916: My dear Ally,   Thank you most awfully for your letter. I went up yesterday evening and this morning. Yesterday it was awfully bumpy so I did 'aerial' which simply consists of unwinding a reel, (which looks like a cinema spool,) of copper cable with a 2 lb weight tied on to the end. It is for wireless but we don't have a transmitter on the bus and it is only to practise winding the thing gently, if you jerk it the weight may come off. Altogether I have had 1 hour 50 minutes. 6 flights. So far I have been in the back seat but I am going in front on my next flight. Hicks (our instructor) says that I seem to have got hold of it. I am orderly officer to-day and have to inspect everything and take names of fellows and numbers of their machine if they land here from another aerodrome. I have just had to send a tender out to a chap who came down here on a BE2b about the most antique bus I have ever seen, and who has had a forced landing $\frac{1}{2}$ mile West of Angmering or some place like that due to a broken throttle control. I hope everyone is well. I heard from V. yesterday. I am glad 'Tales of Hoffman' was good.

There is absolutely nothing to do here when the wind is up. There are a few lectures and some soccer, which I don't attempt to play as the mechanics who play us are very hot stuff.

love to Grannie   Your loving brother C. T. Travers.

Again to Alie, this time from RFC Beaulieu, Hants.
11/12/16.

... Congratulations on the rise. It is jolly fine of you to stick to it like this ... (Alie was working as a temporary clerk at the Admiralty by day, and caring for her Grandmother in the flat, 32, Evelyn Mansions, the rest of the time.) ... They are not giving Christmas leave, or leave of any sort for that matter, except for special reasons. If H. O. comes back at Christmas I am almost certain to be able to get leave.

Perhaps I told you that when I came I was in 'A' flight, the Avro flight.

I am a dud pilot and have been kicked out of A flight. Parker, flight Command of 'B' flight, the Curtiss flight, has taken me on. It is awfully decent of him. He is an awfully good sort. A chap who was in 'A' flight has just crashed one of his Curtisses, he has only got one solo bus left.

The rotten part is that I am perfectly sure I can fly an Avro, I never even had a shot at a solo. You see an Avro is very sensitive on the controls, especially the rudder. A Curtiss isn't.

My only consolation is that a chap who has just come from Shoreham says that Hicks said that I did the best first solo he had seen. Don't tell Grannie that I have been kicked out of 'A' flight. You see it probably makes the difference between my getting on to Scouts or not, if you understand my bad English. I think that there is a chance if I do well on these machines. . . .

And again to Alie, on the 18th December:

. . . Thank you most awfully for sending the Blackwoods. I had nothing to read before. I have only been up once this week, that is since Tuesday. It has always been too misty. Frost at night and mist by day. This morning I went to see the Abbey, which is near to Lord Montague's place and only a few hundred yards from the village. It is a ruin, there is nothing left of the Abbey itself. The refectory is now the parish church but has been restored inside quite recently and has a lot of high church things inside . . . The Cloisters have only got the outer wall standing. The place to the East of the Cloisters contains the graves of the father and grandfather of the present fellow. It is in ruins . . . I think that I may get special leave if H.O. comes back for Christmas. . . .

To Alie on the 8th January 1917:

. . . Thank goodness Vaughan Lee is going. It's about time, isn't it? I suppose Paine is up to the job? He is the chap at Felixstowe, isn't he? . . . I hope Jimmy gets a decent job. I wish he was in the RFC in command of this show here, but it is not much of a job. . . .

They mended two Curtiss some days ago and yesterday and to-day I have had flying. I made rather a rotten landing the day before yesterday and broke a cross strut in the fuselage, but nothing else was damaged and it only took about half an hour to mend.

Yesterday I went up for half an hour, over to the Hamble River and up a little way to Bursledon. I was up to 4,000 ft it was quite cold, but absolutely glorious. I simply had to hold the machine up. (These machines are nose-heavy) – with my hands resting on the bottom of the wheel and the bus went straight ahead. Nothing simpler. It was jolly fine. You could just shift her course a few points to have a look at something on the ground, and then back again. I am sure you would have liked it. . . .

And to Alie again, still headed RFC Beaulieu, on the 20th January 1917, in which the death of Aunt Olive Prescott, great-aunt to Charles, is referred to:

I am afraid I haven't written for ages. I did a solo on a BE2C yesterday morning but the weather has been rotten and I haven't been up since.

What do you think of J's idea of going on a farm. Mum just mentioned it in a letter but beyond that I have not heard anything about it. Do write and let me know.

I am afraid I hardly knew Aunt O.

I remember going to see her once with Mum. I am sorry for Grannie.

I went for a walk this afternoon to Bucklers Hard. They used to build ships there, but now there are only rows of houses and the remains of the yard left.

It is like Blakeney.

The weather has been rotten but even when it is fine we can't do much because of the lack of machines. The BE I did my solo on is the only one of its type (2C) in the flight and it is the dual bus. Besides that bus there are 2 2bs, without engines, and a BE12, which is a more advanced bus.

Good luck. . . .

His training must have proceeded, following that letter, at a faster rate, for he wrote in cheerful vein on the 2nd February, again to Alie:

. . . I am afraid I never answered your last letter. I have done $23\frac{1}{2}$ hrs solo and my graduation papers have gone in; but I have several tests to do before I can 'put my wings up'.

I did my cross-country on Wednesday. I did it on a Curtiss as the BE2C has only fuel for an hour and a quarter ditto the BE/2 and the 2bs were being used. I went to Netheravon and Upavon. It is quite a simple cross-country but I had not got a compass on the machine and it was too misty to see the sun when I got to Salisbury. All you have to do is to follow the railway from Brockenhurst to Ringwood and the river from Ringwood to Netheravon. At Salisbury you take the centre river. Salisbury Cathedral looked tophole. I came down to 1,000 ft over Salisbury to pick up the right river and got an A1 view.

It took me 2 hrs to get to Netheravon – there was a strong N. wind blowing. I went on there at once as they only have Rumpety (Shorthorns) at Netheravon and heaps of interesting machines at Upavon.

I found a good many fellows there that I knew at Reading and the R M C.

I beat my own height record this morning by going up to 10,000 ft on the 2C. As I was climbing I saw a 'remarkable phenomenon'. I was about 6,000 ft, about 2,000 ft above the clouds, when a bank of mist, fairly 'smooth', it wasn't 'lumpy', came drifting along, 1,500 ft below me. As I crossed this I saw a circular rainbow, not very large, and plumb in the centre was the shadow of the great 2C.

It was very distinct.

I have seen the shadow of the bus on a cloud before but not like the last time. I did my night landings this evening. They are an awful farce. You simply land in the dusk with the flares out. I expect it will be at least ten days before I get my wings, then I shall either go to France, or go Zep. Strafing, or go on to I R S for scouts.

I hope Grannie is well. . . .

Not having access to Charles' log-books one cannot say how much training he had before leaving for France; but he seems to have had considerably less than his brother; whereas H. had been prepared 'ready for Service abroad' with practice on 'all types specially scouts', 42 hours solo and a gunnery and bomb-dropping course, Charles, by his own letters, had $23\frac{1}{2}$ hours solo and practice on 5 or perhaps 6 types only. But pilots were at a premium in early 1917 and five days after his first cross-country Charles had his wings up, had been appointed to a Squadron and had crossed the Channel. He was appointed Flying Officer on the 1st February, 1917.

After crossing the Channel he wrote to Emmie:

Grand Hotel du Louvre Boulogne sur Mer 7/2/17. . . . Just a line to let you know that I got over here all right. Quite a decent crossing. I didn't feel any the worse for it.

It took us all hours to get our luggage out of the boat, but I have got it all. I had to report to several people here and am going to *No 10 Squadron* to-morrow.

My address is No 10 Squadron, B.E.F. France.

Bibby and several others will be quite near me and I will travel there with them. I hope you got back all right. Will let you know how I am getting on soon. . . .

There was a family tradition of always seeing people off on an important journey as though such a courtesy were a talisman for their safe return.

When Charles' letter reached Emmie she relayed the news to Alie in her best telegraphese straight away: 'Horton. Feb 11th. Letter this morning from Charles dated 7th Boulogne. Good crossing – baggage all right. Address No 10 Squadron RFC B.E.F. France. Going there on 8th. Bibby and several others travelling with him. Letter from Herbert yesterday he had been there a week. He has found a new 'dope' for his face. Yrs E L T.

Charles wrote to Alie on the 15th February:
    . . . I got over here all right. Mac went to 7 Squadron and Bibby to 16 which is close.
    Please excuse my writing, and the pencil, which is unnecessary, because I could write in ink in my room if I chose to do so. It is warmer in the Mess. We are in a 'chateau'. In italics because it is really a large country house. It is not very old. But it looks quite nice from the outside, as it has a moat, and a round tower with a spiky top. We are very comfortable here. They never shell us, partly because we are out of range of any but the big guns but chiefly because they don't know we're here.
    I am very lucky to have a room with another chap at the top. I may have to clear out for someone senior to me but I think that I shall (be able) to stay. The fellows who are in the Chateau are in Armstrong huts (canvas things) or in billets. Billets are rotten as they are nearly all in farms. Farms are smelly. They have a courtyard in the centre with a manure heap.
    I went up for 2 hours this afternoon on a practise reconnaisance. I took the senior observer up and he showed me the country round here.
    I saw the lines for the first time.
    I kept our side most of the time and wasn't archied but saw some of our machines being potted at. I also saw shells and things bursting on the ground.
    The trenches are a most wonderful sight from above. Of course the

Charles in France

photos you see are very good, but they don't show the contrast between the trench lines and the normal ground. I went to a show in xxxx yesterday evening. It was a pierrot troupe of about 6 men and N.C.O's and 2 officers. It was quite good, and the audience jolly fine. The place was packed. There is another show in the same town called the Whizz-Bangs but it was full up when we got there. It is supposed to be a better show, but this one was certainly good.

This town is sometimes shelled but they never seem to hit much except the central square and everything goes on much as usual. All the tradespeople are very flourishing because the place is packed with men. . . .

The weather was atrocious and Charles seems to have had little flying. He wrote to Jim on the 2nd March:

. . . H.O. turned up here after lunch much to my surprise. He came in a tender and had left a friend at 25 Squadron on the way. It was great to see him. His nose looked all right but he said that it wasn't quite so yet. He is about 45 miles away, so it was a fairly long run and the roads were rotten . . . I showed him the machines etc., I wonder if I shall have a chance of getting down there to see him again. Congrats on getting Port Victoria. How shall I address you?

I haven't been up for ages and I am getting rather bored, but I think the weather is improving at last. . . .

(Jim had been given Command of a Test Flight on the Isle of Grain.)

Nobody who lived through the winter of 1916–17 ever forgot it. Although the greatest horror was the horror of the trenches, there were many lesser struggles which, although infinitely minor by comparison, served to give a slight hint to those at home just how much the Armed Services were enduring across the Channel. Emmie, walking her weary miles in connexion with her S S F A work, knew a great deal about the practicalities of the 'home front.' She was no longer a young woman, in her 6oth year during that longest of all winters, but she was a stalwart and a soldier's daughter and her family were unable to restrain her from undertaking the work she felt so proud to be able to do. It was not a question, then, of lifting a telephone or of hopping into a car but of walking, always walking, visiting servicemen's families in their homes whenever possible, taking them their allowances and in writing letters and making representations on their behalf.

There is a sheaf of letters from men in France thanking her, often in the most moving terms, for all that she had done for their families while they were away.

'Sometimes she would come home quite exhausted,' Jay told me, 'her little shoes all muddy and her legs swollen like puddings and I would try and make her rest . . .'

In early March, with what she called a 'cold', Emmie at last gave way for a few days, entrusting Alie with some messages.

She wrote to Alie on March 5th from Warlingham: '. . . I cannot find the number but Egbert George Lincoln stoker H.M.S. *Gurkha* (which was blown up mine or torpedo in the Channel in February) Alexander Lincoln stoker 29 mess H.M.S. *Leviathan* is the elder brother.

I can't find any more particulars so do not worry. . . . The family promptly seized me & by brute force put me to bed & kept me there til this afternoon. I am now in the drawing-room & feel all right – but a bit groggy from being in bed. There is a bitter cold East wind – which I hope will dry the trenches. Dad heard from Herbert yesterday and Vera from Charles, both well. but Charlie had not had any flying owing to the mist. . . .

Strangely different to Emmie's war-time days were those of her Mother, Grannie Gardner – 91 on the 14th February, 1917, and who, after years of semi-eclipse, was now once more like a rising sun. Her years of traipsing rheumatically from one spa to another were over: she was back at the hub of things and what was more important to her, was once again tremendously useful to her family.

32 Evelyn Mansions was now practically a Command Post for the family; it was, moreover, haven, billet and dumping-ground; meeting-place, postbox and point of departure for the War.

The Zeppelin raids which caused distress to so many were often dismissed by her with her typically Georgian: 'It don't signify.'

She was indeed a Georgian. When she had been born, in 1826, Jefferson still had a few months to live, Jane Austen was a recently published novelist and Florence Nightingale was six years old.

Whether it was her age, or whether her own horrific experiences during the Indian Mutiny, she seemed to have a sense of proportion which enabled her to treat the Zeppelins, when they came, with an indifference untypical of elderly Londoners: the Zeppelins were a nuisance, that was all, and deserved only the slight attention which was appropriate.

She wrote to Emmie in March:

... Another raid last night but we did not go down – it was later very foggy this morning. I have just found this letter which I thought I had lent you. Emily wanted you to see it. We all feel rather dazed to-day from disturbances last night again but no damage done. (What we hear of the night) before we were invited from the drafty stairway by the curiosity gentleman and his wife and had to stay quite late – quite a party in their room. I had an easy chair by the fire while the others and the boy amused themselves with round games and we did not get up here til after 11.30. Then the creatures came back but I was sound asleep – it is a nuisance. Do please take care of yourself and catch no more colds ...'

On other nights when 'the creatures came back' Grannie Gardner sometimes played cards with the boy downstairs. More often she remained 'sound asleep.'

In early April Emmie, leaving her Mother in the care of her daily maid, went off with Alie for a happy short holiday to Bath. On her

return to the flat, to stay with her Mother for a day or two, she wrote
to Charles. It was just the quiet sort of letter such as any mother might
write to an 18-year-old son whom she believed to be still serving in
France.

April 10th.

My dear Charlie, I started to write to you in the train but it shook
too much. Alice had a week's holiday & persuaded me to go with her
to Bath & I think she quite enjoyed it. We kept on the hills a good
part of the day & there are heaps of things to see & we were only
once caught in a snowstorm. I expect she will be getting others
to go with her. Perhaps you & she may go some day. On Saturday
which was quite fine we found our way to a very fine castle Farleigh
Hungerford on the Frome river which is a tributary to the Avon.
We did not see many primroses out. Herbert mentioned the wood
he was in, big trees & heaps of daffies & primroses. Did you hear
he was in command of his flight. ... A letter from Jessie this morning. They (in Kent) had just seen a flight of 13. just going out she
thought.

Grannie is very well but will not be going out to-day as we planned.
It is snowing. They say it is the longest winter for 800 years. I expect
to find Vera at home taking care of Dad. (She) is fond of cooking, so
he is well looked after. He is still lame but that is due to the weather.
He is quite well otherwise.

Much love   Your loving Mother E. L. Travers. Gran's love to
                                                                      you.

Emmie's letter, posted in London SW on the 10th, was stamped on
arrival at Charles' Squadron: 'PRESENT LOCATION UNCERTAIN.'
Then on the 13th April it was forwarded to 'BASE HOSPITAL.'

Charles, coming in a bit steep into one of those 'small and bad and
dirty' aerodromes, had, by his own later account, tipped forward.
Others said that he had cartwheeled. He had suffered facial injuries,
particularly to his nose, which had been almost severed. He received
excellent first-aid treatment at the dressing station and was then shipped
home to the London Hospital for further repair. He was already in
London on 10th April, when Emmie had written to him, the accident
having happened on the 5th.

He wrote to her from 'Charrington Ward, London Hospital:

... Just a line to say that I am all right. We had quite a decent crossing in the '*Newhaven*', a 24-knot boat. It took us some time to get across, though, as we waited outside Calais for an escort for quite a long time.

The C.O. and Robeson (H.A.K.) both said they would write & say how it was I crashed.

I expect I shall be out of here in a week's time or so, then I may go to a Convalescent Home such as the Great Central Hospital. ...

It was a pity that Charles should have been thus disfigured, as he had been particularly good-looking before the accident.

Between hospital and his next posting he was given a short leave; he spent one day of this in visiting Jim and Nancy on Grain and spending an enjoyable afternoon with them on the Medway. Later they all met Jay for tea in Maidstone, a happy afternoon which she remembered long afterwards.

He was posted to No 84 Squadron on the 23rd of May. First, he may have gone to C.F.S. at Upavon, as he referred subsequently to Upavon and he may well have been given a refresher course there before being sent to Lilbourne, near Rugby, where he joined No 84 Squadron. His first letter from Lilbourne, which was to Emmie on the 2nd June, suggests that he had only just arrived: '... I got down here all right. All the Curtiss were on cross countries and it was too bumpy for the 2b so I didn't get a flip yesterday. I was on E.M.F. this morning & I tested the air, but it was not good enough for instruction on the 2b. One of the Curtiss came back after breakfast but the other two are still at large ... We have had some rain, but it is clear now ...'

Flying instruction is now so carefully regulated that it may seem surprising that the RFC should use a pilot as relatively young and inexperienced, as was Charles, as an instructor; They were of course using him to do some instruction: he was not appointed 'Instructor.' His civilian counterpart might be that of 'working pupil.' At any rate he settled down to do as much flying as possible during his time at Lilbourne, the summer of 1917, before being sent back to France. He celebrated his nineteenth birthday on the 3rd July.

To Alie, on the 5th July:

Thank you very much for your letter and good wishes etc. ... I have just been thinking – last birthday was at the RMC, quite an eventful year, judging from previous standards.

I haven't seen H.O.'s promotion. I missed that list. It is jolly fine. I am awfully glad because he told me that some fellows who had acting command of flights in France had lost them when they got home: if you follow me.

I have had some jolly good news. One Sutton, as Freddy would say, arrived here the other day. He was assistant A E D at Beaulieu and knew me and Stocks. He has been ill and in the same convalescent home as Stocks, who can walk and hopes to fly again soon.

Sutton says that Stocks was attacked by 3 Albatros Bii. He shot one down and was hit directly after by about 6 bullets. He got back to his aerodrome after having fainted once in the air, landed and fainted again. They picked him out and at the clearing station (I suppose) was given up as dead. The M.O. knew him and had another look as he thought he moved and found he was alive. He was some time in France, then they brought him over here. I also heard from Middleton, an observer in 10 Squadron, who gave me Turner's address. Turner was my observer. I looped the Mono Avro the other day, she went over quite well and came out quite square. I twisted the passenger some because I stalled and spun directly afterwards. He enjoyed it every much. I was sure he wouldn't mind or I wouldn't have done it.

I was up on the Mono yesterday when she dropped 50 revs and vibrated badly.

I closed off the juice and she was making a rotten noise. I glidied in and taxied her to the sheds.

It was found that a ball race had gone dud and the bits had mucked up the turning gear. So our wonderful Mono has been out of action. I think she will be ready tomorrow morning.

We have got a Gnome Avro.

It is the rottenest old dud I have struck for ages. The oiling system went wrong last night and did in an engine. We fitted a new one and this morning I took her up to test her. I got into a field close to the aerodrome at 7.30 a.m. and we tried to get her to go til 5 p.m. when she consented to take me back to the aerodrome. She wants about 50 things doing to her and then she may be fit for some unfortunate soloist to crash, but I don't suppose he'll have a chance. She is quite safe, of course, but everything seems wrong. . . . It is jolly fine about your promotion. . . . It is awfully nice of Dad and V. I have got some goggles. . . .

H. P. Gardner's steady stream of letters continued throughout the War, mainly to his Mother, often to Emmie. He kept himself, and was kept, well-informed. He wrote to Emmie on 7th July: '... We are anxious to know how Jim is getting on ... (Jim had broken his arm cranking his car). ... It must be very annoying to get damaged when one is so busy, and how is Charlie, he must have had a wonderful escape. Did he fall far. ... H.O. seems to be getting on well. I envy the boys. ... We are having a long and cold winter and enjoy our big log fires. There is not a blade of green stuff anywhere but long dry dead grass that we are always afraid will catch fire at any moment. Fortunately we have a large crop of pumpkins. It is the only thing that keeps our cattle and horses going. I was in Brisbane yesterday for a Rabbit Board meeting. One hears of a lot of shellshock among the returned soldiers, some were off their heads, others lost their nerve and are frightened by any unexpected sound. ... They have stopped the Red Cross people making garments as they have such a tremendous stock of them and want them to give money instead which is not so easy to get. ...'

Charles to Alie on the 17th July:

Thank you very much for the cake. It is A1.

How is Jimmy's arm?

We have several Sopwith bombers here now, they are almost exactly like the 2-seaters and very easy to fly. I had my first flip on one last night. The idea is that they are something between an Avro and a Pup, but I don't think they are good practice because you can't stunt them, and they are easier to fly than an Avro, really. There are very few machines now and it is very hard on the few we have got, with the result that we have a good deal of trouble with the engines. We have an 80 Gnome Avro, a Mono-Avro (which is out of bounds for the time because of trouble with engine bearers) and the $1\frac{1}{2}$ Strutter bomber in 'C' flight. ...

To Emmie on 17th July:

... I flew a Sopwith bomber ($1\frac{1}{2}$ Strutter) yesterday. They are very easy to fly but you can't stunt them. The French use them but I don't think we do any longer. They carry heaps of juice and are nice busses for cross country flying. I should like to bring one to Croydon but they wouldn't let me. I am afraid, because when it is fit for flying I am needed here to instruct.

It has been raining all day & there is not much to do. I might try to get over to Wells House this afternoon. The trains are quite good I believe. . . .

The attraction to Charles of visiting Wells House was not so much that of a young man re-visiting his old preparatory school as the fact that his eldest sister, V., to whom he was devoted, was now employed as Secretary at The Wells House. (It was her first paid job, although she had worked as a dietician, putting her Macdonald College home economics training to good use, as a voluntary Red Cross worker in one of the hospitals not far from Warlingham.)

Charles to Emmie on the 12th August:
   . . . I had a fair amount of flying last week – a good deal of instructional work on the Avro – I flew the Nieuport several times.
   We have got a new C.O. Maj. Douglas & the flights have been reorganized. 'C' flight has the Avros 'B' the Sop. bombers & Nieuports and 'A' the Bristol Scout & Sop. Pups.
   I was transferred to 'A' flight to fly Scouts. I have flown the 'Pup' twice, it is a topping little thing. Now I have got to take charge of 'B' flight while O.C. 'B' flight is away and get in some flying on Scouts at the same time.
   We have had a lot of rain & I am afraid the crops are damaged badly.
   We have a lot of sheep on the aerodrome: a chap was landing the other day & a sheep ran in front. He 'yanked' the machine up but caught it on his tail skid & killed it. . . .

To Emmie on 12th September:
   Last Saturday a chap called Park & myself were sent to collect machines from Farnborough. As it was too misty to start, I went to see Peggs. I saw him & several O.Gs. also a chap called Ashburner who who went there the same time as I did. He was crocked on a cross country run but is all right now & is now a Sgt. in 'E' Coy. Peggs passes out to-day, Wednesday, but they have just stopped all attachments to R.F.C. I think it is a rotten dirty trick because they only let him know about a fortnight ago & he has been there 10 months. Peggs is going to the Sherwood Foresters. I got the bus up here all right though I had to land at Oxford with eng. trouble. Park crashed his bus on the aerodrome here. We have had several crashes on these S.E.5's which

is sickening, because they are easy to fly, easier than the 'Camel' which everyone here has flown.

We are sending 4 machines out from each flight to start with and are going to make a move soon, about the 19th I expect. We will then train in France for some time.

Pennell, myself, Larson (the Swede/English/Canadian) and Brown, a Canadian, are taking the machines in 'B' flight.

All leave has been stopped but I will try to get home one evening.

Could you send these things up?

Long Flying Boots.

Any thick underfugs.

1 Big towel.

It would be topping if you could get these sent off.

I heard from H. yesterday.   love to all. . . .

And an undated letter from Grannie Gardner added some more vital information:

My dear Emmie,   I wish you had stayed – Charlie made his appearance 8 o'clock on his way to Portsmouth to see abt stores of some sort – has to arrive there in small hours & no idea where to sleep – he and Alie studied Bradshaw & finally settled he had better sleep here & leave by 5.30-something (from) Waterloo this morning which he did getting some breakfast at station. He expects to fly across some time next week, I understand the wing is to go, 4 of each squadron to fly – he was very happy about it. I expect he will turn up to-day on his way back to-day but he did not know. . . .

Charles wrote of the flight across:

Clouds were very low 1200–1600.

Pennell went down at London Colney & we other two followed. I went down because my map of S E England had blown overboard and my engine was missing.

Larson hit a rut in landing and broke his undercarriage. Pennell and I didn't start until 4.30 it was clearer than before but we struck a bank of mist over the river. We followed the river to Chatham then went across to Maidstone & so to Folkestone. We were rather low so we climbed to 6000 & crossed. Of course you could see the French coast clearly from 6000 over Lympne (Folkestone). It looked very pretty.

We arrived here about 6.5. I expect we shall have a look at our aerodrome to-morrow.

When we got here we found we were the only members of the sq. to complete the journey bar the C.O. The rest have landed safely, bar Larson.   love to all. . . .

He wrote again to Emmie a week later:

. . . I hope you got my letter all right. We are gradually getting into shape but there is an awful lot to be done. There are crowds of fellows here in the other Squadrons who were at Lilbourne and the Recording Officer of one was the adj. at Beaulieu while I was there. 'Cheesmite' otherwise Heathcote, who was at Wells House, is here too. My address is 84 Sq. B.E.F. . . . I went into Boulogne with another chap to get a piano and other things for the mess. He met a friend of his in the 19th, so of course I asked him if he knew Bucknall, & it turned out that they were in the same squadron. As he wanted to get back we gave him a lift & I saw Beaky. Going very strong. He has been out since the middle of Feb. but hasn't had any scrapping yet. . . .

And on 31st October:

I hope everyone is well. I am going strong. I was on early patrol this morning and there was not another show for me to-day so I took the opportunity of going over to 10 Squadron. It is only a short distance and it didn't take long. . . . It was fine to see the place again. They have enlarged the aerodrome a little bit & I got in easily. How is H.O.? Have you heard from him.

I am fairly warm in my machine and have not been cold yet. My machine is very warm really, a lot of fuel comes back from the engine and the exhaust pipes come back each side of the fuselage.

I hope J. is getting on well. . . . (Jay had for some months been an agricultural student at Greenway Court, Hollingbourne, Kent.) '. . . The watch Dad gave me,' Charles letter continued, 'is going finely. The watch in my bus conked the other day & it came in awfully handy. . . .'

From the Official R.A.F. History:

During the autumn of 1917, when the ground troops were making rapid advance, a novel form of low reconnaissance was tried by No. 84 Squadron (S.E.5). Communications from the front were bad, and General Rawlinson, the Fourth Army Commander, was often uncertain as to the position of his advanced troops. At this time No. 84 Squadron was making a series of low-flying attacks on the retreating enemy, so that pilots became very familiar with the lie of the land over which our troops were advancing. It became the custom, therefore, for pilots to report on the position of enemy troops. In foggy weather, which prevailed on several days about this time, it was only possible to fly about the height of the tree tops. Air reconnaisance became almost impossible, and the situation on the front became uncertain. Under these conditions No. 84 Squadron adopted an ingenious plan. As it was impossible to fly across country without getting lost, pilots decided to follow the roads by flying along them just above the tree tops, carefully noting enemy troops either directly, or indirectly on being fired on, and pin pointing the position. Where several roads radiated from a centre as, for example, Le Cateau, the various roads would be prospected in turn, and by this means sufficient points would be obtained to enable the enemy's line in the neighbourhood to be plotted.'

The pilots called it 'country chasing.'

Charles to Emmie on 24th November: '... It has been very dull and all flying we have done except to-day has been very low. It is quite good fun, as long as it is clear on the ground: no fog or mist. They can't Archie you low down, or not so that you would notice it, anyway ...'

And to Alie, on the same date: '... You must have had a great time doing all the shows with Freda the other day. I should like to see 'Dear Brutus'. I expect it will be on for some time and I will see it when I get leave. I saw H.O. just before we moved. He came to see me with a friend of his, Morris, I think, in a motor-bike and side-car. I don't think that he has gone to Italy but it is possible. The last two or three days we have been flying very low because the clouds are very thick and close to the ground. ... This is supposed to be the leader of a formation ...' – (he illustrated his letter) – 'from the point of view of the machine on his L. rear and a little above, over a town that has been under fire. ...'

Low-level reconnaisance, 'country chasing', whether Archie-d or not, may have been 'quite good fun.' But 'low-flying attacks on the retreating enemy', or strafing, was not.

Forty-six years later Charles remembered, with renewed horror and chilling clarity, exactly what it was like to do low-level strafing and to see the young faces upturned.

The meetings which he had from time to time with H. when both of them were in France, must, one feels, have been supportive and helpful to them both; sometimes they landed at each other's aerodromes, sometimes turned up by push-bike or motor-bike; the visits were usually brief and were always mentioned in letters home. Thus, when H. was back in France again in the late autumn of 1917, he called to see Charles on his way down to Paris.

Charles wrote home on 7th December:

... I saw H.O. again. He was taking a quick down South to Paris & landed on his way. It was misty & we got him to stay the night. Larson who shares my ½ hut is on leave so he had his bed. Unfortunately my oil stove chucked his hand in, & H.O. froze all night. It was bad luck as we are very comfortable as a rule.

I expect I shall get leave soon. The exact time depends on whether one of the flight commanders goes or not. It is too thick for a patrol at present unless they want us badly. We are standing by in the mean time.

We have got a few of the new flying suits issued. I have got one, but I have had to hand in my leather coat in exchange. ... We have got a great cinema show in the mens canteen. It is a great success. ...'

After his 1917 Christmas leave, Charles flew back to France. Once again the Squadron had moved.

He wrote to Emmie from Boulogne on 30th December: '... I got over in great style yesterday. I went above the clouds and it was nice and warm. I can't find out where the Squadron is so will have to go over to our old aerodrome and find out there ... I couldn't get my bag at Charing X. I will write to Jimmy and he may be able to find out whether it has been sent off. ...'

After the turn of the year there was a rapid increase in enemy air activity.

From the Official R.A.F. History:

'As soon as the enemy began to realise that defeat on the ground was not only probable but inevitable, his air force made strenuous efforts to prevent his ground troops from becoming completely demoralised by British attacks from the air. He put up all his available aeroplanes, and to deal with these, systematic sweeps of the sky by several squadrons combined were carried out. ... The scheme had occasionally been tried on the Somme front by the V Brigade. At first a squadron of S.E.5's flying at 15,000 to 17,000 ft. was accompanied by a squadron of Bristol Fighters at about 18,000 ft. The Bristol Fighters being as good in defence as in attack could thus protect the rear of the whole formation.

On the 9th March, Nos 23 (Spad), 48 (Bristol Fighter) and 54 (Camel)

Squadrons, supported by Nos 24 (S.E.5) and 84 (S.E.5) Squadrons, attacked the hostile aerodromes at Bertry, Busigny and Escaufort. No enemy opposition was met with and no casualties were suffered. An attack on Mont d'Origny aerodrome on the 14th March by Nos. 24, 48 and 84 Squadrons was also unopposed; but an attack on the 18th March by No. 5 Naval Squadron (D.H.4) on Busigny, with the support of Nos. 54 and 84 Squadrons, met with fierce opposition. Enemy aircraft, estimated at between forty and fifty aeroplanes, were encountered and in the resulting fight four enemy aeroplanes were destroyed and eight driven down out of control. Eight of our aeroplanes failed to return. On the 3rd April Nos. 65 (Camel and 84 (S.E.5) Squadrons, twenty-seven aeroplanes in all, engaged a formation of some thirty Pfalz and Albatros scouts at about 1,500 ft over the German advanced landing ground at Rosieres. A fierce fight ensued as the result of which seven enemy fighters were destroyed (four by No. 84 Squadron and three by No. 65 Squadron) and two others were driven down out of control. Two Camels of No. 65 Squadron did not return.

So runs the Official History.

The minutiae of life in the air went unrecorded. The cold, such a terrible enemy to H., flying, as he was, with head and shoulders well above any protection from it, did not affect Charles to the same degree. In almost every letter he stresses the fact that he was 'nice and warm' in his machine, or at the very least 'not cold'. The difference between the two brothers lay of course in the difference in their height, a good seven inches. But Charles had other difficulties and since his accident in April 1917 had had some difficulty in breathing at all through his damaged nose. It was probably on account of this that he was invalided home to Ely Hospital on 6th April 1918, from whence he was transferred to his good friends in the London Hospital on the following day.

After some leave he was posted, on the 6th May, 1918, to Central Flying School as a flying instructor.

His combatant war was over and his days with 84 Squadron gone for good. Many years later he was to meet, and to remain lifelong friends with, some of his fellow pilots. That was years later and thousands of miles away.

The following snatch of a letter, for which I have no date, is in Emmie's hand and was written to Alie. It was probably written in the winter of 1918–1919, since it refers to the 'Paris bus' for that was the period when the excitement about a regular air service between London and Paris was at its height.

... On Saturday (25th) it was clear & bright & H.O. on a Sopwith

Pup & Charles on an S.E. came over Swish over the house. I ran out at the back door & Dad at the verandah & they gave us a wonderful display. Charlie said they only started to fly in formation but H.O. started to Huff & Charlie followed suit. H.O.'s machine more suited to it but C.T. put in a fine show. They turned & looped & dived under each other & H.O. came down in a spinning dive & then they went off to Kenley & I went in to have tea ready. In the evening Jimmy turned up – so we had all three. On Sunday about 2 o'clock they went up to Kenley & H.O. got off but Charles was just too long & the fog came down.

The Paris bus was expected and the press were there in swagger motors – but it was put off for weather. On Monday Charlie tried again but met a snowstorm which damaged his prop. so he returned & it has been 'dud' ever since.

He has wired for orders but to-day had a wire 'why had he not returned' so he is off to London by train. On Monday a man a good pilot was caught in a snowstorm over Marden Park & crashed. ... Dad is going to London (if the railways are not held up by the strike) to-morrow. . . .

Peace had returned.

Charles, much to his suprise, was awarded the Air Force Cross.

6

THE ISLE OF GRAIN

1914–1919

Sopwith Bat-Boat – Bomb-dropping experiments – East Coast – to Calshot as
C.O. – Cuxhaven – Norddeich – Felixstowe – The Isle of Grain – peace

ONLY scant reference has so far been made to Jim's work during the
Great War: the work on his bomb-sights; the instruction and training
at Calshot; the experimental and construction work on seaplanes and
flying boats, particularly on the latter with Commander Porte at
Felixstowe, all became part of the history of the Royal Naval Air
Service. The old days at Hendon must have seemed long ago and far
away. Hendon kept up their Meetings until the war – the 'Sundays at
Hendon' – with the polo ground and tennis courts and garden party
atmosphere, with published lists of distinguished visitors, amongst
whom Emmie's loyal cousins, the Droghedas, were often mentioned
as having been present – all that must indeed have seemed like life on
another planet as, down at Calshot, Sub Lt. Travers, blissfully happy,
was flying his Bat Boat.

Maurice Allward, in his enthralling book: *History of Seaplanes &
Flying Boats*, gives a description of Jim's bomb-aiming experiments
from the Sopwith Bat Boat.

'A more significant development in Britain was the famous Bat Boat,
designed by T.O.M. Sopwith. Outstanding features of the Bat Boat was its
beautifully finished, hand-sewn mahogany hull built by Sam Saunders, a boat
building craftsman of Cowes. The Bat Boat was Europe's first successful flying
boat and the world's first successful amphibian.

A Bat Boat was used in a series of pioneer bombing experiments by Sub Lt
J.L. Travers and Lt Bigsworth. During these Travers sat beside Bigsworth
the pilot, with a bag of potatoes on his knees. On reaching a pre-selected field,
Travers dropped the potatoes overboard one at a time, carefully noting the
speed and height of the Bat Boat and the speed and direction of the wind at
the moment he dropped each potato. On the ground Navy ratings observed
the fall of each potato and marked the point of impact with a flag. As experience

was gained, the potatoes were superseded first by specially shaped darts and then by 'bombs.' In this manner Travers gained valuable data on the behaviour of objects dropped from aircraft, which formed the basis of the bomb-aiming techniques developed by the Royal Naval Air Service. A Bat Boat was exhibited at the 1913 Aero Show at Olympia. It so attracted the attention of the First Lord of the Admiralty, Mr Winston Churchill, that he issued instructions that it be purchased for the Royal Naval Air Service.'

The Sopwith was an inspiration to Jim and a delight. In letters home he constantly referred to it as 'his' bat boat although it was, of course, the property of the Navy. No matter that all his own early experiments on sea-going aeroplanes had been with 'flotation bags' – essentially transforming aeroplanes into seaplanes. Tom Sopwith had attacked the problem from another and more effective direction, by concentrating on the ship, or boat, and then making the boat capable of flight.

In June of 1914 Jim had been off sick and at home for a spell, almost certainly with one of the chest infections or heavy colds to which he was prone – he was, after all, constantly chilled when flying. Longmore, then in command at Calshot, sent a telegram to him at Warlingham at 1.15 p.m. on the 12th June, as follows: 'If well enough please attempt to return by first boat to Calshot Monday morning. Next inspection taking place.' After that important inspection great changes took place. At the end of June the Royal Flying Corps was 'split in twain', divided into Navy or Army. For the Navy, the Admiralty announced the formation of the Royal Naval Air Service, consisting of Air Dept. (Admy.), the Central Air Office, the R N Flying School and the R N Air Stations. On the 1st July, 1914, Jim was transferred to a commission in the Royal Naval Air Service as a Flight Commander; and it was in this capacity that he took part in the famous 1914 Spithead Review and the fly-past over the Fleet. The *Aeroplane* of July 22nd reported:

> ... The last flight to leave was the 'home' flight under Squadron Commander Longmore (Lieut.-Commander, R.N.) In effect, the Sopwith gun-carrier (200-h.p. Salmson) which the commanding officer was to have flown refused to get off the water, chiefly owing to a defective propellor, but partly because an experimental alteration had been made to the tail and partly because the engine took a fit of sulks, and there was no time left to get things right. It was uncommonly hard lines because Squadron Commander Longmore had had all the work of organizing things at Calshot for the other flights, and had superintended the departure of all the other machines that morning, so that by leaving his own start till last he deprived himself of the chance of starting

at all. Consequently this flight was under Flight Commander Bigsworth, who started first on the Short gun-carrier (160-h.p. Gnome), a huge machine which seems able to lift anything. . . . The last machine to start was the Sopwith bat-boat (90-h.p. Austro-Daimler), one of the most extraordinary craft in the Navy, and quite the most comfortable thing to fly in I have yet come across. The huge hull, the comparatively low power, and the apparently small planes would lead one to expect a clumsy, sluggish machine very hard to get off the water, and awkward to bring down properly. In practice she gets off easily, provided there is not too much sea – for she is small, considered as a boat – and flies very well indeed.

On Friday night, just before midnight, Flight Commander Travers had taken this Sopwith bat-boat out over the Fleet. He had an ordinary electric headlight off a car fitted on the bow, and a mass of accumulators as well as a passenger, and with this he flew from Calshot right out to the other end of the Fleet by Southsea, reaching about a 1,000 feet as he came to the first ships and getting to 1,500 feet at the other end of the line. This performance rather 'wiped the eye' of the airships which are supposed to be particularly the weapons of darkness.

On returning Flight Commander Travers had an experience which demonstrated the use of a self-alighting machine. After leaving the last of the Fleet, at 1,000 feet or so, he started to come down by throttling the engine so that he was just sinking slowly. His dash-board was illuminated as usual and he was taking his height from his aneroid, intending, when it showed he was getting near the water, to alight in the usual way. Suddenly, when the instrument showed a height of 200 feet, there was a bump and a crash and much splashing, and he found himself on the water. What had happened was that, as the aneroid indicated in 200-foot jumps, he had reached the bottom of the last 200 feet before the indicator moved, just as in a taxi one may be on the verge of ticking up another tu'ppence without actually doing so. The boat fetched himself up quite easily without a particle of damage, and was moored out for the night, doing her trip on Saturday as well as anything in the air. Before this night-flying business the same machine had taken half-a-dozen or more Naval passengers, one at a time of course, round the Fleet. She is, I think, the oldest machine at Calshot, and certainly one of the best fliers, now that triangular fins have been fitted under the tail and forward of the rudders. Of course, she is too small for real sea work, but a similar kind of machine in a really large size – say a 500-h.p. twin-engine job – is something like the beginning of the real flying ship. . . .

One cannot help feeling that Jim's sentiments may have been exactly those of the author of those words. C. G. Grey continued: '. . . One thing that will be altered in such a type of machine will be the tail-booms. At no time have I liked the idea of a heavy propellor and engine buzzing round inside four little sticks which one could break with one's hands, and in the big, powerful, fast machines of to-day it is positively terrifying to see the tail-booms whipping about when the engines are running on land or water, and it is not good for one's nerves to watch them when in the air, for some of them bend visibly when the rudders are put full over. . . .'

At the end of July, 1914, things began to happen with the 'war scare.'

Jim wrote to Emmie from Calshot on 29th July: 'There has been a war scare on since Monday last; all our machines are being flown round to the East Coast Stations. I started yesterday but had engine trouble at Hayling and was towed home. I start again early to-morrow on another machine and will fetch my old batboat Sopwith afterwards when the engine is repaired. I hope Dad is better and that you and everyone at home is quite well. . . .'

He wrote again a week or two later, from Melrose Private Hotel, Felixstowe: '. . . I am quite well and kicking, we are not doing a great deal.

I flew my Sopwith to Yarmouth the other day and I believe it has since been flown on up the coast by someone else. I have been out on patrol flying several days this week. We saw the destroyers coming in here after the action off Heligoland the other day. One or two of them were a little bit battered about but most of them were absolutely untouched. Shotley is full of German wounded. Have you got any news of Herbert. I suppose he will get a chance of going to the front, lucky dog. I heard from Sammy offering his car and services but I don't think there is much chance of him coming here as we have already got 2 cars on the Station. He ought to enlist. . . . I am keeping very fit and wish I could do more . . .'

And again to Emmie from Felixstowe: '. . . I am very fit, we are not doing much, but are all ready to do more when told to.

I hope aircraft will show up well in this war, it will have done some good. . . . Every one is very confident and I hope not over-confident, that we will show up well. We have had two alarms of Zeppelins at night and turned out and got machines out etc. But each time proved to be a false alarm – we sleep at the Air Station, we do patrol 20 to 30 miles out to sea, but have not done much to the present.

I hope everybody is well and that you have good news from Herbert and Vera. . . .'

And again to Emmie from Felixstowe: '. . . Thank you for your letter of 20th. Herbert is a lucky dog going to the front. I expect he is going there. Major Risk has left for the front in charge of motor transport, he has been in command here since the station started, he joined the Flying Corps at the same time that I did. He is Major of Marines and Squadron Commander R N A S. 'We are wondering who is going next. Rathborne, a Captain Marines is C O here now. He flew one of our machines to Eastchurch to-day so I am in command until he returns. It is my turn for the patrol to-morrow, we can't start before 5.15 now as it is so dark and it is very cold so we have started a thermos flask of coffee which is filled overnight.

The S N O Harwich, Capt Cayley, came over here to-day and told us we were to have Service on Sunday in one of the sheds. A parson is coming over with a supply of Hymn Books – and the crews of the T B D's are to come too.

Our electric light installation is getting on well and should be finished soon.

I have just had to order some more uniform, overcoat, boots, etc. We have just had news that 4 of our cruisers have been torpedoed by the enemy off the Dutch Coast. I expect they did some damage to the enemy, though we have not had a full report yet. I heard from Longmore to-day in reply to a letter I wrote him – he says they are hard at work training pupils in Seaplane work. ...' On the 29th September he was sent to Calshot, in command. He wrote to Emmie from Calshot on 4th October:

Thank you for sending the shirts etc. Will you send me some service boots (black without toecaps), some towels, sheets, pyjamas, socks (black) and handkerchiefs if any – please send them to Flight Cmdr. J. L. Travers RNAS Calshot Naval Air Station Warsash. I have got an awful lot to do but I never felt better of happier in my life. There is absolutely not a moment to spare all day. There is one Lieut. RN. Bromet by name who I have as 1st Lieut. (to run the hands etc.) the rest are all Flight Sub-Lieuts., some on probation, some not.

One of them, Elsdon, used to be a pilot at the Vickers School and he instructs them in Seaplane flying.

I take them up occasionally but I am chiefly in the office and all over the station. I do a bit of experimental flying when opportunity serves.

New machines are coming every day, they pass their tests and when the new pilots are proficient I send them off to the East Coast on new machines.

Longmore and Bigsworth are at the Front and so are Chambers and Grosvenor. Edmonds is at Grain, Staff Surg. O'Connell is here and Mr Scarff the Engineer and Mr Hancock the Carpenter.

I spend at least 4 hours a day in the office and the rest in interviewing constructors, passing machines and fitting things in. We are probably going to train a squadron of land aeroplanes at Fort Grange near Portsmouth. I had to go there to see about it. Our Quarters at Calshot have just been painted and are very comfortable now, the food is good. . . .

One of the numerous things which Jim 'fitted in' was the following proposal sent to the Central Air Office from H M Naval Air Station, Calshot on the 16th October 1914:

Proposal for an advanced base for seaplanes attached to Calshot on the Eastern point of the Isle of Wight.

Reason for proposals:

It is considered that seaplanes would be nearer to the possible scene of attack by both submarines or airships.

It would also be of use in the saving of fuel (about 60 lbs) in shortening the necessary radius of action, especially in the event of a torpedo-carrying machine being available. Regular patrols or patrols continually changing in direction could be made every morning, starting just before daybreak. The seaplanes could be under the order of the C-in-C Portsmouth, and should be in the air within half an hour of the receipt of a signal from him.

If anything hostile was observed the seaplane could land in Portsmouth Harbour and report direct, thus saving much time.

Bembridge is chosen as it provides a sheltered position with good command of the Channel.

Personnel

The organization would be as follows

1 Flight Cdr. (or 1 Flight Lieut.)

1 Flight Lieut. (or 1 Flight Sub-Lieut)

1 P.O. Mechanic (E)

2 Air Mechanics (E)

2 Air Mechanics (C)

2 Motor Boat Hands.

Accommodation of Personnel

The officers and hands should find no difficulty in finding suitable lodgings in Bembridge.

Duties of the Officer I/C the Base

1) To be in a state of readiness to send a seaplane out within half an hour of receiving a signal from the Commander in Chief.

2) To carry out a Daily Patrol if required.

Seaplanes

Two seaplanes to be provided from Calshot. If any trouble occurs with these m/c's they can immediately be replaced by others from Calshot.

The advanced base would only be used for very small adjustments and repairs.

It is proposed that one of these seaplanes should be fitted with anti-aircraft armament, such as Lewis Gun or rifle or TNT Grenades.

The other m/c might be either a scouting m/c or alternatively fitted with a torpedo for attacking submarines.

Housing of seaplanes

One Bessonean tent would be required, it is believed that one could be obtained from Sheerness Dockyard. The question of the size of the tent will be carefully gone into by C.O. Calshot and a report will follow.

A sheltered position would probably be chosen well inside Bembridge Harbour, and situated as near as possible to a telephone, but, failing that, a temporary telephone could be run to the tent.

Trolleys would be required for transporting m/c's from beach to the water.

Moorings

These can be obtained in the harbour.

In fine weather m/c's could be moored or anchored in the harbour in instant readiness to go out.

Covers could be provided for the engines and instruments.

Fuel supply

> Stock of petrol 500 gallons.
> ＂ ＂ oil 150 galls (Condor)
> ＂ ＂ ＂ ＂ (Gnome).

This stock could be replenished from Calshot by the Calshot Steamboat.

> signed J. L. Travers
> Flight Cmdr.

He wanted aeroplanes to show up well in this war.

He wrote home again on 11th November: '... Thanks awfully for Herbert's letter, he seems quite cheerful. I am sorry he did not start flying sooner, but I don't think anybody realized he was so keen on it. It is blowing up a bit from the SW but we did an early patrol all right.

My pupils are doing splendid work. There is a tremendous lot of work to do. I have to test the Sopwiths myself now as M*** smashed that one up the other day and the Admiralty are nervous about him (he is not very experienced) and Sopwiths have no other pilot. Hawker tests their land machines...' (Hawker was an Australian, a man of very great skill as an engineer/designer/pilot and a man much liked by his contemporaries. Tom Sopwith was saddened by his early death and commemorated his name in his post-war aircraft construction company.)

Jim's letter continued: '... My office work takes me 2 or 3 hours a day and signals and telegrams are continually coming through which I must see and reply to, so I am kept very busy.

I had a letter from V. and one from Grannie for my birthday and Jess wrote to me.

Herbert's reference to Jezzi's favourite game, it is dominoes, I think.

I applied the other day to join an aeroplane squadron and go out to the front but Longmore squashed it as he said I was doing work here and they could not spare me. We have continual scares of German submarines here but never see any ...'

He wrote again on November 20th:

... I have been very busy the last few days a lot more pupils have arrived. and new machines coming along while several fellows have flown away on machines.

The wind is now blowing very strong and I can neither send pupils out or try new machines. So everybody is employed in the sheds.

Friday is always a busy day because I always have to send in all the weekly reports and pay the hands as well as the other work, Correspondence takes about 2 hours a day. ... I will write again when I get a bit more news. ... I have not seen anything of Ben yet? perhaps he will come here as a pupil.

Ben was about Jim's age, and their birthdays, in early November, were close; there was great affinity between them and they had always got along famously, ever since their boyhood days, when they would occasionally go over for the day to each other's house – Jim and his sisters returning to Woottonga with such noisy whoops of laughter at all the wild times which went on in the Frank (that silly ass Frank) Travers' household, as to make Emmie wonder, sometimes, whether the children should see each other quite so often. Ben, by his own later account, admired Jim and had been inspired by him to learn to fly. He did not, in the event, go to Calshot as a pupil but to Hendon. He has written most vividly of his own R N A S experiences in his first autobiography, *Vale of Laughter*, published by Bles in 1957.

*   *   *

Jim had been fretting, all through the autumn, to see some action. He had more than once referred to H. as a 'lucky dog' to be going to the front. Longmore was out. So, too, was Bigsworth, his old colleague from the potato-dropping bomb-sight experiments. One way and another Jim was ready and eager for the 'stunt' which was now afoot.

The idea to raid Cuxhaven had been ebbing and flowing for months. Indeed, the germ of the idea may have been planted in thoughtful minds as early as August, 1914, when Erskine Childers had arrived at Felixstowe as a Volunteer Officer in the R N A S. As is well-known, Erskine Childers was the author of the classic thriller *The Riddle of the Sands*. Jim had been much impressed with *The Riddle of the Sands*. Everything about the book had appealed to his sense of adventure: it was knowledgeable, prophetic, intensely exciting and beautifully written, a masterpiece both in itself and in a glass, darkly. And now, some of the challenge which it contained was going to be taken up. The very name of Cuxhaven invited battle.

At what stage Jim was brought in I do not know, possibly as late as November or early December, although he would, of course, have met Childers at Felixstowe in the summer.

He had hoped that the Admiralty would build his bomb-sight but, even if they had done so in time for the raid, it is unlikely that it would have been used; for the raiders were defeated more by the weather than by any other single factor, the weather which had been so central to the plot of *The Riddle of the Sands*.

Alie wrote to Emmie from 32 Evelyn Mansions on 8th December:

... Jim has been here this afternoon. He had come up by an early train and had spent three hours at the Admiralty – bomb-dropping or talking bomb-dropping and he seemed quite pleased about it. After lunch I went to the Stores with him to get some fur gloves and some collars. The gloves were a present Grannie had been longing to give him so it was a grand opportunity. His hair was horribly long (he got it cut afterwards) but I thought he looked quite well. He has been tremendously busy and too much office work....'

The idea had been to carry a number of float/aeroplanes or seaplanes, loaded with bombs, on warships and when sufficiently near the target, to fly off the 'bombers' and destroy the Zeppelin sheds at Cuxhaven. When I talked to H. about the raid his whole countenance would light up; he would say that it had been a wonderful idea, not entirely successful, but a wonderful idea. It is only recently that I have read accounts of the raid and have learned how unsuccessful it really was, in spite of being led by that very brave man, L'Estrange Malone. Erskine Childers, too, went as observer/adviser; Jim as observer/ bomb-dropper. Unreliable aircraft and the weather defeated the raiders. Several pilots were lost. It was, in modern parlance, a shambles.

'What's the glass doing?' (Carruthers had asked in *The Riddle of the Sands*) and Davies had replied: 'Higher than for a long time. I hope it won't bring fog. I know this district is famous for fogs. . . .'

The blustery autumn weather had caused postponement of the raid until late December. And then the fog had come down. It was probably after his three hours at the Admiralty on 8th December 'talking bomb-dropping' that Jim knew he would be going on the raid. Jay remembered that he had told them all at home that he would be having some Christmas leave and that he would be at home on Christmas Day. That was all they knew. 'We waited and waited,' said Jay. Emmie had not seemed unduly worried. Perhaps that was partly because her own Mother, Grannie Gardner, had told her many years before that as Jim had been born in a caul he would never drown.

Jim had certainly expected to be home for Christmas for Cuxhaven had originally been planned for mid-December, the raid then postponed on a day-to-day basis until, at last, it took place on Christmas Day.

'Eventually he turned up,' Jay told me, 'days later than we expected him and looking perfectly ghastly. He had come down in the sea and had been rescued.'

That was all she could remember about the Cuxhaven Raid. That it had taken place over Christmas and that the fog had come down and all the plans were spoiled. Since Jay often mentioned that he had served in *Engadine*, it is probable that he was aboard *Engadine* at the start of the operation.

Failure or not, Cuxhaven was a most audacious idea.

Jim returned to Calshot and set about, among his other work, the building of new hangars on the Isle of Wight.

His next adventure was again, as Cuxhaven had been, with the 'Special Service' of Harwich Force. This time it was the operation against Norddeich of the 3rd May, in which three carriers, *Engadine, Riviera* and *Ben-My-Chree* took part.

Norddeich was the home of the enemy's powerful wireless transmitter, equivalent to those which we operated from Clifton and from Poldhu. At 6 p.m. every evening Norddeich started up, – so punctual, according to the Chief Petty Officer Wireless Telegraphist serving aboard the battle-cruiser HMS *Lion*, out from Scapa Flow, that you could set your watch by him. Norddeich had been a nuisance to the Navy for months as, loud and clear, he sought to spread alarm and despondency among the listening British Fleet. The broadcasts were a forerunner of the sort of thing put out by Lord Haw-Haw in the Second World War. The aim of the expedition was to knock out Norddeich.

Jim wrote to his mother – a note which surely reads like a letter of farewell. He wrote from Brown's Hotel. He would not have thought it wise, so near the time of departure, to have stayed with Grannie Gardner at the flat as he normally did when in London and thereby to have run the risk of questioning about his movements.

'Brown's Hotel. 30th April.

'. . . I am off to sea on Monday night for a week.

'I go to Harwich first thing to-morrow – don't say a word to *anyone*.

'I have a good machine a Sopwith and hope to have good weather.

'Just had a long talk with the D.A.D. at the Admiralty.

'Give my love to Dad and Jess & Alice.

'Your loving son, Jim.'

(The term 'the D.A.D.' normally referred to the Director of the Air Department, at that time Rear Admiral Sir Murray Sueter, K.C.B. The initials 'D.A.D.' also stood for: Director Armaments Division.)

The attempted raid on Norddeich was to cause further disappointment.

A choppy sea made it impossible to launch seaplanes. Three days later the Force set out again but were defeated by fog. The squadron set out once more on the 11th May, their third attempt, but lost two of their three machines and the pilot of one.

The scheme was beyond the technical capability available. Jim was back in Calshot from his North Sea activities with the Harwich Force in late May and the next letter he wrote to Emmie was an altogether different one, for in April he had become engaged to be married and the wedding was fixed for June.

He wrote from Calshot Naval Air Station on 26th May: '... if there is anyone wanting to give me anything so nice as a suitcase it would be very acceptable.

My wardrobe is fairly good, really. I am going to be married in frock coat and sword, not cocked hat and full dress as it is war time. Everyone is showering presents and good wishes, it makes me feel quite bashful.

I am absolutely full up with work ... all the same, things are going very well and I am getting my own way with most of my pet ideas. I really think my bombsight will be made at last....'

The work at Calshot: building, testing, instructing – and always the daily patrolling, continued.

In July, Jim had a chill and wrote home: '... luckily it has been blowing & raining so I have not missed much. ... Elsdon went up to the Admiralty last week and drove back a new Talbot car, but it is not a very good car, it is so badly finished. It goes fairly well....'

As CO of Calshot Jim was promoted to Squadron Commander. His work included lecturing on elementary engineering subjects, and testing and reporting on new types of seaplane. The more he worked, the more there was to do. He was only stopped, from time to time, by chills or heavy colds. He persevered with his sighter, convinced of the soundness of his idea. The original thought had been for a method of dropping signals, maps or messages quite as much as for dropping bombs, but, being war time, the bomb-dropping aspect was the only one on which it was taken seriously.

Walls (?Wallis) a 'bomb man', and Wimperis, had spent the first ten days of September, 1915, at Calshot, Walls staying with Jim and Nancy at Church Farm, Fawley, Wimperis putting up at The Falcon.

Admiral Vaughan-Lee, then Director of Air Services, came down to inspect at Calshot and stayed for three days. Calshot was a flying School, and Jim wrote home on October 15th: '... I have been doing a good lot of flying. We have a lot of Canadians here now, they are very good pilots with plenty of go....'

Jim wrote home on 7th November: 'I am making a sight here (at Calshot) but I have not lost all hope of the Admiralty having one made. It is very cold flying now and is either blowing or calm and foggy....'

In December of 1915 he was on the move again and again he was back to the East Coast where Commander J. C Porte, Royal Navy, CO of Felixstowe, had asked for him. 'Bigsworth is coming here,' Jim wrote home from Calshot, 'I don't know what my new job will be like. . . .'

Jim was appointed to Felixstowe on the 20th December. His new job was to investigate problems connected with the handling of seaplanes on ships. Soon, however, the work was to change. Jim was second-in-command to Porte: '. . . Porte is away for a week,' he wrote home a little while later, 'so I am in charge here . . .'

Commander Porte was a true pioneer and a man of great vision and courage. He had been flying, initially on gliders, since 1909. He had been invalided out of the Navy due to tuberculosis before the War and had gone out to the United States of America to work with the great American pioneer, Glenn Curtiss. Porte returned to England, and to the Navy, soon after the outbreak of War. It was he who had recommended the import of a number of Curtiss flying boats into this country. It was Murray Sueter who had supported and authorized the plan.

With the arrival of the Curtiss boats Jim's brief was now to assist Porte in their modification, improvement for local conditions and part re-design. It was work after Jim's heart. Ever since his early experiments at Eastchurch, his waterplane summer flying for Grahame-White or, more recently, the innovative flights on 'his' Sopwith batboat, he had felt that the role of the aeroplane in Naval aviation must be either amphibian or wholly waterborne. In Commander Porte there was a fellow enthusiast and a man who probably knew more about flying boat design at that time than anyone else in the British Isles. It was perhaps Jim who knew more about the practical difficulties of flying over the North Sea, in war time. The disasters of Cuxhaven and Norddeich had proved the appalling hazards of ship-borne aircraft: the flying boat was the thing and the larger the better. Porte asked Curtiss for a much larger boat than the H4 SMALL AMERICA and the H12, 4-(Curtiss) engined LARGE AMERICA was shipped over to England during the summer of 1916. Among the improvements which the Felixstowe team made to the Curtiss boats were the substitution of Rolls Royce 'Eagle' engines for the uncertain Curtiss engines; they also re-designed the hull and gave the boats increased armament. The boats, both LARGE AMERICA and SMALL AMERICA, were of course still essentially Curtiss boats.

There was also in 1916 and to a quite new design the F.1., Porte's own PORTE BABY, which was a very large boat indeed. The BABY was a three-engined machine, with two tractor and one pusher engines — (shades, there, of Jim's Triple Twin) – a crew of five, an all-up weight of 18,600 lbs and a wingspan of 124 ft.

The BABY was built by May, Harden & May of Southampton and Jim may well have been overseeing some work on her when he wrote home: '... I have been staying at Hamble all the week doing some tests and keeping an eye on a Woolston Southampton job at the same time ...' in April of 1916.

As a result of the improvements which Porte and his team were able to make to the Curtiss boats as well as the amount that was learnt during the design and building of the Porte Baby they now continued the series of their own, Felixstowe, designs. These boats were to become legendary and were to start a family of subsequent speci-fications which might be loosely compared, a generation or so later, to the land-aeroplane family of Comet/Mosquito/Dove from the de Havilland factory.

The second and possibly the most successful of the Felixstowe boats was the F.2a, which was a most splendid boat, with a wingspan of almost a hundred feet, an all-up weight of some 11,000 lbs and a forest of seven Lewis guns.

There were further members of the same family, notably the F.2b, F.2c, F.2d and the F.5. Many of the boats were built by Short Brothers, who had moved to Rochester in 1914, under Admiralty contract. Short's were to base their own boats on the classic Felixstowe lines in later years, – the Empire flying boats of the 1930's and the Short Sunderland's of the 1940's being direct descendants of the Felixstowe founding family.

The Official History of the Royal Air Force states that:

At the beginning of the year – 1916 – in conjunction with the formation of the Second Air Board, various changes also took place in the administration of the Naval Air Service. Amongst the more important was the appointment of the Director of Air Services to the Board of Admiralty as Fifth Sea Lord for air matters, and to represent naval interests on the Air Board. Rear-Admiral C. L. Vaughan-Lee, who had up til this time held the office of Director of Air

Services, was relieved by Commodore G. M. Paine, who, on 31st January, 1917, was appointed Fifth Sea Lord.

Further, as it had been decided by the Government that the supply of aircraft should be handed over by the Admiralty and War office to the Ministry of Munitions, the air staff at the Admiralty hitherto dealing with this work were transferred to that Department, the design staff being transferred to the Air Board.

From time to time, throughout the family letters during the latter part of the War, there was reference to Jim having 'gone to London' or 'gone to town' for a meeting of the Air Board. He was up and down to London throughout the war, using whatever transport was available. I have a scrap of a letter written in April, 1916, in which it was mentioned that 'Jim went up to town on Thursday to the selection committee and then down to Grain. . . .' He completed his journey that day by flying a Schneider around the coast from the Isle of Grain to Felixstowe. Almost all his war time journeys were made by train or by aeroplane. Occasionally, not always successfully, he attempted to travel by car.

Once more one must turn to the Official History of the Royal Air Force, not only for the information so concisely expressed but for the extraordinarily vivid way the situation in the North Sea and Britain's perilous position in 1917 is described:

> R.N.A.S. Home Waters . . . the year 1917 stands out as one of marked progress and achievement – a culminating period when the patient and often disheartening work of research and experiment of the two previous years was brought to fruition.
>
> . . . an outstanding feature of these air operations against the submarine was the success of the flying boats which, unaided by surface craft, destroyed no fewer than 5 hostile 'U' boats in the course of as many months. These boat seaplanes, the development of which had been carried on at Felixstowe under the direction of Commander J. C. Porte since the first days of the war. gave to the Navy, at a time when the life of Great Britain was being threatened, a craft capable not only of extended patrols over large areas of water, but also of rapid manoeuvre into an attacking position once a hostile submarine was sighted. The boats proved their value, too, against Zeppelins. Capable of flying across the North Sea from the bases at Yarmouth, Felixstowe and Killingholme, the flying boats were able to surprise and engage the Zeppelins in their own waters; during 1917 two hostile airships were shot down in flames and a third damaged by the flying boats.

Naval warfare had come a long way since Cuxhaven and Norddeich.

Jim flew throughout the war, most of his work being that of testing machines; in addition he went on the two raids across the North Sea already mentioned and survived them without worse harm than submersion in the cold waters of the North Sea. The only injury he suffered during the war was as a result of cranking a car – few of them then had self-starters – probably when attempting to return from Rochester, where Short's were now building on the Medway, – to Felixstowe. He was taken to the Royal Naval Hospital in Chatham. Emmie wrote to Alie at 32 Evelyn Mansions on the 27th April: 'Just heard ... that Jim has fractured his forearm and dislocated his wrist starting a car, on the 25th. In Chatham Hospital. Is it not sad for him? He will be wild. They have X-rayed it. Love to Grannie....'

He was wild, the more so when the doctors told him that he would not be able to use his arm for at least six weeks. For a pilot/ engineer/draughtsman his right arm was everything to him, as valuable as was his eyesight. By the 12th May Jim was fuming to get out of hospital, but they sensibly kept him there and began giving him massage. The arm set well and he made a good recovery and was soon back at work.

In June, 1917, Jim was appointed to the Air Department, Admiralty, to assist Wing Commander Sedden in the testing of new types of flying boats. On conclusion of this work he concentrated on work of a nature which had specially interested him since his earliest days at Eastchurch – that is, experiments with new wing sections. At Eastchurch in 1910 many of his experiments had been in the pursuit of the thick wing. They had at that time been unsuccessful, but much had been learnt meanwhile.

Although Jim's dream of all-metal machines of monocoque construction had not yet been realized in this country he continued to work towards it. The notion of the thick wing, with its inherent economy, was undoubtedly part of the overall vision. He assisted Commander Sedden for some months until, in the autumn of 1917, he was appointed to the Isle of Grain and given command of his own test flight.

'Congrats on getting Port Victoria,' wrote Charles from 84 Squadron, in France. Those five words said immeasurably more than the youthful phrase might suggest.

Congrats on getting Port Victoria.

Port Victoria was a small deep-water port, originally intended as a cross-Channel ferry port of major significance, with a good rail link to London Bridge. On another shore of the Isle of Grain lay the gentle slope of Allhallows sandy beach. The varied shoreline with both deep water and shallow water accommodated ship, flying boat, seaplane and amphibian with equal facility. Jim's work on Grain included the organization and standardization of testing methods. He also carried out a large number of tests on seaplanes and on aeroplanes for ship use.

The Isle of Grain was subsequently designated R N A S Test Depot and Jim was promoted to Wing Commander (E) R N A S on the 31st December. He was 34 years old. It was a busy and a happy time for him. Almost twenty years later, when Alie was building her own small house in the parish of Bredgar, she sited it on a rise of land in order to have a good Northerly view of the Isle of Grain: '... where Jim had his test flight and did so much work....'

In 1918 and while still at Grain he was elected an Associate Member of the Institute of Civil Engineers, being proposed by the following Members: L. A. Legros, D. S. Capper, John J. Thornycroft and B. Hopkinson.

He had long been a Member of The Royal Aeronautical Society and in 1918 he was elected Fellow of the Society, an honour which gave him much pleasure.

He was also awarded an O B E.

In 1920 *Aeronautics* Journal were to write a full-page appraisal of his work, classing him among the first twenty of the leading British aviators of the day.

Commander Porte, who had returned from the health-giving California sun to serve his country, died of tuberculosis before the Armistice.

As is well-known, The Royal Flying Corps and the Royal Naval Air Service were unified to become the Royal Air Force on the 1st April, 1918. Jim's rank was changed to that of Lt-Colonel, R A F and it was in that Rank that he lodged an application for a Patent on the following Provisional Specification on August 30th, 1918.

Improvements in Flying Boats.

I, James Lindsay Travers, Lieutenant-Colonel, R.A.F., of Central House, Kingsway, London, W.C. 2., do hereby declare the nature of this invention to be as follows:

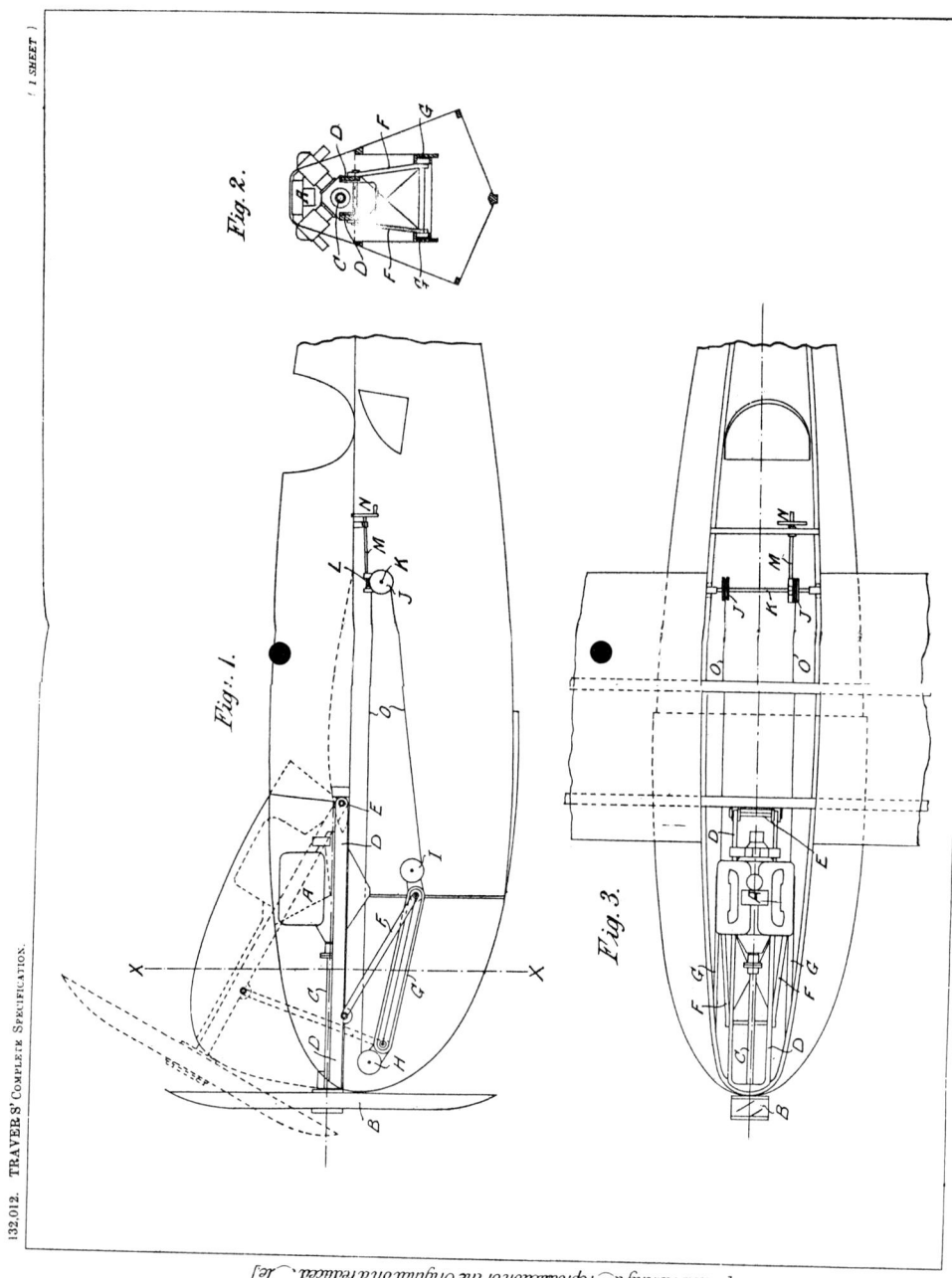

132,012.   TRAVERS' COMPLETE SPECIFICATION.

Fig. 2.

Fig. 1.

Fig. 3.

[This Drawing is a reproduction of the Original on a reduced scale]

Malby & Sons, Photo-Litho

Travers' Specification for Improvements to Flying Boats

This invention relates to improvements in flying boats having a tractor propellor, and the object of this invention is to mount the engine and propellor so that they are in the best position when the boat is in the air to give the maximum effect, whilst they are moved so that the propellor is above the water level when the boat is in the water.

According to this invention the engine and propellor are carried in a frame which is hinged to the boat so that the frame can be turned upwards when the boat is in the water. The frame may be moved in many ways, as for instance, by means of two links whose upper ends are pivoted to the frame whilst the lower ends run on guides or by means of racks and pinions.

The boat may have one or more planes.

Dated the 29th August, 1918.

The Complete Specification, (no 132, 012) and several line diagrams followed, the Complete Accepted on September 11th, 1919.

He was living in his London flat, 15, Bedford Gardens House, Campden Hill, W.8. when he made his next application on a Provisional Specification to the Patent Office. This time it was a joint effort, with Major Archibald Reith Low, R A F, of 22, Avondale Road, Croydon, the Provisional Specification being for

'Improvements in Instruments for Recording the Field of View or Fire from a Fixed Point. . . .' After the preamble it continued:

This invention relates to an instrument for recording by means of stereographic projection the field of view or fire from any fixed point on an aircraft or on any other appliance of which a number of nearly similar types are in use.

A plane table mounted on a known form of universal joint capable of being clamped in any position is arranged to receive and hold immovable a chart and is provided with a fixed arm of suitable length and curvature terminating in a fixed socket provided with ball bearings, the axis of the said socket in the simplest form of the instrument being in a line passing through the centre of the table and at right angles to it.

A rod is rotatably carried by the socket and is provided with two hinged connections one immediately above the socket and the other at a suitable distance below the socket in the direction of the table.

A sighting arm is hinged to the rod above the socket so that the hinge and the socket together form a universal joint. The sighting arm carries a sighting tube coaxial with it attached thereto by a socket joint so as to be rotatable about the common axis and capable of being clamped. The sighting tube is provided with cross wires at its outer end and near its inner end carries an adjustable internal mirror rotatable on an axis at right angles to the axis of the tube, the said mirror being marked with a central spot. The material of the tube is cut away to allow the observer by means of the mirror to see any object

(2 SHEETS)
SHEET 1.

135,631.　LOW & another's COMPLETE SPECIFICATION.

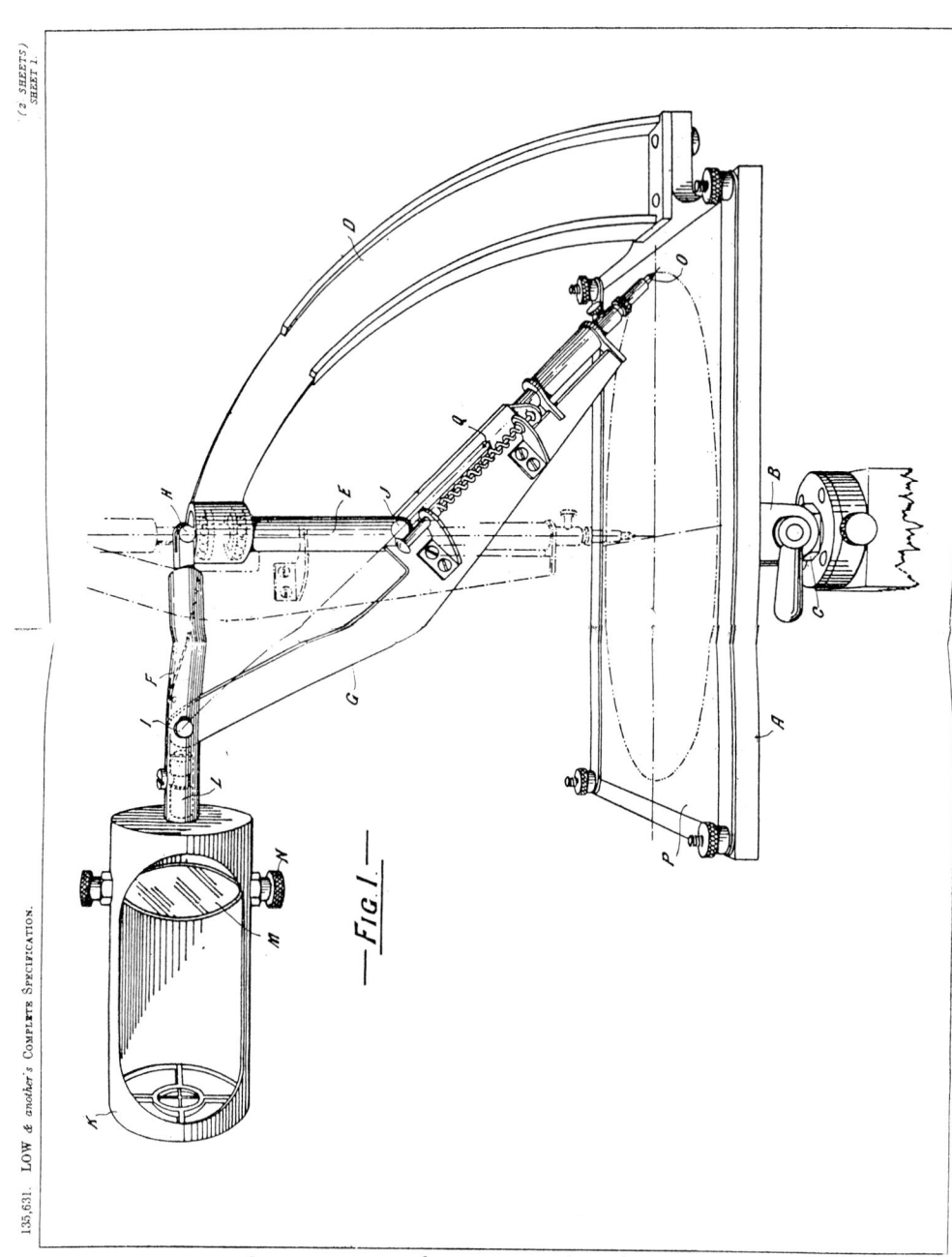

— Fig. 1. —

Malby & Sons, Photo-Litho.

Low & Another's Specification

[This Drawing is a reproduction of the Original on a reduced scale.]

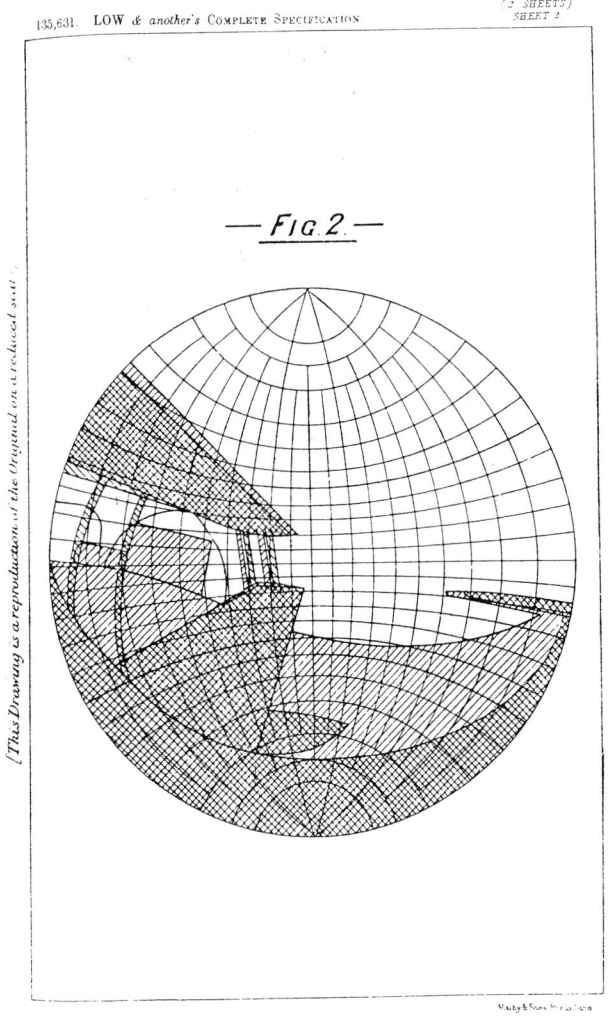

— FIG. 2. —

[This Drawing is a reproduction of the Original on a reduced scale.]

at a distance along the axis of the tube and to align it with the cross wires and the central spot.

A scribing arm is hinged to a suitable point on the sighting arm and is provided with a slot which slides on the hinge pin at the lower end of the rod before described. The scribing arm is provided with a spring mounted style operable at will. In using this arrangement the observer by means of the mirror causes the cross wires to follow an outline and in doing so describes a path on a sphere and a stereographic projection of the said path is produced on the chart. The chart will be a graph of the obstructions to view or fire from the point selected and may be compared with charts obtained in a similar manner from other aircraft or appliances.

Dated the 4th day of December, 1918.'

L. A. S.

Engineering experience subsequent to training.—Draughtsman under   1909
Lieutenant-Colonel Capper (M.), at the Balloon Factory, South Farn-
borough, chiefly working on wind balances for wind tunnel. Assistant to
Professor A. K. Huntington in aviation experiments at Eastchurch.

Private aviation experiments on rotary petrol motors having a single   1910
valve, and experiments on monoplane construction. Early flying experiments.

Took Aero-Club Certificate No. 86. Worked as Assistant and De-   1911
signer with Messrs. Short Bros., of Eastchurch, on aeroplanes and floating devices, and also on the first twin-engined aeroplanes. Experience in
flying seaplanes and night flying with the Graham White Company.

Joined the Naval Wing of the Royal Flying Corps; gained maximum   1912-1913
marks for theory in qualifying examination at Central Flying School,
November, 1912. Pioneer work in flying and testing seaplanes at Calshot.

Appointed Engineer Officer and Workshop Officer at Calshot. Early   1914
experiments in flying boats and night flying experiments. Promoted to
Flight Commander on outbreak of war, and appointed to Felixstowe on
Patrol duties.

Appointed in command of Calshot Air Station (Flying School), and   1915
promoted to Squadron Commander. Work included lecturing on elementary engineering subjects, and testing and reporting on new types of
seaplane.

Appointed to Felixstowe to investigate problems connected with   1916
handling of seaplanes on ships. Later assisted in experiments on large
flying boats under Commander Porte. In June appointed to Air Depart-   1917
ment, Admiralty, to assist Wing Commander Sedden to test new types
of flying boats. On conclusion of this, assisted in experiments with new
wing sections.

Appointed to Grain, in command of testing flight, afterwards Test   1917
Depot. The work has included the organisation and standardisation of

testing methods, and the carrying out of a large number of tests on seaplanes and aeroplanes for ship use.

Promoted to Wing Commander, Royal Naval Air Service, 31 Decem-   1917-1918
ber, 1917.

Extract from Jim's Candidature Notes

The Air Board/Air Council/Air Ministry found work for Jim including
his assistance with the plans for the formation of 'the Imperial Air
Service' and, according to H., some important experimental work at
Boscombe Down, but with peace came a rapid run-down of resources
and neglect of new ideas. Tired – but more than tired, dispirited – by the
waste of the fine aircraft factories which had been built up during the
war, Jim eventually left the Royal Air Force and found work abroad.

His time on the Pacific Coast will be described in a later chapter.

7

THE SPIDER WEB & OTHER PATROLS

1917–1919

Killingholme – the Spider Web – back to Dunkerque – No 11 Squadron –
Navigation School – London/Paris passenger route opened – London/Cologne
mail route opened

THE early part of H.'s second log-book shows an altogether different
view of the war than that which he had so far experienced. No longer
does he record scrapping with Albatros or Fokker, no longer does he
log patrols over those straight French roads around Cambrai,
Bapaume, Le Cateau or Albert, littered, as they were, with wrecked
materiel of war and dead horses. No longer does he fly in the piercing
cold of 18,000 ft., high above the embattled armies, in their trenches,
or clustered in the villages and farms of the ravaged countryside.

His work, for a few months when he was stationed at Killingholme
in 1917, was closer to that which one might imagine a naval pilot to
undertake, starting with his instruction on, or conversion to, seaplanes
and flying-boats.

Many R.N.A.S. pilots and crew flew a great many North Sea
'spider web' patrols; H. went out on comparatively few, but they were
logged, and as interesting in their contrast to Expeditionary Force
flying as they are in content.

The Spider Web was an idea of beautiful simplicity.

It was essentially an anti-submarine patrol and was centred on the
North Hinder Light, which enemy submarines were known to pass.
It was put into operation on the April 13th, 1917, and in the same
month it was also decided to use the Large America flying-boats from
Felixstowe, Yarmouth and Killingholme, for attacking hostile airships
while they were engaged on reconnaissance.

The Spider Web was an octagonal figure, sixty miles in diameter,
with eight radiating arms thirty sea miles in length and three sets of
circumferential lines joining the arms, ten, twenty and thirty miles out

from the centre. Eight sectors were then provided for patrol, and all kinds of combinations could be worked out.

Here are some extracts from H.'s log-book:

'20/7/17. Wind: N.E. SMALL AMERICA 1232 2 × 80 HP Anzani Killingholme Seaplane Station. Local. Instruction on seaplanes. Partial control.' His instructor was F.S.L. Vincent as 1st Pilot, H. as 2nd Pilot, Lt. Lees as Wireless Operator and A.M. Verrall as Engineer, took off on submarine patrol. H. noted 'partial control;' their course was Spurn Head Flamboro' Head out to sea – South to Inner Dousing.

On the following day, 21st July, F.S.L. Vincent gave H. further instruction on SMALL AMERICA 1232, flying locally, and H. made three landings, this time flying SMALL AMERICA 1234; On the 22nd July, in still air, he flew SMALL AMERICA 1234 with Lt Scott as 2nd Pilot and made some practise landings. On the 26th July, again in still air, and with Lt Scott as 2nd Pilot, he flew SMALL AMERICA 1232, 'taxying mostly.' He continued to practise, recording that on 7th August SMALL AMERICA 1232's engines were 'not running well.'

On the 13th August he had a new machine, SMALL AMERICA 1235. Remarks: 'Local. New machine. no pitot. gets off & handles well. 6 landings. good.' Later that day he flew as 2nd Pilot to Flt Cmdr Hards on H12 8669: 'Grimsby & return. Weather too thick for patrol.' He flew again the same day on H.12 8685 with Lt Scott as 2nd Pilot. On the 14th August, in still air, he flew Schneider Baby Sopwith locally for an hour solo. On the 16th, with Wind: W.4. he was 1st Pilot on H.12 8669 (2 × 275 Rolls) for a patrol of 3 hours 25 minutes. 'Spurn, Flamboro' out to sea, back to War Channel – Spurn.'

Later on the same day he flew as 2nd Pilot, with Flt Cmdr Hards as 1st Pilot, on H.12 8669 for an hour and 40 minutes. 'Kilnsea Flamboro Hd. and return. In search of wreckage from *Manchester Engineer*.'

On the 18th August, the Wind still W.4. he flew H.12 8685 with Lt Robertson as 2nd Pilot, locally. Remarks: 'attempted submarine patrol. Port engine not revving.'

On the 19th August with Wind: W.5. he flew H.12 8669 for three and three-quarter hours, with Lt Scott as 2nd Pilot, A.M. Bartlett as Wireless Operator/Observer and A.M. Verrall as Engineer. 'Spiders web off Flamboro' Submarine patrol.'

He made a number of other practise flights and on 27th August took off on H.12 8685 (2 × 275 Rolls) on a flight of 2 hours 25 minutes. F.S.L. Vincent was 2nd Pilot, P.O. Curtis 'as gunlayer' and Air

Mechanic Hawes was Engineer. Their course was: 'Spurn – Triangular off Flamboro 15 miles NE Flambro.' Remarks: 'Port engine revs dropped to 1250 dropped bombs "safe" just got to Killingholme. M.2. allowed us to drift in shore. Machine eventually got off with very little damage done.'

He was given a few days leave after this flight, probably only a long week-end leave; but he enjoyed himself as the whole family liked to do, by a visit to a London theatre and a meal. It sounds like a particularly happy party, with all available Travers pilots present.

Cousin Frank Travers, (that ass Frank) – now quite a sobersides and senior at 119 Cannon Street, wrote to Emmie:

... I heard from Ben and his wife of a meeting with most of your family at some eating-house – not so very long ago. Quite a festive meeting apparently ... And H. wrote home thanking his Mother: ... it must have been jolly to have seen everyone at home all at once. I can imagine that as more & yet more turned up you wondered where you would put us all.

Am very glad that Charles (who was among the London party) ... has had so much good practise on lots of types of modern scouts. It's the best thing that could possibly happen.

This is a funny out of the way place as regards people – but I never go off the station now. ...

H. flew on 3rd September, on H.12 8685, with Flt Cmdr Hards as 1st Pilot, and A.M.'s Bartlett and Hawes as crew. Course: 'Spurn, Flamboro, Scarboro', Whitby, Hexagon course 4 times & zigzag back to Scarboro. Remarks: Torpedoed ship in tow of destroyer. Flt Lt Pearse down on water near Witternsea.' The flight lasted 5 hours and 35 minutes.

Later the same day he flew SMALL AMERICA 1232 locally, with F.S.L. Alexander as 2nd Pilot. Remarks: 'Taxying unable to rise.' He made another practise flight on the following day, with the same 2nd Pilot and on the same machine, and on the 5th September he was out on H.12 8685 (2 × 275 Rolls), with F.S.L. Nightingale as 2nd Pilot and A.M.'s Hughes and Hawes as crew. Course: 'Spurn, Flamboro, Filey, Flamboro out, in Hornsea, out Spurn. Remarks: V. thick off Filey, no submarines. Sea smooth. Spent 45 minutes trying to pick up moorings.' The flight was of 3 hours and 40 minutes duration.

On the 7th September he was out on 8685 again, with F. S. L. Vincent as 2nd Pilot, out to Spurn. Remarks: 'Very thick. Aileron wire carried away at 500 ft. F. S. L. Vincent made a good save. Machine partly crashed.'

On the 10th he was out on H.12 8669 with F.S.L. Cutler as 2nd Pilot and A. M.'s Bartlett and Verrall as crew, flying for 3 hours and 25 minutes off Spurn, Flamboro' Scarboro' Hexagon to Flamboro' and Return. Remarks: 'Escort to special duty ships.'

He flew again on the 23rd September, again patrolling Spurn and Withernsea; then he flew some land machines on local test on the 24th and 28th and on the 28th flew as passenger in Porte Boat 9805 for an hour and a half, with Flt Lt Mackenzie as 1st Pilot. Remarks: 'Test & practice. Centre engine cut out.'

On the 1st October he took off on H.12 8669, with F. S. L. Madge as his 2nd Pilot and A. M.'s Bartlett and Kibble as crew. They were out for an hour and forty minutes. Remarks: 'Search for C.26 airship adrift. 25 miles S E from Spurn sighted wash 4 miles away made for it losing height and attacked from about 800/1,000 ft. observed ripple on surface & smooth patch behind. Climbed to 3,000 ft. returned home at dusk.'

It was an unconfirmed submarine kill. He saw no sign of C.26. On the 2nd and 3rd of October, by way of contrast, he tested Avro 9873 locally, taking up C.P.O. Johnson and A.M. Whiteheart respectively on two of the flights.

On the 5th and 6th of October he made a large number of short flights on B E 2c 9998 and Sopwith Pup N.6472, flipping about on various tests between Killingholme – top of the Wolds – Lincoln – Cranwell – Huntingdon (stop for lunch) – Chingford. From Chingford, on the 6th, he flew on to Brick House, Allhallows, Grain, where he was greeted in most hospitable fashion by Jim and Nancy. He continued on to Eastchurch, where he delivered 9998 to Eastchurch School & Gunnery Flight.

On the 8th October, with Wind: W.3. he flew Fowsey, (Fowler & Pizey Morane Shorthorn) 160 h.p. Renault from Eastchurch to Grain. On the 9th he flew a Clerget Nieuport 130 h.p. Clerget locally at Grain. Remarks: 'English Nieuport fin fitted. Machine not so sweet as old Nieuport with balanced rudder.'

*   *   *

Back at Killingholme, he flew an un-numbered Maurice Farman Longhorn 90–100 Curtiss locally. Remarks: 'Not a good specimen.' On the following day, 14th October, he was patrolling the North Sea again on H.12 8669, eventually landing at Bridlington as 'Gland in pump leaking.' He flew back to Killingholme in the evening.

It was during October, one Saturday, that he had the happy experience of going to Buckingham Palace and having the Distinguished Service Cross pinned on him by his King. It was the fourth time that he had seen the King during the War: when marching out of London with the H. A. C. in September, 1914; at the front with the H. A. C. in 1914; at Dunkerque in 1917; and formally, in his very best blue uniform – how H. hated to get out of his khaki! – at the Palace. It was little wonder that King George V was so much loved by his subjects. For it must have been apparent to many that he thought very highly of them and understood only too well many of their difficulties and dangers.

Grannie Gardner brought Emmie up to date: '... Saturday Charlie came for night met H. O. and Eastbourne friends at Palace. Wire came for H. O. from Felixstowe ... been identified ... for some one knew him to go down ... no one to go ... another urgent one from Eastbourne!! he got down there all right and came up last evening about 7 o'clock had another chat with Charlie who went off 8 o'clock last night for Waterloo parade 6.30 this morning. H. O. off for Eastchurch 9.20 train this morning. They fitted quite nicely in boxroom. H. O. has gone for course, guns or bombs. Eastbourne seems to have wanted to keep him instructing. It is very fine having them turn up ...'

H. made one more long patrol on 8669; the patrol, of two and three-quarter hours, was on 27th October.

He took F. S. L. Alexander as 2nd Pilot and A. M.'s Aird and Hawgood as crew. Wind, during the flight, veered and filled from W.3 to N. W.6. Their course was 'Spurn. Flamboro' out to sea back to Filey – Scarboro' Flamboro' Home. Cut home across Skeffling. Remarks: Clear off Flamboro'. very thick indeed on way home: until we got to the river where it improved somewhat.'

It was his last North Sea patrol.

Jim was right in thinking that H. was not really happy on anything except fast scouts.

From the 29th October to the 3rd November he was up many times each day on Clerget Nieuport (110 Clerget) 9250, with a succession of passengers, doing aerial gunnery practise locally. Then he was transferred back to Dunkerque. As he usually did, as they all usually did, he stayed overnight at the 'Command Post,' Grannie Gardner's flat, to collect his gear together before leaving for France. If there was any play or show of any kind on in London which he had not seen, then the pauses at 32 Evelyn Mansions afforded him the opportunity to make good such a deficiency. He saw Chu Chin Chow many times. Then, with affectionate farewells, he was off to France. His great-uncle, Henry Prescott, wrote to Emmie from Brantyngeshay on November 11th: '. . . Such a beautiful St Martins Day, though it don't feel exactly summerlike – the larches and birches are getting very bare – there's quite a soft carpet of larch spines in parts of the drive. I am so glad you made out your journey all right, though it was troublesome at the end. You must have enjoyed seeing Herbert but what a bustle! I can see it all, and your Mother hovering over it all. I am glad there is someone to whom your Mother can go in case of a raid, but I hope there may be no further need to want a shelter . . .'

H. flew locally at Dunkerque for a week or two, mostly on Camels, B E 2 C's and D H 4's. At the end of November he was given a short leave, perhaps of a week, to go down to Paris. He flew down on a B E 2 C on the 25th November, staying with Charles in his ½ hut, as already described, on his way down. He had a wonderful time in Paris; Spenser Grey took charge of him and guided him around the city, taking him to some interesting places; and in the evenings, Sassoon, (later Sir Philip) 'who knows lots of people in Paris,' he wrote home, 'took me in the evenings to some very jolly private houses . . .'

He wrote to Emmie again on 17th December, from Dunkerque:
. . . So glad to hear the dud Gotha went clear. It would have been funny if Dad had succeeded in bagging a Hun also.
I can quite imagine Dad with a Winchester and three Huns trotting along in front. So sorry you were without letters for a week or two. But I have not been flying much. Except down to Paris. The weather is becoming colder and I feel the need of my fur coat. Can you send it to me c/o Marine Parade, Dover? I enclose some English money as the postage may be high. . . . Could you put my skates inside? With their little screws. The weather will probably go cold and frankly, I

have little to do at the moment. An occasional odd job here and there ...'

He wrote to Emmie again on Christmas Day:

There are so many good things to thank you for. Firstly for the wrist strap which I shall only wear when I am likely to put a heavy strain on it in cold weather ... Secondly for sending the goat coat. It arrived on the 23rd mid-day & your letter inside was dated 21st – so it must have travelled quickly. Thirdly for my B's socks. The stockings I tried on first of all are excellent, the socks I haven't tried yet.

For ten days I have been put in charge of a camp of A.M.'s while the regular man is on leave. It is not supposed to be a stunt job but is quite interesting. My first experience as a C.O! They have had the day off to-day and a footer match in the morning.

Then dinner – mostly pork! – & another match (different team) against some French troops in the afternoon. It is snowing and blowing 30/40 mph to-night, quite an old-fashioned Christmas.

It must have been jolly seeing Charles.

Am afraid I shall not get any leave.

Have not applied for it as I had only just come back to France – also my trip to Paris made a great change and break ...

H.'s log-book entries, during the time he was at Dunkerque Command in early 1918, show that he flew a variety of aircraft, most of them locally, some of them to Dover, (it was a Joint Command); he flew mostly Camels, B E 2 C's and D H 4's, but on 3rd March 1918 he records flying; 'Boat. White & Thompson' for $2\frac{1}{2}$ hours. This would have been a White & Thompson Flying-Boat with 120 h.p. Beardmore engine; the duration of the flight suggests that he was making a submarine patrol, although it is not recorded as such.

Dunkerque seems to have kept him pretty busy, but it was activity that lacked the cohesion of belonging to a squadron. He was all over the place.

He must have been delighted to have been promoted Acting Squadron Commander and to have been posted once again to a Squadron, this time in Command.

Emmie wrote to Alie, still in the flat with her Grandmother, on 5th March 1918:

A telegram was brought to Dad and me while in church waiting for the funeral of Dame Swan. It was for Herbert to say he was appointed to a Squadron and to return at once and acknowledge to Dover – We told them to repeat (meaning to 32) & now I begin to think we did not give that address & they would have repeated to Dover I suppose. However I expect he had left for Dover so I hope it will be all right.

What a flip H. O. had to Martlesham in that gale.

Dr Greenish played the organ to-day.

He knows how to bring out the tone.

He wears a beautiful hood two points.

Do you remember what University

Cambridge Mus Bac is blue and sheepskin I think but the Mus Doc may be red and gold.

I could not make out what he played for recessional. it had clash of arms & trumpets in it ... Love to Grannie ...

H. had been posted to No 11 Squadron, in command. He was at the Depot at St Pol and at first flew only locally. On the 15th March he flew Capt Lambe, R. N. across to Dover R. N. Aerodrome from Petit Synthe. He noted: 'V. fast passage.' The flight took exactly 30 minutes. Later on the same day, still on DH D1751, he flew Capt Lambe from Dover: 'over Biggin Hill, Warlingham, Kenley etc. to Hendon.' Flying him back to St Pol on the same machine on the following day.

After that he made a succession of patrolling flights, up and down the French coast, until the 22nd March, 1918.

Then the line was drawn.

The Royal Naval Air Service came to an end.

On the 1st April, 1918, Naval Squadron No. 11 became No. 211 Squadron, Royal Air Force. Acting Flight Commander H. G. Travers became Major Travers, Royal Air Force. (Captain, temporary Major.) Inter-Service rivalry, that handicap to efficiency, was now officially abolished.

The idea was sound. Some of the inter-Service rivalry had been petty beyond belief. Even H., easy-going and tolerant to a fault, had had some slight experience of how childish some of it was. One instance being the matter of his khaki. Most of his R. N. A. S. colleagues wore khaki in France. It was the normal thing to wear. In addition, H. had been given, by his father, a pair of buckskin breeches half-an-inch thick, impervious to most of the weather and extremely comfortable. J. L. T. had had them made for his visits to Warwick Priory forty years earlier, to wear out hunting. 'They just match the local sand,' H. had written in delight. The R. F. C., when H. was at Vert Galand, objected to naval pilots wearing khaki. 'I will continue to wear it until ordered not to,' H. had written home; but the pettiness of worrying about such a matter, in that winter of all winters, when they were fighting for their lives and when the Navy was helping the Army so wholeheartedly, had seemed extraordinary. Now that sort of nonsense would be stopped forever. They would all be in the Royal Air Force, wearing the same uniform, under the same banner.

But of course it did not happen like that and some Squadrons were still, officially and very firmly, under Army control. It was really the only way to finish off the War.

All the naval air units were re-numbered, the squadrons from 201 onwards and the wings from 61 onwards.

The German spring offensive of 1918, which brought with it the tremendous step-up in all aerial, but particularly in bombing, activity, made it an exceptionally busy time for the pilots; the five squadrons, Nos. 205, 206, 207, 211 and 214, which comprised the 65th Wing at Dunkerque, were transferred to the command of the Field-Marshal Commanding-in-Chief, and formed the VII Brigade of the Royal Air Force.

Each Squadron had special responsibility: Nos. 204 and 213 were fighting squadrons; No. 217 was an anti-submarine squadron; No. 202 was a reconnaissance squadron under naval administration; No. 214 was a night bombing squadron under Army control and H.'s squadron, No. 211, was a day bombing squadron, also under Army control.

Not a minute was wasted.

At 6.15 a.m. on the 1st April, H. took off on DH9 D2782. Remarks: '*Bombed* Schudlebengz.' The name Le Mesurier is written above the line, which suggests that it was Le Mesurier who actually dropped the bombs.

Later on the same day, at mid-day, he flew Lt Powle, U.S. over to St M Capelle, delivering DH9 B7615 there. On the 2nd April, at 5.40 a.m. he took off on DH9 D2782, but the oil pipe broke and he made a forced landing. Subsequently Hoogstaede 'Bomb raid.' On the 3rd April he took off at 5.15 a.m. on DH9 B7614 and '*Bombed* Hun billets Westende.' On the 5th he flew a DH4, D1757: 'To beach at Gravelines; later the same day flying another DH9, B7598, from Gravelines to

Guines. He was kept very busy for the rest of April, mostly flying DH9's, bringing 'machines off beach,' flying Brig-Gen Lambe from Synthe to GHQ RAF, – and back again. He made his next bombing raid on the 22nd, on DH9 D2781 'Bombing Thourout.' He was testing, on DH9 B7620 on the 30th when he had a forced landing at St Pol, collecting the machine later the same day. He set out on the 1st May on an 'Attempted bombing raid.' But 'oil pipe broken.' But later the same day went on a bombing raid: 'camouflaged object in dunes.' He continued to fly many times each day, having, on the 6th May, the unpleasant experience of bursting a tyre while taxying. He made his next bombing raid, (his sixth,) on the 9th May, but the target was unspecified.

On the 20th May, he took off on DH9 B7581 at 9.50 p.m. Remarks: 'Test. night flying landing with white V's lights.' He continued to test and do weather tests for several days, brought a new machine over to No. 211 Sqdn, shewed the lines to a new pilot, (2nd Lt Dickins,) and on the 24th May, on DH9 B7603, flew: 'Spec. mission. bombs on (?)Slypering.by Howitzer.' The following morning, he reported after a weather test flight on the same machine: 'unsuitable for Bombing, will be better later.'

On the 26th May he reports: 'To locate missing machine. Le Mesurier. Landed on old Furnes 'drome and 'phoned A. A. Battery.' A couple of hours later, Le Mesurier now safe and sound, H. recorded: 'Return to Squadron.'

On the 28th May, again on B7603, he flew for 1 hour 40 minutes. Remarks: 'Bombing St Pierre Capelle. Landed at La Panne. La Panne to Petite Synthe.'

Then he handed over 211 Squadron to Major Loraine, D.S.O., M.C.

H. was posted to Home Establishment on the 29th May. This was, in fact, the Navigation & Bombing School at Stonehenge. One cannot help wondering if he was ever particularly keen on bombing. Navigation was his deepest and his abiding interest. He had located other missing machines, as well as Le Mesurier's, but does not ever appear to have lost his own way; it was as though, years and years earlier, as a schoolboy, he had developed his own latent sense of direction, which his father would have called 'an eye for a country.'

He seems to have bought a new pen, or a new bottle of ink, with which to write the next few pages of his log-book, for the writing has a strength and clarity not hitherto present. It is almost as though he is happier and more confident.

On the 15th June, with Wind: 33 mph he flew a D H9 from Stonehenge to Kenley, in 50 minutes: 'By compass course & watch. Exact.' He returned the same afternoon, with the Wind against him at 10 mph, in 1 hour 10 minutes. The course was by the same method and again exact.

The next day he flew locally on a Mono Sop. Pup, landing at C. F. S. Upavon. And at noon had his 'first flip' on a B E 2 E. Remarks: 'Head in bag. best time 7 mins without spin. bag flapped badly & set up period of vibration.'

On the 17th he flew a Maurice Farman Shorthorn for three-quarters of an hour: 'Local 3 landings hedge hopping & station name reading.' Flew a Pup again in the afternoon and at 10 p.m. that night, took off on a F E 2 B: 'Night flying & landing. by landing l. & ground control & Holt flares.' He made two flights that night, of 25 and of 50 minutes respectively.

He did not fly on the 18th June and on the 19th was posted to the Gunnery Experimental Station at Orfordness.

Although his flying time at Stonehenge School of Navigation had been only 6 hours and 10 minutes it had been an excellent start to the 'head-in-bag' or blind-flying which was to become the pre-requisite for so much later navigational instruction. He called at Warlingham before leaving for Orfordness.

Emmie wrote to Alie '... on Saturday Herbert paid a "flying" visit for some gear. He landed at Kenley & came over to lunch & was fetched by a Service car with a nice young lady chauffeuse. I gave her a cup of tea but she was terrified lest the Major shld find her gone. ...'

H. caught a train to Orfordness, a fact which he thought sufficiently unusual to record in his log-book.

He flew a D H9 F I A T on the 20th, on a local 'compass trip,' and at 3 o'clock on the same day flew R. T. 1 on a 50-minute cross country by 2 point system. 'error 1 in 22 m.' At 4.20 p.m. he flew a 'small A. W.' for 10 minutes local practise. (Armstrong Whitworth).

On the 21st he flew R. T. 1 for 20 minutes. 'Attempted X-country by A. A. Signals mistaken. wash out.' In the afternoon he flew a B E 2 E for an hour and twenty minutes. 'Head in bag practice. 10 minute spells. improving.' And at 5.30 on the same day was given 40 minutes instruction by Lt Bousfield on a small A.W. On the 22nd he flew R.T.1 for a cross country of an hour and a half. 'Cross country by 2 point. error $1\frac{1}{2}$ in 25 miles.'

On the 23rd he flew, with Lt Bousfield as passenger, on a cross country of 2 hours 10 minutes. 'x country to Sudbury by A A burst above clouds. error 1 in 25.' On the 24th, on the same machine but with Lt Thompson as passenger, 'x country to Newmarket by 2 point. very bumpy. error 1 in 50.' On the 25th, on a B E 2 E, he flew for 35 minutes: 'x country Hadleigh. Head in bag by 2 point. 1 m. short. line O K.' And on the afternoon of the same day made a 50 minute flight on the same machine, when he returned to Orfordness: 'x country to Orfordness. Head in bag by 2 point. both O K.'

On the 26th, he flew R.T.1 for an hour and twenty minutes: 'Cloud penetration. A A burst above clouds. Wireless jambed by ship.'

On the afternoon of the same day he flew a Bristol Bullet (80 Le Rhone) for the first time, a flight of 25 minutes, locally. 'Too big for machine.'

On the 29th June he flew a D H 9 (240 b.h.p.) on a compass course from Orfordness to Hendon, a flight of 1 hour 50 minutes. 'Came down thro clouds at Elstree when on correct course. Inside compass melted & became too thick to read.' He called on Jim at 'the office' before returning, at 8 p.m. in the evening, to Orfordness. He clipped forty minutes off the return flight.

Emmie to Alie: 'Jim has had another sharp go of flue but had been to the office yesterday ... Herbert had just been in. He had flown from Orfordness, Suffolk to Hendon and was flying on to Winchester yesterday evening for his new job. ....' The 'office' was the Air Board. Thus and thus were the sisters kept informed of their brothers' whereabouts, plans and state of health.

When Emmie wrote 'Winchester' she meant, of course, 'Worthy Down,' where H. reported 'to A.I.C.N.S.' He had flown a B E 2 E from Orfordness to Hendon to Worthy Down, total flying time 4 hours and 15 minutes, and he continued to fly the same machine locally; then to C.F.S. and back, (at Upavon,) then to 'Stonehenge. Hedge hopping.'

On the 2nd July, with Lt Villiers as passenger, he flew D H 9 E.609, from Worthy Down to Orfordness 'above clouds,' a flight of two and a half hours. On arrival he went for a thirty minute flight on an Arab Bristol (220 Arab) 'Local Orfordness – Very nice machine.' Later again the same day he flew D H 9 E 6 o 9 from Orfordness to Hendon 'above clouds', clipping fifty-five minutes off the journey, when completed, to Winchester.

His official list of postings record that he was at the Air Ministry from June 13th, 1918, which suggests that the flying which he and his colleagues did at Orfordness, Hendon and Worthy Down still had an element of research within the practice.

On the 6th July he flew D H 9 E 6 o 8, again with Lt Villiers as passenger, from Winchester to Hendon. 'To Air Ministry.' He may well have been making a report to them. He flew back in the afternoon, first of all 'to Stonehenge (to find Gribble)' and thence to Winchester. On the 8th July he flew a Bristol Fighter for 30 minutes. 'Local. First flip on B. F.'

On the 9th July he flew D H 9 E 6 o 8, with Lt Peacock as passenger, on a flight of 1 hour 45 minutes duration. 'Worthy Down to Southrey Lines. 150 miles. compass course.' And a further flight of 20 minutes: 'Southrey to Cranwell. – Radiator burst on landing.'

On the 11th July he flew a Pup from Cranwell to Freiston 'To see Kirby & Fall. very bumpy.' He returned a few minutes later 'Freiston to Cranwell return. Rain. no windscreen.' Later the same day he flew the D H 9 E 6 o 8, again with Lt Peacock as passenger: 'Cranwell to Worthy Down. 7 miles Ermine Street for 2 point above clouds. O. K.'

For the ensuing fortnight he flew a B E 2 E on local and on short flights too numerous to mention in detail; amongst the flights were several local Worthy Down flights with American Army personnel as passengers; a local Worthy Down flight 'landing – carb. full of water.' 'Worthy Down to Hendon. thick haze near London.' 'Hendon to Farnboro. Rain.' 'Farnboro to Worthy Down. Very heavy rain. Hit wing tip landing.' 'Worthy Down to C. F. S. Upavon.' 'C. F. S. Upavon to Bournemouth. Bournemouth to Worthy Down.' 'Worthy Down to Hendon.' 'Hendon to Worthy Down.'

On the 31st July he made six flights on D H 9 6 o 8, with Major Kingsley as passenger on the first four flights: 'Worthy Down to Old Sarum. Old Sarum to Netheravon. Netheravon to Worthy Down. Worthy Down to Hendon. arrived after dark.' He then concluded the day's flying with a flight which must surely have given him very great pleasure. Still on 608, he had as his passenger 'Lt Col Travers' on two

25 minute flights, from 'Hendon to Kenley' and from 'Kenley to Hendon.'

One can imagine the brothers talking far into the night after their return to Hendon, comparing notes, and, as usual, exchanging a few 'A.1. ideas,' on how flying, or in H.'s case, perhaps navigation, could be improved. On the 1st August H. flew Major Kingsley back to Worthy Down, and after making some solo flights on a B E 2 C the following day, he collapsed with influenza. It was the dreadful 'flu which raged, in varying forms, for more than a year.

H. was 'down with influenza' for a fortnight and on his return to Worthy Down, on the 15th August, resumed his many cross country flights, on Avro 2924, D H 9 608, B E 2 E 8820 and B E 2 C 9966, flying to Orfordness on the last-mentioned machine on 31st August.

For page after page after page the record of his cross country flights continued, and the ever-changing names in the passenger column suggest that many of his 'passengers' were, in fact, some of the first of his cross country pupils.

On the 3rd September he flew from Orfordness to Worthy Down, via Martlesham, where he landed and Chingford, where he also landed; on the following day he flew to C. F. S. and in the afternoon, with 2/A M Hudson as passenger, flew 'To Warlingham landed behind Jarvis Farm'.

Emmie wrote to Alie:

... We really have quite a lot of excitement. I was beginning to write – about 4 o'clock – and heard a quick step in walked H. O. by the garden – landed in King's field by Ridley Rd. – B E 2 C mechanic guarding it from a crowd of small children. So Dad and I went to have a look. Then came back for tea I sent some to the mechanic by Sales. Then we went back, H. O. bringing a Shot Gun he wanted. Quite a crowd by this time but they cleared off to the fence, only Sales in his glory assisting.

They turned the Propellor turned the machine round facing the village, (it was at this end). Then the mechanic climbed in, took out the clutch, and she taxied to nearly the end of the field. 'She won't rise, she'll come down again.' 'She's rising, she'll strike the telegraph wires, no she's just turned' very slowly she rose and circled and came down lower and banked – then rose again took a wider circle looping as she came over and went off ... On Saturday Jim was going to fly to Charles from Hendon on an Avro with a dicky engine. On Sunday he had not come back and (we) heard he had come down with engine trouble at Newbury. On Monday morning a telegram from Jim from Marlboro' that he would not be home that day. But he got to London Monday mid-day. It seemed Charles had flown over from C. F. S. and salved him at Newbury but I don't know any more. ...

H. flew mostly B E 2 E 9966, D H 9 E608 or Sopwith Pup C431. Some of the flights, some of the aeroplanes, and sometimes even the passengers, as well, were out of the ordinary and one is at a slight disadvantage, for a moment, on reading that he flew E608 from Worthy Down to Martlesham, on 24th September: 'To fetch Col Blount's Pup,' until one realizes that the capital P was by habit and that the flight had been, not to collect a privately-owned Sopwith, but to fetch Colonel Blount's young dog. The fact that H. took 1 hour 20 minutes for the flight to Martlesham and 2 hours 15 minutes for the return to Worthy Down, was probably because the return journey was against a rough head wind; but the slowness of the return journey may also have been partly because the youngster was, as H. P. Gardner liked puppies to be, – 'not altogether obedient.'

On another occasion, although nothing to the effect was recorded in H.'s log-book, he had a forced landing near Newbury. Emmie reported to Alie, in a letter of Oct. 13: '... Herbert brought a pheasant which looks nice cold. He had a forced landing near Newbury and was welcomed for the night by Lord and Lady xxxxxxx– very pleasant people ... I caught the 6 o'clock when Harriette came & I found H. O. here. I think he had not meant to stop the night but waited to see me – Sales said he cut his Didos over the house which I missed but saw him next morning but it was getting thick. I had only just time to scramble out of the bedroom window onto the ledge – as I was upstairs. He says Charles is very fit. ...'

In October H. did a certain amount of night flying. It was a good month for night flying, 'the dinner party season,' Jane Austen called it, when you could travel by the light of the moon. On the night of 27th October he made a night cross country flight 'To Andover & return.'

*   *   *

In early November he had two forced landings, the first with a Pup C431, the second with a DH9, H.4237, but that same day, 9th November, flew Gen Groves to Hendon on a Bristol Fighter and that same night made a $2\frac{1}{2}$ hour cross country night flight on BE2C 9966.

After the Armistice on 11th November the Allied Armies in Europe became the Army of Occupation.

The Peace Conference took place in Paris and it was decided to open air routes between London and Paris to enable members of HM Government to attend the Peace Conference, also so that the Headquarters Staff of the Air Ministry could travel back and forth quickly.

H. had been given the job of scouting the various routes. He seems to have been particularly fond of BE2C 9966 and he flew 9966 daily over possible routes until 30th November. No. 1 (Communication) Squadron (86th Communication Wing) was established at Hendon, with a detachment in Paris, but with the increase of passengers and mails to be carried a second squadron, No. 2 (Communication) Squadron was later formed at Buc and No. 1 Squadron was then moved from Hendon to Kenley.

The following excerpt is from AIR/1/162 PRO Kew: '... In all 934 passengers, excluding crew, and 1,028 mailbags or despatches have been carried in 744 trips over the route since the commencement of the service up to the end of August last. It will be noticed therefore that the nature of the service differed largely from that carried out on the Folkestone–Cologne route, as on the latter service practically all the flights were made for mail carrying purposes only ...'

It was not only the cargo that differed between the London–Paris and the Folkestone–Cologne routes. There was a marked difference in the accident rate.

On February 3rd, 1919, H. was transferred to GHQ St Andre, as Navigating Officer I/C Postal Squadrons, and in that capacity soon arranged for Weather Stations to be set up en route between Folkestone and Cologne. The Weather Stations, which now seem so common-sense, were innovative at the time; they were remembered and referred to many years later by 'Peterborough' in his column in *The Daily Telegraph*. 'Peterborough was always kind to me,' H. said.

Quite as important as his Weather Stations was H.'s decision – very much a pilot's decision – to schedule the air departures shortly before the scheduled steamship/train departures, thus releasing pilots from the pressure to – perhaps – make a flight against their own better judgment, (bad weather or any other reason), for if a pilot preferred not to take off the mails would not be held up but would proceed by the surface route. Admittedly the statistics show that the London–Paris route operated from late November, 1918, until August, 1919, and the Folkestone–Cologne service only from March 1st, 1919, until late August, 1919, so that the longer duration of the London–Paris service alters the comparison as well as the fact that the service covered all the winter months; but both services were operating in March and April and the weather in April was particularly bad.

There were five accidents on the London–Paris route, as follows:

1. 1 pilot was killed and a passenger injured when a machine was caught in a sudden squall of hail and wind and crashed on the roof of a building.
2. 1 pilot and 1 passenger were killed when a machine came down in the Channel owing to bad weather.
3. 1 pilot was killed owing to complete engine failure immediately after taking off. The passenger in this instance escaped uninjured.
4. 1 pilot and a passenger were injured in a forced landing owing to weather.
5. 1 pilot was slightly injured in a forced landing owing to engine trouble.

The above details were taken from AIR/1/162 PRO Kew. Their Air Historical Branch Report described the Folkestone–Cologne service as follows:

The through service from Hawkinge to Cologne commenced on the 1st March 1919, and was carried out by three squadrons, one at Folkestone, one at Maisoncelle and one at Cologne. The squadron at Maisoncelle was removed at the end of June to Marquise in order that it should be in a more direct line between Folkestone and Cologne. Neither Maisoncelle nor Marquise can be regarded as half-way stages, as both these places are considerably nearer Folkestone than Cologne, the average time of the trip between Folkestone and Maisoncelle being one hour and between Maisoncelle and Cologne two hours and a quarter. Marquise is even nearer to Folkestone.

The return cross-Channel service from Cologne to Folkestone commenced on the 18th March. The mail service had therefore been running both ways for nearly six months when the aerial mail service was discontinued at the end of August.

Newton & (H.G.) Travers at
Marquise, abt 7/6/19. Polishing the
goggles

The usual procedure was for pilots to fly over one of the stages i.e. Hawkinge
to Maisoncelle (67 miles) or Maisoncelle to Cologne (229 miles). Success was
however obtained in a number of non-stop trial flights between Hawkinge
and Cologne (250 miles) and squadrons were accordingly instructed that all
through flights could be undertaken at any time at the discretion of the pilots
themselves. Many successful through trips were subsequently completed and
in the latter part of July the intermediate station at Marquise was abolished. As
mentioned above, the intermediate station had been shifted from Maisoncelle to
Marquise at the end of June . . .

Types of machine used:

Nos. 18 and 110 Squadrons were each equipped with 18 DH9A machines
fitted with Liberty engines. No. 120 Squadron principally used DH9 machines
fitted with Puma engines, but a few flights were made on DH4 machines fitted
with R.R.6 engines . . .

A very marked feature of the Folkestone to Cologne service is the extremely
small number of casualties to the flying personnel engaged. During the six
months under review 1,842 trips were made, the total flying time being about
3,000 hours: the casualties to personnel recorded were one pilot and one
passenger injured in the same accident.

Sometime in the early summer of 1919, somewhere in France, H. was struggling to crank his car. Not, I think, his own car, but a car that he was permitted to use by somebody at St Andre. He was having some difficulty, as he always did, for his right arm was a dull stick and the wrist not flexible, as they are supposed to be. Straightening his back and then stooping once more to seize the starting handle, he heard a voice call to ask whether he wanted any help, and turning, saw a slim, dark girl, leaning out of the driver's window of a Red Cross ambulance. Thus they met.

The Royal Air Force offered him, in due course, a Short Service Commission. In later years he may have wondered why he had turned such an offer down. But at the time his decision seemed to them both sensible. They were both weary, war-weary – more exhausted, I suspect, than either of them knew at the time; it was not the time to make such a vitally important decision.

He would really have liked to continue flying.

She had other plans.

BOOK TWO

For war either hardens or softens. It never leaves a man as it found him.
                H. Seton Merriman: *Barlasch of The Guard.*

8

THE PACIFIC COAST

1920 – 1923

H & H. emigrate to Canada – Jim to the Air Ministry in charge of Technical Information – Jim to Chile as Technical Adviser to Chilean Naval Air Service – Valparaiso – Quintero – Coquimbo – expedition to the South – Jim's plans for large all-metal flying-boat – homeward bound.

J. L. T. had aged a great deal during the four years of war. Perhaps if he had succeeded in 'bagging a Hun' he might have felt that he had been of some use to his country, but 'the dud Gotha went clear' and J. L. T. had returned indoors, frustrated, and had put his Winchester away against another opportunity. It was not only the feeling of not being a lot of use but the sheer muddle of war-time life which had aggravated and annoyed him. During the war his house was no longer the comfortable, well-ordered place it had once been. All routine had been quite blown away. Emmie had been out at odd hours and at short notice, attending meetings or trudging about, seeing people. When at home, she was writing notes and letters constantly. Warlingham had changed, too, and there was talk of a regular omnibus service from London, another possible source of irritation to J. L. T. He and Emmie decided to leave Horton, a house which they might both have liked much more had it not stood next-door to Woottonga, the house which they had both loved.

J. L. T. was confident of Jim or H. being associated with Grain or Eastchurch in the future, so he and Emmie decided to move into East Kent, settling eventually and after much house-hunting in the small village of Bredgar, South of Sittingbourne.

The family moved to Bredgar House in May, 1919, when the village – such a small village in those days – swam in a perfect blizzard of fruit blossom. The one pony remaining at Warlingham was driven over in her trap, Alie at the reins. *Daisy* had pulled the lawn-mower at Horton and, leather-shod for the work, continued to pull the lawn-mower at Bredgar House for many more summers.

They settled in comfortably, Alie now remaining at home, for Grannie Gardner had lately died.

Grannie Gardner had not been ill, or scarcely so, just tired. Alie had gone to the Army & Navy Stores on some errand, leaving the old lady sitting in an armchair, reading. When Alie returned she had at first thought her Grandmother only asleep, for her book rested on her lap.

Jay used to say that she thought Grannie Gardner had died of boredom, now that her grandsons no longer blew in to see her so often – to 'have a doss', to look up Bradshaw or to leave their gear – those war-time visits which had held all the uncertainty, excitement and sniff of danger and on which Grannie Gardner had thrived.

A page had been turned and a new chapter was started.

As for Bredgar House being near Sheppey or Grain – neither Jim nor H. were ever stationed at either Air Station again.

H. married Hermia Fraser on the 6th August 1919. She was the younger of Lt. Col. and Mrs Fraser's two daughters and described herself always as 'a cosmopolitan Scot' – for although born in Dumfriesshire had spent most of her childhood in Switzerland until, her father retiring from the Indian Political Service, (he had been the first British Resident at Leh, in Ladahki Province) – the Fraser family settled in Shropshire. She was a talented girl, a gifted linguist and musician, an excellent shot with a rifle, a fine horsewoman and a good swimmer, altogether a girl to be reckoned with. But the war had changed her as it changed everyone it touched. She had, early in the war, gone to work in a shell-filling factory, soon being put in charge of a shed of twenty girls. It was dirty, poisonous work. The picric acid affected the complexion. Much worse, it affected the liver. Nobody was truly well for the rest of their lives who had worked in such places. From then on Hermia suffered bouts of jaundice, frequently severe, for the rest of her life.

After severe illness in the winter of 1915-16, – jaundice, measles and complications – she was told to do no work of any kind for six months. During convalescence she stayed with her life-long friend, Sibell Cromartie, at Tarbat, and while there Colonel Blunt-Mackenzie, Lady Cromartie's husband, taught her to drive a car. She learnt on the 'Chinese' Rolls Royce, a magnificent car, and then came South again, enrolled in the Oxfordshire 22 Detachment of the Red Cross and, on her dress allowance, took herself off to France as an ambulance driver.

After she and H. married they lived in Camden Town for some months. He had been demobilized on the 23rd August and their plans were, to say the least, uncertain. They were weary of everything to do with the Great War. They had both lost countless numbers of friends and several cousins. They were tired of Europe, tired of England, tired of Scotland – even. Old Scotland – particularly Invernesshire where Hermia had spent long summers with her father's Fraser-Tytler cousins – old Scotland, civilized, leisured and magical, had gone for good. But across the Atlantic lay Nova Scotia.

They decided to emigrate.

They had no plan, and certainly no contract, in Nova Scotia. Yet they were not aware of being particularly rash, for they knew that in the event of being unable to find an opening in Nova Scotia Hermia's numerous Bell-Irving cousins in British Columbia would always 'find them something to do.'

They remained in Nova Scotia for a matter of weeks only.

They could find nothing. The memory of the beauty of the place remained with my Mother for the rest of her days: 'Oh – those Nova Scotia houses!' she would say, for the proportions, the colours, the gingerbreading, all delighted her. She longed to stay there, but there was nothing, nothing.

They headed Westwards arriving in British Columbia in the middle of the deepest depression that that Province has probably ever known. A friend has recently told me that he knew of someone who, being lucky enough to have a job in a jobless city, kept a pair of gaping, cracked shoes, the uppers almost separate from the sole, with which to slop along from home to the office and back again in the evening and in order not to be importuned, poor as he was, by some old friend now quite destitute.

At first they settled on Vancouver Island and their first child, Daphne, was born there on 30th May. There were difficulties with her feeding from the start and she did not thrive: 'nearly dying as a baby,' – but she was a brave little soul and a great fighter. In spite of all manner of infant ailments and severe glandular disease she battled on and survived.

The Bell-Irvings were experiencing many difficulties themselves, the casualties amongst them had been heavy and they had their own wounded and limbless to care for; they had no very inspiring job to offer, although H. was employed by them for a few months, when he worked as a lumberman up at Powell River. Then H. bought land on Point Grey and built some excellent houses there on spec.

We lived in one, on Collingwood Street, where I was born. He had designed and was building another, for his father-in-law, when he and Hermia heard that her Mother had died and that her father was now ill.

It was doubly unfortunate that he had just put every spare dollar of capital into a saw-mill for the word soon went round that he was thinking of returning to England.

He was to lose very heavily on the saw-mill.

1920 started well for Jim.

He had remained in London, at 32 Evelyn Mansions, in order to be at the hub of things and in a position to hear and apply for any interesting job that might be going. In late January he was lucky and wrote to Emmie describing his new job on the 31st January:

I have just heard that I have got a job in the Civil Aviation Dept of the Air Ministry.

I shall be in charge of Technical Information, it is a very interesting job.

I make a start on Monday.

I am very pleased about it as there was lots of competition for the post and there was no question of influence. – I answered an advertisement for an engineer with certain qualifications and I believe that they had hundreds of applicants …We did not come down this week end because I was expecting to hear about this job.…'

They moved to 15 Bedford Gardens House, a flat which they were all to use, especially Charles, for some years. Jim's job was varied and, as he had written, interesting, taking him all over the place: to Brooklands in June, to Antwerp for a week at the end of July, representing the Civil Aviation Dept of the Air Ministry, to Martlesham in September to judge various flying competitions. But he was restless and, one suspects, missing his flying and in particular, his flying-boats.

He began to cast about for some less office-oriented job. In early 1921 various interesting jobs were on offer. Trinidad. Chile. Both countries where the sea and the sky met and where flying-boats might come into their own.

In the event Chichester Smith took the Trinidad job and Jim closed with the Chileans.

His resignation from the Air Ministry was accepted from 28th February, 1921, and he entered the employ of the Chilean Government in early March, his designation being that of 'Technical Adviser' and his brief being to organize, train and expand their own Naval Air Service.

He sailed in RMS *Ortega*, Nancy accompanying him. They made a slow voyage out, through Panama and down the Pacific Coast. There was a man on board who worked for Cousin Tim Baily's firm in Lima; there were other friends of friends on board, too, who helped to pass the hours and the days as the old *Ortega* made her slow, slow way down past the barren coast of Equador to Callao and then on down the coast to Valparaiso.

Although Chilean society was then somewhat polyglot it was strongly pro-British and pro-American. Commercial activity helped to foster such feelings; for example - Pearson's had the contracts for the new harbour at Valparaiso, a tremendous amount of work.

There was, for Jim, the encouraging presence of a British flying instructor, Major Scott, who, with two other British flying instructors to assist him, was in charge of tuition at the Army Flying School near Santiago.

There were comfortable Pullman cars on the American-built railway system and everywhere, wherever there was any road or any track resembling a road, there was the ubiquitous Ford car.

The Chileans gave Jim the rank of Captain in their Navy and he wore his old R N A S uniform with amended stripes.

Chile delighted them: from the clean, wide streets of Santiago to the bustle of the crowded suburbs and the variety of transport all around: high covered carts drawn by yoked oxen, Ford cars – driven at reckless speed over the rocks and potholes of the minor roads – donkeys, llamas and everywhere people 'darting about on skinny little ponies.'

They took the train from Santiago to Valparaiso and all down their $9\frac{1}{2}$ hour journey they saw, not far inland, the beautiful snow-capped peaks of the Cordilleras.

In Valparaiso they moved into an Hotel.

Jim and other N. O.'s in Chile

Jim began his service to the country diplomatically. On the day of the fiesta, 21st May, which commemorated the anniversary of the Battle of Iquiqui and the death of Admiral Prat, (who was to Chile as Nelson was to England,) Jim flew over the monument to Admiral Prat and dropped flowers at the Admiral's feet. It was a popular action, much liked by the crowds assembled at the nearby Altar for a High Mass.

Captain von Schroeders was appointed aide-de-camp to Jim. He was most helpful. He was a man of good nature but of deep moods, – deeply cheerful or deeply gloomy; but always a friend.

At the sheds at Valparaiso, things moved as they had done in the past; if the men needed spare parts, they took them from an existing complete machine. For instance, all visible screws were removed from the flying boat, because the men wanted them in order to erect the

Avros and Shorts. Such expediences of action were changed eventually.

Jim to Charles on June 14th:

Thank you for your letter written from the C. F. S. – You must have enjoyed getting into the air again and I don't suppose the work suffered very much - (Charles had by this time enrolled as a Matriculated student, probably War-Service Matriculation – in the Engineering Faculty of King's College London) – 'and you will now be back at Maths and Physics with renewed energy. I hope you had a good time at Howden – I saw Maitland at the Air Ministry a little before I left - he is a good chap and a great enthusiast on airships.

When I arrived in Valparaiso I reported to the Naval Authorities and later on went to Santiago (the capital) and stayed with Major Scott, who runs the training at el Bosque the aerodrome. They have a scheme on paper in which the Naval Flying comes under the Chief of the Inspeccion at Santiago. At present this C of I is a rather cheery general under Scott's thumb. He knows nothing and cares less for Naval Aviation

Scott has his hands full with his training (Gosport system). So nothing has been done on the Naval side. The Head of the Navy the Director General of the Armada is a dear old Admiral who hates anything new and dosen't want to be troubled with aviation. However, unless I can get some of the senior Naval people to support me I shan't be able to do much. The junior officers are quite enthusiastic about it.

We have got quite a nice little house in the residential suburb in a quiet street. We found the Hotel in Valparaiso so very noisy with the trams and cars all night beside being very stuffy . . . I catch a train at 8.50 which gets to the office at 9.15. After looking at anything important in the office I get into a sidecar and am transported at a furious speed over an atrocious road to the 'Base des Hydriaviones de los Torpederos' otherwise a ramshackle, leaky corrugated iron shed with earthen floor and no illumination, in which are being erected the seaplanes presented to Chile by Great Britain in 1918. – It is a matter of considerable difficulty. – Moreover, when erected it is a hazardous business to launch them and to get off near the sheds owing to the big swell which almost always exists there. So we have to taxi into shallow water some three-quarters of a mile away.

Every morning I lecture the Officers on Theory of Flight and inspire them to further efforts in the erection and preparation of the machines. I have not started instruction yet because the authorities have not yet sanctioned the purchase of a motor-boat which I consider essential for safety. I catch the 12 o'clock train back for lunch and return to the office by 2 o'clock when I devote the afternoon to visiting Admirals, sending urgent telegrams and dictating letters. At 6p.m. I catch a train home and arrive at the house at 6.30.

The weather is wonderful here. We have had a month of weather with cloudless sky and hot sun. It is cold at nights. It may rain again fairly soon – when it does it comes down solid, every path and street is a watercourse full of brown, rushing water, and the drains, although large, are soon full of sand and rocks. It rains solidly for two or three days. Of course when it blows a Norther the sea gets very rough and very often does considerable damage on the quays and to shipping etc. (Valparaiso is unprotected from the North.)

Chile has very few harbours. The best is at Talcahuano but the weather is worse there. Some people say that Coquimbo is good. The other day I went to Quinteros about 20 miles North of Valparaiso. It seems very good but some people say it gets very bad there when it blows a Norther.

Everybody speaks English in the upper classes so we don't get much practise in educated Spanish only in ordinary Spanish.

By the time you get this letter you will be at Shoreham perhaps – if so please remember me to Evans ... remember me to anyone you happen to see. . . .

And again to Charles on 'Julio 4 1921' from

'Aviacion Naval Direction de Artilleria, Valparaiso, Chile.

. . . Perhaps you will be down at Shoreham when you get this – if so remember me to Evans. I suppose it is possible your plans have been altered owing to the strike. I have been doing a little flying here on an Avro seaplane 130 Clerget and on an old Short 270 Sunbeam. The air conditions are good here, there is a steady South Westerly wind every day except when it blows very hard from the N.W., the latter always brings rain.

The Pacific always has a long swell which makes it hard to land on as you may land 10 ft too high or too low without making what would be a bad 'amarisage' on calm water.

The air is generally clear except for a little low-lying fog in the mornings. The mountains and the colour of the sea and rocks are wonderful, almost every day I see Aconcagua 23000 ft the second highest mountain in the world standing up above peaks 15000 ft high ... The country is really wonderful but undeveloped ... The time is inopportune for spending a lot on a Naval Air Service, but we have a 'promise' from the President of a million pesos (£30,000) for the construction of a Naval Flying School by the unemployed. Whether I shall be able to get them to come to a decision on the site is very doubtful. I have seen a very good place 20 miles North of Valparaiso but they won't decide yet and keep on raising objections. I am trying to get them to place an order for some new machines for instruction but there again they won't make a decision ... the climate is wonderful and there are a lot of decent people ... Living is a very little more expensive than it is at home. This afternoon (Sunday) we drove to the 'Caucha' and saw a Rugger match which was quite good – also some sports running – throwing the discus etc., Most people play golf here but we haven't started, the club is very crowded and I don't think it would be much fun. To-morrow I and Schroeders are going up North to inspect and report on Naval Air Stations and policy etc. .... Please write when you have time. ...'

Jim and von Schroeders took passage in the *Maipo* (returning in RMS *Essequibo*) and Jim wrote to Emmie on the return voyage in late July:

I am just returning to Valparaiso from Arica where I have been for about 5 days. I left Valparaiso about 3 weeks ago on a coasting steamer and we called at all the small ports up the Chilean coast, Coquimbo, Caldera, Taltal, Antofagasta, Iquiqui, Gatico, Tocopillo and Arica. I and Schroeders are making out a long report on the suitability of the various places as seaplane bases. The *Maipo*, the steamer we travelled North on, was a small boat but quite comfortable. We carried quantities of cattle, fodder and chickens etc. so we smelt like a farmyard and were wakened by cockcrow every morning.

At every port we were met by the local maritime Authority (who had been warned in advance) and we went all round looking for sites for stations and aerodromes. This is a wonderful country full of possibilities ... They love making elaborate 'projectos', that is plans. I think they will be quite happy if I supply them with new projectos at intervals. ... Most of the ports to the North of Caldera depend on the nitrate industry. At present this is in a bad way but it may recover next year.

The hills sometimes rise sheer out of the water to 2000 ft and there is not a speck of vegetation, all the hills are just brown sand or rocks … The towns are all built with straight streets at right angles except for a few houses round the plaza or central square … Arica is an exception, this is the most Northerly port of Chile and has considerable military value. When the Chileans fought the Peruvians in 1880, they captured and took the fort by storm and drove the Peruvian defenders over the cliff, capturing a lot of guns. The fort is on the top of the cliff like Gibraltar only more accessible from the land side.

I was taken up to inspect the fort and I rode round the surrounding country. I find it is of great value to be able to ride as it is often the only way to get about. Arica is a pretty little town under the cliff, a small river comes out here so there are masses of fruit and flowers.

Yesterday Sunday 17 July we went on a Ford car, fitted so as to run on the Railway line, up to Tacua. This is near the frontier and is full of Chilean troops although the population is 60% Peruvian. It stands on a small river so there is some irrigation of the surrounding valley. With irrigation anything will grow in this country. . . .

This (*Essequibo*) is a most luxurious steamer compared with the *Ortega* and especially compared with the *Maipo* on which we travelled North. . . . I shall be very glad to get back again after 3 weeks. . . . . I hope they won't send me to Talcahuano just yet, although that is possible. . . .'

Although Jim often referred to things 'moving slowly' it would appear that they moved quite as fast as anything at home which had to have Official or Governmental approval. It was weeks only until he got his motorboat and as soon as this important 'air sea-rescue' craft was manned and standing-by, he sent his first pupil up. The pupil went up on an Avro. The date was 25th July.

Things were really moving at last.

As well as pressing on with the tuition of his pilots, Jim was up and down the Coast, exploring the possibilities of suitable safe havens, mooring facilities and sites for training areas and a flying school.

In late August and early September the Fleet was up at Coquimbo. Jim decided to fly up there. He took von Schroeders as passenger and he was accompanied by two other machines, one of them piloted by Francke. They were all on Shorts. They took off from the Torpederas

Jim (dark flying suit) and pupils in Chile

photo: Hans Frey

by nine o'clock in the morning, but unfortunately flew into a thick coastal fog. They were without wireless and the situation could have been critical. However they all hugged the Coast in prescribed fashion and landed safely, one of them at Coquimbo, Jim and the third machine further North still. They were lost but safe; true to Naval tradition they 'stayed with their boat', and spent the night in their respective machines. Jim and von Schroeders had sandwiches and a bottle of drinking water with them. The next morning the missing men were rescued by the search ship, a destroyer, none the worse. The following day all three machines did formation flying over the Chilean Fleet at Coquimbo.

They had been posted missing and back in Valparaiso there had been considerable agitation and, as it turned out, unnecessary worry.

Soon after this Jim made a number of trips South, all of them interesting; he particularly liked Talcahuano, but 'not for a school, as it is too far away.'

The picnic at Quintero

By the middle of October the flying boat was ready for launching. In proper Naval tradition she was launched just like any other ship, with the senior Admiral's wife smashing a bottle of champagne over her bows, a Priest to bless the sea-going craft and a wonderful champagne breakfast afterwards for the assembled guests, amongst whom were 'all the Admirals, Captains and Commanders...' Jim, of all people, would have appreciated the respect and affection with which the Chileans treated their flying boat. They, and he, were of like mind.

After having a little trouble with one of the engines Jim finally got it going – she was in the surf, – then took off and flew, the boat flying beautifully as he circled the town.

He was still pursuing the possibility of further seaplane bases to the South and in this context wrote to Emmie: '... My pupils are getting on with advanced training and I have started some aerial photography to get the authorities interested in surveying work, as there is a lot of the South part of Chile only half explored and not surveyed. They have a hydrographic department but it can only just keep pace with

Island in Lake Todos los Santos
photo: Collection Th. Schenck

the ordinary routine – so it should be a good thing if they did some photography. . . .'

There is a boyish quality about the delight he took in exploring Chile; any pretext to holiday or to paint or to survey; one feels that he was aware of the Islas Juan Fernandez not too far Westwards into the Pacific Ocean and of the MasAtierra or Robinson Crusoe Island. He bought a car and he and his wife and their friends made journeys whenever time allowed: to Jahnuel, to Quintero, where they enjoyed the mineral baths: '. . . they have . . . a factory for bottling the water – which is drunk all over Chile like 'Perrier' is at home. . . .'

Although the mails back and forth to England were slow, taking many weeks, they were regular and as a result there was a regular flow of news. Apart from private letters, J. L. T. and Emmie sent *Blackwood's Magazine*, batches of *The Morning Post*, the *Weekly Times* and of course, always: *The Aeroplane*. Jim wrote: '. . . We are very interested in the recent flights in Germany and France on gliders and in this evening's paper it says that the *Daily Mail* is giving £1000 prize for competitions this year – it makes me sorry that I am not at home to compete! It will have to be 1923. . . .'

He wrote to Charles on the 22nd January 1922:

'Thank you very much for sending the medal ribbons which have arrived safely and which are quite correct. I also owe you a letter in reply to yours about the show, thank you for sending those catalogues.

The Barr and Stroud engine has the same type of valve gear as the old sleeve-valve Argyll. I suppose the patent has run out by now. It should be a very good thing but it is probably heavy for Horsepower? as the sleeve has to be of cast iron I suppose. Everything here is very quiet owing to the exchange, the peso is worth only $5\frac{1}{2}$d now and is expected to go to 4d within the next few months. I am keeping my pay in gold for the time being and by so doing I cannot lose, although if the exchange does improve I don't stand to gain anything. I have not heard anything definite about staying on here. But it seems possible I may stay until December next.

I hope you are geetting on well with maths, physics and mechanics.

You, like me, will be all the better for a thorough grounding in the elementary subjects. I am sure you will find the other things will come easily to you afterwards.

I have been doing a fair number of tests on glue, timber and wire cable. There is a little testing machine at the Arsenale, Naval Dockyard is called the Arsenale, and as I very often have to use local material it is always as well to test samples. The workshop at the Arsenale is very useful and they are always ready to do do any little job for us.

We have been doing a little practice with a camera gun but the results are not very good. I think that the films suffer from the heat. With our proper mapping camera we have taken some quite good photos of parts of the town and harbour and of the forts.

We got the loan of a German Aero camera for oblique photos the other day and got some extraordinarily good ones of the town, harbour etc. and of other machines in the air.

The Shorts are still going strong but are suffering from float trouble a good deal.

As you can imagine I am quite in my element getting bombsights fixed up and speaking tubes and all that sort of thing.

The Army people at Santiago had another crash the other day on an Avro, 1 fellow killed. I think they were stunting low down and hit a tree. When will fellows learn sense....

And to Emmie on 2nd February:

We have just got your letters written about Christmas time.

The car will be fine for everybody. What jolly little jaunts you will have exploring round the country.

We have great fun on our Ford although the roads are rather bad.

The naval flying is going on very well here and everybody seems pleased at the progress made.

I hope to be able to send you more copies of the photographs that we have been taking from the air, they give a very good general idea of the place.

I do appreciate *L'Aeorphile* very much it's better technically than the *Aeroplane*.

If we stay out here after April, and it seems as though we shall, I should like you to send *Flight* as well as *The Aeroplane* and if *Aeronautical Engineer* is still going, I should like that but I think they have stopped it.

Will you let me know how much all these will cost as I would like to pay for them. The one thing I miss here is somebody to talk to about technical things. Perhaps you could get a German Aero paper if all the others have stopped. It would be interesting.

I get a certain number of catalogues from firms at home and people write to me occasionally and tell me the news, from all accounts things are not very bright in England, as far as Aviation is concerned.

Civil aviation here is practically non-existent, there is a Chilean Aviator who flies an old Morane and some Italians in the South but there are no regular services and no modern machines.

I hope Charles will finish his cycle-car in spite of the counter-attractions of the Citroen and the Triumph, because I am sure he will learn a lot by making it himself.

We often wish we could just see you all at home. Give my love to Dad and Alice and Charles. . . .'

Jim wrote to Charles on the 1st April, 1922, describing his work and his enjoyable life:

Thank you for your letter of Jan 10th written from 61 Palace Gardens Terrace. I hope your digs there are still pretty comfortable . . . We are still having a lot of beautiful fine days but it may start to rain any day now. . . .

We have been carrying out an instructional programme at a place

Elicura. Supermarine and F. boat. View from our balcony

photo: Jim Travers

Short taxying. Supermarine boat. Jim & Briseño

Picking up moorings

photo: Hans Frey

called Quintero about 20 miles North of Valparaiso – it is a very small village but there is a beautiful sheltered bay, they are making some protecting moles and quays and in about 2 years it will be a fine little harbour.

There is a good beach of hard fine sand which is suitable for working the Shorts and the Avros, the boat is anchored. We have a small gun boat the *Elicura* which serves as a store for petrol, oil and spares and as accommodation for mechanics and seamen. We have the loan of a house for some of the officers and I and one or two others live in the Hotel. I find my Spanish sufficiently good ... but when it comes to talking in polite society with slang and fine shades of meaning it's much more difficult. Our work at Quintero has consisted of firstly teaching one officer to fly an Avro Seaplane (the said officer being 38 years old and never flown,) he crashed the said Avro by stalling on a turn during a glide without hurting himself or his instructor, Espisiora.

Secondly, teaching an officer to fly Avros and Shorts and other officers who had flown these machines to fly on the F2A boat. Then we have made them each fire two trays from the Short machine gun,

Flying Boat, Chile, April 1922

in the air at a target on the water as a sort of preliminary to camera gun work which got held up through bad film. The other subjects were bomb dropping, photography formation-flying, navigation: the bomb dropping consisted in about 10 runs each over the mirror both as pilot and observer, and then practice on a target with dummy bombs made of concrete.

The photography consisted in the preparation of a scale map of the Quintero peninsular with a view to discovering submerged rocks. This will be of great use to the Harbour company.

The formation flying consisted in getting off in formation, flying boat and 2 Shorts with sometimes another Short and Avro. The navigation was rather elementary as all our flights were in sight of the coast, but they practised getting wind speed with bombs and steering courses from point to point, also using bearing plates.

We have had a remarkable absence of engine trouble, the Sunbeams on the Shorts and the Rolls on the boat have been going like clocks (touch wood.) The Short Floats have given a lot of trouble as they were made in 1917 and the 3 ply is all coming to bits, the only 3 ply we can get here is oak outside and poplar! inside and the glue is very bad – also we can't get the right size of brass wood screws or any sandow shock absorber or flexible cable or washers or rubber tubing or anything other than the most ordinary materials. For instance the only steel we can get for making bolts is 18 ton stuff, $\frac{1}{2}$ the strength of the most ordinary aircraft stuff.

The mechanics work under the worst possible conditions but knowing no better they don't worry. After a short patriotic harangue they will do wonders but they don't always finish an ordinary routine job, unless watched. . . .

I was awfully interested in your description of your visit to Shenfield and the progress of the H A W K monoplane – I am very glad Arthur is going on with it, I thought perhaps he would get fed up with it – It should be ready for test when we get back about the beginning of next year. The trouble will probably be to find a good aerodrome near by, unless he takes it to Grain or Martlesham.

The Citroen must be great fun. I suppose Saunders will drive it eventually. Our Ford is still going well and the more I see of the Ford the more I admire its peculiar good points. Write and tell me what your ideas are as to your own future and any brainstorms about machines or engines.

Landing at Zapallar

Now that Bagnall Wild is in charge of the Research Department at the Air Ministry we may expect to see engine(s) and materials pushed on, he is a good man and a R E A L engineer. He was responsible for the Aeronautical Inspection Department during the war.

It appears to me that the 2 stroke engine should be experimented with more – especially with fuel injected during the compression or explosion stroke so that the scavenging can be done by pure air. Junkers seems to be experimenting on those lines and although it may be impossible to make a Diesel engine, it should be possible to make a simpler and lighter petrol engine.

Another rather fascinating problem is a combination Internal Combustion and external combustion engine in which a pressure engine (like a steam engine) could be worked from some fuel say petrol which is heated in the jacket of the Internal Combustion engine, the exhaust from the pressure engine provides the fuel for the Internal Combustion engine – In this way the heat normally lost in the radiator could be partially recovered as useful work – the pressure engine would have to weigh not more than Radiator and weight equivalent to resistance saved and weight equivalent to power gained.

engine would be started as simple 2 stroke and pressure engine cut in when hot. Perhaps there is some snag in this that has not occurred to me. . . .'

To Emmie:

We are staying on here (Quintero) for a fortnight longer & are then returning with the gunboat and 4 machines to Valparaiso, where we hope to find a new slipway ready for us and the roof of the Shed repaired.

Yesterday Espinoza one of the pilots and von Schroeders had a crash on the Avro No 1 it was their own fault but I think it taught them a lesson as they were getting a little over confident. No damage done to either pilot or passenger but machine will take 2 or 3 months to repair. On the whole the work is going as well as can be expected when it is remembered that they have spent practically nothing on essential supplies & spares and we have no workshop or decent Sheds even. . . . I have not yet heard if my contract is to be renewed at the end of next month or not but I think that it is certain that they will renew it for a month or two at any rate in order to give me decent notice. . . .

To J. L. T. on the 9th April:

We have now returned from Quintero for good and are at our house in Vina – (he wrote home consistently from his address at Direction Artilleria, Valparaiso, as it caused less confusion and re-direction of mail than writing from the various Hotels or rented houses in which they lived – Ed) – We got through a very good training programme with only one accident in which no one was hurt and the machine can be repaired in time.

'They seem very pleased with the progress made during the year I have been here and Admiral Langlois has asked for my contract to be renewed for another year; this would suit me perfectly well, but the delay in getting the contract ready etc. is causing me some worry as, if we stay, we must look out for another house. This one will be available only until the end of May. . . . I shall probably be going to Coquimbo in August for a month or so and later on in the year to Quintero again for some more training of new officers.'

And to Emmie:

... We are quite pleased about staying on for another year although we both get a bit home sick sometimes. I think we are very lucky when one thinks of the difficulty some people have in getting jobs

Herbert has not written to me lately but I hope his saw mill scheme will go all right if he really has gone into it. ...

And to Emmie again, on 6th May:

Thank you for your letter of March 22nd enclosing a cutting about French tests with gliders. The Germans started doing these sorts of tests after the war and the French are now doing the same – Much can be learnt in an economical way by these trials. I wonder if anyone in England is doing anything?

It's the sort of thing that ought to be made a sort of game or competition and then it would appeal to the average young Englishman perhaps. Merely as a scientific test it will have very few supporters.

We are still expecting rain here but are having delightful weather in the meantime. All our machines are safe in the Sheds as, when it blows a Northerly gale, there is no sheltered place for them afloat.

A certain Capt. Tomlyn has just arrived her to take charge of the Naval War College for 2 years, he is about the same seniority as Capt. Lambe, whom H. O. served under at Dunkirk. ...

And to Emmie again, on 14th May:

I enclose some photographs which I don't think you have seen. ... The one of the seaplane was taken at Quintero it's an Avro. The one of us standing on the beach is taken at Quintero, Mrs Schroeders, Schroeders, Lieutenant Silva and myself, the machine in background is a Short. ...

After returning to Valparaiso from Quintero and hearing that he was to stay on, they looked about for another house to rent and found, at Miramar, one that they really liked; it was neat and small, with a pretty garden and a real fireplace, which last was what they particularly wanted.

'We are getting some lovely roses from our garden.' Jim wrote home, 'there are also some fine violets. The chrysanthemums are almost over and so are the delphiniums. This afternoon I walked to the shore with Dennison' (Dennison was one of their many English neighbours-Ed) during a lull in the rain. The sea was very fine and it looked as though it would blow up worse. They say that it will probably rain for 8 days on end.

As it has been such rotten weather we have been sitting at home both yesterday and to-day (Sunday) and we are really enjoying the charms of the fireplace with a wood fire. It smells so nice and looks so cosy. I have been typing out some lectures which I am going to give to the Naval War College here, and also a specification for a new type of flying boat, which I hope they may be persuaded to get tenders for?

We are engaged in overhauling our machines, but are badly in need of the necessary materials.

I am quite firm and say, 'no materials, no flying in August.' In the end I shall get them.

Love to Dad, & Charles & Alice. . . .'

To J. L. T. on 11th June:

...I am glad to see that J. T. & Sons is doing so well. We are both quite well and have got settled in our new house. It is very comfortable and cosy and we enjoy the fire as the weather has set in really wet and it pours night and day with short intervals. The roads are seas of mud and in some cases roaring torrents tearing down the hillsides. We have had 20 inches since it started about 10 days ago – and more is expected. I go every day to the office and then on to the 'Torpederas' where the seaplane Shed is. I walk round and inspect everything and 2 days a week I give a lecture to the officers....

Winter was the time for overhauling the machines but there were delays in accomplishing this.

It is not hard to uncover the reason: the country was in dire financial difficulty 'The Government here are awfully hard up,' Jim wrote home, 'and don't know which way to look for money. ...' Chile imported so many essential items: 'They import a lot of agricultural and other machinery, motorcars, and every conceivable class of manufactured material ...' he wrote. The needs, modest but essential, of the blossoming Chilean Naval Air Service came a long way down the Government's shopping list even though they were proud of their Naval Air Service and keen that it should continue to grow.

'We are still overhauling our machines,' Jim wrote to Emmie on 3rd July,' – which is a very slow job as the material which we had hoped had been ordered we find had never been ordered at all. So we are in difficulties. We are trying to get some from Buenos Aires but now the railway is snowed up we may not be able to get it that way soon enough.

'We had planned a flight up to Coquimbo with 4 machines but it may not come off now. . . .'

On the 1st August, again to Emmie:

My work is going on steadily, next week I am going to read some lectures (in Spanish) on Naval Aviation before the new Naval War College staff which Tomlin is training. I think that with the aid of some diagrams and drawings on the Blackboard I shall be able to make myself understood all right. .' Jim had improved his Spanish with a course of twice-weekly lessons. '. . . The machines are still held up for certain essential material which has not arrived as it should from London and Buenos Ayres.

We heard from Charles the other day and he said he had been down at Shoreham. I hope he did well in his exam. Tell him not to take it TOO seriously if he did not pass but to carry on and work for the AMICE exam later on, same as I did.

I am wondering what I will do when I get back in May or June next year? I may have saved a bit which will pay expenses while I am looking out for something else, and perhaps there will be more jobs going by that time. . . .

Their social life was pleasant: 'a fine amateur performance of 'Peg O' My Heart' it was very good indeed and so interesting to know the actors and actresses in private life.' One Sunday 'We went to the Caucha (Sporting Club) and watched a Rugby football match between France and England.' There were plenty of bridge-parties, too, for those that wished: 'I have been attempting to play bridge and seem to get on fairly well,' Jim wrote home, 'but I find it awfully hard to keep up interest. Most of the people here play it as if it is a serious business and I find it hard to look upon it quite in that light. . . .'

Although Jim tremendously liked his Chilean colleagues, for they were 'full out for Naval Aviation,' he mixed less, socially, with them than with the numerous and mostly friendly and hospitable British contingent as 'the Chileans keep rather late hours.'

It is not surprising that Jim found it 'awfully hard to keep up interest' in a game of bridge. In every idle moment his thoughts would have turned to his flying boats. Ever since he had first flown the

Sopwith bat-boat in 1914 his interest had been in the boat rather than in the seaplane. 'I wish I had my old bat-boat out here,' he had written home.

The Chilean Navy's F2A boat, one of Commander Porte's and Jim's Felixstowe boats, carried a complement of six. She was one boat only on a coastline which stretched from 18° to 55° in the Southern Latitudes. (There were also six seaplanes and two new Supermarines.)

He had mentioned his own design specification of a large flying boat in an earlier letter. Then, writing to Emmie on the 6th November, 1922, he referred to it again; one has the impression that he was thinking of a really large flying boat. And why not. After all, as early as 1910 the Russians had built an aeroplane capable of carrying sixteen people; and one could increase size substantially on a boat. Jim would have exchanged many such fruitful ideas with Commander Porte during their time at Felixstowe. Many were thinking along such lines.

In Italy, Signor Caproni had designed a mammoth eight-engine, 100-seat triplane, but it had crashed into the water on testing and had not been rebuilt.

I have never seen the specification for Jim's flying boat but it is most unlikely that he was thinking along quite such experimental lines as Signor Caproni and his Ca 60; yet, on the other hand, he referred consistently to his 'large flying boat Policy,' and one guesses that he may have been thinking of something four-engined and with a seating capacity of 20 or so, plus crew. 'My large flying boat Policy has now been officially recommended by the Select Committee which was appointed to decide,' he wrote home on 6th November, 'I hope that they will now go ahead and ask for tenders so that something may be settled before April.' Later he wrote: 'My specification for a special type of large flying boat has been officially approved and so I hope that tenders will be asked for soon so as to be opened before I leave Chile in April...'

Meanwhile he had ordered 'two new Supermarine boats'. These were probably the Supermarine Sea Lion 11 flying boats, of the type with which Britain had won the 1922 Schneider Trophy at Naples. Jim simply referred to them as Supermarine boats.

His letter, to Emmie, of 10th December, starts with a list of their happy social engagements, continuing: '... sometimes we fit in picnics on the little car, just taking our tea or lunch out and I try my hand at sketching. Next Sunday that is the 17th (Dad's Birthday) we are going to Santiago and taking the night train from there down South to the Lakes. We should arrive on Monday night or Tuesday morning at Puerto Varas on Lake Llanquihua (pronounced yankewer). We hope to spend a few days going steamer trips on the lake and may get across to the Argentine Border. I shall have to go to Puerto Moutt and Valdivia and Concepion on our way back to Santiago.

We expect to be back here on or about New Years Day. After that I expect to be going to Quintero with some seaplanes including the two new Supermarine boats which should by then have arrived and been erected. There are some more officers who have already been trained on aeroplanes and who will go through a course of seaplane flying, and we will carry out a course of instruction in bombing with live bombs. (The latter I am having constructed from some old shells).

My specification for a special type of large flying boat has been officially approved and so I hope that tenders will be asked for soon so as to be opened before I leave Chile in April. I hope Dad is keeping well and that you won't be having a very severe winter. . . .'

He returned from the South early in 1923 and wrote to Emmie on 28th January:

. . . I am afraid I have not written home for 2 or 3 weeks – last week I wrote to Arthur Cooper and the week before to Charles.

I have been rather seedy with a gastric attack but not sufficient to prevent going to work each day for a few hours just to keep an eye on things. It's been very hot and the doctor says that fruit especially peaches often cause this gastric trouble among English people – it might also be caused by the dust.

Our training camp at Quintero is not ready yet so our departure there has been put off from one cause or another – It is rather hard for me to make arrangements in view of the continual delays.

Added to this I have had to test the new Supermarine training machines which have just arrived and it needs some patience to wait for good enough conditions of wind and sea for their first flights. . . .

There were other matters in connexion with the Supermarines, too, which also taxed his patience.

Among the mechanics there was among the Chileans one Englishman. He was not one of this country's better exports to Chile, and was as crude in his manners as in his work.

He had erected the Supermarines whilst Jim had been away in the South and had done a 'very bad' job of the work. This had led to Jim having to check all the weights and angles himself; Jim had, moreover carried out all this work under primitive conditions, with the machines out of the sheds and on the beach.

By early March all was ready for the departure for Quintero. Jim wrote to Emmie on 4th March:

... Don't trouble to send me *Who's Who in Engineering* as I shall probably see it at the Club and it seems rather an expense to you. I appreciate the kind thought of sending it however.

We are at the moment at our house in Vina but go back to the training camp at Quintero on Monday, 6th March.

Our Ford car still goes very well – but we are troubled for a garage and leave it in the open. . . .

...Charles wrote me a splendid letter which I will answer by this mail. ... If he makes a study of economical flying now he will be in a fine position in a few years. Tell him not to lose sight of the business side of the subject. Organizing expenses, overhead charges and insurance are the big expenses to-day in commercial flying.

Of course as an engineer he is interested first of all in the technical problems, – but he should study the other part, too.

I am sure Charles will do well as he seems to have good ideas – and enough perserverance to carry them out. . . .

He was typing out a specification and wrote that Nancy was helping him:

'. . . it's rather a long thing about 7 pages of very close typewriting. We are taking it in turns to type a sheet ... it's rather tiring work, such a close concentration required as it must be accurate ... I tried to get the clerks at the office to do it but they made an awful hash of it ... They have done the Spanish copies. . . .

We are going to ask for tenders in England, U.S.A., France, Italy and Holland, but of course I hope that an English firm will get the contract.

It is for a large flying boat, specially built for Chilean conditions.

We were very interested to hear about Laurie and the Faithfulls and

Tindals. One loses touch so with cousins and they seem to grow up so fast and make me feel old when I really feel about 25 or so. ...' Jim was, in fact, 39 years old and would not be 40 until November – '... Give Dad my love and thank him very much for the *Blackwoods* and *Times*, also for the *Aeroplane. Flight* and *Aerophile,* which arrives still and which I greatly appreciate. ...'

In March the Chilean Government asked Jim to remain for a further six months beyond his original contract, which would have ended in April, and, being anxious to carry through his large flying boat policy, he readily agreed.

He also wished to improve the performance of the Supermarines or 'S's', as he called them; they were rather heavily loaded and he had had some trouble with them. After some modifications he proposed a further course on them for the flying men, up at Quintero in October or November and before he left Chile for home in December. Meanwhile he was continuing instruction on the F2A boat: such a good boat, Short-built, with a seating capacity for six and fully fitted for instruction.

But in May of 1923, with the approach of another rain-lashed winter, he sounded a little low in spirits. He wrote to Emmie on 13th May from Valparaiso:

We are still without rain here although the weather is cooler and there is some dew and dampness about and quite a lot of cloudy and foggy weather. It may start to rain any day now but it generally gives good warning by being very clear to the north the day before.

Admiral Langlois who has been my chief ever since I have been here has just gone to take command of the Fleet. I am very sorry but I think he will do well in his new post.

His successor is Capitan de Navio Carabantes – a very nice but rather quiet old man.

I have been feeling rather seedy with these boils, which are painful things. – they do not prevent me going in to work every day but my neck and the back of my head is all bandaged up. ...

We have started having fires as the nights are quite cold – we are burning some pieces of old vine which have a peculiar smell. Also some rather pleasantly smelling fruit tree wood. We were pleased to get all your news in a letter from Dad the other day. Your weather seems very treacherous so be careful of these snowstorms in April and May.

We get very homesick at times and wonder why we ever decided to stay on here until December – which seems a long way away. . . .

It was homesickness only which made him long for England, for he loved Chile: '. . . this delightful country' he called it.

After a particularly long drought:

'. . . no rain falling between 20th August, 1922 and 11th June, 1923 . . .' the rain at last came, and with a vengeance. 'It is now raining hard,' he wrote to Emmie on 17th June, 'and as usual all the water channels and main drains in the town get stopped up by the enormous quantity of sand and stones that are brought down from the hills by the sudden floods of water. . . .

'Things are very quiet in the flying way and the machines are just being overhauled bit by bit so as to be ready to do some exercises in August with the Fleet and later on to go to Quintero for a last instructional course before I leave.

'In October the tenders for the big flying boat are due to arrive and I hope that 3 months will be sufficient to decide which firm is to have the order. – So that I may get a part time job of superintending the construction and tests.

'Of course if an American or French firm gets the order they would have to pay me much more to supervise the job. They are talking of sending two of the Naval Flying Officers for a year to England to go through various courses. I hope that they will.

'I have been sitting in by the fire to-day being Sunday trying to do some water colour sketches from memory. This afternoon we snatched an hour between showers and walked to the beach, about a mile.

'The seas were very big and a fine sight. Two steamers had gone outside as being safer than staying in the roadstead. . . .'

After the long drought the rainstorms seemed, by contrast, ever more wild, with 'temporals', when the wind reached 70 kilometres an hour; mercifully the terrible storm 'only lasted 3 hours; otherwise they say every ship in the bay would have gone down.'

At home, Jim worked away at the model of his flying boat, everything as neat as he could make it, the deckhouse windows simulated with washed off old photographic film. July was the month for such things; the Andes often closed and mail from home scarce. He was still working on the model when he wrote again on 6th August. He also remarked that 'We have had rather a busy week in the way of dinner parties and next week we have 3 more ...' He wrote in the same letter, which was to Emmie, of his plans:

I have also been typing out a scheme for Commercial flying on this coast which I am going to propose....

At the Seaplane Base we are overhauling the machines and have now 4 out of 9 perfectly ready for the training course which we hope to start after the 18th September holiday. My chief work is the Handbook which makes steady progress but the reproduction of the illustrations is going to be rather difficult as the money availiable is limited. – anyhow I will leave it all ready when I leave in December.

I am delivering a series of Lectures on the recognition of aircraft to the coast defence batteries and will give another series on 'Naval Aviation' to the War College at the end of this month. (The lectures I gave last year will be brought up to date).

I hope you are having a good summer with lots of fruit....'

He was less sanguine when he wrote again to Emmie on the 23rd August

... We have had some rather bad set backs in the Naval Aviation work. During the big storm the other day the motor boat was swamped and sunk and we have not yet been able to recover the engine even. Every precaution was taken and I don't think anyone was to blame.

This harbour is quite useless when it blows a 'norther.'

Our projected trip to Coquimbo has been cancelled owing to the urgent need for economy – this is very disappointing to the pilots and mechanics who have been working very hard to get the Machines ready. Anyhow it is a good thing that they are all ready for when the weather is better we shall be able I hope to do some further training....

He had a short holiday in September and wrote to J. L. T. on his return on the 21st September:

We have just returned from a few days holiday in the Andes. We went by train from here and stayed at a place called Los Andes and then went trips by motor from there to Rio Colorado etc. Capt. Tomlin lent us his rods and we did quite a lot of fishing ... I didn't fish all the time as I did some sketches. We are now back in Vina . . . for the week end. We are not going to Quintero until the 4th or 5th of October. . . .

My civil aviation scheme for mail carrying is creating quite a lot of interest. And I am getting peoples opinions on it so as to see if I can get someone to take it up in England. We hope to sail on the 8th December – but this is not certain. . . .

The holiday, though short, had been a great success, for the scenery was wonderful: 'masses of wild peach blossom, vivid green of weeping willows, the river burbling over a rocky bed between steep banks and the snow-capped mountains behind it all. . . . ' It was a good river for trout, too, although Jim had caught only a few, for he had spent much of the time in sketching; thoughts that he might not travel that way again for years may well have prompted him in trying to record the beauty of the landscape.

Although Coquimbo had been cancelled the Naval Aviation people seemed to have spent a long time, perhaps longer than usual, at Quintero. Jim had been there in September arranging more comfort-able quarters for them, in a rented house, rather than in the huts of the previous years. He wrote to Emmie from there on 14th October. (Emmie, J. L. T., Alie and Charles having lately returned to Bredgar from a holiday in France.)

Thank you for the letter of the 9th Sept. We are (both) so glad you had a nice time in France.

I went to Le Crotoy in 1912 to inspect and take delivery of a Caudron 'amphibian' but it would not pass its tests. Later on it was altered and was quite successful.

Rather good Charles getting through his flying tests so quickly and well especially on a machine which he had not flown before, but the De Hav's 9's are quite straightforward and of course Charles is really rather a specially good & sensible pilot with a lot of experience compared to most of the ex flying officers.

How splendid getting that wireless arrangement going so well. I should love to help him with it. Our wireless works fairly well in our machines but always needs small spare parts which take a long time to get from England.

We hope to leave here on the 8th Dec by the *Oroya* (I went in the old *Oroya* to Australia about 23 years ago) we ought to arrive on

January 12th – As yet I haven't arranged anything to follow on this contract but it is possible that I may get a fee for doing some work for them in England for 6 months, which will leave me free to do other work and which will enable me to keep in touch with them (the Chilean Govt.), in case other things don't materialise I shall return again here perhaps.

It will take me at least 6 months to get up to date and during that time I can look about for other openings.

If I stayed in this country any longer I should grow lazy and stupid – there is no incentive to ever do anything. ... I really believe one could stay here for ever making proposals and reports and polite speeches...smiling and drinking cocktails.

Unfortunately I still am interested in Aeronautics from the scientific engineering point of view and therefore this job is a means to an end...

There's not a single person who is really interested in Aeronautical work - (and here Jim would have undoubtedly included all his fellow ex-patriates as well as his hosts in such a sweeping statement) – I want someone to have a good technical argument with, it would do me good, my ideas all get in a groove....

Jim got a lot of flying at Quintero that spring; and as usual when he was flying, he was happy. He wrote to Emmie on the 18th November:

Thank you for your letter of the 5th October wishing me happy returns for my birthday – I may be 40 but I don't feel more than 30. Charles sent me such a fine letter and photographs of the Light Aeroplane Trials at Lympne. I will write and thank him.

I am sorry that Dad has been feeling bad with neuralgia, perhaps when the weather is more settled it will be better.

Do encourage Charles in his work – it is important to get through at least the first part of the A. M. I. C. E. exam before he goes to works. The second part is not really so hard, as he can take subjects which are easily read up.

As he is a slow worker it is all the more necessary to concentrate on the first part and get that done and then go on to the other afterwards.

It is practically settled that I shall do some work for the Chileans in England next year for which I will get a fee and with the understanding that I shall be free to do other consulting work. In that way I shall be in touch with the Chileans and if there is nothing in the consulting

Pastoral, Chile

photo: Jim Travers

business I will return to Chile perhaps in 1925 – I expect by then they will have carried out some of my recommendations and things will be able to go ahead.

I am putting forward a proposal for an Air Mail Service as a reserve to the Naval Air Service and everybody including the President is very enthusiastic about it.

But I shant be disappointed if they do nothing.

We intend sailing on the *Oroya* on the 8th December – due at Liverpool about the 12th January....

Please give Dad my love and the very best Christmas wishes to everybody from us both....

The fact that they intended going home in *Oroya*, so oft – repeated, was to allay any uncertainties in the minds of those at home, about their route; for they had been very keen to send their luggage by sea from Valparaiso and travel home themselves by way of the Andes and thence by ship from Buenos Aires. The direct, the cross country, route. In the event they discovered that unaccompanied luggage was costly in transit and that the whole idea was fraught with too much vagueness where time was concerned. They were longing for home and would, after all, travel conventionally by the long sea lanes.

Jim wrote to J. L. T. from Valparaiso on the 25th November:

It is now less than a fortnight to the time we shall be sailing. We are busy putting the finishing touches to our packing. I have been at Quintero for the last week or so with two Supermarine boats and I am glad to say that they are now going very well and the pilots are enthusiastic over them now they are getting more opportunity to practise.

Everything is going very well with regard to my consulting contract in England. And I think that civil aviation developments in South America will justify the line I am taking.

But if things don't develop within the next year or so I intend coming here again in 1925 to the Navy and with that possibility in view I shall be in close touch with the Chilean Authorities in London.

For many reasons it was not advisable to sign another yearly contract with the Government for next year under the same terms as the last three years...

We are staying a few days with the Wedderspoons – they are very kind as is everybody here.

I hope you are feeling better and have got over your neuralgia.

Don't worry over Herbert – I am sure he is absolutely sound really...With more experience he will steady down I am sure. .... Good wishes for the New Year from us both to everybody....

He spent about a week in Santiago before sailing, making courtesy calls and thanking the many, many people who had contributed so much to his time in 'this delightful country' – Chile.

Further up the Pacific Coast things were not going quite so well; yet it is hard to say in precisely what way they were not going so well, for there were few letters home. Extracting what one can from letters and extracting much more from the memory of what my parents told me, it was sad circumstances more than anything else which eventually brought them home. H. had loved British Columbia ever since, as a young man of 19, he had thought of fruit farming there. But too much had happened since those youthful days, too much of his strong right arm had been shot away. He knew that he would never farm in the Okanagan now. He was brave in attempting the life of a lumberman, – too brave, perhaps.

The chance of buying a saw mill had tempted him but no sooner had the purchase gone through, with every scrap of capital that he could lay hands on put into it, than the news in early 1923 of Etta Fraser's sudden death, unexpected in spite of her thirty years of poor health, reached them; to be followed, only days afterwards, by the news that Col. Fraser was ill. The house on Point Grey, lovingly designed and built for the Frasers by H. and H., was now up for sale.

It was early in 1923 that Jim had written, sounding puzzled, that H. had written to him 'here's to a Merry Xmas at home this year.' It was possibly the first news that anyone had had that H. and H. planned to return. My Mother often told me that it was her concern over D.'s (Daphne's) health which had decided her to seek medical help in London.

Probably, therefore, it was the series of misfortunes and sad circumstances which decided them and a rope of many plys which eventually tugged them home.

Emmie, too, may have confided to H. about J. L. T. 'neuralgia', mentioned with increasing frequency throughout 1923. Was it neuralgia? He had a slight stroke in the autumn and Emmie was warned to expect that he might have another, perhaps a more severe, attack.

H. and H. left British Columbia in late October accompanied by their two small daughters, who were well wrapped up in blanket coats for the long journey, by Canadian Pacific Railway, across to Montreal to take ship for England. H. took out a Canadian Passport, on October 30th, for his departure from the country. He was to renew this Passport several times, for he travelled on it right up until the autumn of 1935, which was when the airline he was flying for became British Airways, and he was required to carry a British Passport. He liked his Canadian Passport and he loved Canada. He undoubtedly hoped to return one day.

9

1924 & AFTER

1924–1926

Wanderers return from the Pacific Coast – J. L. T. dies – testing of HAWK –
Jim dies – H. leaves for Korea.

ANYONE who has read thus far will perhaps have gathered that Jim
exerted great influence over his younger brothers; yet he was in no
sense a dominating character, just a natural leader who, by dint of his
enthusiasm, his ability and his zest for life, inspired the others to follow
him. With J.L.T.'s fading influence over his family and H. no longer
flying and still absent in Canada, Charles turned more and more to
Jim for guidance in his career and for companionship through their
correspondence and shared interests. The gap in age of almost fifteen
years would have evaporated to almost no gap at all as they wrote to
each other of their 'brainstorms and bright ideas' where engine function and design was concerned; yet when he wrote to Emmie, Jim's
concern over Charles' career was almost fatherly. The brothers were
indeed the very best of friends and Charles perhaps even more than
any of the others looked forward to Jim's return from Chile.

Charles had been demobilized with the rank of Lieutenant in the
Royal Air Force on the 11th July, 1919. He was subsequently granted
a commission on being temporarily re-employed as a Flying Officer
on the 10th April, 1921 and went to No. 7 Group, going to No. 6
Training Squadron on the following day and to No. 3 Flying Training
School at the Airship Base on the 15th April. He went to Reserve pool
No. 39 Squadron and proceeded on leave on the 9th May, relinquishing
his temporary commission on the 5th June that year. He joined the
Reserve of Air Force Officers, Class 'A' on the 20th April, 1922, being
confirmed in his rank of Flying Officer on 30th November, 1923. He
kept up his flying training. References to this were sometimes made
in his letters home or in letters to Jim. This training was, of course,
arranged as far as possible around the engineering training with which

he persevered for some years. He also went from time to time in the summer to the 'Works' at Shoreham, but the famous Ricardo Engineering Company have no record of him on their files, so although there are numerous cross-references to his time 'at Works' his time there must have been too short to have been any part of a formal apprenticeship.

He enrolled as a Matriculated Student in the Engineering Faculty of King's College London on 6th October, 1920, for a four year course in Mechanical Engineering. He failed his exam. in 1921 and again in 1922. He stayed up for a further year and left in 1923 without quali-fication. He seems to have been quite calm about his studies and to have listened to Jim's advice: not to mind TOO much if he did not pass but to go for A.M.I.C.E. He had enjoyed his time at King's and had made many friends there. He subsequently joined the KCL Engineering Association and kept in touch with them right up until his final change of address, in 1965. In 1923, however, Charles was just 25 years old, with a life time in aviation ahead of him.

He was in digs at Cartwright Gardens, WC1, and when writing home from there on 27th May, 1923, mentioned an enjoyable evening he had spent with Hermia's father, Col. Fraser, now a widower and beginning to be ill.

... I went to lunch with Colonel Fraser yesterday ... the Colonel had seen his doctor and is going to have this special treatment, I think it is with Rontgen Rays. He is not feeling very fit ...

After tea the Colonel suggested that he and I should go to the Coliseum. I thought that it would be too much for him but he was keen to go so he took me to dinner at Lyons' Popular and to the Coliseum after ...

The great hill climb started this morning and went on till tea time. It was a beautiful day and about 12 men turned up. Freddie Wilson was there and took charge of the timing operations ... The best time was put up by an A.J.S. – which did the $\frac{1}{2}$ mile (standing start) in 38 and 2/5's seconds and the end best by a Norton (41 secs.) I went up in 45 and 3/5's seconds (just under 40 m.p.h.) I think I came 3rd, which was good, considering that the A.J.S. is almost new, and the Norton only two years old. It was great fun ...

Emmie, who never missed an opportunity to 'run up to Town', went to the Summer Exhibition with Charles in June. He wrote to her afterwards, on the 17th: 'I hope that you got a seat in the train on Wednesday, it looked rather crowded. I enjoyed the Academy. I hope it did not make you tired. The Fishmonger's dinner was a great success ... Ben and Frank were there, and I had a yarn with them. They were glad to have news of Jimmy and the rest of the family. Ben is not going to try another play just yet but is sticking to novels. There were some good speeches and the music was very good . . .'

In November, 1923, Charles went for his Reserve of Air Force Officers Quarterly Training at the de Havilland Civilian Flying School. While there, he wrote to Emmie from the Royal Abercorn Hotel at Stanmore:

... I have done 2 hours solo to-day, on the D.H.9. They may not allow me to complete my yearly training, but a letter was sent off to the training headquarters at Northolt tonight pointing out that I might be unable to attend again in the Spring owing to impending exams. I have only 7 hours 5 minutes more flying to do to complete my yearly training.

There are about 20 pupils here, or rather there should be 20. About half of them don't turn up.

Broad (one of the De Hav pilots) took the D.H.53 light monoplane up this morning. It flies much better with the 698 c.c. Blackburn than with the 150 c.c. Douglas.

There are two lady pupils in the civilian school. One of them has been learning for 6 months, but the other flies quite well on a Renault Avro.

I can't tell when I shall get away – as I don't know whether they will let me complete my training and the weather is uncertain.

I hope Dad's neuralgia is better.

I came across a man to-day who was at Beaulieu with me in Dec. 1916...

J.L.T.'s neuralgia was not better. As he approached his 77th birthday and the onset of yet another cold winter in Kent, he stayed indoors most of the time, beginning at last, after a lifetime of energetic activity, to feel old.

In the early days at Bredgar he had been well enough to cut down a pine tree which was taking all the light from the dining room and to make an excellent work table from part of the trunk; for as one might expect the work shop or 'the shop' at Bredgar was fitted up with the old workbench from Woottonga, and all tools, as before, were stored neatly round the walls. He loved the garden at Bredgar and although Saunders, the gardener, worked away steadily, J.L.T. had enjoyed pottering about and making improvements.

It was not only his own neuralgia which troubled J.L.T. The illness of Colonel Fraser caused him much sadness; and although, up until his last months. Col. Fraser enjoyed visiting Bredgar, both men knew that there could be only one outcome of his distressing cancer. The visits would soon cease. They were both men of action, now constrained; both fine horsemen and men with a deep knowledge of horses. Colonel Fraser: a crack shot and a versatile linguist, – fluent, it was said, in nine languages; J.L.T.: an average shot and knowing no language other than English. One: a more courtly man; the other: more straightforward and plain speaking. They were both born in the same year, 1846. They had both travelled and had ridden, in their youth, rough horses over rough terrain for many thousands of miles. In old age, in spite of their differing backgrounds, the two men were great companions. When, eventually, Fraser's visits to Bredgar became infrequent, J.L.T. truly missed the stimulating conversation and the company of such a delightful friend.

But there were consolations to 1923.

In particular, J.L.T. was looking forward to the homecoming of his two sons. Jim had written in a recent letter of how much he had liked Bredgar House and that if he were able to find work in England, of how he would like to settle somewhere 'not too far away from you all.' The work was an unknown quantity but with Sheppey and the Isle of Grain both so near, Detling even more close and Shorts barely 15 miles away at Rochester, J.L.T. was confident that Jim would be fortunate in his search.

H., too, was hopeful of finding work in England. The plan was to take a flat in London, leaving the children in the care of Alie and Emmie, and to hunt about for something useful to do. Although the houses which he had built on Point Grey had been successful, he had lost money over his sawmill; for, as soon as it was learned in early 1923 that he planned to return to England, his sawmill partners, (neither of whom were native-born Canadians,) – held out to buy him out at a low price until, on the eve of his departure from B.C., he was obliged to settle on their terms. With the sawmill had gone a lot of money, including his war gratuity. It was a disappointing business, particularly to someone of his innate soundness.

We arrived at Tilbury in November 1923, and I was later told that Charles came to meet us. I remember only suddenly being inside Bredgar House and the warmth of my Grandmother's welcome.

J.L.T. was often in the dining room, sitting at the round library table under the Zoffany. D. (Daphne) and I used to take it in turns to sit on his knee and he would let us blow open his half-hunter watch.

One day, he was not there.

He had had another, and a fatal, stroke. He was semi-conscious for a fortnight, Charles and H. looking after him with the greatest tenderness and care.

Soon the house was crowded with men in black as numerous cousins and old City colleagues, who had come down for the funeral, thronged through the hall.

Jim had come home too late to see his father.

I can remember the excitement over his imminent arrival, with much running to the door, many telegrams. At last he came and everyone's spirits seemed to lift as he entered the house from the wintry world outside. He walked quickly through to greet his Mother. Later on, he came and made friends with D., who was his god-daughter, and with me. He lifted me up and swung me onto his shoulder. In spite of the sad circumstances of his homecoming I have a memory of a vibrantly cheerful and very dear man.

There was, (Jay told me) – an atmosphere of urgency about him as he discussed his immediate plans with his family. Apart from a list of theatres and concerts to visit he had a long list of people whom he wished to see. He was back and he wanted to find out, with all speed, what was being done and by whom. Above all, he would have wanted to know Oswald Short's views on his scheme – the specification on behalf of the Chilean Navy – for a large all-metal flying boat.

Among the numerous invitations which came to him as soon as it was known he was home again was an invitation from Oswald Short to be a fellow guest with him at the Works Dinner on February 15th. Jim and Nancy took a flat in Oxford Terrace. The Frank Travers' had taken over the flat in Bedford Gardens Terrace. Frank wrote to Emmie from his office at Joseph Travers & Sons, 119, Cannon Street, on the 15th January: '... Jim called here yesterday looking, I thought, very well, and as we are to be near neighbours in town I hope I may see something of him ...'

Among the many people in the world of aviation who were looking forward to seeing him, and among the first to contact him on his return, was his old friend Arthur Quex Cooper.

Jim had written home from Valparaiso that '... Arthur Cooper and Charles are now my only Aviation correspondents...' and now that Jim was, at last, back after all the delays and postponements and the extension of the Chilean contract, there was the matter of the little monoplane, the HAWK.

Ever since his earliest days whatever Jim had designed had been designed to advance a theory and to put that theory to the test. His petrol-injection engine, his monocoque fuselage, the bomb-sighter and the flight-recorder, the twin-engine and the better direct-drive twin-engine, the numerous flotation bags and floats and, with Commander Porte, the beautiful Felixstowe boats.

The little HAWK, for which he had done all the design drawings many years before, had been to experiment further with the thick wing: with 'thick high-lift wing sections.' From Jim's allusions to it it was obvious that he had not been thinking about it at all and was surprised to hear that Arthur Cooper had in fact built the small machine; indeed he was now thinking so much in terms of metal that he might well have re-designed it to an all-metal version. But Arthur Cooper had persevered with it and to such an extent that although in its early days it was known as the Travers Monoplane by the time Jim returned from Chile it had become known as the Cooper Monoplane. Arthur Cooper had built it and it was Arthur Cooper who had radically altered the design of the tail section.

In Jim's letter to Charles of 1st April, 1922, he had written: '... I was awfully interested in your description of your visit to Shenfield and the progress of the HAWK monoplane – I am very glad Arthur is going on with it, I thought perhaps he would get fed up with it – It should be ready for test when we get back about the beginning of

next year. The trouble will probably be to find a good aerodrome near
by, unless he takes it to Grain or Martlesham . . .'

Should one wonder why Cooper, owner and builder of the machine,
did not test it himself, – skilled pilot of long standing that he was, (he
had been at Felixstowe with Jim during the war and had taken over
Command at Grain from him), one must, I think, go back to 1911 to
the old days at Eastchurch. Cooper would have undoubtedly known
about and may have remembered Jim's disappointment on being
denied the test-flights on the Tandem-Twin by the owner, McClean.
It may well have been for reasons of courtesy and friendship, therefore,
which decided Cooper to ask Jim to do the full and thorough tests on
the H A W K. The machine, which was fitted with a 90 h.p. Rolls Hawk
engine, had already been flown in very short, straight flights, one
gathers scarcely more than 'hop' flights, by several pilots, among them
Arthur Cooper. It has not been possible to establish the reason for
him taking the machine to Croydon. It will be remembered that Jim
had written of Grain or Martlesham. Perhaps Croydon was the most
convenient 'good aerodrome near by.' (It had been designated Airport
in March 1921.)

Jim was not entirely happy about the machine; nor was he happy
about the change in the design of the tail section and when he at last
agreed to test the monoplane, on a bitterly cold day in a series of
bitterly cold days, it was on the firm condition that the H A W K would
have gone through wind tunnel tests satisfactorily. Jim would be told
immediately on his arrival at Croydon if the H A W K had failed its wind
tunnel tests. If he received no such message then the machine would
have passed the wind tunnel tests.
    The arrangement was clear.
    So he went down to Croydon on Thursday, February 14th, arriving
there over lunch time. His wife had not wanted him to go and had
tried to dissuade him, as he had had a cold.
    There was no message for him at Croydon and he therefore took
the machine up. He took off into a North East wind of about 20 m.p.h.

There was not a big crowd of people but among those who were there
was (Sqdn-Ldr) C. A. Rae, later test pilot for Boulton & Paul, who
photographed the H A W K on take-off.

The brief description section of Accident Report Number R.62 subsequently stated: 'After climbing to a height of a few hundred feet and flying a half circuit of the aerodrome the M/C went into a steep dive from which it did not recover before striking the ground.

The pilot was killed.'

Another photographer recorded the wreckage of the H A W K.

Newspaper reports quoted a number of eye-witness accounts of which the main thread was constant and as follows: On the pilot attempting a steep bank the machine suddenly nose-dived and burst into flames. The machine was entirely out of control. After appearing to struggle with the controls for a few moments the pilot was seen to stand up and, as the blazing aircraft hurtled to earth he jumped 'in a bold bid for life' as the machine neared the ground. His body was found some 15 yards from the machine. He had been killed instantly.

H. and H. – Herbert and Hermia, had been living at 52, Upper Gloucester Place for some weeks while H. was desperately job-hunting.

On the morning of the 14th February he had finally closed with a mining concern who had offered him a job which would take him to the Far East. He was thankful to find anything at all in those grim days of unemployment, even though it meant leaving England within six days. Hermia wrote to Emmie at mid-day on the 14th and in the afternoon H.O. added his love to the letter and took it and a number of others out to post.

She wrote:

'My dear Mum, Many thanks for your p.c. just received. Am so very relieved to hear Daffy is better & am looking forward to seeing them both to-morrow (Friday). We will *both* come down by the train leaving Victoria 3.20 p.m. I don't know whether you will be glad or sorry or both together, but H.O. has got the Korean job & is to sail on the 20th of this month – that is Wednesday next. It leaves very little time for him in England, but I suppose it cannot be helped. He is going out with a pleasant man named Matheson Martin who has spent many years in Yokohama but is not connected with the mines in any way. He gets 2 days in Vancouver if sailings are on time, so will be able to pick up the gun & rifle & anything else he wants from the house there. No more just now. This to catch early post . . .'

On his return from posting the letters, H. met Jim's landlord. The landlord held a telegram in his hand and he was looking for H. Much later that night, after a series of visits, H. wrote to Emmie:

14th Feb 1924 ... Things seem to tumble on us, one on top of another.

I had only gone to post Hermy's letter to you & met the landlord of #39 Oxford Terrace as I came back.

Thank goodness it was absolutely instantaneous.

I saw A. Cooper this evening & will let you know arrangements to-morrow as soon as I know when the coroner can hold the inquest.

Hermy will be with you to-morrow, but I will find my way down as soon as there is no more to be done here.

It is short notice between now & Wednesday.

Hermy asks me to say she will find her own way up to-morrow ... (from the station)

On the way back to Upper Gloucester Place that evening, having been out to send a number of telegrams H. had seen the news sheets at the street corners and had heard the newsboys traditional cry: 'Read all about it!' It was an experience which sickened him to such an extent that he had a fear of the popular press ever afterwards.

In due course H., accompanied by Charles, went to Croydon to make identification of the body: to formally recognize that which was no longer recognizable.

There were many of Jim's old friends from his student days at his funeral, at Croydon. On seeing Arthur Barry among them, hurrying along and almost overcome with grief, Emmie opened the carriage door and insisted that he travel with herself and the family. Jay often told me this: how controlled Emmie was on that terrible day, while she and Alie could not see for tears.

Let no one who has ever thought of writing a letter of condolence or sympathy to the bereaved ever refrain from doing so; the letters which poured in after Jim's death must have been of very real solace to Emmie.

She sat at the little desk, the small Davenport which her Mother had brought from Theobalds seventy years before, and with the miniatures of Jim's great-grandparents and the photograph of his young widow on the wall before her, she wrote letter after letter in her elegant hand, in the writing which seemed to grow more beautiful and more dignified as she tried to thank those who had taken the trouble to write to her of her son.

Arthur Pike wrote from Warlingham: '... I must write this little line to say how much I sympathise with you & with all of you in the cruel fate which has befallen your Jim, after all those years of splendid work on behalf of the nation, who are thus deprived of his skill and genius.

It is terrible also for his poor wife – please convey to her my most sincere sympathy.

I am glad Herbert is with you ...'

L. A. Legros wrote from London: 'Please allow me, though my friend Gascoyne has writen to tell me he has forwarded you my letter to him, to express to you and to Col. Travers' wife the deep sympathy I feel for you in the severe bereavement you have sustained by the loss of son and husband – one of the best.

'As you will remember he was my pupil in the motor car works and his keenness and hard work I knew would soon place him high on the ladder. The aeroplane gave him his chance and he rose to the first rank of experts in his field. It is one of the saddest features of this new arm and mode of travel that blind chance should claim such victims from the best ...'

Eric McKinnon wrote to H. from de Zoete & Gorton: '... I can't tell you how sorry I was to see the news of Jim's death in the papers. I wish you personally could have heard some of the remarks I have heard in the R.A.F. Club about the loss he will be to aviation particularly in regard to his technical knowledge ... Best luck to you in your new venture.'

C. G. Grey, to whom Emmie had written for further copies of the *Aeroplane*, sent them 'hoping that she would accept them....' 'W.H.S.' (*Aeroplane*) had written one of the most accurate of the many obituary notices which had appeared; amongst his remarks were the following: '... During his service in Chile he was responsible for the training and organization of that service which he brought to a high state of efficiency, and had carried out experimental work concerning the use of large flying boats at sea which may have a very important bearing on the future developments of naval air power ... At the time of his death Col. Travers was still in the service of the Chilean Government and engaged in negotiations for the construction of new aircraft for the Chilean Navy to specifications based on the result of his experience with seaplanes on the Pacific Coast.

'The machine on which he was killed was designed by him in collaboration with Major Cooper before Col. Travers departed for Chile and was built by Major Cooper. The machine was completed shortly before his return to England...' The piece ended with an eulogy.

Also reported in the *Aeroplane* of February 20th was 'A SHORT Function.' Mr Oswald Short was the principal guest at a dinner held by the foremen of Short Bros. Ltd. at the firm's works in Rochester on Friday February 15th ... He (Oswald Short) said that they all regretted to hear of the death of their old friend of the early days at Eastchurch, Lt-Col. Travers. It was a great shock to read of his death because he had intended to visit them and they had hoped he would have been present that night. He was a man who saw far ahead with regard to aircraft development and his loss robbed the country of another pioneer. He was sure they would all join in offering their deepest sympathy to his widow and relatives.'

From Cousin Siss Tindal, now permanently settled in 'little' Yattendon, named after a racehorse who was named after their own Berkshire village, came three close-written pages of memories of happy times gone by, of 'dear old Cousin Lindsay' and 'young Jim of whom I have such happy recollections especially during his short time at Wellington when he used to come over to us. He was a very very dear boy...' and Cousin Siss pressed Emmie to come out to the Clarence River for a year or two, saying how comfortable the house was in spite of being small, for it had such wide verandahs and 'I should love to shew you our start of an orchard with its Oranges, Persimmons, Mulberries, Lemons, Pine Apples, etc...'

A sad little note from J. L. Bevir, saying: '... I knew Jim for the short time he was at Wellington & was very grieved to see his death in *The Times* ...' and adding, at the end of his letter 'my boy was killed in the war & my daughter is married and living in Bucharest – so that we are all alone. . . .'

There were dozens more letters. I have not read them all. Jim, perhaps, would have liked the letter from Janet Livingstone-Learmonth best of all, for it was with her that he had enjoyed his happy boyhood days at Groongal, on the beautiful sheep station on the Darling Downs and when he had, for the first time, admired the wonderful Aermotor, all made of iron.

My dear Emma,

Poor dear old Jim. You can't think how we feel for you all. One of the best & nicest of men. Our dearest love to you. Yours ever J. L. Learmonth.

To all of them Emmie wrote reply 'he would not have chosen a different death. It was instantaneous and to the last he had the joy of the experimenter' and 'soon he hoped they would start a seaplane mail service along the Coast' and 'the Chileans valued him but he was delighted to find himself at home and among old friends here' and to all of them she wrote 'but to all of us the loss is very great' and to many of them she wrote 'the widow is very brave . . .'

H. had a strange letter from Jezzi, written from Lombard Street on the 15th February:

Dear Travers, I have just heard of the accident that took place yesterday at Croydon & am writing to say you have our deepest sympathy in this sad bereavement. Of course it came as a great shock to me in spite of the fact that flying men are liable to crash at any time. I was looking forward to meeting dear old Jim shortly & talking over old times with him. For some reason I had a foreboding that Arthur's machine was going to crash, goodness knows why I should have thought so as I knew it was most carefully made.

My wife joins me in wishing to be remembered to all your people. Please drop in & have a chat when you are this way . . .

As for the accident at Croydon: verbal messages are dangerous things and the cause of many disasters or, perhaps, the cause of many disasters not being averted. It would have been so easy, I would have thought, to have chalked a message on or near the H A W K to the effect that it had N O T gone through its wind-tunnel tests. Those who knew that the machine had not gone through satisfactorily and who were responsible for handing on the vital information were 'at lunch' when Jim had arrived from London.

Poor Arthur Cooper, – one's heart goes out to him, for he felt keenly the fact that he may have been, in however small a way, at least partly responsible for the accident. The Travers family, (with the single exception of H. – he and Arthur Cooper maintained a faint dislike of each other and sought to avoid conversation when they met in later years at the Aero Club) – welcomed Arthur Cooper's continuing friendship. Jay, in particular, looked forward to his visits when she was living in her own house in the 1930s and 1940s; it was thoughtful of him to go and see her from time to time and he did so every few years up until about 1950. They would talk for hours and he said more than once how much he regretted altering Jim's design.

Emmie, I believe, took Jezzi's philosophical viewpoint, that: '. . . flying men are liable to crash at any time . . .'

H. duly left England on 20th February, 1924, bound at first for New York, where he arrived on February 26th. He then made his way across North America, probably by what is now called the Soo Line and by Canadian Pacific Railway, – for I have his railway map of the date, to Vancouver, where he would have picked up his 'gun & his rifle & anything else that he needed' from his one remaining house there. With what feelings he would have looked at the houses he had built along Point Grey, less than three months after he had left them for home, one can only imagine.

He sailed in the Canadian Pacific liner S S *Empress of Russia* and wrote to Emmie from her on 14th March, the first of a series of long letters home. '. . . The day before yesterday we saw the Aleutian Islands Great masses of snow covered rock about 15 miles to the North. I had no idea before that there were mountains on those Islands 5000 & 6000 feet high. We have been putting back our watches about 1 hour per day since leaving England. That is, the days have been 25 hours long because the ships & train were travelling with the sun. On Tuesday night the Old World could stand it no longer and we woke up the

HGT in Korea, 1924   his table and stove

photo: Boydell

next morning to find that it was Thursday. We had crossed the International Date Line. The ship is very empty. Half a dozen Japanese, 8 or ten Americans a French family & a dozen English. add a sprinkling of other nationalities & the passenger list is complete...'

In due time, by way of Japan, H. reached Taiyudong, Chosen, (Korea,) where he took up his appointment as accountant and assistant to the manager of a gold mine. There had been a bad earthquake there some years before and the chartered accountant had left afterwards for a spell in England, badly shocked and having lost his wife in the earthquake.

H.'s letters from Taiyudong are letters of such charm and interest that they would make a small book on their own. One is struck by the sense of peace that emanates from them. After the recent events in England it was as though the harsh, abstemious life of the gold mining camp exerted a healing power over him. His handwriting flowed smoothly as he described his small stone house, the table and chair, and the oil lamp by the light of which he wrote his letters home late, late in the evening.

When, on the 24th May, 1924, Hermia gave birth to her third child, and the news was cabled to him, he wrote delightedly home, not at all disappointed, as was poor Hermia, that the longed-for son had not yet arrived. The 'Lilybud', he called my sister Elizabeth Margaretta, (whom we all called Betty,) and he sent parcels of Korean lily bulbs home for Emmie to plant in the garden.

He had a puppy, Spot, who did not survive and the following year a beautiful Irish setter, all long legs and a silky coat, called Ben. There were Englishmen there. Among them, to H.'s amusement, was an old colleague from R.N.A.S. days, Bryan. '... A.H.C. is in Seoul fixing up some business so I am acting as host over at the Big House. We also have Bryan staying there. He was in the R.N.A.S. with me at Dunkirk ... It is quite by chance that he was sent by our friends in Japan to improve the power production of our gas producers. It has been most amusing to yarn with him in the evenings of old days. He came to Japan with Sempill's Aviation Mission. Apparently Sempills was too quick & efficient for the Japanese & in this topsy turvy country incurred their displeasure by training the pilots in one year when he might have spun it out to three years – as he was getting £300 per month it seems a little foolish...'

He described the climate and the landscape to Emmie and when she wondered whether the mountains were at all like those in her beloved Switzerland, he replied: '... the mountains here are certainly full of character but none of them are really high like Canada or Switzerland. We are about 30 miles from the border I think so the mountains here are purely Korean...' and later in the same letter, talking of English fogs, he wrote: '... In the *Punch* this week which Jess so kindly sends me there was a humorous article about some people who started from some country cottage in Sussex & were caught in a fog, also several illustrated jokes on the same subject. So I am not surprised to hear that Charles' train overshot Sittingbourne station...'

Then he described the Japanese floors: '... Of course no Korean or Japanese ever wears shoes in the house & as a result the floors are very smooth & clean. The Kang floor which heats these native houses in winter is nothing more than a series of flues which run under the floor of the room. In this way they have a sort of central heating & can burn any rubbish in the fireplace which is part of the kitchen. You will say the idea is as old as the Romans but the civilization of Chosen

his view

his house

bulls hauling casting for mine

photos: H. G. Travers

goes back 2000 years B.C. & so the Romans were savages when the people of Chosen were more civilized than to-day...'

In February, 1925, a year after Jim's death and thirteen months after the death of J.L.T., Colonel Fraser at last died. He had put up a fierce fight. H. wrote to Emmie: '... I hope Col. Fraser passed without much suffering, though I fear he may have had a worse time than he allowed anyone to know about. He knew he could not last until my time came to return to England & touched me very much by quite frankly saying good-bye. He thought the world of Hermy and I really believe that it was a great comfort for him to see her during this last year – especially when he was so ill last winter ... I think he was very sad to see Dad fall ill & that they had a mutual affection for each other.... I am sorry to think that Daph's illness at Christmas time must have put a severe strain on everyone.... To-night I am sitting up late because I have to open the safe at 2 in the morning to release some bullion (gold) which is going off to Seoul. Usually we send it in little sacks through the Post Office parcel post – but this is an extra shipment...'

February also brought changes to the mine which were to directly affect H. The part-owner of the mine died. The mine was then bought out by a French concern and in due course and by degrees, all English employees were replaced, in the managerial jobs, by French people.

On October, 1925, H. wrote to Alice & Charles: 'This is probably the last letter which you will receive from this address ... the Frenchmen who had already paid for this property have been allowed to regain control in many matters. One of these takes the form of requiring a large percentage of French citizens among the responsible positions here. The company, therefore, have had to buy out Boydell and myself and there are more British and Americans to go in the near future.... This breaking of contracts by the company has been an expensive business for them and they have had to compensate Boydell and myself with a considerable sum of money each.... Much as I wish to see my babies and the rest of the family, I am looking for further work in the East before returning home ... Should I be successful, I will let you know my full address as soon as possible...'

He wrote on the 14th November from c/o Hong Kong & Shanghai Bank, Kobe, Japan: '... it is very hard to find work ... However, things are never so bad as they seem and I feel that within a year or so I shall be doing as well as ever. In the meantime, I hope to keep expenses down ... I wish I had Hermy here – that is as far as going about and meeting people and so on, but financially I thank heaven that I am alone...'

And to Emmie, on the 25th November: '... It was pleasant to have your letter telling me of the children at their little school, it seems a very well run place. I am afraid that if I go for long without seeing them I shall probably grow away from them and yet one must go wherever the opportunity to make a living takes me ... Charles will realize how hard it is to find work and how quickly savings disappear. I hope he lands something good before long...'

He could find nothing in Japan. All was promises, promises. And Kobe was expensive. He decided to return to England and to start again, before all his savings and compensation money was gone.

He returned by the most economical route, continuing his circumnavigation of the globe, travelling as much as was possible by tramp steamer. He had been out of England for two years; the Government had changed yet again but employment was not any better than it had been under Ramsay Macdonald's 1924 Government when he had left home. Once again his search for work began. Once again Joseph Travers & Sons had nothing to offer the young man – he was still only thirty-four years old – whom they had been so delighted to acclaim as one of their number when he had returned as a 'hero' in 1918.

At least he had his Mother's comfortable house as a refuge while he searched. Many another 'war hero' was selling matches on street corners.

During H.'s two years abroad, Charles had been the man of the family, caring for his Mother and sisters, employing himself in a thousand small helpful ways but, I suspect, still quite stunned within.

He kept up some sort of engineering training at a Works in or near London, precisely which Works I have been unable to establish,* and he kept up his flying training. He also attended the Fishmonger's Dinners regularly and much enjoyed them. For some of his time he was in digs in London. At other times he was at Bredgar.

I remember him best as an old man, stooped and serious, unfailingly kind to D. and me and to Betty, to whom he was godfather. It was years later that I realized that the 'old man' was only in his middle twenties during those Bredgar days. He had made and he continued to maintain a particularly nice wireless set, which stood on its own table by the fireside in the drawing room and which gave us all a lot of fun.

His invention was a constant delight: should the shiny table under the window look a little lifeless one day, then, on the next, it might well be enlivened by a clockwork mouse who ran dangerously near to the table edge but who never overbalanced. Should the shade of the table lamp – an oil lamp in those old country days – seem dull, then Charles, with dark paper and his skilled hand with the scissors, would make origami dancing girls, or prowling wolves, pursuing each other in silhouette against the warm yellow light. But of the many delights and amusements at Bredgar – croquet on the lawn, making hook rugs by the fire, or playing in the tipi which Alie had made for us 'young Canadians', (she had lifted the design from Ernest Thompson Seton's

* Possibly the Handley–Page Works.

Two Little Savages,) of the many delights of that happy place, best of all was the lantern slide.

On any pretext or no pretext at all – it was cold, or raining, or dark – the magic lantern equipment was brought out and the square boxes of slides. A sheet was hung against the dining room curtains which covered the tall windows and the show began. Thus one knew well the sad story of Rip Van Winkle, of the Man Who Ate Cheese for Supper and how the Rat came After It!, as well as more serious subjects, such as the Boer War (in 3 parts) and Queen Victoria's Diamond Jubilee. Charles also showed a nice selection of slides of early aviation subjects.

As soon as H. came home the frequency with which the aviation slides were shown increased. It was H. and Charles' commentaries which made the presentations so memorable. They would talk in a language one could not understand and yet, such was their concentration, one was held spellbound.

One day there was particular excitement, for Charles brought two new slides to the lantern show, one of which was of a photograph that he had only lately been given.

Thus we saw on the screen and many times magnified the photograph of a pilot well wrapped up against the cold, head and shoulders and left arm visible as he flew a monoplane not many feet above the ground.

'It's all right *then*,' would say H., or Charles, as they increased magnification until the aeroplane seemed to be almost in the room with us.

'They say she was hunting . . .'

'Must have been the tail . . .'

'She went very suddenly . . .' – then another slide was shown, this time of smoking wreckage on the ground and away and beyond it, a darker smudge.

'Now what is that?'

What was it. A heap of clothes which was mostly a belted coat. One could not see the face.

Between this.

And this.

The two pilots talked and talked and I longed to understand the meaning of what they were saying, for it was clear that they were having their own accident inquiry.

Sometimes there would be a small noise, just a sigh, perhaps, or the sound of a door closing, and then H. or Charles would put the slides of Jim away for awhile because Emmie, or Alie, had entered the room. But if D. or I were there by ourselves then it seemed that they did not tire of attempting to solve the mystery, nor did I ever weary of listening to them try.

Before H. left Bredgar again he salved Jim's engine, the original petrol injection engine of 1908. It had been out in the coach house for some long time; he and Charles cleaned and polished it and it was kept in the hall for a few days, propped up against the stairs. I thought it was beautiful and that it should stay there, eminently right in that room which already held, slung above the hall chest, an unused Nieuport airscrew which H. had brought home from France. But H., whose property the engine now was, had a more far-seeing idea and he offered it on loan to the Science Museum at South Kensington who were pleased to accept the care of it on those terms. I am happy to say that it is still on display as it has been for many years.

10

PHALERON BAY

1926–1928

H. re-qualifies at Brough – joins the Blackburn Aeroplane Co. as test pilot &
seaplane pilot at their Factory at Old Phaleron Greece – Brancker in Greece –
Geddes intervenes in Cobham/Blackburn plans – H.'s job ends abruptly

THE mining company had given H. excellent references and the firm
of Chartered Accountants, who had gone out from London to Chosen
in the summer of 1925 for the handover, were so impressed by the
part he had played in 'turning the company around' that they wrote
separate letters to Emmie and to Alie saying so, in addition to giving
him letters of introduction to a number of businesses in London. All
these kind words amounted to nothing at all, however, when, back in
England, H. was once again job-hunting. There was nothing, nothing.

So he turned again to flying.

It must be likely that it was his long conversations with Charles,
dedicated, as was Charles, to aviation, which prompted H. to re-
qualify. How they talked, those two. It was magical to hear them.
Should H. have felt any hesitation about returning to the air after an
interval, earthbound, of nearly seven years, he might perhaps have
riffled through his old Service 'flimsies' and have found himself cheered
by the kind remarks recorded therein, culminating in his final flimsy
of 1919, in which he was described by his Commanding Officer as 'an
exceptionally fine leader and pilot'.

He applied to join the Reserve of Air Force Officers and was granted
a commission as a Flying Officer on probation in the General Duties
Branch of the Reserve of Air Force Officers, Class 'A', on the 22nd
June, 1926.

Then he went up to Brough to re-qualify.

The late A. J. Jackson, who chronicled the histories of many of
England's most famous aviation companies, kindly gave me his per-

mission, in 1979, to quote wherever I liked from his work. The following extract is from his *Blackburn Aircraft Since 1909*:

The RAF Reserve School, Brough

The North Sea Aerial Navigation Company Ltd was spared the painful effect that the postwar slump had on most joyriding concerns but it was without aircraft and, to keep the company going, Robert Blackburn made it responsible for organizing the Blackburn company's not inconsiderable road transport operations which included communications between the Leeds and Brough factories and ferrying the fleets of buses and coaches for which Blackburns had built bodies. Because of these activities the company styling was changed to the North Sea Aerial and General Transport Co Ltd at the end of 1920, but no flying was done on its own account until some years later when the Air Ministry decided to sub-contract RAF Reserve training to civilian operators.

The four firms chosen were the de Havilland Aircraft Co Ltd at Stag Lane, Edgware, whose contract was signed on 1 April 1923; the Bristol Aeroplane Co Ltd which opened its school at Filton on 15 May; William Beardmore and Co Ltd who began instruction at Renfrew on 23 July; and lastly the North Sea Aerial and General Transport Co Ltd whose contract was signed in January 1924. From the date of its opening in the following May until 1939 the Brough Reserve School was managed by Robert Blackburn's brother, Capt Norman Blackburn, with T. Bancroft as chief engineer and Sqn Ldr A. G. Loton, AFC, as chief flying instructor.

All the Reserve Schools used primary as well as advanced trainers, and the initial equipment at Brough consisted of three Avro 548A two-seat dual control biplanes G-EBIT, 'IU and 'IV, built to order by A. V. Roe and Co Ltd at Hamble and fitted with 120 hp Airdisco vee-8 air-cooled engines driving four-bladed wooden airscrews. There Brough's similarity to the other Schools ended because the advanced trainers which came into service from 1925 onwards were the three Dart two-seat seaplanes G-EBKF, 'KG and 'KH, and the Kangaroo dual conversions 'BONZO, FELIX THE CAT, WILFRED, PIP AND SQUEAK,' otherwise G-EAIU, 'MJ, G-EBMD, 'OM, and 'PK. Brough was unique therefore as the only School offering seaplane and twin-engined training.

The aircraft were housed in one of the two large hangars built in 1917 for No. 2 Marine Acceptance Depot, which for obvious reasons is known to this day as the North Sea hangar. Pupils were accommodated in huts originally erected for personnel of the Depot and their off-duty entertainment was looked after by the Brough Aviation and Recreation Club formed by the Blackburn directors in 1924.

H. wrote to Emmie from the North Sea Aerial & Transport Co Ltd, Brough, E. Yorks, on the 5th July, 1926: 'We have had very pleasant weather here last week and very hot. The machines and instruction seem excellent and everyone very thorough and careful.

The school practically closed on Friday noon until this morning and the few pupils and instructors all went to the RAF display. We left here at 2.15 and arrived in London at 11.45 so had a fast run down and no trouble. I saw Leask for a moment – our cars were moving opposite ways in two streams and he shouted something about having Charles with him; but I did not see CTT as I had to look where I was going there were so many pedestrians. The display was very fine in every way, the Autogiro a little disappointing in performance but it is a marvel that such a great departure from standard lines should fly at all. On the other hand the Hill tailless monoplane the Pterodactyl (something in the line of the Dunne machine of pre-war days) was most interesting and graceful.

I was very lucky to meet several old friends – two of them were my particulars and found them very pleasant after so many years. We came back yesterday afternoon and to-day everyone is recovering from the effects of the "holiday" and the long motor runs.

Best of love to all. . . .'

Hermia went up to join him and they stayed for a while at the Station Hotel. Brough was full of congenial and friendly people but it was, she often said in later years, 'the coldest place on earth', so the hot midsummer days had not lasted long.

H. started his re-qualifying course on the 28th June and completed it on the 13th July, having flown a total of 13 hours and 20 minutes, on Avros and Kangaroos. Arthur G. Loton, his instructor and the Chief Instructor of the school, remarked on H.'s Form 1416 on Pupil's Ability as a Pilot: 'AVRO At first had difficulty in landing, but improved rapidly and finally flew very well. KANGAROO A very sound pilot who flies and lands well and shows good judgement.' He placed H. in Category 1.

From their earliest beginnings and up to the time of their absorption into Hawker Siddeley, Blackburns had been builders of naval aircraft. East Yorkshire was not only bitterly cold. It was often beset with blanketing fogs which drifted in from the North Sea. Blackburns were, therefore, an ideal company to take advantage of the Greek Government's request for an English firm to build a factory for the construction of aircraft for the Greek Navy at Old Phaleron and to train Greek personnel there. In Greece they could test all year around.

A. J. Jackson wrote: 'During the second half of 1925 the Blackburn company had taken over and completed the construction of the Greek National Aircraft Factory at Old Phaleron, obtained a five-year contract to run it and, using local labour, began to manufacture further Velos aircraft. . . .'

Col. the Master of Sempill had gone out to Greece for Blackburns in 1925 to test for them, but he wished to return to England and when Robert Blackburn met H. up at Brough in the summer of 1926 he almost immediately asked him to join the company as their test pilot and seaplane pilot in Greece.

H. and H. had returned to their flat in London while plans were going forward and letters exchanged, but in mid-August they were up in Yorkshire again and Hermia wrote from The Station Hotel at Brough on the 24th August, to Emmie:

. . . We dashed up here on Sunday, or rather, to Leeds, & H. has a contract with Blackburn for the Greek job, subject to his seaplane flying here being all right, which of course it will be. So that we expect to be pushing off for Athens very soon if all goes well. H. is to do five hours here, and then we get back to the flat, & if everything is all right, shall be very busy settling up things, collecting gear etc. We are, of course, highly delighted as it will be very interesting & a wonderful climate & the children will be able to come out later on. . . . No more just now. We shall know rather more about things when the flying here is finished. . . .

All that H. recorded at the start of his third log-book was that, from the 24th to the 31st August, 1926, he flew Blackburn Dart seaplanes G-EBKF and G-EBKG for a total of $5\frac{1}{2}$ hours: 'Practice at Brough – E. Yorks.'

He left England on the 7th September and travelled out by the quickest route, which was then by cross-Channel to Calais and down through Switzerland and Italy to Brindisi and from Brindisi by boat to Piraeus. His log of flights in Greece opened on Tuesday, the 21st September, 1926 and each page of his flights for Blackburns was headed 'Tests of machines built or rebuilt at Phaleron, Greece'.

He first flew Velos seaplane /450 Napier/ Greek Navy T.13 at Old

Phaleron for 35 minutes. His passenger was C. H. Wylde, a name often revered in aviation circles in England for he was, or he became, a great exponent of the motorized glider. In 1926, however, Low Wylde was the designer/owner of an aeroplane which he had commissioned Blackburns to build for him at Old Phaleron. He remained in Greece for the duration of H.'s time with Blackburns. So far as I know only one of his aeroplanes was built, although he had a second design on paper lodged in the Workshops.

H. flew Velos T.23 (dual to C. H. Wylde) on the 28th September and on the 6th October flew Velos T.14 for 40 minutes for her acceptance test, 'with 10 hrs fuel in special tank. observer Lt Cdr Falkinaikis. boisterous weather. O. K. accepted.' And on the same day flew Velos T.15 for her acceptance trial 'dropping torpedo. throttle slack. passenger Lt. Voulsamis.' On the 7th October he flew T.15 again from Old Phaleron: 'passenger Turnpenny. Without torpedo.' And flew the seaplane again the same day for 35 minutes for her acceptance trial: 'landing with torpedo. O. K. accepted. passenger Falkinaikis.'

H. had gone on ahead to Greece as fast as was possible, leaving Hermia to pack and follow. He had found a flat for them in Athens but she found another that she liked better and they moved soon after her arrival. She was expecting her fourth child in December and the new flat had a small garden.

They both loved Greece and found the cosmopolitan society much to their liking. For H. there was the added interest of being at a land and repair point for many of the long distance flights of the day. Whether at Phaleron Bay or up at Tatoi, (the military aerodrome about 15 km from Athens), he was usually busy and he seems to have written few letters home; his log-book tells the greater part of his story.

On the 8th October he flew D. H.9/Puma N. A.85 from Tatoi aerodrome: 'Reconditioned engine rough & stiff. passenger Fisher.' And on a longer flight on the same day: 'engine still rough. passenger Rudolph Klich (Czech mechanic.)'

Still on the 8th October he flew the Greek Navy's D. H.9 aeroplane N. A.94 from Tatoi: 'reconditioned. machine O. K. Engine rough & stiff. passenger Fisher.'

On the 13th October he flew D. H.9 aeroplane N. A.85 from Tatoi:

H. at Tatoi

photo: Hermia Travers

'Claudel carburettor tests in air.' He continued to make short flights on the same machine, noting: 'O.K. on ground but not in air.' They must have finally ironed out the problem, for he recorded a flight of 15 minutes on the same machine on the 15th October with merely: 'passenger Fisher.'

On the 21st October he flew Velos T.16 'Phaleron Bay/Voulimeri

T.16 on the water

photo: H. G. Travers

T.16 at the Factory

60 minutes Speed & climb private trial new Velos passenger Major (?) Buerl landing with torpedo.'

On the 22nd October he flew Velos T.16: 'Phaleron Bay. Piraeus. Voulimeri. Piraeus. 55 minutes. Official type trial for Velos. passenger Lt. Cmdr Boukas. 5000 ft in 23 minutes. 80 knots at sea level with torpedo.'

On the 1st November he flew T.16 on a flight of 2 hours Phaleron Bay Hymethos Mt etc speed level 79 & 82 knots with torpedo 86 k without torpedo. plus 5% adjustment for atmosphere.

'5000 ft in 30 mins with torpedo.

'7000 in 47 mins.

'8400 in 75 mins.'

On the 10th November he flew D.H.9 aeroplane N.A.74 from Tatoi, with an un-named 'Greek sailor' as passenger: 'Prelim. test flight. Machine & engine O.K. & ready for acceptance.'

On the 13th November, H. wrote to Emmie from 'c/o Blackburn Aeroplane & Manufacturing Co., Old Phaleron, Athens, Greece…'

... The elections all passed off without any fuss & every one is I think relieved that the same government is in power as before. It means a continuity of policy & a steadying influence on everything.

Here we are all very well and the weather holds out. It is very pleasant & cool at nights but we do not yet need blankets.

Thank you very much for sending me the *Weekly Times* with the '*Litt: Supp*'. It is always full of interesting news & free from excessive partisanship.

I wonder what Charles is doing & how things are in England generally. I am much afraid that it will be a very hard winter for many people.

What strides the German commercial air lines are making. How (in England) we are hampered by the Air Ministry – or perhaps it is just by the conservatism of our designers. The big 3 engine all metal Junker which came here (before I arrived) made a big impression on the English as well as the Greeks.

I was up at Tatoi aerodrome last week & saw an interesting incident. When our lorry arrived at the aerodrome there was a large group of army people and French around a Breguet X1X which is the type on which so many long distance records have been made. Then I saw that

photo: H. G. Travers

Cobham on his way South. His DH50 rests on Phaleron Bay

the whole machine was one big tank. The engine out in front & the 2 pilots near the tail!

It may possibly have been Coste & the other fellow returning from Djack. The most impressive thing was the way the 'send-off' was backed up by French consul etc.

When Cobham arrived & departed there were only a few of us from Blackburns to look after him. No sign of consuls! lots of love to you all....

On the 23rd November he again flew D.H.9 N.A.74 up at Tatoi, this time for her acceptance flight, which was 'O.K.' He also flew N.A.94 on the same day for 30 minutes for her acceptance flight, remarking: 'V.G. minor adjustments to be made.'

Also on the 23rd November he flew D.H.9 N.A.85 remarking only: 'Acceptance flight O.K. v. good engine & machine.'

Hermia went into hospital in Athens for the birth of her fourth child and a daughter, my youngest sister Christina, was born there on the 14th December. It was, Hermia told us all later on, the best hospital with the kindest nurses she had ever known. Soon the little family were comfortably at home in their flat once again with, one gathers, any amount of help, if one can make out who Helene and Marie and some of the other girls were, nurses and maids. It was an ideal place to have a baby. Everyone was happy.

On the 17th December H. flew Velos seaplane T.18 at Phaleron Bay for 40 minutes: 'O.K. accepted. good torpedo drop. passenger King.'

On the 30th December he flew Velos seaplane T.17 at Phaleron Bay for 35 minutes: 'O.K. accepted. good torpedo drop.'

His first flight of 1927 was on the 4th January: 'D.H.9 seaplane (Puma) N.A.97. Phaleron Bay. 20 minutes. First flight in D.H.9 on floats in Greece. O.K. Good speed range with half load. Unstuck in 14 sec. light head wind.'

He flew the same machine again on the 13th January: 'Phaleron Bay & Kalamaki & Phaleron Bay. 30 minutes. Acceptance trial. Machine O.K. & landed. On taking off again for 2 hours flight float chassis collapsed before leaving water.'

H G T in the garden of his flat at Odos Pindaros, with
Christina
photo: Hermia Travers

H G T in the garden at Odos Pindaros
photo: Hermia Travers

The name of Low Wylde has already been mentioned. It was to become
only too familiar as the months rolled by. On the 5th February, H.
took the controls of the HELITHON for the first time: 'First trials.
Taxying. T skid bracket broke. repaired.' '7th: Taxying. Tail skid
broke. replaced.' '9th: 2 straights. 05 minutes. O.K.' '20th: 1 circuit.
05 minutes. Undercarriage O.K. shock absorber cross arms bent.
machine has strong tendency to swing landing.' '23rd: Windy. rain.
Rt & left turns. 10 minutes. 60 lbs ballast.' '24th: HELITHON first
trials. HELITHON/ 130 Salmson. Tatoi. Phaleron. Tatoi. 55 minutes.
131 lbs ballast in front seat. readings

Knots dial		kilom dial
top	80	145
climb	60	100
stall	50	77?

lateral control goes first – engine 2000 revs level. Empanage forwards – positive.' Later again the same day: 'HELITHON first trials. 30 minutes 131 lbs ballast in back.' 'First trials. 15 minutes. Flew from front seat. 1900 revs level. top 77 knots climb 58 knots. Empanage middle position.'

On the 25th February he continued to test the HELITHON. 'First trials. Tatoi etc. 30 minutes. Climb to 5000 ft in 15 minutes.

Clouds from 2000 to 3500 ft	0 to 3500	60 knots
	3500 to 5000	55 knots
	74 knots level at 5000 ft	
	self front	200 lbs
	HEMT back	161 lbs
Tanks full		361'

It was of course typical of Hermia to volunteer as ballast.

On the 26th February, Saturday: 'HELITHON. first trials. 1 hour. flying for demonstration(?) Could not make machine roll or spin. As in every previous flight m/c swung badly on landing. damage aileron slightly.'

On the 2nd March he flew the HELITHON again on 'first trials'. 'Cut plywood to give stick more movement.' Then he took the HELITHON, the SEAGULL, up again for a further 15 minutes: 'Undercarriage having been lowered and set back $1\frac{1}{4}''$ another trial landing was made. Taxying was easier & m/c did not swing on landing. Rudder movement is still insufficient. On attempting another flight engine failed completely at 10 ft. m/c safely landed in aerodrome. aileron cable frayed 3rd attempt cut out.'

On the 10th March the first trials of the HELITHON continued: 'New aileron cable fitted. Rudder king posts shortened to give more rudder movement. Control on ground improved. Engine very bad in air 1600–1800 revs & cut out completely twice. Increased stick movement in cockpit is improvement.'

The Helithon

photo: H. G. Travers

The Helithon

photo: H. G. Travers

On the 23rd March he flew D. H.9 landplane N. A.98 from Tatoi for
15 minutes: '1st test. warm engine.' And later the same day flew Bristol
landplane N. A.132 for 15 minutes: '1st test O. K.'

On the 1st April, his 36th birthday, he flew N. A.98 again for a 10
minutes reception flight: 'Engine boiling.' And later the same day flew
N. A.132 again for a 40 minute reception flight: 'O. K.'

The Helithon

photo: H. G. Travers

The Helithon

photo: H. G. Travers

On the 6th April the HELITHON once again hove into view, and once again 'First trials' are recorded. '120 Salmson. Tatoi. 10 minutes. new Salmson installed. new local prop. solo.' And later the same day he flew the machine again for 15 minutes, with Comdr Michael of the Inspection Service as passenger.

He flew the machine again on the 14th April for 15 minutes, to: 'To try new prop for climb. air rough. climb poor. passenger Fisher.'

On the 15th April, Good Friday, he persevered with the first trials of this unpleasant machine. Once again he flew from Tatoi. He made a number of flights, of 40 minutes, 35 and 25 minutes respectively and with her designer, C. H. Wylde (Low Wylde), as passenger. Some of the problems must have been solved as a result of these flights for on Saturday, 16th April, H. recorded in his log-book: 'HELITHON. Acceptance trials. Tatoi. 40 minutes. Weather good. light air from S. W.' And '4 take offs & landings. 40 minutes. passenger Phillipas.' and '5 speed test runs. 15 minutes. passenger Phillipas.' and 'loop $\frac{1}{2}$ roll & spin at 3000 climb to 4000 & landing without engine from 4000. 35 minutes. Passenger Falkinaikis.' and 'Officer from British Mission. 10 minutes. passenger Sqd. Ldr. Brooke R. A. F. to feel controls.'

On the next page of his book the record still runs: 'Sat. 16th April. HELITHON. Trials for acceptance continued at Tatoi. Climb to ceiling & 3 hrs duration trial. 3 hours. Total acceptance trial 4 hrs 40 minutes. Passenger Phillipas. Apparent ceiling 8400 in 50 minutes.'

On the 25th April he was back testing on Phaleron Bay. This time another D. H.9 seaplane with Puma 5403 N. A.89. Remarks: 'Engine boiling though throttled down to 1100 revs. Radiator very cool. Is water circulating?'

He tested N. A.89 again on the 3rd May for a flight of 30 minutes, with Capt. Lamplugh (Insurance) as his passenger. Remarks: 'New baffle in radiator O. K.' And on the 13th May flew N. A.89 again off Phaleron Bay on her acceptance flight of '3100 ft. Accepted O. K.' Later the same day he flew D. H.9 N. A.97 for 25 minutes: 'Preliminary flight after repairs. (new engine). Engine warm but not boiling. Controls stiff.' On the following day he again took N. A.97 off Phaleron Bay for 45 minutes: 'Acceptance flight. Controls eased. now O. K. Machine accepted O. K. Passenger Lt Boucas.'

On the 16th May he flew D. H.9 Seaplane N. A.101 from Phaleron Bay for 10 minutes: 'Engine boiling.'

On the 23rd May he was up at Tatoi, again flying the HELITHON: 'Solo. With top plane 3° bottom 2° stagger reduced by $1\frac{1}{4}''$. Still slightly tail heavy. Get away improved.' And later the same day took her up again for 15 minutes with 'Passenger Wylde & full tank. stalls at 43 knots. off in 10 secs. Flew from back seat.' And later again on the 23rd took the machine up again for 30 minutes: 'passenger Wylde in back seat. climbing as near 50 knots as poss. 4000 ft. 17 mins. Machine still a little tail heavy. Revs only 1400 climbing. stalls 43 knots.'

So much for the HELITHON. There is no record of H. ever flying that particular machine again.

When, in England again, Low-Wylde died at the controls of one of his own machines, there was nobody less surprised, or more relieved, than was Hermia. Her 30 minutes in the back seat of that 'nasty little machine' had convinced her that if Low-Wylde persisted in designing aeroplanes he should be ordered to test them himself.

In May of 1927 Hermia brought Christina home to England; not, as we three girls at boarding school fondly hoped, in order to gather us all up and take us out to Greece with her but the reverse: to park Christina on 'the healthy coast of Kent' at school with the rest of us. When taxed about the matter in later years she would mention such unpleasantnesses as earthquakes and revolutions; whatever the reasons were I have no doubt that they were valid ones at the time.

Hermia wrote from Walmer: 'The journey was a bit of a nightmare I should not like to do it again. The take off was a bit porpoise like ... However we got here, & Christina looks blooming to-day – from Marseilles we were 3 a side sitting up nearly all night. No couchette to be had. It is a farce booking them in advance. ... They' (D., E. and Betty) 'were very excited over the HELITHON snaps – most interested ...'

She and Christina had flown by Dornier Wal to Brindisi and thence had travelled by train and boat, a journey of two or three days, quite a journey to be undertaken alone with a six month old baby.

Charles drove down to Walmer in the old Citroën and took her back to stay with them all. Hermia wrote again to H. on Tuesday, 3rd May: '... here I am at Bredgar. It seems very odd. ... Charles makes one sad. He doesn't seem to have any go at all – is feebly learning Spanish from a Pelman book because Henderson said he would look out for a job for him but it sounds very vague. What good that would be as regards aeronautical engineering I don't know. ... I was afraid Helene & Maria wd not help you much over Easter but hope they have recovered & that all goes well & you get fed. Christina was flourishing when I left & had taken to her new Nanny. All the children were thrilled about a new baby. . . . Daph's scar is fading a lot & one doesn't notice it much. . . .'

It is obvious from the above that Hermia, usually so sympathetic to those in distress, quite failed to understand Charles and the depths of his bereavement. He was quiet, as he always was, but he was also quietly making plans and seeking to re-build his life after the desolation he had known following Jim's death. After that sad day (on the 15th February, to be exact) – he had resigned from ICE, thus cutting himself off forever from Associate Membership. Now he was thinking of ways of returning to aviation. There was never anything 'feeble' about him. Just thoughtful.

As soon as Hermia returned to Greece she and H. were once again in their whirl of social activity. They both played bridge. And golf. He bought a Ford car, a Model T Ford, and they became members of The Greek Touring Club and explored for miles along the dusty roads. She bought an Alsatian puppy, Tinker, whom she exercised on the airfield up at Tatoi.

They swam, often for miles, and they made boat trips to Skyros and to Nauplia.

They walked in the hills and were impressed by the courtesy and hospitality of people, country people, whom they chanced to meet and who would invite them, total strangers as they were, into their homes for refreshment of wine and cheese. They saw much and they enjoyed much about Greece. After their two years of separation, while H. had been in Korea, it must have been a happy time for them both.

They constantly met new people in connexion with H.'s job and here Hermia's gift for languages was useful. She had grown up trilingual English/French/German since childhood days in Switzerland and she soon learnt a smattering of Greek conversation, enough, she would say, to 'speak a few civil words to people'. H. had only the remains of his schoolboy French so her fluency was helpful.

There were dinner-parties too numerous to mention and a fancy dress party, one in particular, that H. was never allowed to forget. Briefly, the story was this:

Hermia had had the whole day to get ready and had made herself look thoroughly glamorous. H., who knew that he would only have a short time after work to bathe and change had opted for a fancy dress which would be speedy to adopt and for which he already had the requirements.

The arrangement for the start of the evening was that she should go on ahead by car with a crowd of friends and that H. should catch a bus from not far away, in Athens, at a terminus and join the party as soon as he was able to do so.

In due time he came home from the aerodrome and changed into his party clothes: his old brown Jaeger dressing gown, floor-length; no socks; his large and bony feet in open sandals. By arranging his thinning hair, snipped with nail scissors, across his forehead he gave a very fair imitation of a monk. He then set out for the bus.

Hours and hours later Hermia became worried. Telephones were not the ubiquitous instruments that they are to-day. A search party was started. The aerodrome. The flat. At a quarter to midnight H. was found. Tired out after his day's flying, he had fallen asleep in the bus, which he had not known was not being driven anywhere else that night and which had no driver nor any other would-be passengers. Any Athenians who had passed by had respected the weary 'monk's' wish to sleep. What anyone else who may still have been about at that hour have thought of a crowd of home-going partygoers attempting to extract a monk from his sleeping quarters – history does not relate.

'It was a comfortable bus,' H. would protest when, years later and on many occasions, we all teased him about the incident, 'a jolly good bus. Built by Shorts of Rochester like all the other buses in Athens . . .'

(He would sometimes tell us all how Shorts had survived the worst years of post-war depression by skilful diversification. They had built, not only a fleet of buses for Greece but among many other things and when the firm's finances were at a critically low ebb, a roadhouse near Maidstone. He told us that he had heard that Mrs Oswald Short had taken all her savings out of the bank, and in order to keep such a loyal and well-trained work force together and in employment, had commissioned the Tudor House on the main road.

The Tudor House was a thriving roadhouse for many years. It was destroyed by fire in 1983.)

On the 27th May H. flew D. H.9 Seaplane N. A.101 off Phaleron Bay for 2 hours for her acceptance tests: 'Accepted.' On the 15th July he tested D. H.9 landplane N. A.98 up at Tatoi: 'Accepted.'

Blackburn Velos T.15 on the water

photo: H. G. *Travers*

Boat coming ashore from Blackburn Velos T.15

photo: H. G. *Travers*

On the 30th July he flew D. H.9 Seaplane N. A.86 from Phaleron Bay for three-quarters of an hour: 'Accepted.'

There is no record of him flying in August. Indeed, he may have been unwell, for later on Emmie 'hoped Herbert had lost his fever'.

They moved house again, higher up, and settling down – as they thought – to remaining with Blackburns until the end of their contract with the Greek Government – once again planned to 'fetch the children'.

Emmie wrote to them on the 27th September: 'My dear Herbert & Hermy, Thank you for both your letters. I am glad you have moved up higher. I am sure the other could not have been very healthy. I hope Herbert has lost his fever. ... It is very thrilling about Daphne & Eva – They will be wild with delight.

'We are wondering if we could help in any way. It is a great undertaking the journey out with them. Would it help at all if Alice went with whoever fetched them. I would pay her expenses & she is fond of the children. She could manage to be away about 10 days about then ... We expect Charles back from Glasgow in a day or two – I daresay he has written to H. O. ....'

Nothing much came of this fresh excitement, however, for we children remained in England.

On the 6th September H. flew Bristol N. A.133 landplane 'Tatoi/ Phaleron/Tatoi for 45 minutes. Preliminary O. K. easy climb to 5000 ft.' On the 20th September he flew the same machine at Tatoi: 'acceptance test. Passenger Velondis. Accepted O. K. 4000 ft.' On the 29th September he flew Velos T.19 Seaplane off Phaleron Bay: 'Prelim. light. 25 minutes. New m/c O K pass. mech.' And later the same day took the same machine, T.19, up again: 'Phaleron Bay etc. Acceptance tests with torpedo. 1 hour 30 minutes. climbed 6000 ft 1 hour. weather hot. air thin. passenger Lt. Velondis.'

On the 5th October he flew D. H.9 Seaplane N. A.99 off Phaleron Bay for 35 minutes: 'Prelim. & acceptance trials. O. K. accepted. climbs well. 3000 ft in 7 minutes. air rough. water surface good.'

Among the many people who visited Greece that year in connexion with aviation in general and with Blackburn's in particular was the Director of Civil Aviation, Sir Sefton Brancker.

Much has been written of Sir Sefton. The biographies as well as the passing references to him all give him the same ring of energy. He was here, there and everywhere – monocled, observant and full out for British aviation. For many, especially for pilots, he *W A S* British aviation.

He had long been estranged from Lady Brancker and he travelled about the world with his mistress quite openly. She was the enigmatic Auriol Lee, a woman of great wit and charm, and an actress of distinction. In spite of the irregularity of their situation they were generally considered as being something of a special case and the remarkable couple were forgiven, and welcomed, by those not in Lady Brancker's circle.

H. and H. were among those in Greece who welcomed them; the four saw a great deal of each other during Brancker's brief visit to Greece. One day the four of them, with the Blackburn's, went on an all-day boat trip together, landing on one of the islands to picnic. It was a memorable and a most enjoyable day and a day during which much was discussed. Brancker made it clear that he was full out and totally supportive of all that Blackburns in general and Robert Blackburn and H. in particular, were trying to achieve in Greece.

The boat trip with the Blackburns, Sir Sefton Brancker, Auriol Lee & others

The boat trip (*three photos* H. & H. *Travers*)

The boat trip. Auriol Lee seated

They kept in touch after Brancker returned to England; Hermia wrote to Miss Lee and received her reply on the 22nd October, from London:

Thank you so very much for your letter – bless you both. I snort & sniff here! We have 'community coughing' in London. *Sech* weather!

The end of the voyage was swift and thrilling Venice Vienna Berlin – & I found a marvellous airsickness dope – & enjoyed it all enormously.

We were snowed under with work at once – the little man off flying – & myself selling bonds etc. He is in Italy now again – & will be away on & off for the next 3 weeks. I saw the B'burnes again at the Schneider Cup dinner & they were very charming to me. I believe the lucky creatures head for Athens to-day. Isn't it too disgusting for them to have lost the remaining 'Pelican' in E. Africa? I'm so sorry for Gladstone too. The book has not come was it sent at the same time as your letter? Your news about X came as a surprise – He seemed so resolved to keep clear of the political game. Do let me hear what happens & all about it.

I think B ... for *once* was a shade offended at the obvious lack of interest on the part of the representative Mc something in Loraine's absence! He doesn't generally notice! & I think he felt it was a gaucherie & was not 'on the job'. That is not *my* business, but I thought it might amuse you. Your holiday did sound lovely. What a divine country. Will you please give H. my love – & *soon* let me hear you are coming along. It is raining drearily – & I think I shall go to bed for the day. Ever yrs Auriol.

Gossip, perhaps, but informed gossip from a woman of some influence. H.'s last recorded test flight in 1927 was on the 28th October, when he flew D.H.9 Seaplane N.A.65 off Phaleron Bay for 40 minutes: 'Preliminary & acceptance trials O.K. accepted. Climbs well. weather ex. water smooth.'

There may not have been any more machines ready for test but there was any amount to be done.

Confident, after Brancker's good offices, that Blackburns would have at least another year at Old Phaleron, Hermia once again planned to return to England to collect her brood.

*　　*　　*

Robert Blackburn spent a good deal of time in Greece; reference to this was made in a letter to Emmie, written by H. on the 3rd November, 1927, from

Odos Pindarou 36a, Athens ... Blackburn & Mrs B. are back again here now – not unpleased with what we have done during their absence though we were unable to obtain all the programme he gave me in August.

This means that neither Hermy nor I can leave here until they go & he may decide to stay weeks yet. It rather puts off the question of going home this week to fetch the children. Our own future & that of our firm here is uncertain until various matters with the Government are settled.

Since August I have been acting (you know) as his personal representative and as chairman of our small board of management here as well as making the delivery flights of the machines we have built here.

This work has been very interesting – entailing the meeting of many people & a little entertaining in all of which Hermy has been of the greatest assistance to me.

Hermy's presence is absolutely necessary here for the moment both for the firm & myself. Luckily the school bill is paid (by H E M T) until the end of the term & the children do not yet know that we proposed to take them away at half term ... [We did – there was a mole in the nursery – Ed.] Within a few weeks I hope we shall know whether we stay here for another year or two or leave early in the new year.

In any case this has been a most wonderful opportunity for me and the experience will all be to the good.

What a serious letter! Write and tell me please dear Mum how Jess is settling in her new house, how Alie's Institute & Kentish plays go, what Charles is doing and any news you have of V or the children.

Do you still think of letting or selling Bredgar. I might happen to hear of a client ...

It was unlike H. to be so much on the defensive and one can only imagine that in addition to the preoccupations of his work he had been aware of criticism, stated or implied, of Hermia for parking all her children among strangers. But H. & H. both knew that all of us would have been far too much for Emmie and Alie. Besides, the medical advice had been to keep D. 'near the healthy coast of Kent at Deal'.

Although the Blackburns had not yet returned to England, Hermia could be temporarily spared and so she decided to come over and collect us. She arrived in late November and, school term being still in progress, went first to London to stay with her cousin Ella Lefroy. She had planned the return trip to be by rail to Brindisi and thence by Dornier Wal. It would be Christina's second flight and a first flight for the three eldest. Once again, however, her plans came to nothing, for even while she was on her way to England, the Geddes axe had begun to fall on the long-term plans of Blackburns in Greece. Politicians then, as now, interfered in aviation whenever it suited them to do so. Hermia wrote to H. from the home of her Uncle Harry (the Rev. H. P. Fraser), Ryton Rectory, Shropshire, where she had gone for the week end after leaving London. Her letter was headed 'Sunday':

After an absolute orgy of telegrams at the Belgravia Hotel I came here & go back to Ella's on Monday, where I will stay indefinitely. It is no use upsetting the children in term time. I have an idea that we might go to The Fair Maid of Kent (hotel) & have them 2 at a time & you could spend as much time as you wanted in Bredgar – & get up to town fairly easily – but there won't be much doing in the Xmas hols. I feel very annoyed to have left in such frantic haste all for nothing – and you are left with the mouldy business of packing up. Do get my fiddle put in a good strong case. R.B. is a curious unaccountable man. I am wondering if you had a row with him in the end. He really has made an almighty hash of his affairs as far as one can see.

I lunched with Brancker & Miss Lee, (before your *second* telegram had come) & told him more or less how things were. He said Woods Humphery was going out. No one will do any good there unless they bribe heavily in the right places. I suppose you may be lucky & get something with Scaros later on. It certainly would be an advantage knowing the country. Brancker was very cheery & friendly – but I think he is far too much under the thumb of Auriol Lee. According to her, Eric Geddes has Sam Hoare eating out of his hand – as he is just a slightly feeble little banker with no knowledge of aviation & Geddes of course is one of these super business men. . . . I met & made friends with Mrs Wingate, & when your second wire appeared it struck me, from what she had said, that our flat might just suit them –

only of course it will want a bit more furniture. They have one small boy & a nurse. So I wired you, & wrote to her. He sails from Marseilles in the *Lamartine* arriving Dec: 5th. I hope you will enjoy yourself & play lots of golf & get as much fun as you can out of your last few weeks. It will leave a much better impression, apart from being far better for you – but the whole thing is rather damnable.

The kids are flourishing, & the Bredgar folk seemed very fit, but one can almost see the moss growing on Charles. Jess is bursting with pride over her little house, which is charming – but I don't see how she is going to make a living yet awhile & it is really too big for one person alone. Perhaps she will take a partner.

It is lovely up here, but London was nothing but a mass of black & yellow fog – perfectly foul & very cold.

When our stuff comes over, I should strongly advise storing it at Deal with old Roberts. He would collect it from Dover. Everything at Bredgar is eaten up with moth & the books are all mouldy – no one has ever looked at anything or bothered to light a fire. It is a pity ... just going to Church – & Cheadle will post this in Shifnal ...

Robert Blackburn, far from 'making a hash of his affairs', had, it would seem, endeavoured to withstand great pressure from the politicians of both countries. The long and the short of it was that the Greek Government wanted the Greek National Aircraft Factory under their total control and had given Blackburns notice to quit, in spite of the fact that their contract was agreed to run until 1930. All Brancker's diplomatic efforts, and subsequently those of Woods Humphery, were of no avail and the firm's days at Old Phaleron were numbered.

Reading between the lines of Auriol Lee's letter, it would appear that Samuel Hoare would have liked to have oiled the wheels with some finance in the right quarter, thereby enabling Blackburns to continue to use the Factory as arranged. But Sir Eric Geddes, who had 'the little banker' eating out of his hand, had persuaded Hoare for reasons of his own not at first clear to anyone else, not to give financial aid. No one who lived through the 1920s was unaffected by the actions of Sir Eric Geddes and although his motives may have been of the highest and most patriotic, particularly during the time of his Chairmanship of Imperial Airways, he nevertheless was a man of such ice-cold ruthlessness that he managed to destroy and seemed oblivious of the fact that he destroyed – careers, jobs, lives, hopes and a great deal of other people's property along the way.

It was Geddes, after all, who had deprived Shorts of so much of their own property. C. H. Barnes described it in his *Shorts Aircraft Since 1900*:

> After further pilot-training flights at Hythe, SYLVANUS returned to Rochester for a special flight for Imperial Airways' directors and the Press. Sir Eric Geddes attended, and Oswald Short escorted him to the flying-boat at moorings, but refused point-blank to show him round the works; he had not forgotten nor forgiven the Admiralty's high-handed sequestration of his Cardington airship factory in 1919, when Sir Vincent Raven had done the talking and Sir Eric had been present to add silent authority. Oswald Short was within his rights in refusing entry, and Sir Eric had to admit defeat, although he was unaccustomed to being denied anything....

Now Sir Eric was on the warpath again and one can, of course, only guess at his reasons for obstructing Blackburns. But the timing is interesting.

'On 24 April 1928,' – wrote A. J. Jackson in his *Blackburn Aircraft Since 1909*.

> The North Sea Aerial and General Transport Co Ltd merged its African airline interests with those of Alan Cobham Aviation Ltd, a company formed by Sir Alan Cobham to exploit the survey work he had done through Africa in his D.H.50J G-EBFO and around it with H. V. Worrall in the Short Singapore IG-EBUP.
>
> Known as Cobham-Blackburn Air Lines Ltd, and with Sir Alan Cobham, Robert Blackburn, Col. W. Wright and Capt. T. A. Gladstone as first directors, the new company formulated a scheme for permanent services between Alexandria and the Cape via the Nile and African lakes with Blackburn Nile flying-boats. Soon afterwards, however, the British Government ruled that Imperial Airways would be the chosen instrument for operating such a route and so put an end to all Cobham–Blackburn air route aspirations in Africa.

Eighteen months before, H. had written home: '... When Cobham arrived & departed there were only a few of us from Blackburns to look after him. No sign of consuls!' It is almost as though the writing had even then been on the wall.

One scarcely needs a map to realize the importance of Phaleron Bay to any flying-boat service intending to move into Africa. Blackburns would have held a key position and great advantage, with so much local knowledge and so much expert maintenance available. Perhaps they posed a competitive threat to Imperials – such indeed would appear to have been Geddes' thinking: a narrow view, if such it was. Surely there would have been room for Blackburn/Cobham and Imperials.

H. came home for Christmas and D. and I stayed with our parents at The Fair Maid of Kent for part of the holiday. Then H. went back to Greece and we went back to boarding school. H. had not had a row with Robert Blackburn. Far from it. The two men had remained on the best of terms and Blackburn had asked H. to continue to fly for the firm as long as there was still any flying to be done and also to continue to act as his, Blackburn's, representative in Greece for the time being. If Cobham/Blackburn Airlines had gone ahead it must have been likely that H. would have moved into that company from the Blackburn Aeroplane Company.

H. left England on the 13th February and according to his log-book: '14th Feb. 1928. As passenger on Italian Aero Espresso mail line left Brindisi 11 am arrived Porto Raffti E. coast of Greece 3.10 Italian time. 4 hrs 10 minutes.'

On the 16th February he was testing again: 'Bristol Fighter 200 Puma landplane N.A.131 Tatoi local 15 minutes. Engine boils. m/c nose heavy. pass. Fisher. Prelim. flight.' He tested the same machine again on Saturday, 18th February for 20 minutes: 'm/c true Engine still too hot – passenger Howard. prelim. flight.' He tested again the same day, the same machine, for a further 20 minutes: 'adjusted engine. Engine still hot. pass. Capt. Hors/Greek Inspection Service. prelim. flight.'

On the 21st February he tested again: 'Velos 450 Napier seaplane T.20. Phaleron Bay & local. 25 minutes. with light load. pass. Fisher. O.K. Preliminary flight.' And later the same day flew T.20 again off Phaleron Bay for 35 minutes: 'full load. pass. Fisher. cold rain & snow. accepted O.K.'

On the 22nd February he flew Velos Napier Seaplane T.21 'Phaleron local. 55 minutes. 3000 ft. prelim. & accepted flight. O.K. passenger Mr Tsoris. Greek engineer friend of (Cmdr)Michael Inspection Service.'

On the morning of February 29th he was up at Tatoi, flying Bristol Fighter N.A.131 for 35 minutes: 'acceptance flight O.K. Engine 76° cruised to 3500 ft. Passenger Varoili mechanical engineer.' On the afternoon of the same day he went down to Phaleron Bay again and

Their Model T Ford in Greece

photo: H. Travers

flew Velos Seaplane T.22: 'Phaleron Bay local. 35 minutes. accepted O.K. passenger A.R. Howard.'

He sold his Model T Ford and he gave Tinker to one of the Greek mechanics up at Tatoi and who had been caring for him for the past two months.

On the 2nd March H. flew: 'As passenger on I-ADZC Dornier Wal 2X550 Asso Isotta Frascini Phaleron to Brindisi 3 hrs 25 minutes. Flew m/c from Corfu to near Brindisi for about 55 minutes.'

From Brindisi, of course, he caught a train home. A popular way was to take the train to Paris and to fly from there but when Hermia had planned that mode of travel in the autumn, the train she was on 'burst a bit of itself and we were jambed for 2 hours in the Simplon Tunnel and missed the aeroplane from Paris.' H. took the train from Brindisi and then the Calais/Dover boat. After a few days at Bredgar he went up to Brough on the 8th March for his RAFO training, the years of 1927 and 1928 compacted into one year's course.

His instructor was Flying Officer Stockbridge from whom he received instruction on the morning of the 9th March. He flew Blackburn Kangaroo 2 X Falcon Rolls G-EAMJ for 30 minutes while under instruction. Then a similar powered Kangaroo, G-EAIU, for a further 30 minutes, still under F/O Stockbridge's instruction. Then, still on the 9th March, he was sent solo on 'IU: 'To Beverly & back. 1 hour 5 minutes. solo. 3000 ft. snow clouds. v. cold.'

Perhaps there was too much snow to fly for a few days, for he next
flew again on the 14th March, Kangaroo 'M J: 'Brough local. 10
minutes. very cold. With F/O Loton.' On 'M J again: 'Beverly &
return etc. 1 hour. General haze.' He made three more short flights
with F/O Loton, on the 16th, 19th and 20th March and three more
flights of more than one hour solo on those dates, all on Kangaroos
'M J, 'M D and 'I U. The longer flights were 'Practice short compass
course.'

He flew Kangaroo 'M J locally on the 22nd March: 'Weather improving' and later the same day and on the same machine: 'short compass
course. 2 hours 20 minutes. 5000 ft stalls 45 m.p.h.' He made four
separate flights on Kangaroo 'M D on the 26th March, flying to
Waddington and back to Brough on two of them. The last flight of
the day was: 'Height test. 1 hour 5 minutes. ?10000 ft. Engine cold.'
On the 28th March he made two flights on Kangaroo 'O M, the second
flight being: 'General flying. 1 hour 20 minutes. 10,200 ft. Left wire
carried away on return at 3000 ft. port engine rev. indicator failed.'

He then noted 'Completion & end of training 1927/28 at Brough.
R. A. F. O. Annual training. North Sea Aerial & General Transport
Co. Brough.'

He attended the Lympne Light Aeroplane Club Meeting in April and
who should be there but F/O Stockbridge, his instructor of a fortnight
before but this time demonstrating the little Blackburn Bluebird. Of
course he took H. up in the machine. What a contrast after the
lumbering Kangaroo.

'6th April. As passenger. Blackburn Bluebird. G-EBTA. Pilot
Stockbridge. 15 minutes. Somewhat cramped for 2 large men! flew
with dual very pleasant & sociable.'

A private pilot of H.'s acquaintance, Victor Cazalet, also took him
up in his machine, a Westland Widgeon G-EBRM: 'Excellent room
& view for passenger. No dual fitted.'

On the 20th April H. went to Stag Lane, probably to enquire if
there was any job going there although such a thing is not of course
mentioned in his log-book.

'20th April. De Hav Moth G-EBRX. Stag Lane local by kindness
of De Hav Co. 20 minutes. A thoroughly controllable light aeroplane.
This particular machine was of the early series & climb was not so
good as the Type X.'

It is the first record I can find of him flying out of Stag Lane.

Although he had ceased to be employed by the Blackburn Aeroplane Company on the 14th April Robert Blackburn asked him to return to do some more testing in May. He left England on the 13th and flew on the 14th: 'As passenger on Dornier Wal (Aero Espresso Italiana) 2 Isotta Fonchina I-A D Z C. Constantinople to Phaleron Bay. 3 hours & 40 minutes. Following wind from N. E. 15 m.p.h.'

He flew at Tatoi on the 17th May: 'D. H.9. landplane. N. A101. Tatoi local. 40 minutes. Preliminary O. K. Good machine. Passenger Mr Howard A. I. D.'

Later the same day he flew 'Avro 504N. 180 Lynx. N. A.138. Tatoi local. 35 minutes. no passenger. excellent machine.' On the following day he flew the same machine, N. A.138, for 45 minutes: 'passenger W. Fisher. 6600 ft.'

That is the last log record of his days in Greece. His log-book noted, on the 'Employer's' page, that 'test pilot & representative terminated agreement 14th April 1928 by mutual arrangement.' – and 'special visit to Greece for above company during May 1928.'

They had been good days. All too short. 'In any case,' he had written to Emmie six months before, 'this has been a most wonderful opportunity for me and the experience will be all to the good.'

Now he was home again and desperately job-hunting, for Hermia was adamant that H. should not accept the testing job which Robert Blackburn had offered him up at Brough: 'We should all die of cold if we went up there,' she said, 'QUITE the coldest place in the world ...' (I have sometimes wondered since if Brough could possibly have been any colder than Kent.)

Those of us who had remained at home during H.'s days in Greece were reminded often of his time in that country by the treasures which he had sent or had brought home: four rush-seated chairs from Skyros, with carved olive-wood backs, a chair for each child; a Greek-key pattern rug (which was still around in the 1950s); carved soldier-dolls; postage stamps of a most marvellous blue. Other treasures, too, which still remain: a box of Helithon snaps; the small Passport which the Greek Government liked him to carry at all times and to have stamped each time he flew a passed machine to the Naval Base. He had kept the Greek Authorities busy with his exits and entrances. (He travelled internationally on his Canadian Passport as mentioned in an earlier chapter.)

Now they had the Factory to themselves, ably assisted in this by Geddes. Before H. left he went up to Tatoi once more to see Tinker and found him there, as so often before, chasing hares on the airfield.

11

HIGH RIVER

1928–1932

Charles to the RCAF – Camp Borden – Jericho Beach – High River – Cut-
backs in the RCAF – Charles job-hunting.

Charles went out to Canada in 1928.

His reasons for going may have been partly that unemployment was
so bad in England at the time that any reasonable man might have
thought things could only be better overseas. There may also have
been the romantic reason of wanting to see something of the world,
at least as far as the Pacific Coast. Generations of the old Merchant
Venturers, generations of globe-trotting Travers may have been in his
mind or his imagination; the facts were more prosaic.

One has the impression that his original idea was to go out for only
a year or two. Perhaps if life had been easier in Canada, or more
prosperous in England, he would indeed have returned within a short
span. In fact after a short-service commission with the RCAF there
came the slump, followed, like a reverberating echo, by the slump in
England. By the time he had met the challenges of his new country
and had overcome a hundred difficulties he was truly committed to
Canada. 'I count myself a Canadian now,' he told me when I met him
again after many years, in 1953.

A generation earlier, in the old Warlingham days, Emmie had shown
some kindness or other to the Tuzo family. When Miss Tuzo had
married Mr Wilson and had settled in Ottawa the friendship between
the two families and a spasmodic correspondence between Ottawa and
Surrey/Kent continued. The long-ago act of friendship was repaid a
hundred times by the warmth of the Wilson's kindness to V during
her years in Ottawa and now, by giving him a friendly welcome and
sound advice on his arrival in Canada, to Charles. They had invited
him to stay while he took his bearings. J. A. Wilson was Controller
of Civil Aviation in the Dominion of Canada.

'... I am quite all right for cash,' he wrote to Emmie a little later on, 'due largely to the kindness of Wilson in putting me up and helping me (into) this job quickly – but the living is more expensive here than at home and if a man came out here without friends to go to and failed to find work quickly he might soon be hard put to it for a living.

'I hope to be able to save a little by the end of my year in the R C A F and, in addition, gain a knowledge of conditions that will give me something to (build) on when I leave the R C A F.

'There are quite a lot of Englishmen formerly R A F at Borden. I know two and many of us have friends in common, but I hope that I shall not be stuck there for long it is just a big training camp. I am enclosing a map which gives an idea of this bit of the country. It is about 70 miles from Borden to Toronto it gives one some idea of the distances.

'It also shows to some extent how the country is covered with lakes and rivers. ...'

He wrote next from Toronto, again to Emmie:

I am here for the week end on leave for the purpose of getting uniform. It is a nuisance as it is expensive here – but they won't let me use the uniform that I left at home as it is not the correct shade of blue. The only thing that I could use is the blue Burberry raincoat that is in the long chest of drawers in my room in the bottom drawer....

I called on a man this afternoon – Partridge – to whom Arthur Cooper had given me a note. He had served at Felixstowe in the R N A S and knew Jimmy....

His commission in the R C A F was probably confirmed in July for his resignation of his R A F commission was dated as the 24th July 1928.

He was posted to the R C A F Station at Jericho Beach in the New Year and wrote from Vancouver to Emmie on the 1st February:

I landed here on Saturday 26th January after a very interesting journey from Toronto. I enclose some snaps that I took at Niagara Falls the previous week-end. Unfortunately those that I took of the Canadian falls didn't come out.

O'Brien Saint and Arthur met me at the railway station at 7.30 in the morning. They were at Camp Borden in the summer and came out about six weeks ago.

Avro and motor boat, Jericho
Beach
photo: C. T. Travers

Jericho Beach. Vedette moored
out. Stanley Park in distance
photo: C. T. Travers

Fairchild with engine cover on, Jericho
Beach
photo: C. T. Travers

Launching the Fairchild
photo: C. T. Travers

Arthur is married & they took me along to his house where Mrs A gave me breakfast before we went on to the Seaplane Station.

This is the coldest winter that Vancouver has had for 10 years or more. It is not nearly as cold as Winnipeg or even Camp Borden but there is a lot of snow and fog.

Vicker's test pilot, Caldwell, has been flying a new 'Vedette' flying boat for it's acceptance tests but today is the first day since my arrival that the officers on the Station have had any flying.

There are 9 officers attached to the Station. Backer (who was at Borden) is on leave & Morfee is away also.

Another man, Bourke, has just left the Service and has gone to an American concern – the Boeing Co, I think.

O'Brien Saint, Arthur, Spradbourne (Spradbrow?) Ashton, Dougal (who was at Renfrew) and myself make up the list. Hull is the C.O. He is not popular but I have not had any trouble with him so far . . . (he) insists on giving hours of dual instruction to men like Arthur and Saint who are as good pilots as he is & to Dougal Ashton and Sprad who have flown seaplanes on operations for hundreds of hours. It doesn't matter very much. . . . I went up with him to-day for a quarter of an hour. I hope that he won't want to give me five hours dual!

I am living in a very good and moderate hotel until such time that I can fix up digs. I think that I will try for some in Point Grey which is fairly handy for Jericho Beach.

We have only six machines on the Station 3 Avros and 3 Vedettes but I expect that we shall soon get 6 new 'Moth' Seaplanes. About 26 officers are expected to arrive at this station before the end of next month. I expect that most of them will come from Borden.

I was wrong when I said that the railway followed the Fraser. It was the Thompson River.

The mountains look lovely – when one can see them.

Wednesday afternoon is devoted to 'organised games'. These consist of rather feeble Badminton and last Wednesday I persuaded the others to come with me to the big covered rink the 'Arena'. We had great fun. Sprad who is Canadian born is quite a good skater. Arthur & I can both skate a little but poor old Dougal, who looks rather like a younger edition of Harry Lauder, had never skated before, but he is a great tryer.

If I can get leave later on I will go across to Vancouver Island and call on Col. Roome – the father of Jack Tuzo's great friend. I must also look up a certain Mr Bone – whom I met on the train – a Scotchman who has been out here many years and is manager of an insurance company here. . . .

I pass the end of Collingwood Street on my way to the Air Station. I must wander down there and see whether I can spot H.O.'s houses.

I have forgotten the numbers.

Everyone says that those years were very lean ones for Vancouver and all B.C. Arthur was here in 1924–5 & he told me once that he and his wife nearly starved. They had come to their last dollar when an acquaintance gave them a hand. . . . I haven't had time to see much of Vancouver. I leave the Hotel at 8.15 & get back at a quarter to six. It is a huge place & will be very interesting.

love to Ally and Jess & have you got Jessies dog – I want to go shares in it. . . .

Charles was posted to High River Air Station, Alberta, in March and wrote from there on the 19th:

We arrived in Calgary at 1 am on Monday morning where our sleeping car was shunted into a siding. They let us sleep on until 7.30 when the porter woke us up and we got our breakfast in a restaurant in the town, just opposite the big C P R Hotel: the Hotel Palliser.

The restaurant was typical of the newer type of cafe. It had white enamelled counters, lined with revolving stools – the food was in glass cases and the waiters wore white coats. Everything nickel plate and glass and white paint. . . . We ('we' consisted of Dougal, Spradbrow, Sergeant Anderson and myself) decided to catch the bus for High River.

It took us about an hour and a half to make the journey. . . . The bus was very crowded as there were several speculators and mining men who had come to look at the Turner Valley oilfield. They got off at Okotoks which has a small hotel and several shops and a railway station. We reached High River . . . and found that Leitch, our new C.O. had arrived on Friday. (We) started a fire in the mess, which is a private house rented by the Dept of (Air) Defence. We all like Leitch and hope that nothing will upset first impressions. Yesterday the men arrived back, and our luggage came by the same train. It was just as I feared – my trunk that I bought at Dan Eastons had busted out at one end and the books were leaking out; I didn't lose any and nothing was damaged.

This is an amusing little town.

Everyone knows each other & I am now utterly confused by the number of first names I should remember. You walk down the 'main drag' I should say the principal street and Spradbrow will say 'Why here comes old So & So.' 'Greetings' and then we are introduced. . . . They are the doctors, the dentists, bank managers, grocers and plumbers of the town. It is a little centre for the farms round and there are four big grain elevators by the railway station.

The aerodrome is two miles away. We drive in there every morning in the station Ford. The men live in (Quarters) in the town.

The aerodrome is wonderful. It is at least half a mile broad and 500 yards long. There are good hangars and a small well equipped work-

The Rockys and foothills in spring

shop and (there is) also a wireless (Radio) station with tall masts.

The only holes in the surface of the aerodrome are gopher holes –
rather smaller than a rabbit hole. There are very few (of these) holes
and we can fill them up. The gopher is a pretty little animal rather like
a squirrel, but it's tail isn't quite so bushy. . . .

. . . (There are) ten or a dozen horses on the aerodrome to-day but
they will be taken off when we start flying. (They are from the High
Wood Ranch).

We have 5 Moths here now but their wings are down in Toronto
having slots fitted, and being overhauled. We are hoping to have a
Fairchild for transport work and new engines for the Moths.

I don't expect that we shall get any flying for 2 or 3 weeks at least.

The Rockys are at least 35 miles away but they look as large as the
Malvern hills do from 7 miles. They are a wonderful sight – all covered
with snow, pale and ethereal but quite clear cut against the sky. This
morning there are shadows of a deep carmine colour across them.
They stretch from far in the North . . . to the South West where they

are hidden by the Porcupine Hills that is the foothills to the main range. At night we can see the glare from the Turner Valley. They must burn the gas as it escapes.

I hope that you are quite well again.

We are quite warm here and beautifully sunny....

High River Air Station, High River, Alta. Canada March 28th 1928:

I am glad that you are taking care of yourself. I see in the papers that you are having better weather now. I hope that you will have a really good spring.

We have had some beautiful days here but there has almost always been a frost at night time. Last night there was a warm South wind which altered to South west this morning. On the western horizon above the moutains was a sector of clear sky – the sky above this was overcast with clouds. This sky is nearly always observed when this warm westerly wind is blowing. The wind is called 'the Chinook'.

This afternoon we had a dust storm. The wind increased in force suddenly & the barometer fell at the same time. The wind got round to the North and the dust drove past us. It was not a bad storm but it was quite unpleasant outside. It became much colder and this evening we had a little fall of snow!

The farmers all want more rain – everything is too dry. If we do not get some there will be plenty of fires to locate.

Our wings for the Moths have not been returned from De Havs. yet. By the way I got those De Hav 7% preference shares that I applied for. The ordinary shares that were given in with the prefs. are now worth 15 dollars or £3 – each....

I enclose a photo of the Turner Valley showing some of the derricks. I think I told you that I went down there with Spradbrow. It is only 24 miles from here and we can see the glow from the burning gas at night time. My photo of the burning gas did not come out and I think that the smell must have addled the film. I think it must be awful to live near an oilfield.

This one smells like a very large, very bad egg.

Everything is running smoothly here.

We are gradually getting stores and equipment into order.

I am looking after the M.T. and all the tools are unserviceable.

We have 2 Ford trucks 2 Sedans (closed Ford) & we are going to get a 6-wheel (unreadable). One Sedan is a new T-Model Ford – the other is the old type.

Please don't mind about the gas engine. We will have electricity in Bredgar soon – when the new Government gets going.

We have electricity here but it is not as cheap as in Toronto, Ottawa or Vancouver. People in the town use natural gas for cooking and heating to some extent. Although coal is fairly cheap....

In the following letter, of 20th April, 1929, Charles first of all referred to a forced landing which H & H had experienced in March. Then he continued:

... We have started our patrols and I have been over the South Patrol twice, once with Dougall and once with Sgt. Anderson, both of whom were here last year. Dougall has been posted to Borden as they are very short of instructors there this year. He is very fed up about it and Leitch has done his best to keep him here. Spradbrow is going to Grande Prairie in the Peace River district, with one machine and an N.C.O. pilot and will be there all through the summer. So that the two remaining N.C.O. pilots, Barton and Anderson, will be the only ones who know the patrols. We will probably have a new pilot officer here who will have to be taught the patrol. I can manage the South Patrol....

To H, on the 21st April, he wrote:

... We have four Moths working now – one more in reserve and another waiting for some mods to the engine bearers. I have been over the South Patrol twice with the other fellows. The first time we didn't go into the mountains or even as far as the Rangers Stations at Sentinel, The Gap and Colemans and landed at Pincher Creek for lunch.

The flight down there took 2 hrs 40 mins and we had to climb to 7000$'$ (above High River) (or 10700$'$ above sea level) to get a comfortable clearance over some peaks. The scenery is really wonderful.

We are using Cirrus Mk11's. The machines are new last year and are in good condition and the top planes have been fitted with slots at DH's during the winter but of course one is never contented and we feel that we should have some of the new Gipsy Moths instead of the Border people getting them. It is bumpy over the mountains and one loses a lot of height sometimes.

It smells as if three cats have just died about a week ago in my room. It is just a gentle wind from the Turner Valley carrying a little sulphurated hydrogen from the oil wells.

The best job round here is selling oil stocks. I went to have some photos developed yesterday and the fellow tried to sell me shares in Twin dome Oils and guaranteed to make me a millionaire by the fall! . . .

To Emmie he wrote:

. . . Did you pay my Aeronautical Society sub.? I have just had a cheque returned with a note that my sub. had been paid already. Please let me know if you did so and I will send a cheque. Another thing that I want to pay for is my share of J's puppy. So please let me know.

Last night we had a fall of snow but it has all gone now. The main road to Calgary is all right but the road to the aerodrome is very muddy. The roads here as in other parts of Canada run North and South and East and West. The main roads have a gravel surface. When this surface gets dry the gravel is thrown out to either side of the tracks of the wheels and it is difficult to steer a car if one gets off the tracks. This makes passing another car rather dangerous but otherwise one can travel fairly fast. Just as one did on the straight roads of France. . . .

The South Patrol takes us down to the American Border but both times that I have flown over it I have cut it short and landed at Pincher Creek. On the way down there we pass over three Rangers Stations, at Sentinel, The Gap and Colemans.

The mountain scenery is very fine. We fly down at about 7000′ which gives us a comfortable margin when crossing some of the peaks on the Livingstone Range. I had lunch with the Forest Supervisor and his wife at Pincher when I landed there the first time. They are very nice people, named Alexander. Alexander was a pilot in the R.F.C. but I had never met him before. . . .

. . . On the return journey from Pincher we take a straight course for High River across a range of foothills known as the Porcupines. There are a good many ranches there and one can see hundreds of head of cattle. The cattle like (to) shelter in the coulees which are dried up watercourses, sunken deep between high earth cliffs. There are some fine waterholes in these coulees as a rule. . . . I have found out that Spradbrow's people came from Loose near Maidstone! His father has been out here since he was a young chap and lives in Toronto. . . .

Thank you very much for the copies of *The Times*. . . . It was nice to see a photo of Jones Williams and the Fairey Monospar. J W was in 'E' Coy at the R M C with me but I have only met him once or twice since. He is a very nice chap and did well at Sandhurst during the latter part of the War. . . .

We finished our inquiry into that crash thank goodness, and it will be sent to Ottawa as soon as possible. The typewriters broke down, both of them, and that delayed the report.

Tudhope left for Cranbrook on Thursday. On Wednesday evening we attended a meeting of the H. River Board of Trade to consider (unreadable) Air Race. Guy Wiedicks who is the chap that runs the Calgary Stampede tried to enthuse the audience into backing up the idea. There was not much enthusiasm as it means some $5000 in prize money. Wiedicks has the promise of $10,000 if (unreadable) can be found.

They were all waiting for Leitch to give his ideas on the subject. Very wisely, he refused to commit himself or to serve on any committees. He put out that he would have his work cut out in enforcing aerodrome rules and keeping the crowd back.

He said that he would have no objection to any of his officers serving on the committee. So I said that I would be willing to fix up programmes, handicaps etc. but that I would (and could) not have anything to do with the financial side or serve on ways and means committee.

I find out now that half the people in the town have no wish to run the show at all. So I am going to make it clear to the Board of Trade that if they can't guarantee the prize money and expenses within a week, I am going to turn the whole show down and advise them to call the race off.

Unless they have the money in the Bank it would be foolish to have anything to do with it. I am sure that they can get the money if they want it, from the Turner Valley people. . . . However that is no affair of mine, and we would all be glad if the race were called off, as we have our own job to do.

I went on the North Patrol with Leitch on Thursday. It took us two hours and ten minutes to get to Rocky Mountain House.

I had to run nearly full out all the time to keep up with Leitch, as I had a wireless aerial and generator and 10 gallons extra gas in the second tank. . . Leitch went on to Edmonton and Grande Prairie via

Slave Lake that night and I returned to High River. It took me hours to get back, and I had only 2 pints of oil left in my sump at the end, as I couldn't fill up with oil at Rocky Mountain House. It took 20 gallons to fill the machine up with gas at this end.

My machine is a MkIII Cirrus and I have a m/c with steel fuselage and split axle undercarriage. H.O. might be interested in this if he happens to be down. My average height on the North Patrol was 4500 ft (i.e. 8000′ above sea level).

The C.O. didn't wire me to say that he had got to Grande Prairie. I didn't worry yesterday as it was ... a public holiday. They all go through the CPR stations and I thought they might have been closed. To-day I began to think of forced landings and I wired Sprad. at Grande Prairie. I was quite relieved to hear from Edmonton that he was on his way back.

I would have gone up there myself but for the fact that I was the only officer left on the station. I had sent our new officer, Jenkins, out on the South Patrol with Sgt. Anderson and they had been held up at Pincher Creek by the high wind. Ivey, the stores officer, had gone off on week end leave.

Jenkins is an Australian who has been in the States and West Indies on Commercial flying. He was in the Australian Air Force before that.

Sgt. Barton and I are going to take the North Patrol and Anderson and Jenkins the South. The full North patrol is longer and more difficult than the South, but one doesn't go over the real mountains but only over the foothills.

Barton is a nice chap but rather nervous as a pilot and I am afraid is a bit windy about the patrols. There is nothing to be afraid of at all, but he had a bad crash two years ago and I think that he cannot have got over it. I am going to go very carefully with him and not let him fly unless he feels up to doing the patrol. He is a very good man on engines and takes a great pride in keeping all our engines up to scratch.

The Highwood River at the back of the mess is filling up rapidly, and looks fine. It has a very swift current and I am not going to bathe in it this summer as there have been a lot of accidents. It is very cold, too, with the snow water. I am really having a good time here, Mum dear. I have a little responsibility, which is a wonderful tonic.
continued Sunday:

I believe that Mrs Wilson is coming out here early next month to address the National Council of Women or one of her other pet

Societies. I will make a point of going to Calgary to see her. She has been so very kind.

Another distinguished visitor to these parts is Prince Henry, who is coming to stay at the E.P. ranch in a week or two.

The birds all came home to roost last night. Leitch was the first one in. He brought the signaller sergeant with him and landed at about 8 o'clock. He had sent telegrams from Grande Prairie on Friday and Peace River but they have not come in yet – and it is Sunday afternoon.

Sgt Anderson and Jenkins found there was a gale blowing when they reached Pincher Creek and nearly turned the machine over in landing. 'Andy' is a good little pilot, though, but only weighs 112 lbs; this was offset to some extent by Jenkin's mass of nine score. They got back here safely an hour after Leitch. Jenkins and Anderson are off again to-day on the S. Patrol. I want Jenkins to learn it quickly so that they will be able to take it turn and turn about. It is a beautiful day here and we had a good weather report from Pincher, so that they should be back in good time.

Barton went up on North Patrol but had to turn back at Red Deer Rangers Station on the Red Deer River – because of snow storms! Here it is quite pleasantly warm and sunny and Red Deer R.S. is only 70 miles North of here.

Dear old Bognor has taken a step up! I was amused the other evening listening to Denver City, Colorado on a wireless set. The American announcer was giving the news bulletin. He was saying that 'His Majesty, King George, left Craigwell House, BOGNOIR', (pronounced with a beautiful French accent, after some hesitation). . . .

There are several more letters which appear to have been written during the summer of 1929 but for which I have no precise dates. Here are some extracts:

. . . The mail has just come in. A letter from you via Vancouver dated March 10th, also one from Marie [Marian Sherwill – Ed] & one from James . . . & one from a very good chap in Montreal who used to be at Borden . . . James likes being in London. He gets a little more pay and is sent round various aircraft factories.

. . . I bought three new shirts, rather good ones but the price was awful. They are Celanese and guaranteed to last for a very long time. The only shirt that I brought out that has withstood the attacks of

Wong Yen is the old silk one of Dad's, so I thought that these Celanese ones might be better than cotton.

Joe Robertson offered me a horse for the paper chase last Wednesday, so I got away early from the Station & had a great ride across country. I really enjoyed it very much & had no trouble sticking on. It is so *much* more comfortable at the gallop than at the trot. . . .

And from a longer letter:

Andy & I left at 8.30. We had arranged to meet Hutch that evening & we drove up with a High River man that evening. It was the night of the cowboys ball in Calgary.

The police closed one street & the Princess Pat's band played for the dancers in the open air. We met Hutchison & went over to the stampede grounds. He was taking charge of the forestry exhibit for the evening to give his subordinates a rest.

It was a good exhibit – a log cabin with samples of the lumber & photographs of the forest reserves. Also trout of all sizes swimming about in little tanks.

I met several of the forest rangers & if I can find time will spend a day or two with one of them, Freddy Nash, of Bighorn Ranger Station.

There were scenes of general conviviality in and around the Palliser Hotel. it struck me that the cowboys were in a minority & reminded me more of Armistice night or perhaps boat race night in London. The townspeople were making most of the noise, aided by the American visitors.

Yesterday (Saturday) I had the North patrol, & asked Leitch if I could go exploring a bit.

The Clearwater forest reserve is at the Northern end of our beat. It is the largest & I think the most important in some ways as there are fewer ranger stations and only 3 lookout towers.

There are quite a lot of Indians scattered about it and if a fire once started there, it might get away before it was spotted.

It hasn't been patrolled for 3 years (when they had the big D.H.4's) and I want to get to know it while the air is clear.

They usually have some big fires in B.C. later in the year. The visibility is reduced by the smoke which drifts across and if one does not know the country it is difficult to fine one's way about.

I can fly for nearly 5 hours on my machine as it has an extra 10 gallon tank whereas last year's machines will barely last 4 hours.

I flew in a straight line as far as the Clearwater River about 5 miles
west of the Ranger Station then west along the Clearwater & over the
mountains at 10,000 ' (above sea level) until I hit the N. Saskatchewan
between Glacier Lake and Wilson R.S.

I reduced height to 1500 ' (above High River) – that is about 500 '
from the ground at Wilson R.S. & about 4900 ' above sea level &
followed the North Saskatchewan Valley until I came eventually to
Rocky Mountain House. It took me exactly 4 hours, so I had a
comfortable margin – but the weather conditions were ideal. It was a
lovely trip. I saw quite a few Indian teepees with smoke coming out
of the flap they look just like the teepee that Ally made but the poles
are usually peeled and seem to stay white and the big teepees seem to
have a great many poles.

I don't know what tribe they would belong to.

The Blackfeet are about the best of the Indians round here – the
Siwash are of a Mongolian type. . . . The Stoneys are not so bad. Old
Mrs Robinson has told me that when she first came out from Montreal
to the West she learnt to speak Blackfoot and they used to come round
to the ranch. They used to have a chief's daughter in the house – but

Dancing House & drum in centre of floor
photo: C. T. Travers

photo: C. T. Travers

Picking up a crew of fire fighters at the Forestry Base at Cold Lake

they were very proud and wouldn't work & never stole or begged. She said that occasionally the chief would come in – to pay a call, as it were. Her husband would put a decanter of wine on the table. They would shake hands & the chief would polish off the decanter.

They would shake hands again & he would leave. No one would say a word!

Of course it is forbidden to sell or give drink to an Indian & they never gave to any but the chief.

I think that it is awfully sad to think of these Indians going to bits. Mrs Robinson said that they sent some of the chief's children to school and they died of consumption.

They have these huge reserves and some do a little farming but the only ones that make money do so by the sale of oil rights or concessions.

When I was having lunch at Rocky Mountain House on Saturday they told me that there had been a Sun dance about 15 miles North of Rocky Mountain H. that week. There had been about 350 Indians there. They are not allowed usually as the Indians get very excited and are liable to do damage.

9.15 p.m. An American machine has just come in.

10.30 p.m. July 5th.

I am sorry that I can't finish this letter.

The Americans are two vaudeville artists, a man & his wife, who fly all over the continent to keep their appointments. Their name is Hart but on the bills they appear as the 'Haphazards'.

They are acrobats and jugglers. They are quite a decent couple. This is the 6th machine that Hart has owned since the war – it is quite a good 2-seater (a Taper wing WACO with 200 HP Wright Whirlwind).

They had the machine and engine looked over to-day & are leaving for Vancouver tomorrow (via Grand Forks).

It is quite a good trip so I hope they have a good day for it. I have been out all day today from 9 in the morning till 6 at night & was invited over to tennis on my return. I didn't play & made an early escape. I hope that I wasn't rude, but I want to get some maps out for the Yank to-morrow & I must be early in the morning.

I wish that I could take an artist with me on some of my trips although I do not suppose that pictures of this country would interest people in England, for example. They would naturally prefer pictures of

English scenery.... I remember that the Morris used to burn the platinum points of the magneto. it might be avoided by setting the spark plug gaps to 15/1000″ instead of 20/1000″.

The Evans's house sounds interesting but the classical style hardly seems practical in a rainy country &, I think, out of place at home.

Leitch is taking his new bungalow very seriously, he reminds me of Leask in some ways. It is a pretty little place in its way. They think a lot of 'hardwood' floors and most of the small houses have them – usually maple.

Our garden is doing wonders despite the flood & the mud. ...' And from what may have been the same letter he writes:

... We have been badly held up for spare parts for our engines (Cirrus Mk11 and Mk111) & for that reason, I believe that next year this station will use DeHavs own engine, the Gipsy. I do not think that there is much to choose between them. I have not had any experience with the Gipsy but the Mk111 Cirrus is very satisfactory. . . .

Charles was thirty-one on the 3rd July and H, no longer a prolific letter-writer, sent him a telegram. Charles replied with a long letter, dated 26th July:

Thank you awfully for your birthday telegram. I am able to say that, so far, I have landed 'Y Y' safely and softly, but I am glad that she has a split axle undercarriage and big tyres for all that.

I enclose a few snaps that I took last week on the first part of our North patrol. I hope to be able to send you some of a couple of fires I spotted two days ago but I have not had the film developed yet. It is usually bumpy and hard to find time for snapshots.

The weather has been very dry, the crops are spoiling and the risk of fire is considerable. I did my best days flying this season on Tuesday – 8 hours 25 minutes.

I am afraid that we shall be held up for aircraft soon. My machine – new this year – must go into the shop on Monday to have the bolts tightened at the spar root fittings and bracing wires (interplane strut) filltings owing to wood shrinkage. I have a metal fuselage machine so that part is OK. All the others are in the same condition. It is not serious on mine but one can't have a thing like that. We get some dirty days when it is bumpy all the time and that loosens things up.

My machine looks like a patchwork quilt. I was caught in the edge of a hailstorm some weeks ago for from 10 to 15 secs. and found 63

AIR PATROL

The Dominion Forest Reserves are the property of the people of Canada, set aside for the purpose of ensuring a continuous supply of timber for the present and the future. They supply pasture for thousands of cattle; they are the source of and protect the streams which water the prairies; they are the homes of fish and game. They are your forests. Help us to keep them green.

Aeroplane Card C—6M—5-22

AIR PATROL CARD

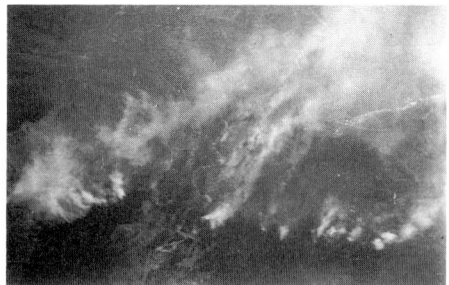

'It is awful to see these forests burn'

photo: C. T. Travers

good holes when I landed. The 64th hailstone hit me on the head! We have Fairey Reed props which is a good thing. The real hold up is with exhaust pipes and manifolds. We have 3 of last years aircraft with Mark 11's. These engines have all done their time and are being replaced by Mk111's but we can't get pipes for the latter although we demanded them 3 months ago.

Then there is a new order that engines have to come out after 200 hrs for complete overhaul at Winnipeg and must be top overhauled after 100 hrs. I've done 120 on my machine but I suppose that she will have to be done next week.

I average about 6 galls/hour cruising at 73 m.p.h. at 5000′ (8400′ above sea level) with 300′ of aerial trailing out behind me. Revs about 1850.

The oil consumption is rather heavy. We use Castrol 'R' and my engine keeps about 12 lb S/A″ oil pressure. I find that 14 pints is the most that I can put in without sooting the plugs on the rear cylinder. I tried 18 and 16 pints but had trouble. She uses about 2 pints/hour.

We have a garage hangar at Rocky Mt. House on the North trip and at Pincher Creek on the South, fold the wings and put the aircraft in under lock and key while we have lunch, and talk to the forestry people.

We also have a cache of gas and oil in steel drums. We usually find someone to pump it up (through a hose) for us. We have made our own tail trolleys similar to the D.H. one in principle, but with 12″ wooden wheels for the rough ground. I saw my first big fire the other day North of the Brazeau River and 200 miles from High River. I had refuelled at Rock Mt. House as a precaution although we carry a 10-gallon tank as usual. I was flying at about 10,000′ above sea level. I think about 800 acres was burning, and the top of the cloud (which forms on top of the smoke) must have been 13,000′ at least. The cloud and smoke stretched for about 25 miles.

Brintnell came in here the week end before last on Western Canada Airways 3-motor Fokker with 5 passengers among them Bracken (Premier of Manitoba) and also Richardsons Secretary. They stopped here for a day and flew across to Vancouver next morning in $6\frac{1}{2}$ hours.

Richardson practically owns Western Canada Airways. I believe that he is now the richest man in Canada. He is very keen on Aviation and on Western Can. Airways owns all the bigger operational companies out here now.

Brintnell is chief pilot and operations manager. He is a very nice quiet chap. He remembered me but I couldn't place him. We found eventually that we had been at the C F S together in 1918.

I remembered him then. He was one of a bunch of young Canadians who had trained in Texas and had come to the C F S for advanced training. He used to play the piano well and accompanied a fellow called Davidson who had a fine voice. I was glad to meet one of my old acquaintances and who knows I may be able to touch him for a job one day.

They have just secured the contract for the Air Mail between Winnipeg Edmonton Calgary and Banff.

Arrangements are being made now for lighting the route and the aerodromes and for wireless service.
They have ordered 6 special Fokkers for the job.
The Banff field is now under construction.
The air mail is due to start in October.

No doubt they will run across to the coast next year. In fact Brintnell told me he was taking this opportunity of looking over the ground.

The new municipal airport in Calgary is about to be opened. They have levelled and gravelled three runways and it should make a fairly good aerodrome.

The Calgary Club has practically closed down since the last crash that I told you about. The Air (ground) engineer and instructor have been suspended and have resigned.

They have taken an agency for American Eagles (110 H P.) and have bought 3 of these awful hacks and a Ryan Brougham. They have some good financial backing from Sollaway Mills, the oil stock brokers; a wealthy firm – Rutledge, the pilot instructor is a nice chap. I wish that he had used better judgment in his choice of aircraft.

He is liable to get into trouble as he has been flying recently in the first of his 'Eagles'. Thank God, we have a Civil Aviation Inspector in the district now. We have enough to do besides chasing up fellows who won't abide by the rules of the game.

Well cheerio H.O! I see that you have been doing your stuff with Ld Thomson. . . . All the best of luck and wishes for further successes in the job. . . .

Charles to Emmie:
High River, Alberta. 27th August 1929.
. . . The fire at Bighorn that I told you about in my last letter has

been going like fun all last week and has now burnt about 15 square miles.

It has been very thick here but we have been over there several times to report on its progress & I found that the visibility improved between the fire and the mountains.

The oil people in Turner Valley were badly scared as they are smothered in smoke as long as the south west or west winds continue, but only one or two wells are in any danger. Hutchinson rang up on Saturday at about 5 o'clock and asked me to meet him as soon as possible in Okotocks (on the Calgary Road).

Hutchinson is the supervisor of the Bow Forest Reserve & is a very nice chap. He is also keen on the Air Patrol as he is an old R.F.C. pilot and was on artillery observation work. He has been most awfully busy organizing for the fire fighting operations and has been single-handed, having sent every available man out to the fire. He has 200 men out there now and wages are 450 dollars per day – nearly £100. He has spent 1200 dollars on blankets and a single trip in there from Calgary for a 2 ton truck costs 45 dollars. He has had to conscript men for the work and obtain cooks and camp equipment, and be at the phone all the time.

There are only one or perhaps two trails in there and the ground is very hilly.

Poor old Hutch is dying to get into the fire, but Saturday was the first time that he had been able to get away.

We met in Okotoks F/Sgt Barton & Hutch & I, and drove in the 40 odd miles to Bighorn Ranger Station.

They were keeping the fire back to the north of the trail but it was right up to it in places.

We had a good look at the hay meadow at Bighorn and decided that it would do in an East or a West wind.

The scheme is for me to stand by with a 2-seater, and when Hutch. 'phones me up to dash up to Calgary, pick him up – and then fly him in to Bighorn, returning with him when he has finished his work there.

This would take him 40 minutes (Calgary to Bighorn) instead of $2\frac{1}{2}$ hours by road. If the wind changes to the north the trail may be blocked also.

I tried it out on Sunday using my own single-seater which carried a load of extra petrol, and wireless equipment equal to Hutchinson's 180 lbs & I had no difficulty in landing or taking off. This is rather a

good 'ad' for the Moth as the field at Bighorn is over 5000' above sea
level and about 450 yards long and 50 broad. The ground rises all the
way over foothills to the moutains 4 or 5 miles to the west. To the
east the foothills lie on either side of the Sheep River Valley.

It is a wonderful place on the ground.

The Sheep runs in a gorge about 50' deep. The ranger station and
the hay meadow lie on the North bank and the steep side of Missing
Link (or Bighorn Mt) rises near the North of the meadow. It is awful
to see these forests burning.

Next Thursday our Director (of Civil Gov. Air Operations), Gordon,
and the Chief Engineer Officer, Stedman, are going to visit the Station.

I hope that they will not expect too much spit and polish about the
Station, although the machines will bear comparison with any that
they have seen elsewhere.

I have certainly got a earful for Stedman if he will listen to me.

I also want to find out – if possible – what sort of chances I have
with the R.C.A.F. or the Dept. of C.G.A.O. I don't think that there
is anything much in the future for me with the R.C.A.F., or for any
other non-permanent officer, and will tell Gordon so. If he agrees with
me I think I will write at once to Brintnell for a job.

I enclose a couple of snaps of this last fire, taken just after it started.
They are rather poor ones but show the different points on the fire.

The other snap is of the incomplete dam on the Bow River. The
Ghost River joins the Bow just above the dam and can be seen flowing
in from the background of the photo.

This dam is called the Ghost River dam and will give about 30,000
h.p. I am rather tired and will turn in now. . . .

It looks as though Gordon persuaded Charles not to abandon his short
service commission and not to write to Brintnell. There was no further
reference to Charles leaving the R C A F that year. Indeed within a few
months all his plans seem to have changed.

He returned to England in November of 1929, on leave to get
married.

His bride was Miss Marian Sherwill, daughter of Mr and Mrs
Sherwill of Harrow-on-the-Hill, and whom he had met before setting
out for Canada in 1928.

Of course he and Marian visited his family at Bredgar during his time in England. They came down to Walmer, too, where we (H. & H. and children) were by then all living as a family again and I can remember a very jolly lunch party.

Early in 1930 Charles, with of course Marian, – was back at High River.

Marian, a plucky girl if ever there was one, threw herself into the new life.

Charles to Emmie:

High River, Alberta. March 25th 1930. . . . Marian and I were going into Calgary to see some folk-dancing one day last week but it was cold that day and we called it off.

April 25th 1930:

. . .We went to a 'Vimy' Dance at the Town Hall on Saturday last. Marian enjoyed it very much although it was only a sort of village dance. . . .

We had intended to call up Mrs Gardner and propose ourselves for this week end at her place in the hills. I am afraid that we cannot possibly get there though as there has been a heavy rain and the roads will be impassable. It is over 40 miles from here. . . .

May 6th 1930:

Many happy returns of the day. I hope that this will be in time for your birthday. It is ripping to get your letters and to hear all the news.

We both appreciate *The Times Weekly* and the literary supplement, also *Blackwood*'s and the *Tatler*.

I will send a subscription to Freddy Wilson's presentation fund. He is a good chap and has done more for old students than anyone at King's.

Marian and I went to Calgary last week end and were most extravagent.

We have not got the Olson's house yet – but hope to do so – and the furniture people have agreed to store the furniture free of charge until we need it. . . .

I have a slightly guilty alarmed feeling that I have bought too much gear, but I think that it is quite wise and I shall not have anything more to buy when we move in. . . .

We went to the cathedral in Calgary on Sunday morning but were unlucky as we did not hear Dean Robinson, whom Marian met when she was in Calgary one day with the Ortons. There was a horrid tub-thumping fellow preaching. . . .

May 22nd:

    . . . I flew up to Grande Prairie a week ago to-day. Leitch took Blefgar a forestry official, in one aeroplane, and I followed in another.

    I took a signaller, Sergeant Hawkins, in my machine, as he was needed at Grande Prairie to attend to the wireless apparatus there.

    It is well over 500 miles by air, about 540 I think, by the route we follow, so that we were pleased to take only 6 hours and a quarter on a slow machine like a Moth. We landed at Calgary – to pick up Blefgar – at Edmonton and at Slave Lake. The country between Edmonton and Slave Lake is not very good for part of the way. After about 50 miles one leaves the railway and heads northwards over the Athabaska River and does not see a sign of anything living for about 60 miles.

    Grande Prairie is a prosperous little place with about 1,000 inhabitants.

    Spradbrow has his flight up there, consisting of 2 aeroplanes and 5 NCO's and men, one of whom is a sergeant pilot. He has three hangars that will each take a Moth easily with the wings folded, also an office building and an oil and petrol store. He has a very comfortable tent and a mess tent. The men sleep in three other tents.

    He has been very busy with fires already.

    A great many settlers are still taking up land but the open prairie is mostly taken up and they are having to clear this land of trees and scrub.

    It is a wonderful farming country. One farmer whose land is next to the aerodrome has been averaging 50 bushels per acre for the last three years and they say that his wheat alone has brought him 20,000 dollars every year. He has been there since 1910 and is one of the first settlers.

    Leitch went back to High River the next day, but I had to wait until the wireless sets were all working before I could take Sgt. Hawkins back, so that I did not leave until Saturday. It took us 7 hours and a half to return, owing to contrary winds, which were very strong at times, but I had a good passenger who did not fuss and who was not airsick like some forestry people I have had out lately.

I think that we have got a house at last. The Olson's fell through ... but some people are moving away on June 4th and I can have their house if I can come to terms with the landlord.... The rooms are light and the walls distempered and the floors are very good. There is gas, electric light and water and a big furnace (gas-fired) in the basement, so that it will be a very easy house to work....

I am still riding Oliver a bit but must try to sell him I think as I am not getting full value out of him.... I am very well and I wish that I could come home sometimes.... The *Times* is fine and it is very nice to get it....

Other scraps of letters:

... We have really got a good collection of books of this sort and I am an Hon. member of the High River Club where they take *Blackwoods* but I have only just been put up and haven't been round there much.

Today was a real scorcher but, as usual, here, the night is pleasant and cool.

I have been invited to play tennis with some people called Nelson tomorrow. I am not much of a tennis enthusiast but I believe that they have a good swimming pool ... (and about a library) ... we have a grant for this purpose. I got them through the *Aeroplane* and they are all to do with aviation, as we are not supposed to buy many novels, but mostly books on aeronautical subjects.

The titles are *All the World's Aircraft* an annual on the lines of *Jane's Fighting Ships. The Third Route* by Philip Sassoon. *The Great Trans-Pacific Flight* by Kingsford-Smith and Ulm and *With the Baghdad Air Mail* by Roderick Hill. I am now reading *The Third Route* which is well written and entertaining and have finished *The Trans-Pacific Flight....*

We have not done so much flying this week as there has been a little rain and we are busy overhauling the machines and changing engines on several of them. Also the smoke has been very bad. It is still coming from the BC side, where the fires have been terrible. Some of the smoke may come from the States. I went up one morning to test the air before letting the patrols go out and climbed to 7000' above High River before I came to clear air ... but at 7000' I could only just distinguish objects directly below me.

Did I tell you about the moose bull that I saw from the air some time back. It was in a muddy little lake (Hoodoo Lakes) eating the lily roots.

Ivey has just been away on a weeks leave and found that the bears were quite tame on the Banff-Windermere road.

They were having lunch in the car when 3 bears, a mother and 2 small ones came up to them out of the trees and they fed them on sandwiches. . . .

I have been for a few flights lately and we have been bringing in the Rangers from their posts before the freeze up. I brought in one from Slave Falls. His name is Harry Smith & he is quite an interesting old chap. He has Indian blood & is very interesting.

Their first child, a son, was born in November.

Although there had now been three generations of 'James Lindsay,' Charles and Marian broke just enough with family tradition to call him James Gardner. The choice of names was very much to Emmie's liking. Charles, having cabled Bredgar at once, wrote delightedly later the same day, to Emmie:

. . . I hope that you received my cablegram and that it was understandable. The baby was born this morning at 7.30. . . . Later on in the same letter he thanked Emmie for a book: Thank you very much for *The Good Companions* which came yesterday. It is awfully nice of you to send it. . . . Isn't it curious that I have just finished reading *Angel Pavement* by the same author. Stoneham, our new (English) stores officer lent it to me and I enjoyed it very much. . . .

In the spring of 1931, things began to wind down at High River. Charles wrote to Emmie on March 10th:

. . . We have definite instructions to place the air station on a 'care and maintenance' basis. Spradbrow and I are to fly the other three aeroplanes 'at our convenience' to Winnipeg which is very nice, as we shall wait until the weather turns fine and warm. We expect to leave High River on the 30th – less than three weeks from this date. Unless I have a good reason to change my plans Marian and Jimmy and the furniture will come with me to Winnipeg and I shall sell the car. . . .

If I am shipped to some rotten little sub-base on the shore of some fly-blown lake in the N.W. Territories I shall have to part from Marian and Jimmy. Rather than leave them in Winnipeg I will send them home to England for the summer and bring them back in the winter. . . .

Next Friday Marian is going to give a bun-fight to aid the Church. Several other ladies are doing the same sort of thing. You ask your friends to come and have tea with you at 25c (1/-) a head. Marian is going to be most original. She is going to give them coffee and cakes in the evening and so get the husbands as well as the wives and I am going to get the little cinematograph down from the air station and show some films which we took of the Turner Valley oilfield and of the mountains, from the air.

These films are quite new – we only took them a few months ago. I am also going to hire a 'comic' and a 'drama' which I can do in Calgary at very small cost. These two will probably be very old films – but they will help out our programme. . . .

I am very well but inclined to put on weight!

I am trying walking out to the aerodrome in the mornings. . . .

From High River, perhaps the last letter he wrote from High River, on March 22nd:

Just a short letter to tell you that we are all well. I have been packing and it is late.

I expect that we shall go to Winnipeg at the end of this week, but we are being kept very much in the dark by our H Q in Ottawa. Sprad. and I took two more of our aeroplanes to Winnipeg last week end. We had a better trip than the time before although I had a forced landing about 50 miles East of Regina. A valve rocker bracket became loose on No 1 cylinder – putting that cylinder out of action. I landed in a stubble field and luckily found the loose nut etc., resting on the top of the cylinder. I had a mechanic with me and he soon had everything tightened up. We were on our way again within half an hour and reached Winnipeg that evening.

Unfortunately Spradbrow, who had not seen me land, but who missed me shortly afterwards, went back to Regina, after looking for me in the Assiniboine Indian Reserve over which we had just passed.

He searched this part of the country for an hour before going back to Regina. He had my suitcase and my overcoat and hat, also all my mechanic's kit. It was rather foolish of us to let him take it, but it was done with the idea of making the load in his aeroplane equal to mine. He came on next day.

I have put in an application for another seaplane course as I may have to fly seaplanes and I have had very little experience on them. I hope that I shall get it. I would like Marian to see Vancouver.... I am going to sell the car as it costs too much to ship to W. I got some English film in Winnipeg for my UPK. It is much better than Kodak film, it is Ilford. I hope to get some good snaps....

Thus, with photographs and letters, letters and photographs, Charles kept Emmie and H and his sisters at home in England up to date. The old schoolroom globe was too yellowed and in any case of too early a date, to assist Emmie in tracking Charles' flights. Even the Black's General Atlas, which had belonged to JLT's father, was early, and showed much of Canada's boundary with the United States as well below the 49th Latitude. But she had enormous fun, with magnifying glass and school atlas, in following some of his travels.

Charles and Marian and young Jimmy lived in various rented apartments or cottages in Winnipeg. Charles wrote to Emmie from 1 Yale Apartments on July 15th 1931

... I was away for 12 days on an 'Air Tour' which visited some of the small country towns in Manitoba. I was detailed to go with the tour as the R.C.A.F. representative, the rest of the pilots being civilians.

It was very interesting to see so much of this province, which is a much nicer part of the world than I and other strangers like myself think it to be. It is not fair to judge it by Winnipeg and the unbroken level of the prairie through which the two railways run on their way to Saskatchewan.

We went to Portage-le-Prairie, Neepawa, Rivers, Brandon, Killarney, Russell, Dauphin, Virden, and back to Winnipeg. I was glad when the trip was over because I wanted to get home and because it was rather a tiring sort of job answering an endless string of questions about aircraft and flying, and listening to the same old speeches at the evening 'banquets' that we had to attend at each place visited. All these small towns are keenly interested in flying, and are putting up the money for 'airports'. They are keen, but at the same time they hope to attract the American tourists, who are using aeroplanes nowadays in considerable numbers....

In spite of the Air Tour to promote flying there began to be talk of cuts in the RCAF. It was a strange contradiction.

*   *   *

Canadian aviation historians K. M. Molson and H. A. Taylor, writing in their classic *Canadian Aircraft Since 1909* described and set the scene in their 'The Background' chapter:

> ... In 1930 a Conservative Government came to power and in 1931 the air mail services were threatened with extinction but in the event were only curtailed. However, in 1932 air mail services between all major Canadian centres were eliminated and only a few northern services retained. This cancellation of valid contracts almost caused the close of Canadian Airways which held the contracts for all the main routes and most of the northern routes. The company had bought aircraft and bought or leased facilities to undertake the contracts and was now faced with paying for these committments with no source of revenue.
>
> This decision by the government to make the infant air transport industry bear more than its proportionate share of economies necessary to weather the depression almost killed it. What prevented its demise was that the price of gold was high and consequently there was considerable activity in prospecting and exploration. For the next few years Canadian civil aviation consisted largely of flying prospectors on their searches for minerals and, when a potential mine was found, flying in men and materials to develop it. A surprising amount of business was generated and by the mid-1930's more freight was being moved by air in Canada than in all the rest of the world combined. All this was the more remarkable because it was being done without a nickel of Government money being spent to assist northern flying.'

In a later paragraph in the same chapter the authors continue:

> Other factors that did not help Canadian civil aviation in its development were the method of its control and the participation of the RCAF in what was termed civil government air operations. Control of civil aviation passed from the Air Board to the Department of National Defence in 1923 and was administered by the RCAF who created a Civil Aviation Branch to deal with it. While placing the control of both civil and military flying under a single jurisdiction was probably convenient to the government, the military control of civil operations has never been satisfactory even though administered with the best of intent. The civil government air operations were a constant thorn in the side of the civil operators who felt, justifiably, that the RCAF was doing work which should have been theirs and which they could do more economically, but protests always fell on deaf ears....

There is no doubt that Canadian aviation, like most other aviation world-wide, was not being given the Government support which it deserved. Soon the RCAF cuts would come. Charles had only another six months of service, a fact of which he was still unaware, for he began to make plans for some long leave and a trip to England with his family. . . .

Charles wrote to Alie on 12th September, 1931, from

c/o Royal Canadian Air Force, 797, Notre Dame Avenue, Winnipeg:

Many happy returns of the day ... (he sent a photograph of Jimmy). . . . I am afraid that it is not a very grand present, but I must make the excuse that I am saving up for the trip home, if it comes off.

I hope to get leave early in November, but if they won't give me any leave at all, Marie and Jimmy will go alone – but I hope that I shall be able to get leave.

We went out on the Red River to-day and left Jimmy with the maid. I rowed from the place where one can get a boat to the Winnipeg Rowing Club's big Clubhouse, and we watched some 'Speedboat' races ... they travel quite fast, bouncing along on the surface of the water. . . .

I have completed the Court of Inquiry that I was working on all last week. Fortunately one of the members trained as an accountant in Glasgow and understands all about book keeping. Otherwise I would have found the job a difficult one. . . .

I have applied for leave from 28th October with the idea of catching the *Duchess of Atholl* from Montreal on the 30th. I may only get 5 weeks but I have applied for a fortnight's special leave in addition. . . .

In the event Marian and Jimmy came over alone.

Charles to Emmie:

Feb. 22nd 1932. 797 Notre Dame Ave. Winnipeg. Canada.

... I expect that you will have heard from Marian that I sent her a cablegram to cancel her passage, because heavy cuts were going to be made in the R.C.A.F. These cuts turned out to be even larger than I expected and the vote for aviation has been cut to less than one third of what it was last year, so that our small air force has been reduced accordingly.

All the non-permanent officers including myself will be sacked at the end of March. There are 84 of us and we include nearly all the most experienced 'photographic' pilots in the service.

The remaining 48 permanent officers will have no flying to do as there is no money available and the various air stations will be put on a 'care and maintenance' basis.

Civil aviation will be hard hit too. Most likely the air mail will be stopped, except the northern route up the Mackenzie River. Poor old J. A. Wilson said 'That is ten years work gone for nothing, Charles'.

The present Prime Minister R. B. Bennett is entirely responsible. The cost of operating the C.N. Railway this coming year is expected to be 85 million dollars and by making the cuts in aviation he will save about $3\frac{1}{2}$ million dollars.

It is an unexpected blow to me and to poor Marian I am afraid. We had hoped that our branch would become a civil service with a guaranteed future.

We were all sent straight back to our Stations and I travelled back with F/O Barclay.

The two of us have decided to do whatever we can to get something started and we are working on a scheme to provide the Alberta Government with an air service on a small scale for the use of their forestry department. I have the advantage of knowing the country and the officials and of being an engineer. Barclay is an accountant, trained in Glasgow, is a very steady pilot, and has done 2 years forestry work in Manitoba and Saskatchewan. We have applied for our commercial licences and air engineers certificates, and have prepared a scheme which is nearly complete. We think De Havillands will help us – owing to the fact that their R.C.A.F. market for aircraft has vanished.

I think that there is a chance of success. I am quite sure that if we could start it, it would not be difficult to make it pay. However, if it does not succeed we can try other ideas.

My idea is to live as cheaply as possible and I think that in a few months time, when the summer comes, I will find something to do.

Do you mind if Marian stays at Bredgar sometimes? . . . Please don't worry or send any money because I have enough to get on with and I have made up my mind to do my best to get started. love to all at home.

Your loving son, Charlie.

He had not signed himself so informally since before the war.

Charles to Emmie from Winnipeg Air Station, 797, Notre Dame Avenue, Winnipeg. 6th March:

. . . I have been taking examinations for my commercial pilot's licence and Air Engineer's certificates and expect to finish them off on

Wednesday next. I will be employed by the R.C.A.F. until March 10th, then go on leave until the end of March.

I am afraid that there is not the least chance of the Government changing its mind with regard to the aviation estimates.

I see that in England the aviation vote has been cut from 85 million to 82 million *dollars* or thereabouts – about $3\frac{1}{2}\%$ whereas ours has been cut from $5\frac{1}{2}$ million to $\frac{3}{4}$ million dollars – nearly 70%!

So far I have not had any replies to my application for jobs, but Malcolm Barclay and I hope that we will be able to start something in Alberta. We have written to D.Havs of Canada and hope that they will back us up.

We had some mild weather but it has turned cold again $-14°$ Fahrenheit yesterday at 9 o'clock in the morning but we get plenty of sunshine! ... My typewriter which I bought in Ottawa is very useful. I will write you a typewritten letter soon....

Charles to Emmie from 797, Notre Dame Avenue, Winnipeg, on 26th March, 1932:

I bought this typewriter while I was at Ottawa, because they made so many nasty remarks about my writing, but since then it has been really useful. I am writing most of my letters with it now for practice. Barclay can type well, and he did all the typing for the Alberta scheme.

I had a letter from Hutchinson, of the Alberta Forestry Service, to-day. It was quite a long one, and although he says that nothing can be done this year, he is very keen to go ahead with some scheme of aeroplane patrols next year.

I hope that next year I will be able to obtain the contract for this work or else get a job with the Alberta Government. In the meantime Barclay and I are thinking of buying a motor-boat and running pleasure trips from Kenora, on the Lake of the Woods. This is the centre of a large tourist traffic from the U.S.A. and from all parts of Canada. It is on the main C.P.R. line and the Trans-Canada Highway will be opened for traffic through it shortly, so that people can drive in from Winnipeg in a few hours.

If I cannot get any news of a flying job, Barclay and I are going over to Kenora next week end, to see how the land lies.

I must say that I am not wildly enthusiastic about the scheme; one can estimate the costs with some degree of accuracy, but it is impossible to tell how much business one would get....

S/Ldr Leitch passed through Winnipeg on Thursday on his way to High River, on leave, but I missed seeing him. I heard, though, that he had good news of his wife and baby girl.

The authorities have not decided whether to close Camp Borden, if they do, he will be sent to the new training centre at Trenton, on lake Ontario.

Tomorrow, Easter Sunday, I am going to lunch at S/Ldr Andersons: They have been most awfully nice, and I am sure, are as sorry as anyone that this cut has happened.

One of our pilots, Weedon, who has been doing photographic survey work for 3 years, is leaving for England next week, to try for a job with one of the air survey companies; but I do not think that he will be successful and I think that it is an easy mistake to make, to suppose that conditions will be any better at home.

My advertisement in the *New York Times* will appear tomorrow. I think that it may do some good, because there are a great many new mining districts being developed in Northern Manitoba, and in the N.W. Territories, and any mining concern in the States that wished to send a geologist into that country, would require a pilot and an air engineer who understood the conditions.

I am glad that Marian and Jimmy are at Bredgar, they will love it, and I am very glad that they will see V. and John. . . . It must be lovely in the garden at home. . . . Love to all at home. I hope that H.O. is better. . . .

The next was a typewritten letter, still from Notre Dame Avenue, on the 5th April, 1932:

Thank you for your letter of March 21st.

I went to Kenora last week and have delayed answering until my return.

I cabled Marie to come out because she wants to come, and because I think she should be out here even if I go up North, as I hope to do for the Harriman interests.

If I succeed in getting that job, I will try to find a small house or bungalow for Marian in Winnipeg. If not, Barclay and I are thinking of taking a Moth sea plane down to Kenora, where we think that we could operate it profitably.

We would do short passenger flights by special charter. I do not think that there would be any competition at all, and if we are able to buy our Moth very cheaply we can make it pay.

The R.C.A.F. is not using its Moths this year, & has several in very good condition, with Short floats. I think that we might be able to buy one for quite a small sum.

We had thought of running a motor boat service at Kenora but found that there were three large firms in that business and several small concerns; their rates are so low that there would be very little profit in running one or two boats.

I have got my commercial pilot's licence, and expect that my Air Engineer's licence will arrive any day now.

I am very well; the weather has turned warm and the snow is melting in the streets. At Kenora, however, we were able to walk across the lake to an island where there are several bungalows to rent and they drive cars across to the Ontario Provincial Air Service base on the same island. They told us that the ice usually goes out quite suddenly at about the end of the month.

It must be a beautiful place in the summer. There are thousands of little islands & rocks all covered with trees. On this island close to Kenora there is electricity and towns water and there is a frequent ferry service to the town; but there are many others with no one on them. There is plenty of game, deer and moose a little way away....

Still from Winnipeg, but this time from 255 Langside, on the 18th April, 1932:

... Thank you very much for your letter and for offering to help me in the Alberta scheme. It would have been of very great assistance & it would have enabled us to do the work.

There is, however, no chance of us doing anything there until next year.

I hope to hear from the N.Y. people but in case that does not come off, I am thinking of getting a Moth if I can buy one of the old Air Force ones for less than 500 dollars with floats as well as wheels. At that price we would be able to make it pay carrying passengers, I think. We have written to Ottawa about it, but have not committed ourselves at all.

I have been getting maps and information about the Great Bear Lake country, in case the Harriman people wanted us to take an expedition up there. It would be very interesting and not very difficult if we had a big organization behind us. Supplies of petrol would have to be flown in or sent by the water route.

The usual water route is up by Slave Lake, and then round by the Mackenzie as far as Ft Norman then in to Franklin and across Great Bear Lake. The Radium and silver etc. is on the Eastern shore of Great Bear Lake. There is also unlimited copper and some gold. There is oil at Ft Norman.

Break up on Great Bear Lake occurs early in April and the lake is clear of ice about the beginning of July or end of June. Freeze up is early in September, but one can operate on skiis, over the whole route, from December to April, and on floats from July to September.

It is rather dark in winter.

We had an idea of starting a small workshop here to do some specialist aircraft work but the equipment is costly and it would be a long time before we worked up the business I am afraid.

Barclay and I answered an advertisement this morning and found that it was a job selling silk stockings & etc. from door to door.... It was rather hard to keep a straight face when interviewing the sales expert. The whole thing seemed so utterly ridiculous, but we were very solemn....

I am looking forward to seeing Marian and Jim....

Charles to Emmie, from 117 Woodhaven Boulevard, Winnipeg, on 10th May, 1932:

Many happy returns of the day.... I wish that we were all at home together....

I think that I have got a job with the Manitoba Forestry Service. It will not be much, a little over half my pay in the R.C.A.F. but still, we can live on it I think.

I would be employed as an Air Engineer (mechanic) and spare pilot. Manitoba are getting 5 Vedettes from the R C A F to form the nucleus of a provincial air service.

The other three pilots and the air engineer at the second base are friends of mine, so I think that it should be a good show. I haven't got the job yet but hope to hear more this week....

And again from Woodhaven Boulevard, on the 13th May:

Marian and Jim arrived safely Wednesday morning.

They had a very good voyage & Marian had a good time and met the Countess of Bessborough and all the suite. The sea was calm but they had to go slow one day because of fog.

I have got a job: the one I told you about and Marian may be able to follow me to Lac du Bonnet in a month or so. . . .

You were naughty to see them off at Southampton, but it was nice for them.

Love to Ally and Jess. . . .

Charles was to fly out of Cormorant Lake and Lac du Bonnet for a number of years.

Extracts from some of the many letters he wrote from those places will be quoted in another chapter.

12

THE SMELL OF PETROL

1928–1929

H. and family settle in Walmer – H. regretfully declines Blackburn testing job – instructs at Bristol & Wessex – instructs at Cinque Ports Flying Club – forced landing on 'NN two weeks before leaving CPFC.

DAPHNE's health had improved so markedly after her operation at the War Memorial Hospital at Deal and Dr James Hall and the other medical staff were so kind and clever there that the logical step, now that H. & H. were in England and likely to remain so, was to find somewhere to live on that part of the coast. There were several leaseholds for sale in Walmer, Hermia particularly liking a pretty house in Archery Square. In the end they bought on the seafront itself, H.'s theory being that if the sea breezes were *so* healthy then the nearer one was to the sea the better. Undeniably he also liked the idea of watching shipping in the roadstead. There was such a lot of coastal traffic in those days. 9 The Beach was Hermia's property. She bought it with part of the legacy from her father, investing every remaining farthing in Baird Television. The matter of Baird Television became part of all our lives. One day, (Hermia was totally confident,) the invention of the brilliant Scot would be recognized, popularised, and – overnight – profitable. It was not until about 1938 that she finally admitted defeat. Television was coming from the Alexandra Palace by then. Not a word about dividends.

9 The Beach was slate-hung on it's open side, beside which a narrow garden path and flint wall separated us from No. 10. On the other side it was joined on to No. 8. It's sash windows, too large for so small a house, faced the sea, and the sea breezes blew around them and through them and rattled the panes incessantly on all but the calmest of days.

Captain Baker – James Valentine Baker – was Flying Instructor at Stag Lane in 1928 but he was keen to move to Heston in the autumn. He asked H. to take over from him at the London Aeroplane Club at

Stag Lane as soon as Heston was ready for him, Baker, to go there.
H. was delighted and planned a move to Stag Lane in due course.
Meanwhile he looked about with some urgency for a job for the
summer. (He had parted from Blackburns in May.)

The Instructor at the Bristol & Wessex Club at Filton had had his
appendix out and had been given leave of absence to recuperate. The
job slotted in with H.'s plans and he took up his duties with the Bristol
& Wessex, his first ever job as a civilian flying instructor, on 17th
July, 1928, flying Moth G-EBVC down from Stag Lane to Filton:

'1 hour 30 minutes. delivery of Hughes' Moth from storage at Stag
Lane.'

Still on the 17th July: 'Engaged as a temporary pilot Instructor to
Bristol & Wessex Club.' He took up G-EBYH the same day, for two
flights of 10 minutes each: 'slotted wing. local.' On the 18th July he
started instructing, making numerous flights with various pupils in
''YH'. In the evening he tested G-EBTV: 'Test. solo. 20 minutes.
Stopped prop. on loop. Forced landing. Restarted & came home.'
Later the same day taking up 'C. Neale. beginner.' on the same
machine.

On the 19th and 20th July he was instructing continuously; among
his pupils were Singh, Warren, Miss Miles, Greenhill, Laws, Chopra,
Dr Lysacht and Neale. He flew ''YH' and 'TV', also testing these
machines variously.

The 21st July, a Saturday, was King's Cup Day and all flying was
stopped from 11.30 to 4 o'clock. In the evening he flew: 'Bristol
Brownie. 35 "Cherub" G-EBJL. local solo. 35 minutes. great fun in
calm.'

He spent the rest of the daylight hours giving joy rides locally on
''TV': '30 landings!!' He also gave a solo show on ''TV' for 15
minutes to end the day.

For probably the first time since the end of the war, Sunday now
became a working day: indeed one of the busiest working days of the
week. On Sunday 22nd July, he continued to instruct on ''YH' Singh,
Chopra, Allinson and a new pupil, Putnam, member of the famous
publishing family: 'beginner. straights & turns.' He also took up
Culverwell, late CFS Instructor. In the evening he took his pupil,
Neale, to Edgecote and return.

He did not fly on Monday; he recorded '23rd: no flying'; it was
usually the custom in flying clubs to have Monday as the day off.

He resumed instructing on Tuesday 24th July on the two Moths, more or less alternately, ''Y H' and ''T V'; amongst his pupils were: 'Bathurst and Laws. Lynas. Byrnes. Evans and Greenhill.' On the 25th July, with the 'Wind too high for school work' he flew Ashley Hall to Stag Lane in '1 hour 10 minutes. shewing route to Ashley Hall.' returning in one hour and fifty minutes. On the 26th July he must have been flying from dawn til dark, starting with a five minute test on ''Y H'; he then instructed Patterson, Evans (landings) Lynas (landings) Chopra (straights & turns) Greenhill (landings) Dr Lysaght (turns & landings) Byrnes (turns & straights) Miss Miles (landings O.K. sent her solo.) Heaven (straights & turns) and Newman (straights & turns), there being many flights with each pupil. On the 27th, the weather still holding, he tested ''Y H' briefly before beginning the day's work: 'Charlton. beginner. Evans/spins & landings. Lynas. landings fair. Singh, won't listen. Miss Miles. approaches good.' Much the same sort of programme continued on subsequent days, but with varying names. He obviously thought highly of Miss Miles. And of B. L. Bathurst who, after being a beginner a few days earlier was now: 'O.K. for solo. sent solo.' Other pupils not already mentioned were Capt. Davie Air Ministry: 'OK for solo.' And Asst Instructor Culverwell: 'very OK.'

Instruction continued into August. On the 1st Aug. he noted 'promoted Flt. Lt. RAFO.'

His log-book is frank and not always kind: 'Allinson. opinionated. slow progress.' 'Lynas. landing a little high.' 'Miss Miles. to correct faults.' 'Lynas. landings progress.' 'Greenhill sent solo. 1st solo (1st solo since 1919)'. 'Allinson. won't flatten out.' 'Singh landings. great improvement.' 'T. H. Clarke. flying more reasonably. sent solo.'

On the 4th August he took Mrs Allinson up for a half-hour flight before continuing to instruct, his pupils for that day and each flying for a number of times: 'Hibbert. Charlton. Allinson. Rodgers. Peters. Miss Miles. Singh and Greenhill.' He rounded off the day with another 10 minute test on the Bristol Brownie G-EBJL. He seemed to have liked the Brownie, for after another very long day's instructing on Sunday, 5th August, he took her up for another 10 minute test. 'Test OK.'

The 6th August was Bank Holiday Monday that year. It was also his 9th wedding anniversary but I do not think that Hermia had then gone down to Filton although she did so soon afterwards. H. flew one of his pupils, Lynas, a compass course against a head wind to Tangmere in 1 hour 20 minutes, on ''Y H'. From Tangmere he flew a passenger, Keith Jopp, to Lympne in 1 hour exactly, returning with the same passenger in the same time. Then in the evening he and Lynas returned to Filton: 'G-E B Y H. Tangmere to Filton. 1 hour 10 minutes. passenger Lynas. cmpass course. weather good but poor visibility.'

On the 8th August, the 7th presumably having been the substitute day off that week, he tested ''T V' first thing, but: 'test m/c O.K. Weather too rough for instruction.' He continued to instruct on the 9th, 10th and 11th August, slipping in what were probably most enjoyable little test flights on the Bristol Brownie G-E B J L. On the 12th August he reported on some of the pupils whom he had instructed that day: 'Peters. Neale. Greenhill. good progress.' There was no comment on Clarke, Allinson or Keeling.

On the 13th he flew 'G-E B T V. Filton to Stag Lane. solo. 1 hour 15 minutes. Very high & boisterous S S W Wind. unpleasant journey.'

He did not record his return trip to Filton but it would appear that Hermia may have accompanied him; otherwise she must have driven herself down independently. She made the entries in his log-book for him from 14th to 18th August inclusively and on later days. She also made herself useful in the office by helping to keep the records straight, as a result of which the owners offered her a full-time job to stay on and become the Flying Club's Secretary. She declined the offer but she was flattered and very pleased to have been asked.

Towards the end of August new names began to appear among the names of pupils in the Remarks columns: 'Kidmore.' 'Dutton.' 'Amory.' (Amory turned out to be a Travers cousin.) 'Mr Rigby, Australian 'B' licence. 2 landings. O.K.' 'Patrick.' 'Pollock.'

On the 21st August H. flew G-E B T V to Stag Lane 'for repainting. H.E.M.T. passenger.' This reduced the Bristol & Wessex Club's fleet to one aeroplane, ''Y H', whose tail-skid scarcely touched the ground for the three days that ''T V' was away. H. collected the repainted ''T V' on 24th August. Still old 'Y H worked hard, spending most of the 25th August airborne, to: 'Wales & return.' 'To Gloucester & return.' and for 30 minutes, amongst many other afternoon flights: 'Putnam. straights.' Last flight of the day, like a spoonful of honey, H. took up the little Bristol Brownie for her 10 minute test.

He learnt a lot about instructing during his brief time with the Bristol & Wessex Club. He had, as already recorded, instructed fellow RAF and RFC pilots in cross country head-in-bag flying in 1919 – but his pupils then were already pilots, often pilots with at least as much flying experience as H. had possessed himself and with whom he simply shared some of his navigational skills. They were, too, all young or youngish men in uniform and used to the normal service disciplines. Civilians, on the other hand, were all fee-paying members of a wide public and of all ages, shapes and intelligences. H. learnt pretty soon what a variety they were and with what variety of ability, self-confidence, or sensitivity to criticism.

Although he made unkind remarks about some of them in the depths of his log-book, he often revised or reversed these remarks when, later on, he mentioned names in conversation. For example, Singh, who 'won't listen' he later described as an absolutely marvellous pilot, ascribing the rapidity with which Singh learnt to fly to the fact that he was already a fine horseman with a horseman's abilities: co-ordination of hand and eye, sensitivity, anticipation and right judgment followed by quick action.

Early in September, still with ''Y H' doing most of the work, H.'s time with the Bristol & Wessex came to an end.

He recorded on the 31st August:

'Handed over to Bartlett he having recovered from appendicitis.

Pupils sent solo – six.

R A E C tests – five.

Own flying time 18th July to 31st Aug 124 hrs 05 mins.

Club time for Aug: 166 hrs 35 mins.

Previous record: 95 hrs.'

He overlapped with Bartlett for a couple of days, his last pupil being: 'Greenhill. landings.' on the 2nd September.

When H. left the Bristol & Wessex, Baker was still at Stag Lane, but he intended handing over there to H. before leaving, whenever required to do so, for the new flying school at Heston. H. therefore arranged to go to Brough in October for his RAFO training while waiting to take over at Stag Lane. Meanwhile he had a few weeks at home with all of us at 9 The Beach.

He bought kites and taught D. and me to fly them above the

promenade and the green between the row of houses on 'The Beach' and the sea. We all went fishing with the Walmer boatmen and were taught to row, with a single oar, and to drop a line over the side for whiting.

He brought a 1926 14 h.p. Armstrong Siddeley, painted black and named *Jemima* and in her we went on picnics above Kingsdown, still uneven with practice trenches from the war; and further afield to Barham Downs, not then fenced or ploughed as I believe much of it is now.

There had been a transition period between the days when Bredgar House was home and when we moved into 9 The Beach in the late summer of 1928.

During the transition period our HQ was The Fair Maid of Kent Hotel, a flourishing establishment who liked to cater especially for families. Hermia had stayed there whilst overseeing D.'s hospital treatment and at other times when visiting us at our boarding school. We had gone out to tea there from school. Hermia was fond of the place. She and H. had spent part of his 1927/28 Christmas leave there.

H. & H. were an attractive couple; she may have been less good-looking than he was but she was much better looking than photographs taken of her at the time suggest; she was slim, straight-backed, very vivacious and witty. They were a glamorous couple and they were asked out a lot.

Among many new friends of those Walmer days was Brigadier General Sir Reginald Ford, Commandant of the Royal Marines at Deal.

Sir Reginald Ford kept permanent apartments in the Hotel as a home for himself and for his grown-up daughter, Primrose, and for his two sons when they came on leave. The Hotel was so handy – it was nearly opposite the Main Gate of the Barracks – that he could be summoned to the Barracks at a moment's notice. A widower, with three grown children, he was typical of men who have been successful in their own careers and who in later life often find themselves a little lonely. He was immensely sociable, a conversationalist and a keen chess-player. He and H. & H. got along very well, played a bit of chess and were altogether interesting company for each other. Primrose was a dear, a girl of great character and the kindest of friends to Hermia, in spite of the difference in their ages.

There were invitations to the Officer's Mess and H. & H. spent a number of enjoyable evenings there. One of the amusements after a really good dinner party was to 'ride the horses', particularly to ride the horses blind-folded.

The Royal Marine 'horses' were slippery mechanical metal monsters, so cleverly constructed and operated that they were hard to stay on at the best of times and almost impossible after wining and dining and being blind-folded.

H. thought a great deal about those horses.

If, as he had been told, they were often used as practice mounts before riding instruction was given then the next step, for him as a flying instructor, was to devise something similar to them to be used in pre-flight training. So, in 1928, he began thinking about and drawing plans for his own blind-flying flight simulator. He was searching for something better than the 'head-in-a-bag' in-flight instruction: an instrument-only flight simulator.

He went up to Brough in early October, recording in his log-book: '3rd Year. 1st $\frac{1}{4}$'s training. Reserve training at North Sea Aerial & General Transport Co. Brough.'

Chief Instructor Arthur Loton was still there – sound as ever and a fine instructor. He took H. up dual on Blackburn Kangaroo G-EBMD on the 6th October for 40 minutes; then again on the 8th October for 15 minutes. Still on the 8th H. took up G-EBMD for an hour and five minutes solo.

There followed further dual with Loton on the 9th after which H. went solo again for 30 minutes. On the 10th, dual with Loton, followed by H. doing a solo cross-country: Brough – Sherburn – Beverly – Brough, of 1 hour and 25 minutes; all his flying having been done on the same machine, Blackburn Kangaroo G-EBMD.

It was during this October visit to Brough that Robert Blackburn asked H. to rejoin Blackburn's at Brough. H. later regretted – so Hermia said – coming south to discuss it with her before accepting. He came south on the 11th October. It was her birthday, her day, and he was always gallant. She wanted to live in Walmer.

On the 12th he was appointed as a temporary Instructor at the Cinque Ports Flying Club at Lympne and on the 13th began his flying there. His time with the CPFC started badly.

His first flight from Lympne was in their newest Moth, DH60X G-

EBSS, which he took up for a 15-minute test. Then he took up Bain for a joyride on the machine. Then he went up, still in the same machine, 'SS, for 30 minutes: 'dual to Brett.' Then he went up, still in the same machine, for 15 minutes: 'dual to Skinner.'

After he stepped out of 'SS Skinner took her straight up again, flying solo. H. recorded: 'Skinner then was killed owing to belt breaking he fell from machine which was totally wrecked.'

The brief words did not diminish the tragedy.

There had been, as I recall, something of a fuss about him taking the job at Lympne at all. H. had maintained that there was absolutely nothing for him down on the Kent coast. All the worthwhile jobs were elsewhere – at Brough, where he had been offered an interesting testing job, – or Edgware, where he had a job (he kept assuring Hermia), which was being kept open for him but which would not be so indefinitely. Really, – if he was not to take the Blackburn job – he wanted to be nearer London. He wanted to be able to attend meetings and see people.

Hermia, who had infinite confidence in H.'s ability and a determination to stay put in Walmer with her children, assured him that he would of course find something nearby. So he had found a six-months' instructing job at Lympne, but it was of an unsatisfactory and temporary nature only; if he had bowed to Hermia's wishes over test-flying for Blackburn's he was not prepared to give way to her on the matter of going to Stag Lane instead. He would, he said, go there when Baker gave the word. Meanwhile: he was not a man who ever gave anything less than his best. He settled down to work hard for the Cinque Ports Flying Club.

Moth DH60 G-EBNN had been overhauled and he tested her on the 15th October. Then there came a spell of bad weather, after which he tested 'NN again, on the 19th October, then instructing on her for the rest of the day until it was time to go over to Hawkinge to collect Moth DH60X G-EBYJ for Mr Law and fly her back to Lympne. He tested 'NN repeatedly on the 21st as well as giving a number of half-hour lessons. Amongst his pupils were Worsell, Clematson and young Martin, recorded as being 15. On the 23rd he flew Law's machine, G-EBYJ, to Stag Lane to have a compass fitted, a flight of 1 hour and 10 minutes; he returned to Lympne the same day with the owner, Law, as passenger. Tony Law, son of Bonar Law, the former Prime Minister, had bought 'Y J and now wished to learn to fly her. There was much before-breakfast instruction on 'Y J on the 25th, 26th and again on the 31st October. Law was an adept pupil and became a fine pilot, winning a King's Cup Race one year. Apart from instructing Law on his own machine, 'Y J, the early Moth, 'N N, appears to have been the only other machine to which H. had access, for he instructed on her exclusively right up until the 8th December. Among his many pupils such names as Douglas, Barham (prospective member), Clematson, Worsell, Crammond, Sargent and Swinnard appear with great regularity. So also Harrison, Wanliss and Somerset. He recorded taking D. up for a 3 minute flight after doing a short test on 'N N on the 18th November. Other than that and numerous short tests his flying was all instructing, even when making what sound like enjoyable trips. Such an one took place on the 9th November:

'D H60X G-EBY J.   Lympne to Hawkinge to collect Law. 15 minutes.
  „   „   Hawkinge – Farnboro 1 hour 5 mins to lunch with
                    Dolly Gray.
  „   „   Farnboro – Brooklands 15 mins To Guards Air Meet.
  „   „   Brooklands – Lympne 55 mins. returning to Lympne.'

A new pupil, Armstrong-Payn, arrived on the 26th November. The Armstrong-Payns were near neighbours of ours at Walmer, having a beach house, a secluded and weather-tight bungalow sitting behind hedges and walls right on the green. I remember them as rather jolly P. G. Wodehouse sort of people – very friendly and absolutely mad on flying.

I have an idea that they lived in London during the week and came down for the fresh air and the flying at week ends.

On the 8th and 9th December H. recorded having flown Spartan G-EBY U, but whether this was a visiting aeroplane or one acquired by the C.P.F.C is not mentioned.

On the 16th December he went up to Stag Lane to collect a new Moth, one of the new series: D H60X G-EBRI. No doubt 'RI was a replacement for the wrecked 'S S.

16th Dec. D H60X G-EBRI. Stag Lane to Lympne. 1 hour 30 minutes. High Southerly wind. low cloud. Rough!'

On the 17th he took up a pupil in old 'N N again and on the 19th tested 'R I for half an hour and being pleased with her took a passenger,

Somerset (one of his pupils) to Camberley and return in 20 minutes. It was foggy when he tested 'NN again on the 21st, but he was instructing Somerset on her on the 22nd, later taking up another pupil, Parks, on 'RI.

'RI's popularity began to spread and on the 23rd he took up a number of joyriders on the machine, among them Miss Douglas, Hon. Mrs Douglas and Mrs Douglas.

He tested 'NN regularly before taking up pupils and often reported difficulties of a various nature. On the 27th Dec. after a 5 minute test he recorded: Test. missing badly.'

He tested her again on the 30th December and reported 'Test O.K.' but in between and whenever possible he instructed on 'RI.

H. flew 'RI throughout January, 1929, and many names of new pupils began to appear in his log-book then: among them Parks, Adkinson, West, Story, Boyes, Calvert, Everden and Miss French. On the 12th January he flew 'RI to Croydon, taking 45 minutes for the trip: 'to ADC for Cirrus Spares.' He flew to Croydon again on the 14th January with one of his pupils, Calvert, as passenger. 'RI was doing all the work. After instructing on her all the 20th and 21st January he flew: 'Douglas to Barham Downs. landed on stubblefield' on the 23rd January and after returning to Lympne instructed Calvert locally for 55 minutes. Then he tested 'RI on the 24th January and noted: '30 minutes. 3 tests. rev. counter erratic. replaced.'

'NN had been a long time in the shop but in early February she was back again. H. Reported on the 3rd February: 'G-EBNN. 30 minutes. Test after o'haul. O.K.' So he took up a pupil, Evernden, on her on the 4th, reporting: 'forced landing in aerodrome.' He then tested 'NN for half an hour and on landing took up Calvert for 10 minutes but reported: 'Engine knocking.' So he transferred to 'RI and took up Calvert again for a proper 20 minute lesson.

Hermia had enjoyed the short amount of instruction she had had at the Bristol & Wessex and so, hearing about the joys of the new machine, she asked for a few more lessons. H. took her up on 'RI locally at Lympne on the 5th February and she liked the machine and flew her well.

On the 7th February H. and his pupil Calvert flew 'to Croydon and return via Penshurst,' taking 1 hour and 50 minutes for the trip. He flew 'RI for the rest of the 7th, instructing, and throughout the 8th, 9th and most of the 10th February. The last flight on the 10th was on 'NN, a 10 minute flight: 'Test after engine overhaul.' It is obvious that H. had been unhappy about 'NN, because he tested her repeatedly on the 14th, 15th, 16th and 20th February, eventually taking up a pupil, Sargent, on her for 45 minutes on the 20th before transferring to 'RI again.

He flew both machines alternately for the next few days, taking up 'West adv. dual' on 'NN for 45 minutes on the 1st March. Enter commercialism.

It is noticeable how all the joyrides were on 'RI, for joyriders were prospective pupils, yet many of the more hardworking lessons by already committed pupils, were on 'NN.

Halley had two joyrides on 'RI on the 2nd March but on the same day Shaw-Kennedy had 30 minutes instruction on 'NN, Story had advanced dual on 'NN and Parks had dual on 'NN.

He was instructing on 'RI on the 3rd, Shaw-Kennedy, Took and Brett and took up as passengers Hunt and Crammond. Then it was back to 'NN for the rest of the day. At one point landing 'NN: 'to have oil pipe repaired.'

On the 5th March, after giving Somerset advanced dual instruction on 'RI, he flew 'RI to Stag Lane: '1 hour. 5000 ft above haze.' He returned the same day: 'Stag Lane to Lympne. 55 minutes. On C.Co, 225° 10 mins. 180° 5 mins. 130° to Lympne. In clouds as far as Headcorn.'

So H.'s days continued, instructing on 'RI whenever possible and when not, making do as best he could with 'NN. On the 8th March he reported: 'G-EBNN. 15 minute. Test after engine repair.' and again: 'Test after rudder adjustment.' He gave advanced dual to West on her on the 8th March and on the 9th, after a long day's instructing, during which Hermia had been hanging about all day waiting for a lull in the flying to have a short lesson herself, he took her up for her first half-hour on 'NN. Hermia did not like the machine. 'Heavy.' 'Lop-sided.' 'Doesn't seem to answer the controls properly' were some of the remarks she made. H. assured her that aeroplanes came in all degrees of niceness; she would get used to 'NN; he had flown many worse machines. However, on the 10th he was able to get hold of 'RI and Hermia had a short lesson on her which she enjoyed. But she was in for 'flu and the lesson was cut short. She did not fly again for some weeks.

Other pupils, Woods, Parmiter and Clematson among them flew 'RI and they and other pupils continued to learn on both machines. On the 17th March, Braddell's name first appeared in the log-book. He had two 30 minute lessons on 'NN on that day.

On the 18th he had a 30 minute lesson on 'RI and later the same day was sent solo on 'NN for 15 minutes. Either he was an especially gifted pupil or he was not an ab initio pupil, for it was the Gosport system par excellence to go solo on the second day. But not impossible. He was a delightful man, Maurice Braddell, a film star and an actor of some distinction. Maurice Braddell went solo again on 'NN on the 19th March and on the 23rd March he had 15 minutes advanced dual instruction on 'RI.

Still 'NN continued to be a worry and was in the shop for something or other every second day. H. brought a new machine down from Stag Lane on the 24th March and since it was not recorded as being anyone's private aircraft it was probably a new machine for the Cinque Ports Flying Club.

H. recorded: 'DH60X G-EBTZ. Stag Lane to Lympne. passenger Story.'

Towards the end of March V.'s husband, Jack Frederick, died at Malvern Wells. Although he was in his late '70's and had been ill with cancer for months it was, as such occasions are, both a shock and a great sorrow. H. was most anxious to support his sister and to pay his last respects to Jack Frederick by attending the funeral. But the Cinque Ports Flying Club were busy. They agreed, therefore, to lend him a machine so that he could be there and back in a day and only lose a day's instructing time. They lent him the new machine.

H. recorded: '26th March. DH60X G-EBTZ. Lympne to Malvern Wells. 2 hours 20 minutes. to Jack Frederick's funeral.'

The return flight did not go according to plan. He recorded: 'Malvern to Croydon. 1 hour 30 minutes. stopped by fog.'

Hermia had accompanied him and they spent the night at Croydon. On the afternoon of the 27th March, when the fog had lifted, they completed their journey, taking an hour from Croydon to Lympne.

On arrival at Lympne H. took up 'RI and then 'NN for a 5 minute test of each aeroplane. It was a good opportunity for Hermia to have another flying lesson. Another pilot must have wanted 'RI. H. and H. took off in 'NN.

The accident report stated that the accident (civil accident C – 137) to Moth G – EBNN with a 60 h.p. Cirrus 1. No. 4 engine occurred on an instructional flight at about 17.00 hours on March 27th, 1929. Their 'Brief Description' stated:

A sudden and complete failure of the engine occurred when the aeroplane was at a height of about 150 feet, having just taken off after a practice landing on the aerodrome. The pilot attempted to execute a forced-landing in a small field, but the machine fell heavily to the ground and was wrecked. The pilot and passenger escaped injuries of any consequence. In the 'Facts Established' section they stated: a) the aeroplane was built by Messrs. The De Havilland Aircraft Co. Ltd., and was sold to the Yorkshire Aeroplane Club in 1926. It was acquired by the last owners in September, 1928, when its total flying time amounted to a little over 1000 hours, and to the date of the accident it had been flown for a further 103 hours.

The engine had run for about 35 hours since last top overhaul, and for about 219 hours since complete overhaul by the makers. and later c): The weather conditions for local flying were good. There was very little wind. d) The aircraft was passed as serviceable by the ground engineer and was tested for about 5 minutes by the Instructor just before the flight in question. The petrol tank was last replenished on the morning of 25.3.29, six gallons being added, and, according to the statements of the ground engineer, it was then full. The aeroplane was not in use during that, or the following day, the test flight on the afternoon of the accident being the first flight since 24.3.29. e) On the flight in question the aircraft took off under the control of the pupil in the rear cockpit and flew in a normal manner with the engine running satisfactorily for 7 or 8 minutes. The pupil then executed a practice landing on the aerodrome and at once proceeded to take off again, but when the aeroplane was 150–200 feet from the ground, and some little distance beyond the boundary of the aerodrome, a sudden and complete loss of engine power occurred, the engine apparently ceasing to fire. The pilot was in telephone communication with the pupil, immediately took over full control of the machine and, after first satisfying himself that movement of the throttle lever had no effect on the engine, prepared to land. Having insufficient height to regain the aerodrome or to reach any suitable landing ground the pilot attempted to land in a small and narrow field immediately below him, but during a final turning manoevre the aeroplane stalled and fell heavily to the ground. The undercarriage collapsed and the machine turned over on to its back. f). The pilot, who was pinned under the wreckage for a time, states that his first fear was an outbreak of fire, but although his head was immediately above the petrol tank he did not see or smell any escaping petrol. The pupil, who at once went to the assistance of the pilot and attempted to lift the wreckage off him, saw no petrol running from the tank and smelt no fumes. g) The aircraft had crashed about one mile to the North East of the aerodrome. From the marks on the ground and the structural damage to the machine it was evident that the aircraft had stalled and fallen to the ground from a very low height. The damage to all parts of the structure was attributable to impact with the ground. h). All petrol pipes and connections were intact and contained nothing to obstruct the normal flow of petrol to the carburettor. The filter was clean and the petrol cock (latest type) was fully open. The carburettor was in serviceable condition.

'The petrol tank (lying upside down) was intact but slightly crushed. The screw-in plug at the top of the tank (for auxiliary feed pipe connection) was missing and it was evident that this had not been in place at the time of the crash. The tank was empty but there was remarkably little discolouration of the grass under and around the tank. i). There was no defect in the ignition system. The switches were 'On'. j). Apart from the exhaust manifold being crushed, and one valve rocker bracket being broken, as a result of impact with the ground, the engine was practically undamaged. All internal working parts were in serviceable condition and adequately lubricated.'

In the Inspector of Accident's 'Opinion' he stated that (a) That the accident was due to the aircraft stalling in a turn near the ground while the pilot was attempting to execute a forced landing, on account of engine failure, in somewhat difficult circumstances. (b) That the cause of the engine failure could not be determined after the accident but the evidence strongly suggests a shortage of petrol in the tank.

Hermia's own account was the one that stuck in my mind for a good many years. She, like H., had expected the machine to blow up at any moment and she spent an unpleasant time trying to lift the machine off him, sniffing all the while for the smell of petrol. At the time she had thought him more seriously injured than, in fact, he was, as he was pouring blood from his mouth and face. She could not get the machine clear partly, perhaps, because she had broken her wrist when 'NN hit the ground and it was not functioning properly. Eventually she ran to get help but others who had seen 'NN come down were there to help H. and he was freed by the time she returned.

H. recorded in his log-book: '27th March. DH60 G-EBNN. Lympne local. 10 minutes. pupil H.E.M.T. turns & landings. soon after 2nd take off motor cut out m/c badly damaged in subsequent forced landing from 150/200 ft while avoiding cattle. Sustained loss of 2 front teeth & cut lip.'

He had been more irritated than anything else at the mishap, for he had got out of far tighter corners without a scratch. The field straight ahead and in his glide path was full of cows, (he told us all later), and he had been afraid of frightening and stampeding them, so he had made the turn which had caused further loss of height and a toe, as it were, caught on some telegraph wire so that the aircraft then pitched to the ground. He had so very nearly got away with it.

H. was used to forced landings. He had experienced literally scores of them. From the first one, on his seventh solo when, on returning from Bexhill on M.F. #3007 the engine had stopped at 2800 ft; he had 'come down over Pevensey. machine dismantled' and he had stepped out of the wreckage without a scratch, way back in January of 1916; – to losing Warneford's 'very old but good' engine, still attached to it's airframe, in the Channel off Dunkerque later the same year; to forced landings on the 'small, bad, dirty' little aerodrome at Marieux; to at least seven of them in the summer of 1919, during one of which he recorded that he had 'knocked over a brick wall. m/c undamaged.'

Down to more recent days in Greece, when he had put the HELI-THON down fast on the Tatoi turf more than once to still more recently, on 4th February, 1929, the date of his last forced landing on 'NN prior to the one on the 27th March.

A forced landing, he used to explain, only means: landing sooner than you meant to and not always where you meant to; but he had never hurt himself before as a result of one and it was a very long time since he had damaged an aeroplane.

'Congrats on what must have been skilful handling in a rotten situation,' wrote Charles from High River in his letter of 21st April, '– I hope that you have nothing serious in the way of cuts and that you will soon be none the worse for the accident. Also that it will not hold up your job with the London Club for any length of time. I wondered what it was that you had up your sleeve! That is great work and well done ... Love to all. I hope that Hermy is none the worse for the shaking ...'

Hermia often flew with H. again but only as a passenger. Her own log-book closed on the 27th March that year. It had all given her a bit of a jolt, she said, and she had decided that she was not cut out to be a pilot. Which H. said was a pity as she had made some very nice landings.

*   *   *

Dr Hall had advised H. to stay in bed for at least a week to rest and to recover from any concussion; but after a couple of days H. was up and about again for he had much to see to. First of all he went along to Mr Sturdee, dental surgeon and family friend, who was in practice from his house close by Deal Castle. Mr Sturdee did wonders for H.'s appearance with some temporary false teeth. Then H. went back to the Cinque Ports Flying Club to face the music.

The music, after what had seemed to him only a rather heavy forced landing, was louder than he had expected. Moreover he found it hard to believe that they were still prepared to trust the Ground Engineer for although it was of course H.'s absolute responsibility to check his petrol supply before taking off, there was also an equally strong unwritten law that the Ground Engineer is supportive of the pilot. The Ground Engineer in question had been nothing but trouble to H. throughout his time at Lympne and more than once there had been a query about there being less petrol in tank than there should have been; which was why, on 27th March, H. had queried whether 'NN had been filled up and had been assured that she had. Then, too, there was the matter of 'NN herself. H. thought that she was easily repairable. Cinque Ports said that she was a write-off. The managers of the Cinque Ports Flying Club held a meeting at which half of them thought that H. should stay. The other half, equally, thought that he should go. H. therefore resigned. It was in many ways painful for him to resign under such unhappy circumstances and in the face of lack of confidence.

He had been due to leave the CPFC in the middle of April when his six months was up, in any case. He just left a couple of weeks early.

'How lovely!' was the concensus at 9 The Beach, 'now you'll have a holiday.' 'The trouble with holidays,' he reminded us all, 'is that one doesn't get paid for holidays ...' However he and Hermia had several days of fishing off Deal with boatmen Beauchamp and Bushell, one of whom was the owner of H.'s favourite boat, *Lady Beatty*.

Many years later, four or five at least, H. was reading his morning paper at the breakfast table one day when a delighted grin spread over is face: 'They've got him!' he said, 'they've got him at last!' And when the chorus of 'Who?' and 'What?' went up amongst us all he said, (mentioning the name), that the Ground Engineer at Lympne had at last been caught red-handed, having been 'suspected for some time' of dishonestly defrauding the CPFC of petrol and other supplies and that he had been summarily sacked.

Not all events during the winter and spring of 1929 were unhappy, however: the formation of the Guild of Air Pilots and Air Navigators of the British Empire was one of the most important events of the day in British aviation. I will quote from official records about the Guild in the next chapter. H. had been at that famous overcrowded Meeting on February 1st, when all had been still in embryo, and only a day or so after the mishap to 'NN, a couple of months later, had received a letter – I think it was from Brancker – which was the greatest possible tonic to his spirits and help to his speedy recovery – for he was invited to a Dinner at Rules Restaurant in early April.

L. A. Wingfield, MC., DFC, first Solicitor to the Guild, telephoned me as recently as September of 1986 in response to a letter of mine, remembering H. at that famous Dinner and from subsequent Dinners and Meetings of the Guild. They were both Founder-Members; the list of the first eighty Members reads like a roll-call of the aviators of the day.

The London Aeroplane Club wanted H. to start for them as and when arranged, but in view of the accident to 'NN, thought that it would be wise for him to do his RAFO training before he began instructing for them. He was piqued at this, just a little, but agreed. Hermia was much more annoyed than he was at this implied criticism. 'Any other pilot and we would have both been dead,' she said, for she agreed wholeheartedly with Charles' viewpoint, that it had been 'skilful handling in a rotten situation . . .'

H. therefore went up to Brough on the 23rd April and put in a total there of 9 hours dual, solo, height tests and cross-country practice and thus completed his 2nd, 3rd and 4th quarters of his 3rd year's training for the RAFO. He flew Blackburn 'Dart' landplanes throughout his training, G-EBKH and G-EBKF, and Chief Instructor Arthur Loton reported on him: 'This officer flies this machine very well and his landings are excellent' and once again placed H. in Category '1'.

He went down to Stag Lane early on the 27th April and flew from Stag Lane on that day: 'Gipsy Moth Coupe. G-AAGM. Stag Lane.

local. 10 minutes. first flight on Coupe Gipsy. good for cruising but unpleasant when air is full of m/cs!'

H. had been asked to start instructing on the 1st May, so he fixed up about digs in Edgware and then came home to pack his bags and bring us all up to date with his plans.

As for 'NN: she was not repaired and perhaps it was as well. She was almost as nasty as the HELITHON.

A recognizable section of her fuselage was cut from what remained of her and was hoisted high on a roadside hoarding at the entrance to Brooklands: 'Learn to Fly at Brooklands!' – or words to that effect – were splashed on the brightest of bright notice boards: 'IT'S SAFE AND EASY AT BROOKLANDS!' They had not troubled to paint out the registration letters, though, and when Hermia drove past and saw them 'G-EBNN' she said that they gave her such heebie-jeebies that she never drove by Brooklands again if she could help it.

Easter Meeting at Lympne, 1929

photo: H. G. Travers

13

STAG LANE I

1929–1930

H. starts instructing at the London Aeroplane Club – extract from Guild of
Air Pilots & Air Navigators history – the matter of Amy Johnson – Jean
Batten enrols as a pupil

'I see that his appointment to the London Club is mentioned in *Flight*
in the Club Notes,' wrote Charles to Emmie on the 20th April, 1929,
'I am glad that he has got the job as it is one of the most important
clubs in the world . . .'

Important it may have been: it was certainly one of the busiest and
was becoming, at the time H. took up his job there as Chief Flying
Instructor, busier every day.

The London Aeroplane Club was under the aegis of the Royal Aero
Club, then in Piccadilly. Anyone who wished to learn to fly and who
enquired at the Royal Aero Club where they might do so, was directed
towards Stag Lane, only ten miles from the Marble Arch and down
the road, so to speak, at Edgware.

Stag Lane had been a success from it's inception, although it was
about as different as it could possibly be to Lympne. Stag Lane had
no long sweep of chalky, well-drained downland or open sky, which
was such a feature of Lympne. Stag Lane was low-lying, uneven,
inclined to mists and vapours, a hollow square within an approaching
army of houses.

Victor Doree is a former Stag Laner with whom, due to the kindness
of Stuart McKay in putting us in touch, I have lately been in correspondence.

Victor sent me an article which he had had published in *Vintage
Aircraft* in their THE GOLDEN AGE series of articles, together with
his permission to quote from it. The early passages give an idea of the
smallness of the enterprise in the London Aeroplane Club's first years.

The London Aeroplane Club was inaugurated at Stag Lane on 19 August 1925. It's headquarters were a wooden shed leased from the de Havilland company and the two Cirrus 1 Moths, G-EBLI and 'LU, were kept, wings folded, in a tiny hangar alongside. Instruction was provided by the CFI, Capt. G. F. M. Sparks, and an assistant, Mr G. T. Witcombe. The enthusiam of the members was overwhelming and in the first month of operation 72 pupils put in over 100 hours on the two machines, daily utilization figures of between five and six hours being achieved on both. In fact bookings were so heavy that it was most difficult to obtain instruction unless one could be on the spot at the time. As far as I can recall, no licence was necessary for the purpose of giving flying instruction other than the 'B' licence which was required when flying for 'hire or reward' and consequently it appeared to me that both Capt. Sparks and Mr Witcombe had their own individual styles of instructing, which I found to be confusing.

   Instruction was only carried out in reasonable weather but even without a clubhouse the social side was most enjoyable. Every weekend many members turned up and if there was no flying then other activities were indulged in. During the winter months skating was very popular on Elstree Reservoir. . . .

   Needless to say, it was only a year or so after the opening of the club that a first rate clubhouse with bar was built. This, however, seemed to make no difference to the flying enthusiasm and members came to the club to fly whenever possible. . . .

By the time H. took over from Baker the Club was firmly established, busier than ever, and 'one of the most important clubs in the world'.

Stag Lane Aerodrome and its hangars, workshops and sheds were all the property of the de Havilland Aircraft Company. So, too, were the machines on which instruction was given. They were leased to the London Aeroplane Club. The fuselages of the LAC machines were painted yellow, their wings and tail-sections only being finished in the more usual silver dope. Thus Club machines were readily identifiable. The machines were in the care of the de Havilland staff and they were maintained to a high standard. There scarcely ever seemed to have been anything wrong with them and forced landings were few and far between.

H., still assisted by Mr Witcombe during that first summer, had a stable of five Moths, 'ZC, 'BL, 'EX, 'BN and 'XS. A sixth, 'WY was added on the 26th June and a seventh, 'HO, on the 29th June. The hours flown on those Moths were largely dependent on the weather and as, during the hours of daylight, there were always pupils waiting for lessons, the hours were long.

Stag Lane. The hangars and clubhouse, 1929

photo: H. G. Travers

The weather in May, 1929, was good and a lot of flying time was recorded. The number of landings made was not recorded, however, and one can only deduce that whereas in poor weather there might be only three or four landings on any one day, on a good flying day such as the 16th May (7 hours 15 minutes flying) or the 25th May (7 hours 40 minutes flying) there might be easily forty or fifty landings a day.

On the 12th May H. recorded a short flight 'with Alliot' in a Klemm Salmson; other than that flight he instructed right up until the 1st June on his fleet of Moths and never a word of complaint or criticism about any of them. On the 2nd June Sir Sefton Brancker visited Stag Lane. Whilst he would no doubt have had conversation with Geoffrey (later Sir Geoffrey) de Havilland, it seems likely that he also wanted a word or two with H. about the state of the art in civil flying. H. recorded: '2/6/29. Moth. 'EX. Weather test. 10 minutes. Sir Seft. Brancker.' To take somebody up for a 'weather test' was an euphemism, in H. & H.'s vocabulary , for having a quiet word with them; there were opportunities for discreet talk on a weather test and afterwards. What was said between the two men on the 2nd June is not, however, on record.

Stag Lane, 1929. H. G.
Travers talking outside
clubhouse

Stag Lane, 1929. 'W Y warms up

Stag Lane, 1929. 'W Y warms up

Among the hundreds of Stag Lane pupils there are a few names which
one cannot forget.

One man, Nathan, was among H.'s pupils on his very first day there,
the 1st of May. Major Nathan had been a keen skier. He had been
caught in an avalanche and had lost both feet as a result of frostbite.
His efforts at walking were both difficult and painful and his splayed-
out stagger, as he stepped from his car and walked out to his aeroplane,
was dreadful to see. He was a delightful man. When he qualified as a
pilot he bought his own aeroplane, a de Havilland Puss Moth. (The
following summer, 1930, he took D. and me up in this Puss. It was
not D.'s first flight as she had been up in 'NN from Lympne but it
was mine. I remember going out over the cliffs at Dover and watching
all the colours shift and change under the English Channel.)

Another of H.'s early pupils was a young fellow called Chichester,
cousin of the Chichester Minor who had been in Bevir's Dormitory
at the same time as H. Chichester had already begun to learn to fly and
he wanted H. to teach him some navigation. Since navigation was H.'s

first and best love it was a task that he found pleasurable, the more so because of Chichester's natural bent for the subject.

'I had just a few lessons with him in 1929,' Sir Francis Chichester wrote to me in 1971, in response to my query.

Another pupil was young Fauchette O'Connell, such a pretty girl, who became a great favourite with us all. A few years later she married another extremely well-liked Stag Laner, Malcolm Ogilvie-Forbes.

Another pupil was a woman who became a life-long friend, Burse Scaramanga. (Mrs John Scaramanga.) She was an immensely talented, even a brilliant woman, but of uneven temperament and always restless. Although wealthy in her own right and married to a successful stock-broker she was not in the least careful of her money but loved to spend, to buy, to give presents, to travel, to share everything with all her friends. Fond of music and very musical herself, she was distraught that Hermia could no longer play her violin – 'my beloved fiddle' Hermia called it – since the accident on 'N N, when Hermia had broken her wrist, and disdaining medical attention, had allowed it to set in it's broken state, deformed, a series of jutting angles. Burse brought us a gramophone of the newest His Master's Voice make and a stack of records, among them Richard Tauber – then a new discovery in England – and Paul Robeson, Ernest Luff and lots of Viennese waltzes, and sea-shanties. I have an idea that H. never sent Burse Scaramanga solo; but she had a great many flying lessons and brought further pupils to Stag Lane in her wake.

H. recorded his flying time for June, 1929, of 364 hours 45 minutes 'beating May by 27 hours'.

H. G. Travers & others outside hangars,
Stag Lane, 1929

On the 8th July he flew home for his day off, the first of many
occasions on which he did so. He recorded: '8.7.29. Moth. 'E X. Stag
Lane/Bredgar 40 minutes. Bredgar/Manston 20 minutes. Man-
ston/Walmer 10 minutes. Walmer/Stag Lane 1 hour 10 minutes.'

On the 11th July he made an interesting flight with Hubert Broad,
de Havilland's test pilot, Broad being the pilot, on 'T D. 'Endurance
Moth' – a flight of 20 minutes, during which they made a speed test.
On the 19th July he gave 'Mrs Scaramanga X country Instruction,
'B N. Stag Lane/Lympne. Lympne/Stag Lane. 2 hours 15 minutes.'
And on the same day, till on G-A A B N, gave Lord Somers 'X country
Instruction stag Lane/Marsh Court. Marsh Court/Stag Lane. 2 hours.'

On the 20th July he recorded: G-A A E X. Stag Lane/Brough. 1
hour 45 minutes. Dual X country Mrs Scaramanga. Brough to Heston.
2 hours 20 minutes. Heston Rally. Heston to Stag Lane 10 minutes.
return home.'

He disliked keeping any pupil 'hacking round the aerodrome' as he
called it and took them off on cross country flights just as soon as he
could. The minute they had done a little solo he liked them to go on
short cross country solo flights. He could see no point in endlessly
beating the bounds of Stag Lane.

Towards the end of July the weather improved and there were
several days of six and a half hours' flying over that period. On the
31st July he came home for August Bank Holiday, flying down to
Manston on 'B N in an hour and ten minutes and returning to Stag
Lane on the 2nd August on the same aeroplane. He would undoubtedly
have flown home for days off a great deal more often than he did if
there had been safe hangarage nearby. As it was, he was always
dependant on either Manston, or Bekesbourne, at either of which
airfields he could leave his machine in safety. Otherwise he would
come home for just a few hours, bringing a passenger, or a mechanic,
with him, in which case he usually landed at Ripple Mill, a couple of
miles from our house along the Dover Road.

As he had of course taken his car to Edgware, Hermia bought one
of her own, a 1922 Talbot-Darraq, which she painted grey and named
Susan. *Susan* was a great car for picnics – lots of room for children,
rugs, hampers and so forth.

He spent the 14th August at Heston, doing some instructing there
for part of the day on Moth G-A A C Y, so perhaps Baker was single-
handed and had asked for some help. There was such a friendly

interchange between instructors and other pilots that such a thing was likely. He also recorded on the same day: 'Avian. G-AAIX. Heston local. 10 minutes. with Baker.' After a further 10 minutes with Baker he went solo on the Avian and then instructed on her: 'Winch. 15 minutes. Sinclair. 20 minutes.'

On the 20th August he was back at Stag Lane and hard at work.

On the 31st August he took a pupil cross country on 'BN, undoubtedly the favourite of his fleet at that time, to 'Stockbridge & return. 1 hour 45 minutes.' Putting in more hours of instruction on 'WY, 'BL, 'BN and 'XS on his return. On the 12th September he flew 'WY throughout the day, including a cross-country to Bekesbourne & return, a total of five hours flying, the following day instructing for almost as long on 'WY, 'EX, 'BN and 'ZC. On the 25th September he flew 'EX, 'ZC, 'XS and 'BN all day, including 'Ld. Apsley to Hanworth & return' amongst the instructing. On the 29th September he flew 'Lamp. to Radlett' on 'BN in 30 minutes. This would have been Lamplugh, whom he had first met at Phaleron Bay and whom he met and piloted on numerous occasions thereafter. The daily instructing continued on the same fleet of excellent Moths but as the pupils are seldom named I will not quote from every page.

On the 1st October he flew as passenger in a Hawk Moth for 20 minutes and flying continued until the 5th October. On the 6th he took 'BN and 'WY up for tests but 'Gale rose' and there was no further flying that day. On the 9th October he took a pupil cross country to Bedford and return and on the 20th October recorded: 'Moth. 'BN. Stag Lane to Skegness. 1 hour 15 minutes. passenger Mr Montague Under Secy for Air.' continuing the journey with the distinguished passenger: 'Skegness to Wittering. 1 hour. 15 minutes. Wittering to Stag Lane. 30 minutes.' On the 23rd October he organized something very much after is own heart: formation flying. It was something he had not attempted since 1919 and never with civilian personnel. But why not? It was a short, successful flight: ' 'WY. Stag Lane/Croydon. 20 minutes. Croydon/Stag Lane. 20 minutes. formation X country.'

Although the majority of pupils at the London Aeroplane Club were men there were a scattering of girls there. Some of the girls were not, in fact, pupils, but were 'me-too's' – such a withering collective noun for the girls who could not afford flying lessons or who, perhaps, simply wanted to see what was going on and be a part of the general flying movement.

There were two aviatrices there, Winifred Spooner and Dorothy Spicer, who were not H.'s pupils but who were often at Stag Lane during his time there. They had been flying for some while before he joined. They were both first rate pilots. A third, Pauline Gower, joined the LAC during H.'s early days there and was one of his many ab initio pupils. She became one of the best pilots this country had produced and was a most charming girl. She had family connections with Kent, with whom she often stayed at week ends. She kept a bay mare in Kent, not far from Walmer, an elegant thoroughbred called *Vogue*, and was a skilled horsewoman, thus giving further support to H.'s pet theory that good pilots often come from the ranks of the good horsemen/women. 'A good pilot', in his view, was of course a pilot who could find his way across country as well as someone capable of making quiet landings. Another first-rate pilot was Joy Muntz, also a member of that select band known as the Beauty Chorus.

Of many good things which happened in civil flying in 1929, the formation of The Guild of Air Pilots and Air Navigators was among the most important. It had been first mooted in 1928. The following passages are from the Guild's History, kindly sent to me by Captain P. Wilson, Clerk to the Guild.

As in so much else, Brancker had given the lead.

Chapter 1. The Formation of the Guild.

The Guild was formed in 1929, at a time when civil aviation was beginning to develop on a world-wide, rather than a parochial, scale ... pioneering flights such as that of Alcock and Brown across the Atlantic from Newfoundland to Ireland in 1919 served to emphasise the significant advances in the design and performance of aeroplanes which had been achieved during the war years and to indicate something of their potentialities in the civil field. Nevertheless, from the international point of view, the development of civil aviation during the 1920's was sporadic.

In France, the Government was very much aware of the potential importance of air transport and had sought to encourage its development immediately after the end of the war. In 1920 eleven independent companies offered services as far as Warsaw and covered approximately 3,250 miles of air routes, carrying a total of 6,697 passengers and almost 150 tons of mail and express freight. The development of air services in the French colonies was soon to follow and during the 1920's the French, like the Germans, playing an important part in the introduction of air services in Latin America.

The growth of civil aviation elsewhere in Europe was also rapid, particularly in the Netherlands and Germany itself, KLM being formed in 1919 and Deutsche Lufthansa in 1926.

In Australia and Canada the story was much the same. Scheduled air services between outlying settlements in the Australian outback were introduced as early as 1921 and aircraft were being used for forest survey and patrol in Canada immediately after the war.

In the U.S.A., on the other hand, progress in civil air transport as a whole had been noticeably slower, being concentrated on the carriage of mail rather than passengers. it was not until 1927, when Lindbergh made his solo crossing of the Atlantic from New York to Paris, that substantial public interest in air travel was aroused. Nevertheless, once aroused, it lost no time in getting down to business and as the decade drew to a close a number of operators who were subsequently to emerge as the big names of American air transport were beginning to expand their activities on an impressive scale.

After an uncertain start, progress had been remarkable in the United Kingdom. Services between London and Paris were inaugurated in 1919 and within a year three British companies and two French were operating scheduled services across the Channel, carrying passengers and mail. Competition was naturally severe and within another year it became obvious that a Government subsidy would be necessary to enable the two British carriers which had so far survived to continue operations.

The high cost of subsidy and the extension of operations to other European cities had led, in 1924, to the amalgamation of the existing carriers into a single national company, Imperial Airways, which was entrusted with the responsibility of developing British overseas air transport. Within three years plans for long-distance commercial routes had been translated into reality and early in 1927 a de Havilland DH.66 Hercules three-engined biplane carried ten passengers, including the Secretary of State for Air, from England to India on a proving flight prior to the introduction of scheduled services on that route.

In passing, it is interesting to note that, as a background to this record of achievement in air transport, there was a significant sense of true enthusiasm for flying in Britain during the later 1920's: the appearance of the de Havilland Moth; subsidies for flying clubs ... the seeds from which rich harvests were to grow. And a Secretary of State for Air who had been accused of having been 'bitten by a mad aeroplane'. A refreshing thought, indeed.

Thus, towards the end of the 1920's air transport was becoming established as in industry of world-wide significance. . . .

Nevertheless, this was still only a beginning, particularly from the technical aspect. The 'craft' of flying and navigating aeroplanes was still very much a matter of seat-of-the-pants and rule-of-thumb, using rudimentary flight instruments and navigational equipment. As the potentialities of aircraft as a means of public transport began to be exploited on an increasing scale by day and night and, as far as humanly possible, despite the weather, so did the responsibilities and necessary qualifications of their pilots increase accordingly.

In the United Kingdom, captains of commercial aircraft were warned that, in 1929, they would be legally required to become certificated navigators. At that time there were no facilities for studying before undertaking the qualifying Air Ministry examination and it was therefore necessary to arrange private navigation courses. These were set up largely as the result of the efforts of Captain A. G. Lamplugh, then the Chief Assessor of the British Aviation Insurance Group. Under this arrangement Squadron Leader E. L. Johnston, the Chief Air Ministry Navigation Examiner – who, incidentally, had been the navigator on the Hercules proving flight to India – taught small groups of pilots at the Royal Aero Club.

Towards the end of 1928, on December 5th, those who had voluntarily qualified assembled at Rules Restaurant in Maiden Lane, London, to celebrate the fact at a 'Veteran Air Navigator's Dinner'. The dinner was also attended by Sir Sefton Brancker, at that time Director of Civil Aviation, who suggested in the course of an after-dinner speech that the time would seem to have come for pilots who had attained high professional status as holders of a 'B' Licence and Air Navigator's Certificate to form their own Company on lines similar to the great City Companies of London.

This suggestion, backed as it was by semi-official blessing, was well received. Immediately after the dinner it was discussed further by a small company including Brancker, Johnston and Lamplugh and it was decided that all 'B' Licence pilots and certificated air navigators of the United Kingdom should be invited to attend a meeting at Rules on February 1st, 1929, to consider the proposal and vote upon it.

The attendance at that meeting left little doubt as to the outcome of the vote. Professional pilots and navigators throughout the United Kingdom answered the call and gathered in that delightful old restaurant not far from Covent Garden, standing several deep because there was insufficient room for seats for all of them. The suggestion was quickly approved and it was decided to call the association The Company of Air Pilots and Air Navigators of the British Empire. A Drafting Committee was thereupon elected to work out the details. The members of this Committee, V. H. Baker, Sir Sefton Brancker, W. L. Hope, N. Macmillan, H. G. Brackley, G. L. P. Henderson, E. L. Johnston and A. S. Wilcockson, including pilots and navigators who flew as instructors, transport pilots, test pilots and airship officers. A solicitor, L. A. Wingfield, agreed to assist the Committee.

The Drafting Committee advocated two departures from the original lines of thought upon which the association had been formed. Firstly, it changed the name from 'Company' to 'Guild' and so linked it with the ancient title of association of English craftsmen. Secondly, it was decided that membership should not, as originally intended, be restricted to those who were in the air transport industry, but that it should be extended to all who served aviation professionally, provided that they held a professional, rather than a private, licence.

Two months later, on April 10th, 1929, a second open meeting approved the work of the Drafting Committee and elected a Foundation Council to supervise the formation and registation of the Guild. The Council consisted of seven members, all of whom held the full qualification: H. G. Brackley, E. L. Johnston, N. Macmillan, W. L. Hope, O. P. Jones, C. R. McMullin, A. S. Wilcockson.

The Foundation Council held three meetings, all at Rules Restaurant, and elected Sir Sefton Brancker Master of the Guild. The Reverend D. P. Robins was invited to become Chaplain and L. A. Wingfield was appointed Clerk. Rules were drawn up and the first fifty members were approved. . . .

1929 was a bad year in many bad years for the stockmarkets of the world and more than once, watching over my father's shoulder as he sat in his armchair on a day off I would hear him say how bad things were.

He had various shareholdings including shares in Joseph Travers & Sons which had been left to him by his father, but they were not I think a vast quantity and they were, in any case, a sheet anchor. 'Those are stocks and those are shares,' he pointed, in answer to my questioning, 'and they are all going down, down, down.'

But he had a job, as many had not, and although it is unlikely that it was a job which he would ever have aimed for, he was delighted to have it and found it extremely interesting; and as he cared a great deal about what became of civil flying in England he did his level best to try and keep it going forward on a sound basis.

'The Government hate us,' he sometimes said, 'and would like to put a stop to civil flying.' He meant civil Club flying. The Government were supportive, surprisingly supportive in view of the disarmament views of many, of the training of Reserve Officers at the Civilian Flying Schools.

Partly because of the attitude of many in power, he constantly exerted himself to promote the safety aspect. He had, in early days at Walmer, obtained permission from Sir Hereward Wake, Colonel ffrench-Blake and others to land hard by Dover Castle, playing fields of the Duke of York's School at Dover; he also had the kind permission of the man who owned the filling-station and level field at Ripple Mill to land there; and to land at Martin Mill; and of the Earl of Guilford to land at Waldershare Park. Sir Gerald Wollaston, Garter King-at-Arms and then in residence at Walmer Castle, told him when they met socially: that he was most welcome to land on the Castle Meadows. It was an offer H. never took up, as the Castle Meadows were marshy and were bisected with a drainage dyke or stream which made the Meadows an unsafe landing ground.

These were all generous permissions given to him personally. He sought a wider choice of 'emergency landing grounds' to be made known to all aviators and he wrote to the Press to suggest that golf courses should be marked on all aviation maps. There was an outcry at this. He had to write afresh and explain in a detailed way that he had not meant that golf courses S H O U L D be used as landing grounds, just that they should be marked so that they could be used in an emergency.

He still perservered with his flight simulator and made many modifications and refinements to the drawings he made of his invention.

In the autumn of 1929 W. Gordon Store joined the London Aeroplane Club as Instructor.

Not only was he a first-rate pilot and instructor, he had the advantage of having been bitten by a mad aeroplane at a very tender age in South Africa. He was a great addition to the L A C and he and H. got along very well. Mr Witcombe left, I rather think, some months after Gordon Store took up his duties.

When Gordon Store left Stag Lane about a year later to further his flying career, he gave H. a great treasure: his own *Swallow in the Flower-bed*, a four-motor high wing amphibian of considerable seating capacity, something along the lines of a Savoia Marchetti, every bit of which he had carved with a penknife and to his own design. The *Swallow* was finished in a livery of crimson lake, with white wings.

She was too precious to stay downstairs and be mauled about by inquisitive fingers and she remained on H.'s chest of drawers for many years, beside his Toc H lamp.

One pupil during that first winter was a man called, I think, Clouston. (He was no relation of the famous A V M A. E. Clouston.)

H. brought him home to stay overnight one Sunday/Monday and they drove down together in Jemima, the Armstrong-Siddeley open tourer, which was still giving steering trouble.

Although they were not expected until late, Hermia said that I could stay up and answer the door, and when I did so, in response to the fierce knocking, there were two giants out there in the storm of rain and gusting wind. You could not see which was the taller of the two. It was dark. Beyond them the Channel tore at the shingle and the breakers were so high as they hit the top of the beach that they caught the light from the wide-open front door.

H. and Clouston were drenched from head to foot, water was literally pouring from their clothes and they had had a long, cold journey, but they were laughing and smiling as, bringing half the storm in with them, they entered the house. They were clutching their overcoats or Burberrys and they hurried through the hall saying 'Quickly, out of sight' or something like that. Hermia greeted them and they all trooped to the kitchen, which was in a semi-basement downstairs.

The next day we all heard the whole story.

Driving along one of those winding woodland roads which carry the motorist from the Ashford Valley road to the Dover road, (in modern parlance – from the A20 to the A2) they had hit a pheasant as it blundered into the headlights. H. had stopped the car at once and had got out to lift the bird into the roadside covert, but Clouston had grabbed it and immediately wrung its neck and flung it into the back of the car.

'My W O R D! – and there's another one!' – he was Australian and told the story to perfection: another bird, caught and held in the glare of the headlights, was standing in the road. Once again Clouston moved fast and a second bird was soon lying beside it's companion on the back seat of the old Armstrong.

H., who had been brought up in the knowledge that a pheasant is a preserved species who may only be killed by permission of the owner of the preserved land, was at first genuinely shocked at Clouston's action. But as their journey to Walmer continued he began to be amused and then delighted. Poachers! The country roads were little used by cars at night in the winter in those days. Not a soul had seen them. Poachers! No wonder he was keen to hurry through to the kitchen as they clutched their hidden booty. So the two pilots told the story of their journey down from Stag Lane. They had to return on Monday evening, after tea and so Hermia made one of those large family high-teas of which she was so fond, for it was a meal she was used to having with her cousins in Scotland when she was a girl, and we all sat around the table for hours talking and listening to Clouston as he told us something of his story.

Born and bred in Australia, he had qualified out there as a pilot. He had been too young for the war. He had joined the Flying Doctor Service, which he described at length, as one of their pilots. As it was the first we had heard of that great service we listened spellbound; every time he paused H. prompted him with further questions and comments and he told of the men who had started it up, of the aeroplanes they flew and of how they hoped to expand it nationwide. To do so they must first of all improve their navigation and this task they had entrusted to Clouston. He was to study the subject and then go home and instruct his fellow-pilots. He had been sent to England to enquire at the Royal Aero Club where he could learn some air navigation and obtain his 'B' Licence and they had sent him to: 'the best in the country' and here Clouston beamed around the table at us all.

Dry, no doubt, after his long talk, he reached across Hermia and lifted the teapot: 'I'll help myself this time,' he said.

H. was happy among Australians. He had loved the year he had spent out there and knew, by railway train, motor-bike and horse, some parts of that vast country very well indeed. Whether they discovered mutual friends out there I do not know. They certainly had a lot of shared interests and enthusiasms. Clouston was given a standing invitation to return to 9 The Beach during his time in England, but he was on a tight budget and had been asked to learn whatever was necessary as fast as he could and then to hurry home.

We never saw him again at Walmer.

Although H. worked long hours they were variable hours, largely dependent on the weather, and he found time, occasionally, to accept one or two of the social invitations which constantly reached him and Hermia. They both enjoyed going out and always looked rather glamorous.

They had met – possibly through Victor Cazalet but I do not know – the 'other' Cazalets, the famous Cazalets of Fairlawne, who were most kind and hospitable and who took them to see a performance early in the London run of R. C. Sherriff's *Journey's End*. Hermia came home able to talk of little but the play for days.

It was not only on the London stage that people thought again about the Great War. Reminders of 1914–1918 were all around us. One did not have to go to a play in London to be aware of how those terrible days had affected the country and the people. The Royal Marine ceremonies on Armistice Day were the formal reminder, a distillation of the bugle calls we heard each day, from Reveille to Sunset; and the War Memorial Hospital at Deal, with it's Pound Day, to which every adult and many children subscribed, reminded us continually by it's very presence. So, too, did the Memorial to the Royal Naval Air Service on the greensward at Walmer. The turf on the Downs at Kingsdown had only lately grown over the war-time trenches and bunkers and the white-painted word DEPOT had not faded much on one of the wooden huts there.

On warm sunny days, along the row of shops and houses called The Strand, a strong-looking, cheerful girl would stand proudly beside a sort of high bench or high chair, to which was strapped a man limbless except for – I think it was – one arm. 'This is my Dad,' she would say to anyone who paused to speak, and she would point to the medals pinned to the swaddlings on his wheezing chest, 'it's nice for father to see the sunshine. We like to give father an airing while Mother's doing out his room.' What was left of father would roll his head round and smile a ghastly smile while his fine brave daughter stood to attention beside him in the open doorway.

On some days, such as Bank Holiday Monday if that day was fine, open motorized charabancs would roar along The Strand, up Drum Hill and all the way through Ringwould to Dover and Folkestone, changing gear all the way, a burgee on the bonnet proclaiming: BLIGHTY and the occupants singing that it was A Long Way To Tipperary.

In my parents' room at home, on H.'s chest-of-drawers, his Toc H lamp burned with it's quiet flame.

No one forgot.

D. was seventeen months older than me and a better worker, so that, although our day school gave us a roughly equal amount of prep. to do each evening, she always finished hers long before I finished mine. She was then free to go where she wished – such as over the wall to No 10, an empty house, where she was cleaning out the stables there ready for the pony she was saving to buy. It was weeks before she let me into her secret and told me why she finished her prep. so rapidly each evening and where she went for an hour or more while I stayed at the dining room table, schoolbooks, ruler, Japanese pencil-box and insoluble problems to myself.

One evening in the spring of 1930 I was there as usual and as usual was struggling with my prep. It was a gloomy evening, still light, but dry and cold, with a gusting wind.

Through the folding doors which separated the small drawing room in the front of the house from the even smaller dining room at the back, where I sat at the table, I could hear my parents' voices. I heard their voices rise and wane and by the restraining sound of Hermia's voice and the soaring sound of H.'s, I guessed that they were talking flying. I loved it when the house was filled with flying friends, and the windows rattled to flying talk, so that the drawing room seemed no bigger than a cockpit, the flailing wind outside no more than the whirr of an airscrew, the narrow, shaking house under stress, under strain, buffeted until one almost fancied that it would push it's chocks away of it's own volition, detach itself forever from number 8, and take off over the alarming sea.

There were no friends at home on this particular day, however, just my parents talking most interestingly just out of hearing. Just out of sight. I finished my prep at last, did up my satchel and opened the folding doors.

In front of the fire, on a low chair, sat Hermia. There was a book, open about half way through, on the arm of her chair, and at which she occasionally glanced. (She 'read' at a fantastic rate, appearing to skim or only glance through a book, yet in any later discussion of the work would appear to have read every word) – she was also smoking, the ash on the end of her cigarette almost as long as the amber holder which held it. Her fingers flew as on five or six steel needles a sock for some member of the family descended lapwards with earthworm determination. She was talking and as I entered the room she scolded me for barging in during their conversation, for I had greeted them with the classic remark of the day: 'What's up?'

H. had been pacing the room, three steps into the bay, three steps back, his left hand running through his fair hair, his right claw-hand clutching the bowl of an unlit pipe.

'Let her stay,' he said, 'she might as well hear it all.'

'What's up?' I repeated.

'Only a tiresome young woman,' cut in Hermia, tapping her foot irritably, 'who wants to fly to Australia.'

'The same one?' I asked, for we had all heard a good deal of the lady in question.

'Same one,' said H. – 'Come on, now, E., what do YOU think?'

Hermia gathered up her knitting and her novel, told us that as she had rather a lot to do, she would leave us to our discussion. – H. knew HER views on the subject which subject had now become too tedious for words. She then suggested – indeed recommended that we stop talking about the wretched girl and have a game of chess. She left the room, shutting the door firmly, just short of a bang.

H. and I took out the chessmen and the board which went on top of a cardtable and began to set the pieces out and as we did so the conversation continued.

Events, which had been rumbling along for months had now, apparently, reached a climax. The following is a mixture of what H. told me on that day and of remarks that he and Hermia made on other occasions.

Baker had left some unfinished business at Stag Lane. His unfinished business was the matter of Miss Amy Johnson, whom he had taught to fly and who was now seeking further adventure. She had been a nuisance to Baker. Now she was fast becoming a nuisance to H.

The faint dislike which H. and Miss Johnson appear to have felt towards each other on their first meeting had increased sharply as the months went by and as she persisted in stating her intention of flying to Australia, pestering H. for his approval of her plans and generally badgering him on the subject. She and H. were poles apart, thinking and speaking from premises so different as scarcely to be founded on the same language. It appeared that she considered him, with his pleasant, well-modulated English voice and cheerful countenance, to be a typical product of a sheltered South of England public school upbringing, – a man who had never done a day's work or known hardship or difficulty in the course of his easy, pain-free life.

He considered her to be a grim and unattractive young woman with a chip on her shoulder as thick as three cubic feet of best B.C. lumber.

She considered him to be 'against' her because she was from Yorkshire and was a woman for she was thinking of herself and so took his rebuttal of her plans personally.

He considered her to be too crass to be able to take no for an answer and that on a subject of such vital national importance as was civil aviation.

The war between them dragged on.

H. won the early battles: 'She can't go, I've told her again and again, it is quite out of the question,' he said. But in the spring of 1930, just when he hoped that he had heard the last of it, she brought up some heavy artillery in the form of Lord Wakefield.

Lord Wakefield, as reasonable as he was generous, had promised her both financial and material support for her proposed venture, support without which she could not afford to go, provided that the Director of Civil Aviation, Sir Sefton Brancker, thought that she was able to undertake such a flight.

Brancker, loyal friend from the old Blackburn days in Greece, lost no time in getting in touch with H. and sounding him out about Miss Amy Johnson.

They talked long.

H. gave his opinion – that it was a brave idea but that she was unfit for such a journey. Her navigation was non-existent – she would lose her way – she relied too much on luck in her flying – she had no idea what such a journey entailed.

Of course: if Brancker was prepared to assume full responsibility for Miss Johnson then that was another matter. He, H. G. Travers, would not do so. As a matter of fact it was a considerable relief, he said, to have the wretched business off his hands. Memories of those five young pilots who never reached Vert Galand with him in the autumn of 1916 may well have been in his mind as he handed Miss Johnson's fate and future over to the Director of Civil Aviation. Let him bear the burden.

Sir Sefton lunched with Lord Wakefield and put the case.

Wakefield did not, of course, miss the point and the matter, which was to have been decided that day, remained unsettled for a further twenty-four hours. H. had been sadly mistaken in thinking that he had handed over responsibility to Brancker. Lord Wakefield had been counting on H.'s approval as a matter of course and it had not been forthcoming.

Now Lord Wakefield wanted to see H. alone, without Brancker, and had asked him to lunch the next day. As a result of this summons H. had twenty-four hours to consider and to decide Miss Johnson's future for that no longer lay with Sir Sefton but, via Lord Wakefield, with him.

No wonder he paced the room, up and down, up and down, three steps into the bay, three steps back, irresolute, worried, trapped.

Of course I do not remember every word that was said between us, but there were snatches of our talk which I have never quite forgotten, possibly because H., again and again, stressed the necessity of reaching the right decision.

'She doesn't realize the importance of such a flight ... no woman has made such a flight before ... the Press will fasten on to it ... if it is a failure (and she's unlikely to succeed) it will be such a bad advertisement for civil flying ... she seems to have no idea of the importance of what she is contemplating ...'

All this was new to me. In my ignorance I had thought that people flew back and forth to Australia as a matter of course. Jim and Australia. Jim and flying. 'Jim A L W A Y S flew to Australia,' I asserted with the confidence of the hopelessly wrong. (He had of course done nothing of the kind.)

H. told me a little about mileages and fuel stops and oceans and weather. 'A few men have gone,' he said, 'a very few. And no women.'

He asked again: 'What do Y O U think, E.?' I asked if it was a good thing to do. He said: 'Very good, if she ever gets there ...' I said that she ought to go. 'You've made up my mind for me,' he said.

We then played our game of chess.

When I next spoke to him on the subject it was some days after his lunch with Lord Wakefield. He described the scene, in the big room looking out on London River – London River, the hub and the heart of the Universe. Beside that same river, from whence the Travers ships had sailed to the four corners of the earth, Miss Johnson's flight began at last to fall into the scheme of things and before they parted H. told Lord Wakefield that, if she would undertake to learn some navigation, he would let her go.

As was usual with H., once he was committed to an idea or to a task, he gave of his very best. His task was now to do his utmost to instil a little navigation into Miss Johnson's repertoire of knowledge. He did what he could and Brancker – with his usual skilful diplomacy – advised her to accept all the tuitions he could on the subject. As a result of his tactful intervention her manner became less abrasive to H. and he, consequently, more sympathetic to her. She had much to learn, however, and as the numerous other Stag Lane pupils also had claim on H.'s time, he arranged for her to have a Navigational course in London. I think that he arranged this for her through the Royal Aero Club; she certainly had tuition at the Royal Aero Club.

As already described in the earlier chapters, it was a family tradition to see people off on any long journey. No matter how poor the health nor how pressing the prior invitation, everything was dropped in order to obey the ritual attendance on an important departure. It was the talisman to ensure the traveller's safe return. So it was H. who led the small group of well-wishers who gathered at Croydon early on the morning on May 5th.

At home, we read the papers.
    'She's gone,' I said when I saw him next.
    'She's gone,' he said, 'she's on her own now. Quite alone. Perhaps she won't like it quite so much, on her own . . .'
    Mr Johnson, Amy's father, appreciated more than anyone else, (except of course Hermia, Brancker and Lord Wakefield), how much H. had done to enable her to attempt the flight – that it had all hung on a hair's-breadth decision which had been H.'s alone – and he wrote to H. a letter of friendship and gratitude soon after Amy's departure; it was a warm-hearted letter from a generous-minded man. Looking in on my father to say good-bye before school one morning I saw him smiling delightedly as he read the letter at his breakfast table.
    'A wonderful letter from Will Johnson,' he said.
    He was immensely cheered by that letter.
    Whereas before he had only hoped that Amy Johnson would escape with her life now he began to wonder if there was even a slight chance that she would succeed. But he rated her chances very small and when that brave woman finally touched down with her famous splintering landing in Australia there were few more surprised, or more deeply glad, than was her recent instructor.

At home, we read the papers.
    'She's got there,' I said, when I saw him next.
    'She's got there,' he said, grinning broadly.

'There's a fuss,' I said, 'in the papers.'

'There's a tremendous fuss,' he said, 'and it will go on and on. She'll get sick of it all by the time they've finished. There's even a perfectly frightful little tune . . .'

A handful of people had seen her leave Croydon on 5th May.

On her return to London in August there were mounted police out to help restrain the adoring crowds who thronged the streets through which she made her triumphal progress. Among many other honours she was made an Honorary Member of G.A.P.A.N. 'Six months ago,' she said, in response to their toast, 'I would have queued up to shake hands with any one of you . . .'

Her otherwise excellent response was spoiled, for H., by her statement that 'she had never believed in safety first.'

'Unfortunate,' remarked H., 'very unfortunate. Just the sort of remark which does so much harm . . . and she will be listened to now.'

A week or so later, I found on returning from school one Monday afternoon that H., who had been home for his day off, had already left for Stag Lane. As he normally stayed until late on Monday or sometimes, in the summertime, left home at four or five o'clock on Tuesday in order to be at Stag Lane early on that day for the morning's flying, it was disappointing to have missed him.

I fired questions at my Mother.

'How was Daddy?'

'Very well.'

'Really well?'

'Very well. Very cheerful.'

'Anything happening?'

'Yes. He's got another one.'

'Another one?'

'A new pupil. Another girl. Another girl who's really going to DO something. This one is different, though. She's an absolute charmer.'

'What is her name?'

'Her name,' repeated my Mother slowly, 'I think it's Batten. Miss Jean Batten.'

14

STAG LANE II

1930–1931

H. takes Navigator's Certificate (2nd Class) – R.101 – Jean Batten – some pupils and personalities at Stag Lane

ON THE 24th, 25th and 26th March, 1930, H. took his Navigation Examination. He was granted Air Navigator's Licence (2nd Class) No. 85. Other than that break of three days he was instructing, including a good deal of cross-country instructing, (to Amy Johnson and others,) throughout all the flying hours of daylight on his stable of Moths. He also recorded flying Breda X V G-A A V N on the 9th and again on the 13th of April.

He was busier than ever, often leaving Stag Lane late on a Sunday evening to drive down to Walmer for his day off. In good weather he sometimes broke the journey at Bredgar in order to call on his Mother and his sisters, leaving the Ashford Road (A20) at Hollingbourne and cutting up Hollingbourne Hill. One night he was making just such a journey when, driving under the railway bridge at Hollingbourne, which is on a right-hand bend in the road, the steering finally went on the old Armstrong-Siddeley. The car veered sharply to the right, running into the deep drainage ditch beside the road.

Nowadays there is a housing estate at that point, 'Troy's Mead' and the ditch has long since been filled in in order to widen the road, but in those days there was just the ditch and a hedge beyond and no house on that side of the road. There were no public telephone boxes, either, nor nearby breakdown services. It was late and dark and H. was tired out after a long week's flying. He wrapped a travelling rug around his shoulders, hoped that the night would remain fine, and settled down where he was, to sleep. At about midnight a bull's-eye lantern was shone in his face and the local policeman enquired if he was hurt. H. explained what had happened and that he was not hurt, just sleepy. 'You just stay where you are, sir,' said the kindly bobby, leaving H. to his rest. Not one car passed in either direction for the remainder of the night.

Poor *Jemima*, who, if she had survived, would have added lustre to any motor car museum, was now just so much wreckage. Hermia suggested that he should buy an aeroplane and when H. demurred, muttering about expense and what we could, or could not, afford, she became keener than ever that he should buy one 'just for the summer.' She was a powerful persuader.

On the 2nd May his log-book records flying Lamplugh down to Cowes, in one hour from Stag Lane, in 'VZ. On the 17th May he recorded: G-AARE. Stag Lane. 15 minutes. Test of own aircraft.' 'RE had been on floats when he saw her and it is probable that the flight with Lamplugh on the 2nd May would have included looking her over. She would have been on wheels, of course, by the 17th May.

She was a good one. Amongst the numerous high-quality Moths available to him, there were always those which he liked better than others. 'BL and 'BN of the London Aeroplane Club's machines and now 'RE of his own. He flew 'RE down to Bredgar on the 19th May with a pupil, Jan Oliver, and took Jay up for a five-minute flip from The Warren, then on to Bekesbourne with Jan Oliver where we all gathered to admire 'our' aeroplane.

H. had made an equitable arrangement with Geoffrey de Havilland and with the LAC that 'RE should be treated like the other Club machines: the Club would have full use of her except for one day a week or by other, prior, arrangement; de Havillands would maintain her; other than that she was private property and could therefore have her own coat of paint. Hermia, who was a flamboyant character herself, like to have quiet colours around her, muted colours of stone, beige or grey. The new machine was named by her *Grey Goose* and was painted in a grey livery, (not quite the very dark grey Hermia would have liked) – and which was possibly the most unsafe colour imaginable; but it looked very nice and showed off the silver dope on the wings to perfection. It was a happy day for both H. and H. when, on the 31st May, they flew down to Bristol for the Bristol Air Pageant in her, taking 1 hour and 20 minutes: 'leading Club formation. passenger H.E.M.T.' H. recorded more soberly that they returned the same day in 1 hour and 25 minutes: 'weather thick.'

Grey Goose on the Hamble May, 1930

Another enjoyable jaunt, on time off, was to call on Hermia's parson uncle, Harry Fraser, at Ryton in Shropshire.

16.6.30.	Moth G A A R E.	Stag Lane to Walmer. 1 hour. alone.
16.6.30.	Moth G A A R E.	Walmer to Stag Lane. 55 mins. H.E.M.T. passenger.
16.6.30.	Moth G A A R E.	Stag Lane to Ryton Salop 1 hour 25 mins. ,, ,,
16.6.30.	Moth G A A R E.	local at Ryton 20 minutes.
17.6.30.	Moth G A A R E.	Ryton to Stag Lane. 1 hour 25 mins. heavy rain.

On the 19th June H. was instructing at Stag Lane as usual, so Hermia must have returned to Walmer by train.

19.6.30.	Moth. E X, X S, B L.	Stag Lane local 5.35 mins. Instructing.
20.6.30.	Moth 'B L.	Stag Lane local. 10 mins. test.

Grey Goose over Kent, 1930

Grey Goose over Kent, 1930

1.6.30.　Moth. BL, XS, EX. Stag Lane local. 5 .hours. 20 mins. Instructing.

22.6.30.　Moth. BL, VZ, WY. Stag Lane local. 5 hrs. 10 mins. Instructing.

24.6.30.　Moth. BN, VZ, WY, XS. Stag Lane local. 4 hours 50 minutes. Instructing.

And so on.

Of course *Grey Goose* did not solve the problem of hopping down to Walmer for his day off, as H. had known that she would not; she was a delightful aeroplane and one that he and Hermia enjoyed flying in, but she was a flippancy and he knew it. After a while he sold a half share in her to a well-known Stag Lane personality, Charles T. Tutt. Tutt was pleased with the arrangement, but as he seldom took up his option to fly her it is likely that it was Hermia who derived more pleasure from her beloved *Grey Goose* than did anyone else.

H. then bought a motor-bike for the weekly trip down to Kent, a gorgeous BSA, a great thrumming, brumming monster on which he was very happy. 'The most economical form of motorized transport yet devised,' he used to say of motor-bikes. Unfortunately for his effort at economy, Hermia viewed the B.S.A. much as Emmie had viewed one of its many predecessors, that: 'I am afraid he will smash himself up on his own mo-bike' and the BSA, on which I had enjoyed pillion rides along Liverpool Road and Archery Square, was banished.

Apart from the occasional flight down in 'RE, he came down by train for a while, but Southern Railways on the line to Walmer were slow. He occasionally borrowed *Susan*, the 1922 Talbot-Darraq, but she was a poor starter who needed cranking as a matter of course, a task that H. found both difficult and painful.

One day he arrived home in an extraordinary little fabric-covered buzzing bee called a Wolseley Hornet. She was given full marks and allowed to stay. In fact Hermia sometimes borrowed her, the Hornet having a self-starter, in order to dash up to Stag Lane or into London for some social occasion or to meet H. for dinner at the Aero Club. She was a saloon, rain-proof and cosy in the coldest of weather.

If shortage of time, or transport difficulties, forbad H. coming down to Walmer he would sometimes make the shorter journey to Bredgar, landing at Swanton Court or in the small, head-of-the-valley pasture at The Warren. On a cross-country, particularly when taking a pupil on a cross-country, he often made a point of changing course over Bredgar House, thereby making a courtesy call on his Mother. Emmie thoroughly enjoyed such fly-pasts.

'We thought it was you on the very lovely monoplane yesterday morning,' she wrote to him on the 23rd July, 1930, 'it was so like a great bird sailing up to the house that men in the orchard might have thought you were after the cherries. Jessie said the wind was very high at The Warren, not suitable for landing ...'

Yes, it was H. He had flown Major Nathan and Hermia down to Dover during his lunch hour one Tuesday in Nathan's 'very lovely monoplane', Puss Moth 'Y C and was returning in a hurry but not in too much of a hurry to call on his Mother. He was back at Stag Lane, via Bredgar, in 50 minutes for the afternoon's instructing, putting in another three and a half hours instructing on 'Z C at Stag Lane.

That was a good flying week, with 5 hours 5 minutes flying on the 25th and 7 hours and 10 minutes flying on the 27th July. In addition he took up Peter Hoare's Moth G-ABBD for a 10 minute flight on the 27th: 'Windscreen test. Draughty.' On the 31st July he gave a 'joyride. pass. Frith' on 'GAARE *Grey Goose*'. The name certainly appealed to H. and he often entered it in his log beside her registration letters. He flew her exclusively for the first fortnight in August, during his holidays, as follows:

1/8/30 Moth GAARE *Grey Goose* Stag Lane/Bekesbourne. 55 mins. to fetch H.E.M.T. Bekesbourne/Stag Lane. 45 mins. passenger H.E.M.T. Stag Lane/The Warren. 45 minutes. To supper with J.T. (Jay) solo. The Warren/Bekesbourne. 20 minutes. solo.'

Grey Goose must have been safely hangared at Bekesbourne for a few days, while H. came home. As so often when he had a little time off, he and Hermia went fishing with the owner of the *Lady Beatty*. 'I can't understand,' said the Deal boatman, 'how that aeroplane stays up in the sky. I think it's a marvel. It's something I'd like to try more than anything.' – I may not have remembered his precise words, but that was his drift. H. promised him a flight in the near future.

5/8/30. Moth GAARE *Grey Goose* Bekesbourne/Lympne. 20 minutes. With Hall to escort Miss Johnson. Lympne-/Maidstone/Bekesbourne 1 hour.

12/8/30. *Grey Goose* 'RE Bekesbourne/Warnock 50 minutes. H.E.M.T. to lunch at Eastbourne & return. War-nock/M'stone/Bekesbourne. 50 mins.

15.8.30. Moth. GAARE Bekesbourne Deal B'bourne. 45 minutes. passenger Beauchamp. The owner of the *Lady Beatty* had experienced at first hand the marvel of flight. He often mentioned it if he saw any of us along the beach. He still could not understand, he used to say, how an aeroplane could stay up in the sky. He was not the only one to enjoy a flight that day.

15.8.30. GAARE. B'bourne. local. 15 minutes. Daphne Travers. Bekesbourne local 15 minutes. Eva Travers.

He left 'R E at Bekesbourne for a few days, perhaps Charles Tutt wanted to fly her, and was back at Stag Lane on the 19th and thereafter, instructing as hard as ever on 'X S, 'B L, 'Z C, and 'E X. He took a lift down with Hofer on 'E X on the 22nd August and collected 'R E from Bekesbourne, making a slowish flight of an hour back to Stag Lane. The following week must have been good flying weather, and he instructed for 5 hours 5 minutes on the 27th and 5 hours and 40 minutes on the 28th August.

He was back on *Grey Goose* again on the 29th and brought a pupil, Miss Ogilvie-Forbes, down to Deal on her in 50 minutes, taking an hour and ten minutes for the return flight to Stag Lane. Miss Ogilvie Forbes probably came down to lunch, for H. spent the rest of the 29th instructing at Stag Lane on 'Z C and 'B L. Beauchamp had spread the word in Deal on the joys and marvel of flight. The next excitement was the Deal Hospital Air Rally on the 30th August.

It was perfect weather, it must have been, for I can remember the excitement of the open tourer, the runaway 'bride and groom' speeding across the landing-ground at Deal, with such shrieks and cries as they saw the 'bride's' father pursuing them in his aeroplane. Perhaps that was not the story. At all events a great chase ensued, and some precision bombing of the car with bags of flour eventually stopped the elopement. The bombing aeroplane was not *Grey Goose*, as she was giving joy rides all afternoon. H. and Jan Oliver had flown her down from Stag Lane in 50 minutes, had joy-rided on her for over four hours, then they had taken her back to Stag Lane in an hour and ten minutes.

She must have needed a top overhaul after all the work that she had been doing, for H. instructed for the next five days on the other Club machines. The War Memorial Hospital at Deal, a hospital of which all of us locals were proud, had profited handsomely from the Air Rally. It had been a good day's work. The log continues:

6/9/30 G A A R E. Dual to Major Harvey. U.S. Army Air Corps. 25 minutes. Instruction.

6/9/30 Moth V Z. To Leicester & return. 2 hours 40 minutes. X country. I think that Major Harvey was the cross country pupil.

7/9/30 G A A E X. Practise & heats at Leicester for Grosvenor Cup. 1 hour. just beaten for 2nd place by Jackson.

Then it was long hours of instruction again, until the 22nd September, when H. recorded: 'G A A R E. Stag Lane   Ipswich   Stag Lane. 2 hours. fetch Lawrence.'

The matter of R101 occupied H.'s thoughts greatly during 1929 and 1930. He had been horrified when he had read that the Government were, after much attempted dissuasion by many people, going ahead with her.

H. felt in duty bound to speak up on a subject on which he felt so strongly for, as always, he took the long view that flying must be established as a safe mode of transport before it could make much further appeal to the civil population.

He had been temporarily lulled by Lord Thomson, who had assured him that he would listen to expert advice, until the newspaper report announcing the revival of the plan of a long-distance flight for R101 made H. groan in despair.

('I see that you are doing your stuff with Lord Thomson,' Charles had written to H. from High River in 1929, probably after reading the report of H. piloting Lord Thomson to the official opening of the Heston Air Park in July, which coincided with the finish of the King's Cup Air Race at Heston.)

'They're going ahead after all, this Government always want to cash in on things,' he complained, 'why C A N ' T they keep out of it all. Because R100 has been so successful they want to go one better ...'

He must have been privy to conversations with the R100 designers, or with their associates or friends, or have heard a whisper from someone with knowledge of airship design in order to be so emphatic, for H. had never claimed to know very much about airships.

He became increasingly agitated about R101 as 1930 wore on. Lord Thomson's name was blackened in our household and was to remain so, perhaps unfairly.

Sir Barnes Wallis wrote to me on the subject (in answer to a query of mine), in February, 1974: '... Lord Thomson paid the penalty for his ill-judged enthusiasm for the R101, but I suspect that he must have been strongly influenced by V. C. Richmond her designer. It is evidence of their powerful influence with the Government of the day that the three men – Richmond, Colmore & Rope, who had never built a rigid airship, should have been entrusted with that work – in which past experience was all-important ...'

On June 28th, 1930, however, Lord Thomson was still in triumph and at the 11th Royal Air Force Pageant at Hendon on that day there were a number of interesting flights billed, including amongst others 'Individual aerobatics by three slow-flying aircraft: the PTERO-DACTYL, the AUTOGIRO and the Handley-Page GNOMME' and the star attraction

'A I R S H I P R101 will fly over the ground.'

Excitement about the proposed flight of R101 to India mounted. At first it was said that Brancker was to be among the distinguished party on the trip. Then that he was not going. Rather at the eleventh hour, it was announced that he was definitely going to be aboard. The eleventh hour was late September.

H. and H. became very distressed at this news and one evening, (probably the Monday before the departure date), H. telephoned Brancker at his home in London. It was almost unheard of in those days to make what was in effect a business call to a man's private house out of office hours, and H. paced up and down, up and down, whilst Hermia urged him to make the call. To do such a thing went against his code, yet he agreed with her that he must do so. Time was running out. H. would be flying all week and even were he not, he could not possibly speak confidentially from the office at Stag Lane, nor from the Aero Club. There was no telephone at his digs in Edgware.

But from Deal 255 he could make one final plea for caution. He made the call. The manservant asked him to ring back in about an hour as Sir Sefton was still at dinner. He was expected home soon. H. sat with his head in his hands and for once I was silent as my parents talked. Colmore was the name I heard again and again. Not the other two names. When H. returned to the telephone my Mother and I remained in the drawing room, where I was holding a skein of knitting wool for her to wind into a ball. She was nervous, tap-tapping her foot and telling me not to talk. She kept the door ajar so that she could hear what was being said.

'No good,' said H. when he rejoined us. His conversation with Brancker, the last he was to have, was short. 'He likes Colmore ... thinks very highly of him ... it's no good.'

Hermia was kind, telling him that he had, nevertheless, done the

right thing. She hoped that Brancker had not been annoyed by the
call. H. said something to the effect that he had seemed surprised but
was awfully jolly and had told H. that he was looking forward to the
trip, that he had every confidence in Colmore. . . .

Brancker must have been surprised at such a call. He might well have
been irritated by it; but he was a diplomatic man and a cordial friend
and his reaction was that of one reassuring a fuss-pot.

One may only guess at the delayed reaction that he might have felt,
particularly if he had discussed the matter further with Auriol Lee, for
he would have remembered that H. was not easily alarmed and that
he had knocked about the world and flown all manner of aircraft in
all kinds of weather. Sir Sefton Brancker might well have pondered
all this in the few days between the unusual telephone call and the
moment when he left his home for it was noted that, normally urbane
and confident though he was, he looked, when boarding R101 on that
fateful October day, as white as a sheet.

Although H. said little about the loss of R.101 it was obvious that
the tragedy had affected him deeply. He would pace about or walk out
of the room if the subject was mentioned. The unnecessary loss of life,
particularly loss of men of the calibre of her navigator, E. L. Johnston,
and of Brancker – and for what? To satisfy the vanity of some
Government Minister. After Beauvais a new phrase came into his
own – unwritten – manual of instruction: 'Always have the courage
to turn back.'

A slim slip of a girl, doing her first solo one summer evening in 1930,
had seen R.101 through the mists that arose around the Welsh Harp
and the vale in which it lies.

The girl, Jean Batten, described the occasion in her autobiography
Alone in the Sky.

> 'It was a calm evening with little wind and after a final three-point landing,
> just as I had commenced to taxi towards the hangar, I heard Major Travers'
> voice on the speaking-tube that was connected to the ear-phones on my leather
> helmet, 'wait a moment, Jean' he said, and started to climb out of the front
> cockpit. As he stepped down off the wing, I saw that he was clasping the dual
> control column under one arm. He held it up and said with a smile, 'she's all
> yours Jean', then he began to walk back towards the club house.
>
> 'As I watched the tall figure trudging away, I was conscious of being very
> much alone for everything seemed unnaturally quiet and the silence was only

punctuated by the staccato note of the propellor as it ticked slowly over. The large doors of the De Havilland factory were closed for the night and all the workers had departed. The aeroplane in which I sat was the only one on the aerodrome for all the others had been wheeled into the hangar and Mitch, the ground engineer, was no doubt waiting impatiently to put it away and hurry home.

'Apart from the receding figure of Major Travers there was not a soul in sight, and a light evening mist was advancing slowly, like a sluggish milky tide, from the adjoining fields across the aerodrome towards the dip in the centre.

'No time to waste, I thought, and taxied the Moth back to the boundary and turned it in to wind. This was the moment I had been waiting for; a milestone in every pilot's career and, like all those who had gone before me, and those who would follow, I knew it was one to remember forever. I sat quite still savouring to the full this moment that could only occur once in a lifetime; and looking at the panel in front of me on which were four instruments, the engine revolution counter, airspeed indicator, altimeter and oil pressure gauge, and in the centre above them, a small horizontal glass tube of liquid with a bubble in it to indicate lateral stability in flight. The first golden rule for the pupil was, to keep the nose on the horizon and the bubble in the centre.

'I reached out my gloved hand and gave the engine full-throttle and as the Moth taxied swiftly forward gaining speed and the tail rose, eased the control column gently back and with only my light weight aboard, was airborne after a very short run. I was conscious of a great surge of joy and exhilaration that seemed to flood through my whole being like an elixir as the little biplane left the ground and, responding like a live creature, seemed to share my feelings and soared into the sky as joyously as a lark.

'I missed the familiar head and shoulders of Major Travers in the front cockpit but knew that he would be watching critically, as I banked the Moth in a graceful left-hand turn to circle the aerodrome. Just as I looked over the side of the cockpit towards Harrow which was no longer visible, I caught my breath for in the misty twilight I could distinguish the dim silver outline of the R.101 flying very low over Northolt. It's flight was a majestic progress and the great airship, moving slowly through the mist resembled a huge whale swimming in a calm sea, and seemed just as vulnerable, with a cruising speed of a mere 80 miles an hour, and too little reserve power to enable anything so large to challenge the elements.

'I watched the great airship fascinated, until it disappeared into the gathering dusk making it's leisurely way northwards towards the base at Cardington. That was the last time I saw it for only a few weeks later it lay, a blazing mass of tangled wreckage near Beauvais in northern France ...'

Jean Batten has become a legend in her own lifetime but it is also true to say that she was a legend in our family before she had ever gone solo. The rest of the family other than H. had not met her, yet that is so.

It was not just that she was a pretty girl, although she was; nor that she was an especially apt pupil, although she was that also: it was her whole philosophy which was so perfectly in accord with H.'s, often unexpressed, ideas; and her ambitions which seemed to follow everything that Jim had so often described as his goals. It was almost as though Jim had come alive again.

The wheel of nations, turning on London River; the family of nations, world-wide, who could be linked by regular passenger, mail and freight services, a vast network of friendly trade and communication.

Travel, transport, trade.

That one so young should have the vision to appreciate that pioneers must keep opening up – and keeping open – more and yet more air route possibilities and that one so young and charming, having this vision, was willing to pick up the gauntlet. Such a gauntlet! The far-sighted courage of the girl is still, more than fifty years later, quite staggering.

Before the world had ever heard her name, Jean Gardner Batten was a legend with us. I was deeply disappointed not to be able to meet her then, in 1930, before she was famous; and then to hear that she had returned to New Zealand to get some finance together.

But H. smiled. 'She'll be back,' he said, 'next year.'

When I discussed this Stag Lane chapter with Bill Oliver recently, he warned me: 'You won't get it all.'

How right you were, Bill Oliver.

Only a handful of the old Stag Laners have survived and I have been in touch with just a few of them. Others one remembers, or remembers by name.

Had H. flown fewer hours or put less care and effort into the instruction which he gave, he might have had time at the end of his long day to have made the sort of detailed record of his pupils that he was able to make when in his first civil instructing job at the Bristol & Wessex. Such details were now quite out of the question. For page after page, the aircraft registration letters were followed by the one word 'Instructing.' Sometimes even the hours flown were in doubt, or were entered by another hand. He certainly flew many more hours than are recorded. Some of my kind correspondents, therefore, can now pick up the story:

From Jean Batten's letter of 24th May 1966:

The days at the L A C Stag Lane in 1930 are deeply etched on my memory. I can see Travers so clearly even now a tall slim figure very fair with deep set blue eyes – trudging back across the aerodrome after sending a pupil solo – the dual control column tucked under his arm & the hood of the duffle coat which he wore in winter thrown back to reveal an old leather helmet which rumour had it was very lucky & which he had worn in the Royal Flying Corps. He was a very practical man – 'don't forget the three C's' he used to say to anyone setting off on a first cross-country flight. Clock – compass – & common sense!

His pupils used to wait for their lessons sitting outside the tiny office on a wooden bench. If it were fine & we could see the church spire at Harrow all was well & he would take off with the first pupil. If the mist was thickening or snow flakes starting Travers would say 'to-day no see – no fly' & we all made a dash for the small club house where Ben would have a roaring fire & steaming cups of tea & ham sandwiches for the cold hungry pupils.

My own most vivid personal memory of Travers is my first cross-country night flight for my commercial's pilot's licence one misty night in November. Just as I was about to take off from Lympne he thrust a torch into the cockpit – 'you might need it' he shouted above the roar of the engine & of course I did for all the lights failed although the instruments were luminous. I arrived over Croydon & circled flashing Travers' torch over the side of the open cockpit. In those days civil planes carried no radio with the exception of the few Imperial Airways Airliners. Night flights were very rare & the signal to land at Croydon was a green flare fired on that occasion from the control tower by Commander Jeffs!

The aerodrome at Stag Lane was very undulating so much so in fact that from the club house it was impossible to see even one of the L A C's distinctive yellow D.H. Moths in the centre if one had not seen it land first. It was therefore not an easy place to instruct from. It was said that if you could fly at Stag Lane you could fly anywhere & because it was difficult may be one reason why the L A C turned out so many good all round pilots. The other reason was certainly Major Travers – a born intructor with the rare gift of divine patience. . . .

One of his pupils, Elsie Faulconer, (The Hon. Mrs Rob Faulconer), was a great favourite with all of us and she and her husband were most hospitable and kind, inviting D. and me to stay at their glorious house, Nottlers, on two occasions. Her younger son, Mr Ivor Faulconer, answered my letter when I appealed to him for memories of the '30's. The following extract is from his letter of 1979:

... Yes of course I remember your father and doing my first loop with him. I remember him landing in the field at Nottlers several times and it was largely from that that I got my love of flying. I only gave it up about 10 years ago, having been in the Fleet Air Arm during the war and kept it up after. The last thing I had was a Tiger Moth which I shared with a farmer friend & we kept it in a cow shed in a field at Cranleigh – quite like the old days. I also had a lot of fun with a float Tiger Moth in the Tiger Club at Redhill. I have got a photograph of you and Daphne standing beside me on a pony called Ginger at a meet which I remember was at Ashridge ... I do remember your father and my Mother bombing us with bags of flour while we sped round the Welsh Harp in a speedboat, and I remember speeding down the Watford by pass at the great speed of 60 in our old Wolseley, keeping station with the yellow Moth flying alongside! I always remember your father waving me away so that I didn't get decapitated by the propellor when I rushed up to greet them! ... I remember coming to see you at Deal, too. ...

Although Hermia often used to say that H. had no head for business, many of his Stag Lane colleagues thought otherwise. Victor Doree, in particular, remembered that on one occasion he had just sold a small yacht and had a handsome cheque in his pocket. H. showed him a very attractive Moth at Stag Lane and before sundown the cheque was in H.'s pocket and Victor was the proud owner of an aeroplane. 'I never regretted it,' he said, generously. Victor had in fact qualified as a pilot when in Australia, a year or so after becoming a founder-member of the London Aeroplane Club, but H. gave him some cross country instruction later on.

Victor Doree remembered Jim Mollison before Mollison's famous East-West Atlantic flight. Mollison was watching his aeroplane being fuelled and he was chatting unconcernedly with Victor and others as he watched. 'A very brave man,' wrote Victor. Jim Mollison was drunk on the first occasion that H. met him. H. was of the opinion that any man was entitled to be drunk once or twice in a lifetime, particularly if he had recently had great success or great failure, but when Mollison was drunk on their second meeting and again on their third and aggressive in his drunkenness, H. dismissed him as a bad advertisement for civil flying. He was disappointed in Mollison as he knew well of his reputation as being one of the best pilots of the age.

Bill Oliver spoke to me of Mollison (roughly as follows): '... all that is ever remembered about Mollison is his drunkenness. I wish people would sometimes remember the great skill and achievements of the man, that such flights as his East-West Atlantic crossing was one of the finest flights ever made and made a record that held for decades ...'

Later on, Bill Oliver wrote: '... Last week I wrote to Hugh Bergel, a Stag-Laner from our time. He was a captain in A T A and wrote a book about his experiences entitled *Fly and Deliver* which I considered to be good. What I particularly liked was that here at long last was somebody who had something good to say about Jim Mollison. Like Hugh, I always found him approachable, modest and kind. As for his flying ability, I have never heard *that* impugned even by his detractors ...'

Mollison was not a Stag Laner but he was such a famous pilot in his day that it is worth recording that plenty of pilots remember him down to the present day as being 'approachable, modest and kind.'

Bill Oliver's Mother, who died quite recently at the age of one hundred years and who was the famous romantic novelist, Bertha Ruck, wrote of her son and his friends in the *Flight and Fliers* chapter of her autobiography; quoting from her own letter she wrote:

> ... At this moment even if it is only for this moment, I am the mother of the Youngest Certificated Pilot in Great Britain. (Since that date there have been only one or two younger).
>
> Bear with me while I quote my letter to his grandparents, for flying was to them, even then, what the first landing of the first Interstellar Liner on the planet Mars will be perhaps to our grandchildren.
>
> B. came home yesterday evening to say that he had got his ticket. This A-Licence-and-Aero-Club-certificate is of course only the first stage, the B licence being much more difficult to get. All last week he had been practising for the height test. He had to go up and practise approaches without engine from 6000 feet. He also had to describe five figures-of-eight. This he did, taking as

his objective Harrow School at one end of the Eight and a building at Stanmore as the other. Thank Heaven he's got over his seventh solo, said to be the most dangerous. You shall see his Pilot's Log Book later.'

Continuing the text, the author continued:

Another letter to my father in Wales, with trivia which I knew would be unfamiliar to him who had not then even seen an aeroplane: 'Yesterday afternoon to the Aerodrome, driving through Wembley, Gunnersbury and all those suburban avenues which you find depressing; as one of the men with us remarked: 'Fellows must often make mistakes about which house they go into, their own or their left-hand or right-hand neighbours. However, it can't make much difference, as the furniture, the meal and the wife (especially the wife) would be practically identical.'

'The Flying Club was full of people, including little Miss Amy Johnson. During tea, machines buzzed about outside, people going up for twenty minutes at a time to practise flights. Amy Johnson was taking up in turn a covey of what looked like nephews and nieces. Before tea, Bill put his name down for a machine. He was given a gaudy-looking Moth, painted bright yellow, like a tie he made me get for him at Devereux. When he zipped on his leather flying-waistcoat and climbed into the Moth you cannot imagine what a baby he looked, though so tall. You know they have to take off into wind, so first he ran along the ground away from us, and then, returning, we saw his machine take off like a little yellow canary. He flew several times round the aerodrome and then made several practice-landings. He seems at home. He seems already one of this rough-haired, crazy-eyed confraternity who all appear to be called Alan, to wear the same zipp-fastened clothes, shout 'Ha-ha' at the same jokes, and talk a language of their own, which you have never heard, any more than they heard your Regimental shop. We left Bill with them. Slam, our dog, was with us. How he must puzzle about these doings of his grown-ups, never knowing if he is to be left with one or with the other, and now one of them has taken to vanishing into the very sky!

Arthur and friend who had been on a visit to Shrewsbury in friend's bright green Alvis, returned twelve o'clock at night. At eight o'clock this morning they were on the road to Oxford. What a restless generation! (As each generation says of the next one.) But I am so glad I have seen Bill fly, going up straight off the ground as he did the first time he walked across the room as a baby, without any hesitation. All this week I was crashed with over-excitement. It is a weight off my mind now that I can visualise it, and I have made up my mind to take flying, as we all should, as a matter of course.'

I borrowed Stuart Hill's studio to throw a party, chiefly for Bill's aviation gang and met the man who had taught him to fly; Major Travers. ('Don't call me Major; call me Trav.') He was six foot four, with large, blue eyes and white teeth to correspond; he begged me to believe that he 'wouldn't lie to me about his Job,' and that Bill, 'as soon as he got into the air, was quite as responsible as if he was thirty.'

At the end of the party there turned up to take me out to dinner my old friends Arthur Watts and Jimmie Horsnell, and we, after all the jazz – racing – and aviation chatter, enjoyed sentimental reminiscences about the dear dead Well Hall days....

Arthur Watts said: 'We thought the wine flowed then, just because one was given a glass of claret at dinner; do you realise we'd never tasted a cocktail?' (Drinks of which we had not heard the names – Sidecar, Green Goddess, White Lady, Bosom Caresser, Dawson's Quick Death.) Passed unanimously that we in our youth were much more harmless, simpler, and of sweeter natures, than this loud rapid air-minded outfit.

But wasn't this being disloyal to my new friends whom I so liked?

How helpful have the flying-folk always been to me, as a story-teller.

At Stag Lane a young Pilot (Mr. W. T. W. Ballantyne) hearing I wanted data about skywriting for my novel *To-day's Daughter* (in which the male lead in search of his inamorata takes plane and writes her name in the sky) gave up an entire evening to explaining this procedure to me, and later sent me invaluable diagrams, as well as pages of helpful stuff, all clearly written out.

In Berlin the Chiefest Boss-man of the Luft-Hansa, who signs himself simply Wronsky, was extraordinarily kind to me; so was his Adjutant, Mr. Angermunde, in whose office I was allowed to sit listening to a long and illuminating telephone conversation between him and some brother pilot. Mentally I was translating this German into all the English 'Right you ares,' the 'So long, chaps's,' the 'God bless's'....

Years later Victor Doree still remembered Bill Oliver's aerobatic, the 'Oliver Twist', which was, he said, really clever: the rapid air-minded outfit were by no means all talk.

Bill himself wrote to me: '... I was sixteen when I first went to S/L and the fact that I recently retired from a lifetime of flying (which included six years on active service with the RAF in WW2) without putting a scratch either on myself or on an aeroplane demonstrates the advantages of having been Travers-trained. On my wall here' (Hawaii – Ed) 'there hangs a picture of your father and me. He is exhibiting a blind-flying hood such as was used in those days and the same picture appeared in a November 1932 issue of *The Aeroplane* ... I must have been something of a handful but at no time did your father ever lose patience with me or fail to put out his best while initiating me in the fundamentals of my future profession ...'

Hugh Bergel wrote to Bill Oliver in 1984 and the following is an extract from his letter:

My publishers forwarded your letter a few days ago. Very many thanks for it, & for the kind things you say about my book ... How well I remember those golden days at Stag Lane – in particular Travers & Gordon Store as well as Baker & Matthews. Thank you for telling me the sad story of Matthews end – I never knew what had happened to him. And here's a coincidence! At the end of my never-to-be-forgotten very first Spitfire flight, after landing at Abingdon I had the great pleasure of meeting the Station Commander – who was my one-time (but only very occasionally) instructor – Travers! I seem to remember that he looked a bit surprised, even shocked, that I had progressed as far as a Spitfire. (H. must have been temporary Station Commander only – Ed.)

I left Stag Lane in 1933 – about the time the London Club moved to Hatfield – to save money by switching to Gliding, a move that I never regretted, if only because without my 85 hours of gliding I don't know if I'd ever have got into A T A. ...

('Matthews,' wrote Bill Oliver, 'was extinguished in a mid-air collision which I witnessed at Gravesend in 1939 ...')

Other old Stag Laners with whom Bill Oliver remained in touch with were Richard Clarkson, John Saffery and Malcolm Ogilvie-Forbes. He wrote to me:

... I told John Saffrey that I was in contact with you and I enclose a photocopy of his reaction plus an anecdote concerning H G T as a bonus. Outside my family, J H S is my oldest friend. We met at Stag Lane 55 years ago and have been mates ever since. During the war John was C.O. of a P R U Squadron at Benson and got a very good D.S.O. for photographing Leipzig by daylight after a Lanc raid. ...

John Saffery's reaction to hearing that Bill had been in touch:

... Delighted to know that you have located Travers daughter. My best Travers story is of an afternoon when I had made what I reckoned was a very creditable approach and touch down when he shouted 'I've got her' swung round back to the fence and jumped out. He fumbled about in the long grass and returning carrying a mushroom about 10″ in diameter & said he spotted it as we came in. We shared it for supper & very good it was. ...

As Jean Batten said, Travers was a very practical man! He certainly was not one to ignore a 10″ mushroom.

Although most of H.'s log-books during his years at Stag Lane were, as already stated, largely filled with the one word 'Instructing,' there were occasional references to aeroplanes other than the Moth or to flights other than 'Stag Lane local' which are perhaps worth noting. Here are a few of them:

6.10.30. Moth. 'R E. Stag Lane/Cowes. 1 hour. 15 mins. 2nd pilot M. O. Forbes. 'R E Cowes/Croydon. 45 minutes. Croydon/Walmer 30 mins. (alone).

7.10.30. Walmer/Bekesbourne/Stag Lane. hr; 15 mins.

16.10.30. G A A Z W. Puss Moth. 15 mins. Major Davey accident dept. joy ride.

16.10.30. 'Z W. (deH. demonstration.)

19.10.30. Puss Moth. G A A X X.

23.10.30. 'R E. Stag Lane/Water Eaton/Stag Lane. 1 hour 10 mins. M. O. Forbes. X-country.

17.11.30. Brought a Klemm from Heston.

2.12.30. Puss 'Y C. 20 mins. John Nathan & friend (John Nathan was Major Nathan's son.)

18.1.31. Puss Moth. G A B H C. S/L to Radlett. 45 mins. Instr. Lamplugh.

18.1.31. Puss Moth. G A B H C. 20 mins. Inst. Bulstrode.

19.3.31. 'Z C. When testing had a forced landing at Heston. 10 mins.

22.3.31. Blackburn Bluebird. A A B F. 15 min. test.

26.3.31. Instructing on 'J Z, 'E X, 'R E, 'B N, 'J C, 'J J. Flying 'J J on a x-country to Abingdon/Reading & return.

26.3.31. Moths 'K I, 'K N, 'J W, 'J J. Reading local. 1 hr. 20 min. Tests for purchase.

28.3.31. Bluebird 'B F 20 min. test. To Reading 30 min.x-country. Reading. local. 15 min. Test.

30.3.31. 'J Z. Stag Lane/Hamble? Cowes & return. 2 hrs. pte. hire from Club.

5.4.31. Robinson Redwing. 15 minute. Test.

13.4.31. 'J W. Stag Lane/Bricket Wood/Stag Lane. 15 min. private. (That was the occasion, I seem to remember, when H. flew Maurice Braddell over to visit the Faulconer family at Nottlers.)

24.4.31. Desoutter E I A A D local & Heston 1 hour. 8 landings, light & loaded.

5.5.31. Moth. 'V Z. Tredington Glos & return. 2 hrs 05 mins.

7.5.31. Moth. 'J W Norwich & return. 2 hrs 40 minutes.'

13.5.31. Moth 'J Z local & cross country Rutland with Combi. 2 hours. 40 minutes.

26.5.31. Moth 'A V Walmer & return 2 hrs.

H. and Charles Tutt sold *Grey Goose* to the London Aeroplane Club in 1931, where H. continued to fly her as often as she was available for she was still a great favourite of his. She was repainted in the yellow livery of the L.A.C. and her name was painted out. The fact that H. flew 'A V down to Walmer on the 26th May suggests (though does not confirm) that he had sold 'R E before that date.

29.5.31. 'R E, 'Z C, 'B N. Instructing. To Leighton Buzzard. 3 hrs 40 mins.

30.5.31. Moth. 'A V. dual to Beaumont. 15 mins.

31.5.31. 'A V. 2 hours 35 mins. Insured in Club.

7.6.31. Salmson Klemm (Scott Taggart's.) Moths 'V Z, 'J C, 'J L. $1\frac{1}{2}$ hrs film test.

12.6.31. 'J C. 'J Z West Wittering. 4 hrs 20 mins.

17.6.31. 'J J C. of A. 'Z Z. 'J C.

18.6.31. Sports Hermes Avian. Heston. 20 mins.

18.6.31. Moths 'J C, 'L W. 'Z Z to Halton & return.

19.6.31. L W, J C, J Z, R E, Z Z, E X. Instructing.

26.6.31. Moth Gipsy II G A A Y Y. Test after C of A.

It will be remembered by all who have followed the life cycle of the Moth (Gipsy type) that while the design of the airframe changed little the engines were constantly being improved: the Cirrus 1 being replaced by the Cirrus I I, then by the Gipsy I. Now, in Y Y, by the Gipsy I I.

Throughout July of 1931 H. did a good deal of night flying in addition to his daytime instruction. His night flying was usually in V Z and took him and his pupils to Croydon and Penshurst, or to Croydon and Lympne. A typical entry, on the 22nd July: 'Moth. R E, J J, L W, J Z, V Z. 2 hours 50 minutes. Instructing Moth V Z. Stag Lane. Croydon Penshurst 1 hour 15 minutes. night flying instruction.' The following day he was giving flying instruction at Stag Lane for 2 hours and 20 minutes and the day after for 4 hours and 20 minutes. Fatigue was a hazard of the job. There are blanks in his log book at

'A variety of close-fitting helmets.' Map-reading and Course settings Stag Lane.

photo: courtesy DAILY MAIL

about this time. I can remember Hermia reminding him to write it up and H. saying he would of course yes he would.

The night flying entries refer to only a fraction of the operation. *Flight* described H.'s method thus:

> Major Travers, the present Chief Instructor, is a man of ideas, and he has incorporated some extremely sensible and practical methods in his night flying syllabus. The old Service method, which is still followed in many training schools, is to send a pilot to make dusk landings alone and let him go on until the last two landings are made in the dark. Major Travers believes in taking the pupils on cross country flights with night landings at the end, so that they are first accustomed to the difference between day and night conditions. He then takes them to some aerodrome, usually Lympne, where night flying equipment is available and gives them dual instruction in night landings until both he and the pupil are confident that the latter can fly and land in the dark. Major Travers then leaves the machine and the pupil flies solo from the aerodrome to some other recognised night landing aerodrome, usually Penshurst, leaving his instructor to return by train. A practical and painstaking method, but one which will recommend itself more to the pupil than to the instructor!

9.9.31. Moth 'R E. 'J J. 'V Z 1 hour 20 minutes. Instruction.
9.9.31. Puss Moth 'X X & to Croydon & return 50 minutes to meet Miss Johnson.

20.9.31. Puss Moth. A A X X Stag Lane/Hanworth 15 minutes dual to Lamplugh. To breakfast at Hanworth. return to Stag Lane 25 mins.

26.9.31. Moth 'R E, 'J J, 'J Z Stag Lane local 2 hrs 35 mins. Instruction & Blind flying Instr.
1.10.31. Gipsy Klemm (Amherst's) Stag Lane local 20 minutes. Test.
1.10.31. Comper Swift A B J R. Stag Lane local. 20 minutes. Test.
1.10.31. Monospar twin Salmson. Croydon. 20 mins. with Scholfield. (Scholfield was Monospar's test pilot.)
1.10.31. Moth. 'J Z, 'E X, 'V Z. Stag Lane. 2 hours 05 mins. Instruction.
1.10.31. Moth 'V Z. Stag Lane/Croydon/Penshurst etc. 1 hr 15 mins. night flying.
2.10.31. Moth 'J Z. attempt to fetch. 45 mins. Clouds in ground at T ... turned back.
3.10.31. Moth 'J Z, 'V Z, 'E X, 'R E. Stag Lane local. 3 hours 40 mins Instruction etc.

27.10.31. Moth 'R E. Stag Lane Hamble Stag Lane 1 hr 35 min. Foggy at Stag Lane.

8.11.31. Moth 'J J. 20 mins. Test. fog.

9.11.31. Moth 'J J. 10 mins. Test. Heavy rain.

22.11.31. Moths V Z. J Z. Stag Lane local. 30 mins. Tests. foggy.

7.12.31. Moth J Z. 1 hour 50 minutes. x country instruction.

13.12.31. Klemm 80 H P Argus 'D1220' Stag Lane local 10 mins. Badly balanced for rudder torque.

14.12.31. Moth J Z. Stag Lane/Bricket Wood/Radlett/Hatfield/Broxbourne/Maylands. 2 hours 10 mins. Instruction.

21.12.31. Puss Moth 'X X. Stag Lane etc. 20 mins. demonstration.

History does not relate whether he was able to sell X X on that day. As Victor Doree said: he usually had an aeroplane for sale and it was always a good one.

15.1.32. Klemm, Pobjoy. Stag Lane etc. 20 mins. amazing take off.

It would appear that 'X X was still on the market, for on 23rd January, 1932, he recorded: 'Puss Moth X X. Stag Lane local.' 20 mins. demonstration Hall Caine.'
Successful? She did not appear again in the log-book.

6.2.32. Moth A B S H Stag Lane local. 30 minutes. Reid Turn Indicator.

On the 8th February, after instructing for 2 hours on E X and V Z, he recorded 'went sick flu.'

His next recorded flight was on the 14th March, when he began instructing as hard as ever. On the 21st March he recorded flying for a total of 1 hour and 40 minutes 'Instructor's Tests. Reserve at Hatfield.' Presumably flying J Z back to Stag Lane the next day, as he was instructing on her again at Stag Lane on the 23rd. '25.3.32. Moth R E. Gatwick etc. 2 hours. In April he began a programme of blind flying instruction.

At the end of April Sir Alan Cobham brought his circus to Stag Lane. H. recorded: 3.4.32. Moth V Z. Stag Lane local 50 minutes. joyriding for Cobham's circus.

To Emmie, he wrote:

2.5.32. The Royal Aero Club, 119, Piccadilly, London W1

Thank you very much for the fine birthday present. I am going to make a start in the morning & shall try the Austin Reed people – another of my young friends told me to-day that he went there & he always looks clean & well turned out, so its going to be rather fun, I think.

On Saturday and Sunday we had to stop ordinary Club flying by order of our Landords the de Havilland Co., for the convenience of Sir Alan J. Cobham and his air circus, termed National Aviation Day.

Saturday was a frizzle and Sunday was better and we joined in the joy-riding and formation flights.

There were an amazing number of m/c's in the air & yet we were all on the look out and the flying was very safe and sane.

It is a complete circus, with 'TOWED-off' gliding by Lowe-Wylde, parachute descents and beautiful aerobatics by Turner-Hughes.

Towards the evening the rain came along but the day was nearly over. Now it is all a sea of mud again. What a country!

Friends just over from America tell me that things are in a worse mess there than here & one of the curious outcomes is an increased friendliness towards this country, especially among the more thinking people.

I hope we get some fine weather soon or the summer will be over before it starts. The children will love to come I feel sure: I am sending your letter on to Hermy to-night.

Your loving son   H.O.

Betty's birthday was on the 24th May, the day after Emmie's; it was not only this that made those two have a special relationship but the fact, I think, that Betty had come into the family so soon after the deaths of J.L.T. and of Jim. Emmie liked her to stay, above all others, – she would I believe have had her to live at Bredgar if Hermia would have allowed it; as it was, she contented herself with birthday remembrances.

H. to Emmie:

28.5.32. The Royal Aero Club ... Betty was completely happy all day and greatly appreciated the cake, candles, and prayer-book, and personal letter from you ... I suppose one's 8th birthday is very

Two Members of the BEAUTY CHORUS at Stag Lane

photo: courtesy DAILY MAI

important. She spent the afternoon on the downs with the others and myself and was riding in the morning. . . .

What rain we have had – the aerodrome and all fields so wet and sometimes drag on the wheels & turned machines on their noses taxying.

I have been busy since last I was at Bredgar, because Tangye has been away sometimes, both for well-earned leave at Whitsun and with his teeth giving trouble, the result of a motor smash nearly two years ago.

The soft warm weather is making all the grass and things grow very quickly, yet fields all over the country are soft and treacherous. You will be wanting to go into the garden but please do not do so yet. The days are very damp and the ground will take a long time to dry after all this rain . . . I forgot to say I flew over Cheshunt yesterday and saw a house and lake which might have been the one you knew. . . .

On the 6th May H. recorded:

6.5.32. Fox-Moth. 25 minutes. new type. 3 landings light & 3 loaded.

Then more Moths again until

25.5.32. Waco. 300 WRight. 3 place ship! Stag Lane local. 20 minutes. new type!

26.5.32. Moth J Z, J J. x country. 2 hrs 35 mins. Instructing.

18.6.32. Moth A B, A S. Eastbourne, Horton, Bangor, Birmingham. 7 hrs 45 min. X Country.

23/24.6.32. Moth V Z. night flying Croydon/Lympne etc. 1 hour. 50 mins. Instr. night flying.

24.6.32. Moth V Z. Stag Lane X country. 1 hour. 40 min. Instr.

2.7.32. Moth J J. Portsmouth & return. 1 hour 50 min. Portsmouth Meeting.

3.7.32. Moth V Z, J Z, E X. Stag Lane etc. & Portsmouth. 5 hours 10 mins. Instr.

8.7.32. J J. J Z. To King's Cup start etc. 2 hrs. 45 min.

11.7.32. Moth. R E, J J. Stag Lane & Poole. 2 hrs. 45 minutes. Instr.

12/7/32. Moth. J J, E X, R E. Return from Poole & Stag Lane. 6 hrs. 15 min. Instruction.

16.7.32. Moth J J, V Z, J Z, R E. Stag Lane & Hawkinge. 2 hrs. 05 min. Instruction.

23.7.32. Moth R E, J J. Stag Lane & Colchester etc. 2 hrs. Instruction.

30.7.32. Moth R E, J J, E X. Stag Lane Pershore etc. 4 hours 10 mins. Instr.

31.7.32. D H60G Moth J J, R E, E X. Stag Lane Hornchurch etc. 2 hrs. 05 min. Instruction.

10.8.32. J Z, E X, R E. Stag Lane & Birmingham & return. 4 hours 20 min. Inst.

10.9.32. Fox Moth A B X S. 1 hour 30 minutes.

11.9.32. Fox Moth X S. Heston Gatwick 2 hours 30 minutes.

14.9.32. Fox Moth G-A B X S. 3 hours.

9.12.32. D H60G V Z 1 hour 40 minutes. Night flying.

H.'s fifth log-book closed on the 14th December, 1932.

Stag Lane was an enjoyable place to visit; sometimes H. took D. and me there together; sometimes, if it fitted in with a visit that one or other of us had made to London, or to Bredgar, – separately.

She and I both went to the 1931 Christmas Party. The tables were put together down the centre of the Club house to form one long table, paper hats and paper decorations enlivened the scene, and Nigel Tangye showed us how to form small wine glasses out of silver paper and flip them up so that they stuck, by suction, onto the ceiling.

Outside in his trailer caravan, Old Etonian Gilbert Elliott waited to give his magician's show. D. and I had used every wile we could think of to persuade him to let us into his caravan to see him practising his magician's tricks. He was adamant. He was, he told us, a member of The Magic Circle and would be excommunicated by them if he allowed us to step inside the door.

It was a wonderful Christmas Party, but the Stag Lane I liked best was the Stag Lane of a working day, the sky alive with Club Moths, with visiting aeroplanes, and constant activity around the Club house. As soon as we reached the crest of Kensal Rise, (for H. loved to take new routes and short cuts to enliven the familiar journey,) one could feel the excitement beginning to mount and when at last the turning was reached, (the sign Stag Lane fastened high on a corner wall in those days and not close to the ground, as now,) – one turned up a winding road to the left, – not a 'hill' but against the collar nevertheless, – then through a wide gateway to the right and down a small slope to the roped-off cinder-covered car park of the London Aeroplane Club.

The L A C consisted of two small wooden buildings. They stood immediately beyond the car park. Beyond them were the hangars which housed the Club machines. The de Havilland factory was mostly to the left. It was astute thinking on the part of the founders of the Club to separate the two operations so clearly, for it meant that all Club personnel and members were kept to the right, grouped together, their cars, their Clubhouse, everything; and the Club Moths in the hangars just beyond.

There would be no intrusion into the de Havilland factory.

When H. let us see the hangars and workshops he gave D. and me instructions that we must on no account run about, but walk quietly with him. More than once he said: 'The Club is only here on sufferance. de Havs don't like us much. None of us must give them cause for complaint.'

*   *   *

A well-known figure at Stag Lane was the artist, Stanley Orton Bradshaw. A dapper little man, very quiet, drawing board under his arm, yet never too aloof to show an eager nine-year-old his drawings. And they were so good. Lovely clean portraits of aeroplanes, (H. had one done of *Grey Goose*,) and witty brush and ink drawings of some of the Stag Lane habituees.

My own especial favourite at Stag Lane was Tom Campbell-Black; he and H. shared a tiny office and I was allowed into it occasionally and watched Mr Campbell-Black writing up his reports. (He was among other things the Prince of Wales' pilot). I think he did some testing for de Havillands for a while, in addition to Hubert Broad and before Geoffrey de Havilland junior took over. Campbell-Black was the man who had found the German air ace, Udet, when Udet had been lost, forced-landed on a tiny island in the Nile; for which action Campbell-Black was officially thanked by the German Nation.

It was Tom Campbell-Black, too, who had experienced one of the most unusual flying escapes then recorded.

The story went that when he was flying over the desert somewhere his aeroplane had gone out of control and was spinning to earth. He opened, or had already opened, his canopy preparatory to baling out but his foot was stuck under the rudder bar. Struggling and contorting to escape, (he was a very short man,) – he accidentally pulled the ripcord of his parachute, which opened through the cabin roof. His parachute then pulled him free of his aeroplane as it plummeted to earth. He escaped with nothing more than a sprained foot and ankle.

He was an extraordinary pilot. Bill Oliver told me a story of how, one evening, he (Bill) had been walking back to the Club house at Stag Lane, across the airfield, at a late hour, when he heard the distinctive whispering sound of a light aircraft landing. He looked about him in the dark but could see nothing. There were no landing lights nor any other lights on the aerodrome. Quite soon a Puss Moth stopped nearby and Tom Campbell-Black stepped out. He was looking for a drink. Bill O. told him that the L A C Clubhouse was closed for the night. The nearest watering hole was The Bald-Faced Stag.

On reflection the bar at Heston seemed more attractive. So Bill O. stepped aboard and Campbell-Black took off. No hesitation. In the dark. They landed at Heston a few minutes later and toddled off together for a friendly jar.

Such a landing was 'simple,' apparently.

You made an approach on instruments and then gently let your aeroplane down the last few feet, judging height by the gradual increase in the scent of the summer grasses coming up to meet you.

Simple.

There were a number of Stag Lane pupils whom we did not, as a family, meet, but of whom we were all aware; they were so generous and kind to H. and to all of us.

Hamish Hamilton ('his real name is James') the publisher, learnt to fly at Stag Lane, and although most of his lessons were with Nigel Tangye, Gordon Store's successor, he remembered H., when he took his ticket, by the gift of some novels newly out of his publishing house. The two I remember were *Swings & Roundabouts* and *Pebble in the Pond*. They both epitomized the 1930's.

Cyril Mills, son of Bertram Mills, was another pupil; he was generous to a fault with ringside seats for us all at Olympia to see the great Bertram Mills Circus. It was a fabulous circus. Jobling Purser, maker of Pyrex oven-to-table ware, gave H. and H. a massive amount of bowls, dishes and plates when he took his ticket; we were all taught to look for the initials J P on the underside of any Pyrex we might subsequently buy ourselves, to keep a good product going. Another pupil was Jack Armour son of the war artist, sporting artist and humourist, G. D. Armour. G. D. A. gave D. and me one of his own beautiful books.

Of course not all the pupils were prosperous; most were not; but as Victor Doree wrote to me: 'Flying in those days was fun and cheap. Petrol at 1/6 gallon (7½p a gallon) and if you took a friend this was usually paid for. You just got into your plane and flew where you wanted ...'

There was one man, I forget his name, who went around the flying clubs canvassing support for his one-man ex-serviceman's association. He supplied, among other things, cuff-links, and H. bought a pair, one of which I still have, enamelled on good quality steel with the magic intials 'AOFB' which, as anyone could guess, stands for 'Ancient Order of Froth Blowers.' The price was not fixed. People gave as much as they could afford.

Likes and dislikes abounded then, as they do now. There were jealousies and rivalries. H. sometimes said that 'manners and customs change; human nature – never.'

Although H. liked Geoffrey de Havilland junior and found him to be thoroughly agreeable, there was often a slight and inexplicable frost between de Havilland senior and H. Natural warmth on H.'s side was frozen off by de Havilland, although this did not decrease H.'s respect for the man or his aeroplanes or the business success which he had achieved.

De Havilland had admittedly been lucky.

Soon after the war, when de Havs were just about broke, a young man with a bright idea and money to back it, (the Coupe Monoplane was nothing if not the right idea at the right time) – had walked into the de Havilland office, had liked what he had seen and had put down his money. A brave action that had paid off. Alan Butler was everything that de Havilland was not, for he was cheerful, out-going, and easy in conversation. The dilettante appearance was misleading for he was immensely thorough, a skilled pilot and astute man of business.

As for de Havilland, one may perhaps guess at long-ago rivalries at the IRIS Works. Jim had joined the Works before de Havilland and had been in the team which had discarded Ivon de Havilland's cruder design in favour of the better braced and stronger chassis. So much had happened since, that those old IRIS days might have seemed to be in another century, yet they were only twenty-five years or so earlier.

Or one may guess at a more recent rivalry between Geoffrey de Havilland and H., but if there was any competition between them then I cannot discover when it might have taken place, as de Havilland had qualified long before H. and had remained continuously in aviation ever since, making an early reputation as a designer at Farnborough. Most of his war work had been designing, not fighting. They had held the same rank during the war and both had dropped the use of their rank afterwards. H. had resumed the use of his at Hermia's insistence. She was so proud of him. She thought that people ought to know that, although he had lived abroad for years, he had served his country during the Great War. He, on the other hand, thought that the use of rank was quite unnecessary in peacetime. He had been plain Mr in Canada, in Korea, in Greece and when instructing at the Bristol & Wessex and at the Cinque Ports. It was only on his appointment to the London Aeroplane Club that he had become 'Major' once more;

possibly this was the act that had irritated de Havilland; possibly they simply had incompatible temperaments. H. summed him up by saying that 'de Hav W A S a bit stuffy'.

Other people were well known to us as children, mostly by reputation.

Handley-Page: he was 'an awful good chap, most likeable.'

Handley-Page was a large, generous-hearted man who liked to design large aeroplanes. He was almost too fair and open-hearted a man to be in business. H. would have been sad to have lived to have seen the day when the firm of Handley-Page's was obliterated by Governmental clever-Dick's and Handley-Page, the firm who had built the huge Hannibal, was no longer on the list of constructors. Commander Perrin, the Secretary of the Royal Aero Club, was known in our family as 'little Perrin.' I have no idea why. He was not little, nor remarkably short. He was very solicitous of my Mother, I remember, and I have a vision of him rushing down the steps at 119 Piccadilly to greet her, while we all waited in the old tourer for H. to call and collect some expected messages: '– My dear Mrs Travers, – and all the family, I see. And how are you? ...'

She thought him rather gallant, if fussy.

He was an energetic Secretary and, in the parlance of the day, 'full out' for the Royal Aero Club.

Best of all was A. V. Roe, (Sir) Alliot Verdon-Roe.

I saw him once, a lone figure walking down the grass slope towards H. and me one windblown summer evening, hands in pockets, the crowds all gone from the air circus which was near Martin Mill in Kent. He stood for a while, studying an autogiro among the parked aircraft, which had been left unattended. Perhaps the autogiro was his for he had built an early one. Then he wandered along the line to look at something more apparently prosaic but which he said was 'interesting, very interesting ...' Only H. and I were there with him and he and H. talked for about 10 minutes. Later my father told me that that W A S Avro. A V R O of the 504. So quiet, so unassuming.

By such shorthand labels the great names of aviation were known to us all when young.

Ever since he had gone to Stag Lane on 1st May, 1929, H. had wanted Hermia and all of us to join him at Edgware.

She had pleaded for time.

She wanted us all to grow strong, living by the sea, largely on fish, and becoming tanned by wind and sun. She had been horrified to find, when she had retrieved us all from our boarding school in 1928, that none of us were thriving. Now we three were fit and well. D.'s health was a perennial worry, but after the first-rate care at the War Memorial Hospital followed by the healthy seaside life and diet, her glandular trouble had subsided and she was fitter than she had ever been, with more energy than the rest of us put together.

It was natural for Hermia to want us to stay in a place wherein we were so obviously thriving and where kind Dr Hall could continue to care for us, especially as her fifth child, my brother Lindsay, had now been born and she considered him to be a delicate baby. It was equally natural for such a family-loving man as H. to want to have his family near him and more than reasonable for him not to want to make an 180-mile round trip in all weather, – rain, frost, fog or snow, in unheated transport, once a week, particularly on what was supposed to be his day of rest.

There was a running battle between them, still unresolved by the summer of 1932; although I now have great sympathy with Hermia's viewpoint, at the time I fumed at her determination to stay put.

I could imagine nothing more delectable than living in one of those Edgware houses which she so disliked, and as near to Stag Lane as possible, so that one could watch all the arrivals and departures, the innumerable bouncy landings and swerving take-offs, one could run in and out of the Club house, joining in the gossip of who had just landed – and how, and in what – or playing the fruit machine – 6d a go – and waiting for H. to have a spare ten minutes to take one up for a flip.

Nigel Tangye took D. and then me up one day when H. was too busy and H. did whenever he had a free ten or fifteen minutes. In the summer of 1932 I was flying with H. at Stag Lane when he began to give me instructions. I was in the front cockpit. '. . . Forward a little . . . E A S E the stick back . . . gently . . . forward slightly . . .' We met the turf smoothly and taxied to the Club house. 'Well done, E.,' he said, helping me down off the wing, 'you've landed a Moth. Very nicely, too.' Of course I had done no such thing as I had merely obeyed instructions. But it was a nice feeling. He promised to teach me to fly as soon as I was legally old enough, in seven years' time. 'My' Moth was, I think, 'SC.

Hermia began to dislike H.'s flying job more and more and he to dislike the winter journey down to Walmer more and more.

There is no doubt that Brancker's death had shocked her terribly, indeed, she often said that it had done so. Now she was fearful the whole time for H.

Their nadir was reached sometime about the winter of 1931/32. H. often arrived at home with a blinding headache. As he had seldom had headaches before he put them down to excessive fatigue or eyestrain. Then one day he discovered the cause: a leak somewhere in the Wolseley Hornet which was shovelling monoxide fumes into the cosy, compact, rainproof little car. They could have killed him. He sold the Hornet at once and bought an Austin 12 tourer. Hermia now made a further effort to make him give up flying. A farm, she said, was the thing. There were not, H. explained, very many farms along the coast, let alone any for sale. But he would give the question of a farm some thought. He would look about on some of his cross-country flights.

In due course he came up with a farm. It was on the slopes of the North Downs in Kent and one cold day we set off en famille in the open tourer to look at the place. We drove for hours and at last climbed a hill. The farmhouse stood near the top of the hill and back a hundred feet or so from the road. We opened the farm gate and looked across a shallow, muddy depression in the farmyard, from which a stinking vapour was rising.

'It's a midden,' said my Mother in horror.

We skirted the midden and approached the house. Fragments of wet, khaki-coloured stucco had fallen from the walls. Narrow concrete steps led up to a narrow, faded door. H. had viewing permission and a key, but no one wished to enter. It began to rain – a light, cold drizzle. With less talk than was customary amongst the young in our family we returned to the car and drove the long miles back to Walmer.

The next time a farm was discussed, years later, it was H.'s idea. By then it was a different farm, in a different county and once again, nothing came of the idea.

15

STAG LANE III

1932–1933

H.'s Royal Aeronautical Society Lecture on Civil Primary Training November
1932 – H. & H. move into Hertfordshire – last days at Stag Lane – de
Havilland's depart for Hatfield

WHEN Emmie sent press clippings out to her brother, H. P. Gardner,
at Dingyarra in Queensland, she sometimes took copies of them first;
thus, in her own hand, one may read what PETERBOROUGH wrote
about H. in an August, 1932, copy of the *Daily Telegraph*:

> At Stag Lane Aerodrome yesterday I was glad to renew acquaintance with the
> popular and energetic head of the London Aeroplane Club, Mr H. G. Travers.
> For $3\frac{1}{2}$ years he has been in charge of instruction and the Royal Aeronautical
> Society have paid him a high tribute in asking him to lecture in November.
>
> The London Aeroplane Club is fortunate in having Mr Travers in charge,
> for he is not only a first class pilot, but an excellent administrator. Many of
> the people who he has taught to fly are unaware of the interesting things he
> did during and immediately after the war.
> In the spring of 1919 he took in hand the Folkestone Cologne air mail which
> was used in connection with the Army of Occupation. It was not functioning
> at all well for there were several crashes owing to fog. Mr Travers promptly
> got to work on the provision of wireless telephony and by means of five field
> stations, long since out-moded, supplied pilots with weather information for
> the whole of the route. He can afford to smile at the talk of the novelty of
> *flying blind*, heard of late, for in 1918 he might have been found at Worthy
> Down giving instruction in instrument flying but no one called it by that name
> then. It was simply 'Head in a Bag' flying for the pilots went up with a bag
> over their heads and did remarkably well.

H. took a tremendous amount of trouble with his lecture, writing and
re-writing it. He delivered it before The Royal Aeronautical Society
on Thursday, November 3rd, 1932, at 6.30 p.m., in the Lecture Hall
of the Royal Society of Arts, 18, John Street, Adelphi, W.C.2.

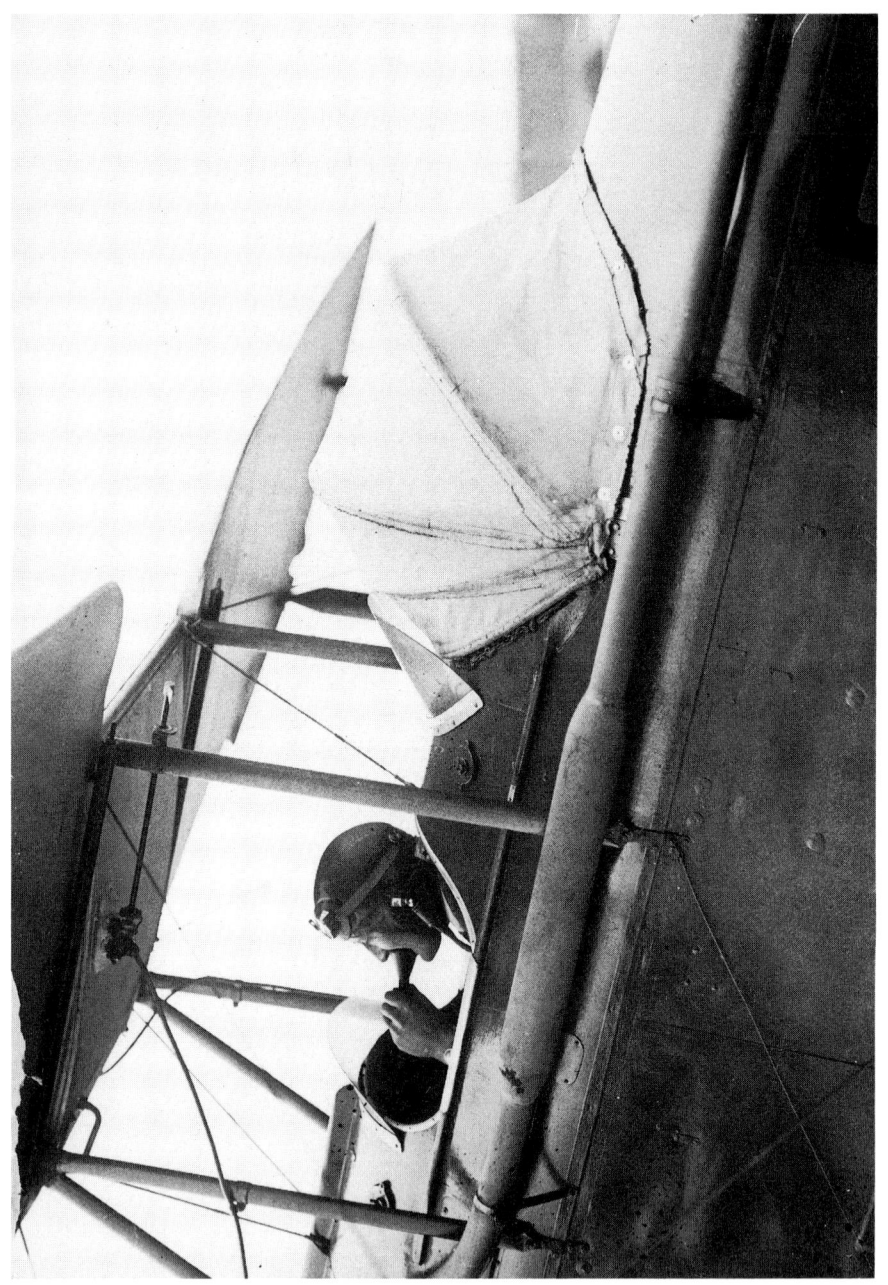

Blind Flying Instruction. H. G. Travers. Instructing on 'JZ in 1932

photo: courtesy Universal Pictorial Press & Agency

Blind Flying. ']Z takes off

photo: WIDE WORLD PHOTOS

'CIVIL PRIMARY TRAINING.
by H. G. Travers, D.S.C.

Part I.

The views expressed are my own at the time of writing the paper and may or may not be shared by others. As any living thing such as aviation must be constantly growing and changing slightly, I expect to have to modify my opinions in the future. Civil primary training should endeavour to train the whole able bodied civil population to use the air as their lawful occasions demand.

Historical

In the beginning there was no departmentalisation of flying. The pioneers designed, financed, built, flew, crashed and repaired their own aircraft. There was no official military aviation. New-comers visited the pioneers, bought machines and taught themselves as the true pioneers had done.

Quite early and long before the Admiralties and War Offices of the great nations could be induced to take any interest, some of the pioneer firms started schools of their own, where their customers could learn to fly.

Foremost among these were the Wright Brothers in America and the Farmans in France.

It is of very great interest to note here that the Wright Brothers had graduated from gliders, and that they fitted dual control to their first and later school machines; while the Farmans devised the other system under which the pupil was put alone to rolling practice, then hops, straight flights and finally circuits. The English, influenced probably by the outstanding achievements of Bleriot's first Channel crossing and the proximity of France, seem to have adopted the French method in the beginning and it was several years before Mr. Beatty opened a Wright School of Flying on Graham White's aerodrome at Hendon. Dual control was originally adopted in England to economise aircraft.

Much mud has been thrown at pre-Gosport instruction, but to obtain a just perspective we should divide the history of Flying Training into several periods. The first may be called the true pioneer era when all were groping in the dark. This ended about 1910 and was succeeded by the second period when those who had gained some rule of thumb knowledge imparted it to their pupils.

The military services were at that time represented in the flying schools by individual officers of vision who were learning there all that was then known about the handling of aircraft. During the third period, 1912–1914, the military started schools of their own, but added nothing to the common fund of knowledge for many years.

It may interest admirers of super-aerobatics to be reminded that the Chute de Chevillard (a sort of stalled turn), the loop and the bunt were all first performed by civilians and for show purposes. Civilian schools did good work up to and after the outbreak of the German War.

Fourth Period. Although this is a paper on civil training, it is not out of place to say that the quality of flying training reached its lowest during the years 1914–1917. Most of the pre-war instructors had been called up, and replacements followed one another so rapidly that much valuable knowledge both in actual preliminary training and in cross-country flying was lost. The fifth Period was entirely military and is that of the much-needed Gosport reform. But, being devised to train war pilots, aerobatics were at a premium and cross-country flying at a discount. The sixth is also military and is that of the present day Central Flying School. Almost coincident with this period is the renewal of civil instruction which began in a small way at Brooklands under the late Colonel Henderson and at the five subsidised clubs – London, Bristol, Norfolk, Midland and Lancashire.

Present-day Training.
I would like to suggest that for civil primary training we are now entering a seventh period, which may be described as Wittering sequence adapted to civil conditions.

The C.F.S. sequence is too well known to need repeating here, and so to a lesser degree is the C.F.S. sequence for blind flying. It is generally acknowledged to be the finest military flying training in the world. But when it is remembered that the civil schools have to deal with some young men in perfect physical and mental condition, but also with old men, busy business men and young women, the halt and the maimed and the very nearly blind, all of whom are paying their own good money to learn to fly and most of whose attendance is irregular, it will be sympathetically understood that the very excellent C.F.S. sequence must be modified for civil schools.

At the London Aeroplane Club we have done this by abbreviation of those paragraphs which do not apply to modern civil aircraft (aileron drag for example) and by spending more time on the separate use of the controls.

To many beginners the use of the feet to create a yawing movement is strange at first, so with the instructor working the stick and the throttle the pupil is drilled in rudder work on the ground and in the air at various throttle openings. He learns how to suffer the minimum of inconvenience from the bad forward view of to-day's tractor aircraft. Similarly, with the instructor working the throttle and rudder, he is drilled in use of the stick at all speeds and attitudes.

When he really knows what he is doing with the controls separately he is allowed to use both together. The extra time spent on a thorough understanding of the use of the controls plus real care in insisting on a comfortable flying position and good helmet is well repaid in later stages.

By this method the pupil has been unconsciously taught to preserve an accurate attitude during the take-off and landing. 'Operative' and 'optical' landings begin during his early lessons. Taught this way, stalls, spins and loops seem natural. 'Hacking round the aerodrome' has ceased. To avoid any chance of going stale, map reading and compass flying are given as weather permits.

Fog and gales alone stop instruction. There is something to do all the time. The drill sergeant bullying and cursing of the pupil is a thing of the past.

Qualities of Instructor.

Civil primary training nowadays calls for a type of instructor who has had to deal with a wide variety of human, and, if possible, of aircraft types. His own flying should be easy and unselfconscious. He must be able to analyse the movements of the aircraft while the pupil is apparently in sole charge, to fly the machine through the voice-pipe, to encourage a fluid swing of the controls and create an alert but happy state of mind in his pupil. He must be a very quick judge of the probable home life and habits of new pupils. Their character does not long remain a secret. Masks and veneers slip readily away when in the air. It is this human side which makes civil training so interesting and turns what would otherwise be a drudgery into something akin to membership of the world's greatest library – the infinite variety of men's minds and characters.

I like to believe that the standard of civil flying is steadily improving. If that is so it is because we are getting a better type of instructor.

The quarrelsome, boasting, swaggering, drinking pilot is fast disappearing, if he has not already departed.

Voice Savers.

Those who have had to instruct foreign pupils have often used a system of signals, and most instructors find that they can save their voice in this way.

Two hands held up with open palms means that the pupil has entire control.

Two clenched hands raised, with index fingers describing little circles means 'hold her nose up.'

A single hand on edge means straight ahead, and inclined to the right or left means 'ease her off' in that direction, while a full turn or use of the control is indicated by the hand held out in the required direction.

It follows, therefore, that when teaching the operative side of landings by means of 'normal glide and horizon landings' at 1,500 ft., the instructor holds up both index fingers and moves them from side to side.

Public Safeguards.

In spite of all the 'red tape' the Government control, flying would be much more dangerous to the general public if it were not for the influence exercised by the schools on their members and by the British Aviation Insurance Co. On the private owners. I would like to suggest that the Air Ministry could be of great assistance to the safety of flying if they entirely revised the issue of licences, which might in future be as follows:-

'A.' – Eight hours dual, under licensed instructor, plus three hours solo – for private solo only.

'B.' – 'A,' plus further dual and 50 hours solo for private passenger carrying and also for mail or goods for hire or reward. Flying test as for present 'B' at Northolt.

Assorted civilian pupils. Drawn for H. G. Travers by Stanley Orton Bradshaw

'C.' – 'B,' plus a further 150 hours, plus night flying and practical navigator's exam. – limited commercial.

'D.' – A 'C,' plus a further 500 hours on a variety of types – instructors and unlimited commercial.

At present the Government 'A' licence is only a certificate that the holder has done three hours solo in the last 12 months. Some private schools rush their pupils into the air with insufficient experience. But the best clubs, such as the London, at Stag Lane, and the Lancashire, at Woodford, require at least eight hours dual before the pupil is sent solo, and at the London Aeroplane Club we have a local rule which allows no soloist to carry pasengers until he has at least 50 hours solo flying and has passed a general flying test similar to that set at Northolt for 'B' licence candidates.

During his 50 hours solo flying he is checked over from time to time and allowed to go on carefully graduated cross-country flights alone.

It is a great mistake to allow pupils to hack round an aerodrome doing nothing.

But before they go cross-country the civil pupil should be given (on suitable flying days) short personal talks on the four great C.s of cross-country air pilotage – COMPASS, CLOCK, CHART and COMMON-SENSE.

He is shown the triangle of velocities and told that the course always lies between the track and the wind. He may then be taken on a dual cross-country, along a route marked on the map, and asked questions at intervals of a few minutes.

'On what course are we flying now?' (Compass.)

'What is that town on the left?' (Chart.)

'How long since we left "X"?' (Clock.)

'When do you expect to reach "Y"?' (Common-sense.)

If he is seen to be chasing the compass he is told to take an outside reference point, such as a cloud or distant hill, and only glance down at his compass from time to time to check the bearing of his aircraft's head. Suddenly the engine stops, it has been cut off by the instructor. The pupil must select his field and reach it by easy curves of constant speed, ending with a flat side-skid. When the visibility is poor and there are no outside reference points it is necessary to provide one inside the aircraft. The most popular method of doing this is by a turn and bank indicator with a separate pitch indicator, thus providing three dimensional references. The fact that it is possible to teach people to fly entirely by this method opens up great possibilities for civil training.

Maintenance Lessons.

Those who are going to keep their own aircraft far away from a competent ground engineer should certainly do a course of aircraft maintenance under a practical instructor.

They will learn to check systematically from propellor to tailskid, to clean filters and lubricate controls and chassis.

I strongly emphasise the importance of employing a practical instructor with a good record for maintenance.

Theoretical instruction and an excess of book learning are a weariness of the flesh. I would rather have a pupil who could change a plug in the dark than one who knew 50 facts about the heat treatment or metallurgy of the engines' insides.

Health of Pupils.

Flying provides plenty of fresh air, but no exercise. Pupils and instructors tend to become fat and livery.

To counteract this, and to help to create good 'hands,' my daughter suggests that all flying schools should be provided with ponies. N.F.S., at Hanworth, have done this in a small way already. But I submit, however, that to get the full exercise value from horses the pupils should groom as well as ride them.

Part II.

On the Vital Importance of Cost and a Review of Views.

The object of civil primary training being to produce the maximum number of safe and sane pilots it follows that they must be produced at the lowest possible cost per head since, as they are themselves paying for their instruction, a high training cost will seriously reduce the number of candidates. Training costs can be divided among:–

(a) Wages of instructors.
(b) Rental value of aerodrome and hangarage.
(c) Aircraft costs (prime and running).

(a) It does not pay to employ a too low priced instructor. If he is incompetent he will produce inferior results and fail to economise aircraft. If he is a good man, but temporarily hard up, he will leave at the first chance of a better job.

BUT, the very clever and showy pilot is not necessarily the good instructor. Under present conditions of training at Clubs, and allowing for the irregular attendance of civilians, twenty-five complete 'A's per instructor per annum is very good.

There are always a certain number partly trained pupils who go abroad on business, or terminate their training for reasons of unexpected financial difficulties.

It must be remembered that the instructor's responsibilities increase when the pupil goes solo. In fact they only cease when the pupil leaves the flying school.

Therefore the instructor should be paid either in proportion to the total flying hours of the school or at a fixed wage. He should not be paid for his dual hours as such. Improved organization and equipment should result in a far greater production of pupils per instructor and increase his wages if possible.

(b) Rental of aerodrome and hangarage. From a costing point of view this is a fixed amount per annum whether the land is freehold or leasehold. The rent varies immensely according to locality.

Wonderful aerodromes and hangarage may be had away out in the country, miles and miles from any centre of population. On such sites 'rental per acre per annum' may be low, but as flying hours will be few, 'rental per flying hour' may be very high. On the other hand the huge rentals per acre charged near a big town may, under the energetic management of a competent instructor, work out at a very small charge per flying hour, provided always that the town or district contains a big proportion of potential pupils and that the school is equipped with a sufficient supply of suitable aircraft.

I have not yet suggested a possible method of reducing aerodrome rental charges per flying hour. Some of the American schools have apparently tackled it by planting their aerodromes on cheap ground not too near the cities. Simple dormitory accommodation is provided and pupils attend for standard courses starting at fixed dates. The system should have many advantages in that a set schedule can be prepared, simplifying attendance and discipline. To produce maximum economy under such a system pupils should make their beds, sweep the dormitories, perform all unskilled and some semi-skilled hangar and tarmac labour. The only paid staff need be instructor-manager, ground engineer, storekeeper-accountant, and cooks.

Such a school would be divided into red, white and blue watches, so that the equipment and classrooms were in continual use. That is the only way in which the standing charges can be well distributed.

Even in the London Aeroplane Club we have been running a seven-day week for some time past, with the result that our flying hours have been nearly 600 per machine per annum for the last two years.

(c) Aircraft Costs. These can be divided into two parts, the standing charges and the consumable stores.
Standing Charges:–

(1) Interest on capital.
(2) Obsolescence.
(3) Insurance (if at a fixed rate per annum).

From a costing point of view these standing charges are similar to aerodrome rental in that they can be fixed for the year. Therefore the greater amount of flying per machine per year the lower will be the standing charge per flying hour.

Consumable Stores are:–
Insurance (if paid by the hour).
Engine overhauls.
Petrol, oil, tyres and tail skid shoes, and the thousand and one maintenance items whose consumption increases in direct proportion to the hours flown.

Type of Aircraft to be Employed

The would-be operator of a civil school run on a scale to satisfy the demand for popular flying is faced with as many conditions for compromise as any engineer.

He must (without subsidy) reduce the costs of training and at the same time increase the comfort and safety. To reduce the standing charge we must have airframes and engines of lower first cost.

(1) I am informed that a large part of the factory cost of aircraft is charges for design to Government standards, control and inspection. (Farnborough, Martlesham and A.I.D.)

The 'material-and-labour' cost of the aircraft varies in direct proportion to the weight of the finished aircraft. The cost of inspection varies in proportion to the number of component parts of which the aircraft is built. In other words reduce the size and weight of, and number of parts in, an aircraft and you reduce the cost to the operator. The inspection cost could be still further reduced if a new class of light aircraft were created between the glider and the 'power-drive military machine,' for whose design and airworthiness not Farnborough but Lloyds would be held responsible.

(2) Aircraft built to satisfy Lloyds would probably carry a low insurance rate.

(3) Strength, simplicity, ease of maintenance, would please both Lloyds and the operator.

(4) Low-fuel consumption is much to be desired.

(5) To reduce the accidents from collision on the ground and in the air a forward and sideways view as good as the F.E.2 b, or a modern glider, is absolutely essential.

The present tractors are terribly blind and unless we revert to the 'pusher-view' a big increase of flying will result in more collisions. A decrease in the collision risk should result in a decreased insurance rate.

(6) For the instructors and pupils the following points are important:-

Freedom from vices, sudden stalls, hunting on elevators or tendency of machine to take charge.

Freedom from oil throwing, fumes in the cockpit or draughts down the occupants' necks.

Freedom from propellor swinging.

Instructional machines should be designed to be reasonably flyable without springs on elevator or rudder, particularly rudder. Besides the virtues demanded above the operator will expect to find a really comfortable position for pilots of all heights, widths, ages and sexes, and easy communication between instructor and pupil.

Colossal climb, top speed or diving power or ability to fly inverted will not be expected or required of the future civil training aircraft. The small proportion of pilots who wish to learn and perfect themselves in advanced aerobatics or train as mail pilots will attend one of the semi-military schools, and will wear parachutes.

I have tried to indicate a method by which the prime and running aircraft costs may be reduced in the near future, but that alone will not suffice to reduce civil training to the point where the general public can afford to be trained.

To be really popular, training costs must come down from about £45 (unsubsidised) to £10 per head. As far as possible office and other workers must be prepared in the dark winter evenings. We can bring to our aid help from a variety of outside sources:-

(i) The use of the feet to create and correct yawing movement can be taught in lighted drill halls or flood-lit school yards by mounting pupils on small petrol engine trolleys, hand throttle controlled and steered with a rudder bar or pedals. Obsolete airframes can be mounted free to swivel on posts in exposed and windy situations in which young pupils may amuse themselves moving the controls and trying to steer compass courses, as done by Squadron-Leader England at Lee-on-Solent.

(ii) Air Service Training at Hamble have a device in their classroom which resembles internally the hooded cockpit of an instrument-flying instructional aircraft. There is no reason why this should not be used to familiarise a pupil with stick and rudder movements.

I have made the experiment at the London Aeroplane Club of taking a member of the ground staff who had received no flying training and placing him in the hooded cockpit of the blind flying machine. His reactions in the air were better than the average pilot trained by normal methods. This is possible because he had no preconceived ideas of flying the machine from the sensations of his deep muscle. I believe the Air Force have carried the idea further. Perhaps there is someone here who can give me further news on the subject.

(iii) The third aid from outside should come from the Gliding Clubs. The London Gliding Club, at Dunstable, in particular have displayed an originality and resourceful invention which make the conventional school or club look like a canal boat beside a sailing dinghy.

They have brought communal co-operation to a fine art, built a village of huts and hangars and devised an effective means of hauling gliders to the hill-top, all at a very small cost. From a flying training point of view they are interesting in that they start their pupils on what are virtually long landings by pulling them over the surface of the flat ground on a half-stretched elastic.

This method might be interpolated between the A.S.T. instrument device and dual on the low-powered aircraft.

They have also a wide variety of types. I do not know if this is as valuable to glider training as it is to power training, but 20 hours solo on eight different types of power machines are worth 50 hours on one type.

Unfortunately, a variety of types and engines does not help to keep down costs.

Co-operative or Group Flying.
Such a school as I have visualised would be of no use for those in regular employment. But for such people the last two years have seen the beginnings of a new type flying club.

The examples which occur to the mind are the Household Brigade and the 'Bus Drivers' Clubs.

In both cases a weekly or annual amount per head is levied on all members of the particular profession or occupation. I believe I am correct in stating that all officers of the Household Brigade pay 10s per annum, and those who happen to be stationed near Heston obtain flying at very low rates. Similarly, all the members of the London General Omnibus Company's Sports Club pay 6d. per week and those near Broxbourne fly for a nominal charge per hour.

This type of group club should become very popular. We need not only cheaper aircraft but a better forward view. Where hostility to the single engine pusher exists to-day in the present generation of pilots, the attitude of mind is not the result of sane reasoning but has been sucked in with their bottle-milk at second and third hand from the descendants of Gosport. It is one of the more evil relics of the Smith-Barry revolution.

Pilots who have never seen a pusher except in a photograph, inform one solemnly that at the slightest hint of engine trouble the propellor bursting into a thousand pieces cuts the outriggers, and the crankshaft comes through one's back. Why not use a modern forged-one-piece metal propellor and why have outriggers? If I may be personal for a moment I should like to mention that my first forced landing took place after about two hours dual and 20 minutes solo. The aircraft was a Maurice Farman Longhorn. The landing was made on an earth dyke wall across a ditch. The propellor and the tail-booms were broken. The engine did not hit me in the back.

The machine was flying again in a few weeks.

Later, on another occasion at Vert Galand in the winter of 1916–17 I saw an F.E.2b, make such a tail high landing that it practically flew into the frozen ground. The undercarriage was wiped off, the propellor and tail-booms broken; the nacelle skated along the ground on its forepart; the engine, a 160 Beardmore, weighing over half a ton, did not push the crew in the back and they stepped out completely unscratched.

Remembering that false landings from engine failure are to-day the exception rather than the rule, pilots should free their minds of bias and ask themselves this question:–

'Is it better to have 100 per cent. speed, 100 per cent. climb and full aerobatic performance and suddenly leave this world by hitting a factory chimney or a flagpole?'

'Or is it better to have 95 per cent. speed and climb and limited aerobatics and always to be able to see where you are going on the ground and in the air, have freedom from oil splashes, exhaust fumes and icy eddies of the slip-stream and go on flying until you are too old to leave the fireside?'

The other party who are accused of resisting the return to the pusher appear to be the senior design and works management staffs of the factories.

After all they have become experts in their own lines, the design and production of fighters, flying boats or whatnots and one cannot expect them to change at their time of life.

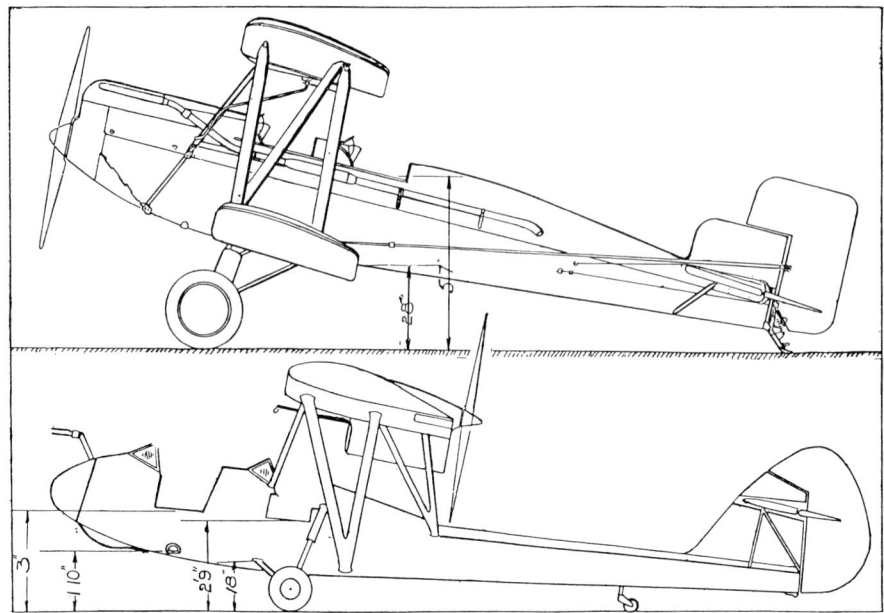

IMPROVING VISIBILITY.—The upper picture shows a conventional tractor and below a light training machine of
the pusher type which is now being built.   The pusher type also has the advantage of easy access.

Improving visibility. Two drawings on one sheet by Stanley Orton Bradshaw to
illustrate H. G. Travers' Lecture

Therefore the popular light aeroplane for cheap civil training will probably
come from a firm yet unborn whose staff will be picked and trained for the
new work.

The requirements outlined above seem to indicate a pusher of small horsepower and light loading quite unlike the machines which have served us so
well for the last six years.

It is quite possible that in order to keep down the frontal area, concentrate
the weights, and simplify the communications and dual mechanism, the
designer will have to mount the instructor close behind and astride the pupil-
pilot's seat, as was the custom on the Longhorn and Shorthorn Farmans.

An alternative is side-by-side as done by the Wright Brothers.

For better civil primary training we require:-

More sanity from our constructors.

More sanitation on our aerodromes.

More equity in our regulations.

More equitation in our spare time.

More levity in our lectures.

More levitation by our legislators.

I wish to acknowledge assistance from Mrs. Cockburn-Lange for the photo-

graph of head-on collision of two tractors (taken by her late husband); Mr.
S. O. Bradshaw for preparing cartoons and black and white sketches; and to the
following for slides:- London Gliding Club, Air Service Training, Westlands,
R.Ae.S. from their collection.'

The Lecture was illustrated with slides, mostly of photographs, Bradshaw generously giving H. the cartoons which he had drawn especially
for the occasion.

The Royal Aeronautical Society had given H. a platform for his views
and a packed audience had listened to them. Response was mixed and
varied from the chilly to the ecstatic. Among those who spoke in the
Discussion afterwards: Group Cap J. E. A. Baldwin, D S O, O B E, was
generally critical, agreeing only with the lecturer on the importance
of fitness among the pupils.

Sq Ldr Tom Harry England, D S C, A F C, supported Group Captain
Baldwin in his support of the Gosport system. He added the suggestion
that, as the mercantile marine formed a reserve for the Navy, so civilian
aviation should form the reserve for military training, to which C. G.
Grey, in *The Aeroplane*, remarked: 'Which is exactly what it does...'
Sq Ldr England said that there was no logical reason for training
pilots on the type of machine advocated by the lecturer as they would
have to fly entirely different machines in time of emergency.... ('On
the contrary, a few years hence everybody will be using twin-engine
tractors or pushers...' C. G. Grey).

Flt Lt H. F. Jenkins (A S T Ltd) spoke favourably of teaching the
controls separately. But he was not optimistic about the possibilities
of using training apparatus before starting flying. ... He agreed with
the lecturer about the possibilities of the pusher type. He thought that
the wide use of Farman machines in 1916–17 made considerably less
training necessary than would have otherwise been the case. The good
forward view and general comfort probably made these machines easy
to land.... Flt Lt W. E. P. Johnson, A F C, discussing the advantages
of flying a variety of types, said that he would rate this higher than
the lecturer did. Flying five types for five hours was better than flying
one type for fifty. A training machine should be able to vary its
characteristics. He spoke of the advantages of the Fairey 111F in this
connection as the flap-gear could be used to alter its characteristics.
He suggested that an intelligent pupil could benefit more from one

hour on this machine than say a DH9a.... The present obstacles to this better forward view might be summed up by the code-word 'failed,' which meant 'Farnborough,' 'Aeronautical Inspection,' 'Legislation' and 'Departmentalism.' He pleaded for a business control of aviation instead of the rather disinterested and chilling gaze of those whose livelihoods are pensionable.

Mr. C. H. Lowe-Wylde (the revivalist of powered gliders) said that the air must be regarded as a means of transport for everyone. Flying at present was too difficult. Our aim should be to train everyone to fly, rather than concentrating on the production of Service pilots and air chauffeurs.

Mr W. O. Manning (designer of the Wren light aeroplane which did 87 miles to the gallon) spoke on behalf of the designer. He said there was no reason why the pusher should not be built. The user had really to decide. The pusher certainly had the best forward view, except for the twin-engined tractor and this type was probably not suitable for training. ('Why not? If it can be produced cheaply enough to be operated at reasonable cost it is a better and safer machine.' C. G. Grey.)

Others who spoke in the discussion were Mr E. C. Gordon England, Mr. M. L. Bramson, Mr Rupert Preston (Household Brigade Flying Club) Mr Lee Murray and others, including 'Freddie' Guest. In his reply to the discussion H. said among other things that he thought eight hours' dual was necessary to provide a variety of experience in all weathers. He suggested that if large enough sheets of water could be found, people might go solo after very short instruction and then practise alightings all over the place in a power machine on the lines of the Lowe-Wylde boat-glider. He added that the lecture was not written for the man in the street.

Most of his critics lifted one point to criticise. Only one dealt with the complete lecture and that was Air Commodore The Right Hon F. E. Guest, who suggested that the paper ought to be regarded as the foundation of civil flying. Its scope was enormous and there was enough in it for at least four lectures. He suggested that a further three debates on the matter of the lecture should be organised.

Freddie Guest seems to have been the only one present who had followed the length and breadth of H.'s thought and who really understood that H. was advocating a totally new approach to civil primary training and that he cared, very deeply, about the subject.' 'Freddie' Guest was the only one who had the slightest idea what I was driving at,' H. said afterwards, 'and C. G. Grey was kind.'

Among the scores of Stag Lane pupils who must sadly remain anonymous, there were three whom I would like to mention before the close of this chapter. They were at Stag Lane during the last twelve to eighteen months of H.'s time there.

One was Roland Falk and the other two were the brothers R. P. and F. A. (later Sir Frank) Cooper.

The Cooper brothers had been glider pilots and active on the gliding scene for years and had been founder-members of the London Gliding Club at Dunstable. The London Gliding Club was itself very much the brainchild of Dr Slater and of brilliant Kit Nicolson. It was Mr Nicolson, an architect, who had been largely responsible for the innovative training to which H. had referred in his R.Ae.S. lecture. Mutt Summers, the test pilot, was also early on the scene at Dunstable.

'Wanx' Cooper, as all of us soon learned to call the youngest of the (three) Cooper brothers, had been horrified to hear that H.'s home was at distant Walmer, and the friendly concern of both Phil and Wanx Cooper did much to strengthen H.'s own resolve to move nearer to his work.

It was customary when taking a pupil on a cross country flight to fly, if possible, to the home of his family, or to some building that he/she knew well. Thus, on early cross country flights with Philip and Wanx Cooper, H. and they made course for Felden, where their parents, Sir Richard and Lady Cooper, lived. Then they flew to another large and beautiful, though much newer house on Berkhampstead Common, where Mrs Emil Deen lived. (Wanx Cooper and Miss Deen were soon to become engaged. They married in 1933.) Circling Berkhamsted Hill one day with Wanx Cooper, H. noticed a small house nearby, sitting in an acre or more of garden, all surrounded by a high hedge and on a Southerly slope at the edge of Berkhampstead Common.

'What's that little house?' he asked.

'That's the old Pest House,' Wanx is reputed to have answered, 'it's been empty for years....'

H. struck while the iron was hot and before returning to Walmer for his next day off called on the agents in Berkhamstead and registered his interest in the house. In due course we went on a family expedition to see over Moor Cottage, as the Old Pest House had been more conventionally called for many years.

It was one of the last days of October, 1932.

While the agents showed H. & H. over the house we children explored out of doors. Conkers the colour of old furniture were bursting out of their shells among the leaves beneath the five tall chestnut trees. The stables – two looseboxes and a pine-lined saddle-room – were just waiting to be filled up with ponies and saddlery and the garden was a wild untidy riot of fallen apples and faded Michaelmass daisies. I doubt if any one of us four girls ever forgot that first glimpse of heaven.

D. and I moved in with H. on Monday, 28th November, and Hermia, the nurse and the rest of the family drove up in the Talbot-Darracq on the following day. The minute they arrived to take charge, H. dashed off to Edgware, a mere 18 miles, to do his day's instructing. And so we settled in.

Because of their key role in deciding our removal into Hertfordshire, both the Cooper and the Deen families became very dear to us; their kindness then and subsequently was quite unforgettable. We were made very welcome into Hertfordshire and when H. told us all something of our old Prescott forbears, and that our long-ago link with the county gave us a definite entitlement to live in it, I felt more than ever that I had now come home.

Within a few weeks a score of friendly neighbours had called: before the New Year we children went to a party at Whipsnade Zoo and a fancy dress dance and midnight supper at Ashridge.

We settled in for a thoroughly enjoyable winter.

The third pupil, Roland Falk, was among the last of H.'s pupils. He was also among the best, if there is such a thing as best in that great art.

'Quite extraordinary,' was how H. described the young man who had come to Stag Lane, straight from school, to take his ticket.

At first H. found it hard to believe that his latest pupil had not flown before, but he had not done so, and was ab initio. My Mother referred to him as 'young Falk' as though she were trying not to be too impressed. But we were all impressed by H.'s description of the speed of his comprehension and of his lightning co-ordination of hand-

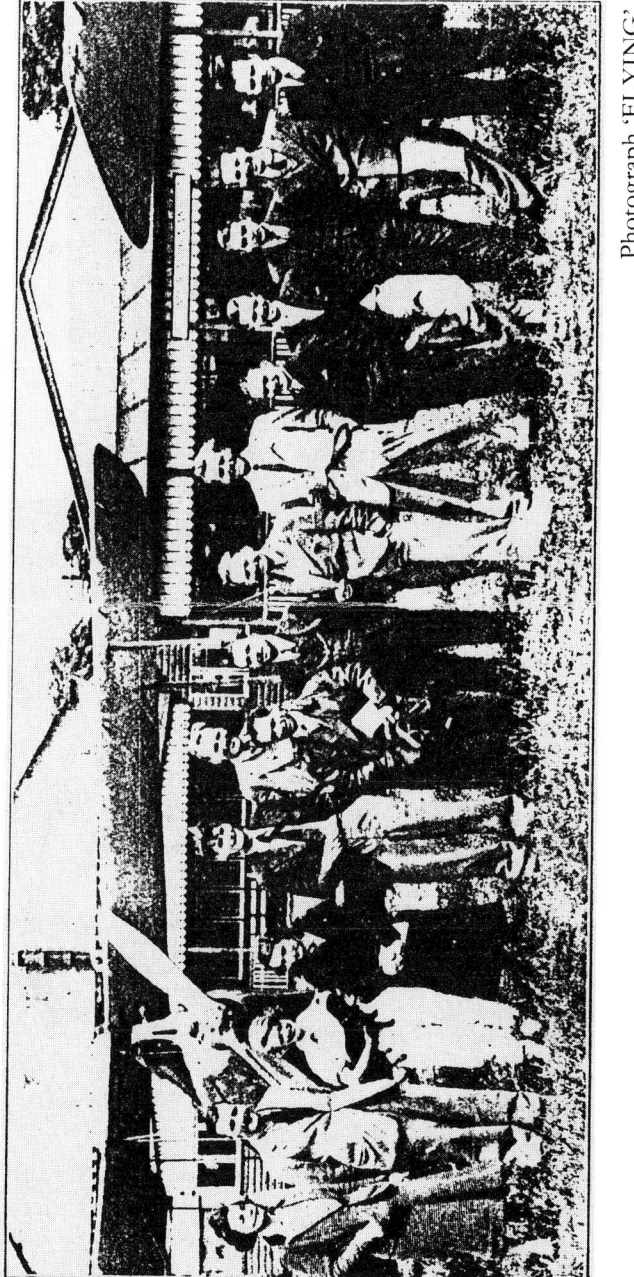

Photograph 'FLYING'

From left to right they are: Miss L. E. Holland, R. C. Pearse, Miss B. Scott (and Peter), Miss F. O'Connell, R. V. Wrighton, Major H. G. Travers (above), L. Lipton (below), C. Goldsmith, Flt.-Lt. W. F. Rimmer, Geoffrey de Havilland jr., E. A. Croft, Peter de Havilland, T. C. Place, W. R. Oliver and F. H. Matusch

and-eye. He came to lunch with us at Moor Cottage one cold winter's day early in 1933 and I have a memory of a very quiet and correct young man, with the fine-boned hawky face that often bespeaks the ability to make rapid judgments. He came to Berkhampstead again in May but I was staying away with friends deep in the country and missed that visit. However my Mother wrote to me: '. . . Young Falk came back with Da for the night & they went off after 6 a.m. breakfast this morning to take about 5 or 6 machines to Reading. The aerodrome they were going to have machines circling the aerodrome at irregular intervals and heights, & any visiting machines that got through without being seen were to get a free breakfast! but if they *were* spotted, they had to pay for their own & the spotting pilot's breakfast. Rather amusing. . . .' I only saw Roland Falk fly once. It was at Farnborough, in 1951, by which time he was A V R O's most famous test pilot.

de Havillands had been moving themselves across to their new factory and their large new acreage at Hatfield over a period of years. Their own D H Flying School had been transferred and set up there in 1931. It had been generally understood that the London Aeroplane Club were going across, too, when Stag Lane finally closed. That was indeed partly the reason why Berkhamstead was so eminently suitable, being six or seven miles closer to Hatfield than it was to Stag Lane. Since H. was employed by The London Aeroplane Club, 119, Piccadilly, the home of The Royal Aero Club, and since his employers had expressed themselves pleased with the success of so many of his pupils and of the L A C in general, he was of course, expecting and expected to go to Hatfield.

Geoffrey de Havilland was, by all accounts, a kindly and paternalistic figure to those who worked for him; to some, indeed, he was almost a demi-god; but to those outside the firm, no matter how closely involved with aviation or how knowledgeable of the subject, he could be cold, often harsh. Knowing H., knowing his record and experience, – knowing, too, how much he had done through Stag Lane to teach the gospel according to the Moth, ('the aircraft which have served us so well for the past 6 years,') – even though H. wanted designers to make a change in primary trainers, – de Hav's treatment of H. was waspish, spiteful and insulting. He had played a clever trick on H., allowing him to believe throughout the years of transition, that he would be moving to Hatfield with them as a flying instructor.

It was a shock to a man of H.'s age and calibre to be offered a job as a draughtsman at Hatfield, de Hav knowing perfectly well that H. was not a trained draughtsman. I seldom admired my father more than when, after the first chilling shock of the letter, he turned down the offer; particularly as, in almost the same breath, he assured us that sooner rather than later we would all be on a diet of stone soup.

He obeyed the chorus of requests that went up around the breakfast table and gave us the receipt for stone soup.

Stone soup. it will be remembered, was what some French farmwives were good enough to make during the hungry winters of the Great War. Soldier: 'Any soup for a hungry soldier?' Farmwife: 'No – no soup. Nothing to make into soup.' Soldier: 'Nothing? Not even a stone?' Farmwife: 'A stone? Soup from a stone?' Soldier: 'But of course! It's delicious.' etc. etc. The soldier fetches stone from his pocket. The charade continues, the farmwife being persuaded to add further flavourings to the stone. It is a superb dish, infinitely variable, and one that can be warmly recommended. Hermia cooked the best stone soup in the world, so good that one might be forgiven for imagining that it had leeks, potatoes, celery, an onion or two, sometimes even a real beef bone in it, as well as the statutory gallon of water and handful of cooking salt with which to release the full flavour of the stone.

The many who knew H. at Stag Lane, amongst them Nigel Tangye, Hamish Hamilton, Roland Falk, Victor H. Doree, Bill Oliver, Jean Batten – and many others – and who have written to me about him in response to my letters all tell the same story: H. was a calm, patient, exceptionally sweet-natured man; yet I remember that as he sat, reading and re-reading Geoffrey de Havilland's plan for the future of flying training at Hatfield he became extremely cross. It was not, I think, only the crossness of his own acute disappointment but a worry that once again civil flying had lost an opportunity and was taking a wrong turning. I cannot remember his precise words but what he said, in effect, was – let de Havs have all the flying schools they want but don't pretend that it will be, as de Hav had written 'just the same.' Their instructors will be their instructors, no longer under the aegis of, the wider view of, The Royal Aero Club. All the goodwill, built up over seven or more years by the London Aeroplane Club had been bought out and taken, by de Havilland, unto himself. They've got rid of me, if that is what they wanted to do, but, by this letter, they have also got rid of the London Aeroplane Club.

My Mother moaned that we could have stayed at Walmer all along!

H. was to have the grim consolation of having been right about the de Havilland 'London Aeroplane Club.' No matter how many good pilots they produced and, of course, there were many, civil flying had lost an opportunity and had taken a bye-way, for it became more, not less, exclusive and was never quite the same again. Many Stag Laners never transferred allegiance. Joan Meakin, Hugh Bergel and others concentrated on gliding. Some pilots were never seen in flying circles again after the closure of Stag Lane. The Golden Days were almost gone.

Joan Meakin came to see us one day, bringing her fiancee, Ronnie Price. What a darling she was, with her glorious red-gold hair and cheerful courage in adversity. She was earning a little money by painting parchment lampshades which Harrods were buying as fast as she could make them and she showed D. and me how to form and cut the lampshades and trim them with thonging. She cheered us all up, not least with her terrifying tale of an adventure which befell her when she was gliding from Sutton Bank.

As I recall it, her story ran roughly as follows: She had lost all lift and had landed in the evening in a remote district far from any country known to her. She had landed near a hamlet containing a pub, or inn, and a couple of cottages. She went to the pub, which had a telephone, and arranged with Sutton Bank friends for retrieval of herself and her glider the following day. The pub had a room and she stayed there overnight. During the night she had a nightmare so terrible that it woke her up and although she was tired after a long time in the air, she could not bear to close her eyes again, but lit her bedside candle and stayed alert in terror. For her nightmare had been that of a girl murdered by a young man, screaming as she could not open the window to escape and as the knife plunged into her neck. It was the girl's screams which had woken the peacefully-sleeping Joan Meakin.

In the morning the landlady, an ancient widow, asked Joan if she had had a comfortable night. Joan made polite remarks about the room, adding that she would have slept very well had it not been for a stupid nightmare. A description of the nightmare was asked for, and given. Such a murder, apparently, had taken place some twenty or so years before.

There have been versions of this story around for years, but the other versions have all concerned friends of friends. Joan Meakin's story had been her own experience.

Hatfield became quite plushy, with squash courts and swimming pool provided by Alan Butler. Although such exercise was a very good thing indeed for the pilots as well as being a great joy to the de Havilland workforce and their families it did, undeniably, slant the place more towards being a country club; it all tended to have a different emphasis. As Victor Doree wrote: (Stag Lane was) 'Rather different from the later Hatfield club where social members seemed to be far more numerous than the flying members. . . .'

H.'s last days at Stag Lane were in September; he had been flying as hard as ever throughout the summer; on the 7th August, 1933, he brought DH60M GAASL Gipsy II 120 h.p. from Stag Lane to Potten End, (a village on Berkhamstead Common,) for 4 hours 'joy-riding for Conservative Fete.'

Instruction hours of three, four and five hours flying continued, on EX, SL, VZ and JZ. On the 11th September he flew VZ from Stag Lane to Croydon 'night flying. $1\frac{1}{2}$ hours. flying dual Miss Bennett & Oliver.'

On the 14th September 'VZ. Gipsy 90 HP Stag Lane local 4 hours 15 minutes. Instruction. On the 15th 'VZ, SL. Stag Lane to Croydon. Instruction & to Croydon night flying.'

'16.9.33. VZ, SL. Stag Lane & Croydon night flying. Oliver passed O.K.'

Bill Oliver's own log-book recorded:

13/9/33. Puss Moth G-AAYC Gipsy III 120 h.p. Sherburn-in-Elmet to Hatfield. 1 hour 50 minutes. Major Nathan as passenger.

13/9/33. Puss Moth G-AAYC Hatfield to Stag Lane & local. 30 mins.

16/9/33. Moth G-AAVZ. Gipsy I 85–100 HP. Stag Lane – Croydon. 15 minutes. Pilot Travers. Night flying instruction.

16/9/33. Moth G-AAVZ. Croydon – Lympne. 45 minutes. Self. NIGHT FLYING passed O.K.

Bill Oliver remembered that night very well indeed. He wrote:

... I remember only one exchange of conversation during the flight in question which involved dual-instruction from Stag Lane to Croydon and three landings by the Chance Floodlight there before I departed solo for Lympne. It was when we were over Battersea Park and I had just observed a glow from an opening furnace-door when HGT asked me if I knew where we were. 'Lot's Road Power-Station below the starboard wing,' I said. 'Well, I'm not going to worry about you!', he replied. ...

They both flew at Stag Lane on the last day of all, 17th September. Bill O. recorded:

'17/9/33. Moth G-AAVZ. Lympne to Croydon. 40 minutes. Returning barograph to control tower.'

'17/9/33. Moth G-AAVZ. Croydon to Stag Lane. 15 minutes. Very foggy.' H. recorded that he instructed on VZ and on SL for 3 hours and 40 minutes. Then he ruled a line under the entry and wrote, in capital letters: END OF LONDON AEROPLANE CLUB-STAG LANE.

I believe that he would have preferred the sack to the way he had been shouldered out.

His log-book recorded a total of 3994 hours and 15 minutes flying time up to the 17th September, 1933, but remembering the numerous flights that I know for certain he never recorded, he may well have flown half as much again.

When the blow about Hatfield had fallen he had called on Emmie, an unrecorded flight, to tell her the news in person. She was 76 years old now and quite frail, but as clear in her thought and affectionate of her family as ever. She offered a sum of money as a gift or as a loan. He thanked her and refused. It was the very last thing he wished. She wrote him a note the same evening, addressed to him at the Royal Aero Club:

My dear Herbert, I am sorry for your worry. It will come all right in time. In the meantime there may be pressing emergencies. Let me know how the land lies & if a sum like I mentioned would be any good.

'I think you are all so splendid & so much happier than if you were scattered. Love to Hermy & the 5. Your loving Mother.

Emmie, as usual, had summed up the situation. We were all much happier than if we had been scattered. In fact, although we all knew that H. and H. were worried about finances and the future, I remember the winter of 1933/34 as being a wonderfully happy time.

H. did what many unemployed men do – he dug the garden and put in some more fruit trees; he did a hundred and one carpentry jobs about the place; he also wrote dozens of applications for jobs, some of which I typed out for him, and he constantly saw people, sometimes at the Aero Club – 'some view of a job.' It was then that he regretted having no engineering qualification, for it was a lack which often tipped the scales in favour of another applicant. It was a buyer's market in those days.

He was in correspondence with Airspeed, a firm he enormously admired, but I think they wanted him plus a little capital and capital was the one commodity in short supply; H. had no idea how long his meagre supply of capital was going to have to last.

During the winter, and subsequently, he made several attempts to find a backer for his flight simulator, but without success. I went with him on one occasion to an old Warlingham friend, Dr Ross-Todd, who had retired to a house with a long garden – such a beautiful garden, at Aston Clinton. Dr Ross-Todd, like all the others, was sympathetic but not in a mood to back anything so uncertain of success as a flight simulator. We called, on that same day, at a garage in Aston Clinton. I believe that the man who owned it, Mr Martin, had teamed up with H.'s old instructor colleague, Baker, to make escape systems. Once again, nothing came of the proposal. They liked the scheme, but had no spare cash.

The time was ripe for a flight simulator. The time came and went.

Among H.'s experiences on his youthful round the world trip, the journeyings in the *Atua* from New Zealand and around the islands of the South Pacific had been one of his most enjoyable times. Travelling very cheaply he had travelled with a vaudeville troupe returning to the States. From them he had learnt a repertoire of songs, monologues and barber-shop ballads.

They surfaced once more in that winter of unemployment and made many a meal that might otherwise have been gloomy quite riotous with laughter. There were such variety. A typical song ran:

'Now – our little Billy is getting very stout

And his pants he daily splits,
So –M U T Her sewed the piecrust on
To the place just where he sits . . .' etc. etc. . . .

Other songs to which he knew all the words included 'I won't Let you Play in my Yard' and the Cockney favourite 'It Weally is a Werry Pretty Gardin'.

Hermia, whose own repertoire ranged from Schubert's Winterreise to Shenandoah, Tom's Gone to Hilo, or Ye banks and Braes – she had a beautiful contralto voice – said that she thought H.'s recitals were incredibly vulgar, but she obviously enjoyed them quite as much as we children did.

It was a winter for parents to put on a brave face. Privately, H. and H. were not hopeful. They both confided in D. and me at various times just how bad the outlook really was.

Yet I still remember it as being a happy winter; for once, we were not scattered.

Charles was a faithful correspondent, the best, by far, in the whole family. H. and Charles exchanged letters and in discussing the grimness of the situation perhaps felt better for having unburdened their thoughts.

In the autumn and winter of 1933–34 H. at last had time to write more fully than he usually did, although it must be said that even with all the time in the world he would never have matched Charles' fluency.

Hermia often said that Moor Cottage was too cold for human habitation. When Charles' letters arrived from Lac du Bonnet, H. sometimes read aloud passages from them which mentioned, in Fahrenheit, the temperature BELOW FREEZING. It served to remind us all just how very snug we really were.

Hermia cheered everybody up, particularly herself, by saying that it was only a matter of time, only months – probably, before television, BAIRD television, caught on, became fashionable and made her, and our, fortune.

16

LAC DU BONNET

1932–1934

Lac du Bonnet – Cormorant Lake – Lac du Bonnet

CHARLES' letters describe his work so well that there will be little need for comment. I am only sorry that many have had to be shortened. Charles' words have not been altered. It will be noted that the letters start in May, 1932, continuing the sequence which ended with his letter of 13th May, 1932, in Chapter 11.

To Emmie:
'BOOST THE PAS HIGHWAY'
On to the Friendly North.   Hotel Cambrian, The Pas, Manitoba.
                                                          May 17th 1932.
    ... I left Winnipeg yesterday morning with Barclay and Kennedy. Uhlman and Phinney have not yet arrived in Winnipeg from the East, but are motoring through and may have been delayed by bad roads. We arrived here at 7 a.m. and are going to have some breakfast and then catch the train to Cormorant Lake, only about an hours run.
    We were met here by the forest ranger who had come out early to meet us.
    This little place is quite prosperous just now owing to the mining development that is taking place.
    It is also on the Hudson Bay Rly to Churchill.
    I didn't like leaving Marian and Jimmy.
    I expect to fly one of the Vedettes back to Lac du Bonnet in a few weeks time – Lac du Bonnet is much closer to Winnipeg – only about 70 miles – and is quite a small summer resort for Winnipeg people . . . it is a beautiful sunny day and quite warm. . . .

Levelling our Air Base, Lac du Bonnet. Paterson & Paul Jensen.
photo: C. T. Travers

Making the road. Lac du Bonnet
photo: C. T. Travers

To Emmie:

c/o Manitoba Government Air Service, Lac du Bonnet. June 9th.

... I heard to-day that you have been ill but that you are better now. Mummy dear do take care of yourself.

I hope that the weather is warmer now & I wish I could send you some of our sunshine.

I have been flying a good deal during the last few days as there have been a great many fires. The country is dotted with lakes and we always have a good landing place for our small 'Vedette' flying-boats.

I went out yesterday at 5.30 in the morning, from Lac du Bonnet, with two Indians and their bed rolls. I left them at a very pretty little lake called Gordon Lake, which was several small islands in it. The shores are rocky – rounded rocks and boulders, and marshy where a stream comes in. After that I flew up towards another lake, but it was too cloudy and I returned to Lac du Bonnet at 9.15.

I went out again in company with the other machine, at 11.15, and we found a way to Upper Eagle Lake where there was a camp of about 6 men. Two Icelandic, three Indian and the sixth was the camp boss, a young Canadian.

We had to take these men and their camp equipment to other points, but my engine would *not* start and I spent the night there with the passenger in the other machine, who is the district forestry supervisor. He is a great cook and made a wonderful supper of bannock (dampers), eggs & bacon, rice pudding, bannock & honey & coffee.

The mosquitoes were bad but we put our heads into our mosquito bar which is a sort of small tent made of muslin.

I fixed the engine up and we left this morning.

Marie and Jimmy are going to come up here to-morrow from Winnipeg. I have a small shack here for the summer....

To Emmie:

22.6.32. c/o RCAF Sub-Station, Lac du Bonnet, Manitoba.

... I was so very glad to have a letter from you and to hear that you are feeling better ... be very careful and keep the nurse on....

I have done a good deal of flying and feel that I am quite an experienced seaplane pilot now.

The last few days have been better – and wetter – not so many fires. The forestry work is different to that in Alberta as far as flying goes, because we can carry men and supplies to the fires and away again.

On the 17th and 18th I carried about 18 men and a quantity of supplies away from the scene of a fire at a place called Owl Lake to various points from which these men had been obtained.

The men were mostly ½breed Indians or else Swedes, Poles, Russians etc. There are some full-blooded Indians too.

They are willing, cheerful fellows although they all look very ferocious after a few days in the bush.

Some of these men lived at a place called Manigotagan on the shore of the big lake (Winnipeg) at the mouth of the Manigotagan River and I landed on the river there. Others came from Upper Rice Lake where there is a big gold mine, the San Antonio mine, and we disembarked them at the dock belonging to the mine.

The aeroplanes are all going well and I have been able to spend more time on them the last few days.

Mrs Barclay is staying with us now – she came up from Winnipeg two days ago. Her husband is still up at Cormorant Lake and I am afraid will not be able to come down.

We have not done anything but forestry work so far but of couse we are not directly controlled by the forestry service. We are called the Manitoba Government Air Service – and we may have to do any other work for the Govt.

Forestry cabin on an island in Lake Sasaginnigak, Manitoba

photo: C. T. Travers

The Inn at Berens River. The Ranger, G. Wilson, in front

photo: C. T. Travers

This country is so covered with lakes and rivers that one is nearly always within reach of a good landing place.

We carry ample emergency supplies of food, matches, blankets and a mosquito bar (or net) so that we could stay out for weeks – until found in case of a forced landing. We usually arrange to follow certain routes and that makes location of anyone lost far easier and we also have carrier pigeons.

Another plan is to set fire to a small island if there is one in the lake (there are very often one or more of such islands). This would attract other planes or the notice of men in the watch towers. I am glad that H.O.'s show went well at Brooklands. I am sure that he would be interested in aviation out here.

When I called in at Rice Lake the first time the mine manager said to me: 'I wonder why Roy Brown is late to-day. In case he doesn't come in to-day please 'phone him up and ask him to bring up 10 5-grain tablets of quinine etc. etc. to-morrow'

Brown is one of Canadian Airways pilots who makes a daily trip into San Antonio mine which would take a week or ten days by canoe.

The little 'Vedette' is not fast but it will lift 4 good sized Indians and pilot and packs; equipment etc.

I will try and get some photos soon. With love to Jess & Ally....
(Roy Brown was perhaps better known as Captain A.R. Brown,
D.S.C., the war-time pilot who shot down Baron von Richtofen.)

To Emmie:

c/o M.G.A.S. Lac du Bonnet July 7th 1932.

... Last Monday I flew up to Berens River, 150 miles north of here
on the eastern shore of Lake Winnipeg.

It is about half way to Norway House, which is the important
trading post at the northern end of the lake and like Norway House,
is a Hudson's Bay Co. post.

There was a strong wind blowing onto the dock when I landed
there and I was lucky to avoid damaging the aircraft badly when
bringing her up to the dock.

As it was, I dusted the wing tip and the elevators slightly, but that
was easily fixed up when I came back next day.

To Emmie:

c/o Manitoba Govt. Air Service, Lac du Bonnet. Sept 20th 1932.

... I hope that you have had a good holiday and enjoyed the change.

We will soon be on the move again to our winter quarters because
our little summer bungalow will be getting cold at night time. We
have found two cottages which are well lined and insulated and I hope
will get one or the other....

I have been walking the $1\frac{1}{4}$ miles 4 times a day and enjoy the exercise
but that would be too strenuous in the cold weather. We will be here
this winter – not at Cormorant Lake, I am glad to say....

We spent two nights in Winnipeg last week and stored all our
furniture and locked up our house.... It has been rather a white
elephant but at the same time we both enjoyed having it and it has
made us want to settle down, we are both rather tired of moving. The
Air Force are giving a dance to-night. It is not a smart affair at all but
one given by the men on the station. I expect that Andy and some of
the other officers will be down from Winnipeg and also the two officers
on this station, and the Forestry rangers. In fact everyone is invited
so I expect that we will have fun.

I was flying to-day and it was quite chilly. The trees are beginning
to turn and look very pretty.

Did you have fireworks for Ally's birthday? We had some forest fires to celebrate it. . . .

To Emmie:

M.G.A.S. Lac du Bonnet. 25th September 1932.

. . . I have been for a few flights lately and we have been bringing in the Rangers from their posts before the freeze up. I brought in one from Slave Falls. His name is Harry Smith & he is quite an interesting old chap. He has Indian blood & he knows the Indians well, but to a stranger at any rate he talks about 'dose Indians'. . . .

It is raining to-night but it is mild.

I hope to be able to rent an old frame building for 8 dollars a month. It is on Air Force property at the corner of some land which they are clearing for an aerodrome. . . . It is really a nice little place. . . . The attic is boarded in and lofty. It would be a fine place for Jimmy to play in, in the winter, when it is too cold out of doors. It has big windows. (It is only $\frac{1}{4}$ mile from the Hangar) The only other place I can find looks like a cardboard box. I think it would be warm and easily heated but it is not beautiful. . . .

To Emmie:

M.G.A.S. Lac du Bonnet. Oct 6th 1932.

. . . You must have had a wonderful summer. It is turning cold here although we have some fine sunny days. We have not had the usual early snowfall yet but must expect it to come soon. We have not heard that we can rent the little house on Air Force property yet, but we expect to hear soon. We think that we are sure to get it because the Director of the R C A F, who was here on his annual inspection of Lac du Bonnet Sub Base last week was asked by Sq. Ldr Anderson if it would be in order to rent the two cottages and the Director said "Why not?" . . .

Emmie had written to Charles about moving for the winter, from Bredgar.

To Emmie:

Manitoba Government Air Service, Lac du Bonnet. Oct. 24th 1932.

. . . It is very interesting to hear about the house. I think that it would be a splendid thing to move for the cold, wet months if you knew of a good place to go to. If you cannot find anything really attractive I would set about making Bredgar a little bit more snug. So that you can enjoy the run of the place and not have to keep to one or two rooms. I am afraid that my mind runs to the things on which it has been working a short time before. I have just bought a very satifactory wood-burning heater for my "new" house. It stands a foot or two from the wall and is connected by a sheet iron flue pipe to the brick chimney. The iron pipe isn't very ornamental but it is the usual thing in the country places in Canada and it has the advantage that more heat is transmitted to the room than with an ordinary fireplace. . . . One of these in the hall. another at the end of the drawing room . . . you could keep the house warm and dry. . . .' In the event, Emmie did no such thing. She really would rather have frozen than ruin her beautiful drawing room.

Charles continued in the same letter: . . . I wonder what the Salcombe House is like. it might be worth a look over. It is a lovely part of the country.

We have been very busy yesterday and to-day changing an engine because the old one was giving signs of approaching trouble. The commercial operators have been doing well lately because of some gold discoveries at Island Lake several hundred miles N.E. of Lac du Bonnet. Prospectors have been flying out there and some rich 'finds' have been reported.

I hope that Hermy will like her new house. At any rate H. will have a chance of seeing her and the family sometimes.

The fruit must be lovely. We find that the Ontario apples & plums have a better flavour than the B.C. ones very often and people say that that is due to the harder climate in Ontario. . . .

To Emmie:
Manitoba Govt Air Service Lac du Bonnet 21st November 1932.
. . . I am bad at writing nowadays. I know that I haven't written for a fortnight.

I think it is just that long ago that we had our first big snow storm. It lasted for three days and then it became very cold – thirty below one night. On the following morning I looked out at about 6.45 and the lake had begun to freeze along the shore. It was the sort of weather that we often have in the winter, perfectly calm and clear, and very deep contrasts between the snow and the trees. The water of the lake

The Air Force Point, Lac du Bonnet

photo: Marian Travers

was glassy and reflected the very pale colours of the sky just before sunrise. By 11.30 am the whole lake was frozen except in the places where the current is strong.

There was a little fall of snow that night but the next morning I was able to go to work along the shore on the ice which was from 2 to 3 inches thick. It is now very easy to get to work and only takes me five minutes although we have had more snow....

To Emmie:

Lac du Bonnet Manitoba Dec 9th 1932.

... I hope that your cold is better and that you will be quite well by Christmas.... Please thank Ally very much for "Farmer's Glory". I am reading "The Fountain" by Charles Morgan, that I got from Eaton's lending library. It is rather heavy going, if well written. It doesn't seem to have a plot that is worth while. I have been reading of H.O.'s very successful meeting at the R.Ae.Soc. I think it is great work. He has evidently stirred up opinion against the interference of the Air Ministry in Civil Aviation.

I always remember the rotten Oculist who turned me down for a
"B" licence in 1928. I passed my $\frac{1}{2}$ annual medical exam. A.1. a few
weeks ago! – and have been earning a living in Aviation since I came
here. I feel sure that they were wrong. . . .

To Emmie:
  Lac du Bonnet, Manitoba, Canada. March 18th 1933.
  . . . I hope that you have quite got over your chill and that the
weather is pleasant. I see that you have had a real blizzard. The snow
actually began to melt here about a fortnight ago but it turned colder
again and we have had some beautiful days. Very cold some mornings –
but clear and calm.
  Marian and I went up to Winnipeg on the 11th (Friday) and left
Jimmy with Gerda the Swedish girl. . . . I went up for the purpose of
seeing Canadian Airways as I thought that there is nothing like a
personal interview.
  Roy Brown took me along with him (he was also up in town), and
he introduced me to the Western Manager & Thompson, and to Jack
Moore, one of their pilots, who is also in charge of their sales dept. I had
a long talk to both Moore & Thompson. I liked Moore particularly – as
a matter of fact I had met him previously & we discussed semi-
technical subjects until Thompson could see me. He was also very
pleasant & we found a good deal in common as he was in the next
B.E. Squadron to No.10 which was the first one I served in, in France.
He is English & was at Bedford School, but had been out in Canada
before the war.
  Roy Brown told me later that after I had left the office Thompson
said to him something very nice about me & showed him a letter that
he had written to the Head Office in Montreal asking permission to
take me on as soon as the first opportunity occurred. He is also going
to write to J. A. Wilson & Wing Commander Anderson for some
references. I know that they will give me good ones so I hope that we
shall not be going up to Cormorant Lake after all. If I have to do
"Bush Flying" for Canadian Airways I think that Marian & Jimmy
had better stay here or in Winnipeg. I incline to Winnipeg, where she
is in reach of Dr. Mc Queen & the Hospital at a minute's notice. . . .
I might be put on a mail run: in that case Winnipeg would also be a
good centre.
  The wish to be near Winnipeg and the concern that Marian should

be close to medical help was because she was expecting their second child in July.

Charles' letter continued: We felt much happier after my interview with Canadian Airways and quite enjoyed ourselves in a quiet way. We saw some acquaintances – we don't feel that we have any real friends in Winnipeg – and they welcomed us. We admired their babies, some huge & fat & some skinny and active but all, of course, very beautiful indeed. . . .

. . . Please don't bother about the flying suit if it costs a great deal to send out or if it is very mothy.

I haven't taken any more snaps.

"*The Times*" & "*The Aeroplane*" are very much appreciated. What a frightful mess "Yurrup" is in. I hope they won't scrap & if they do that we won't become involved on any consideration except that of National security.

I hope that H. & H. have got over their colds by now. . . .

To Emmie:

Lac du Bonnet, Manitoba, Canada. March 28th 1933.

. . . It must have been very alarming when your chimney caught fire. I do hope that you have quite got over your cold by now. It would be lovely to see the crocuses.

. . . I have not heard any more about the job I applied for in Canadian Airways – except that my references were taken up by the manager in Winnipeg. I had given Wing Cdr Anderson's name. He was my last C.O. and I had mentioned J. A. Wilson: that I knew him.

The manager told Roy Brown that he had obtained my references and that they were the best he had ever had for any pilot. That is encouraging, but if they haven't got a job for me it won't help. . . .

. . . I think that the crisis in world affairs has not come yet. The League of Nations is a "bluff" as they say here, and Japan has "called their bluff" knowing that none of the European nations would start a major war against her on China's behalf. I think that this has given the Japs so much confidence that they would tackle the U.S.A. now if the U.S. won't give them their way with the Chinese – and the mandated islands in the Pacific, that the League wants back from Japan. I only hope that Europe stays peaceful. Surely the Germans aren't sufficiently united to start another row, even with Italy to help them?

Marian and Jimmy with a Vedette beached near our house

photo: C. T. Travers

Wasn't it good about the Fairey Long Range beating the world's record.

I am glad that Ally is going ahead with plays. All great playwrights have to put up with the oddity of their actors. . . .

(The Fairey Long Range Monoplane had been flown by Squadron Leader O. R. Gayford, D.F.C., R.A.F., & Flight Lieutenant G. E. Nicholetts, A.F.C., R.A.F., from Cranwell, England to Walvis Bay, South Africa, a distance of 5340 miles, non-stop. The aircraft was fitted with Napier L I O N engines.)

Charles did not hear any more about the job he had applied for with Canadian Airways and by July he was once again up at Cormorant Lake. Marian and Jimmy went with him.

Their second son, Joseph Sherwill, was born there in early July, his birthday close to Charles' own birthday. The news of his arrival was relayed around the family.

'. . . another boy at Cormorant Lake,' Emmie wrote to Hermia.

Joseph Sherwill, her youngest grandchild, was the only grandchild whom she was never to see. His arrival gave her her fourth grandson. She already had four granddaughters. The family remained up at Cormorant Lake until mid-October. Charles wrote to Emmie on the 7th:

Mile 42 H B Rly Cormorant Manitoba 7th October 1933.

... What a great trip to Berkhampstead you had. It sounds lovely to us, the old inn, seeing H. & H. and all the kids. I would like to see them and I wish he would write more often to me but he is a busy man and feels as I do, I expect, that he would like to be able to say "Charles, I know of some people who are looking for a man like you to run their ginger beer factory." I hope that he will have better luck this time than he did with the London Club who will realize some day what a hard worker they have lost.

I would like to see Betty and Tina. Betty is my godchild but I have never done a thing for her. Would she like some moccasins I wonder? I will get a pair here: there is a man who makes good ones.

His name is Joe Buck & he is always in jail, poor fellow, but he is very clever with his fingers and his silk work is good and I think rather better than the bead work. We are having a beautiful Indian summer, & there are no flies or pests now....

To Emmie:

Lac du Bonnet 18th October.

... We left Cormorant on Thursday last (12th Oct) and had a rough trip to Norway House.

Marian was airsick but Jim and Joe slept. We spent two nights at Norway House. The weather was too bad to go on but the Ranger and his wife (Durants) made us very welcome.

We stayed on the Forestry Island.

On Saturday we came down the Lake shore to Lac du Bonnet in perfect weather. We landed at Berens River after the first $1\frac{1}{2}$ hours and had tea with Mrs Paterson the H B Co station manager's wife and then flew on to Lac du Bonnet another $2\frac{1}{2}$ hours....

We have a little house in Lac du Bonnet town.

To Emmie:

Lac du Bonnet Manitoba Sunday Oct 29th 1933.

... When we came down here we found everything very disorganized. There is no money in the Provincial Treasury apparently, and as a result they have put off building a workshop and hangar here until the present time. The RCAF cannot spare any space in their hangars this year, so we have to move our base to a point $2\frac{1}{2}$ miles away in the town of Lac du Bonnet.

Jim Uhlmann (in charge of this end of M G A S) whom we all dislike, has made a mess of the job. He also seems to have antagonized the Deputy Minister for the Interior – Attwood – who has the control of any large expenditure of this sort.

The result is that we have had to dismantle the aircraft at the Air Force base, send them down here on trucks etc., and store them in temporary shelters and in the back of a garage. . . .

To Emmie:

Lac du Bonnet Manitoba 10th Dec. 1933.

. . . I would like to have the "*Aeroplane*" still, if you would not mind, but please do not send *The Queen* or *The Weekly Times* any more. . . . We can frizzle along on my pay and I cannot throw up a job which, at all counts, is a fairly secure one. I haven't the least doubt that I should have done so long ago if I had only myself to cater for. None of us like Uhlmann – who is out for himself. On the other hand I might still be looking for work which is as scarce as ever out here. . . . Canadian Airways have been very busy here and had three aeroplanes on the lake on Saturday. There is a lot of freight going into the mines, which are going strong.

The God's Lake freight is not flown in from here but from Ilford Lake mile 286 on the H B line.

There is a winter road being built up there too for the heavy Linn tractors which drag a train of freight behind them. It must be a cold job, it was quite bad enough building this workshop and I am glad that it is done now. . . .

To H.:

Manitoba Govt. Air Service, Lac du Bonnet Manitoba. 5th Feb. 1934.

My Dear H.O.

Thank you very much for your letter which was full of news. I had only vague references to your doings in letters from Bredgar and I was anxious to hear from you.

I do envy you your cottage in the country. Every time we move we think enviously of people with some permanent residence. But we must wait some time for that.

You will be better informed of conditions in Canada than I am of those at home in England.

It seems that policies of "economic nationalism" that operate in many countries are responsible mainly for the reduced market for Canadian wheat which sold at one time last year for 45c per bushel. It has risen recently to about 68c but this is due to alterations in the exchange I believe. In any case the demand is limited and we have agreed to reduce the production of wheat at the recent London agreement.

The result must be continued poverty and hardship on the prairies until farmers have changed their "wheat ranches" into mixed farms.

Mining has now taken the place as Canada's second industry. The production of gold last year was $85 million and nickel production was three time that of 1932.

Under the present favourable gold prices there is great activity in prospecting and development work in the North.

Lumbering is doing much better but I am not well informed about it because the Manitoba Industry is a small one – the product is only good enough for local use and cannot compare with B. C. Lumber in quality. There is a big pulp mill about 20 miles from here for the production of newsprint etc. but it cannot operate at present prices.

As far as aviation goes which is all over Canada the prospects are good.

Over 30 emergency landing grounds are under construction between Winnipeg and Ottawa – following the CN line roughly for the Air Mail which is to be re-started on the prairie run Winnipeg – Lethbridge (and Calgary and Edmonton) in the fall this year. Winnipeg-Ottawa, Montreal, Toronto will be started soon afterwards and the Lethbridge-Vancouver finally in 1935 and 36.

J. A. Wilson was in Winnipeg last week attending the Annual Convention of the Canadian Flying Clubs Association. Actually he was inspecting the work on these emergency landing fields, but only had time to see as far as K(unreadable) about 2/3rds of the way – as he ran into bad snow conditions. He left his pilot (Sq. Ldr. Tudhope) and came on by train.

I went up to see him and had a long talk with him at his hotel. He

is a great old chap as game as they make them and full out and genuine
too.

I would like to have a shot at the mail run. The pay will not be as
good as it used to be not more than $4,500 a year, but that will be a
lot better than I am getting now.

I have an application in for it anyway.

There is a powerful rumour that Imperial Airways are making a
strong bid to get the whole Trans-Canada run and that they are buying
landing grounds and securing options on them. I think that this is
doubtful.

Canadian Airways look upon the job as their own.

They have tendered for the prairie run and are considering
Lockheeds I believe.

When I first heard of this about 2 months ago I heard that H.P.'s
were pushing a low wing monoplane with a top speed of 175 m.p.h.
I wrote at once to David Williams and told him to get busy. He replied
saying that we had approached the directors who were very interested
and hoped to do something about it.

J. A. Wilson told me that in addition to the beam and 2-way radio
they intended to use robot pilots. – Theirs has worked O.K. except
that it worked too hard on the ailerons.

Of course there will be visual beacons, so with no passengers it
sounds O.K. to me.

The small operators are cutting in on Canadian Airways bush flying.
There are 3 private operators at Sioux Lookout. There are none here
thanks to the energy and reliablity of Roy Brown, who is dissatisfied
and (wants to) start on his own. There is a lad with 2 machines at The
Pas and Flin Flon and Lee Brintnell is giving them a run for their
money up the Mackenzie.

Canadian Airways have made too many mistakes. Their overhead
and debt is large and their equipment is getting old. If I had $20,000,
even $10,000 I would buy a couple of Stinsons. Hire an engineer and
a junior pilot and get to it – Passengers and freight into the mines.

I think that Roy Brown will do this. He has a wonderful connection
with the mines here and will get all their business.

The F.C. 51–71 costs $12,000 with Wasp Junior 345H or Wright
975E or 350HP – with floats and skis say $14,500 or $15,000. The
Stinson with Lycoming about $9,000 with floats and skis. San Antonio
(which is going to pay a dividend in April), Central, Gunnar Gold,

Rio Grand etc., are only 70 air miles from Lac du Bonnet. There is a mail contract Freight at say 6c/lb and passengers. I wonder how the Airspeed would do on Floats or on skiis. Of course the performance would be much reduced, but it seems the sort of job that might be very useful in the bush.

We are getting satisfaction out of our old Lynx.

With the new Cheetah the Airspeed Courier should out-perform any Stinson, or the smaller Fairchild.

I do not know how the wood construction would stand up in a sea plane.

Cost is all important. The small operator finds it hard to raise the capital and many companies sell their aircraft on an hourly basis, after investigating their clients records, of course. It is unfortunate that the D H products do not fit in with our requirements for bush flying.

I hope to get a rise shortly, but it remains a mechanics wage or little better.

Canadian Airways run a weekly service from here to Gods Lake, but their freight is all flown in from Ilford – which is mile 286 on the Hudson Bay Rly.

The Great Bear Lake area is going ahead and shipments of pitch-blende have started from La Mine, The Eldorado.

If silver and copper come to anything they have all sorts up there. Canadian Airways have bought 3 Junkers with P & W Hound engines, lately. They carry over 1 ton, on skiis.

I think that there is a small but growing market here for a *really very cheap* bush flying aircraft with wheels, skiis and floats. Not less than 250 H P single engine, preferably metal fuselage structure low or high wing monoplane.

(2) For a really high performance mail carrier – single engine – 650 lbs. mail full instrument flying equipment no passengers, about 60 cub. feet compartment. To cruise not less than 200 m.p.h. Or at any rate to compete with the best U.S. mailplane. I think therefore that there is a job for someone to demonstrate the above.

We are all well here. I hope that you are too.

I wish that you were within calling distance. I would like to have a yarn and I think that we might hatch something that would turn out well. I do not know for certain whether I shall go to Cormorant or stay here next year.

I wish that you could give this country the once over. There will be big developments in purely commercial aviation soon. Already some areas are dependant on air transport for their existence.

If only British interests would see ahead they could have the market. It's nothing now, but will be good in five years, but one can't buy an English aeroplane in Canada except a Moth. No matter what people say the Stinson is a good little aeroplane for the money. I have seen one take off 1000 lbs of fish and that engine ran for 700 hours. without an overhaul. That aeroplane cost $7,000 (on wheels) in Canada. It was overloaded and the engine burnt up at the end of 700 hrs.

Nevertheless it was a good performance.

No more of this rot now H.O.

I think I am half asleep and argumentative. It is too bad you won't answer me back!

Please give my love to Hermy and the family – thank Daph and Eva very much indeed for their letters and illustrations which I will answer some day.

Your affectionate brother,
Charles.'

Charles wrote to Emmie on the same day, 5th Feb. 1934:

'I think that I shall be stationed here this summer. Barclay has got a job with Canadian Airways so that now we have only Uhlmann, Phinney, myself and young Paul Jensen as pilots. I am not keen to go bush flying for Canadian Airways at their present rates of pay, but I might be tempted to join them in the autumn when they restart the Airmail Service. I would like to join Roy Brown (one of their senior pilots) who wishes to start on his own, but that is all in the air. . . . I saw Thompson who could not give me any encouragement. He is an old Bedford School boy. . . . He lost his nerve flying mail and thinks consequently that anyone over 30 will do the same. As a matter of fact, I liked the little night flying that I have done and on the new run there will be no passengers carried. Consequently if one got into a real jamb with bad weather – snow or fog – one would have no compunction in jumping out with one's parachute. There will be two-way radio – beam radio – visual beacons – landing grounds – also robot pilots, blind flying equipment and landing lights.

As they say here – "It sounds like a cinch", by which is meant that it sounds easy. Well I don't think that it would be easy but I do think that it would be safe.

J. A. Wilson was awfully nice and wanted news of everyone. He had been inspecting some of the 33 landing grounds that are being completed between Ottawa and Winnipeg. He had to leave his pilot after he had seen about 20 because they had had bad weather and snow, conditions which delayed them and caused a broken skin. I do not know for certain whether I shall be here next summer or at Cormorant Lake again. Phinney wants me at Cormorant but at the same time Uhlmann is more or less running things & he wants me here. Uhlmann is not so keen on flying now, he loses his temper in the machine & hits it, (or so Jensen says) so he will want me here to do most of the flying. I am not going to press for either. I like Phinney and Cormorant Lake and I will probably have a row with Uhlmann if I stay here. However it is a long way to take a family, and expensive, and I may be able to keep in touch with development better down here. . . .

I had a good letter from H.O. who gave me interesting news of himself and aviation affairs at home. . . .'

To Emmie:
'Lac du Bonnet, Manitoba. 7th March 1934.
'. . . I shall be doing most of the flying down here this year and will probably have to make a long patrol once a week. Visiting the Ranger Stations at Burns River, Little Grand Rapids and Sasaquinqak. . . .'

He vowed not to buy a car, for numerous good reasons, and continued: '. . . However I think that I shall build myself a small rowboat and buy an "outboard" motor such as we used last year up at Cormorant Lake on our canoe. Building a boat will be simple after repairing the hull of our Vedette! It is only a question of finding the time to do it. . . .'

To H.:
'Lac du Bonnet, Manitoba. 16th March 1934.
My dear II.O.,
Would you mind buying me a pair of goggles. I can't get a decent pair in Winnipeg under $12.50 and thought that too expensive, and I went through last season with a borrowed pair but have had to return them.

"*The Aeroplane*" has some advertised on the back page at 24/-. I would like them with that "smoky" tint, but not too dark, the yellow tint will do as well.

I enclose a money order for $7.50. Let me know if that is not enough.

Many happy returns of the day H.

I hope that you will have a good year and lots of luck.

I have been too broke and too scared to throw this job up and tell the world just what I think of J. C. Uhlmann and the Provincial Government.

Conditions have improved for me and I have agreed to stay with them through the summer, provided I get a rise. I think that I have told you about our new base and workshop. I shall be stationed here next summer and will do most of the flying I expect. Jim Uhlmann is tired of it.

Paul Jensen (his father came from Norway) is our other pilot. He is young and very keen – a good lad.

Phinney will be up at Cormorant Lake again – with Hollingsworth, our new pilot engineer. Hollingsworth was a sergt. pilot in the R.C.A.F. He had a row with his instructor and left the service, and has been with the Winnipeg Club and Northwest Airmarine, as Air Engineer and spare pilot.

He is a very capable mechanic and a good, but inexperienced pilot. Malcolm Barclay, my half section, was lucky enough to get into Canadian Airways about 2 months ago, and has been freighting from mile 286 on the HB Rly. into Gods Lake Gold mines. He gets $125/month and 3c a mile. Apart from the fact that we are all trying to get out I am not sorry that I did not get the job. His wife and child cannot go to Ilford – He may be there all summer or he may be sent to Aklavik or McMurray.

Canadian Airways are in rather a hole. They are having to meet the competition of smaller operators who can undercut them every time. There is plenty of business for all at present, but whereas the Airways can hardly operate at a profit owing to overhead office expenses, the small man flies, digs up his own business, and makes a good thing of it in many cases.

Brintnell is doing very well up the Mackenzie Valley – Labruie is giving him all his business (into Gt. Bear Lake), and he has two first rate men flying for him who are well known in that country. (Brintnell used to be manager of Western Canada Airways). Roy Brown, Jack Moar, Ashton and Ted Stull (don't publish this) were "all set" to leave Canadian Airways this spring. I suppose that they are among the six or seven senior Canadian Airways pilots in the West. The scheme fell through. Moar wanted a big concern and the control – and he had least to offer – but they had the backing up to $100,000 I believe.

Now it seems that Stull will leave to go on his own. Financed by Bob Jowsey, a successful mining man who is also an honest man, they say. He will get the freighting into Gods Lake Mines, one of Jowsey's finds.

Roy Brown, whom I know well and lives here in L du B has the money promised for starting on his own here. It is really "his" run now, because he is so well known and liked in the district.

I do not think that I can describe the development that has taken place in the northern bush as a result of flying. I do not imagine that it is realised in England. Very few people there can have seen that vast stretch of Pre-Cambrian rock or they would surely have done something about it! I have a belief that it is one of the richest countries in the world in minerals. It has only been scratched, at a few accessible points, yet it is the second largest producer of gold, the largest of nickel and contains enormous known deposits of copper, silver and lead.

Supplies for the mines are carried by rail to the nearest railhead, then by tractors, drawing sleighs which carry up to 10,000 lbs. The tractors are extremely large, powerful and costly. If the ice on the winter roads is not good (as is the case this year and last) they sometimes fall through the winter roads where they cross lakes. I have heard of two cases (at Gods Lake) this year. Gas consumption is usually 3 or 4 m.p.g. and gas may cost anything according to the locality.

The tractors travel all night and average 8 m.p.h. in good going, but they often fall by the wayside.

Still the tractor on a winter road is often the only way available for carrying in heavy mining machinery.

Dog teams owned by Indians carry about 500 lbs. a load. They do not travel at night.

In the summer there is the canoe route with the limitation that your mine may not be accessible by canoe. I do not think that the canoe

will be used in the future, whenever time has any value. Water transportation pays on some of the very large lakes of course. I am very
long winded H.O.

As far as I can make out, Commercial Air Transportation did not
amount to much in the bush before 1927–28.

Since that time there has been a little improvement in equipment,
not a great deal. The old stand-by, the Fairchild 2W or 71 is still the
best all round bush flying aircraft. The Wasp still the best engine. It
still takes anything up to 2 hours to get an engine going in cold weather
warming engine, warming oil etc. Skiis have not been improved, they
still crack, stick, break check cables and sandows.

The olio gear goes solid.

Floats are a little better Edos are good – and strong.

There is one thing, prices are down.

The Fairchild 51–71 with the 340 P & W Wasp Junior, *Floats,
Wheels and Skiis* cost about $1650 in Canada.

Is there any possibility of an English manufacturer producing an
aeroplane to compete with the above?

It has occurred to me that there is a possibility of getting going in
this way.

Offer (say the Airspeed Co.) to purchase one of their Courier aircraft
on the following terms.

1.   That the aircraft be fully equipped for Canadian flying conditions,
     floats and skiis and wheels, and winter gear, anchor, etc, etc.
2.   That on making a deposit (of say 10%) the aircraft is shipped and
     delivered without further charge to Montreal.
3.   That I should be appointed Canadian agent.
4.   That in the event of damage to aircraft I should (be) absolved
     from any blame by Airspeed Co.
5.   That I should be allowed to ply for reward with the aircraft.

For my part I would agree:

1.   To endeavour to promote the sale of this make of aircraft.
2.   To devote a proportion of the profits from the operation of the
     aircraft to repayment of any debt.
3.   To report at regular intervals upon all technical points dealing
     with the behaviour of the aircraft under operating conditions.

It sounds like asking for a lot.

However, if they could be convinced that the market is worthwhile it would not be a bad deal.

Otherwise they would have to find a man who knows the layout here and pay him a fee and expenses.

Roy Brown is thinking of getting two aircraft.

One good 2nd hand F.C.71 with C type Wasp, and a new Stinson or Waco for light loads. He will employ a junior pilot, probably his young brother, and a good air engineer.

The Stinson will cost about $1150 with floats and skiis. I think that the payload, about 430 lbs, is too small.

Anyhow, H., tell me what you think of the scheme, remembering that it could be put in a more convincing manner, supported by facts and figures of successful operations out here. I am rather tired now, it is about 2 a.m., but it struck me that if you were at a loose end we might spend a profitable winter 1934–5, freighting into Red Lake or Central Manitoba or Gods Lake districts, or to go further afield up the Mackenzie or into Great Bear Lake. Gas is easier to get up there now, and I do not think there would be any difficulty.

The Lynx or Cheetah works all right out here.

No more now

Your affectionate brother,

Charles.'

To Emmie:

'Lac du Bonnet, Manitoba. 11th April 1934.

'... Yesterday I got a day off and he' (Phinney – Ed) – 'and I flew up to Winnipeg with Roy Brown who offered us the trip. It took us only 35 minutes but the return journey, by bus, took $3\frac{1}{2}$ hours.... I expect that the ice will break up about 25th April if this mild weather holds. Malcolm Barclay came in from Ilford – 286 miles up the Hudson Bay Rly from The Pass – to-day.

He is taking his Fairchild in to Winnipeg for repairs to the fuselage.

Freighting heavy loads in the winter puts some strains on the framework. The surface of a lake may be drifted, the prevailing winds blow the dry snow like so much sand particularly on the large lakes. The ice may be cracked in various ways and there are the winter roads which build up a hard ridge through the passage of horse-drawn sleighs and the drifting of snow against the sleigh tracks. Then near a settlement there are water holes and sometimes places where ice has been cut for storage until the summer.

Most of our aeroplanes are of American design and intended for use with wheel or float undercarriages. So that skiis are usually made in Canada and attached to existing undercarriages. These are not always flexible enough to absorb the shocks. I expect that we will start flying early next month. The forestry rangers who are engaged for the summer only will start work next week putting equipment in order for the coming season. Sharpening axes and counting shovels, mattocks, tents, blankets, pots and pans.

They are going to put their log house in order. It was dragged 2 miles last winter over the snow to our new base. It was an extraordinary sight to see this good sized log building being dragged along the road by a tractor.

I am glad that you like the Barrs (new neighbours in Bredgar – Ed) 'and that the Woodham Smiths may be pleasant neighbours too. I read The Story of San Michele the other day. I had had it by me since Al sent it at Christmas. What an extraordinary book. I thought that the author must be a very clever man but rather unpleasant.

love from Marian ... love to all. ...'

(Mr and Mrs Woodham Smith had bought The White House, Bredgar, from Paymaster Admiral Holmes. They lived there only a few years. Mrs Woodham Smith published her life of *Florence Nightingale* in 1950.)

To Emmie:

'Lac du Bonnet, Manitoba. 18th May 1934.

'... I have had two flights, both for the Mines Department, not for the Forestry. I took Mr Cole the Minister for Mines and McColl, Director of Surveys of this Province up to Wallace Lake about 70 miles from here. They wanted to look over some claims – which are in dispute.

The claims are on an island about 3/4 miles long and $\frac{1}{2}$ mile wide in the middle of this lake. They were staked by a man named Ross about two years ago, but he allowed them to lapse while he was on a prospecting trip in the Gods Lake district last fall. A young engineering student named Klempner was the first to restake these claims. The snow was on the ground when he went in.

A week or so after a man named Robinson staked over the same ground. Robinson contends that Klempner failed to comply with the regulations regarding staking, that his posts were not numbered correctly and swore that he did not put any posts in the interior of the islands but only on the shore.

We spent two days, Friday and Sunday, at Wallace Lake.

They found that Klempner had made a few minor errors but they actually found Klempner's posts in the interior.

Cole and McColl were cheerful passengers.

Cole weighs 230 lbs. They call him "Old King Cole" and he looks just like his Majesty, a merry old soul.

The case has not been decided yet.

I have bought an old car, a 1928 Hupmobile ... it has a straight-eight motor, rather a powerful one, but it has six tyres (2 spare wheels), all in good condition – and I can have the old oil from our aeroplanes for nothing. It has to be changed every 25 hours and is otherwise thrown away, but is still quite good for a car....

'... Malcolm Barclay came back from Ilford to-day by train. He said that there was no sign of the ice moving there. It was below zero there on the morning that he came away. He will have to go back either to Ilford or Norway House when the ice goes out. He is hoping for Norway because he will be able to take his wife and little girl there....

It seems that all three aircraft will be here this year....'

To Emmie:

'Lac du Bonnet Manitoba June 6th 1934.

'... The Phinneys – their maid and baby – left on Monday (4th) for Cormorant Lake, which they reached the same day.

Hollingsworth, the new pilot – who took the other machine, had a little trouble & had to spend the night at Norway House but went on yesterday.

This sudden move followed the news that we were to have more Vedettes. Col. Stevenson has been to Montreal & obtained two from the makers (Canadian Vickers) for $5000.

That is actually all he had to spend as the Provincial Govt. is almost bankrupt. One is unused & the other has done 50 hours flying.

The engines & Propellors have been promised by the RCAF who wish to get rid of some of their old equipment.

There is one thing to the good & that is that we understand this type thoroughly & can get the best possible results from it. I am going on a trip to-morrow with one of the forest rangers. . . .'

Emmie had been less than well for several years. Her trip to Berk-hampstead with Alie in 1933 was the last visit she was to make to any of her family.

After his Mother's death in 1934 Charles' stream of letters home did not diminish, for he then wrote almost exclusively to Alie; she always answered his letters with her own long replies.

17

THE AIR-LINE BUSINESS

1934–1938

Unemployment – H. flies for Cobham's Circus – for the Duchess of Bedford –
for United/Hillman/Spartan/British Airways – as Supernumerary Captain
Imperial Airways scouting Empire Air Routes – illness & convalescence –

IF H. was tempted to join Charles in Canada the temptation can have
lasted for no more than a few minutes.

He read Charles' 'Airspeed' letter aloud to us all at the breakfast
table. Paused. Read aloud again: '... if you were at a loose end we
might spend a profitable winter 1934–5, freighting into Red Lake or
Central Manitoba or God's Lake district, or to go further afield up the
Mackenzie or into Great Bear Lake. ...'

The Mackenzie. Great Bear Lake. The names were thrilling. 'Oh –
let's go! Do let's go!' went up the cry. Hermia, however, was silent
and her silences were powerful. Freighting into Red Lake or Central
Manitoba ... the romance of the scheme would surely have attracted
H., for he would have heard tales of the North during his trans-Canada
journeyings in 1910 and again in the 1920's when he had lived in B.C.
He would have heard tales of the Mackenzie, which flowed North and
West from Fort Chipewyan, by Lake Athabasca and on past Great
Bear Lake on it's way to Fort Good Hope and the Mackenzie Delta.
He would have heard stories, and have read others, of Fort Chipewyan,
important assembly point for the Fur Brigade and from whence those
same voyageurs of long ago had raced their bark canoes down to
Grand Portage and thence, by way of the north shore of Lake Superior
and Lake Huron into the Ottawa River and down to Lachine and
Montreal.

The canoe. The snowshoe. The dogsled. Now the aeroplane – trade
and transport – transport, travel and trade. H. would have been in
great sympathy with Charles' idea, the tug of adventure would have
been strong, but reason prevailed and he shook his head slowly: 'I'm

not going to Canada again,' he said. He had observed something of the fallacy of believing that prospects were better in another country. Charles' colleague from High River had thought that England would be easier than Canada – perhaps England was easier than the United States, where the depression still roared. As for poor Chile, the Bolsheviks, it was said, had flooded the country with counterfeit U.S. dollar bills in 1932 and the economy was in a desperate state.

'... A friend of mine writing from Chile ... says that England is a paradise of prosperity by comparison with that country,' H. had written to Emmie.

Taking it all in all, there was a good deal to be said for staying put in the modest comfort of Moor Cottage and in continuing to apply for any likely-sounding job that came up; and Berkhampstead was beautifully near London for interviews. But by the spring of 1934 he still had not found anything.

'What will happen,' I asked him one day, 'if you *don't* get a job?' 'I'll find a job,' he said, '*some* sort of job. It's just that it is such a pity to do so much less than one is capable of doing.' The unhappy decision to do just that was forced upon him eventually, however, for he had no intention of waiting until he had run through every penny of his capital. When April came and still nothing he went to see Cobham. Sir Alan did not forget old friends, particularly not old acquaintances such as the former Blackburn's pilot who had been helpful and courteous to him in Greece.

He could not offer H. anything very inspiring but if H. would care to join the National Air Display as a temporary pilot he could start at once. 'Keep on flying!' was Sir Alan Cobham's motto and it was not such a bad one.

H. joined the National Air Display on 12th April, 1934, at Ford in Sussex. He flew an Avro Cadet 3-seater (Genet Major 130 HP): 'landings for inclusion on "B" and practice.' On the following day, 13th April, he started his summer of flying for Cobham. He had originally been engaged for a fortnight.

He wrote to Emmie on 21st May: '... Many happy returns of the day. What wonderful weather you must be having in the South. Don't let the warm days keep you out too late. The evenings and winds are still cold. We have had a wonderful tour in Scotland though it was cold in the North and high winds nearly everywhere. Since starting we have visited Daghenham (Essex), Guildford, Alton, Devizes, Weston-super-Mare, Bath, Gt. Malvern, Leamington, Birmingham, Leek (Staffs), Lymm (Cheshire), Bolton, Cockermouth, Whitehaven, Carlisle, Barrow-in-Furness, Penrith, Dumfries, Kelso, Lanark, Kirklintillock, Glasgow, Edinburgh (Davidson's Mains), Dundee, Macduff, Huntley, Peterhead, Aberdeen, Inverness, Thurso, Wick, Lossiemouth, Berwick-on-Tweed & here, Tynemouth. We go on to Chester-le-Street, Scunthorpe, Doncaster, Sunderland and so on.

In this year 1934 flying is no novelty but people turn out for a good show of flying as they would for a flower show or a circus. I should say that Cobham and Eskell – the two proprietors are doing well out of it.

I only came into it as a stop gap for 2 weeks and have been here for 5.

The pay is not bad but the personal expenses are very high as one stays at a different hotel every night, and it is not a job which takes me anywhere or has any future.

The aircraft are new and good and well looked after.

It is a great opportunity to see the country but at my age that cannot be one's first consideration.

If I stay with them we shall be in the South of England during the height of the summer season.

Love to you all at Bredgar. . . .'

He flew the Avro Cadet G-ACPB throughout April. Amng the comments in his log-book are:

13th April. Ford to Dagenham, (thick on hills) to opening Display.

14th April. Dagenham local. 3 hours. (28 trips) mostly 2 passengers.

15th April. Clandon local. 2 hours 30 minutes. (31 trips mostly 2 passengers.)

20th April. Gt. Malvern local. (19 trips) mostly 2 passengers (including V. and John.)

At Leamington he made 24 trips, at Birmingham 57 trips, at Leek 28 trips and at Lymm 19 trips. At Lymm he noted: 'New propellor no revs.' At Bolton, where he made only 5 trips 'Bad field, foul spot.' Bolton to Cockermouth was a: 'rough trip.' Carlisle local: '18 trips.' Carlisle to Barrow: 'a memorable journey over lakes.' Penrith local: '19 trips, a grand day in sunshine among the hills.

On the 1st May, still on the same Avro Cadet he flew locally at

Dumfries: '19 trips.' And on the 2nd May, flying to Kelso, he flew: 'over Milkbank & lowlands.' Four years earlier, when he and Hermia had taken a much-needed holiday, they had toured Scotland, travelling up the East Coast and on up to Cape Wrath, descending down the West Coast and staying with many of her kinsfolk and old friends on the way.

Now he was seeing the house and the river Milk once again; perhaps the sight of the river reminded him of quieter pleasures; later on in the summer when he rejoined Cobham's Circus after a short break, he remembered to take his trout rods back with him for the rest of the tour.

At Lanark on the 3rd May be recorded: '36 trips, tail plane damaged by rock thrown up.'
On the 4th May, doing only 6 trips, he borrowed Avro Cadet 3-seater G-ACOZ while repairs were being made to the tail plane of '-PB.'
 At Glasgow he made 44 trips and at Edinburgh 36 trips, noting: 'very strong wind, gale in evening.'
 At Huntley on the 11th May he made 14 trips and at Thurso on the 15th May he made 17 trips, noting: 'wind rain sleet & snow.'
 Ay Lossiemouth on the 18th May he made 40 trips. Once again: 'tail damaged by rock.' And at Berwick-on-Tweed he flew 'evening Display only, repairs to tailplane.'
 At Darlington he made 30 trips and at Sheffield on the following day, 24th May, he made 63 trips. On the 25th May he came home. He was still looking for other work and had been asked to fly as accompanying pilot with Victor Cazalet M.P. in a Monospar.
 He acquainted himself with the machine on the 3rd June: 'Monospar G. 2 × Pobjoy R.'s, each 75 hp. Heston local. 20 minutes. self-landings in B. Law's 2nd Hd. Monospar.'

He flew with Cazalet on the 9th, 10th and 12th June, from Heston to Wexford, Fermoy and Killarney, returning from Wexford via Bristol to Heston. They flew in Cazalet's own Monospar; total flying time 8 hrs. 05 m. On the 15th June he flew as passenger, the pilot being Piper, in a Short Scion from Rochester to Southend and back to Rochester. He was seeing as many people as he could, including Shorts. He wrote to Emmie, from Moor Cottage, on 31st May: '... Thank you very much for the cheese and the Kepler. the cheese we are enjoying. The Kepler will I hope keep to the next batch of colds.

I left Cobham's Air Display for a week to interview some people in London, who had asked me to come down and manage an aeroplane for them. But I cannot find anything but talk.

All through the north of England, and Scotland, people are becoming very interested in air travel and the airlines which have started have made a small profit in several cases. Especially successful is the Highland Airways from Aberdeen – Inverness – Kirkwall which saves about 3 days for the travellers to the Orkneys.

He ran through last winter with surprising regularity. I am now trying to enter the air line business but it is not easy. I do not wish to go back to Cobhams as it does not pay very much after one's day to day expenses and leads nowhere. ...'

But Cobham was keen that H. should rejoin the National Air Display. Although the work itself was rather hackwork the National Air Display was a well-organized concern and one which H. much admired; particularly the thinking behind it all. Aviation was being brought to the people in a most popular way. Scores of people saw their first aeroplane at close quarters and hundreds more had their first flight through Cobham's Circus. Amongst the number who had their first flight with the circus was Miss Sheila Scott although not, by her own description of her pilot, with H. H. was patient with his hundreds of joy-riders and answered their questions with care. It was true that Cobham's showmanship sometimes amused him, but if Cobham had not been such a good showman the National Air Display would not have been the tremendous success which it undoubtedly was. The drive of that one energetic and patriotic man was reminiscent of Grahame-White 22 years earlier. Cobham, like Grahame-White, did much to WAKE UP ENGLAND.

Cobham was only with the Display from time to time, for his lively brain was already busy with his flight refuelling scheme. H. piloted 'Sir A. J. Cobham' from Speke to Hatfield on the 21st July, but apart from that he is not mentioned in the logs.

(It will be remembered that Sir Alan made his first attempt at a long flight, using flight re-fuelling, on the 22nd September, 1934, flying an Airspeed Courier which was refuelled from a Handley Page tanker. The flight broke at Malta.)

When H. rejoined the Circus in late June he determined to keep more of his pay for himself and his family instead of it going on overnight hotel expenses, so he took his little bivvy tent back with him, as well as his valise, Primus stove and Hardy rods. I wrote him long letters during the summer, giving him news of the animals and the garden, and in return H. sent me postcards: a picture of Highland cattle, the mountains behind them, 'By the Loch Side' '. . . After the last mountain Ben Morven we crossed miles & miles of bog cut up by small streams and then Thurso.'

A coloured photograph of the Menai Suspension Bridge posted in Manchester on 28th July: 'Very high. We flew under it with lots to spare – to the surprise of the motor van driver on the bridge.' And late in the summer, from Cornwall, a photograph of a field near which he had pitched his tent the night before and where, at dawn, he had seen a fox steal by.

On the 22nd June he was on Avro Cadet G-ACPB again, joining the Circus at Nottingham. From Nottingham they went to Woodford, Leamington, Ramsey, Blue Barns, Norwich, Blue Barns and via Romford to Penshurst; then Penshurst to Herne Bay, then Petersfield and from Petersfield he took his machine to Woodford on the 29th June: 'for inspection at Avros.'

He remained away from the Display for several days and while the machine was being inspected at Avros he went for his six-monthly medical, which was: 'O.K.'

On the 1st July he was passenger in an Avro 642 18-seater (2 × Jaguar V1 D 430 hp each) from Woodford to Heston. Tompkins was the pilot. They returned to Woodford on 3rd July, again with Tompkins as pilot; and from Woodford H. took Avro Cadet G-ACMG to Sywell – Loughton: 'ferrying Wilson. To fetch Desoutter, not ready.' So returned to Woodford with just Wilson as passenger. On the 4th July G-ACPB was ready again and he flew via Sywell to Southampton: 'returning to N.A.D.' The following day he flew to Havant: 'to fetch Tiger,' and then continued display flying for a further week, at Whitchurch, Bournemouth, Ryde, Shanklin, Wimborne, Blandford; He made two trips from Blandford to Wimborne, fetching: '1). Vickers. 2) Chissell (farmer at Wimborne.)' Then he continued flying at Newbury, Trowbridge, Hanham (Bristol): 'exceptional rising air currents.' From Hanham to High Posts to Southampton, five separate flights, all on 14th July, he recorded: 'searching for Miss Meakin who glided from Hanham to Near High Posts.'

'We were worried about her,' H. said later, 'there were several of us out looking for her . . .' In fact Joan Meakin was found safe and well, much to everyone's relief, late the same day. Her flight, from Hanham to near High Posts, was a British Distance record for a glider pilot.

Then Brooklands, Hanham, Wolverhampton . . .

It was probably from Wolverhampton that H. made one or two courtesy calls on Hermia's uncle Harry Fraser, who subsequently wrote to his neice on the subject from Ryton Rectory: '. . . The friendly plane was here again Monday evening, when I was in the house, I heard it's roar overhead as if it were going to fall upon us. I rushed out & saw it disappearing to the N.W. The servants rushed out & saw it just above the yard close down coming over the trees which are not high. The inhabitants waved their hands, & went on, luckily not toppling down one of my tall chimneys.

I know no one in the air likely to give me a visit except Herbert & yourself. . . . Just round us is now like a bird cage – not agreeable to airmen. There are many pylons – one only 300 yards off, at the end of the field you lighted on when you came.

About the same distance is a transformer with high tension lines & two or three low tension connexions, one to my house. So an over venturesome airman might come to grief . . . Did I tell you I was having a cocktail party? I had one a fortnight ago – & about 50 came, & I was told those who were not invited were very much disappointed. It seems to wake up the neighbourhood, as a change from the dreary tennis parties one has to attend . . .

Earlier in the summer, probably on the flight from Penshurst to Herne Bay, H. had flown over Bredgar. Emmie wrote to him on the 3rd July:

'My dear H. We saw you overhead but I do not know where you are now. . . . I think Alice will perhaps collect some "deeds" at Mr Hovendens & try to fix up to bring Daphe here. To-day the car is having an overhaul at Pullens. I want you to tell me your Bank because when I have a scheme I like to carry it through – so don't forget – I rather liked the snap of Lindsay . . . Much love to all . . .'

One will never know what her scheme was: perhaps the offer of capital towards starting a ferry service of his own, perhaps some help in buying his way into an existing small airline; whatever it was it would have been some scheme that was generous, thoughtful and with H.'s best interests at heart.

Soon after the letter was written she became ill; then somewhat better, exchanging letters with her children and grandchildren as energetically as ever before and making plans for them to visit her; she was so often less than well that when she grew slightly stronger anxiety once more faded. Then, in early September, Alie was taken seriously ill, probably from an untreated appendix; she was always too stoical. H. was still touring and in between Frinton, Yarmouth, Cromer, Hunstanton, Wakefield, Saltburn, Stockton-on-Tees and so forth he was dashing to Bredgar whenever possible or telephoning Moor Cottage for relayed news. Emmie, once again, was very ill.

Worry is no friend to the pilot.

On the day that Alie was undergoing surgery and at a time when V., Jay and a trained nurse were caring for Emmie, H. recorded in his log-book: '12/9/34 Sutton, local, failed to unstick & ran into hedge.'

Another pilot, Bebb, gave him a lift in his Cadet to Ford, where H. collected Avro 504N G-ACPV (Lynx 180 hp), flew her to Sutton and rejoined the Display. On the 14th he was back on another Cadet, G-ACOV, and flew her from Sutton to Northampton. He flew G-ACOV at Northampton, Tunstall, Lincoln, Mablethorpe, Burton-on-Trent, Leicester, Kettering, Coventry, Halton and Slough. On his way from Slough to Hereford he noted: 'Landed in Cotswolds. v. low clouds & poor vis.' After Hereford the Display was at Barry, Port Talbot, Chepstow, and thence to Staines. On the 29th September he flew Avro Lynx G-ACPY from Staines to Brooklands, where he collected the Cadet which he had damaged on the 12th: 'fetch Cadet after repairs.'

The news from Bredgar was very bad indeed and relatives not already there were being sent for. H. flew from Staines to Potten End on the 30th September and came home for a few hours; Hermia had been wondering whether to enlist the services of the British Broadcasting Corporation to make him hurry to Bredgar, since she had been unable to contact him by telephone. Fortunately such a public fuss proved unnecessary.

After flying for the whole afternoon at Romford on the 30th the NAD tour of Cobham's Flying Circus ended.

He flew to Coventry on the 1st October to collect the Avro Cadet G-ACPB and recorded: 'returning Cadet to Woodford for NAD. Forced landing due to bad weather between Coventry and Woodford. Delivered Cadet to Avro's, Woodford.'

Then he went, for the last time, to be at Emmie's bedside.

The eager girl who, in the 1870's, had written to her own Mother '... when Georgy asked why we couldn't get away at the North Pole I could only wish we were able ...' had lived to see her three sons flying and flight itself being a matter of no particular moment; had read of the 1933 flight over the summit of Mount Everest and knew that, in 1934, it was no longer so rare just to fly to Australia for once again men were going to race each other there.

Less than a decade after her death it was generally known in aviation circles that men would be able to reach the moon.

On the 19th October H. & H. went up to Mildenhall for the start of the Mildenhall–Melbourne Air Race.

The race was for the MacRobertson prize of £15,000 given by Sir Macpherson Robertson to mark the centenary of the founding of the State of Victoria and to be a part of the general celebrations.

H. & H. left Moor Cottage at dusk on a bleak autumn evening, taking rugs and Thermos flasks for their overnight drive in the open tourer.

H. had heard from Tom Campbell-Black and from Hubert Broad that de Havs had something very very special in the COMET. He also wanted to see the new passenger-carrying machine from the Douglas Aircraft Company.

The competitors left Mildenhall at dawn on the 20th October and the winner was the de Havilland COMET, the DH88, flown by C. W. A. Scott and Tom Campbell-Black, in a time of 70 hours and 54 minutes.

Although H. had been unemployed since the end of the National Air Display he was kept pretty busy sorting out and helping to oversee the disposal of property and the contents of his mother's house. It was a bitter-sweet day when our share arrived in the Carter Paterson pantechnicons at Moor Cottage; everything which arrived was a treasure from the past, every treasure a reminder that the past was gone for good. The Zoffany went up in the drawing room, the J. F. Herring in the dining room, less beloved pictures everywhere else; the cupboards filled up with silver, much of it uncleaned and never used; and furniture, books and book-cases crowded all the rooms. To Hermia's eternal shame, H.'s treasure, the Nieuport propellor, the spare airscrew from his good friend the Nieuport, was banished to the boxroom. The fact was that Hermia had become excessively nervous lest any of us should show any interest in flying.

Property all settled to the family's satisfaction, H. returned to job-hunting.

One day in late January, 1935, I happened to be near the telephone when it rang. I answered 'Berkhampstead 559.' A woman's voice at the other end of the line announced that it was 'The Duchess of Bedford speaking,' and that she would like to talk to Major Travers. He was in London for the day, seeing people at the Aero Club, still looking for a job. Hermia took over and explained and the Duchess rang back in the evening, spoke to H., and asked him if he would pilot her. A tentative plan was made but the weather closed in and the proposed flight was postponed.

The Duchess wrote to H. on 1st February:

Woburn Abbey, Bletchley.

Dear Mr Travers,

Your address was given me as 'Major' and the telephone calls you 'Mr' so I am giving you one of each until I know better.

I am afraid the weather is not at all promising for the particular purpose for which I wanted to go to Littlestone viz a little sea bird watching, but I had also done very little flying lately and the birds were really an excuse for the flight.

I must ring you up in the morning – also if we go, learn whether you would like us to send for you or whether you would prefer to motor yourself over.

Yours sincerely

M. Bedford.

The mist lifted the following day and there was quite a wind, but not too much to fly. H. recorded:

2/2/35. Gypsy Moth Gypsy 90 h.p. engine. Woburn – Littlestone. 50 minutes. Self for take-offs. With the Duchess of Bedford. Her Grace flew most of the way.

Littlestone – Woburn. 1 hour 55 minutes. Self and landings. Very strong NW wind.

The wind had cleared away the sea birds but the flight had been a success and the Duchess asked him to fly with her again; he expressed himself delighted to do so; she was a tremendous character and it had all been rather an adventure. The Duchess wrote again on 6th February: '... I have been hoping to hear how much I am indebted to you for flying with me on Saturday. Please may I hear?'

As no payment had been discussed when they met this was a nice sequel and after much heart-searching and bearing in mind that they were using the Duchess' own aircraft, fuel, etc. he finally decided on what he thought was a fair sum to ask. She wrote again on the 8th February: '... In view of what others have asked me for similar services in the past, I really cannot accept the estimated value of your own and have ventured to double the amount of the cheque....'

'She is a brick,' said H. The cheque that the Duchess sent him would seem small in modern values, but in 1935 it would have bought at least a ton of best coal, or would have paid a quarter of the yearly rates. Her thoughtful action touched him deeply. When autumn came the Duchess telephoned again two or three times, but although H. would have really enjoyed flying with her again (self for take-offs and landings) – he was by then flying for an airline and could not get away.

He was genuinely very sad when in March, 1937 she was lost. He too had experienced fierce and unpredictable air currents, thermals and draughts on that part of the coast surrounding The Wash and over which she had disappeared: 'they toss you about like a cork,' he said, adding that he had never found such dangerously unpredictable conditions anywhere else around our coasts. Another possibility and one he considered even more probable was that the Duchess, an old lady, had been taken ill. She did not like to fly alone partly perhaps because she may have thought of such a thing happening.

Although the rest of us had never met her we had most of us spoken to her over the telephone from time to time. When she was lost we were all aware that someone rather remarkable had gone for good. I have sometimes thought of her since and have hoped that she was unconscious when she went in.

H. was angry when some newspaper reporters suggested that she might have deliberately taken her own life: H. was perfectly sure that she would have done no such thing.

Throughout the spring of 1935 H. hunted for a job. There is no longer any record of how many jobs he went for and came home without. Bill Oliver remembers meeting him in the outer office of one of the ferry services. They were both after the same job. Neither of them were lucky that day. They never met again.

There was a fete in aid of the Conservative Party before the general election, and H. borrowed a Spartan to give joy rides at the fete. Mrs Deen asked him to lunch on the day, so it was arranged that he would land in one of her fields first of all before taking the aircraft on to Potten End, where the fete was to be held.

The field at Berkhamsted Hill, where he was to land first of all, was a long, rather narrow field, stretching along roughly to the South of the New Road, (which runs from Berkhampstead Castle to the Inns of Court Monument). He had telephoned us before take-off to say that he would be landing by about 1.30. Christina, Betty and I went over to the field, a scant quarter of a mile away, to greet him there. The Bedworth twins, Pat and Pam, who were about my age and who lived in a tall, brick house close by the Golf club, joined us at the stile to wait for him.

I could not see how he was going to get in. The field was like a narrow shelf; one can only suppose that to a pilot of nerve and experience it had its advantages, very short taxying distance on take-off being the most obvious.

A little way into the field from where we girls waited there stood a water-trough for cattle. It was a permanent trough with water piped into it and was a thoroughly heavy-looking and immovable object.

After circling the field H. brought the machine in from the North. We saw the top of the Spartan coming up the side of the shelf towards us. He began zig-zagging as he taxied towards us but as he drew nearer Pat Bedworth became alarmed in case he had not, after all, seen the water-trough. She bounded over the stile, she shouted and jumped about and waved her arms. 'Come back!' I yelled, thinking of the propellor, but she would not do so until she was sure that H. had seen her and noticed the danger. After he had switched off and picketed the Spartan he spoke to us. He had seen the water-trough from the air and had observed it all along as he zig-zagged towards us: there was no need for Pat to be so anxious. Still he was impressed by her presence of mind.

Later on he remarked to us at home that if there were more Pat Bedworths there would be fewer taxying accidents.

He lunched with Mrs Deen that day and then flew to the field at Potten End to give joy-rides for the afternoon.

None of those flights were logged.

The first flights to be logged (after flying from Woburn to Littlestone Woburn in February), were in late July.

He made a couple of flights in a privately-owned Puss Moth G-ACYT, from Heston to Ford and return.

Then he took a blind flying refresher course.

He did 2 hours and 5 minutes dual and then three separate 30-minute solo flights on the 27th July, from Redhill, on Gipsy Moth G-ABZE. Bulstrode is mentioned and was almost certainly H.'s blind flying instructor. Bulstrode also took him up for a '5-minute joyride' in 'Autogiro. Genet Major 130 h.p. Redhill. Local.'

H. went to Hanworth on the 29th July:

'BAM Eagle. Gypsy Major 130 h.p. Hanworth. Local.' He made a number of flights on this machine, after a demonstration by Vaughan Fowler, then flew the Eagle (G-ADGJ): 'self with and without load. Working retractor gears and landings for "B".' This is the first record of H. piloting a machine having retractable undercarriage; although still unusual on British machines, the Douglas Aircraft Company had introduced such gears on their DC1 in 1931 and that machine, which had first been seen in England in 1933, had been much admired by the Airspeed Company.

The Airspeed Company were probably the first British designers to introduce retractable undercarriage.

H. joined Spartan Air Lines on the 6th August, on a temporary basis, and having familiarised himself with a type new to him, the DH Dragon (2 × Gipsy Major 130 h.p.), G-ACNI at Heston on that date: '3 landings light and 3 loaded' he began flying for them on the 7th: 'Southampton–Cowes–Sandown' all the flights in ballast and with numerous landings. On the 9th he flew Spartan Cruiser G-ACVT 3 × Gipsy Major 3 × 130h.p. locally at Southampton and later the same day made the first three of many ferry flights that he was to make for Spartan Air Lines, in the Dragon G-ACNI, from Southampton.

He had entered the air line business.

He flew the Spartan Cruiser and the Dragon alternately, flying anything from 1 hour to 8 hours per day. It was a local ferry service – but already beginning to expand its business. H. wrote to Alie on the 19th August: 'c/o Spartan Air Lines, Cowes, I. of Wight.

My dear Sloper.... 'Yes I have been busy here we work on a rosta and I am off this afternoon. At present very easy work in the fine weather just Sandown Cowes Southampton and return. sometimes as many as eight Ferry trips per day. Engagement only temporary in the beginning. As soon as I have my W/T licence I am to go to Blackpool for the I. of Man service....

He was given his W/T licence on the 22nd August, 1935. It was number 265.

He continued on the same route, flying the same aeroplanes, (except for once when he flew a different Spartan Cruiser, G-ADEL,) throughout August and into September. On the 24th August, when piloting Dragon G-ACNI, he recorded: 'delayed at S'ton by bird sucked into air intake after taking off. Landed with one engine.'

Although one has read of birds attacking aeroplanes, – an Italian pilot was attacked by eagles as early as 1912, it was sufficiently unusual, (to have a bird sucked into the air intake), for him to recount the incident to several of his flying friends. I cannot find a record of the first occasion when such a thing happened.

He continued to fly the scheduled ferry services as before until the 6th September, when he flew Spartan Cruiser G-ADEL on the London service: 'Lea–Cowes–Heston–Bembridge–Cowes–Lea' returning to the local 'Lea–Cowes–Southampton–Cowes Lea' service on the Dragon G-ACNI on the 7th September and returning once more to the London service on Spartan Cruiser G-ADEL on the 8th September. There appears to be no further talk of the I. of Man Service for a while. It was the mixture as before, with the London Service once or twice a week. On the 13th September he noted that: 'Operations base transferred to Cowes.'

He wrote to Alie on the 24th September, on Spartan Air Lines Limited writing paper, which gave their address as 'Somerton Aerodrome, Cowes, Isle of Wight.

'... I do not know whether I shall be taken on more permanently by these people. It is a small job and when I was taken on originally it was made very clear that it was only temporary – a lot of hanging about now that holiday makers are gone home and fewer services running so v. little flying pay. But no definite notice of termination yet. I should not write on the firm's paper but it is the only available. Hope J. is feeling better. Love to both. I did a London service on Sat. returning Sunday morning and saw Hermy and the family. Hope the little rose trees arrived safely. Change them if not suitable – HO.

There was little variation in the routine of the scheduled ferry services except that he was, as he had written to Alie, doing less flying now that most of the holiday makers had gone home. Two or three hours a day was now usual.

On the 25th September he flew 'Spartan Arrow GABOB (1 Gipsy III × 120 h.p.): Cowes–S'ton–Cowes 25 minutes. Self. Special charter with keys to *Majestic*.' How I wish that I could remember the long and complicated story, one worthy of P. G. Wodehouse, which lay behind the special charter to *Majestic*, but I cannot.

On the 26th September he took G-ACNI up for 15 minutes 'to shew McIntosh landing of Dragon.' He probably then handed over to McIntosh, for he left the Isle of Wight service of Spartan Air Lines. It had, after all, been only a summer job. He went to Redhill and flew there from the 28th September to the 4th October inclusive flying a total of over 10 hours: 'Self and Bulstrode. Course of instruction as Instructor in blind flying.' For the course he flew either Moth G-AAVV or Moth G-ABZE 'Redhill local.' On the 5th he flew a Blackburn B2 Trainer locally at Hanworth: 'Norman Woodhead & self. Test for Instructor and Blind Flying Instructor.'

Following that successful test he became 'attached to United Airways Ltd.' at Blackpool. United Airways was part of or was itself attached to Spartan Air Lines. He began flying on United Airways scheduled services on the 11th October, but he only flew for them for a couple of days before there was a further change of plan by his employers. He flew Spartan Cruiser 'G-ACZM (Gipsy Major 3 × 130 h.p.) from Blackpool–Liverpool. Liverpool–Blackpool. Blackpool–

Ramsey' on the 11th flying 'ZM back from Ramsey to Blackpool on the 12th. Then, later on the 12th, he flew a DH Moth G-AAYY (Gipsy 11 120 h.p.) from Blackpool down to Stapleford, then on to Brooklands. On the 13th October he made his first trip on Hillman Airways scheduled run from Stapleford to Paris, flying as 2nd pilot to Wilson in a DH86 G-ADEB (Gipsy Six 4 × 200 h.p.). It was the first of many such flights. Hillman Airways, too, were attached to, or were a proliferation of Spartan Air Lines. Hillman's had three DH 86's: 'EA, 'EB and 'EC and he and Wilson flew them all in turn and as required.

He wrote to Alie on the 20th October, from Moor Cottage:
My dear Sloper,

I was only a few days in the north and then loaned to Hillman's who are short of holders of navigator's licences which must be included in the crew of machines going abroad over 100 miles journey.

So I have been 2nd pilot on the 4 engine DH86 running from Stapleford (Essex) to Le Bourget (Paris). When on the morning service we come back the same afternoon. On the afternoon service we stay the night and come back next day. When in England I have driven home but 40 miles is a longish trip to have to make frequently. When in Paris we get £1 a night which covers our expenses. I have been at this new job since the beginning of the week. Friday last week in fact. Last Thursday we had the afternoon when arrived at Stapleford on Friday morning went out again but brought the afternoon service home on Saturday so had last night at home – am just off again now.

Thank goodness the m/c's are fast so the big head wind last night only made us $\frac{1}{4}$ hour late. i.e. 2 hrs for the journey instead of 1 hr.45. We frequently make it in 1 hr. 30 if the wind is favourable.

The route we take is Stapleford, Tilbury, Maidstone, Rye, Le Treport Beauvais Paris and go high if the weather below is rough or cloudy.
In great haste.
Your affect. bro HO.

On the 25th October he familiarized himself with: 'DH89. Rapide G-ACPN. (2 × 200 h.p. Gipsy Six) at Stapleford for 30 minutes.' There were some aeroplanes in H.'s flying days that were just so good as to be hard to compare with those of lesser design; a smile would flood his face when he spoke of the Rapide, that aeroplane of such happy design.

Later on the 25th October he flew a Puss Moth G-ABVX with a Gipsy III (120 h.p.) engine down to Reading and back to Stapleford on a 'special charter', then on the 26th he began taking the Rapide G-ADAJ out on the daily scheduled service from Stapleford to Brussels. He flew 'AJ until the 4th November, Rapide G-ACPO on the 4th and 5th November and Rapide GADAG from the 7th to the 18th November.

(The DH89 Dragon-Rapide was usually known as the Rapide.)

On the 11th November he wrote to Alie from Moor Cottage:

My dear Sloper and Jess,

Thanks for the Hovey letter and amended a/cs which I return herewith.

Back from Brussels again today & as the afternoon service had no passengers, I did not return thither this afternoon but came home for the night.

I never know before hand at which end I shall spend the night. It depends on bookings by passengers. There are only two pilots in this service and we start from opposite ends at approximately the same hour. So though I do not always fly both ways in the day yet I have not yet had a day off.

There is a lot of shuffling about with the amalgamation of United, Spartan and Hillman's Air Lines. I do not have any hopes of profit as to myself as I am a bad lobbyist. . . .

H. was careful of those who flew with him; not only from a normal sense of responsibility but, equally, from an awareness that they were the thin stream who would, one day and if all went well, turn into a flood-tide of airline passengers. Aeroplanes would continue to become larger and with a longer range; weather stations, wireless and other navigational aids would be improved. Development may not have been at the phenominal rate of the first twenty years of the century but steady progress was still being made.

Meanwhile he continued to 'gang warily.' One of his own safety dodges, while supervising refuelling of his aircraft, was to ensure that all petrol was strained through the chamois leather which he kept solely for the purpose, washing it out and drying it carefully each time he was at home.

One day in November 1935 he had a macabre adventure. He recounted it to me soon afterwards when we were driving home from Berkhamstead, where we had been doing a little shopping. Briefly, the story was this: There was a house which was being built close to the aerodrome. (I have a memory of him mentioning that it was at Croydon, but as his logs show him to have landed more frequently at Stapleford, it may have been by the latter aerodrome.) It was an attractive, well-built house and H. had watched it's progress with interest. The houses which he had built for himself on Point Grey some fifteen years earlier had given him some knowledge of construction. He liked the way they were putting the roof on. He liked the colour of the tiles. He knew, every day or so, the exact state of the work and what stage had been reached.

Coming home one day from Brussels, fog closed in. He had passengers on board. He arrived over the aerodrome on time and began to circle it. He knew where he was over the surface of the earth and he knew how many feet up he was. He was not, technically speaking, lost, but he was in a dense white-out and might as well have been blind.

Round and round he went. Round and round. 'It was unpleasant,' he said, 'things looked rather shaky for a time.'

He said that he would have taken a chance of getting down had he been alone, but he had three passengers on board, fare-paying air line passengers.

Then through the swirl of white he caught a glimpse of the partly-tiled roof on the nearly-completed house before it was once more blanketed out by fog. As he knew the exact relationship of house to aerodrome he was safely down within minutes, his passengers unaware that he had been in any difficulty. The house had been like a guiding hand. It had made him think again, he said, about an idea that had been in his mind for some time. Now the plan was firming up. At home he had often said: '. . . if only there was someone on the ground to talk to. . . .' Now he went on: 'How reassuring it would be, to have someone on the ground, telling you exactly where you were, someone on the ground who knew where the aircraft was and who could say over the wireless to the pilot – forward a little, left a little, down a little. . . .' Even as he spoke he was developing the plan further in his mind: 'One would have to have people at two separate points,' he continued, 'but I'm sure that it's an idea that could be workable . . . to have someone on the ground as you were coming in. . . .' The following year he mapped out his plan, the plan which somebody else, not he, was to label 'talk-down', and tried to sell it to the Air Ministry. But they were not then interested.

Hillman's operated four Rapides during the months that H. was with them, G-ADAJ, G-ADAG, G-ACPO and G-ACPN, all with two Gipsy Six engines, and he flew them all at different times; they were all good, well-maintained aircraft and he had no trouble of any kind with any of them. He loved the Rapide.

His last flight for Hillman's was when he flew G-ACPN back from Brussels to Stapleford on the 22nd December. Then he wrote at the foot of the page: 'End of service with Spartan att'd United att'd British Airways att'd Hillmans' and came home for Christmas.

Opening his mail one morning, he said: 'Geddes wants to see me.'

'Geddes?' repeated Hermia slowly, 'Geddes? – I hope that you won't think it necessary to go?'

'I may as well hear what he has to say,' replied H. cautiously.

When he came home from London after his meeting with Sir Eric he looked like the cat that took the cream.

Sir Eric was Chairman of Imperial Airways. As was well known, Imperials were planning to open their Empire air routes the following year and although Imperials had plenty of good and experienced pilots, many of them were weak on their navigation.

Sir Eric offered H. the job of giving advanced navigational instruction to the existing Imperial Airways pilots. He offered H. £700 per annum, and the rank of Captain, to fly as supernumerary Captain with the existing Captains and give them navigational training in flight.

Over the evening meal Hermia began a long diatribe against Geddes.

'Now, my dear,' said H. gently, 'no man quarrels with his bread-and-butter.'

'Nor with his wife's bread-n-butter nor with all his little bread-n-butters,' chipped in Betty, earning for herself one of those glittering glares from Hermia which her ability to hit the nail on the head so often provoked.

H. was joyous, determined not to be made miserable while he was still basking in his good fortune at having been offered such an interesting job, and when Hermia persisted in her hymn of hate against Geddes, H. rejoined with a surprisingly tuneful rendition of 'I won't let you play in my yard, you can't climb my apple tree, I won't let you play in my yard if you won't be nice to me. . . .'

H. would have no doubt seen old colleagues, such as Major H. G. Brackley, DSC etc. (also an ex-RNAS pilot,) as well as other Imperial Airways people, before or at the same time as his interview with Sir Eric, but it was Sir Eric's name only which caused Hermia such annoyance. Undoubtedly the underlying cause of her being so upset was the fact that H. was continuing to fly when she wished so fervently that he would give it up. She came round, of course, and although she had wandered about muttering 'Geddes! How COULD you!' for several days, by the time H. had been up to London and had come home with six new shirts from Austin Reeds, of a pleasant and practical grey-blue colour and with soft collars, (comfortable on long flights,) and with a handy new Course & Distance computer which he put away, to be ready, in his well-polished old leather briefcase, she gave every appearance of being reconciled to Imperial Airways in general and to their Chairman in particular.

There were four spaces in the pages of a pilots log book for 'Name and Address of Present Employer.'

In H.'s sixth log-book the entries ran thus:
1. London Aeroplane Club 119 Piccadilly W1.
2. Nat. Aviation Day (temporary).
3. Spartan Air Lines (& associates).
4. Imperial Airways Ltd. (and subsidiaries).

He was entering the service of the premier, flag-carrying, airline of Great Britain and the Empire. They would soon be crossing the Atlantic on a regular scheduled run. The prospects looked good and he was very happy.

He had made four flights with them, presumably before his contract was agreed, on the 4th January. These were:

Vickers Vellox. 2 × 800 h.p. Pegasus engines. Croydon. Local. 10 minutes. Youell and self. Circuit and landing.

Short Calcutta. G.EBYG. 3 × 850 h.p. Tigers. Rochester local. 20 minutes. Major Brackley. Self as crew.

Short Calcutta. G-EBYG.ditto.ditto. 30 minutes. Major Brackley and self as 2nd pilot and crew.

Short Calcutta.G-EBYG. Rochester–Hamble. 1½ hours. Middleton Armstrong. Self as passenger.

He began flying and instructing regularly with them on the 1st February, but if his earlier methods of instruction are anything to go by, he had probably already given a short course of lectures to the pilots on the ground. No such lectures are mentioned in his log-book, of course, and their existence can only be guessed at.

The log-book, once again, can take up the story:

1/2/36. H.P. 42 G.AAXD* 4 × Jupiter. Croydon–Paris. 2 hrs. 08 min. Capt. Horsey – self as supernumerary captain. (Handley-Page 42. Built at Radlett. Metal biplane. 4 × 550 h.p. Jupiter engines.)

2/2/36. H.P. 42. G.AAXD. Paris–Croydon. 0935–1216 2 hrs. 41 mins. Capt. Horsey. Self as supernmry captain.

8/2/36. H.P. 42. G.AAXC. 4 × Jupiter. Croydon–Paris. 1900–2143 2 hrs 43 min. Capt. Tweedie. Self as supnmry captain.

9/2/36. H.P. 42. G-AAXC. Paris–Croydon. 0930–1104. 1 hr 34 min. Capt. Tweedie. Self as supnmry captain.

11/2/36. H.P. 42. G-AAXC. 4 × Jupiter. Croydon–Paris 0900–1202. 3 hours 02 mins. Capt. Walters.

11/2/36. H.P. 42. G-AAXC. Paris–Croydon. 12.32–1426. 1 hr. 54 min. Capt. Walters. (Self as sup. captain – made landings at Paris and Croydon and take-off at Paris.)

On the flights on the 12th, 13th and 14th February, the aircraft used was DH86 G.ACUF. 4 × Gipsy Six engines. His pupil was Capt. Holmes. Together they flew: Croydon–Paris. (Detained by weather south of Paris). To Marseilles 3 hours 12 minutes. Marseilles to Rome 2 hrs 48 min. (They stayed overnight in Rome.) Rome to Marseilles 2 hours 55 min. Marseilles to Paris 2 hrs 47 mins. Paris to London (Croydon) 1 hour 17 minutes.

He was home, then, for a couple of days, bringing with him a cluster of Christmas fruits, tangerines. The tangerines were not in a silver paper wrapping, which was the only way any of us had seen tangerines before but were on their own twig and still, as it were, alive, with their leaves still on. He had picked them in Rome the same morning; it seemed to us almost unbelievable. 'There will come a time when such a thing will be thought quite commonplace,' he said.

On the 19th February he flew with Acting Captain Oliver at Croydon, locally, in DH86 G.ADFF; he also made a number of light landings with himself as pilot. On the 20th a number of landings loaded on the same machine. On the 22nd he was away again:

22/2/36 DH86 G.ADVE 4 × Gipsy V1 Groydon–Paris. Paris–Marseilles. 5 hours 40 minutes.'

23/2/36 G.ADVE. Marseilles – Rome 2 hours 45 minutes. Captain Wilkins piloted on these three flights: Self as passenger. From Rome he must have caught a train across to Brindisi. The next flight were instructional ones:

25/2/36. Short Kent FB G.ABFC. 4 × Jupiter. Brindisi–Athens 3 hours 40 minutes. (1 hour). Capt. Bailey. 1st Off Stacey. Self as supern. pilot. flew boat for 1 hour.

They then took the boat, Short Kent S C I P I O from Athens to Mirabella (Crete), a flight of 1 hour 40 minutes, of which he flew the boat for 30 minutes and then on from Mirabella to Alexandria, a flight of 3 hours 10 minutes, of which he flew the boat for 1 hour.

On the 26th February, with Capt. Messenger as pilot, they flew Handley P. 42 Hengist GAAXE 4 × Jupiter from Alexandria to Heliopolis a flight of 1 hour 20 minutes and on the 27th took the same aircraft, this time with Capt. Egglesfield as pilot, from Heliopolis to Luxor. 1st Off. Klein joined for that trip which was of 2 hours 35 minutes duration. The same crew continued from Luxor to Wadi Halfa, a flight of 2 hours and 25 minutes, and then there was a change of crew as they changed aircraft once again. Capt. Algar was the pilot, accompanied by 1st Officer Hoare, who took Handley Page 42 H E L E N A G.AAXF on the 3 hour flight from W. Halfa to Luxor. H. had taken a turn at the controls on each of the earlier flights and he flew for an hour and fifteen minutes of H E L E N A's flight to Luxor.

On the 28th the same crew took G.AAXF H E L E N A from Luxor to Heliopolis, a flight of 3 hours, of which H. flew for an hour and a half. At Heliopolis the crew changed and Capt. Foy, with H. as passenger, flew G. AAXF from Heliopolis to Alexandria, a flight of one hour and fifteen minutes.

29/2/36 Short Calcutta GEBTZ 3 × Jupiter Alexandria–Crete (Mirabella) 3 hours 24 minutes (1 hour) Capt. Gurney. 1st Officer Stacey.

Self as supernumerary. Crete–Greece 2 hours 12 minutes (40 minutes).
Greece (Elensis Bay)–Brindisi 4 hours 16 minutes (40 minutes).

The figures in brackets record the length of time that H. flew the boat.

He travelled by train from Brindisi to Paris, a journey surely reminiscent of those he had made ten years earlier when he had been with Blackburn's; and then made his way home from Paris by air:

5/3/36 Scylla. 'JT 4 × Jupiter Paris–London. Capt. Horsey. 1st Officer Woodhouse. Self as passenger.

His job with the Captains completed he then began a new job for Imperials: navigation instruction to the younger, or more junior, Imperial Airways pilots at Croydon; and assessment of new or better navigational systems. Imperials had bought some Westland Wessex aircraft and H. found these excellent for the work he was engaged on. Nowadays 'Westland Wessex' more usually describes a helicopter but in those days the Wessex was a six-seat, three-engined high wing monoplane. An ugly, sturdy-looking beast.

12/3/36. Wessex. G.ACHI 3 × Genet 7 Majors 3 × 125 h.p. Croydon local 44 minutes. 3 landings light and 3 loaded.' It was his usual familiarization flight on a type that was new to him. On the afternoon of the same day he recorded: 'DH86a GADFJ 4 × Gipsy Six 4 × 185 h.p. 41 minutes. self giving 1st Officer Jeffries landings.'

One day in March when I spent a couple of hours at Croydon (in transit to stay with V. at Malvern Wells), H. shewed me over the Wessex. The one we looked at was in a hanger. I climbed into the cabin and sat, as directed, on the single seat behind and midway between the two side-by-side seats which was where the pilots under instruction sat. The single seat, which was slightly raised, left little room for one's head. 'Isn't it excellent?' said H., 'one has a good central view of the instruments and yet one is not in the way of the pilots. One is able to instruct without getting in their way. You see how good an arrangement it is?'

I was 14 years old and not of excessive size for my age, being about 5′ 4″ and about 8½ stone; yet I was conscious of being very much squashed up in that single seat, my head bent forward just underneath the cabin roof, and when H. asked again what I thought I replied with my usual tactlessness that there did not seen to be much room.

He laughed and said that there was plenty of room, plenty. . . .

His flights down through France to Rome and from Brindisi on down to Alexandria had given him a good idea of present conditions and facilities on part of the route that the Empire Flying Boats were going to take. He had also improved the navigational skill of those pilots already mentioned. Later on there would be crossings of the Atlantic by gentle stages.

For the time being he was to continue to instruct in navigation and he would do that from Croydon.

'I hope that your new job is going well and that you like it,' wrote Charles from The Pas, Manitoba, at the end of January. . . .

D. C. Bennett joined Imperials at about that time.

H. liked the frankly-spoken young Queenslander and was, both then and in later years, one of his greatest admirers.

One of the machines on which H. was to instruct was 'GW. I had remembered that her six seats were divided (3 and 3) by an especially constructed bulkhead; and on inquiry to Westland Helicopters (formerly Westland Aircraft Co) recently, have been told that such a bulkhead was unusual and not normally made. The probable reason would have been to separate pilots under instruction in the 3 forward seats from any passengers, or other Imperial Airways personnel, in the 3 aft seats.

Before 'GW was ready H. took a pupil, Capt. J. Oliver, on a flight of 1 hour 20 minutes in 'Viastra. G-ACCC 2 × Pegasus engines. Croydon–Slough–Croydon.' On the 24th March he made a number of tests on 'GW, the re-built Wessex: 'Self. 1st test after rebuild. No load.' 'Self. Full load. Defective instruments.' Further tests followed, one flight with a pupil having to be stopped because 'C of A missing.' However he eventually got into his stride and settled down to instruct for the spring and summer.

Although he flew Wessex G-ACHI occasionally, it was the rebuilt G-AAGW who did most of the work. Some pupils were rapid learners, others more slow – if the frequency with which their names appeared is anything to go by. Among H.'s pupils were many of the finest pilots in the land; it was a rewarding time for him to be among so many like-minded and able pilots. Among the names of his pupils are those of V. G. Parker, E. G. Reed and M. Sorbie; Brunton, Riley, Coulson, Bennett, Lines, Dykes and Andrews; D. C. Harrison, Abrahams, Banks, Garner and Kyrke-Smith. When flying with Garner, on the 5th May, he recorded: 'Self and Garner. Child's kite at 2,000 ft over Clapham common.'

Other pupils included Hill, Movatt, McGinn, Messiter.... W/T operators are often mentioned as being aboard and he and they were no doubt trying out different systems. On the 15th May he flew DH Rapide, G-AEAJ locally at Croydon for an hour and eleven minutes: 'Self and W/T op + 2 Marconi Test. Overload to 1,400 lbs.' On the 18th May he flew Rapide G-AEBW locally at Croydon for half an hour: 'self and 2 W/T op. Acceptance Test.' And the same day flew Rapide G-ACPR for nearly half an hour: 'self and operator acceptance test.' Then on the 19th he was back on old Wessex GW again, instructing as he did most days of the week. This time giving Hanbury two flights to Redhill and back and many landings at Redhill.

He made an odd sort of entry on the 27th May, flying Wessex G-AAGW for 1 hour 35 minutes: 'self Hatchett and operator. Test of Plessey. (*Queen Mary* leaves for NY).' It was almost unknown for him to have put any extraneous note in his log; perhaps there was some wireless significance? Or, more remotely, the notion that Imperials were going to have to hurry up with their Transatlantic run. How amused they all would have been to see how cleverly Cunards have adapted to modern times and have made a feature of the *slowness* of a crossing by the QE2, pointing up such leisurely journeying by advertising a return Atlantic flight by Concorde.

There were numerous further tests of Plessey equipment, some when accompanied by 'Imps' some when 'Plessey' were on board, some when Engineer Atkins and/or W/T oerator were on board. It would appear that they were between them ironing out problems, for various tests, which involved some long flights, to Cardiff or to Belfast, for instance, or 'Croydon, Shoreham, Ryde, Bristol, Liverpool, Manchester' and so forth continue to have been undertaken during the first part of June.

On the 12th June he flew 'GW from Croydon to Selsey, Southampton and back to Croydon with Hatchett, Haggar and Carning (Plessey) also on board.

Other pupils during June were Needham, Frost, Nicholas, Greenshields, and on the 16th June, made two flights of over two hours on 'GW Greenshields and Robson (AMEDO) making further W/T tests. On the 18th he made a number of flights on the same machine, to Bristol, Exmouth, Bristol local and then home to Croydon again with 'self. Nicholas. 1st Off. Finch and Carning. W/T and DF test and practice.'

It was undoubtedly very important work but one can only guess at the sustained discomfort of their conditions during those longish flights. The third seat in the forward compartment of the Wessex was only suitable for a child; yet it was where H. sat throughout the W/T and DF testing flights. True, they did not always go as far afield as Bristol, Liverpool or Manchester, but flights to Hatfield and Rochester were quite common. H. began to feel a few twinges of rheumatism across his shoulders. We were all so used to seeing him rub away at the top of his right arm, in which any remaining lumps of metal must long ago have become encapsulated, that we did not think it so very unusual that he should ask, now and again, to be helped into his overcoat. He grew quieter in manner and often seemed worried. One day, when I was at Croydon with him, he took me to see Jim's grave.

Croydon Airport was an interesting place in those days, truly international.

I once stood beside H. in the long bar at the Aerodrome Hotel and heard him exchange greetings with pilots from the airlines of Holland, France, Germany and Switzerland. All the pilots – save occasionally the French, who were often rather reserved – seemed to be on the very best of terms. There was a professional camaraderie born out of mutual respect. Jolliest of all were the pilots of Swissair.

Hearing how interested H. was in the Douglas, (he had admired the one that he had seen at Mildenhall in 1934 very much,) – they invited him on a flight with them. His log-book records:

30/6.36. Swissair Douglas HB.ITA 2 × Wright Cyclone 2 × 800 h.p. Croydon–Zurich 3 hours (30 minutes) Ackerman, Mittelholzer, Xell and self.' (The Douglas would have been a DC2.)

'1/7/36. Swissair Douglas HBITO 2 × 200 h.p. Wright Cyclone engines. Zurich–Basel–Croydon. 3 hrs 20 mins. Heitmaneck op.' Mittelholzer was a great character, by all accounts, and was a most enthusiastic advocate of airlines in general and Swissair in particular. H. had a memorable flight to Zurich and back in the Douglas with him and saw (I gathered for the first time) the automatic pilot or 'George the robot pilot' in action and on the Douglas as part of standard equipment. He talked often about Mittelholzer and his enjoyable flight in the Douglas.

(When I was hoping for a flight to Switzerland with Swissair in 1947 H. wrote to me: '. . . my old friend Mittelholzer was killed in the Alps some time ago.')

On the 2nd July he was back on Wessex G-ACHI and instructing again. 'Self and Klein', 'Self and Klein and Hill', and 'Self and Hill' on the usual navigational training flights to Redhill and back, later the same day taking Wessex 'GW down to Cardiff with 'Greenshields self and operator' on board.

He was instructing on a DH86a, G-ADUF, all the 5th July, locally at Croydon: '1 hour 37 minutes. Self, Klein, Nicholas, Reid, Greenshields.' '49 minutes. Self and Nicholas. 6 landings.' '40 minutes. Self and Klein. 5 landings.' '08 min. Self and Reid. 1 landing.' '21 min. Self and Nicholas.(Full load. 2 landings.)'.

On the 6th July he spent what must have been some enjoyable time at Rochester. The Empire flying boats were the great new project for Shorts, commissioned by Imperial Airways in 1935. The first of these new boats, S.23 C-Class boats, was 'HL, later named *Canopus* and she first flew on the 3rd July 1936.

He flew over to Rochester on Wessex G-ACHI, with Stone as a pupil and Mrs Robson as passenger. After landing at Rochester, to call for a cameramen, they flew locally at Rochester, no doubt up and down the River Medway: 'photos of Empire boat.' Then they landed again at Rochester for more photographs and to land the cameraman before flying back to Croydon.

I have sometimes wondered which of the many beautiful photographs of *Canopus*, some of them from little more than river-height, were taken on that particular photographic run for Imperial Airways. I cannot remember details of H.'s conversation with Major Brackley and with Lankester Parker that day, but he was very excited about the Empire boat. When Hermia saw one of the photographs which had been taken ashore on that day she said: 'How good it is of you!'

'That's not me,' said H. in amusement, – 'that's the young Queenslander, the Australian I was telling you about – Bennett.'

Bennett and H. were not really alike. It was an illusion caused by similar height, regular features and Imperial Airways uniform. There was a difference, too, of at least twenty years in their ages.

Instruction continued on that day as it did on most days, with mostly local flying which included numerous landings.

On the 10th July, in Wessex GACHI, he flew from Croydon to Barton: '2 hours 20 minutes. Self. Frost Greenshields and operator Newton.' – flying on the same day from Barton to Speke with 'self Matthews and Greenshields,' returning again with 'self and passengers'. On the 11th, in an hour and 53 minutes, he returned in 'HI to Croydon: 'self Frost and operator Newton.'

He flew locally at Croydon and Redhill until the 14th July, when he took 'GW down to Roboro' in 2 hours 30 minutes: 'self and Stone and W/T op. Gronan.' The three of them continuing on to Haldon in 25 minutes and then returning, from Haldon to Croydon, in 1 hour 25 minutes.

A new pupil, Derrington-Turner, is mentioned on the 16th July and he and W. Hill seem to have been the only pupils for two of three days until, on the 21st July, Cash is mentioned, his name continuing for a week or so, mingled with the names of Garner, May, Woodman, Robins, Garside, and Capt. Alderson. If any of these names have been miss-spelt, I hope that their owners or their descendants will be forgiving. The fact is that, beginning in July and continuing through August and into early September, H.'s handwriting, which was once so beautifully clear, became indistinct and weak as though the very effort of moving pen across paper was too much for his aching arm and frozen shoulder.

In August the names of I. G. Ross and of Thomas also began to appear among the earlier names; on the 9th August 'self and Capt. Alderson', on the 10th 'self and Capt. Wilson and Capt. Phillip', on the 11th 'self and Capt Phillip, I. G. Ross J. Woodman', on the 17th 'self and Richardson', on the 20th, in DH86a G-ADVI, 'self and Capt. Bailey, Capt Phillip, Madge and Mountain', on the 21st on DH86a G-ADFF 'self and Capt. Phillip and Mountain', later the same day and back on Wessex 'HI a further hour and five minutes 'self and Mountain.' On the 23rd on two further DH86a's: 'VF and 'AP and on the 24th, with 'Phillip and Madge as passengers', he flew Short Scion Senior GAECV (4 × Niagara 111) for 40 minutes. On the 1st September he instructed in Wessex 'GW from Croydon to Barton, with pilots Madge and Ross piloting, flying Dragon G-ACVD (2 × Gipsy Major 260 h.p.) from Barton to Speke 'self, Madge and Ross'. On the 2nd September 'Madge and self' brought Wessex 'GW back from Barton to Croydon. On the 3rd September 'Madge and self' flew 'GW from Croydon to Hatfield, returning the same day and then presumably flying over to Hatfield again the same day as he records: '3.9.36. Dragonfly. DH Demonstration. 2 × Gipsy Maj 260 h.p. Hatfield local. 40 minutes. Buckingham and self.' On the 4th September, back at Croydon again and on Wessex GACHI 'Croydon–Redhill 12 mins. Madge and self'. 'Redhill local. Self and Robins. 10 mins.' He must have brought 'HI back to Croydon, although that is not mentioned, the last entry on that page being '4.9.36. Wessex. GACHI. 10 mins. Self and May.'

Months later, when he was convalescent, he ruled a line under that last entry and wrote in his usual clear hand: 'Fell ill with rheumatic poisoning. Put under care of Sir Wm. Willcox and Dr Porteous.'

When Jim had come home from Chile in 1924 he had been tipped (so said Jay) for an important job with Imperial Airways. His death had intervened to prevent any such appointment. There can be little doubt that H., too, would have moved into the senior administrative ranks of Imperials when his instructional days with them came to a close.

He had written to Emmie, in 1934, 'I am trying to enter the air line business' and when, eighteen months later, Geddes had asked him to join Imperials, H. was almost certain of staying with them for the rest of his working life. He would have loved to have done so, the whole concept of the Empire Air Routes being so close to his heart. It may well have been his very keenness on the job which was to contribute to his physical collapse; the cause of which, of course, dated from December, 1914. When, in the summer of 1936, his shoulder began to give him serious trouble, he went to see a doctor, the same doctor 'who had treated Col. Fraser years ago.' So V. wrote later on to Alie, '– and I believe he told H. to take 3 months holiday. Which H. said he couldn't do. The old man then put him on a diet of Ryvita and weak tea. . . .'

The idea of anyone working as hard as H. had done all year being put on a diet of Ryvita and weak tea is quite unthinkable. He became increasingly weakened and in pain as summer progressed, eventually being quite unable to climb into or to leave the cabin of his aeroplane although up to the very last entry, on the 4th September, he was capable of flying it.

His fellow pilots were the epitome of loyalty and friendship; they lifted him into the Wessex or the DH86, and carried him as gently down after they had landed. They knew what the job meant to him. But there came a day when, without telling him, they called their own doctor to see him.

At this point there were a series of lucky coincidences which, if I remember correctly, were as follows: their own doctor was on leave or away on business and his locum knew – or knew someone who knew – Dr Porteous. On seeing H. at Croydon Dr Porteous asked his old chief, Sir William Willcox, of St Mary's Hospital, Paddington, to see his patient.

Sir William had just retired and saw almost no patients but he agreed to see H., and on their meeting told him that he would do all that he could for him if H. did not mind being experimented upon. He brought H. into his 'Inoculation Ward' at St Mary's and treated him as a private patient, although he made no charge. The Inoculation Ward was a single ward or, rather, the side ward to a public ward. H. was an in-patient for six weeks or so. Sister Hyde, kind, expert and thoughtful, cared for him.

The treatment, by modern standards, may seem humdrum, but it was quite advanced for those days: autogenous vaccine, infra-red heat treatment of his shoulders and right arm, removal of some bad teeth, bed rest, warmth, a careful and restorative diet in which nothing, ever, was twice-cooked or warmed up. There were none of the anti-biotics in those old days which would probably, had they existed, cleared up the toxicity quickly, but the treatment did at least give some relief to his pain. His overall exhaustion remained. It was explained to him that his illness was not only the result of his old shrapnel injury, it was as much the result of open cockpits and intense cold across his shoulders for many years, it was flying out of Vert Galand in the icy winter of 1916–17, it was overwork, overstrain – Sir William told H. much that he already knew; trouble had all been building up slowly over the years and was unlikely to be resolved quickly. The cramped conditions in the Wessex had possibly speeded up a process which was already taking place.

Imperials were generous. And patient. They wanted H. to return to work as soon as he was well again, meanwhile they paid him his full salary and would continue to do so until the end of the year.

V. invited him to do a trip to Droitwich with her and to be her guest at 'The Worcestershire Brine Baths Hotel' for some weeks. As soon as he was strong enough for such a lengthy drive Hermia took him up to Droitwich. The cure was a modest success. H. felt much improved after his swims in the warm and buoyant waters of the Spa and his 'electrical' treatment there, presumably more infra-red heat treatment.

He sent me a postcard postmarked '13 NO 36' from Droitwich, a pretty scene of an old farmhouse in a wooded valley, his handwriting on the back of the postcard clear and firm once again: 'A gloomy day yesterday but that does not matter when one is up to ones neck in it! Love Da.'

Up to ones neck in it! – The pun in that remark was lost upon me then; I thought that he referred only to swimming in the healing waters of the Spa baths; yet when he came home and sat wrapped in blankets, grey with cold and unhappiness, in a corner of the drawing room, other meanings became apparent. He was deeply depressed. It would have been strange had he not been so.

'I know that you have been working too hard and that's agin Union rules,' wrote Charles from Lac du Bonnet, all cheerfulness, 'This is a great place for holidays....'

H. was much too down to think of taking a holiday.

A sea voyage to Canada, a carefree time with his much-younger brother, yarning about flying, yarning about old Woottonga days – what benefits a change of that nature might have brought! He huddled over the fire. He read the newspapers and grew cross with the politicians. We played a great deal of chess. He helped me with the air navigation passages of a thriller I had almost finished and he told me that, even in a thriller, I could not fly a string of polo-ponies across the Atlantic in 1936, for there was no aeroplane yet large enough. Bye and bye he began to read or to re-read some of the books which had come from his old home: Montaigne's essays, Washington Irving, Captain Marryat, Smollett (in 7 volumes), Prescott's *Philip the Second,* Grote's *History of Greece*, Napier's *Battles,* and lives of some the great navigators of the past, Vasco de Gama, Prince Henry the Navigator, and Drake. Many of these books had been annotated by their original owner, the lonely old bachelor, great-uncle Archie Travers, as he had sat in his rooms at St Swithin's Lane or in Cannon Street sixty and seventy years before. Uncle Archie had not so much annotated his books as corresponded with them, conversed with them, engaged

them in endless small talk, for such phrases as 'I quite agree!' 'What
nonsense!' 'The gallant young ensign!' or 'Such want of discipline!'
litter the margins of the pages.

Alie had always been a generous book-giver to all her nephews and
nieces; along our shelves at Moor Cottage were numerous collections
of boys adventure stories, sea-stories, highwaymen's stories and Ernest
Thompson Seton, Arthur Ransome, John Masefield and Hugh
Lofting. The last-named was H.'s favourite children's author and when
he read *Dr Dolittle* he beamed with pleasure at the description of the
'pushme-pulyou'. 'It's Jim's engine!' he said 'Jim's aeroplane that he
built for Shorts was a pushme-pulyou.'

Imperials gave H. another month to recuperate and another month's
salary, hoping that he would be able to return to them in early
February. By early February he was only just able to bath without
Hermia's help and he was still unable to wrap the Shetland shawls and
blankets around his shoulders without assistance.

He was forty-five years old. He looked ninety.

'You MUST write to Imperials,' Hermia kept on telling him, 'you
MUST write.' For Imperials telephoned her constantly for news. At
last, reluctantly, he wrote. He would not be returning to them in
February; they replied, asking: when would he be able to rejoin them?
Could he give them a firm date? He could not. They sent a young man
down to see him, a pleasant young man who was cheerful on arrival,
disbelieving and quite distressed when he saw the huddled figure of
the Imperial Airways Captain. He left, looking pale.

So Imperial Airways slipped through H.'s grasp. It was the end of
a dream.

Of the many neighbours who looked in to see him, it was probably
Philip and Wanx Cooper who cheered him up the most; they told him,
their old friend and instructor 'Trav', all their news and views and
being many years younger than he, were just the sort of jollying
influence to lift his spirits; besides, they talked flying the whole time,
or gliding, and that in itself was just what he needed – to be kept in
touch. They helped to make him feel that his usefulness to aviation
was not a thing of the past. Apart from their cheerful talk they lent
him the latest P. G. Wodehouse books from time to time and when

he read these we saw his happy smile again. Thus and thus went his convalescence until, with the warmer spring weather, he was allowed into the garden for short spells and gradually he regained further mobility.

In about 1936 a new cinema had been built in Berkhamstead. The Ritz had reared it's ugly asbestos roof in competition with the modest little Court, which was not originally a cinema at all but was a theatre where films were shown.

Ever since H.'s visit to the open-air bioscope in Ipswich in 1910, when he had broken his journey on the way South from Dingyarra to Gunjan on a cool, green day, he had loved the bioscope, the flicks, the cinema. Now he and Hermia began visiting the Ritz, or the Court, quite often. They had a lot of fun. Sometimes we 'barged in' as well. There was *Pygmalion* that year. And an even better one, *Juarez*. They went by themselves whenever they could shake the rest of us off.

There were many pilots living in and near Berkhampstead.

The pioneer aero-engine designer and aeroplane designer, F. M. 'Fred' Green, lived at Little Gaddesden. It was he who had worked in the very early days with O'Gorman and it was he, who, with de Havilland, had designed the BE No 1.

Hubert Broad, de Havilland's brilliant and famous test-pilot, came with his wife Margot to live in a pretty cottage in the hamlet of Nettleden in about 1936 and the following year an old chum, the glider pilot Philip Wills, built a house, Martins, at Potten End. Philip and Kitty Wills were frequent callers and were a great tonic to us all – lovely, cheerful people.

While down the road, so to speak, and perhaps nearest of all, was a young man who was then still making his name as a singer. He and his wife and baby had just moved into an old house on the edge of Ashridge Park. When H. and H. were dining at Lady Cooper's one evening they met the young couple. Keith (now Sir Keith) Faulkner had been an RNAS pilot. He and H. got along well at the dinner party – although they could not claim to have ever met in the RNAS. Sir Keith must have joined up at an even younger age than Charles had done and have been little more than a boy even at the end of the Great War. Nevertheless H. much enjoyed talking to someone who knew the same language.

Hertfordshire people were the kindest and the most thoughtful in the world in those days.

The Sydney Dwight's, of The Pheasantries, next-door, sent baskets of pheasant eggs and the Arthur Dwight's, of Great Farm, sent game. Lady Knutsford, within a week or two of hearing of H.'s illness, catechized me for more than half an hour out cubhunting one October day as to his illness, treatment and progress; and reminded me of her connexion with the London Hospital, telling me to promise to let her know if she could help in any way. Lady Cooper asked H. and H. to dinner several times during his convalescent months in the spring and summer of 1937.

And in that same spring Sir Granville Ram told us that he hoped that the Travers family in general and H. and H. in particular, would avail themselves of the use, for a month at a time, of the Ram's cottage in Cornwall. 'Whenever you like,' he said. We never went. But it was a wonderful offer.

Thus and thus went his convalescence until he was better. He began to map out his safe landing system and one day when I was doing some typing for him he dictated his whole plan, with a covering letter to the Air Ministry, in which he offered to teach his system to pilots, both Royal Air Force and civilian, for a salary of £600 per annum.

I think that his letter was acknowledged but I cannot remember whether or not he heard anything further on the subject.

In the autumn of 1937 he felt cheerful enough to go to Croydon to meet his favourite ex-pupil, Jean Batten, on her return from her record-breaking Australia–England flight. He was filmed greeting her, I remember for he and I went to the newsreel of the occasion on the evening of the same day at a cinema in Edgware.

H. sometimes mentioned interesting landmarks which he had seen from the air; now that he was looking about for something to do, (for he doubted if he would ever fly again), he spoke once again of Well Farm.

Well Farm: he had noticed it for years from the air when flying over Dunstable before he had ever seen it from the ground. It was the site and the setting in its own land which had appealed to him so much, tucked, as it was, under a shoulder of the hillside – beyond Little Gaddesden and only 6 or 7 miles from Moor Cottage.

When he heard that the derelict old place was for sale he drove us all over to look at it. All, that is, except Hermia, who had been so horrified by the seeping stucco of the 'midden' farm down in Kent that she (quote): 'never, *never*, NEVER wanted to see a farm again.'

Well Farm was not stucco but, if I remember correctly, a mellowed brick; even so it did not look half as nice to us as our beloved Moor Cottage. We were not enthusiastic and when H. called on the agents and heard the ridiculously high price which was wanted for the old place he said that he would wait a bit, for the price was sure to come down eventually. Sadly for him it did not do so, for, war being imminent, many people were moving out of London at about that time and prices held. Well Farm went to auction in 1938 and was bought by the most surprising purchaser of all, Alan Butler, Chairman of de Havilland's.

H. was pleased for the Butlers, whom he had always liked. If he could not have Well Farm himself he could not think of anyone else who would appreciate it as much, for they were both pilots who had probably first seen it, as he had done, from the air. (They were in fact both pilots of great skill and had won a number of important races. Yet they never sought the limelight. All that they did was done very well and with great elan.)

H. asked Hermia to call on them as soon as they were settled in but, before she could do so, they drove over to see us in the most affable and friendly way, turning up one sunny afternoon in a shiny little black car, Mr Butler at the wheel. He was obviously pleased to renew acquaintance with H. They had always got along well when they had met at Stag Lane.

Although they had arrived at an hour suitable for a social call there was more to their visit than neighbourliness. Mr Butler indicated that he would like a word with H. and the two men paced the lawn by the rose-beds for some minutes in quiet conversation.

When we said good-bye to Mr and Mrs Butler, after all sorts of invitations from them both to visit them at Well Farm and so forth, I thought H. looked weary.

What was it?

Alan Butler had asked H. to join de Havillands and as soon as possible. In 1938 the aviation world was quite a small world and even though Mr Butler and H. had not met for several years the former would have been well aware through their many mutual acquaintances, especially perhaps from Sir Philip Sassoon, of H.'s recent career.

'– If you change your mind,' said Mr Butler, as they left.

'No. I have a job,' said H., untruthfully.

'I wish you could go to de Havs,' I said to H. later on.

'No, no, E.,' – he sounded as though he was perfectly clear and decided on the subject, 'one cannot go back. It doesn't do to go back. . . .' And the matter was settled.

In July, 1938, Luton Airport was opened.

The Mayor and Corporation of Luton invited H. and H. 'and family' to a place of honour in the grandstand with them for the occasion. In the event H. and H. took Lindsay with them up into the grandstand and us four girls sat on the grass with the rest of Luton and watched the flying.

H. O. robs his bees. Summer of 1938 at Moor
Cottage
photo: Burse Scaramanga

It was a wonderful display, the most breathtaking flight of all being that of the little Mew Gull – so close above the grass at over 300 m.p.h. that the machine should have been invisible. But that lovely top line of the Mew Gull: cowling, canopy and tail-fin, was clear and unforgettable: what a good day that was.

The day after the opening of Luton Airport the Mayor of Watford wrote to H. Watford, also, wanted an Airport. They would like one within ten miles of the Town Hall and would H. find a site for them, please?

He had not flown since September, 1936, and he had no aeroplane; but he had scores of friends who were still flying and one of them took him up in a Spartan on a lengthy cruise over Watford and its environs, a veritable 'spider web patrol' in its thoroughness. There were main roads, the canal, the LMS 4-track main line from Euston to Scotland; a great deal of scattered building, remnants of woodland, Roman camps in abundance such as those around Berkhamstead and to the South on Grove Farm. There were the Chiltern Hills, in fact, and on the river land to the south and east towards London there were Radlett, Elstree, Stanmore ... Watford wanted their own Municipal Airport, not the landing-with-permission on anyone else's aerodrome.

There was a pretty view to the South from Moor Cottage: over the roses, the box-bushes, the white-painted wicket fence by the ash tree, over a thorn hedge to the Dwight's pasture field which sloped away on down, the valley beyond hidden from view, the land rising again a mile away, all the land and the varying fields folded and re-folded, as compact as the leaves of a cabbage.

He knew this view well from his bedroom window.

'There is one field, just one field ...' he repeated, when any of us asked him about Watford airport, 'I can see it from my room, I've seen it from the air ... now I must go and look at it from the ground. . . .'

We went to look at it. All of us in the faded old tourer, a Humber this time and a bad starter. It was a dry, cold day in a summer of dry, hot days and Hermia began to worry that he was doing too much again: that he would be too cold as he crawled about the long field close to Bovingdon village, visuallizing approaches, looking at levels and surfaces, pacing distances. . . .

'If you could buy the field next to it as well,' he explained to us all later on, over tea, 'and take out the intervening hedge – then it would be possible. Not good. But possible. Certainly for the Airspeed, they can get in and out of almost anywhere ... other aircraft could use it in some winds. I'll write to the Mayor and let him know what I think. He certainly ought to buy that land straight away, both fields if he can and if the farmer will sell, and register it quickly as a landing-ground. If I can find anything better no harm will have been done ... if not, then at least Watford will have their landing-ground. . . .'

Poor Watford.

They took all the actions that H. had advised, but the year was 1938. No sooner had Bovingdon been registered than it was commandeered by the Air Ministry. In due course the U.S. Army Air Corps, under Colonel, later General, Curtis Le May, took it over. The first Flying Fortress Squadron to touch down in England touched down at Bovingdon. And how the pilots hated it. And who could blame them for hating it. A narrow strip of land on the side of a hill in a shallow valley, where H. had envisaged the agile Airspeed nipping in and out, was used by the massive Boeing bombers. To any US Army Air Corps pilots who may chance to read these lines I say again: it was not meant for you. Navigation was the bogey which made the authorities decide to order the Fortress Squadron into Bovingdon. The pilots would fly non-stop across the Atlantic, a first Transatlantic flight for them all and they would arrive in a strange and very small country, unused to the weather conditions, in (possibly) the black-out, weary after their long flight, (even though it took the remarkably fast time of under 12 hours for most of them,) and they would somehow have to find their way down. Bovingdon was a navigator's dream, with the canal, the main road, (A41) and the gleaming rails of the four-track main railway line heading just about true North West. Those three shining visual aids would have helped many a worried pilot or navigator home.

(The Liberators came in first a few miles further along, at Cheddington.) Poor old Watford. It would really have liked its own airport.

Luton, on the other hand, goes from strength to strength.

Much had happened in aviation since the start of H.'s crippling illness. Mrs Beryl Markham had made her superb Atlantic flight. Tom Campbell-Black had lost his life. Lost it in surely the stupidest of all taxying accidents, for he should not have been where he was on the apron. The Royal Air Force pilot had the right of way and had no idea that the Mew Gull was there until his propellor ploughed into it. Of course he was absolved and rightly so but how one's heart goes out to him.

Amelia Earhart was missing. And fifty years later – is still missing. More strange, even, than the *Marie Celeste*, which mystery has been partly solved.

At home gliding, at last, really began to come into its own, after early days at Itford, Detling, Sutton Bank and Dunstable. Wolfe Hirth brought a team of glider pilots, fellow Germans, over to Dunstable. He stayed with Philip and Kitty Wills at Martins and H. & H. were invited to meet him. Hermia thought him quite charming and they both thought him courageous to achieve so much for German aviation. H. was wary, however, perhaps having more idea than Hermia what was afoot, in spite of the camaraderie of the gliding meets.

H. read the news of Imperial Airways with delight. It was all going so well. Long distance scheduled flying-boat services: it was Jim's dream come true: Empire Air Routes, mail-carrying and passenger-carrying. Short-built boats which might soon encircle the globe.

18

LIGHT THE BLOWPOTS

1935–1940

Charles flying out of Lac du Bonnet – joins the support team for the Govt
Survey Party putting a Base Line across Canada – Alie visits at Lac du Bonnet –
visit of King George VI and Queen Elizabeth – outbreak of War – death of
Lord Tweedsmuir

CHARLES was by now in Ottawa. He had moved, as all good pilots
should eventually move, into the administrative side of aviation. It is
only former pilots who ought, ever, to administer aviation. Although
his letters may have become more domestic as he wrote to H. from
his comfortable home in Ottawa, they were read as eagerly as the
earlier bush-flying letters had been read.

Canadian Aviation, too, which arrived regularly as a gift from Charles,
was very popular with H., giving as it did a fresh slant on the
international subject. Fifty years on, *Canadian Aviation*'s azure photographs of the lovely Armstrong Whitworth ENSIGN, or the black-
and-white picture of that hardy and good-looking workhorse, the
American BARKLEY-GROW T8P 1 CABIN TRANSPORT, do not
seem to me to be so *very* old-fashioned.

Before Ottawa, however, and when he was still with the MGAS,
Charles had spent some rugged months, from January to May, 1936, flying (along with Jim Uhlmann), for a Government survey party who were
putting a Base Line across the Canadian continent from West to East.

They flew, for the work, out of The Pas. But in 1935 he was still
flying out of Lac du Bonnet and I shall take up his story there.
To H.:

Lac du Bonnet, 29th May 1935.

Dear H.O.,
Thank you very much for your letter of 17th May. I was glad that
you saw Marian and Jimmy – it was very good of you to fetch them

from Harrow. Marian said it was the only time anyone did and she very much appreciated it.

She and Jimmy arrived yesterday morning (28th) having spent a night in Ottawa on the way with some friends. She also called on Mrs Wilson, and saw J. A. – as usual they were extremely friendly. I am very interested in all the news of yours and it is great to hear that the family is fulfilling its early promise. . . . I would like to see them again – I will have to make some dough and take a trip myself. . . .

I enclose a cutting from *The Aeroplane* written by a man, Ayres. He has not been in the West and is unknown to me . . . he has collected a few ideas and I have pencilled a few comments which may be hard to read. I think they answer some of your questions, but to take yours in turn:

The Junkers (Wasp and Hornet engined) has been very successful as a freighter, both with Can-Airways and Wings. It's low wing is not a serious disadvantage as it is high enough to clear low docks.

The airframe maintenance is probably lower than that of any other civil aeroplane in Canada. The metal skii is less frequently damaged by broken ice or by spray than is the fabric or plywood covering of other makes.

The Junkers appears to lift its load very easily compared to the F/C and has a good rate of climb. It has a good door and cabin space.

On the other hand the first cost is high, it is rather slow and the cabin is dark and uncomfortable.

For our freighting and for commercial freighting I suggest an all up load of about 6,000 lbs., an engine of about 500 H P, payload of 1,750 lbs on floats, good loading doors, staggered.

The above is more or less what the new F. C. 82 is going to have. We hope to get one soon. It has a 4′ wide cabin.

I think the Gipsy 6 looks a fine job. I would like to see the Monospar with the 2 Gipsy 4's out here on floats as a small passenger carrying job. It might replace the Waco's and Stinsons and give better service.

The Lycoming on the Stinson is *good, not so* their Smiths variable pitch prop.

The Continental on the Waco is not very satisfactory, high cyl. head temps and valve trouble. The take off on floats (with a 300 lb overload) is horrible to witness.

Why not get after General Aircraft Co. (David Williams is designing for them now) and if at a loose end bring a Monospar out here on floats.

It is a bit small but might go over big. They know the Gipsy out here.

Cheerio H.

Please excuse this hasty scrawl.

Your loving brother, Charles.

'Lac du Bonnet, Manitoba. 15th December.

My dear H. O.,

Thank you very much for your letter from Brussels which was very interesting. It gave me a bird's eye view of some of the rapid developments in British Aviation which are rather confusing to me because of their rapidity their origins and their motives. Now I see, as you explain, that the big money has come into the show & is scrambling for the front seats. I do hope that the people behind it do not confine their efforts to local air lines but compete in all the great Empire and International Trade Routes. I am thinking at the moment of the Atlantic & Pacific and the Trans Canada link. It looks as if we are running a bad fourth to the Yanks, the Germans & the French there: but I expect that old Imperials are doing pretty well elsewhere and are not so dumb after all.

How do you like the DH89?

It has a wonderful performance & there are one or two out here but there is an idea current that they will neither stand the trying winter conditions nor the punishment which the average seaplane freighter has to take in the summer. The bush operator is prejudiced against multi-engines because of the extra labour in winter time & the slightly higher maintenance cost.

We all expect that the Trans Canada mail run will be resumed next year and I hope that they will use multi-engined British aircraft. I wonder what the new S. T. 18 Monospar will be like. I mean to put in for an Airways Inspector's job as soon as they are advertised: because there would be some chance of getting on in the Dominion Civil Service: also I might have a chance later to switch to the mail run which would be quite good pay I expect. That is all 'castle building' though, and I would be content here but for three things – our chief pilot, Uhlmann, and living & school facilities here. As for the first, he has learnt to leave me alone, more or less, for the second – I have bought a river 'lot' & may build a small place on it (I think it would be a fair spec. if I keep the cost right down): but the school is an unsolved problem. ... There is a splendid boys school in Winnipeg & I would like him to go there if I can manage it. It is the school problem – in fact the whole business of bringing up the kids that makes me want to go back to England sometimes ... Apart from that I quite think that I am as happy here as I would be in England. I would like very much to see you and yours and the sisters often ... but otherwise I have not got any very close friends there. Perhaps if I hadn't a living to get and the everyday problems to face I would be homesick. It is a very deep seated emotion and we often think and talk about H. & H. & the kids.

Please give our love to them all & tell them that I have been busy or would have written for Christmas.

We have just got the new Fairchild ready for winter flying. Rather a job as it had never been flown on skiis before. We all flew her on Friday 13th without mishap & she handles very well. Jim Uhlmann is taking her away for a short job before Christmas then I expect to be away for a month leaving about the New year. We will be freighting supplies from a point about 150 miles N. of The Pas on the Hudson's Bay Railroad to a series of survey camps. They are putting a baseline across from West to East. to the North of God's Lake. We will also move the camps every 10 days or so. A lot of short hauls.

I hope that we will get small portable W/T transmitters & receivers battery operated; but we have had quite a struggle to get the right winter equipment such as Woods eiderdowns; blow pots and engine covers of correct design so the chances of getting extras is small.

I am awfully glad to hear that you are doing so well H. O. and hope that you will soon be manager of one of their concerns which is where you should be with your ability and experience. They don't know what a navigator is out here. I wanted to study with the idea of working up for a 2nd Class Navigator's Licence, but as they don't issue any here it seemed a little futile. However if you can send me any dope on the requirements or what books to read I wish that you would let me know. I think they may bring one in some day. I have done the Air Pilotage part fairly recently. . . .

To H.:

Opasquai Hotel, The Pas, Manitoba. 30th January 1936.

I hope that your new job is going well and that you like it. It sounds good one and I hope that you will let me know all the latest dope on the Air Ministry requirements for Navigator's licences, etc. I feel sure that we will follow their standards very closely out here.

They have just announced a new type of Pilot's licence here, called a Transport licence. It ranks higher than the ordinary 'B' licence, and calls for instrument flying, night flying, and is issued only for types of aircraft specified on the licence. I have applied for one, but have not had time to obtain the necessary photos this month.

I have been away from Lac du Bonnet for nearly 3 weeks with J. C. Uhlmann, and the new F. C. 82. He has been showing me the job up here and we have been splitting up the flying. It is really straightforward but he is one of the ultra cautious birds and rather windy in bad weather. At the same time he is (a) great worker so I keep my own counsel.

We have been doing 3 jobs and the difficulty has been to fit them in together. The first, which we have finished, was to transport a Dept. of Health Doctor, and a 'radiologist' with about 800 lbs. of X-Ray equipment to the different mines for the purpose of testing the miners for silicosis (miners pthisis). The other jobs were for the Surveys Branch who have two parties cutting Base Line from West to East. One is about 90 miles east of the H. B. Rly. Station at Wabowden. (136 miles from The Pas). The other is about the same distance E. S. E. of The Pas, near the mouth of the Sakatchewan.

There are about 20 men in each party, dog teams, and on the southern one, horses. We feed them and the dogs, flying the food in from Wabowden and The Pas, and the whitefish for the dogs from Gods Lake and Oxford Lake.

We take about 1600 lbs. so that it means quite a lot of heavy manual work loading and unloading, although we get help at the camps.

We also move camp for these parties and we can do that in about 3 or 4 loads.

The worst 'chore' is warming up the machine in the morning. We have breakfast usually about 0645 so that it is dark when we get down to the machine. We have a shack at Wabowden where we can make a fire to warm up the oil – drained the night before. One of us attends to that, while the other unties the bottom of the engine cover and holds it down by means of sticks of cordwood, or other heavy objects.

The old & the new. Aeroplane and dogteam, N. Manitoba, March 1936

photo: C. T. Travers

He puts the two stools and the fire extinguisher under the cover and lights the two blowpots (like big Primus stoves) gets under the engine cover and pulls them after him. They are stood on top of these stools to bring the flame within about 3 feet of the power cylinders.

Our engine covers are a little different from the usual type which is a single one fitting round the engine, not the prop, and heavily padded on top with felt and asbestos.

Ours is different and consists of one inner one round the engine and another light canvas one covering the prop and the cabin windows. It is not very good and blows about rather in a wind.

After about 1 hour she should be ready to start. The blowpots are put out hurriedly and the engine cover opened enough to allow the oil to be poured into the tank. We have special 'tractor buckets' with spouts, 4 galls. each, for the oil.

These can be hung up over the blowpots if there is no other way of heating the oil.

As soon as the oil is in the covers are removed and the engine started.

When run up she can be stopped for a few minutes while the skii cables are attached. (We carry a small block and tackle and stretch the bunjy) and the blow pots, covers, etc. are thrown into the cabin.

In the evening the oil is drained into a 10-gallon can, the skiis jacked up and the covers put on. Any greasing must be done while the engine is warm.

She is refuelled and by that time it is dark, so that it makes a fairly long day, particularly when cold.

We had a really cold snap last week, −36f at Gods Lake, −38 at Hut Lake −46 −57 −46 at Wabowden. We had trouble with frosting of the windows on the inside and we are going to try frost shields when we get back. It begins with an air temp of −20 outside but we didn't fly on the day it was −57 because it had been almost impossible to keep a clear patch on the window the previous day. On the whole we have had good weather, but curiously enough there was a kind of mist on the cold days. It was all below 3000'. It was not all ground drift – but it must have been tiny ice particles. Just now we have run into a streak of bad fog.

Not very much but too bad, I guess. It is much warmer and we may run into snow.

I am keen to get back to L du B and see how they all are, and get

Machine in flight

photo: courtesy Royal Canadian Air Force, Ottawa

a few clean clothes. I bought some rotten ski pants and they are only holding together by a few cotton threads, so I mean to go and brandish them in Mr Timothy Eaton's face and demand my money back.

With love to all at Moor Cottage.

Your loving brother

Charles.

Charles' tour of flying duty – splitting the flying with Uhlmann – for the Base Line Survey Party lasted from January to May. It was bush flying at it's most basic, rugged – and unforgettable. When May came he resumed his fire patrol work for the M G A S.

After Emmie's death and the settlement of her estate, Alie decided to build a small house for herself in Bredgar, but before doing so she was determined to fulfil a longstanding wish, that of travelling round the world. She crossed the Atlantic to New York then journeyed through New York State and so into Canada. After some weeks at Lac du Bonnet she continued on Westwards and made a leisurely voyage across the Pacific and down to Australia.

She visited her Uncle H. P. Gardner in Queensland and the numerous cousins in Queensland, New South Wales, Victoria, and Tasmania. She was staying with the Gardners in Queensland when Charles wrote to her on the 22nd September 1936:

My dear Ally. . . . I expect that you will soon be at Toogoolawah. . . . I have had an acknowledgement of my application for the Department of Civil Aviation job and now must be patient. . . . We had some rain a week after you left but some of the fires are smouldering still. It was quite a job sorting out all the firefighters and their equipment.

I made twenty landings one day all in different lakes – most of them the small rocky kind, picking up scattered crews of Indians with their packs, canvas buckets and packpumps. Axes, shovels and mess kits.

I hope that it cleared up before you left Vancouver, but it is not the best time of year there.

I hope that you were impressed by the Rockies. I was immensely so but I would not care to live among them. I would rather be on the Eastern slopes of the foothills and see them from a distance. . . . I suppose that I must have been rather bad-tempered at times after a day's flying in the smoke. I do hope you will forget and come back this way. . . .

It is odd to read of Charles describing himself as 'bad-tempered', for there can have been few more sweet-natured than he; but, if he was, then, as he says, 'after a day's flying in the smoke' would explain all. It is also true that although Alie had grown up with three flying brothers they had none of them lived at home when they were engaged on flying work. Except (possibly), during the war when she was living with Grannie Gardner in London, she would never have seen an exhausted pilot coming home at night; or leaving early in the morning to fly again.

Lac du Bonnet, Manitoba. 14th Oct. 1936.
My dear H. O.

I hope that you are better by this time and that you will be able to take a full-sized holiday. I know that you have been working too hard & that's agin Union Rules. This is a great place for holidays. We have just had Thanksgiving Day. I can't tell you why. Any way it's a holiday, added to which I had a couple of days off as I cut my face & lip slipping on the wet float of the Fairchild 82 & falling against one of the float struts. It was very welcome. I was able to do some painting inside the new house and to-day I was going to Winnipeg in the old car but it let me down after 15 miles with a shorting switch cable. It was one of those heavily armoured 'thief proof' cables from the dashboard key to the contact breaker casing and I must admit that it stumped me. I had to get a tow back to Lac du Bonnet while some friends gave Marian a lift on to Wpg. where she had some shopping to do.

... I may have a chance for a job in the Dept. Civil Aviation rather better than my present one. There is only one vacancy at present and probably some one down East will get it.

I expect that it will freeze up here about the 8th or 10th Nov. and then we can expect winter flying to start again. It isn't bad if you have good equipment but I hope that they don't keep me out all the blooming winter or I won't see much of the kids or of Marian.

Marian was so very pleased with the welcome you & Hermy gave her when she was over. I don't think that I ever thanked you but it made a great impression for she often mentions it as being a bright memory in what was otherwise rather a disappointing trip. I think that you would like this place. There is plenty of rough fishing & shooting. There is good bathing at the end of our lot and I have a

Vedette 'G-Z over Larder Lake

little cat boat with a centre board.... In the winter time there is badminton in the evenings (rather amateurish) and very amateurish skiing. Then hockey – if you are young and expert enough & curling if you are old enough. I'm a poor sport and hate leaving my own camp heater in the evenings.

There is always a thrill for me in the mining game and if Marian hadn't got a good measure of common sense I think I'd be prospecting now. The country is lousy with minerals, not all precious metals, of course. Not one prospector in ten makes anything.

Wings Ltd. who nearly went on the rocks last spring – losing four machines in rapid succession – have had several wonderful breaks. I still think that it was Roy's (Brown's) personality that pulled them through. He is a great fighter & I know that you would like him.

First Ted Stull staked a new discovery on the Sachigo River in which Wings Ltd. has an interest. They also flew all the drilling machinery in there from God's Lake.

Then they collared a contract for from 500–700 tons freight from the Newmont Co. to be flown from Burns River to Favourable Lake 130 miles. They have to move 100 tons before freeze up which may be difficult as the weather is rather unsettled. The Cormorant Lake detachment have returned and Phinney is staying with us for a few nights while he gets his report written & equipment stowed away. He is a real good fellow and I hope that he will do some good with a prospect he has up North on the Eskimamish River.

Please excuse pencil. I got up to Winnipeg after all, and turned the old car in. I don't want to get another and think that I can do without it. They cost too much to run.

Please give my love to all the family.

Your loving brother

Charles.

To Alie:

King Edward Hotel, Toronto. (undated but date known by contents)

... I really am awfully bucked at the new job. It is a similar one to that one I applied for but that was filled. I decided to come this way through the States and flew to Chicago in one of the new Lockheed Electras. On one stretch – between Minneapolis and Chicago, which we made in the dark we averaged nearly 200 mph. Our airspeed was 175 and we had a good tail wind. The cabin was very quiet and comfortable and we had a good lunch hamper supper on board.

I had a good look at Chicago on Sunday, saw a museum and the Art Gallery – huge buildings.

There were some good rooms in the Art Gallery. One of Dutch and Flemish paintings and another of French and English masters, rather jumbled up, I thought. There were also rooms full of junk, bequests by departed Chicago art patrons.

Anyhow they have some lovely things there and there were a great many people looking at them.

I didn't think much of the city apart from Michigan Boulevard which faces the lake. It reminded me somehow of Brighton Front on a huge and modern pattern.

The back streets are horrible, rapidly disintegrating into slums. The 'plane ride was a bit expensive so I came on through Detroit by bus. It took about 20 hours from Chicago to Toronto and I am going on to-morrow. . . .

To H.:

Ottawa. 5th Feb. 1937.

. . . We have settled down here after rather a hectic move from Lac du Bonnet.

My successor in the M. G. A. S. has rented the house there and I hope will be a good tenant although I hope to be able to sell it next summer. I am on the Air Regulations end of the job – not on the Airways – which is the other branch. It was rather a disappointment to me at first but I am just as pleased now as I have more to do with the bush flying end of the business – and that is the peculiarly Canadian condition that is capable of much greater development in the future.

Just at present an attempt is being made to enforce 'Air Regulations' (based on the I. C. A. N.): particularly as regards overloading.

When you consider how widely dispersed are the bases from which machines operate – the small number at each base – and that one cannot limit operations to licensed airharbours you will realise how difficult it is to enforce Regulations.

Now that we are under the Dept. of Transport, I hope that a better system will be found to regulate the business.

I hope that Hermy and the children are well and that someday before long, I'll see you all again. One thing I feel is that I am 1200 miles nearer to England now & that means that there is a better chance of seeing you too.

Marian and the boys are well: this is a damp messy sort of climate after Manitoba but I think we'll like Ottawa. There is a good school near & Jimmy is going to the Kindergarten.

Young Joe is doing well. . . .

I would love to have a snapshot if you have one of the family. . . .

To H.:
Ottawa. 10th October 1937.

. . . I am getting worse at letter-writing and when I do start it seems hopeless to find anything interesting to say.

There have been several enquiries about you from your old friend Breadner, who is one of the Big Shots in the R. C. A. F. now and is at their H. Q here in Ottawa. He is a Group Captain and I think is next in line after Crois – who is Senior Air Officer.

He has always been keen to hear news of you and was very sorry to hear you had been ill.

Do you remember Swede Larsen in 84 Squadron? He was in the same flight as I was. I had remembered hearing that he was living in Hanover, New Hampshire and Marian and I called in to see him on our way back from a short motor trip to the coast of Maine. He and his wife and family gave us a tremendous welcome. He is a successful architect and is doing fine work. I never knew he had it in him and I am tremendously pleased at his success – because he is so keen on his job. . . .

I have been some time in this job but do not know yet whether I will ever make a Civil Servant. You have tangled with Air Regulations, I think, without infringing them. There isn't a Commercial Pilot in Canada that hasn't done both, yet I am supposed to help administer this same lop-sided offshoot of the Versailles Treaty and the I. C. A. N. under conditions that were never anticipated.

I'm just not prepared to go round the country – like a funny policeman – and 'jack-up' experienced operators for technical infractions. I'm hoping to do what I can by persistence and a flock of 'memoranda'.

Cowley is my particular boss. I didn't like him when I was in Manitoba.

I have changed my opinion completely. Apart from his real friendliness he is one of the fairest-minded men I have ever met. He has an alarmingly good memory (as mine is bad) and he is always ready to listen to suggestions.

My job is mainly in the office here but we make an occasional trip round the area north of Ottawa to Sudbury, South Porcupine, Kirkland Lake, Noranda, Amos, etc.

I always look forward to this trip: we have a Waco with 285 and Edo Floats. We will soon put it on skiis – as the freeze-up will soon come.

To-day is Thanksgiving Day, but Gen. Edwards (who is really a Radio man is head of our department under the political heads (Howe and Smart) wanted to go to a Hunting Camp about 40 miles north. Hollick-Kenyon was one of the party. He has just come back from a search for the lost Russian machine.

He was using a new Consolidated boat with a 4000 mile range. It is a U.S. Service type really. They are going to have another look – with a Lockheed Electra – and are trying at the present time to dig up some suitable skiis.

He told me they made one flight of $22\frac{1}{2}$ hours over broken ice – no place good enough to make a safe take-off after landing. . . .'

The 'lost Russian machine' was an object of concern for many weeks. In August *Flight* had reported: 'Indistinct radio signals have been received on a wavelength which corresponds with that used by Levanevsky and his companions who have been missing in the Far North for a fortnight. Sir Hubert Wilkins and James Mattern have joined in the search.

Down in Ottawa Charles and his family settled into a different sort of Canadian life.
Charles to H.:
385 Hinton Avenue, Ottawa. 1st March, 1938.
. . . All is well here apart from the chance cold and a nasty spill Jimmy had last week end. We took him with us to the Gatineau Hills – skiing. J. A. Wilson was going to show us an easy trail but there was a bad 'crust' on the snow and young Jim slipped almost at the start & displaced the semi-lunar cartilage . . . of course it stops his skiing and skating for this winter which is too bad as he was doing well on skiis and getting around on skates. Joe is skating well . . . I'm afraid I spend a lot on this sort of thing but it has always seemed to me one

of the compensations for the 6 months of winter – that all the winter sports are available* ... continued 15th March: Marian & I have been out skiing, yesterday and to-day. It has been wet and sloppy in town: thawing during the day then freezing at sundown but up in the hills on the Quebec side north of Ottawa river there is plenty of good snow. Mackenzie King has a place up at Kingsmere so the snow plough keeps the road open. It is only 14 miles so it is an easy run in a car. The sunshine has been wonderful and we are all tanned.... I wonder if there is any chance of seeing you or any of the family out here H.? It would be grand to see you again. Please give my love to Hermy and the family....

To Alie:
20th April 1938.
... The machine I had last year has been sent out West to replace one destroyed by fire in a hangar and I have a (similar) new Waco with a new radio compass in it.

To-morrow I have to take the head of our department to Toronto and expect to be away for a night or two. It will be rather a welcome break in the office routine. I hope soon that we can arrange to put this aircraft on floats so that I can visit some of the operators up North.

I have been trying to find out where I can get Pemmican (a kind of dried and produced meal) for emergency equipment and had a very long interesting letter from Stefansson, the Arctic explorer and anthropologist. He has some very refreshing and convincing ideas on diet and laughs at the modern fads for vitamins in everything from soap to soup....

The next letter came A I R M A I L via New York.

The first part of the letter was written on the back of three picture postcards; the postcard pictures were of C N R construction and freighting – Amos to Val d'Or.

To H.:
notification of change of address to 1 Maple Lane, Rockcliffe, Ottawa.
1st July 1938.
Dear H. O.
I thought you would find these p.c.'s interesting. I bought them in Val D'Or, Quebec a new mining camp north of here. I stayed there

* In adult life Joe became National Ski Champion of Canada.

on my way back to Ottawa from a short trip. I was away 10 days with
the Waco visiting the principal operating bases in our district. I had a
mines branch official with me for the first five days. English or B.
Columb. named Eardley-Wilmot – a good sort. He is making a film
of mining activities and we took shots of the Hollinger (South Porcupine) and Lake Shore (Kirkland Lake – camps). He left me before
I got to Noranda which is the big copper zinc producer of this area.

I heard from Scotty Dougall who is in England on leave. I am
writing giving your address as he asked after you. His is c/o R C A F
Liaison Officer, Air Ministry, London. He is still with the same outfit
in India.

The above was all written on the three postcards. The letter continued
on a separate sheet of paper:

I must take this chance of writing a short letter: I can just catch the
New York mail.

Marian and the two boys are well. Marian much stronger than last
year and playing tennis ... I really can't afford to go away this year
but can borrow a tent and I know a good sandy beach on the Ottawa
about 40 miles up the river, where we can camp for a week or ten
days.... This is all about ourselves....

Life is sometimes a bit humdrum in the office but at least we can
get out occasionally and I enjoy my occasional trips north on the Waco
seaplane. The poor old 'bush' operator is not receiving much assistance
these days: all the money is going into the Airways development –
which is enormously costly for the small population of Canada, while
the essentially Canadian development of Northern flying is not recognized at its true value – economic or strategic. The younger pilots and
engineers are being absorbed by T. C. Airways and the cost of aircraft
and repairs is rising. There is a slump in the mining market and less
mining development – net result – hard times for the 'bush' operator.

There are signs of improvement I believe and I hope also of better
policies. There is at least one commercial aircraft designed for freighting but I wish some English firm would come into the picture.

Your loving brother

Charles.

(Paul Jensen was among those of the younger pilots who eventually
joined T. C. Airways.)

Charles' days as a bush pilot were over for good, but his eight or nine years of that hardy life stayed with him for the rest of his career and gave him a deep sympathy with those of his successors who, like him, knew what it was like to fly all day in the smoke of a forest fire; or, in winter, to light the blowpots and heat the engine oil in temperatures so low that the ice particles closed down all visibility and the cabin windows went blind; a fellow-feeling, too, with all pilots who by reasons of cost were deprived of essential equipment and who, as a result, were obliged to think that a two-way radio was an 'extra' and a luxury.

'I think we'll like Ottawa,' he had written home.

A year or so after they had moved to Maple Lane, Rockcliffe, Charles bought a 'lot' in the same area of parkland along the banks of the Ottawa River. They built such a pretty house there, on Manor Road, and stayed there for many years. Rockcliffe was a good place to live.

In wintertime they went off to the Gatineau Hills to skii and after a year or so of exploring the Gatineau Valley they built themselves a summer cottage on the banks of the Gatineau River near Chelsea, later extending the summer cottage into a permanent home.

The hard times were over and they settled down to enjoy the more comfortable life which they had earned.

At about this stage of a book of this period it is customary to make some remark to the effect that 'War clouds were gathering.' But as anyone who lived through the time will recall, they had already gathered and were just sitting there, at a low ceiling, and waiting to deluge the world. As Charles had written to Emmie way back in 1933: 'Yurrup is in a frightful mess.'

The opening round in the bout, it will be remembered, was Munich. 'There was no doubt that we were caught totally unprepared,' H. wrote to Alie on the 30th October:

My dear Sloper,

The House Dinner at the Aero Club was most interesting & what I heard privately next day more so. There was no doubt that we were caught totally unprepared not through the fault of the Air Force nor of the manufacturers but entirely due to the glastly network red tape & *graft* created by the Civil Service Air Ministry & Treasury. I had specific cases given me by several trustworthy individuals & there is no doubt that it amounts to treason (not against the King but against the country).

Quite apart from the fact that not only have they wasted months & years of valuable time but not even spent economically. More details when we next meet

Your affec H. O.

Charles wrote to Alie in an equally serious vein: 'Just a short note to send my love and to say how relieved I feel that the immediate danger to you and all others at home has passed. I hope that we may hope for Peace for many years even if we must purchase it at the cost of compulsory military service and other restrictions of our liberty. I hope that it will bring more active development of our natural resources here. . . .'

Charles, once again dealing with more mundane topics, wrote to H. on the 15th November:

Thank you for your prompt reply to my letter. Please excuse the delay in answering your wire, I had to give it a little more thought. I enclosed the Share Certificate (No 6676 for 534 Joseph Travers & Sons ordinary) in an envelope registered to you tonight via New York and also sent the cablegram.

From your cable I note that there is not much demand but if you don't get an offer of 40/- or thereabouts I think I should hold on for a time. Anyway I know you will do the best and I would like to thank you H. for going to this trouble on my account.

We are having the first flurry of snow. It has been a beautiful late Fall and very mild although the leaves have gone from the trees for several weeks.

Our Waco went on wheels yesterday – It takes about 4 hours to change over from floats as a rule.

We have quite a good civil airport here now with hard surfaced runways.

The Lockheed 14's of T. C. A. run experimentally from Montreal to Toronto & Vancouver daily.

No mail or passengers yet. . . . Your loving brother Charles.

I was looking at an old letter of yours from Korea describing a driving test on a Ford. Very interesting.

Charles to H. on the 8th Dec 1938, the envelope marked by him 'via New York ss *Aquitania*':

Dear H.O. I have just executed transfers of the 534 Shares of J.T. & Sons at the request of your brokers: Cazenove Akroyds & Greenwood & Co. . . . I think the price obtained very good. I had not hoped for as much & thank you very much H.O. for your care and trouble. . . . I hope to go down to New York next week to get a new radio compass for our Waco. The Waco I use for my northern trips has been on floats all summer & has only just been changed to wheels. The radio was not entirely satisfactory & we are going to trade it in for a new one with an 'automatic' radio compass.

This is supposed to give you the bearing of any station to which your receiver is tuned.

I am also hoping to get a trip to Vancouver & back on T.C.A. before Christmas – but the Edmonton Inspector has to go first so I may miss out. I'll write & tell you about it & try to get some snapshots on the way through. . . .

At about that time it was announced that the King and Queen were to visit Canada. It may have been a sensible move. It was without doubt an extremely popular one.

'It is going to be the grandest thing: this visit of the King to Canada. . . .' Charles wrote to Alie as soon as he heard. He wrote to her again on the subject on the 19th May 1939:

My dear Ally. . . . I wish that you could have been here to-day – a great day for us all in Ottawa.

The King and Queen arrived at 10.30 and drove up to Government House on the State Carriage, with the usual escorting troops and followed by our local big-wigs in cars. We had a splendid view and had only to walk round from the other side of Govt. House grounds – where our house is – to the Main Gate.

Their Majesties looked wonderful. The king in scarlet Field Marshals uniform and the Queen in well-chosen mauve and becoming hat. Very smart I understand. It was a sort of bonnet with all sorts of flowers and what nots sticking out of it. cont. 21st. Yesterday and Saturday was a great day too. In the morning there was the Trooping of the Colours on Parliament Hill. We saw very well indeed from the top of the big Bank of Montreal building, the sun shone but it was not hot, it was just comfortable without our coats. The children enjoyed it but they had had a long day on Friday and were getting a little tired.

I think they expected the King and Queen to appear like giants – very conspicuous against the Grenadiers uniforms. The ceremony was well done, the drill was almost faultless and the setting really lovely.

In the afternoon we went to the Garden Party – we nearly lost our tickets – and we all enjoyed it tremendously – ate the King's birthday cake and were overjoyed to find that the King seemed to have dropped his slightly hesitant, nervous manner, and to be having a really good time.

This was splendid because everyone was so taken by the Queen's appearance and manner that there was a feeling that she might have 'stolen the show.'

The only problem for the guests was how to strike a happy medium between their enthusiasm and 'decorum.' They all wanted to get a *real good* look, the probability being that it will be a long time before they would have another.

It may not have been quite a normal garden party but it was certainly a huge success. Their Majesties seem to have been extraordinarily nice to everyone. Presentations were not prearranged – not all of them. One certain lady who is notorious for her talkativeness was presented: she did her curtsy; her jaw dropped and she couldn't find her tongue. They say she'll never get over it – the missed opportunity to talk to the King.

Of course the dresses were amazing.

I don't mean the ladies' only but the gents, however we all did our best to honour the occasion – one old pioneer with whiskers had evening tails – white waistcoat and tie! To-day – Sunday – the King unveiled the War Memorial. We watched them drive out from Rideau Hall (Govt. House) then listened to the broadcast account of the proceedings and service, because we knew it would be impossible to get into Confederation Square.

It had rained during the night but the streets were just drying in the bright sunshine when they drove out. The King made a wonderful speech all about freedom and liberty and after the first opening sentences – dropped the rather stilted jerky style and spoke very steadily and firmly in that deep voice of his.

Immediately after the unveiling and to everyone's surprise he and the Queen spent over twenty minutes talking to the 'Vets' and 'Amps' and War Nurses. Walking practically unescorted through the crowd.

Even over the radio it made a tremendous impression and of course we ran down to see them drive back.... Now they have gone....

We have been stirred by such strong emotions – unusual emotions – that the past 48 hours seem dreamlike.... I am quite sure from comments of our neighbours and friends that they feel this quite as strongly as we do ourselves.

It will be the same in Toronto, I'm sure.

Montreal was a surprise, I think – the French there went crazy and shouted themselves hoarse.

In Quebec there was one small slip. The Royal Party were rather quicker than was expected at one point – with the result that they caught up with some of the escort going in the opposite direction up a very narrow cobbled street.

Just what happened I don't know, but I think the escort had to 'back up'. ...

Charles to H. on the 3rd September 1939:

Ottawa.... I hope you are all well and that you may all come through this war without harm.

We have just listened to the King's Speech and now there is a report that the *Bremen* has been captured by a British warship. I hope this is true.

I expect that you will be busy. I've reported to the R. C. A. F. I'm on the reserve of course but expect that we will be busy for a short time with our own end. I hope that I can be effective before long....

Charles to Alie on the 14th February 1940:

Lord Tweedsmuir's funeral is this afternoon and all Government offices are closed – but we are not going to see the procession. Marian is just over 'flu and the rest of us have had colds.

We mourn his death, – he was very popular all over Canada and particularly in Rockcliffe, here we often saw him and he would always give us such a friendly smile as I took off my hat. I never spoke to him except at garden parties to say 'Good afternoon' – but they all say he was a dear old chap.

... I've had another unsuccessful battle to get back to the R. C. A. F. I suggested that they might be able to use me as an engineer officer and the idea 'clicked'. I saw Steadman and he said they could 'use me' right away. I would have to go in as a Flying Officer but should get fairly rapid promotion to Squadron Leader. They actually held a position for me. I saw all my own bosses. J. A. Wilson would not recommend it to his chief – said he could not spare me. . . .

19

ABINGDON & OTTAWA

1939–1945

H. fails to sell his flight simulator or safe landing system – Charles unable to
get back into the R.C.A.F. – Charles' office job in Ottawa – H. in R.A.F.V.R.
at Abingdon – Bomber Command – 8 Group Pathfinder Force – Charles article
in *Canadian Aviation*

Ever since his recovery from his illness, H. had put in for job after
job. He was too old. Or he was not an engineer. Nobody seemed to
be interested in his two good inventions, his blind-flying flight simulator and his safe-landing system. One day he said, sounding rather
bitter: 'they (the Air M) have bought the Link after all. They could
have had mine for much less. . . .' It was one more blow but one for
which he was not wholly unprepared. He had written to Alie about
the air-line business, in 1935, 'I am a bad lobbyist . . .' He seldom
mentioned his simulator again. At least the Air M had had the sense
to buy a simulator – of whatever make – with the economy of time/pilot
loss/fuel and so forth which it would produce. He was still talking
away about his safe landing system, trying to arouse interest in what
seemed to him such a simple and effective aid. There was discussion,
but that was all: 'I cannot find anything but talk . . .'

He kept in touch, went to Meetings of his beloved Guild of Air
Pilots & Air Navigators, called in at the Aero Club and, as already
mentioned, went to their House Dinner there in 1938. He applied to
rejoin the Reserve of Air Force Officers and on the 5th January, 1939,
was granted a commission as a Flight Lieutenant Operational (Air
Control) Officer in the Reserve of Air Force Officers, Class 'CC'. He
was posted to Abingdon. During the summer of 1939 he made a
number of flights with other pilots: to Boscombe Down and back with
Sqdr Ldr Saye in a Miles Magister – H. 'flew m/c on courses out &
home.' He also made a few solo flights in Flt Lieut Dease' Klemm
Swallow E I A B D and Dease gave him a sealed authority to fly the

Klemm whenever he wished. In August he flew an Anson (?m/c from Honington) on 'three circuits & landings'.

On the 7th October, after war had broken out, he flew as co-pilot with Brent in a D H 86 4 × 4 × 220 engines, from Abingdon to Rheims (Champagne) and back: 'To see practical demonstration of working directional loop.' Once again it was the navigational side of flying which interested him. On the 1st September he had been re-organized into the R A F V R, which saddened him. He had been R A F O. for many years in the 1920's as well as since early January of 1939. But it was so, and he had to put 'V R' after R A F. He was 'Granted a commission as a Flight Lieutenant in the Administration and Special Duties Branch of the R A F V R' His seniority was 3.1.39.

His job at Abingdon became 'Regional Control Duties'.

H., naturally only too aware of the possibility of aerial invasion, wrote to Alie on the 5th June, 1940 '. . . I am so pleased to hear from Hermy that you will be coming to us but I do hope that you will come of your own free will as a normal visitor & not under the pressure of war. In other words I pray that the war does not reach Kent. There is no doubt that the German plans include invasion of this country by parachute troops, tank & troop carrying aircraft. The arterial roads from Maidstone to Charing, Rochester to London, & Herne Bay bypass to Margate are typical of what they would choose to land on; which implies therefore a battle for the North Downs.

The tank carrying aircraft is quite within the bounds of design. I can quite understand your reluctance to leave especially as your high sense of duty would keep you at your post . . . How thankfull we can be for the marvellous show put up by the fighter squadrons and all other units of the Air Force operating over the narrow seas & the Low Countries . . .'

H. had bought a copy of the now-legendary book put out in English pre-war by the publishing house of Lovat Dickson. In *Germany – Prepare for War* Professor Ewald Banse advised and detailed the plan which Hitler's armies were to follow: first landings on the Suffolk coast, followed by landings in Kent and Sussex, the classic German pincer movement. The armies, the invading forces, to link up to the North West of London.

Somewhere to the North West of London, said H., and in eminently suitably landing country, lay Halton, Dunstable, Woburn, Tring. It was a country rich in important houses, too, – Ashridge, Woburn, Tring, Chequers, Mentmore and many others, any of which would be suitable co-ordinating headquarters for the 3-point invasion and, of course, garrisons for the enemy troops. Colonel Haslam, (later Sir Humphrey Haslam), was O/C the LDV later Home Guard at Berkhampsted and it was he who organized the posse, and the daily rota, of riders who, unarmed and not strictly speaking in the Home Guard at all, searched the thousands of acres of Berkhamsted and Northchurch Commons, Rail Copse, Sallow Copse, Ashridge to the Bridgewater Monument and all along the escarpment to the forester's cottage and back through Clipperdown, in our search for enemy parachutists in the summer of 1940. We left home on our ponies in the dark so as to be in all the semi-wild country at dawn. Now at this distance in time the enterprise seems amateurish to the point of folksiness – but at the time it was hard-headed enough and at least we girls all felt that we were doing something even slightly useful in that time of waiting.

Charles wrote to H. on the 6th September, 1940, and it would appear that H.'s 'CC' rating had been improved to 'AB'.

... very many congrats H.O., on getting an A.B. – I think it does you great credit – so many people chuck their hands in when they have a bad illness. I can tell you I often feel down on my luck, there's nothing wrong with me – just too much damned office and I'm a little sore that my Minister won't release me to go back to the R.C.A.F. It is really J.A. Wilson who is holding me. He is an awfully fine old chap but of course has his own point of view which is not always mine.

I'm now doing as Superintendent of Air Regulations. issue all licences pilot's engineer's and control officer's. handle all registration & airworthiness of aircraft administer Air Regs (infractions, suspensions) also the war time Defence Air Regs and the special authority to visiting U.S. aircraft – Prohibited areas. There is a lot of correspondence with our District Offices and some work connected with issue of instructors authorities. There is an awfull lot of interviewing and it seems to be a tradition that one must be accessible to anyone – it is all very democratic & nice and given time I rather enjoy the mental rest given by these interruptions. – but that isn't much satisfaction when there is a pile of work left undone at the end of the day! I met Col Burchall and Capt Wilcockson yesterday and they enquired after you and were very glad to hear of your great improvement and asked to be remembered to you when I wrote. You will have heard of their activities and I suppose I shouldn't discuss them.

That is the hopeless part of letter writing these days. The few interesting events in my day are not for discussion and yet they will be of no interest in a short time. We have a lot of Americans up here anxious to help 'All they can'. A – very few – just want to help themselves. I'm building a house and expect to move in – in a few weeks. My address will be Manor Rd., Rockliffe, Ottawa, Ont. so please write there.

The idea of building is quite frankly as a hedge against inflation & against rising rents and because of my stupidity with regard to ordinary investment. The only good ones I have made in recent years are one gold mine and my house at Lac du Bonnet. . . .

It is a nice looking red brick house in Rockcliffe – which is the best residential district. There are no vacant lots near the house in fact there are very few left in the 'village' of Rockcliffe.

I drew all my own plans & so saved about $.1000 but it took a lot of time at night.

There is living room dining room kitchen study and lav. on ground floor & attached garage. On the first floor there are 4 bedrooms & 2 bathrooms linen closet etc. No attic. In the basement there is furnace room, work shop! & playroom. I don't know if the latter will be much used so I am not going to furnish it elaborately. It will have a fireplace, ping pong table & a sofa of some sort. The whole place is insulated with rock wool batts & heated with a good air conditioning – oil burning furnace. I think I can heat it for the same cost as coal in my present place $125/year.

This all seems so futile when you in England are fighting to keep the whole 'issue' intact. I suppose there will come a time when they can find a use for me . . .

Charles to Alie in October, 1940:
   . . . You ask what my work is. I am afraid that it is neither exciting nor obviously of major importance. However they will not release me to the RCAF although I'm still on the Reserve – and have done all I can to get moved – not all I can – because I could resign – but I

feel my family responsibilities too heavy to do that. I'm 'acting' Superintendent of Air Regulations and under the Controller of Civil Aviation and the Minister of Transport. I administer the Regulations that control civil flying in Canada, issue all pilot's licences and engineers licences, and aircraft registration.

Then I look after Civil flying instructors authority and so have some part in the extra work going on just now. We issue permits required under Defence – a wartime measure. The Chief Aeronautical Engineer works with me and assists in inspections that are necessary. We also do the accident investigations and prosecutions for breaches of Regulations, dangerous flying and all that sort of thing.

We have 14 aircraft and besides using them ourselves for inspection tours – and for calibration of the radio beam system on TCA we have to act as a communication flight for Cabinet Ministers and other senior Govt officials who find it more convenient to travel with us than on TCA or with the RCAF.

Of course these machines have to be maintained, overhauled and we keep a small staff of mechanics – whom I have to keep an eye on. We have just done a job of ferrying for the War Supply Board. About 14 aircraft were built for the Mexican Govt. at the time of the Spanish Civil War.

Curiously the Mexicans didn't want them when the Spanish war ended, and the machines have not been finished. So they have just been taken over as trainers by the RCAF. They had to be flown about 1200 miles over bad country and they asked us to do it. I am glad to say the job has been finished without losing anyone but the pilots did a good job because the machines were not designed to run in cold (artic) weather and the carburettors kept freezing up.

There are five district officers in the Air Regs Branch and they have assistants and stenogs and an engineer in each office. All this work converges on our office where there is myself and a chap called Desmond Murphy as my assistant, about half a dozen girls and 3 engineers.

Before the war there were 6 of us: Cowley (now Air Commodore) Abbott (sick) self, Murphy and Saunders (released to RCAF). So that is the story. I can honestly say that I'm busy but I'm dashed if I know whether I'm in the right job. I'm not any sort of a fatalist and if I ever get a glimpse of light and see my obvious duty in some other directions I hope I'll have the strength to follow that course without hesitation.

Jim and Joe are very well ... Marian sends her love ... look after yourself Ally dear.

I forget precisely when it was that H. said to me – words to the effect: 'the Air Force are using my system! – only they've improved on it. We've got Chichester, you see. Things couldn't be better, one of the very best navigators there is and I expect they've put him to work on it. It's even better now than my original idea. ...' He was so happy about it, so pleased for the pilots, and I never once heard him griping that he had never been credited with the idea. It was one of the true advancements in air safety and for once it did not matter in the very least who had originally thought of it. During the winter of 1940/41 H. took the action which earned him a Mention in Despatches in January. Unless the survivors of the aircraft concerned, in terrible trouble over Abingdon, are still around and happen to read this there is no way of discovering his precise action. When I asked him about it in later years he would say: 'I saved the country forty thousand pounds one dark night and the country always likes it when anyone saves them money ...'

Charles wrote from Rockliffe on the 26th February 1941:
... I've been told that you were mentioned in despatches recently and although I missed that Gazette I want to add my congratulations to the many you must have received. I was speaking on the 'phone to a lad at R.C.A.F. H.Q. yesterday & he said that Bread. had brought back good news of you. I was very glad to hear this and it bucked me up no end as I was feeling a bit lousy and useless....

Charles to Alie on the 8th March 1941:
This country and parliament is waking up to the fact that the forecasts made eighteen months ago of enormous aircraft production in Canada were just bad guesses by ignorant politicians – and there is a lot of mud being thrown around. My own impression is that there has been more stupidity than dishonesty, that there has been a great deal of fine preparatory work done and that false prophets and critics alike have not considered that:—
Canada is not an industrial country.
Canada has no surplus of skilled engineering labour.
Canada has only two or three men possessing any knowledge of aircraft production.

Canadian a/c plants were very small, imported nearly all their processed material *and* components from the U.S., a small proportion coming from England.

Canadian a/c manufacturers imported all engines and metal airscrews. British and U.S. domestic orders have caused shortages of all essential components and engines. Manufacturers of U.S. type trainers has therefore been held up in Canada, and manufacture of British designs made all the more difficult owing to the differences in standard specifications and gauges!

I needn't elaborate on this theme and as I have no part in this work I am not competent to do so, but you will easily see reasons why production is delayed.

I think they are getting on with the job now, but the shouting in Parliament isn't over yet. . . .

. . . Sigurd Lockeberg is one of the 'fathers' of skiing in this part of Canada. He is over 60 and is such a fine simple old chap.

He has a brass factory and small plant in Ottawa and works about 14 hours a day making buckles and other fittings for Army equipment.

Last war he made bugles. He is still a good skiier but 'owing to an old injury' doesn't do any racing *now*!

. . . The Wheelers have just built a good runway here and the big 22 passenger Douglas 'planes fly up from New York via Montreal in $3\frac{1}{2}$ hours.

It is a great success and everyone's very pleased about it because it helps the exchange to get American tourists up here and so aids the purchase of War supplies.

The tourist trade is about the 3rd largest industry in Canada so it is treated with proper respect.

Breadner is now Chief of the Air Staff in the R.C.A.F. I was speaking to one of his staff on the 'phone about a week ago and this chap said: 'Oh you'll be glad to hear that the Chief saw your brother recently and said that he was looking very well. . . .

And later the same year:

. . . Marian saw to the sale of the Lac du Bonnet house. . . . The Molloys are still there. Roy Brown is in Winnipeg. He was running an A.O.S. for a time and testing Ansons. Jim Uhlman and the M.G.A.S. are still guarding our Natural Resources, or what is left of them. . . .

I forget now who first told me that Amy Johnson was missing – it may have been Pat or Pam Bedworth, or Heather Craufurd. We four, all in Hertfordshire Detachments of the Red Cross, were billeted on the Hon. Mrs George Murray at Highfield House, Hemel Hempstead. We were all four on night duty and we had been on night duty for months. During the day we slept, or tried to sleep, in a room that had been the night-nursery of the young son of the house and who had now been sent to safer quarters further North. He was about seven years old. Outside the room in which we tried to sleep there was a stable yard. Beyond the stables, in the parkland and about 50 yards from our windows, the ack-ack battery was relentless. The battery gave round-the-clock protection to the hutted hospital where we worked, to Highfield House and much of Hemel Hempstead and to Brock's Firework Factory, now making munitions and whose huts almost filled a large field nearby.

In that half-world of physical exhaustion and dark and noise it was hard to remember who had said what – and when.

Amy Johnson was missing. Amy Mollison – Amy Johnson was missing.

It was true.

The next time my night off coincided with H.'s leave I asked him whether he had heard? Yes. He had heard. He changed the subject. I said that I thought it was very sad about Amy Johnson. H. spoke for several minutes about the fine young men who had gone, who were going every day, so many of them. So very many. I know, I know, I persisted. Still it was sad about Amy Johnson. Did he not think it was sad?

'Of course it's sad, E. dear,' he said, adding, sotto voce, 'I'm only surprised that she lasted so long. She had a tremendous amount of luck to last as long as she did.' He went on to say that she had probably gone down over The Wash, as the Duchess of Bedford had done. The turbulence there was unaccountable and violent. (It was only in recent years that I read that Amy Mollison had been lost over the Thames Estuary.)

Nothing has ever been able to alter the sense of responsibility I felt for Amy Johnson. Nothing at the time lifted the deep sadness I felt at her loss. We had never met, although she had glared at me out of angry eyes, as she sat crouched over the fireplace in the Clubhouse at Stag Lane, poking at the small fire and whispering to another pupil who sat on the opposite side of the fire. I had stared back until H. called to me to go out with him to a waiting Moth.

That was before she was famous. Now, early in 1941, she was gone. Only eleven years. I remembered the discussions, the arguments, about her: that tiresome young woman who wants to fly to Australia.

Tiresome – she may have been. Prickly. Hypersensitive. Angry. But surely one of the very bravest there have ever been.

Charles to Alie 11th May 1941:

(Marian) has been working hard at the Blood Donors Office that has just opened here, also at the Womens Auxiliary Red Cross and working on a refresher course of shorthand, too. The Red Cross is pretty hectic, apparently … I've been doing a little flying lately. I was told off for the odd transportation flight and I realised that I wasn't doing as much as I should: but my very stuffy job is almost entirely an office one and although I am learning the Ritual of the Civil Service I have not become a devout Civil Servant.

Continued June 9th:

… I decided that I was feeling a bit too stale and 'ossified' so made up my mind to go myself to fetch the rest of our small Beechcraft which had been to the factory in Wichita for some alterations. I had to hurry but could not get a seat on Trans Canada's 'plane to Windsor (which is just across the river from Detroit). I went on the night train from Ottawa (and didn't sleep a wink for indigestion) then took a taxi through the tunnel under the St Mary's River to Detroit. It was very hot in Detroit and I had nothing to do until the evening, when the 'plane left at 7.30 for Chicago.

Detroit is busy and prosperous these days but it is most attractive seen from the Canadian side, with it's cluster of skyscrapers and busy shipping.

I wandered. In and out of the big hotels and stores but couldn't as a loyal subject buy anything beyond a meal owing to the need of conserving our purchasing power for munitions. My 'plane left from the City Airport which is old and not very good. The chief feature being a huge tower for the storage of gas, which does look something like one of our gasometers but is a little taller. It is close to one of the runways and does set up rather bad eddies in certain winds. For years the airminded people of Detroit have tried to get rid of this tower but

the cost has been too great. They have even built a fine new airport
20 miles the other side of the city: but it is too far out. I'm afraid I
rather shocked a fellow passenger when I suggested that one well-
placed bomb would solve the problem very neatly.

Off we went in a large shiny Douglas and flew under a low cloud
ceiling to Chicago over the busy South shore of Lake Michigan.

continued July 17th:

I am including these two earlier attempts at letters by way of apology
and in case this effort is no more successful. I think I left off when
trying to describe a trip to the Beechcraft Factory. It was a very hurried
trip. We were put off the 'plane at Kansas City – two American doctors
and myself – at about 1 a.m. – they were going to a 'convention' at
Wichita. The aerodrome was out of commission at Wichita – but the
airline people gave us 1st class rail tickets instead. I found out that the
Santa Fe Bus Co. ran down there and we all tore off to the bus terminal
and scrambled on board. It took us 6 hours. So after a shave and
breakfast I went out to the factory. There were a few delays but after
lunch I took off and got as far as South Bend that night.

The next day I crossed over to the Canadian side at Windsor and
had an uneventful trip back to Ottawa.

The only other break from office routine has been a trip up to Moose
Factory in James Bay.

It was a very straightforward journey up there and the flight back
uneventful. The country is far from beautiful. Great rivers and mile
upon mile of muskeg and stunted forest of spruce and tamarack and
jackpine. There are very few good lakes in the last hundred miles so
it is wise to follow the rivers. Moosowra (across the river from Moose
Factory) is a famous place for duck hunters and there were some
American professors studying the wildfowl staying at the H.B.Co's
post. There were also some captive Eskimos from the Belcher Islands
up in the Bay. They had been brought in on a charge of murder the
previous winter by the R.C.M.P. An Eskimo, who has not been caught
yet, set himself up as a preacher or prophet and announced that Our
Lord was about to revisit this earth. He based his prophecy upon signs
in the heavens and the ravings of a fanatical Eskimo woman, Mina.

He announced that as a preparation for the second Advent, all
property must be destroyed, the children driven out into the snow and
clothing burned. Anyone disobeying was obviously an unclean devil

and must be shot. About nine men were bumped off and the young H.B. agent managed to get a message over to the mainland.

They got Mina, who has since died in hospital, I believe – and these two smiling round-faced little men who helped load my machine.

I believe they will get 'suspended sentences' which means a life job around the R.C.M.P. post, doing chores, with food, bed and tobacco – about the best bit of luck that is ever likely to come their way.

Thank you very much for your birthday letter. I have been feeling a bit old lately and have just been taking a holiday.

... Marian and I rented a 'camp' from some friends, the Camerons.... The 'camp' or bungalow is on an island in Big Cedar Lake about 90 m N of Ottawa. There is a good road for about 80 m. The last 10 is dirt road.

We came the easy way – by air. J.A. said that we might just as well make our practice flights up this way – so another inspector flew Marian and I and Timmie our spaniel up here last Wednesday.

It has been glorious, only 1 wet day.

We have a home made spring board and you can see the bottom – 10 feet down – the water is so clear. I haven't had any luck fishing but I never had enough patience and besides the boat leaks so badly you have to bale it all the time. There is a birch bark canoe which is beautiful to paddle but is too cranky to fish out of....

Well we have to go back to-morrow but someday we must get a place like this ...

Am back in Ottawa Saturday 19th July. All well.

H. continued at Abingdon as Air Traffic Controller. He had the mixed pleasure and pain of meeting several of his former pupils during that time: Roland Falk and Hugh Bergel amongst them. He was delighted to meet old friends. The painful aspect was that he would have so very much liked to have been an operational pilot once again. The Station Medical Officer had flown with him several times and advised against further flying, except of course on a casual basis, as a passenger.

The King and Queen visited Abingdon. The Officer Commanding had expected a brief, formal visit and inspection. The King wanted to see and to hear and he left the Queen for some 15 or 20 minutes while he toured the Station. H. was detailed to entertain Her Majesty. 'What an absolute charmer,' he said when he told us the story.

Another visitor to Abingdon was Airey Neave. H. said that he gave one of the most inspiring lectures that he had ever heard. Escape was always possible for a pilot taken prisoner-of-war. It was one's duty to try and escape and: Here are a few dodges.

His lectures were so good – and so thrillingly yet quietly given – that he was asked back to Abingdon repeatedly. The losses had been heavy from Abingdon. As an example: of the seventeen New Zealand pilots who had come over in 1940 only four survived a year later.

H.'s record of postings states that he went to 'HQ Bomber Command' for 'Flying Control' duties on the 8th November 1941; 'HQ No 2 Group' for 'Flying Control' duties on the 16th March 1942; 'HQ No 91 Group' for 'Flying control' duties on the 9th May 1942; and to 'No 19 Operational Training Unit' for 'Flying Control' duties on the 5th March 1943. But for most of the time Charles addressed his letters to Abingdon and they eventually reached H. If in doubt Charles wrote to Moor Cottage and Hermia or D. sent them on; and sometimes he sent them over by 'Special Messenger', as he did for H.'s birthday on the 1st April 1941. He referred to this in a letter of 17th July:

... I didn't realize you made your half century. I think that you would qualify for a bat at Ashey's but from what I hear of it you will chalk up a lot more runs.... I'm glad that Col. Robinson delivered my note. He is a most extraordinary man. He is a millionaire & for years has been flying his family around the world visiting the ruling families of umpteen hundred states – spreading goodwill and all that.

H. seldom mentioned any Service matter to any of us but one day, when on leave and at home probably from Bomber Command or after talking to old friends now with the Photograpic Reconnaissance Unit at Benson, he confided to Hermia and me in a voice of quiet excitement: 'The Germans have got a rocket.' Imagining the milk-bottle-and-stick variety of firework I failed to grasp the importance of the news. 'It's a big one, E.,' he said. I asked: what did it mean? – 'What does it mean, E.? What does it mean? – It means that we will be able to go to the Moon – certainly this century – perhaps quite soon after the end of the war....'

At that time he feared that the War might last for another ten years.

Charles to H. 23rd November 1942:

This is just a short note to wish you all a Happy Christmas. It is a long time since I have written and I haven't heard much news of you lately so I expect that you are all busy. We have had our first snowfall and the children were skiing in the Park a week ago. Now it has all gone – we are having cold, dry weather.

The wonderful news of the past few weeks has cheered everyone although I am glad to say that I haven't seen any signs of the over optimism that has been reported from the States. Since my illness I haven't been down there but our Test Pilot – who does most of the transportation jobs for us tells me that the production of the Eastern plants is only just beginning to count.

The recent disclosures of the strength of the British First Army compared with the U.S. Task Force in North Africa has had a sobering effect on some of the noisier American journalists.

The Alaska highway was opened yesterday. Whitehorse has swollen to many times its pre-war population – which – they say – is far from pleased at this revolutionary change. I can quite understand it.

The road was built – regardless of cost – at a rate of 8 miles per day!

The first Canadian built 'Mosquito' was demonstrated here on Saturday by Geoffrey de Hav. (junr). It was a most impressive show and they put the Harvards on the ground for the 25 mins it lasted. The Earl of Athlone came out to see it & the public was invited.

Earl Godfrey (Air Cmdr now!) was there and I saw two of the U.K. inspection board, General Lock and Brigadier Anthony. I know Anthony and took them and their party up to the Control Tower where it was a lot warmer. A lot of people got the same idea – a little later – and we began to wonder whether our control tower and all the Brass Hats would crash through the D. of T. hangar roof on to our nice shiny Beechcrafts & Lockheed below.

The air was damp and we saw some beautiful vapour trails form and disappear as the Mosquito banked vertically – a couple of hundred yards away from our tower. . . .

We can still run our cars here but the amount of gasoline is very limited – the old ration of 5 gallons per ticket being reduced to $1\frac{1}{2}$/We use our car as little as possible and I have about 30 gallons (or its equivalent in tickets) until March 31st 1943. . . .

We have cut out all 'non essential' flying as far as we possibly can but the few remaining 'loose ends' have been cleared up effectively by the 'Oil Controller' who at our instance has refused gasoline permits for unecessary purposes. There is of course a good deal of essential 'bush flying' both to mining communities and to the new airports and defence bases in the north where there are civil contractors at work. The Training Plan Schools – the E.F.T.S's – are now almost entirely military – the instructors being Sgt Pilots 'on leave of absence without pay' who are trainees of the schools. Only the management are civilians and I imagine that before long the transformation will be completed. I think myself it has been too slow although it has not made much difference – one way or the other – to the output.

What do you know about the work of the A.T.A.? I have read the accounts of the history and organization that have appeared in '*The Aeroplane*' & '*Flight*' and as something of the sort may be necessary here I would be glad to hear any comments that are not confidential, of course.

We have a few good women pilots that are eating their hearts out here and I don't see why they can't be used. . . .

Charles put a cutting from *Canadian Aviation* in with his letter. It was of an article which he had written and which had appeared in the October issue of *Canadian Aviation*.

NEGLECTED WEAPONS?
The Skiplane and the Seaplane.
by C. T. Travers.

The great speed and lifting capacity of modern military aircraft have not been achieved without the compromise of conditions that were thought, at one time, to be at the limit for safe operation.

The requirement of speed has driven the designer to a progressive increase in the wing loading; so that despite the provision of every device to augment the lift, landing speeds and take off speeds have been doubled; despite wheel brakes and variable pitch airscrews, the landing run and take-off run of heavy aircraft have increased in still greater measure.

Larger airports with longer runways have been demanded for every successive new military design of outstanding performance. The long range bomber requires a runway over one mile in length in order that it may take-off with a full load, and it is again emphasized that as the maximum speed of that bomber bears a close relationship to its stalling speed, so does its maximum speed and weight depend on the length and strength of the runway from which it must operate.

An air force will, therefore, require permanent airports or air bases, so located that the enemy may be sought out and attacked and so inter-connected that his raiders may be repelled or denied any local superiority or any freedom of movement in their vicinity.

Permanent aerodromes may only be constructed at any expenditure of great quantities of material and labor. In remote, unsettled areas transportation difficulties hinder such construction so that they must be planned many months before their use is contemplated.

These permanent installations have so great a military significance that they will be among the first objectives of any invading force. Should they be captured, the defending army will find itself without adequate air support, now recognized as a vital factor in military operations. It would appear to the writer that the defense of Canada and the maintenance of offensive operations beyond Canada might depend to a very high degree upon the continued possession of our distant and coastal air bases, yet experience has shown that isolated bases are vulnerable to attack from the air and by airborne parachute troops. Serious military consequences might follow should our long lines of communication become interrupted, or these bases be closed to our aircraft, even for a short time. These great air bases may, indeed, be considered by the strategist as factors which limit the range and mobility of his air power in attack; which in defense are fixed, yet vulnerable, preventing temporary withdrawals by the land forces in their vicinity under penalty of loss of air support.

There is good reason, then, to consider whether those natural airports, the lakes and rivers of this country, could be used in support of our present system of air bases, thereby strengthening our supply lines and our defenses.

It will be found from a study of the records of Civil Aviation and of the more accurate maps that there is no land area in Canada out of easy flying range of a lake or river large enough for aircraft operation; indeed, the water area so exceeds that of the land in some sections that a pilot may easily lose his way over the maze of lake and forest.

Lakes and rivers cannot be damaged by enemy bombing in the summer, and in the winter any attempt to destroy the whole ice surface of a lake by bombs would soon exhaust his supply on the other hand, aircraft may be easily dispersed around the shore and hidden in the natural cover of overhanging trees.

The intensive development of the military and civil landplane in the last decade, made possible by the new airports, led to the neglect of the skiplane and seaplane as military machines. The demand for fast mail services came from the great cities where there are few lakes, where the rivers, clogged with barges, are hidden by a pall of smoke and trapped with a network of cables.

Rivalry for control of oceanic air routes and farsighted policies, notably in England and the U.S.A., brought about the construction of great long-range monoplane flying boats of from 20 to 70 tons whose designers abandoned once again the traditions of low landing speed and low wing loading that were characteristic of the biplane boats of from 10 to 15 tons displacement built in larger numbers in 1918. This new trend was not followed in the small flying boats and seaplanes used by the Fleet Air Arm because the requirements for landing speed remained fixed by the special operating conditions in that branch.

The civil skiplane and, in lesser degree, the small civil seaplane and flying boat persisted as a practical device of the northerner, Canadian, Scandinavian or Russian, to adapt available aircraft to his needs. He was concerned with the economics of unsubsidized air travel and was unable to employ aircraft of military performance, although he was successful in finding the most simple solutions of problems which arose in the course of his novel enterprise. The demand for new aircraft, created by the bush operator, was not sufficient to encourage more than one or two firms to construct special aircraft, so that progress was very slow and their effort was devoted to general purpose, civil types.

It is believed that there exists a popular, if tacit assumption, that the skiplane or seaplane is inherently slow and heavy, based on a comparison of commercial types adapted to bush requirements with modern landplanes operating under subsidy. The writer contends that this generally held view is, however, erroneous and that both seaplanes and skiplanes can be produced with performance that is sufficient for Air Force requirements.

It is assumed that for economy of production such an aircraft would be convertible, that is to say, it would be designed to serve as a landplane, skiplane or seaplane, by fitting a suitable undercarriage, fin and other detail components. This arrangement might have the result that any one form would fall short of the ideal engineering solution. The seaplane also must be fitted with floats or a hull big enough to displace a weight of water perhaps twice as great as that of the whole machine yet strong enough to resist impact with the water at high speeds. The additional weight and resistance of these floats would seem to be sufficient to condemn the seaplane for military use were it not for the records of past achievements of these aircraft. The world's speed record has been held more often by a seaplane than a landplane and eleven years have gone by since a seaplane raised that record to 407.5 m.p.h.; today we hope that our fighters will go as fast.

The contest for the Schneider Trophy, which provided the excuse for the high speed aircraft of 1931, also proved that pilots who had been used to flying aircraft which stalled at 60 m.p.h. could be readily trained to land a new type of seaplane at 100 m.p.h. Equally remarkable was the feat of taking these aircraft off the water when it is remembered that fixed pitch airscrews were used at that time.

No special racing skiplane has ever been built, but repeated attempts have been made in Canada and Russia to reduce the drag of the ski undercarriage. Research and experiment at home led to the manufacture of more than one type of streamline ski, which did not require external trimming cables to hold it at the proper angle in flight but, unfortunately, considerations of cost, weight, and relative stiffness with consequent fragility, prevented their general adoption for Civil or Air Force aircraft. The 'bush' aircraft, with its high weight per horsepower, or power loading, experienced difficulty in accelerating to flying speed when the snow was sticky or soft; often running a great distance over rough snow, so that a flexible ski of relatively large area gave the best results. The military aircraft on the other hand, with low power loading and variable pitch airscrew should accelerate rapidly and permit higher ski loadings, to the advantage of the smaller, rigid streamline ski. Retraction of the ski would appear to be a straightforward engineering problem, necessary for the faster types.

Reports have appeared that experiments have been made in Germany with retractable floats but no details are known. The great inland waterways of the dominion – the rivers and the lake chains – have been for centuries the natural routes for war and trade, and the skiplane or seaplane will be able to call at any one of the hundreds of posts and settlements on these waterways for supplies.

The slow laborious methods of freighting fuel over winter roads will not be sufficient for a war of movement and large freighter aircraft will be required to maintain remote detachments with fuel and ammunition, with ground crew, camp equipment and food. The extent to which it is possible to support a detachment in the bush with air-borne supplies will determine its mobility and effectiveness, consequently equipment will have to be reduced to essentials and the ground crews selected with care so that every man may be self-reliant and the whole unit, as far as possible, self-supporting. The foregoing argument is advanced with the full knowledge of at least a few of the objections that might be raised to its propositions, the engineering and production delays, the crew training and organization.

'Where are these aircraft to be used?' – it may be asked. 'As seaplanes on the Somme or as skiplanes in the Libyan desert?' Briefly then: Russia, Norway, Finland, even Burma, every country through which we must advance to defeat the enemy and which is blessed with rivers, lakes or a good snowfall. Think of last winter in Russia, the wheeled aircraft hopelessly immobilized in the deep snow, the snowplows and rollers wrecked or simply not there, where they were wanted. Remember the Gloster Gladiators (fighters) sunk to their bellies in the snow of a Norwegian lake, a present to Hitler! Almost any skiis would have set these aircraft free but those who planned the operations were perhaps not familiar with the use of skiis and may be excused for their error.

The writer makes no further apology for his arguments, believing that the dangers of these days justify a fool in breaking in, where the angels, who are terribly overworked just now, fear to tread.

Charles to H. December 14th, 1942:

... The snow came early this year and today it was 10 below in the morning.

About two weeks ago we had a heavy snowfall and although they worked on it quickly as poss. T.C.A. were held up all the next day. It is great skiing weather but I can't do much climbing yet so I must leave my skiis for the present. I saw my doctor yesterday. My B.P. is up to normal but my pulse is still slow. I've put on 12–14 lbs and there is a good chance – according to records of similar cases – that my heart may cut in on the dud cylinder again.

Anyway the old doctor is very cheerful and I have great confidence in his opinion. The two boys are well.... They both skii very well and play a hard game of hockey. Unfortunately they don't get any properly organized rugger and the Canadian game is usually played here. I have never understood it completely – but I don't let on! They both swim strongly.... We hope to get a foothold on the Gatineau about 10 miles from town for swimming – but that may have to wait for more settled times.

17th:

More cold weather. The street car is about 2 blocks from my house and my long nose – which is my thermometer – told me it was cold enough. Actually it was − 16°F but it is damper here by the river than in Manitoba and you feel it more.... The B.B.C. News and 'Newsreel' is relayed to N. America every day & we rely on it ... The American News hawkers are usually over optimistic. If General Montgomery could hear them and had time to listen I think he would blush! They say he is right at the top of the pile of all Generals – past and present.

28th:

We had a very pleasant time at Christmas. My half section in the Office – Desmond Murphy, his wife, brother-in-law and boy spent the day with us. They had the roof sold over their heads – a common enough experience in Ottawa for Civil Servants with small fixed salaries.

There has been a great influx of people to Ottawa – Civil and Military Staffs have increased enormously and while the Government is able & willing to pay more to its temporary servants – the Treasury (and consequently the commission) refuses to do anything for the permanent staffs. We have been 'frozen' in our jobs. That is to say both Murphy & I cannot leave to join the R.C.A.F. although we've both been on the Reserve for years and he at any rate is still an active pilot.

Please excuse this old 'grouse'. I'm afraid none of us are content to 'be our age' or to realise that office work would be just as tedious in the Service as it is outside. I hope that someday I shall have a chance of hearing all about the War from you, but as one can't write about it now I was wondering whether you would have time to give, briefly, your ideas on Civil Aviation Control. You had many years of experience in Civil Aviation and no doubt see the need for changes in the Law and the International agreements. Here in Canada we adhered very closely to the I.C.A.N. and the English pattern. – but there were a good many modifications brought in to suit our local conditions. More recently we have adapted a whole series of *Airway* Rules from the American pattern and our system of *Airport* traffic control which preceded the Airway Control is similar to that in use in the States.

This all takes us away from the intention of the I.C.A.N. and their legacy (from Marine Law) of 'black balls or shapes' 'pyrotechnical lights' & 'small green or white flags'. At the same time we do not want to make the mistake of the U.S. Authority and attempt to legislate for every possible eventuality.

It seems inevitable that we shall have even more precise control of flight along the airways and at traffic controlled airports and that these areas & routes will be reserved to pilots & aircraft that can meet the requirements. The traffic will consist of scheduled flights almost entirely – there will be a few charter flights, but private aircraft cannot be allowed to delay or endanger aircraft of public utility. Aerodromes open to private & itinerant commercial aircraft will have control of a much simpler pattern. I think that every restriction to private flying must be thrown out unless it can be proved that it is necessary in the public interest – even if there is some sacrifice in safety. I believe that the law should be simple & liberal and the penalties severe. It is hopeless to fine some hardened old sinner $10 – & costs & suspend his licence for a week! ....

To H. on 14th April, 1943:

... I was staying with Fred Larsen – an old friend from 84 Squadron – who became a very successful architect. He has a son in the U.S. Army Air Corps & a daughter of 16 but can't get a job in their Air Corps &, like myself, has recently been rather ill.

His business is at a standstill of course and he has been going in for painting – so I had to try my hand at it too. The results were surprising and most amusing and I have added another item to my list of useless hobbies.

Marian and the boys are well – all three are better at sport than I ever aspired to be – and I am duly thankful for the fact ... There is still a great deal of snow left in the hills and four or five foot heaps of ice and snow on the north and east of our house. A very cold and miserable spring – about a month later than last year.

I am going to see the D.M.S. in a few days to see how I am making out. I believe I am fit – although my pulse is still only 34–36 it does buck up a bit after exercise! B.P. is O.K. again & I don't fatigue so easily. If they would let me do a little flying in our Beech, which is a very good little aeroplane, I would soon find out whether I was good for anything more than throwing 'files' around this – office.

Everyone has been getting all steamed up about the effusions of Mrs Clare Luce and for every book or magazine article published on 'Post War Civil Aviation' there must be twenty 'Memoranda' on the same subject, well buried in the departmental files of the United Nations.

I must admit that I am scared by the lack of realism in most of these writings and by the failure of so many to understand that it will be impossible to return to a pre war state of affairs – because of the necessity for a strict military control of Europe and other great land areas....

I'm a poor letter writer but wish that you were not so far away so that I could see you sometimes....

H. had been posted to Stradishall on the 17th May 1943 again on flying Control duty. On the 7th September he was posted to HQ No 8 Pathfinder Force, where he was to remain until the end of July, 1945.

He was delighted.

He wrote to Alie on the 15th October 1943:

Old Court House, Godmanchester, Huntingdon.

My dear Sloper,

I feel very guilty at not having written for your birthday, but just before 17th Spt I was moved to a new job here. I had the opportunity to exchange and this is much more the sort of work I like doing. In fact I prefer it to any I have had before, still a S/L post.

Godmanchester is a wonderful little place, very very old, this house is modern, William IV or early Victorian, but the cottage which forms one boundary of the garden is 14th cent. and the barn and sheds along the other side may easily be 17th. Huntingdon is also full of interest, though I have not had any time to explore.

On the other hand St Ives, with the single exception of 'Oliver Cromwell's barn' and the farmhouse, which were outside the town on this side, is dreadful yellow brick. Railway Gothic at its worst, except again the wonderful old bridge over the river.

Ol. Cromwell's barn should be listed as a national monument, it is so fine. I was sad to see the roof giving way a bit in one place, but when I passed to-day it appeared to have been repaired, so perhaps someone is looking after it. There is rather a dreadful tin filling station on the corner of the property and some old cars in the farmyard. Dreadful. Sad, too, that the new houses are spreading up the road on this side of the old property.

My work is mostly in Huntingdon and district up to about 20 miles away but sometimes takes me up as far as Norfolk . . .

The constraints of the time and of the Pathfinder Force in particular made it second nature to H. to mention nothing of his work. But as students of the Second War will recall, some of the most successful raids or return matches were made possible by the Pathfinders, under legendary Donald Bennett, for it was his Pathfinders who navigated to the targets and who dropped markers or flares to guide the heavy bombers in their wake. H. was very busy during his time at HQ 8 Group and had he not had so many home worries* it would I think have been one of the best times of his life. He was being more useful than he had been the whole war and was doing work that he 'preferred to any other'. His work took him to many Stations, including that of Tempsford (Group Captain 'Mouse' Fielden, the King's Pilot), – from which Station it will be remembered that the raid on Amiens Jail was carried out. 'You meet all sorts of interesting people at Tempsford,' H. said to me once, but he never mentioned names, other than that of his old Imperial Airways colleague Bennett, now his Commanding Officer at 8 Group.

In the autumn of 1944 Christina, waiting for her call-up papers for the W.R.N.S. to come through, paid a short visit to Godmanchester to see H. Her visit cheered him immensely: '. . . the happiest time I have had for years' he wrote to me.

* Both D. and Betty were very seriously ill during the latter part of the war.

Christina remembered meeting Air Vice Marshal Bennett during her time in Godmanchester, and a number of other pilots. She has told me since that, from various remarks and allusions they made in conversation at the time, she was perfectly sure that H. had recently been on one of the "shows" with the Pathfinders.

Navigation, after all, was his first love and his greatest skill. There was nothing recorded in his log-books.

20

THE OLD FIREPLACES

1945 – 1969

H. & H. buy their first farm – and their second – failure and retirement –
Charles represents Canada at Farnborough – H. dies – Charles to Mexico –
further correspondence with Alie – Charles dies.

TOWARDS the end of the war H. and H. bought a farm: such a
reasonable, such a pleasant thing to do. He had seen it first when he
had been walking up partridges in the stubble in September, 1944. A
little rough-shooting was a courtesy shown to many locally-stationed
Royal Air Force personnel by the sporting farmers of Huntingdonshire
and Cambridgeshire.

On week-end leave at Moor Cottage, he had described the dear old
farmhouse: Queen Anne, modernized in Georgian times, of mellowed
brick; tumbledown barn; numerous outbuildings and milking stalls;
small patch of garden; three hundred acres, (some let to Lady Hunt-
ingfield); pretty copse; a little creek bordered by willows; Eltisley
Church spire in view, Yelling Church a few yards across the lane. A
blacksmith's shop in the village; and a butcher's shop; and a pub and
a post office. All this just ten miles from Cambridge.

Hermia demanded to see it and, when she saw it, fell in love with
the place. 'It calls to me,' she said. Well – it was her turn to have
something that she wanted. We had all had the time of our lives and
years of happiness at Moor Cottage. Now it was her turn and she
moved fast as one should always do when one sees one's heart's desire.

Then H. began to do some sums and he wondered if, after all, he
really had enough capital behind him for such a venture. Hermia
promptly sold the lease on Moor Cottage, (we had the house on a 14-
year lease with option to renew) – thus effectively closing the discussion – for of course a move then became inevitable.

They moved to Huntingdonshire in May, 1945.

'D. was the greatest possible help over the move,' H. wrote to me,
'I could not have managed without her.'

On the 15th August, 1945, V. J. Day, I came on leave and H. met me at Euston Station. He was going to be de-mobbed. We drove in his Ford-10 Tourer, a marvellous little car that had never given a day's trouble over many years, to the de-mob centre; after a couple of hours he re-appeared carrying, among other things, a civilian ration book, a great many cigarettes, – he had almost given up his pipe – numerous bars of N A A F I chocolate and a perfectly frightful suit of clothes, which I vaguely recall as being also chocolate-coloured. 'May be useful when I'm driving a tractor,' he said cheerfully. As we drove out of London and steadily northwards, however, his cheerful manner faded.

He was out of the Royal Air Force, (although he remained on the Reserve until 1954), and he was going in at the deep end. He was 54 years old. He knew little about farming other than that which any country-lover may observe as he travels about, for his first-hand experience had been long ago and in the Southern Hemisphere. He did know a certain amount about accounting, though, and as we drove along he explained about borrowing and mortgages and capital – I could not even begin to follow it all – and how he was afraid that he had gone in too deep. That was the only part that I did understand. My blood, as they say, ran cold.

As soon as we arrived at Church Farm he was all cheerfulness again, bounding out of the car to shew me the barn – he was now quite sure that it was Elizabethan – he had discovered a thatcher in Buckden village and we would go over to-morrow and find out if the thatcher, who had been ill, would be able to come over and make a start on the re-roofing of the barn.

Hermia was, she said, in her seventh heaven. She and H. had discovered that Church Farm pre-dated Queen Anne by many generations and was in fact Caroline on an even earlier foundation. They had found a reference in Pepys' Diary – he of course a Huntingdonshire man: 'My cousin Nightingale hath a very pretty house at Yelling ...' which explained why the narrow, seven-acre field next to the old drove road to the East of the house which ran through the farm – was called Nightingales.

Hermia continued to uncover small pearls of that nature throughout their time there. She had grown so old and ill-looking during the war that it had seemed to me she would never be re-vivified, but now she looked brighter and happier than she had done since 1939. The house, full of familiar and much-loved pictures and furniture, was her home in a way that she had never felt Moor Cottage to be; the view was gentle towards Eltisley spire beyond the willows in the creek. The war and the breaking up and scattering of the family in 1940 now seemed a long time ago. There was, too – and as an unexpected bonus, more congenial society in that quiet Huntingdonshire country than she had looked for or expected and several neighbours called: the Findlay's from the Old Rectory in Yelling; eccentric and amusing Mrs Butler from the Manor House at Papworth St Agnes; David and Angelica Garnett from Hilton Hall – David an old acquaintance from Stag Lane – and the de Wilton's – Colonel de Wilton only lately home from cruel years in a Japanese prisoner-of-war camp.

D., who had long wanted to settle 'and grow a little moss' as she put it and Lindsay, who had said all along that he liked the idea of the farm and farm machinery and leaving school promptly, both came home in due course and worked very hard indeed. But Betty, Christina and I, still aching for Moor Cottage, were less sure. So we came and went, came and went, unable to settle, like swallows who have arrived too late to build and who can hear the North wind and winter coming down.

German prisoners-of-war came to work on the farm, four of them, in the charge of a little corporal, who booted them out of their lorry at the farm gate in the morning and yelled obscenities at them to hurry back aboard each afternoon.

H. told us that he had never met a German in all his life whom he disliked as much as he now disliked the nasty British corporal. 'The men are not criminals but prisoners-of-war,' he explained to us all, 'they have been taken prisoner-of-war quite honourably when they were serving their own country and they should be treated honourably,' and he remonstrated with the corporal, more than once, but the corporal only sneered at him and made foul remarks. H. asked the camp Commandant that a different N C O. be sent and after some delay the corporal was replaced by a sergeant, a reasonable, straightforward man who behaved in a civilized way to the prisoners-of-war in his charge.

After the Germans were repatriated there were two Luxembourgers, – men who had been pressed into Hitler's Army as part of his Labour Corps or Pioneer Corps. Hermia called them her Dwarfs, although they were not that, just wizened, arthritic little men, brilliantly deft with their hands.

'My Dwarfs have made me some lovely egg baskets out of special grasses – not osiers – which they found on the rise of land above the Creek, 'Hermia told me one day 'I never even knew that there WERE any special grasses on that little hill.'

On another occasion they re-veneered the old chess-table with veritable skin grafts of wood and their work endures to this day. It was not good work, they explained, for it was not good wood, only deal.

The greatest excitement was when H. and Betty, playing cribbage one winter's evening, began to speculate about the ugly Victorian fireplace in the drawing room. H. began to tap and to listen for hollows. The next day they brought the Dwarfs in for a consultation. Between them and over a matter of weeks they had restored an ancient fireplace to it's original beauty.

One day in early Church Farm days H. drove me along the side of Gravely Aerodrome. The road that cut off a triangle of land and which entered Yelling village by Farr's Farm has long been closed but then it was a public road and a short cut from Graveley and Papworth St Agnes. I asked him about the strange-looking incinerators spaced on either side of the runway on Graveley Aerodrome. He said that they were the FIDO's – the fog-dispersers – '... and the most useful landing aid ever invented. There is nothing as terrible as fog when you're trying to get down,' he said, still talking as he was still thinking, like a pilot. He was, in fact, never to fly again, not even as a passenger and, as though in recognition of the fact, Hermia at last gave way over the matter of the Nieuport propellor and allowed H. to hang it in the narrow hallway. It was a beautiful piece of workmanship.

When they left Church Farm, in 1949, '– getting out in good order,' he called it for the winter of 1946–47 had been a bad start from which they found it impossible to fully recover – he took the propellor over to a new aviation museum not far away. As that museum sounded as though it might have been the Shuttleworth Trust I enquired and have now been assured that they have it safely there.

H. was out-voted over his wish to retire completely in 1949. He wanted to go and live in a little house or bungalow in Bournemouth, where it was warm. Or better still – in New Zealand. He was out-voted 3–1 against. I asked D. many years later about it. 'Yes, that was true,' she said, 'he wanted to go and live in a bungalow in Bournemouth.'

D. found the next farm they went to: much older house, much smaller acreage. Again there were willows outside, old beams and old fireplaces within. Again, he could not help trying to improve the place, as he had improved Church Farm. He did so like to maintain and to improve whatever he touched. He went in with a returned p.o.w. from one of the Japanese camps, who was setting up as a contractor and between them they bought an almost new C L A A S combine harvester, a magnificent pea-green monster and such as can be seen in every county nowadays. In 1949 theirs' was only the second one to be imported into the U K.

H. also designed, built (with Lindsay's help) and patented an excellent corn drier and he was delighted when D., who had done so much from the start to build up their beautiful small milking herd of pedigree Jersey cows, designed and drew a milking parlour that was so neat and well thought out that it became the recommended design for the County.

In 1949 I was at home for part of the summer. I had planned to do some writing and to start work on the book, to take H. on one side and and ask him to reminisce: about himself, about Jim, about the old flying days. I had come to the wrong shop for that. They were all working so hard and were so wrapped up in the farm that I was swept along with them in the excitement and work of harvest time, of the efficiency of the C L A A S combine, all the talk and work of the place. I told D. what I was planning.

She said – words to the effect – 'I shouldn't bother him with all that now. As a matter of fact a journalist or reporter or something came here a little while ago. He wanted to talk to Pop. He was compiling a book on the twelve men whom he thought had contributed most to the winning of the war. Pop was one of the twelve, I think it was his safe-landing system and some of his other ideas ... there was to be a chapter to each man. Twelve men, twelve chapters ... only Daddy said that that was all ancient history, flying was a thing of the past for him, he was farming now and very busy ... and the journalist or whoever he was went away....'

It was exceptionally bad luck that the second farm did not succeed for they had all worked so hard on it. They were all a lot older, H. and H. looking far from well. H. had another slight heart attack. D. became

seriously ill again and was in hospital for months. There was no one
with her skill to care for the cows properly or to milk them and keep
all the records in order and so they were sold. Yet it was the cows –
the milk-cheque – who were the great cash-producer. As I learned in
odd remarks from H. when he visited his sisters in Bredgar or in brief
allusions to fresh disasters from Hermia, the slow disintegration of the
place seemed to be more and more like a garment unravelling. Or
perhaps like Dunne's early flying machine which, on landing in a dyke
'separated into it's component parts. . . .'

The family separated into their component parts and after many
vicissitudes H. and H. arrived again in Bredgar, where by then my
husband and I had our cottage.

The bank and the vultures had not taken everything and a few
treasures survived. Among the treasure was a silver cigarette box
which Bill Oliver had given H. more than twenty years before as a
memento of Stag Lane days. H., who valued the box as he had valued
the giver, put the box into Christina's hands some months before the
farm finally folded.

Although H. and H. moved in with me early in 1957 I was often not
at home myself but was back and forth to Devonshire with my
husband. Each time I returned to Kent, often for only a few days at a
time, I wondered whether or not to discuss the possibility of doing a
book with H. either about Jim, something I had long wanted to do
or, if H. was agreeable, about all three. Each time I came home I
hesitated to broach the subject, remembering the twelve men and the
twelve chapters. Each time that I went back to Devonshire I wished
that I had done so.

Charles and I wrote to each other from time to time and so it
occurred to me to sound him out first about a life of Jim. If he was
favourable I could take it from there and discuss the project with H.

In retrospect I regret every wasted chance of talking it over with
my father, for what had been true on a hard-working farm in 1949
was no longer the case when he was totally retired – he was not idle
by nature and was fretting for something to do – eight years later. It
was particularly stupid of me as there were several openings. I had,
for instance, read Nevil Shute's *No Highway* and we talked about it.
'Ah!' said H. with sharpening interest, but have you read *Slide Rule*?
That is an absolutely first rate book. . . . He was at Stag Lane you know

... then Airspeed of course ...' his voice trailed into his memories. Still I said nothing. In those wasted months I could have obtained H.'s first-hand account and had his story at a time when he still had safely by him his attache case with those historic letters, letters from Robert Blackburn, Geddes, Sir Sefton Brancker, Will Johnson, Sir Alan Cobham, Geoffrey de Havilland, letters from grateful and often distinguished pupils, all in that attache case before it had been raided and robbed and most of the contents thrown on the fire. ...

Back in Devonshire again in July, I wrote to Charles. His reply was dated the 5th August:

Hotel Vancouver, Vancouver 1 B.C.

I have no excuse for the delay in answering your letter – except the doubt I may have as to the amount of factual material I can supply.

I am delighted that you are planning to write a life of Jim and will send you what I have when I have time to dig it out but I must tell you that my memory, never very precise, is to a great extent limited to the personal sense of affection for a dear brother who had a great enthusiasm for aviation. I have a few of his rough notes and some old letters. A rather poor photograph of his aeroplane that I took in the shed at Eastchurch, and that is all.

I think he filed a Patent Application for his engine – This may be at the Patent Office.

Your Dad might be able to add a good deal that will round out the story of the early days at Eastchurch.

Many of the old timers may be around.

We are all well at home and Marian is able to get around – drive – and do all her chores – swim and play golf. ... (Marian had suffered a badly-fractured leg some months earlier.)

We have a new Government and a new Minister of Transport. Mr Hees. He is a young – a sixfooter – a successful business man and full of energy. He has been rushing all over the country getting to know people in his new job.

So I hitched a ride with his party two days ago in order to visit my own blokes on the West Coast. We left Ottawa at 9 a.m. Sunday and landed at Patricia Bay (Victoria) at 3. 30 the same afternoon. Not bad time.

We have some grand fellows in my branch.

One who is nearly my age, persuaded the Air Force to put him and three mountain climbers down on Mt Slesse by helicopter near the

7800' peak that stopped a T. C. A. North Star a few months ago. They
had to use ropes to reach the wreck but a great part fell 1000' to a
scree that is inaccessible because of avalanches. He wants to count all
the little pieces but I have told him to quit before he breaks his neck. . . .
I shall be over to see you.

Your affectionate Uncle Charles.

After he had returned to Chelsea, his house on the Gatineau River, he
wrote again:

. . . To-day Saturday is the first that I have had time to look through
my old papers and I am sorry that I have nothing that would serve as
'source' material for a life of your Uncle Jim. I know that we all talk
a great deal about him but in retrospect I believe that his personal
charm – affectionate nature and enthusiasm – all rather intangible
qualities - are those that remain in my memory.

As an inventor and designer he never received public notice in any
degree – although I feel that he had great insight. He had a fondness
for sketching & drawing – might even have done something in Art –
though I'm no judge of that . . . I'm sure your Dad would be able to
draw on his memories of those days – rather more direct than mine.

I returned to Ottawa last Saturday from Vancouver and on Sunday
we had the worst crash in Canadian aviation history, not far from
Quebec City. The investigation and endless questions have kept all
my staff here and in that part very busy. You can well imagine the
diversity of technical & legal problems and I hope that you will excuse
my late reply on those grounds . . .

From those two letters I learned the picture: that Charles was delighted
I was going to attempt a life of Jim but that he could not give me any
source material. It did not matter. I would go to official sources for
dates and details and rely on my father for all the rest. He had already
talked to us all so much of Jim when my sisters and I were young. So,
at last, in January 1958 and after months of pointless delay, I talked
about the book to H. The opportunity came by chance. We were
sitting in the kitchen, drinking coffee, and sorting through some of
the packing cases which my parents had brought with them.

It was a gloomy day outside with a cold rain beating on the small
window. Indoors we were very snug by the Aga. As I leafed through
a collection of photographs of the Dutch Masters in the Riksmuseum

I came suddenly on a collection of aviation photographs, circa 1930, tucked in amongst them and asked H. what they were. His response amazed me. As he detailed them – 'that's a Pterodactyl, that's *Grey Goose* – on floats' and so forth all the years of worry and disappointment seemed to have vanished, his voice was confident and cheerful again and his eyes sparkled. So I poured out my idea of a book, about Jim, about them all three. He began to pace the floor. He would look out what he had – letters and so on – he had many memories, particularly of Eastchurch – the Admiralty had all Jim's work on flying-boats and seaplanes. . . .

I was due to rejoin my husband in Devonshire the following morning. So H. and I agreed to make a start on the book just as soon as I came home again in April. He would make a few notes and we would start the book in April. . . . The winter of 1957-58 was no colder than any other in England. In February there was even a strangely warm spell which should have been a warning about the coldness of the approaching spring.

Charles and Marian had made several visits to England since the war. Their first trip after the war was in 1948 – his first visit for almost twenty years, hers' for ten. Thereafter they came over every few years until 1958. Usually they crossed together, holidaying and calling on family and friends but on one occasion he came by himself, on business, and unannounced. The first that any of us in Bredgar knew of his arrival was when I received a telephone call from Claridge's: 'Mr Charles Travers would like to speak to you.'

He came down to stay with us in Bredgar for the week end and told us all the news.

The news was interesting and the news was good. Charles had been asked to choose new aircraft for the replacement fleet of medium-haul machines for TCA. He could shop around the world and he had decided to shop around in 'Yurrup' first of all.

He had spent some days on the Continent: 'We – the Canadian contingent – were treated like Royalty in Germany,' he said, 'when we landed in Dusseldorf they had the Mayor of Dusseldorf and the Town Band out on the tarmac to greet us . . . .'

At Farnborough there had been no such Royal welcome and the quiet-spoken, 55-year-old former pilot may have been scarcely noticed as he

looked with keen-eyed interest at what he saw. In those days, it will
be remembered, Farnborough was a yearly display, exhibition and
market-place.

Charles liked what he saw there, particularly, he said, liking the
Bristol Britannia, but the Britannia was still in blue-print. Whatever
he bought for TCA they would, he said, have to stay with for some
years. An airline could not chop and change and switch at short
intervals. So with much regret he decided against the Britannia in case
of the unlikely event of major problems showing up during flight
testing. All this he told us as we sat before our fireside, eating scrambled
eggs and drinking coffee. His eyes twinkled as he described the Britannia – what a superb aeroplane that was going to be!

Next in preference to the Britannia was the excellent and well-
proven Vickers Viscount. So he closed with Vickers, on behalf of the
Canadian Government, an order for Viscounts that was considered
big enough for it to be excitedly reported over the BBC Radio News
that evening. The order, an important one for the British aircraft
industry, was worth 'over £2-million.' Charles did not have to buy
British: he was briefed to buy that which was most suitable for the
then needs of TCA. It was a happy coincidence that Vickers had an
aircraft that was just right. Reading his old letters 'I wish some British
manufacturer would come into the picture – they could have the
market' – makes one aware just how pleased he must have been that,
in 1953, British and Canadian interests coincided.

When I visited the National Aeronautical Collection at Rockcliffe
in 1982 it came as something of a shock to see a Viscount, one of their
collection, standing out by one of the hangars – a museum piece
waiting for restoration and eventual housing.

In the spring of 1958 Charles and Marian had decided on a holiday,
first to get some of the sunshine and warmth of Spain and then to
come to England in late April.

Charles wrote to H. from Chelsea on the 22nd March:

I daresay the sisters have told you that we are planning a short
holiday in England about the end of April and I am looking forward
to seeing you and Hermy again.

I am afraid that neither Marian nor I have been in the best health –
although I expect that a change will do the trick. We have booked a
round trip – Lisbon & Barcelona so as to take in a bit of sun. We have

had rather a hard winter and there are still feet of snow round our place and on the river in front. My job is going well but there has been rather a panic in the last twelve months over the high accident rate and I now have to organize an Accident Investigation Division and concentrate solely on this rather ghoulish task.

Unfortunately the usual limitations in the Government will slow up the job even with the best efforts of our Personnel blokes. We are in the middle of an Election Campaign but will miss Polling day. We are pulling for the Conservatives. They had a bare majority in the last short Parliament – and I think have a better leader in Diefenbaker than in Pearson as well as a far stronger cabinet. Dief. is full out for stronger Commonwealth ties and should build up trade with England. We are finding out now – to our cost – that in trade affairs the U.S. are fair weather friends who cannot withstand their own internal pressures for protection against Canadian produce.

All the best H. We are leaving to-morrow night from Montreal and will look forward to seeing you soon. C H A S.'

It was the last letter H. was to receive from Charles, for Charles' next letter reached Bredgar after the funeral.

'He will always do what is expected of him,' so wrote J. L. Bevir to Emmie soon after H. had left Wellington.

What was expected of H. on the 15th April, 1958, was that he would go to the village and buy a tin of coffee, that particular item having been forgotten on the morning's expedition.

The wind was like a knife from the North East, slicing over the Isle of Sheppey from the North Sea. It was not a day for an elderly, ailing man to venture out even once, let alone a second time, but he went, in spite of the cough which had been troubling him for days.

He was awake and coughing for most of the night and in the morning Hermia, suddenly worried, telephoned for a doctor to come as soon as possible. She made the mistake of telling H. that she had done so, whereupon he got up to wash and shave and promptly collapsed. He died within about ten minutes. In the circumstances a post-mortem was ordered. It was then established that he had died of virus pneumonia. He was 67 years old.

Charles and Marian stayed over with Alie for a few days after the funeral and we had some bittersweet hours of talk and reminiscence during their sad little visit.

There had been an echo of earlier days, said Charles, while he and Marian had been about to depart from Lisbon. The story went: That there had been one of those elderly, wealthly, bejewelled and befurred ladies of the type who ought never to travel alone. The lady appeared to be in dire trouble about her ticket/flight number/time of departure or something of the sort. 'She was what we call at home a "duchess in distress",' said Charles. He lifted his hat and offered the lady assistance 'I'm Charles Travers,' he said, 'may I be some help?'

The lady's travel difficulties were soon resolved and all the passengers boarded the aircraft. Soon after take-off another passenger, a man of Charles' own generation, came along the aisle to speak to him. 'I heard you say that your name was Travers,' said the stranger, 'I wonder if you are by any chance any relation of the Travers who used to instruct at Stag Lane? My name is Tutt, Charles Tutt – Trav and I used to own a Moth together: *Grey Goose*. . . .'

He and Charles had some enjoyable in-flight conversation and Mr Tutt gave his address, (in Weybridge) and hoped so much that H. would get in touch with him there; he would like to yarn again about old Stag Lane days. . . .

The following morning, at their London hotel, the papers broke the news to Charles and Marian.

None of us in Bredgar had known their day-to-day plans in Spain, nor with which airline they were travelling and so had been unable to let them know by private letter.

Only a month or so earlier there had been the Munich air crash and Charles brought up the topic, wanting to know whether I had heard what opinion had been reached as to it's cause. At that stage – about April 22nd or so – they were still, I thought, trying to blame the pilot.

Charles was almost disbelieving.

It had looked to him, as it had looked to them all in the AID in Ottawa, like slush on the runway.

'We *all* thought that it was slush on the runway,' he said. It will be remembered that it was only after the destruction of the pilot's career and his early death that the official view was, at last, given that the cause of the Munich air disaster was: 'slush on the runway.'

Charles and Marian returned to Canada earlier than planned; and a letter of his to H. arrived after he had gone home; I sent it on to him and he replied:

Chelsea, Quebec, Canada. 20th June 1958:

... Thank you very much for your letter and enclosure. I am very glad to have that letter ...

'... I wish we had more time in England but we did see some of Marian's relatives and visited V. up in Malvern. Our trip was very comfortable in the big 'Britannia' turbo-prop and we flew non-stop to Montreal in $11\frac{1}{2}$ hrs! It has been very cool weather and rather wet – particularly on week ends!..'

Among the handful of old friends whom Charles had seen in England was his old school friend Thurstan James, now Editor of *The Aeroplane*. I had sent a short notice about H. to the paper (as it happens inaccurate in one detail) – but Mr James had already heard the news. He wrote to me on May 2. 1958 from Bowling Green Lane: '... I was sorry to learn from your Uncle Charles of your father's death. It was some time since I last saw him in the Royal Aero Club....'

Later on Thurstan James was to write in the warmest of terms to Christina, telling her that it was Jim who had first of all inspired him to take up a life in aviation....

For many years Charles and Marian had gone down to Mexico to bask a little and refresh themselves in the warmth of the sun and they bought a house along the shores of Lake Chapala, as did so many other Canadians and Americans. There was quite a little colony of them there.

In 1963 they still owned their house at Chelsea and they invited me to spend a few days with them there when I went over for Joey's wedding.

The Gatineau Hills, the Gatineau River and their lovely house, all were even more beautiful than I had expected and the early summer days of late May were alight with the fresh green of the maple. It was a short visit, for Charles had not been well. He said good-bye. 'We won't meet again,' he said. They spent more and more time down in Mexico, eventually settling there permanently. Family letters still crossed the Atlantic at regular intervals, most to Alie, his lifetime and most faithful correspondent. A few came to Jay; or to me.

To Jay from Chapala, Jalisco, Mexico. June 22nd, 1966:

... Marian hasn't had a single reply to her advertisement of our beautiful Chelsea house, but she has sent me a cutting from the Ottawa

On the Gat. Charles at his home at Chelsea, on Lake
Gatineau, 1963

photo: author

paper and it is evident that we were asking about twice as much as we
are likely to get! Marian did so well in selling two of our houses in
the past that we were optimistic – but it doesn't really matter – as they
say in Canada 'we are not feeling any pain'! So she may have to put it
in the hands of a real estate agent and come back to Mexico.

She has seen many of her old friends who have been glad to see her:
then there was the famous Dog Show (which she started). Everyone
brings their family pooch, specially groomed. It lasts two days & is
quite a smart affair. They make a lot of money for charity. Still M.
says its not like the old days and she wishes she were back here in
Chula Vista. . . .

I'm managing to look after myself but we have a daily maid who
washes the clothes & dishes, mops the floor etc. She works very fast
and then comes up with a cup of coffee and a smiling face at about a
quarter to twelve – and says 'Terminado, senior' & I say 'Bueno,
gracias, Bertha' and off she goes.

I do my own shopping & cooking – and that's 'really sumpting'. . . .

Alie wrote to him suggesting that he write a history of flying. He replied.

To Alie July 6th:

... Now why don't you write a history of the W.I. because what you did put life into that rather depressed old Village of Bredgar is an epic in itself. Thanks to Alken the Church did not provide any stimulus for a decent social life for the people – there was no one to give them a lead.

I do hope that you will continue to improve in health, Ally dear, and that the house will sell well. ...

Joe is away on his travels and is going to Australia and New Zealand after South America. ...'

Alie returned to the possibility of Charles writing a flying history, for he wrote to her again on the subject on 30th August:

... Ally dear, I have thought a lot about writing some account of the extraordinary development of the aeroplane within our lifetime, and of your offer to send me valuable 'source' material. My reasons for refusing are confused and that is the point.

Historical fact might be distorted and realities give place to emotional images. If I could write well, in a truly poetic vein, produce an impression of the human enthusiasms of the time – then that would be worthwhile.

In England there are official histories and I believe in the U.S. also.

I know of the two Canadians who are attempting Canadian histories – from the time of McCurdy in Nova Scotia – and one, who is a close friend, has asked me for 'stories'. Then of course there is Hollywood and the film, I've forgotten the name (The Early Whirly-Birds?) I haven't seen it and I don't want to – although they spent millions on its production. I understand that there is the usual hopeless confusion in sequence of time, and in the location of events, although some of the full scale copies and models of early aircraft are well done. ...

Another letter to Alie in which he described fully automatic transmission: ... It is a hydraulic transmission using a kind of light oil. Do you remember Jim's ideas for an 'infinitely variable speed gear'. – This is the nearest thing to it. So you see that is the main problem of a person with gout is getting in and out of the car! ...

To Alie in 1968: '... Marian nursed me for years and although I am now feeling remarkably well and self-confident I suppose that it is – in part – due to my acceptance of a slower easier approach to little daily problems.

Dr Melling, a neighbour from Edmonton, Alberta, persuaded me to buy a TV some years ago. It was a source of constant annoyance until I hid it in a cupboard. . . .

I think that Vietnam has been a rude lesson to the USA and that they will get out as soon as they can, leaving the Vietnamese to sort it out on their own. This goes also for the Eastern Mediterranean. . . .'

And later on: '... Don't worry about the Yanks too much. This is their innings but they are dropping more catches than we ever did.

I thought they were right in Viet Nam and I was concerned about Australia and New Zealand but now I'm not so sure that they didn't walk right into a trap. I listen to the short-wave U.S. broadcasts sometimes and they talk of nothing else but how to get out of the mess. . . .'

To Alie on the 5th June 1968: '... Thank you very much for the bumper crop of '*Illustrated*'s' (*the Illustrated London News*-Ed) ten in all, plus the *Faversham News*. I hope that they keep the new airport away from Sheppey, although it may only be a few years before the aircraft take off vertically and so not require those 10,000 ft runways and extended 'approach' paths.

I read that many of the tactical military aeroplanes are already doing this, through the rise of fantastic 'thrust' developed by the newer engines. What would dear old Jim have thought of it all? He might have designed a super flying boat cum 'hovercraft' that would lift itself gently from the seaside dock and then gain flying speed over miles of open sea. . . .

I am sending a copy of our *News* – not that it contains anything of special interest but rather to show the good all round coverage it provides. . . .'

To Alie, on the 3rd July: '... This house is small so I drive the $2\frac{1}{2}$ miles to Chapala for the mail or groceries and then go into my separate 'Humpy' which is workshop art room – writing desk, lav and shower, all complete. It was a small addition and provided a bunk house for Jim when he stayed with us last year.

Of course it wouldn't do up North. No heat, and single pane windows!...'

In other letters Charles described the wonderful Mexican music, so different to anything he had heard elsewhere. Marian and he enjoyed concert-going. All through the letters he wrote from Mexico there is the lilt of happiness. Getting on a bit – he may be, but he was still, albeit slowly, enjoying life.

On the 9th May, 1969, he was just driving 'the $2\frac{1}{2}$ miles to Chapala for the mail' when the car was involved in an accident. No other vehicle was involved and it was thought that he may have fainted at the wheel. No one other than Charles was hurt.

He died in hospital the following day.

With typical consideration Marian wrote the news to me to relay to Alie, rather than let Alie read such a letter when she might have been, as she so often was, alone. I drove over to Faversham and read Marian's letter aloud and saw the light go out of Alie's blue eyes. She dragged on, in and out of hospital, for another eight months. It was really surprising that she bothered to live on for as long as that. Jay died the following year, in 1971, and so that generation of Travers closed V. having died in 1966.

Through the thoughtfulness of Stuart McKay I met Bill Oliver again and have seen him several times in the past few years when he has been over from his home in Hawaii to visit his cousins in Kent.

Although no longer the youngest certificated pilot in the country Bill O. has changed remarkably little since Stag Lane days of sixty and more years ago. Still easy-going and unflappable with the same sharp mind and kind heart.

We talked of Stag Lane: of Geoffrey de Havilland, of Victor H. Doree, R. M. Clarkson, Hugh Bergel, Jean Batten, John Saffery, Tom Campbell-Black, Edouard Bret – one of the few still around and who now lives in the South of France – so many names, so many pilots.

We talked, just a little, of the War. I told him how, in the depths of winter 1940-41, I had seen London burning; of one night in particular when, on a bus on the way to Hemel, the whole sky to the South East was aflame and it was possible to read a newspaper by the light of that terrible sky. Of how H. had subsequently said: 'It was the Docks – St. Kat's – that was all our sugar going up.'

Bill remembered how he had been flying during the blitz over South West London when the whole air was suddenly fragrant with lavender, the sweetest scent of all wafting up from the ground and all around him — and how he later learned that the Yardley Factory had been hit.

Enough of the war. Much longer ago than Stag Lane, which seemed only yesterday.

I spoke of my book.

'You won't get it all,' he said.

Well, I have not got it all — or even a tenth part of it.

Perhaps one day I shall write a better book, correct any mistakes I may have made in this one and fill in some of the many gaps which still remain.

For the time being this is all.

THE END

ACKNOWLEDGMENTS

I would like to record my deep indebtedness to my sister, Christina Back, for making this book possible, for she generously let me read and copy so many of the letters in her possession. All quotations from Jim's letters as well as the majority from H. and Charles' letters to Emmie and to Alie, are taken from letters in my sister's possession. So, too, are extracts from various other family letters and from the correspondence following Jim's death. I do thank her for her long-term support and encouragement throughout the writing of this book; and for the kindness of herself and her family during my many visits to her home in 1979, 1980 and 1981.

Charles' letters and writings occupy the greater part of five chapters and I would particularly like to thank his widow, Marian 'Marie' Travers, and my cousins James G. and Joseph S. Travers, for the very warm and friendly way they agreed to my using this material.

Most of the letters in Chapter 5 might have been lost without the prompt action of Margaret (D'Albiac) Frederick, into whose possession they came following the death of her husband, my cousin Capt. (E) John Frederick, R.N., who had inherited them from V., his Mother. It was most kind and thoughtful of Cousin Margaret to send me the packet of family letters – out of the blue and unaware that I was attempting a book – and with it H.'s copy of *Wing Tip*, to which by a happy chance her father's cousin, John D'Albiac, was a contributor, he also having been a pilot serving in No 1 Wing, RNAS, in 1916.

To my Cousin Bea (Cornwall) Robson I am indebted for additional information on the Cornwall family in British Columbia; and for her kind encouragement; and I thank Dr. Thomas L. Brock, LL.D., for his thoughtfulness in putting me in touch with Cousin Bea; and for his own help and encouragement over the years.

Earlier on, before contacting the family, I had been accumulating relevant information whenever possible, and with this in mind had written to Jean Batten for any memories of my father at Stag Lane which she could give me for inclusion in a life of H. Her response, typical of her spontaneous generosity, was her superb letter to me of May, 1966, – 'written from the heart' she later told me. When we finally met, at the Guild of Aviation Artists Dinner at the Royal Air Force Museum, Hendon, in 1981 – at which she was joint Guest of Honour with Judith Chisholm – Jean gave me her permission to quote wherever I wished from her writings. Some months later she wrote to me confirming this. It was the last letter which I was to receive from her. She wrote while she was staying with Robert Pooley and his family, friends of hers over many years, in Hertfordshire. Mr Pooley's firm, Airlife, had published Jean Batten's autobiography, *Alone in the Sky*, in 1979. Mr Pooley very kindly sent me a copy in 1985. I acknowledge with thanks Airlife's permission to quote from *Alone in the Sky*.

Other correspondents with between-the-wars memories, particularly Air Vice Marshal Donald Bennett, Wing Commander Roland Falk, Hamish Hamilton, Nigel Tangye, Sir Barnes Wallis and Philip Wills, all wrote to me in the most kind and helpful way; and a postcard from Sir Francis Chichester acknowledged flying instruction from H. early in his, Chichester's career.

During the 1980s I was able to spend more time on the project than formerly and a chance visit to a Lecture given by Gordon Bruce, (among many other things Archivist of Short Bros.,) led me to ask him for help. The practical help which Mr Bruce gave me was to prove invaluable for, apart from giving me a reading list, he put me in touch with a source which I had not previously known was open to an ordinary, non-flying citizen, namely with the Library of The Royal Aeronautical Society.

Mr Arnold Nayler, Librarian of The Royal Aeronautical Society, has over many years been of the greatest possible help and encouragement and I thoroughly enjoyed my visits to Hamilton Place. It was a sad day when the time at last seemed to have come for me to stop reading old copies of *Flight* and *The Aeroplane* and to settle down to typing it all up. In my early studies at the R.Ae.S. Mr Leith was a great help and in recent years Mr Riddle has produced – as though by magic – any book which I thought that I should read. My warmest thanks go to all in The Royal Aeronautical Society Library who gave me such friendly help in my researches.

I am very grateful to Mrs Jean Tsushima, Hon. Archivist, the Honourable Artillery Company, for her information on the London Trained Bands; and for sending photocopies of some pages of the History of the H.A.C., by C. Goold Walker, from which I quoted so extensively in Chapter 3.

I thank Miss Patricia Methven, Archivist of the Liddel Hart Library for Military Studies, King's College, London, for her helpful advice during my inquiries into Jim's time at KCL; and Mr Andrew Mussell for his help in supplying all the books I needed when in the library; and for his several long letters giving me so much useful information on Professor Huntington.

I thank the B P Library of Motoring, National Motor Museum, Beaulieu and in particular Mrs Lynda Springate for sending me photocopies of the articles on the Iris car and the road tests on the car, 1905/06, from *Automotor Journal*. I thank Mrs D. M. Baird, (Betty Baird), and the Editors of the *Canadian Geographic* for their kind permission to quote from 'Alberta Ferry & The Bleriot Connection' in the Dec/83/Jan/84 issue of *Canadian Geographic*; I thank Harald Penrose for his kind permission to quote from his *The Pioneer Years*; I thank the Fleet Air Arm Museum, Yeovilton, for their helpful information on Jim; and the Royal Air Force Museum, Hendon, for much general advice and for permission to quote from the pre-1914 Hendon programmes; I thank the Institute of Civil Engineers for a copy of Jim's Candidature Notes; and for information on Charles; and the Institution of Mechanical Engineers for information on Jim; also Putnam Aeronautical Books and Conway Maritime Press for their kind permission to quote from four of their many fine books: C.H. Barnes' *History of Short's Aircraft*, A.J. Jackson's *History of Blackburn Aircraft* and Molson & Taylor's *History of Canadian Aviation*. Also to Putnam Aeronautical Books for permission to quote from Harold Penrose' *The Pioneer Years*. I thank Mssrs Sidgwick & Jackson for their kind permission to quote from Erskine Childers' *Riddle of the Sands*; the Executors of the H. G. Wells Estate for permission to quote from *An Englishman Looks at the World* and to A. P. Watts, Literary Agents, for obtaining permission for me; to the Public Information Office, House of Commons, for the quotations from Hansard, vol 46 column 2091–2 and to Miss Bronwen Rowlands for digging them out for me.

To the Editors of *Flight* and *The Aeroplane*: thank you.

I join the hundreds of would-be chroniclers who would have been in a dreadful fix without the help of the two great journals; I am particularly indebted to the writings of C. G. Grey who, it now appears, foresaw many future developments as accurately as he described those which had already taken place. I would also like to thank the Editors of *Canadian Aviation* for their kind permission to reproduce Charles 1942 article on the ski-plane.

I am indebted to Mr Andrew Nahum, of the Science Museum, South Kensington, for kindly giving me the technical description of Jim's 1908 petrol-injection engine quoted in Chapter 1. And I thank David Collyer, of the Kent Aviation Historical Society, for information on Eastchurch in 1911.

Westland Helicopters Ltd, to whom I wrote for comfirmation of my memory of the seating arrangments in the Westland Wessex at Croydon in 1936, gave me the information for which I was searching and I am very grateful to Mr Case, Technical Director, Westland Helicopters, for his detailed reply; and to Sir John Cuckney's Personal Assistant for putting me in touch with Mr Case.

I am very grateful to the Royal Air Force Historical Branch, Ministry of Defence, Theobalds Road, for their kind permission to quote from the *Official History of The Royal Air Force*, by C. R. Bullock, originally published in 1920, (revised 1936), in the several war-time chapters. I have also used this master-work as my source of information on the disposition of Wings and Squadrons; and I owe Mrs Isla Hargreaves my warmest thanks for the spontaneous kindness with which she offered to lend me her copy of this invaluable book. (Mrs Hargeaves' father, the late Wing Commander Baseden, was one of several truly remarkable pilots of the Great War for, having lied about his age in the most patriotic fashion, had his wings up and was a pilot serving in the RNAS before his sixteenth birthday).

The P. R. O. Kew have been a great source of information on the period of the Great War, and I acknowledge with many thanks the help and guidance given to me by the staff there.

I thank Governor J. M. Reid of H M Prison, Eastchurch, for his helpful information on the ownership of land at Eastchurch and its' eventual disposal.

Although all the Travers family knew of Jim's potato-dropping experiments, none of us had the dates or details or knowledge of what aircraft was used, so Maurice Allward's *Seaplanes & Flying Boats* was a rewarding find as well as being a fascinating book to read. I thank the Moorland Publishing Company for their kindness in allowing me to quote from Mr Allward's book.

I would like to thank Alan D. Roberts for his helpful information about Port Victoria and the Isle of Grain, which historic place Mr Roberts and his family can see so well from their house on Gossy Hill.

The Guild of Air Pilots & Air Navigators was an organization which H. liked better than any other and the one to which he felt most proud to belong, ever since that first overcrowded Meeting at Rules Restaurant on 1st February, 1929. Captain P. Wilson, Clerk to the Guild, gave me a great deal of information on the Guild's foundation and early days; I am most grateful to him for his time and trouble and for his permission to quote from the Guild's History.

L. A. 'Lawrie' Wingfield, with whom Captain Wilson put me in touch, gave me lots of help in the most jolly way, not sounding like the 90-year-old which he must by then have been, over the telephone one evening in 1986. His final words remain in my mind: "We all loved Brancker!"

As for Stag Lane: apart from Jean Batten I had no other correspondent who might remember Stag Lane until, by extraordinary chance, I happened to see Ivor Faulconer's address mentioned on the social page of a journal and decided, after hesitating for several years, to write to him although we had not met since childhood days. Mr Faulconer's evocative reply has been only a part of the help which he has so kindly given me; for he put me in touch with Stuart McKay, Founder and now Secretary of the de Havilland Moth Club; and Stuart put me in touch with many old Stag-Laners including that dear man, Victor H. Doree.

Victor Doree never boasted of his contribution to aviation but it was he – if my informants are correct – who bought and paid for one at least of Jean Batten's aeroplanes, wanting no return but that she should continue her remarkable career. What a generous and noble thing to have done.

Stuart McKay also put me in touch with William Richard Oliver again, 'Bill' Oliver, and Bill, like Victor Doree, has given me first-hand material for the Stag Lane chapters. I am most grateful to them both; also to Bill Oliver for his very kind permission for me to quote from his Mother's brilliant pictures of life in the 20's and 30's. Stuart himself has been a continuing source of information and encouragement and I thank him and Miranda for their help.

I should also like to thank the Marquis of Tavistock for kind permission for me to publish the three letters from Her Grace the late Duchess of Bedford, "the Flying Duchess", written to my father in 1935 and which are in my possession.

The PRO in Chancery Lane gave me much help in my inquiries into Jim's various Patents registered there and I am most grateful to the staff for their time and trouble in seeking them out and to Mr Tregenza for his advice.

To the many others who over the years have answered my questions about aeroplanes I give my most grateful thanks.

I never did ask Hugh Bergel, John Saffery or Sir Barnes Wallis for their permission to quote from their letters and I hope that they or their families have no objection to my having done so and will accept the warm thanks I now offer for the help which their letters have been to the book. Pilots letters are always the best.

Last and most important of all, I thank my husband, whose unstinting help at a critical time has enabled this book to appear in print.

Illustrations: All photographs are from author's own collection. Photographers where known have been credited.

I would like to thank the Royal Canadian Air Force; the National Aeronautical Collection, Hangar 86, Rockcliffe, Ottawa; the Editors of the *Daily Mail*; and *Universal Pictorial Press and Agency Ltd* for kind permission to print their photographs in my book.

E. Travers. 1990

INDEX OF PILOTS NAMES

Abbreviated list, without decorations, and frequently without rank or initials.